Encyclopedia of E–Business Development and Management in the Global Economy

In Lee
Western Illinois University, USA

Volume II

BUSINESS SCIENCE REFERENCE

Hershey • New York

Director of Editorial Content:	Kristin Klinger
Director of Book Publications:	Julia Mosemann
Acquisitions Editor:	Lindsay Johnston
Development Editor:	Julia Mosemann
Publishing Assistant:	Sean Woznicki
Typesetter:	Deanna Zombro, Callie Klinger
Quality Control:	Jamie Snavely
Cover Design:	Lisa Tosheff
Printed at:	Yurchak Printing Inc.

Published in the United States of America by
Business Science Reference (an imprint of IGI Global)
701 E. Chocolate Avenue
Hershey PA 17033
Tel: 717-533-8845
Fax: 717-533-8661
E-mail: cust@igi-global.com
Web site: http://www.igi-global.com/reference

Library of Congress Cataloging-in-Publication Data

Encyclopedia of e-business development and management in the global economy / In Lee, editor.
    p. cm.

  Includes bibliographical references and index.
  Summary: "This research book is a repository for academicians, researchers, and industry practitioners to share and exchange their research ideas, theories, and practical experiences, discuss challenges and opportunities, and present tools and techniques in all aspects of e-business development and management in the digital economy"--Provided by publisher.

  ISBN 978-1-61520-611-7 (hardcover) -- ISBN 978-1-61520-612-4 (ebook) 1.
Electronic commerce. 2. Electronic commerce--Management. I. Lee, In, 1958-
  HF5548.32.E518 2010
  658.8'7203--dc22
                          2009036871

British Cataloguing in Publication Data
A Cataloguing in Publication record for this book is available from the British Library.

All work contributed to this book is new, previously-unpublished material. The views expressed in this book are those of the authors, but not necessarily of the publisher.

List of Contributors

Contents
by Volume

Section 3: E-Marketplaces

Section 4: E-Business Strategies

Section 5: E-Business Models

Volume II

Section 6: E-Business Management

Section 7: Online Consumer Behavior

Volume III

Section 9: Web Services and E-Business Process Integration

Section 10: E-Business System Development

Section 12: Emerging Trends

Preface

In the early 1990s, e-business ushered in what is now called "the global economy." It revolutionized the process of buying, selling, and exchanging products and services, and spawned a host of business and technological innovations. As globalization and competition pose new opportunities and challenges, firms face increased pressures from stakeholders to create e-business values. They are attempting to find which e-business models and applications will contribute effectively to their sustainability, growth, and innovation. Innovations in technology in the e-business area have constantly encouraged firms to improve existing business processes and to come up with new business models and applications. Recently, advancements of wireless technologies have extended the reach of e-business to mobile business environments. As a growing number of customers utilize mobile devices to exchange information and to conduct business transactions, firms are competing to provide the most value-added, innovative, convenient mobile services for their customers. While large firms have been the early adopters and beneficiaries of most e-business innovations, an increasing number of small and medium-sized enterprises (SMEs) are also rapidly adopting e-business to better serve customers, improve productivity, extend a market base, and stay competitive.

E-business brought about a paradigm shift caused by "disruptive" technology that is radically changing the traditional way of doing business. The global economy emerging from the Internet revolution changed the rules and principles traditionally held by business firms. The paradigm shift was unprecedented in terms of the complexity and magnitude, and pressured firms to be more innovative and proactive to business problems than ever before. Anecdotal evidence of excellent companies such as e-Bay and Amazon.com shows that they understand the dynamics of the complex interrelated internal and external forces imposed on the company, develop comprehensive business plans from multi-layered stakeholders' perspectives, and implement the plans at the right time, magnitude, and place. However, in light of the current lack of comprehensive studies in e-business planning and management, an overarching framework is in urgent need to assist e-business managers in analyzing enabling technologies and the success factors when developing e-business plans.

Although a large volume of literature is already available on e-business, many new ideas and applications are constantly emerging and provide potential opportunities and challenges for further research. In light of this phenomenon, it is high time to take stock of the new knowledge in e-business development and management. **Encyclopedia of E-Business Development and Management in the Global Economy** provides a repository for academicians, researchers, and industry practitioners to share and exchange their research ideas, theories, and practical experiences, discuss challenges and opportunities, and present tools and techniques in all aspects of e-business development and management in the global economy.

This book is divided into twelve sections with a total of 129 articles: **Section 1, Theoretical Foundations of E-Business**, discusses various e-business theories and the impacts of e-business to the economy and society; **Section 2, E-Business Planning and Performance Evaluation**, addresses planning and performance evaluation methodologies for e-business; **Section 3, E-Marketplaces**, discusses various types of e-marketplaces and related technologies; **Section 4, E-Business Strategies**, addresses competition, dynamics, and trends in e-business; **Section 5, E-Business Models**, discusses various business models and their value creating opportunities; **Section 6, E-Business Management**, discusses organizational culture, leadership, management methods, customer management, and practices for e-business; **Section 7, Online Consumer Behavior**, presents e-commerce consumer acceptance models, trust, and psychological perspective on online consumer behavior; **Section 8, Mobile Commerce**, addresses mobile consumer behavior, mobile marketing, mobile virtual community, and mobile services; **Section 9, E-Business System Development**, presents service-oriented architecture, system design principles, quality of service, and e-business applications development; **Section 10, Web Services and E-Business Process Integration**, discusses various web service technologies and issues in business process integration; **Section 11, E-Business: Issues, Challenges, and Opportunities**, addresses digital divide, technological and regulatory challenges, emerging economies, and new e-business application opportunities; and **Section 12, Emerging Trends**, presents new web technologies, Web 2.0, and future trends. A brief introduction of each article follows:

Section 1: Theoretical Foundations of E-Business consists of nine articles. "The Macroeconomic Impacts of E-Business on the Economy" by Daniel Heil and James E. Prieger, Pepperdine University (USA), covers some of the impacts e-business has on the economy, emphasizing macroeconomic effects. It suggests directions for future research and discusses issues that e-business presents policymakers. "The Microeconomic Impacts of E-Business on the Economy" by James E. Prieger and Daniel Heil, Pepperdine University (USA), covers both the predicted impacts of e-business on the economy suggested by microeconomic theory, to understand why e-business has proliferated, and their empirical magnitude, to show the economic benefits. "The Power Laws of Enterprise 2.0" by Jacques Bughin, McKinsey & Company, Inc (Belgium), presents key stylized facts around the adoption, use and success of social software, a phenomenon dubbed "Enterprise 2.0." "Prices on the Internet" by Jihui Chen, Illinois State University (USA), reviews price dispersion and related literatures, and discuss future research directions. "Price Dispersion on the Internet: A Further Review and Discussion" by Fang-Fang Tang, Peking University (China); Xiaolin Xing, Fannie Mae (USA), reviews significant price differences and persistent price dispersions in the Internet markets. "The Electronic Law of One Price (eLOP)" by Camillo Lento, Alexander Serenko, and Nikola Gradojevic, Lakehead University (Canada); Lorne Booker, McMaster University (Canada); Sert Yol, Lakehead University (Canada), tests the eLOP by utilizing two datasets with online price data. Pairwise comparison tests reveals that the eLOP does not hold true for any of the product price categories tested. "Trust in Electronic Commerce: Definitions, Sources, and Effects" by Hongwei Du, California State University, East Bay (USA); Albert Lederer, University of Kentucky (USA); Jiming Wu, California State University, East Bay (USA), discusses the concept of trust, its definitions, and sources. "Avatar Theory" by Ching-I Teng, Chang Gung University (Taiwan); Shao-Kang Lo, Chinese Culture University (Taiwan), presents Avatar Theory to outline fundamental propositions related to avatars. Avatar Theory can provide a background theory for subsequent avatar studies related to online games. "Relationship between Second Life and the U.S. Economy" by Rosemarie Reynolds, Yusuke Ishikawa, and Amanda Macchiarella, Embry-Riddle Aeronautical University (USA), investigates the relationship between the economies of Second Life and the United States, using financial data collected from Linden Lab and the Federal Reserve.

Section 2: E-Business Planning and Performance Evaluation consists of nine articles. "E-Business Adoption and its Impact on Performance" by Sabah Abdullah Al-Somali, Ben Clegg, and Roya Gholami, Aston University (UK), discusses the process of e-business implementation, usage and diffusion (routinisation stage) on business performance. "B2B Website Benefits Realization in Australian SMEs" by Chad Lin, Curtin University of Technology (Australia); Yu-An Huang, National Chi Nan University (Taiwan); Rosemary Stockdale, Massey University (New Zealand), examines the relationships between B2B website adoption readiness, B2B website adoption constraints, IT investment evaluation, and B2B benefits in Australian SMEs. "Lifelong Learning in the Knowledge Economy: An Empirical Analysis of e-Learning Adoption at Firm-Level" by Maria Rosalia Vicente and Ana Jesus Lopez, University of Oviedo (Spain), examines e-learning adoption among a sample of European firms (an area for which empirical evidence is quite scarce), and investigates the factors driving its introduction. "Measuring the Quality of E-Business Services" by Mark Springer, Craig K. Tyran, and Steven Ross, Western Washington University (USA), develops a framework to compare and contrast different models of e-service quality. "Measuring B2C Quality of Electronic Service: Towards a Common Consensus" by Mahmoud Amer and Jorge Marx Gómez, Carl von Ossietzky University of Oldenburg (Germany), proposes a B2C electronic Service Quality "eSQ" model of consensus summarizing the past research efforts. The Business Value of E-Collaboration: A Conceptual Framework" by Lior Fink, Ben-Gurion University of the Negev (Israel), provides a conceptual framework for researchers and practitioners who are interested in investigating and understanding the organizational impacts of collaborative technologies. "A Model on Antecedents and Consequences of E-Procurement" by M. José Garrido, Ana Gutiérrez, and Rebeca San José, Universidad de Valladolid (Spain), analyzes whether different Internet tools are used throughout all purchasing phases and whether the characteristics of the buying situation determined the use of the Internet in that process. "Global Online Performance and Service Orientation" by Anna Morgan-Thomas, University of Glasgow, UK; Robert Paton, University of Glasgow (UK), examines the contribution of e-commerce to SME globalization. The focus here is explicitly on existing firms and their online activities. "Electronic Funds Transfer Systems and the Landscapes of Global Finance" by Barney Warf, University of Kansas (USA), summarizes some of the major public and private EFTS networks and the repercussions for capital markets, stock exchanges, and foreign exchange markets.

Section 3: E-Marketplaces consists of nine articles. "Intermediaries in E-Commerce: Value Creation Roles" by Nirvikar Singh, University of California, Santa Cruz, (USA), examines the evolution and robustness of intermediation in e-commerce, by examining the fundamental economics of intermediation in terms of economies of specialization, scale, and scope. "Identifying the Factors that Lead to a Successful Intermediary in Electronic Commerce" by Margaret Jackson and Marita Shelly, RMIT University (Australia), explores the factors that have led to the success of financial intermediaries and in particular, BPAY Ltd. in Australia. "A Framework for Identifying B2B E-Marketplace Strategies" by George Mangalaraj and Chandra S. Amaravadi, Western Illinois University (USA), reviews existing literature and provides a parsimonious framework for classifying electronic marketplaces. "Electronic Logistics Marketplaces" by Yingli Wang, Mohamed Naim, and Andrew Potter, Cardiff Business School, (UK), defines and describes Electronic Logistics Marketplaces (ELMs) in terms of their architectures, features and functionalities, impact on logistics practice and benefits to stakeholders, and future requirements. "An Agent-Based B2C Electronic Market in the Next-Generation Internet" by Vedran Podobnik, University of Zagreb (Croatia); Krunoslav Trzec, Ericsson Nikola Tesla (Croatia); Gordan Jezic, University of Zagreb (Croatia), presents an agent-based framework for the business-to-consumer (B2C) electronic market, comprising user agents, broker agents and provider agents, which enable Internet users to select an Internet Service Provider in an automated manner. "Concept of Agent-based Electronic Marketplace" by Norleyza Jailani, Ahmed Patel, Muriati Mukhtar, Salha Abdullah, and Yazrina Yahya, Universiti Kebangsaan Malaysia (Malaysia), explains the concepts of an electronic marketplace (e-marketplace) and the types of e-marketplaces in today's computing environment that is facilitated and driven by the Internet. The concept of software agent and the different types of agents which may exist in an e-marketplace application in the current setting of the global economy is also discussed. "Concept of Mobile Agent-Based Electronic Marketplace Safety Measures" by Ahmed Patel, Universiti Kebangsaan Malaysia, (Malaysia), extends the basic concepts of Mobile Agent Systems (MAS) to elaborate on the principles and address the key issues of security, privacy, trust, and audit for normal e-business and digital forensics purposes. "Time Constraints for Sellers in Electronic Markets" by Kostas Kolomvatsos, and Stathes Hadjiefthymiades, University of Athens (Greece), describes a model for the seller behaviour and through this model quantifies the maximum time of seller participation. "Towards Efficient Trust Aware E-Marketplace Frameworks" by Malamati Louta, Harokopio University of Athens, Greece; Angelos Michalas, Technological Educational Institute of Western Macedonia, (Greece), proposes enhancements to the sophistication of the negotiation functionality that can be offered by e-commerce systems in open competitive communications environments.

Section 4: E-Business Strategies consists of five articles. "Assessing Relational E-Strategy Supporting Business Relationships" by Anne-Marie Croteau, Anne Beaudry, and Justin Holm, Concordia University (Canada), develops an integrative construct of e-strategy, mainly focusing on the relationships built between and within companies. "Leading the Organizational Dynamics of E-Business Firms" by Esin CAN MUTLU, Yasemin BAL, and Pınar BÜYÜKBALCI, Yıldız Technical University (Turkey), conceptually discusses the important organizational aspects in e-business firms and supports them with the needed leadership traits. "Adoption of e-Commerce by Canadian SMEs: Defining Organisational, Environmental and Innovation Characteristics" by Lynn L. Sparling, Okanagan College (Canada); Aileen Cater-Steel and Mark Toleman, University of Southern Queensland (Australia), focuses on the definitions of organisational, external, environmental and innovation variables in the organisational context. "E-Business Strategy in Franchising" by Ye-Sho Chen and Chuanlan Liu, Louisiana State University (USA); Qingfeng Zeng, Shanghai University of Finance and Economics (China), discusses how e-business can be "meaningfully" used in franchising. "Exploring the impact of Government Policies and Corporate Strategies on the Diffusion of Mobile Data Services: Case of Economies at Different Stages of Transition" by Tugrul U Daim, Portland State University (USA); Jing Zhang, Beijing University of Posts and Telecommunications (China); Byung-Chul Choi, Samsung Information Systems America (SISA) (USA), explores how governments and businesses impact the diffusion of mobile data services with their policies and strategies.

Section 5: E-Business Models consists of nine articles. "eBusiness and the Resource-based View: Towards a Research Agenda" by Pedro Soto-Acosta, University of Murcia (Spain), provides a review of the adoption of a resource-based view of the firm (RBV) in e-business literature and suggests directions for future research. "E-Commerce Business Models: Part 1" and "E-Commerce Business Models: Part 2" by Khaled Ahmed Nagaty, The British University in Egypt, (Egypt), presents various e-commerce business models and their advantages and disadvantages, and discusses the important issues and problems facing e-commerce web sites. "Creating Business Opportunities Based on Use of Electronic Knowledge Business Models" by Tsung-Yi Chen, Nanhua University (Taiwan); Yuh-Min Chen, National Cheng Kung University (Taiwan), explores the knowledge value chain in the collaborative innovation era, introduces the knowledge commerce model, and analyzes possible revenue streams and opportunities associated with knowledge commerce. "Online Private Sales Clubs: An Emerging Model Of Fashionable E-Commerce at Promotional Prices" by Ana Isabel Jiménez-Zarco, Open University of Catalonia (Spain); María Pilar Martínez-Ruiz, Castilla la Mancha University (Spain); Silvia Sivera-Bello and Sandra Vilajoana-Alejandre, Open University of Catalonia (Spain), identifies some of the keys to success, as well as the growth opportunities associated with the online private sales club. "Business Model Renewal: The TIA-MARIA Framework for Enterprise Realignment" by Rebecca De Coster, Brunel University, (UK), develops a framework for business model renewal based on case study research into firms entering the emerging sector of mobile networking. "Architecture Model for Supply Chain Orchestration and Management" by Marijn Janssen, Delft University of Technology (the Netherlands), discusses the role of Supply Chain Orchestrators, with the aim of deriving an architectural model for the integration of the activities of organizations in the supply chain. The architecture model is illustrated and evaluated using a case study. "Ambient e-Service: a bottom-up collaborative business model" by Yuan-Chu Hwang, National United University, (Taiwan), presents an ambient e-service framework that characterizes ambient e-services with three dimensions (value stack, environment stack and technology stack). Several ambient e-service applications are also exemplified. "Online Auctions: Pragmatic Survey and Market Analysis" by James K. Ho, University of Illinois at Chicago (USA), presents a survey and market analysis of various online auction business models.

Section 6: E-Business Management consists of twenty articles. "Configurators/Choiceboards: Uses, Benefits, and Analysis of Data" by Paul D. Berger, Bentley University (USA); Richard C. Hanna and Scott D. Swain, Northeastern University (USA); Bruce D. Weinberg, Bentley University (USA), discusses the uses and benefits of configurator/choiceboard systems, and how the analysis of its usage can be beneficial to the company. "E-CRM: A Key Issue in Today's Competitive Environment" by María Pilar Martínez-Ruiz, University of Castilla-La Mancha (Spain); María Rosa Llamas-Alonso, University of León (Spain); Ana Isabel Jiménez-Zarco, Open University of Catalonia (Spain), highlights the importance of e-CRM as a key business process for global companies, gaining a better understanding of its benefits from different managerial perspectives, emphasizing key factors for effective implementation, and pointing out challenges and future directions in the field. "Effective Virtual Project Management Using Multiple E-Leadership Styles" by Margaret Lee, Capella University (USA), reviews management concepts for virtual teams that include leadership styles such as control-related models, transformational and transactional leadership styles, leadership that empowers team members to self-manage, and situational and contingency leadership styles. "On-Line Credit Card Payment Processing and Fraud Prevention for e-Business" by James G. Williams, University of Pittsburgh (USA); Wichian Premchaiswadi, Siam University (Thailand), addresses the issue of credit card fraud in terms of how cyber-criminals function and the potential solutions used to deter credit card fraud attempts. "Virtual Stock Markets as a Research Tool in Marketing and Management" by Lorenz Zimmermann, Ludwig-Maximilians-University Munich (Germany), explains the basic concept of Virtual Stock Markets (VSM), describes the potential areas of application, and shows examples of successful implementations in business practice. "Potential Benefits of Analyzing Website Analytic Data" by Elizabeth Votta, Roosevelt University (USA), presents potential benefits of analyzing website analytic data, including: discovering traffic trends, targeting market segmentation, developing best practices, optimizing landing pages, and improving conversion rates. "Teams of Leaders Concept (ToI) and E-Business Operations" by Dag von Lubitz, MedSMART Inc. (USA), presents the concept of teams of leaders (ToL) and its implications to e-business operations. ToL centers on the active, platform independent fusion of advanced IM, KM and high performing leader teams. "Customer Relationship Management (CRM): A Dichotomy of Online and Offline Activities" by

Kelley O'Reilly and David Paper, Utah State University (USA), documents how companies can determine the best blended approach to CRM initiatives that balance both online and offline marketing initiatives. "Understanding E-Payment Services in Traditionally Cash-Based Economies: The Case of China" by Xiaolin Li and Dong-Qing Yao, Towson University (USA); Yanhua Liu, Wuhan College of Economics and Management (China), examines a series of issues pertaining to China's e-payment services, which include China's e-payment growth, mechanisms, characteristics, opportunities and challenges. "Scenario Driven Decision Support" by M. Daud Ahmed, Manukau Institute of Technology (New Zealand); David Sundaram, University of Auckland (New Zealand), introduces scenario as a DSS component and develops a domain independent, component-based, modular framework that supports scenario management process. "e-HRM in TURKEY: A CASE STUDY" by Yonca GÜROL, Yildiz Technical University, (Turkey); R. Ayşen WOLFF, Haliç University (Turkey); Esin ERTEMSİR BERKİN; Yildiz Technical University (Turkey), investigates several specific and critical points that will contribute to a better understanding of E-HRM by illustrating how it is used by a Turkish firm in the health sector. "ARIBA: A Successful Story in E-Commerce" by Zhongxian Wang, Montclair State University (USA); Ruiliang Yan, Indiana University Northwest (USA); James Yao, Montclair State University (USA), review major events and innovations that helped ARIBA to grow and succeed rather than fail. "Integrated Optimal Procedure of Internet Marketing" by Lan Zhao, Chongqing University (China) and SUNY/College at Old Westbury (USA), focuses on how to integrate all the phases of Internet marketing process into a seamless pipeline. "Managerial Succession and E-Business" by Anthonia Adenike Adeniji, Covenant University (Nigeria), focuses on why succession planning is crucial in e-business and in the global economy. "E-business and Web Accessibility" by Panayiotis Koutsabasis, University of the Aegean (Greece), proposes measures for reaching and maintaining a good level of Web accessibility in terms of the specifications, design and evaluation phases of a user-centered approach to systems development. "Understanding the Use of Business-to-Employee (B2E) Portals in an Australian University though the Management Lens: A Qualitative Approach" and "Understanding the Use of Business-to-Employee (B2E) Portals in an Australian University through the Employee Lens: A Quantitative Approach" by Md Mahbubur Rahim, Monash University (Australia); Mohammad Quaddus, Curtin University (Australia); Mohini Singh, RMIT University (Australia), analyse the views of the portal steering committee (who represent the interests of the university senior management) relating to the portal usage behaviour of university staff and identify the key factors which they believe to have contributed to employees' low usage practices of portals. "An Exploratory Study on the User Adoption of Central Cyber Government Office of the Hong Kong Government" by Kevin K.W. Ho, The University of Guam (Guam); Calvin Chun Yu, The Hong Kong University of Science and Technology (Hong Kong); Michael C.L. Lai, Hong Kong Police Force (Hong Kong), investigates those factors affecting the user adoption of the Intranet Portal of the Hong Kong Government, a.k.a., Central Cyber Government Office (CCGO). "An Exploratory Study on the Information Quality Satisfaction of Central Cyber Government Office of the Hong Kong Government" by Kevin K.W. Ho, The University of Guam (Guam), examines the information quality satisfaction of the Central Cyber Government Office (CCGO), which is a communication portal developed by the Hong Kong Government. "Visual Merchandising in Online Retailing based on Physical Retailing Design Principles" by Tony Pittarese, East Tennessee State University (USA), presents effective design guidelines for the creation of successful online stores which are based on the design principles and practices of physical retailers.

Section 7: Online Consumer Behavior consists of thirteen articles. "Internet Consumer Behavior: Flow and Emotions" by Marie-Odile Richard, University of Montreal (Canada); Michel Laroche,

Concordia University (Canada), develops the flow construct of Internet consumer behavior, composed of skills, challenge and interactivity, and the emotions construct, composed of pleasure, arousal and dominance. "Internet Consumer Behavior: Web atmospherics" by Marie-Odile Richard, University of Montreal (Canada); Michel Laroche, Concordia University (Canada), presents six variables of web atmospherics: navigational characteristics, website structure, website organization, effectiveness of its content, website informativeness, and website entertainment. "Internet Consumer Behavior: Behavioral Variables" by Marie-Odile Richard, University of Montreal (Canada); Michel Laroche, Concordia University (Canada), examines the key behavioral variables identified by the literature: exploratory behavior, site attitude, product attitude, site involvement and product involvement. "Internet Consumer Behavior: Major Moderating Variables" by Marie-Odile Richard, University of Montreal (Canada); Michel Laroche, Concordia University (Canada), describes some of the key moderating variables such as gender, need for cognition (NFC) and optimum stimulation level (OSL). "Consumer Information Sharing" by Jonathan Foster and Angela Lin, University of Sheffield (UK), provides an up-to-date review of the practice of consumer information sharing. "B2C E-Commerce Acceptance Models Based On Consumers' Attitudes and Beliefs: Integrating Alternative Frameworks" by Ángel Herrero-Crespo and Ignacio Rodríguez-del-Bosque, Universidad de Cantabria (Spain), describes the main principles of Theory of Planned Behaviour, the Technology Acceptance Model and Decomposed Theory of Planned Behaviour and examines their weaknesses and strengths for the research of e-commerce acceptance. "Effect of Perceived Risk On E-Commerce Acceptance: State of the Art and Future Research Directions" by Ángel Herrero-Crespo and Ignacio Rodríguez-del-Bosque, Universidad de Cantabria (Spain), examines the influence that perceived risk in online shopping has on the process of e-commerce adoption by end consumers. "Third Party Internet seals: Reviewing the Effects On Online Consumer Trust" by Peter Kerkhof, VU University Amsterdam (the Netherlands); Guda van Noort, University of Amsterdam (the Netherlands), presents an overview of findings regarding the persuasiveness of Internet seals and reflects upon possible explanatory mechanisms for these effects. "The Importance of Gender, IT Experience, and Media-Rich Social Cues on Initial Trust in e-Commerce Websites" by Khalid AlDiri, Dave Hobbs, and Rami Qahwaji, University of Bradford (UK), investigates how to increase the perceived trustworthiness of vendor websites. "Using the Internet to Study Human Universals" by Gad Saad, Concordia University (Canada), provides a brief overview of how the Internet is a powerful tool for investigating many human preferences, choices, emotions, and actions which occur in universally similar manners. "The Neurocognitive and Evolutionary Bases of Sex Differences in Website Design Preferences: Recommendations for Marketing Managers" by Eric Stenstrom and Gad Saad, Concordia University (Canada), examines how sex differences in the processing of spatial and perceptual information lead to differential preferences in website design for men and women. "Exploring Video Games from an Evolutionary Psychological Perspective" by Zack Mendenhall, Marcelo Vinhal Nepomuceno, and Gad Saad, Concordia University (Canada), demonstrates how an evolutionary psychological (EP) approach could elucidate why video games have increased in popularity, and how it is related to our evolved human nature. "An Integrated Model for e-CRM in Internet Shopping: Evaluating the Relationship between Perceived Value, Satisfaction and Trust" by Changsu Kim, Yeongnam University (Korea); Weihong Zhao, Jiangxi Normal University (China); Kyung Hoon Yang, University of Wisconsin-La Crosse (USA), develops an integrated e-CRM model by investigating the psychological process that occurs when a customer maintains a long-term relationship with an Internet online retailer.

Section 8: Mobile Commerce consists of eleven articles. "Mobile Communications / Mobile Marketing" by Suzanne Altobello Nasco, Southern Illinois University Carbondale (USA), introduces mobile communication technologies, and discusses various mobile marketing and advertising strategies. "C2C Mobile Commerce: Acceptance Factors" by Lori N. K. Leonard, University of Tulsa (USA), presents a model of an individual's intention to make use of mobile devices for C2C e-commerce which includes usefulness, ease of use, convenience, trust, and security. "Exploring the Mobile Consumer" by Kaan Varnali and Cengiz Yilmaz, Boğaziçi University (Turkey), provides insights into consumers' experience with mobile marketing by presenting a review of the mobile consumer behavior literature in an organized framework. "The Personalization Privacy Paradox: Mobile Customers' Perceptions of Push-Based vs. Pull-Based Location Commerce" by Heng Xu, John M. Carroll, and Mary Beth Rosson , Pennsylvania State University (USA), presents the personalization privacy paradox, and discusses the different impacts of pull and push mechanisms on the privacy personalization paradox. "Mobile Gaming: Perspectives and Issues" by Krassie Petrova, Auckland University of Technology (New Zealand), identifies the determinants of mGaming success and suggests recommendations for mobile game design and mGaming service provisioning. "Role of Personal Innovativeness in Intentions to Adopt Mobile Services – Cross-service approach" by Sanna Sintonen and Sanna Sundqvist, Lappeenranta University of Technology (Finland), contributes to the research on behavioral intentions to use mobile services. The key role is attributed to innovativeness in predicting mobile service adoption. "Service Discovery Techniques in Mobile E-commerce" by Nandini Sidnal, K.L.E.S. College of Engineering and Technology (India); Sunilkumar S. Manvi, Reva Institute of Technology and Management (India), discusses various mobile E-commerce issues with its main focus on the service discovery issue. It also elaborates on various syntax and semantic based service discovery mechanisms and concludes with future directions to service discovery mechanism. "Perspectives on the Viable Mobile Virtual Community for Telemedicine" by Jan-Willem van 't Klooster, Pravin Pawar, Bert-Jan van Beijnum, Chariz Dulawan, Hermie Hermens; University of Twente, (the Netherlands), contributes to Mobile Virtual Community (MVC) in general and mobile patient monitoring and treatment in particular by 1) analyzing in detail the robustness and other requirements to be fulfilled by the technical platform for MVCs, 2) providing guidelines for MVC platform development based on service orientation, and 3) discussing the actors, front-end views and service components involved. "Socio-Economic Effects on Mobile Phone Adoption Behavior among Older Consumers" by Sanna Sintonen, Lappeenranta University of Technology (Finland), evaluates what influences the usage of mobile phones among the aging consumers. "Mobile Agents in E-Commerce" by Bo Chen, Michigan Technological University (USA), highlights good features of the mobile agent paradigm for the applications in e-commerce. A number of selected mobile agent-based e-commerce systems and the agent platforms are introduced. "Mobile Telephony as a Universal Service" by Ofir Turel, California State University Fullerton (USA); Alexander Serenko, Lakehead University (Canada), discusses the need for reasonably priced, high quality telecommunication services to everyone who wishes to employ them and suggests the inclusion of mobile telephony services in the "universal service" basket.

Section 9: Web Services and E-Business Process Integration consists of seven articles. "Web Service Discovery, Composition, and Interoperability" by Duy Ngan Le, Karel Mous, and Angela Goh, Nanyang Technological University (Singapore), presents a brief survey, problems and possible solutions to three Web service operations (Web Service Discovery, Composition, and interoperability). "Case based web services" by Zhaohao Sun, University of Ballarat (Australia); Gavin Finnie, Bond University (Australia); John Yearwood, University of Ballarat (Australia), proposes CWSR: a case-based web service reasoner. It examines the correspondence relationship between web services and CBR and provides a unified treatment for case-based web service discovery, composition and recommendation. "Web Services E-Contract and Reuse" by Marcelo Fantinato, University of São Paulo (Brazil); Maria Beatriz Felgar de Toledo, State University of Campinas (Brazil); Itana Maria de Souza Gimenes, State University of Maringá (Brazil), presents a two-level e-contract metamodel. This metamodel is designed to promote the reuse of e-contracts during e-contract negotiation and establishment, taking into account contract templates. "Situational Enterprise Services" by Paul de Vrieze and Lai Xu, SAP Research (Switzerland); Li Xie, GuangDong Polytechnic Normal University (China), investigates how to apply new Web technologies to develop, deploy and execute enterprise services. "Social Networks and Web Services-based Systems" Zakaria Maamar, Zayed University (U.A.E); Leandro Krug Wives, Federal University of Rio Grande do Sul – UFRGS (Brazil), defines a social network in the context of Web services and shows how this network is built and used to discover Web service. "Interoperability Issues of Business Processes-Key Issues and Technological Drivers" by Ejub Kajan, State University of Novi Pazar (Serbia), gives an overview of the main obstacles in system integration, a critical assessment of existing approaches and recent research efforts in order to overcome interoperability problems. "Integrated Business Process Designs and Current Applications of Workflow Systems in E-Business" by Mabel T. Kung and Jenny Yi Zhang, California State University at Fullerton (USA), shows a comprehensive list of the structural integration of workflow models and designs that are currently applied to e-business.

Section 10: E-Business System Development consists of thirteen articles. "Facilitating Interaction between Virtual Agents By Changing Ontological Representation" by Fiona McNeill and Alan Bundy, University of Edinburgh (UK), presents the Ontology Repair System, which is designed to be a tool for automated agents acting on behalf of people or systems. "Modeling Collaborative Design Competence with Ontologies" by Vladimir Tarasov, Kurt Sandkuhl, and Magnus Lundqvist, Jönköping University (Sweden), applies ontology engineering to modeling competences of individuals, including different competence areas like cultural competences, professional competences and occupational competences. "Event Driven Service-Oriented Architectures for E-Business" by Olga Levina and Vladimir Stantchev, Berlin Institute of Technology (Germany), provides an introduction on the event- and service-oriented technologies, their origins and application areas. "Speeding up the Internet: Exploiting Historical User Request Patterns for Web Caching" by Chetan Kumar, California State University San Marcos (USA), discusses proxy caching approaches that exploit historical user request patterns in order to reduce user request delays. "The Effect of User Location and Time of Access on Ecommerce: A Long Tail Study of Website Requests" by Chetan Kumar, California State University San Marcos (USA), discusses how user location and time of access affect website visitations, and the resulting implications for e-commerce. "Incorporating Knowledge Management into E-Commerce Applications" by Sandra Moffett, Martin Doherty, and Rodney McAdam, University of Ulster (UK), reviews how knowledge discovery, corporate collaboration and rapid decision making challenges can be incorporated into e-commerce applications, and presents tools and techniques which should be incorporated into a fully functioning web commerce application. "Application of Semantic Web Technology in E-Business: Case Studies in Public Domain Data Knowledge Representation" by Sotirios K. Goudos, Aristotle University of Thessaloniki (Greece); Vassilios Peristeras, National University of Ireland (Ireland); Konstantinos Tarabanis, University of Macedonia (Greece), presents a flexible and scalable framework of an information system for complex cases and shows the advantages of the semantic web technologies application to e-Business. "Design Elements and Principles for Maintaining Visual Identity on Websites" by Sunghyun R. Kang and Debra Satterfield, Iowa State University (USA), examines design factors and determines which of these factors affect people's ability to identify and perceive information on web sites. It will discuss how design elements can cross media boundaries and create a consistent and effective user experience between the physical business and its presence on the web. "Designing e-Business Applications with Patterns for Computer-Mediated Interaction" by Stephan Lukosch, Delft University of Technology (The Netherlands); Till Schümmer, FernUniversität in Hagen (Germany), discusses aspects common to e-business collaboration applications and presents an approach to capture the best practices within these applications by means of patterns.. "A SOA-Based Framework for Internet-Enabled CRM" by Wei-Lun Chang, Tamkang University (Taiwan), identifies the significant elements and value of Internet-Enabled CRM and provides a roadmap and practical and managerial implications for future CRM. "Building Context-Aware E-Commerce Systems: A Data Mining Approach" by Anahit Martirosyan, Thomas Tran, and Azzedine Boukerche, University of Ottawa (Canada), extends usage of context as compared to previously designed context-aware e-commerce systems. While in previous work, context was mainly considered for mobile e-commerce systems, it proposes to build and use context for e-commerce systems in general. "Efficient Service Task Assignment in Grid Computing Environments" by Angelos Michalas, Technological Educational Institute of Western Macedonia (Greece); Malamati Louta, Harokopio University of Athens (Greece), uses an Ant Colony Optimization algorithm (ACO) for service task allocation in Grid computing environments. "Policy Driven Negotiation to Improve the QoS in the Data Grid" by Ghalem Belalem, University of Oran (Es Senia) (Algeria), integrates into consistency management service, an approach based on an economic model for resolving conflicts detected in the data grid.

Section 11: E-Business: Issues, Challenges, and Opportunities consists of nine articles. "Understanding the dimensions of the broadband gap: more than a penetration divide" by Maria Rosalia Vicente and Ana Jesus Lopez, University of Oviedo (Spain), focuses on the analysis of the European broadband gap by means of multivariate statistical methods, and in particular, factor and cluster analyses. "E-inclusion: European Perspectives Beyond the Digital Divide" by Bridgette Wessels, University of Sheffield (UK), outlines the background to the emergence of the term 'e-inclusion' and its definition and provides the policy response by the European Union. "Importance of Electronic Record Preservation in E-Business" by Helena Halas, SETCCE, Slovenia; Tomaž Klobučar, SETCCE and Jožef Stefan Institute (Slovenia), analyzes electronic records preservation for business organizations from an organizational perspective. "Electronic Commerce Prospects in Emerging Economies Lessons from Egypt" by Sherif Kamel, The American University in Cairo, (Egypt), addresses the development of the digital economy in Egypt focusing on the challenges faced relating to a number of social, technological, financial and legal issues and the road map formulated in collaboration between the different stakeholders, including the government, the private sector and the civil society to diffuse e-commerce in Egypt. "Using Assistive Technology to Ensure Access to E-Learning for Individuals with Disabilities" by Hwa Lee, Bradley University (USA), provides an overview of technology access for E-Learning for individuals with disabilities including legislations relevant to technology access for individuals with disabilities. "A Holistic View of the Challenges and Social Implications of Online Distribution: The Case of Pensions" by Tina Harrison, The University of Edinburgh, U.K.; Kathryn Waite, Heriot Watt University (UK), critically evaluates the extent to which use of the Internet has facilitated and promoted pension distribution in the UK, as well as identifying the forces that are constraining or facilitating further change. "The Global Telecommunications Industry Facing the IP Revolution: Technological and Regulatory Challenges" by Harald Gruber, European Investment Bank (Luxembourg), unravels the interplay between the evolution of technology, market performance of the telecommunications sector and regulation in order to put the role of telecommunications for e-business into perspective. "Evolving e-Business Systems: Transgenic Forces in International Realpolitik Space in 2050" by Denis Caro, University of Ottawa (Canada), posits that transgenic governance forces are evolving and will engage future international e-business professionals in a multi-polar world of 2050. "E-recruiting: Sources, Opportunities, and Challenges" by In Lee, Western Illinois University (USA), classifies the various e-recruiting sources and discusses opportunities and challenges in developing and managing e-recruiting.

Section 12: Emerging Trends consists of fifteen articles. "Emerging Trends of E-Business" by Pengtao Li, California State University, Stanislaus (USA), presents the emerging trends of e-business in various areas, including Web services, Web 2.0, Mobile Commerce (M-Commerce), and corresponding ethical and social issues. "Virtual Commerce" by Suzanne Altobello Nasco, Robert E. Boostrom, Jr., and Kesha K. Coker, Southern Illinois University Carbondale (USA), presents virtual commerce in the context of virtual reality by illustrating how people buy and sell products and services in virtual worlds, and discusses how companies can incorporate virtual commerce into their existing marketing and overall business strategy. "The Web 2.0 Trend: Implications for the Modern Business" by Michael Dinger and Varun Grover, Clemson University (USA), introduces the use of Web 2.0 technologies in contemporary business environments, and presents a value oriented framework designed to guide firms in the development of Web 2.0 initiatives. "Web 2.0: The Era Of User Generated Content on Web Sites" by Jos van Iwaarden, Ton van der Wiele, and Roger Williams, Erasmus University (The Netherlands); Steve Eldridge, The University of Manchester (UK), looks into the role of user generated content (UGC) in purchasing decisions, and explains the strategic implications of UGC for online management of service quality. "Web 2.0 Concepts, Social Software and Business Models" by Matthes Fleck, Andrea von Kaenel, and Miriam Meckel, University of St. Gallen (Switzerland), provides an overview of the most prominent definitions, basic concepts and applications of the term Web 2.0, and investigates the Anderson's long tail concept, issues of transparency and the effects of an interconnected user base on e-business. "Grounding Principles For Governing Web 2.0 Investments" by Steven De Hertogh, Vlerick Leuven Gent Management School (Belgium) and Amsterdam Business School (The Netherlands); Stijn Viaene, Vlerick Leuven Gent Management School and K.U. Leuven (Belgium), proposes a set of grounding principles for governing web 2.0 investments. These grounding principles refer to attention areas and key choices that management ought to pay heed to if it wants to successfully invest in Web 2.0 for the enterprise. "Web 1.0, Web 2.0 and Web 3.0: The Development of E-Business" by Tobias Kollmann and Carina Lomberg, University of Duisburg-Essen (Germany), highlights the characteristics of Web 1.0, Web 2.0, and Web 3.0. "The New Generation of Knowledge Management for the Web 2.0 Age: KM 2.0" by Imed Boughzala, TELECOM Business School (France); Moez Limayem, University of Arkansas (USA), introduces, defines, and clarifies the concept of KM 2.0 compared to the traditional KM in terms of scope, nature of knowledge, place of the individual, process, and technology. "Recommender Systems: An Overview" by Young Park, Bradley University (USA), presents a brief overview of recommender systems as an effective and powerful personalization tool in the e-commerce environment. "A Linguistic Recommender System for Academic Orientation" by E. J. Castellano and L. Martínez, University of Jaén (Spain), develops OrieB, a Web-DSS for Academic Orientation based on a Collaborative RS (CRS) for supporting advisors in their student guidance task. "Wireless Technologies: Shifting Into the Next Gear?" by Simona Fabrizi, Massey University (New Zealand), provides a theoretical explanation for an apparent paradox of why some Mobile Operators (MOs) postpone upgrades while others do not. "Search Engines: Past, Present and Future" by Patrick Reid, AstraZeneca (UK); Des Laffey, University of Kent (UK), covers key issues in the area of search engines and looks at emerging issues in search, including rich media and mobile, and privacy issues. "E-Government – Status Quo and Future Trends" by Tobias Kollmann and Ina Kayser, University of Duisburg-Essen (Germany), provides an overview of current findings in the realm of e-government and presents future directions of research. "Blog Marketing: Potential and Limits" by Călin Gurău, GSCM – Montpellier Business School (France), investigates blog members' perceptions and level of acceptance of blog marketing, and discusses findings and implications for blog marketing communications. "RFID Enabled B2B E-Commerce Technologies and Applications" by Ygal Bendavid, Ecole Polytechnique de Montreal (Canada), focuses on the emerging phenomenon of Radio Frequency Identification (RFID) technologies and the EPC Network by examining how it enables innovative B2B E-Commerce applications.

The Encyclopedia of E-Business Development and Management in the Global Economy is an excellent collection of the latest research and practices associated with e-business theories, strategies, management, technologies, applications, and trends. This encyclopedia is the first comprehensive book that presents aspects from the research, industry, managerial, and technical sides of e-business. As leading experts in the e-business area, the contributors did an excellent job of providing our readers with extensive coverage of the most important research topics, concepts, business practices, technologies, and trends. The projected audience includes policy-makers, e-business application developers, market researchers, managers, researchers, professors, and undergraduate/graduate students in various academic disciplines. I expect this encyclopedia to shed new insights for researchers, educators, and practitioners to better understand the important issues and future trends of e-business research and technologies.

In Lee, Ph.D.
Professor in Information Systems
Western Illinois University
Macomb, IL, USA
August 2009

Acknowledgment

I would like to acknowledge the help of the 225 expert reviewers involved in the double-blind review process for the 129 accepted article of the encyclopedia, without whose support it could not have been satisfactorily completed.

I sincerely thank Ms. Kristin M. Klinger, Julia Mosemann, Heather A. Probst, Jan Travers, Mehdi Khosrow-Pour, and other members of the IGI Global, whose contributions throughout the whole process from the inception of the initial idea to the final publication have been invaluable. I also thank my family for their understanding and support for this book project.

In closing, I would like to express my gratitude to the 234 authors for their invaluable contributions and collaboration.

In Lee
Editor

About the Editor

In Lee is a professor in the Department of Information Systems and Decision Sciences in the College of Business and Technology at Western Illinois University. He received his MBA from the University of Texas at Austin and Ph.D. from University of Illinois at Urbana-Champaign. He is a founding editor-in-chief of the International Journal of E-Business Research. He has published his research in such journals as *Communications of the ACM, IEEE Transactions on Systems, Man, and Cybernetics, IEEE Transactions on Engineering Management, International Journal of Production Research, Computers and Education, Computers and Operations Research, Computers and Industrial Engineering, Business Process Management Journal, Journal of E-Commerce in Organizations, International Journal of Simulation and Process Modeling,* and others. His current research interests include e-commerce technology development and management, investment strategies for computing technologies, and intelligent simulation systems.

Section 6
E–Business Management

Chapter 42

Configurators/Choiceboards:
Uses, Benefits, and Analysis of Data

Paul D. Berger
Bentley University, USA

Richard C. Hanna
Northeastern University, USA

Scott D. Swain
Northeastern University, USA

Bruce D. Weinberg
Bentley University, USA

INTRODUCTION AND DEFINITION

This article discusses the uses and benefits of configurator/choiceboard systems, and how analysis of data from its use can be useful to the company having such a system. Dell and other companies have greatly improved, if not perfected, the art of product customization by using a system of choiceboards or configurators (used here as interchangeable terms) that allow consumers to customize their products. A popular term for what is being accomplished by the use of choiceboards is "mass customization," a term that not long ago may have been thought of as an oxymoron. We always had "job shops" that produced to order for individual consumers or companies. However, relatively speaking, individual

DOI: 10.4018/978-1-61520-611-7.ch042

customization did not occur on a large-scale basis, and was quite distinct from what was called mass production, and surely, was not routinely available online even when there was first an "online."

A choiceboard is essentially interactive online software that enables customers to choose a basic product and then customize it by selecting from a set of product features. For example, on Dell.com, the consumer chooses a basic computer system such as the E510 and then customizes it by specifying an operating system, memory capacity, monitor, video card, keyboard, etc. Each of these choices has an incremental price that increases or decreases the overall price. The base price combination is not necessarily the least expensive possible combination of features. If the consumer chooses a less costly feature than the option included in the base price/ feature combination, the overall price indeed goes down. The price is continually updated as the choices are made. Several choices offer only a yes-or-no response, with "*no*" indicating a choice of the default option. Features also may include services options such as shipping and warranty. Clearly, the choiceboard system does not offer an infinite number of possibilities. For example, Dell.com offers from two to five levels of hard-drive capacity.

Other companies that have made good use of this choiceboard approach include Travelocity. com and VermontTeddyBears.com along with many others, including automakers. Indeed, although the vehicle is generally purchased from the dealer, automakers report that the vehicle configurators and model pages are the most used sections on their Web sites. Configurators are also in frequent use in Business to Business (B2B) contexts when one business is ordering from another. In B2B, far more numerous options are presented and the Website design is too complex to be cost-effective in a B2C context.

Choiceboards can differ greatly in terms of what they offer. Some allow consumers to actually experience different options; a well-known example (although not usually thought of as a choiceboard by the consumer) is choosing a cell-phone ringtone. The consumer can sample each tone option for ten seconds or more. Lands' End lets customers create custom clothing by providing pictures of clothing options and measurement information.

USES AND BENEFITS

A choiceboard system serves many purposes. First, it lets consumers customize their products or services. At one time, such customization was possible only for high ticket items like automobiles. Rather than buying a car off the dealer's floor, customers have long been able to select a color along with other options—air conditioning, automatic or manual transmission, sunroof, etc.

There is clear evidence that consumers enjoy the opportunity to customize their products as long as the process is painless—ideally offering perfect orders and super service (FastCompany, 2000). A perfect order "…gets shipped on time and complete, and arrives at a customer's desired location within a precise time window and in excellent, ready-to-use condition." Super service has the flexibility to handle last-minute customer changes and still provide the same level of service. Consumers can balance priorities, deciding whether they care most about price, delivery time, or various special options.

A second use for, and benefit from, a choiceboard system is relatively invisible to the consumer: inventory control. Dell, for example, uses a pull-based system, in which customers initiate orders and only then do order processing, inventory decisions, and production kick in. This compares favorably to a push-based system in which a company decides what consumers are likely to want and delivers that merchandise to distributors and retailers months in advance of actual sales. This can leave stores with large inventories that end up moving only after the distributor offers rebates, dealer incentives, and giveaways. Dell's pull-based approach has allowed it to integrate its production line with its suppliers, so that neither Dell nor its suppliers get overburdened—or underprovided—with inventory (Slywotsky and Morrison, 2000; Bharati and Chaudhury, 2004).

A third use and benefit of choiceboards is that they save money on labor costs. They also, by definition, eliminate most transcription (e.g., order taking) and other human errors. A seller's Web site can potentially generate thousands of customer quotes per day, which can be delivered instantly, 24 hours/ day, 365 days per year.

All these are significant pluses. However, developing a choiceboard system is expensive, so the benefits must justify the cost. People who can write for the Web cannot necessarily construct choiceboard systems. All but the largest companies have to outsource that task, and it may not be worth it. Lane Bryant, for instance, once had a choiceboard system. However, they suspended the service, possibly because the cost of its maintenance or improvement was not warranted by the benefits it provided.

Finally, there may be a long-run benefit to having a choiceboard/configurator system. Companies can use choiceboard data to measure—and perhaps to predict—consumer buying patterns and preferences. This, in turn, may support the implementation of superior marketing strategy. All of this can be done through the use of conjoint analysis.

CONJOINT ANALYSIS OF CONFIGURATOR / CHOICEBOARD DATA

Conjoint analysis is a technique used to determine the utility values that consumers place on various levels of a product's attributes. Usually consumers are shown different product scenarios (i.e., product configurations), each a combination of levels of its different attributes. At a typical Dell Web site, visitors can choose among at least three levels of processors and three levels of operating systems. Going more deeply into sub-menus then allows choices of levels of many other attributes.

Consider three attributes of a product—price, warranty duration, and degree of customer-support services. The company is interested in the purchase intent that accompanies different combinations of levels of these attributes. If the customer can consider five prices, four warranty durations, and four levels of customer support, there are 5x4x4 = 80 scenarios possible. If demand for each combination could be predicted, a cost/benefit analysis would tell the company which configuration is most profitable. This might seem to imply that the company wants to choose one scenario, but that is not necessarily the case. The cost/benefit analysis might lead the company to eventually give the consumer a set of special bundled choices—

probably not an 80-option choiceboard, but maybe four popular combinations.

The usual mechanism for conducting a conjoint analysis is to gather a set of respondents—ideally representative of the target market—ask them to examine and evaluate different scenarios, and then indicate their purchase intent for the one they choose. The precise methodology of a conjoint analysis is not clearly defined; there are several methodological variations lumped together under the term, conjoint analysis. The company can ask respondents to rank-order the scenarios shown,[1] producing ordinal data. Alternatively, respondents can be asked to indicate purchase intent for every scenario (i.e., possible combination). The most popular rating method is the 11-point Juster Scale: 0 indicates no chance at all that the responder would purchase the product in that form, 1 indicates a 10 percent chance, 2 a 20 percent chance, and so on up to 10, which indicates a >99% chance, virtual certainty. This is generally considered a superior method to simple ranking. However, self-reported purchase intents do need to be rescaled,[2] since it is well known that self-reported purchase intent values are overstated. For example, perhaps only 80% of those who check off "10" actually would actually make the purchase, and perhaps only 62% of those indicating "9" would actually make the purchase, etc. Many companies have proprietary data concerning how these adjustments should be made for their product category. Nevertheless, the resulting information is rightfully treated as interval-scale data and offers a richer set of appropriate statistical tools for data analysis than does rank data.

This "full-profile" technique allows an assignment of a "utility," or relative value, to each level of each attribute. It is referred to as "full profile," since each evaluation by the consumer is made with his/her seeing a product that has *some* level of *every attribute in the choice set* – in essence, a "complete" or "full" profile of the product.

How can a company use the principles of conjoint analysis to analyze configurator/choiceboard

Table 1. Simplified choiceboard

ATTRIBUTE 1 – MONITOR*	
1) monitor A	($-150)
2) monitor B	($0)
3) monitor C	(+$300)
4) monitor D	(+$500)
5) monitor E	(+$800)
ATTRIBUTE 2 – PRINTER**	
1) no printer	($0)
2) printer A	(+$200)
3) printer B	(+$300)
4) printer C	(+$550)
ATTRIBUTE 3 – RECOVERY BACKUP CD	
1) none	($0)
2) include	($10)
ATTRIBUTE 4 – VIDEO CARD	
1) card 1	($0)
2) card 2	($75)
3) card 3	($125)

*Note that monitor B comes with the system, but the customer can choose a more or a less expensive monitor.

**"No printer" is the default: the base price does not include a printer.

information and determine consumer buying habits and preferences in a way that enhances profit? Consider:

1. Typically, a company using a configurator/choiceboard has a large amount of data on actual customer-choices, which means that the data indicating these preferences are very accurate.
2. Typically, a customer has been exposed to all available choices, which means that there is no need to choose only a subset of the possible attributes.

Example

The Dell case can be simplified for illustration purposes. Suppose for a certain basic computer configuration, customers are presented with four features (see table 1), one at a time, each incor-

porating a certain number of choices and each choice's associated incremental price:

Let us assume that customers see these four sets of choices if they begin with a certain basic computer configuration. There are 5 x 4 x 2 x 3 = 120 possible combinations. However, the choices are not presented as full profiles. Full profiles would have to appear as 120 specific combinations. For example, one profile might combine Monitor 1 (i.e., "A") + Printer 1 (i.e., no printer) – no backup CD + Video Card 1; this combination (i.e., "profile") would reduce the base price by $150. Another profile could combine Monitor 5 (i.e., "E") + Printer 4 (i.e., "C") + the backup CD + Video Card 3, raising the base price by $1485. If the customers were asked to evaluate all 120 scenarios, the scenarios would be shown in random order.[3]

Under a full-profile scenario, each option offers one choice for each feature (printer, CD, etc.). In an actual choiceboard, each choice set appears "monadically," i.e., one feature at a time. Still, by going back and forth among the choices, the customer can technically consider all 120 scenarios.[4]

So how can an analysis of configurator/choiceboard data enhance company profit? In this example, Dell has actual behavioral data, which is far superior to intentional data. The relative frequencies of purchase for a particular configuration reflect the purchase probabilities. Suppose that Dell finds that all three video card choices are equally popular. This implies that the pricing of the different cards is appropriate. Suppose that 95 percent of the customers choose to include the backup CD. That indicates that Dell may be "leaving money on the table," and could increase profits by raising the price above $10. In any case, it strongly indicates that Dell should conduct some marketing research to determine the demand curve for the backup CD.

This concept extends to other features such as the monitor. Suppose that the default is a 15-inch flat-panel monitor and the other options, in order of increasing price, are a 15-inch wide-screen flat panel, a 17-inch flat panel, a 15-inch sharper-vision flat panel, and a 17-inch sharper-vision flat panel. What if many customers choose to upgrade to a 15-inch wide-screen flat panel, but relatively few choose the 17-inch flat panel? In that case, maybe Dell may want to raise the price of the 15-inch wide-screen flat panel and/or reduce the price of the 17-inch flat panel—or both. Naturally, optimal prices depend on the production costs of each option. The choiceboard data could also lead to profit-enhancing bundle pricing for the most popular combinations. Indeed, there are probably several significant correlations among the various choices.

Clearly, analysis of configurator/choiceboard data can also be a great boon to Dell's suppliers in terms of inventory needs and order quantities. This cost savings to suppliers should be passed on, at least in part, to the focal company, that is to say, Dell.

FUTURE RESEARCH DIRECTIONS

Future research should investigate two primary issues. One is the proverbial cost/benefit issue. As noted, it can be quite expensive to construct a configurator/choiceboard system that is sufficiently user-friendly to both the consumer and different members of the supply chain. Further investigation and refining of the configuator/choiceboard process may lead to a large increase in the benefit/cost ratio. The second primary area for further investigation is the additional potential benefit of superior marketing decision-making that can accrue from selected, perhaps more complex, analyses of configurator/choiceboard data, especially if the buyer's demographics can be captured and related to purchase choices.

CONCLUSION

The use of a configurator/choiceboard approach makes the purchase process easier for the consumer and more beneficial to the vendor. In addition, an analysis of configurator/choiceboard data can suggest pricing strategies, promotional strategies, determination of the customer lifetime value for each of several different customer segments, and applications for CRM and other key management information-systems, as well as a whole host of other marketing decisions.

REFERENCES

Bharati, P., & Chaudhury, A. (2004). Using Choiceboards to Create Business Value. *Communications of the ACM, 47*(12), 77–81. doi:10.1145/1035134.1035137

Hammonds, K. (2000). Value Propositions. *Fast-Company*, *37*(1), 38.

Slywotsky, A., & Morrison, J. (2000). *How Digital Is Your Business?* New York: Crown Business.

ADDITIONAL READING

Addis, M., & Holbrook, M. (2001). On The Conceptual Link between Mass Customization and Experiential Consumption: An Explosion of Subjectivity. *Journal of Consumer Behaviour*, *1*(1), 50–66. doi:10.1002/cb.53

Dahan, E., & Hauser, J. (2002). The Virtual Customer. *Journal of Product Innovation*, *19*(5), 332–353. doi:10.1016/S0737-6782(02)00151-0

Delbert, B., & Stremersch, S. (2005). Marketing Customized Products and Striking a Balance Between Utility and Complexity. *JMR, Journal of Marketing Research*, *42*, 219–227. doi:10.1509/jmkr.42.2.219.62293

DeShazo, J., & Fermo, G. (2002). Designing Choice Sets for Stated Preference Methods: The Effects of Complexity on Choice Consistency. *Journal of Environmental Economics and Management*, *44*, 123–143. doi:10.1006/jeem.2001.1199

Duray, R. (2002). Mass Customizations Origins: Mass or Custom Manufacturing? *International Journal of Operations & Production Management*, *22*, 314–328. doi:10.1108/01443570210417614

Duray, R., & Milligan, G. (1999). Improving Customer Satisfaction Through Mass Customization. *Quality Progress*, *32*(8), 60–66.

Fiori, A., Lee, S., & Kunz, G. (2004). Individual Differences, Motivation, and Willingness to Use a Mass-Customized Option for Fashion Products. *European Journal of Marketing*, *38*(7), 835–849. doi:10.1108/03090560410539276

Fogliatto, F., & da Silveira, G. (2008). Mass Customization: A Method of Market Segmentation and Choice Menu Design. *International Journal of Production Economics*, *3*, 606–622. doi:10.1016/j.ijpe.2007.02.034

Franke, N., & Schreier, M. (2008). Product Uniqueness as a Driver of Customer Utility in Mass Customization. *Marketing Letters*, *19*, 93–107. doi:10.1007/s11002-007-9029-7

Goldstein, D., Johnson, A., & Heitmanm, M. (2008). Nudge Your Customers Toward Better Choices. *Harvard Business Review*, *86*(2), 99–105.

Huffman, C., & Kahn, B. (1998). Variety for Sale: Mass Customization or Mass Confusion. *Journal of Retailing*, *74*(4), 491–514. doi:10.1016/S0022-4359(99)80105-5

Liechy, J., Ramaswamy, V., & Cohen, S. (2001). Choice Menus for Mass Customization: An Experimental Approach for analyzing Customer Demand with an Application to a Web-based Service. *JMR, Journal of Marketing Research*, *38*, 183–196. doi:10.1509/jmkr.38.2.183.18849

Michel, S., Kreuzer, M., Kuhn, R., & Stringfellow, A. (2006). *Mass-Customized Products: Are they Bought for Uniqueness or to Overcome Problems with Standard Products?* Working Paper, Garvin School of International Management.

Ogawa, S., & Piller, F. (2006). Reducing the Risk of New Product Development. *Sloan Management Review*, *47*(2), 65–71.

Peppers, D., & Rogers, M. (1997). *Enterprise One to One*. New York: Currency/Doubleday.

Pine, B. (1999). *Mass Customization*. Cambridge, MA: Harvard Business School Press.

Pine, B., Victor, B., & Boynton, A. (1993). Making Mass Customization Work. *Harvard Business Review*, *71*(5), 108–122.

Prahalad, C., & Ramaswamy, V. (2000). Co-opting Customer Competition. *Harvard Business Review*, *78*(1), 79–87.

Randall, T., Terwiesch, C., & Ulrich, K. (2007). User Design of Customized Products. *Marketing Science*, *26*(2), 268–280. doi:10.1287/mksc.1050.0116

Schreier, M. (2006). The Value Increment of Mass-Customized Products: An Empirical Assessment. *Journal of Consumer Behaviour*, *5*, 317–327. doi:10.1002/cb.183

Simonson, I. (2005). Determinants of Customers' Responses to Customized Offers. *Journal of Marketing*, *69*, 32–45. doi:10.1509/jmkg.69.1.32.55512

Slywotsky, A. (2000). The Age of the Choiceboard. *Harvard Business Review*, *78*(1), 40–41.

Terwiesch, C., & Loch, C. (2004). Collaborative Prototyping and the Pricing of Custom-Designed Products. *Management Science*, *50*(2), 145–158. doi:10.1287/mnsc.1030.0178

Ulrich, K., & Ellison, D. (1999). Holistic Customer Requirements and the Design-Select Decision. *Management Science*, *45*(5), 641–658. doi:10.1287/mnsc.45.5.641

Wind, J., & Rangaswamy, A. (2001). Customization: The Next Revolution in Mass Customization. *Journal of Interactive Marketing*, *15*(1), 13–32. doi:10.1002/1520-6653(200124)15:1<13::AID-DIR1001>3.0.CO;2-#

KEY TERMS AND DEFINITIONS

Choiceboard: An interactive online-software that enables customers to choose, for a variety of features, a single option from a list of options. Used during online purchase, a customer can take a basic product and then customize it by selecting from a set of product features.

Configurator: Another word for Choiceboard

Conjoint Analysis: A set of statistical technique used in market- and marketing research to determine how people value different features that make up an individual product or service.

Full Profile: In conjoint analysis, a product combination being evaluated that has *some* level of every attribute in the choice set (vs. a *partial profile*: a product combination being evaluated with only a subset of attributes in the choice set being specified).

Mass Customization: A term used in marketing and manufacturing, representing the use of flexible, computer-aided manufacturing systems to produce custom output. In other words, it combines mass production processes with individual customization.

Self-Reported Purchase Intent: Respondents provide their best estimate for their likelihood of purchase in the future.

ENDNOTES

[1] It is very likely that the scenarios evaluated are not all possible combinations, but only a carefully selected subset chosen by applying principles of experimental design. See, for example, Berger, P. & Maurer, R. (2002). *Experimental Design with Applications in Management, Engineering, and the Sciences.* Pacific Grover, CA: Duxbury Press.

[2] Self-reported purchase intent values are widely agreed to be exaggerated, the degree of exaggeration differing for different product categories. For example, for a particular product category, experience may indicate that only 72 percent of those who indicated virtual certainty actually bought the product,

only 59 percent who indicated a 90 percent purchase probability actually bought, and so on. Marketing research firms often consider information about these conversion values to be proprietary.

3   As a practical matter, the order would be random, equivalent to a shuffle of a deck of cards. It would be impossible to rotate through all orders, since the number of orders is $120! = 6.69 \times 10^{198}$.

4   There may or may not be a significant difference in what an analysis concludes depending on the difference in presentation. The authors do not know of any study that has focused directly on this issue. The key aspect of any difference in analysis would probably lie in the validity of inferences about interaction effects.

Chapter 43

E-CRM:
A Key Issue in Today's Competitive Environment

María Pilar Martínez-Ruiz.
University of Castilla-La Mancha, Spain

María Rosa Llamas-Alonso
University of León, Spain

Ana Isabel Jiménez-Zarco
Open University of Catalonia, Spain

INTRODUCTION

As competition and the cost of acquiring new customers continue to increase, the need to build and enhance customer relationships has become paramount for businesses. The building of strong customer relationships has been suggested as a means for gaining competitive advantage (Mckenna, 1993) so, in today's marketplace, a growing number of firms seek to develop profound, close and long-lasting relationships with their customers since it is much more profitable to keep and satisfy current customers than to manage an ever-changing customer portfolio (Reinartz & Kumar, 2003; Ross, 2005; Llamas-Alonso et al. 2009).

This one is a consequence of many paradigmatical changes in the marketing field during the past decades, such as a transition from a focus on the product, transactional marketing, acquiring clients (responsive marketing approach) and market share towards a customer centric approach, relationship marketing, two-way communication, retaining customers (proactive and holistic marketing approaches) and share of customer. Thus, in this fast-moving and highly competitive scenario Customer Relationship Management (hereafter referred to as CRM) emerges as a business philosophy devoted to enhance customer relationships and consequently create value for both the company and the customer.

CRM has become a cornerstone issue not only in off-line buyer-seller relationships, but also in on-line customer-supplier relationships. The impact of information technology in the fields of marketing and management has emphasized the importance

DOI: 10.4018/978-1-61520-611-7.ch043

of re-arranging a new plan for marketing that gets benefited from new technologies. With the rise of e-business applications and the use of electronic channels, CRM has expanded the capacity of the organizations to interact with their customers and suppliers using e-technologies such as the Internet, which is termed as e-CRM. The availability of information on real time, interactivity and personalization, as characteristics of the Internet as well as of other e-technologies, are furthering e-CRM functions fostering a closer interaction between customers and business organizations (Chandra & Strickland, 2004).

The aim of this chapter is to highlight the importance of e-CRM as a key business process for global companies, gaining a better understanding of its benefits from different managerial perspectives, emphasizing key factors for effective implementation and pointing out challenges and future directions in the field.

CUSTOMER BASED ADVANTAGES AND NEW MARKETING ORIENTATIONS: PROACTIVE AND HOLISTIC APPROACHES

The development of competitive advantages based on the continuous creation and offer of value to customers, contributes significantly to the business success. Thus, firms that aim to achieve these advantages need a market oriented corporate culture which boosts customer knowledge and learning, as well as customer communication and cooperation (Slater & Narver, 1999) in order to: (1) give an effective response to customers' needs (Matthing et al., 2004) and (2) gain a competitive positioning in the market.

Customers can exhibit two types of needs: manifest and latent. Manifest needs are defined as those ones that the customer is aware of, and they are clearly and directly manifested while latent needs are those that are not expressed by the customer, either because he/she has never

previously experienced them or because he/she has never planned on responding to them (Matthing et al., 2004). In this context, marketing oriented firms can implement two types of actions with the aim of meeting customer demands. The first type, called **responsive marketing orientation**, focuses on understanding the manifest needs of customers in order to develop products and services to meet them (Slater & Narver, 1999). The second behaviour, termed as **proactive marketing orientation**, seeks to learn about and understand customers' latent needs with the goal of offering them proper and satisfactory solutions (Slater & Narver, 1999; Matthing et al., 2004).

Some studies highlight the direct and positive relationship between proactive marketing orientation and business success (e.g., Kuada & Buatsi, 2005; Slater et al., 2006). A proactive marketing orientation will help the firm to get to know the customer's needs (both latent and manifest) and so, it will be able to offer products and services that increase the value that the customer receives (Grönroos, 2000), providing the firm with a sustainable competitive advantage and improving business results in the long term.

No doubt that, as suggested by Dipak et al. (2002), among others, marketing needs to evolve quickly, especially in order to provide customers with adequate responses to their requirements. This will increase the success of the firm, considering the current scenario characterized by globalization, new technologies −especially the Internet − and hyper competence. In this context, the holistic marketing implies to take an step further in the marketing field (Keller & Kotler, 2006). Thus, in order to create and deliver value, the firms seek to interact in all potential areas with all agents (clients, employees, partners, stakeholders and communities). As pointed out by Dipak et al. (2002), this new marketing approach makes it necessary to the firm: (1) adapt a more holistic perspective regarding the customers needs, trying to offer more than a specific product or service; (2) develop a more holistic perspective about how its behaviour affects customer satisfaction; and (3) develop a more holistic view about the sector –especially taking into account emergent developments, representing new opportunities and drawbacks –.

The latter two marketing approches constitute the foundation of CRM initiatives. In this scenario, CRM emerges as a business approach that combines strategy and technology with the aim of managing knowledge about the customer and establishing two-way communication and effective interaction between the firm and the customer in order to improve the efficiency and effectiveness of the business processes. This focus involves a win-win approach by increasing value for both, customer and firm, since it helps to improve customer retention and loyalty, cross-sell and up-sell solutions, reduce operating costs, and increase sales revenue (Llamas-Alonso et al., 2009).

The wide deployment of the Internet and other e-technologies during the last decades has encouraged firms to take steps towards the development of marketing strategies in an e-world. In most of the cases, technologies like mobile phones, game consoles or web sites have been used with commercial purposes. Nowadays, a high number of companies use applications below the line, such as product placement, advergaming (and advergaming 2.0) as communication tools, drawing the attention of their customers (Moore, 2006). Thus, with the shift of business applications towards the Internet and other e-technologies (e.g., mobile phones, PDAs, customer call and contact centers, voice response systems, etc.), CRM has enhanced organization's capabilities by providing access to its customers and suppliers via the Web. This business strategy using these e-channels is termed as e-CRM –*electronic CRM* –. Through the integration of both technological and marketing elements, e-CRM covers all aspects of the customer's online experience throughout the entire transaction cycle (Lazakidou, Ilioudi & Siassiakos, 2008).

E-technologies have become a key touch point in the interaction between customers and companies, so the interest in managing customer relationships through these applications has grown parallel with the rise of e-CRM as a sub-field embedded into the general discipline of CRM. No doubt that the Internet is furthering e-CRM functions since it provides features that are attractive to both customers and organizations (Chandra & Strickland, 2004). E-CRM intertwines traditional CRM solutions with e-business applications. In this vein, Bradway and Purchia (2000) suggest that e-CRM is the intersection between paramount shifts like the growing Internet market and the prevailing focus on customer-centric strategies.

Therefore, e-CRM strategy involves taking advantage of the revolutionary impact of the Internet and other e-technologies to expand the traditional CRM techniques by integrating technologies and new electronic channels such as web sites, wireless, and voice technologies and combining it with e-business applications into the overall CRM strategy (Pan & Lee, 2003). Hence, the main differences between CRM and e-CRM are related to the underlying technology and its interfaces with users and other systems. In this particular respect, it is important to highlight that the additional capabilities that e-CRM systems provide to customers (e.g., self-service browser-based window to place orders, check order status, request information, etc.), offer them freedom in terms of place and time. All e-CRM applications are designed with customers in mind, giving them a complete experience on the e-technologies. Each different user has a different view of the array of information, goods, and services available to him/her (Chandra & Strickland, 2004) according to his/her individual profile.

In addition, it is important to outline that e-CRM is not the same as web-enabled CRM. On the one hand, while web-enabled CRM is usually designed around one department or business unit, e-CRM applications are built for the whole company, including customers, suppliers and partners

(Chandra & Strickland, 2004). On the other hand, e-CRM can also include other e-technologies and channels, such as mobile phones, customer call and contact centers as well as voice response systems. The use of these technologies and channels means that companies are managing customer interactions with either no human contact at all, or involving reduced levels of human intermediation on the supplier side (Anon, 2002).

Finally, e-CRM helps on-line businesses to better manage interactions with their customers using the Internet as the focal touchpoint. The web can represent the initial means through which CRM business actions, like targeted cross-selling and personalized product offers based on analysis of a customer's behaviors and preferences, take place but other channels are also appropriate to get in touch with current customers and prospects, enhancing their loyalty in the first case and attracting their interest for the company in the latter one (Dyché, 2001).

E-CRM OBJECTIVES AND BENEFITS

The main objective of an e-CRM system is to establish a double-way communication between the company and its customers via the web and other e-technologies driving to a close and long-lasting relationship. These technologies enable the improvement of the customer service, by providing analytical capabilities within the organization (Fjermestad & Romano, 2003) and so, retaining valuable customers.

Two of the key words defining society today are mobility and flexibility. The contact between customers and companies is no longer limited to a personal contact or a contact through a computer, instead a wide range of tools can serve the customer to interact with firms. In this regard, e-CRM applications foster customer focused philosophy since they provide firms with completely new avenues to maintain and attract customers, improve transaction and service capabilities, and develop

integrated, customer-centric infrastructures that enable businesses to provide the customer with a level of valuable end-to-end service impossible to achieve less than a few years ago.

Due to the additional possibilities that the use of e-technologies provides, in contrast to CRM, e-CRM allows the organization to dynamically change its marketing efforts to adapt them to market demands. It means for example that, as business conditions change, an organization with e-CRM capabilities implemented can design and release specific campaigns to targeted customer segments (Chandra & Strickland, 2004). In order to do this, it is important that the information obtained through the web site is integrated with the information from the rest of the channels to provide the managers with a holistic view of the customer.

As a managerial tool, e-CRM is a sound platform for putting into practice relationship marketing, even if some limits still (and will) continue to exist for engaging firms into individual on-line relationships with innumerable customers. E-CRM goes an step forward from CRM initiatives since it allows:

- Do (real-time) personalisation to degrees it is not possible with CRM.
- Interact with customers in ways, at speeds and through channels that it is not possible through CRM.
- Track behavioural trends in ways it is not possible with CRM.
- Empower customers in ways it is not possible with CRM.
- Exploit the benefits of an internet-based rather than client/server technical architecture.

E-CRM can be viewed as a business process in which customer equity is continuously created, enhanced and managed by interacting with customers through electronic touch points fostering close relationships with customers, improving customer retention and loyalty rates, creating opportunities for cross-selling and up-selling operations and generating benefits for both the company and the customers.

According to Kimiloglu and Zaralihigher (2009) e-CRM implementation involves high levels of improvements in customer satisfaction, transaction amounts and frequency, brand image, effective database management and customer targeting, efficient business processes, technology utilisation, excellence and innovation in services, improved sales, profitability and decreased service support costs.

KEY FACTORS IN A SUCCESSFUL E-CRM IMPLEMENTATION

The infrastructure supporting e-CRM requires knowledge of customer data capture, storage, selection and distribution. While several tools may be employed to capture data, the approach to what data are collected, stored and used in reporting and analysis requires skills and techniques similar to those used in the offline world (King & Tang, 2002).

Many companies are currently working on the implementation of e-CRM systems. To efficiently do this they should understand and respond to the following critical success factors for e-CRM initiatives (King & Tang, 2002):

- Accurately assess e-CRM needs: Prioritize e-CRM initiatives based upon a gap analysis between the current and the future states and use this road map to plot progress over the next several years. Spending several weeks upfront understanding the current situation may reveal areas where the need for traction in e-CRM is great, and the rewards for progress in these areas will be commensurate.
- Understand customer requirements: Some efforts to understand customer requirements

are necessary. To prioritize e-CRM projects, the firm needs to understand which changes will be enthusiastically welcomed by customers and which ones will not place the company any closer to better fulfilling customer´s needs.

- Don't view e-CRM as a technology initiative: Every e-CRM initiative has technology components, but e-CRM is not a technology initiative. It is a business initiative requiring the project discipline of technology groups during implementation and the process focus of the business teams throughout the initiative.
- Quantify expected returns from e-CRM: Given current market conditions, no firm would embark upon an initiative with the scope of an e-CRM project without quantifying expected returns. At least, that would seem to make good business sense. With any large-scale initiative, the measurement of returns should include interim reviews of expenditures and cost savings along with monthly tracking of revenue changes. Quantify expectations upfront and maintain constant vigilance of results constitute a critical aspect.
- Make e-CRM an enterprise-wide initiative: Whether the firm opts to take a comprehensive journey or a series of targeted road trips, an e-CRM road map for the firm should exist. With an e-CRM road map, each road trip can be seen in the context of an enterprise-wide initiative and be treated as part of a larger whole. If the firm truly views e-CRM as enterprise-wide, even minor successes exclusive to a single channel will be communicated and celebrated widely.
- Ensure integration across all distribution channels: In the same way, whether the firm is involved in a comprehensive or targeted implementation, integration plans must take into account all distribution channels.

- Employees will make or break e-CRM efforts: e-CRM efforts are people initiatives. The smallest e-CRM effort incorporates changes to technology, processes and people, with people as the variable with the greatest range in the equation. People changes may include the need to learn new skills, to work with different functions or even to eliminate positions entirely. Clear communication in the beginning about potential outcomes for each individual as well as their department and the firm can lead to greater buy-in and higher likelihood of a succesful implementation.

- Be willing to change the processes: Business processes are the third leg in the technology-process-people triangle that is affected by an e-CRM implementation. Many firms do not take full advantage of the benefits of newly implemented technology because they are unwilling or unable to change their business processes. A true e-CRM implementation will result in changes to three; and, often, the process change has a greater impact on cost savings than the introduction of new technology.

- Recognize that e-CRM is a change effort: e-CRM implementation involves a change effort with all the cross-functional team meetings, corporate communications and multiyear planning of any enterprise-wide attempt a reformulating the business approach.

CHALLENGES AND FUTURE DIRECTIONS IN E-CRM

E-CRM is understood as managing relationships with customers through the web site and other e-technologies. A key issue is to integrate the information about the customer obtained from these channels with the information from the rest of the channels in order to provide the managers with a holistic view of the customer and his/her relationship with the firm. A 360° customer view constitutes the foundation to understand customer needs so that the company can manage a cost-effective system that contacts the right customers at the right time with the right solutions to meet their needs.

The use of e-CRM tools and systems yields in an improvement of the marketing performance by introducing new opportunities to companies to enhance their effectiveness and to deliver customer value (Scullin et al., 2004). It offers additional opportunities to lower die costs involved in communicating with customers, optimize work flows as a result of the integration with other enterprise systems, facilitate better market segmentation and enable optimal customer interactions, relationship and customization opportunities (Adebanjo, 2003).

One of the main challenges in adopting e-CRM initiatives comes from managing the myriads of interactions taking place in a network firm, dealing with all the information holistically, and using that information in a dynamic, flexible, effective and interactive way to provide customers with a close and personalized treatment. The first step is to record and store the logs regarding the customer trackings but the true challenge is to be able to analyze all these logs and transform these data into knowledge. This in-depth knowledge should be the base for a customized relationship with every customer.

Another challenge comes from the need of a holistic cross-functional integration of processes, people, operations, and marketing capabilities that is enabled through information, technology and applications. According to Harrigan, Ramsey & Ibbotson (2008), e-CRM should move on to a more strategic and integrated level particularly in SMEs. Only if the e-CRM implementation takes place on a company-wide level the pay of will be optimal. Future trends point in this direction.

Finally, the adoption of an e-CRM approach implies a high level of involvement, a great challenge for the firm, since it means a different way of understanding the marketing strategy, the market and the approach to the customer and communicating and aligning the organization around this strategy. It also requires an important investment in ICTs and an intensive use of these ICTs, in order to improve the efficiency of the internal processes and the management of the relationships with customers.

REFERENCES

Adebanjo, D. (2003). Classifying and selecting e-CRM applications: an analysis-based proposal. *Management Decision, 41*(6), 570–577. doi:10.1108/00251740310491517

Anon., (2002, February). Unravelling e-CRM. *CRMMarket Watch, 8*(28), 12–13.

Atuahene-Gima, K., Slater, S. F., & Olson, E. M. (2005). The Contingent Value of Responsive and Proactive Market Orientatations for New Product Program Performance. *Journal of Product Innovation Management, 22*, 464–482. doi:10.1111/j.1540-5885.2005.00144.x

Baker, W. E., & Sinkula, J. M. (2005). Market Orientation and the New Product Paradox. *Journal of Product Innovation Management, 22*, 283–502. doi:10.1111/j.1540-5885.2005.00145.x

Bradway, B., & Purchia, R. (2000). *Top 10 strategic IT initiatives in e-CRM for the new millennium.* Retrieved from http://www.financial-insights.com

Brown, S. A. (2000). A case study on CRM and mass customization. In S. A. Brown (Ed.), *Customer relationship management- a strategic imperative in the world of e-business.* Toronto: John Wiley and sons, Canada.

Chandra, S., & Strickland, T. J. (2004). Technological differences between CRM and E-CRM. *Issues in Information Systems, 2*, 408–413.

Chen, Q., Chen, H. M., & Kazman, R. (2007). Investigating antecedents of technology acceptance of initial eCRM users beyond generation X and the role of self-construal. *Electronic Commerce Research, 7*(3-4), 315–339. doi:10.1007/s10660-007-9009-2

Dyché, J. (2001). Getting ready for CRM: A pre-Implementation checklist. *CRM Guru.* Retrieved from http://www.crmguru.com/features/ect/jdyche.html

Fjermestad, J., & Romano, N. C. (2003). Electronic customer relationship management: revisiting the general principles of usability and resistance: an integrative implementation framework. *Business Process Management Journal, 5*(9), 572–591. doi:10.1108/14637150310496695

Franke, N., von Hippel, E., & Schreier, M. (2006). Finding commercially attractive user innovations: A test of lead-user theory. *Journal of Product Innovation Management, 23*(4), 301–315. doi:10.1111/j.1540-5885.2006.00203.x

Frishammar, J. (2005). Managing Information in New Product Development: A Literature Review. *International Journal of Innovation and Technology Management, 2*(3), 259–275. doi:10.1142/S021987700500054X

Grönroos, C. (2000). Relationship Marketing: Interaction, Dialogue and Value. *Revista Europea de Dirección y Economía de la Empresa, 9*(3), 13–24.

Harrigan, P., Ramsey, E., & Ibbotson, P. (2008). e-CRM in SMEs: an exploratory study in Northern Ireland. *Marketing Intelligence & Planning, 26*(4), 385–404. doi:10.1108/02634500810879296

Hult, G. T., Ketchen, D. J., & Slater, S. F. (2005). Market Orientation and Performance: An Integration of Disparate Approach. *Strategic Management Journal, 26*, 1173–1181. doi:10.1002/smj.494

Keller, K. L., & Kotler, P. (2006). Holistic marketing: A broad, integrated perspective to marketing management. In J.N. Sheth & R.G. Sisodia (Eds.), *Does marketing need reform? Fresh perspectives on the future* (pp. 300-306). Armonk, NY: M. E. Sharpe Editor.

Kimiloglu, H., & Zarali, H. (2009). What signifies success in e-CRM? *Marketing Intelligence & Planning*, *27*(2), 246–267. doi:10.1108/02634500910945011

King, R., & Tang, T. (2002, January 18). E-CRM in the Post Dot-Com Age: Nine Critical Factors to Success. *DM Direct Newsletter*. Retrieved from http://dmreview.com/article_sub.cfm

Kuada, J., & Buatsi, S. N. (2005). Market Orientation and Management Practices in Ghanaian Firms: Revisiting the Jaworski and Kholi Framework. *Journal of International Marketing*, *13*(1), 58–88. doi:10.1509/jimk.13.1.58.58539

Lazakidou, A., Ilioudi, S., & Siassiakos, K. (2008). Electronic Customer Relationship Management Applications and Consumer Trust in E-Commerce. *International Journal of Electronic Customer Relationship Management*, *2*(3), 262–275. doi:10.1504/IJECRM.2008.020411

Lee-Kelley, L., Gilbert, D., & Mannicom, R. (2003). How e-CRM can enhance customer loyalty. *Marketing Intelligence & Planning*, *2*(4), 239–248. doi:10.1108/02634500310480121

Liu, Y., Zhou, C., & Chen, Y. (2006). Determinants of E-CRM in influencing customer satisfaction. In *Proceedings of the 9th Pacific Rim International Conference on Artificial Intelligence* (LNCS 4099, pp. 7-776). Berlin: Springer.

Llamas-Alonso, M. R., Jiménez-Zarco, A. I., Martínez-Ruiz, M. P., & Dawson, J. (2009). Designing a Predictive Performance Measurement and Control System to Maximize Customer Relationship Management Success. *Journal of Marketing Channels*, *16*(1), 1–41. doi:10.1080/10466690802147896

Matthing, J., Saden, B., & Edvardsson, B. (2004). New Service Development: Learning from and with Customers. *International Journal of Service Industry Management*, *15*(3), 479–498. doi:10.1108/09564230410564948

McKenna, R. (1993). *Relationship Marketing: Successful strategies for the age of the consumer.* Boston: Harvard School Business Press.

Moore, E. (2006). *Advergaming and the on line marketing on food to children.* Fundacion Kaiser Familia.

Padmanabhan, B., Zhiqiang, Z., & Kimbrough, S. O. (2006). An empirical analysis of the value of complete information for e-CRM models. *MIS Quarterly*, *30*(2), 247–267.

Pan, S. L., & Lee, J. N. (2003). Using E-CRM for a unified view of the customer. *Communications of the ACM*, *46*(4), 95–99. doi:10.1145/641205.641212

Reinartz, W. J., & Kumar, V. (2003). The impact of customer relationship characteristics on profitable lifetime duration. *Journal of Marketing*, *67*(January), 77–99. doi:10.1509/jmkg.67.1.77.18589

Richard, J. E., Thirkell, P. C., & Huff, S. L. (2007). An Examination of Customer Relationship Management (CRM) Technology Adoption and its Impact on Business-to-Business Customer Relationships. *Total Quality Management & Business Excellence*, *18*(8), 927–945. doi:10.1080/14783360701350961

Ross, D. F. (2005). E-CRM from a supply chain management perspective. *Information Systems Management*, 37–44. doi:10.1201/1078/44912.22.1.20051201/85737.5

Scullin, S., Fjermestad, J., & Romano, N. C. (2004). E-relationship marketing: changes in traditional marketing as the outcome of electronic customer relationship management. *The Journal of Enterprise Information Management*, *17*(6), 410–415. doi:10.1108/17410390410566698

Slater, S. F., & Mohr, J. J. (2006). Successful Development and Commercialization of Technological Innovation: Insights Based on Strategy Type. *Journal of Product Innovation Management*, *23*, 26–33. doi:10.1111/j.1540-5885.2005.00178.x

Slater, S. F., & Narver, J. D. (1999). Market-Orientated is More than Being Customer-Led. *Strategic Management Journal*, *20*, 1165–1168. doi:10.1002/(SICI)1097-0266(199912)20:12<1165::AID-SMJ73>3.0.CO;2-#

Srivastava, R. K., Shervani, T. A., & Fahey, A. L. (1998). Market-based assets and shareholder value: A framework for analysis. *Journal of Marketing*, *62*(January), 2–18. doi:10.2307/1251799

Zehrer, A., & Fenkart, S. (2008). Electronic customer relationship management, a new approach to self-evaluate a tourism destination. *Journal of Technology Marketing*, *3*(2), 169–182. doi:10.1504/IJTMKT.2008.018863

KEY TERMS AND DEFINITIONS

Advergaming: The product placement in video games (advergaming) objective is to enhance the familiarity of the customer with the brand. The placement, the role, the scene and all the details related to the appearance of the brand in the video game are important since they contribute to position the brand in the mind of the customer. Una evolución del concepto es lo que se conoce con el nombre de advergaming 2.0. It takes a step forward achieving a high degree of customization of the advertising on real time. This is a dynamic formula which adapts to the user and to several characteristics of the game such as the time of the day or the profile of the customer.

CRM: CRM (Customer Relationship Management) is both a business approach and a management tool concerned with the generation and maintenance of long-lasting relationships between the firm and its customers by increasing knowledge about customers and establishing two-way cooperative relationships between the firm and its customers.

E-CRM: Since e-CRM (electronic customer relationship management) relates to selling, serving or communicating to customers via the Web, e-CRM can be regarded as a subset of CRM, meaning that e-CRM is one channel through which a company can deploy its CRM strategy.

Holistic Marketing: "Holistic marketing is the design and implementation of marketing activities, processes, and programs that reflect the breadth and interdependencies of their effects. Holistic marketing recognizes that "everything matters" with marketing —customers, employees, other companies, competition, as well as society as a whole –and that a broad, integrated perspective is necessary (Keller & Kotler, 2006, p. 300).

Proactive Marketing Orientation: Proactive marketing orientation, seeks to learn about and understand customers' latent needs with the goal of offering them proper and satisfactory solutions

Responsive Marketing Orientation: Responsive marketing orientation focuses on understanding the manifest needs of customers in order to develop products and services to meet them.

Chapter 44
Effective Virtual Project Management Using Multiple E–Leadership Styles

Margaret R. Lee
Capella University, USA

INTRODUCTION

The field of organizational behavior defines leadership as "the ability to influence a group toward the achievement of goals" (Capella, 2005, p. 294). Leadership styles have been well studied and researched. Early leadership studies were developed using traditional, co-located work arrangements in mind. Later studies expanded to include traditional project team environments. In the current business environment, however, nontraditional virtual work arrangements are becoming more popular. Virtual project teams are increasing in business today and will continue to become more common in the future (Martins, Gilson, & Maynard, 2004).

Managing nontraditional work involving virtual teams is becoming a necessity in the current business environment. The type of leadership e-

managers must demonstrate for successful virtual team management is different from traditional project team management (Konradt & Hoch, 2007). Understanding appropriate leadership styles for virtual project teams and the transition toward new leadership styles is an important part of managing human resources in organizations and successful virtual project management. Emerging e-leadership roles and management concepts for virtual teams include multiple leadership models, and their application is an important part of our evolving virtual organizational behavior.

This paper reviews management concepts for virtual teams that include leadership styles such as control-related models, transformational and transactional leadership styles, leadership that empowers team members to self-manage, and situational and contingency leadership styles. In the virtual project environment, the effective manager needs to use

DOI: 10.4018/978-1-61520-611-7.ch044

as many different styles as needed to bring the project to a successful completion.

BACKGROUND

Introductory Definitions

Virtual teams reflect the ever-increasing non-traditional work environments of the 21st century, with members collaborating from geographically distant locations (Lee, 2009). Ariss, Nykodym and Cole-Laramore (2002) define virtual teams as a group of skilled individuals who "communicate via computer, phone, fax and video-conference" (p. 22). Virtual teams involve individuals who are geographically distributed and use technology to communicate and produce results (Duarte & Snyder, 1999).

The term e-leadership describes leadership in today's nontraditional virtual business environment. The need for e-leadership in virtual project teams has become increasingly relevant as businesses move toward more non-traditional work. Virtual project teams are increasing in business today, and understanding e-leadership styles of virtual teams is an important part of e-business. E-leadership styles for virtual project team managers may be different from traditional project team managers, and how they might be different is still an emerging study. E-leadership styles is an expanding topic for developing the knowledge and practices necessary to determine the most effective leadership styles for virtual project managers.

Leadership Styles

Control-Related Leadership

Control-related leadership is defined as leading by tasks and includes motivating, providing role clarity, setting clear goals and priorities, and by giving good directions. Control-related leadership has been linked to effective virtual team management. Konradt and Hoch (2007) examined leadership roles and showed that the task leadership function was "rated as significantly more important to virtual team effectiveness than people leadership function" (p. 25) and "that managers in virtual teams viewed control-related roles as more appropriate for virtual team success and performance than non-control-related roles" (p. 26).. Similar goal-related concepts can be found in management by objectives (MBO) studies. Previous studies found that control-related leadership strategies were positively related to virtual team success (Hertel, Konradt, & Orlikowski, 2004). Control often has a negative connotation when linked to management behaviors, but leadership involves some degree of responsibility for influencing the behavior of workers (Hersey, Blanchard, & Johnson, 2001, p. 17).

Transformational and Transactional Leadership Styles

Transformational and transactional leadership characteristics are common management styles for virtual teams. Transformational leaders are defined as leaders who inspire followers to work (Capella, 2005). Transactional leaders are defined as leaders who motivate followers to complete goals by clearly identifying roles and setting vision (Capella, 2005). In a study by Hambley, O'Neill and Kline (2007) to determine virtual team leadership behaviors, the results were divided into five major behaviors closely related to transactional leadership characteristics: (1) ability to provide role and expectation clarity and good communications, (2) working along with the team; (3) relationship building skills; (4) effective team meetings; and (5) strong project management. Many of the e-leadership behaviors identified in the Hambley, O'Neill and Kline study (2007) can be linked to the transformational and transactional leadership styles. They found that leaders setting goals for virtual teams reflected the transformational style motivational skills. Providing role and expectation clarity for virtual teams reflected the contingent reward factor of transactional style leadership.

Leadership through Empowerment

Effective leadership through empowerment involves self-management within virtual teams. Bell and Kozlowski (2002) report that virtual leaders need to implement a system that will allow virtual project team members to self-manage. Self-managed work teams are defined as teams that "take on many of the responsibilities of their former supervisors" (Capella, 2005, p.234). It is important for virtual team leaders to distribute leadership functions to the team itself, making it self-managing (Bell & Kozlowski, 2002). Bell and Kozlowski suggest that many virtual teams are composed of individuals who already have virtual team experience and expertise in their area of work. Leadership roles can be shared by team members who are not co-located (Pearce & Conger, 2002). Similar to empowerment, the leader-participation theory "provides a set of rules to determine the form and amount of participative decision making in different situations" (Capella, 2005, p. 309) and could be applied to e-leadership. However, a truly empowered leadership style will free the virtual team from organizational constraints and encourage proactive action and accountability (Hersey, Blanchard, & Johnson, 2001).

Situational Leadership Styles

The situational school of leadership models assume that effective leaders can develop and adopt certain styles or behaviors. Tannebaum and Schmidt (1958) presented a framework to help explain an effective leader in their continuum of leadership behavior. Their theory analyzed the different patterns of leadership behavior and how this range of behaviors determined the type of leadership, leadership pattern, and effect on short- and long-range objectives. Blake and Mou-

ton (1964) proposed a behavioral management theory that suggested that many behaviors and motivations affected leadership. They established five key managerial styles: do nothing, country club, task/production, mundane/middle of the road, and team. However, Blake and Mouton's main limitation was that their model assumed that there is one consistently sound style of leadership across all situations. Hersey and Blanchard (1969) contributed to the emerging situational school of leadership, proposing that effective leaders adopt certain styles or behaviors to be successful. Hersey and Blanchard proposed a life-cycle theory of leadership suggesting that leadership could be adjusted to the maturity of the subordinate. They used multiple dimensions - task/production oriented and people-oriented – and the variable "maturity" scaled from most mature to most immature. Building on existing research, they developed a situational style leadership model (telling, selling, participating, delegating) dependent upon workers' maturity.

Contingency School of Leadership

The contingency school of leadership models further developed situational leadership ideas to encourage matching the leadership style to the activity or work. In Fiedler's (1967) seminal book, he identified three major variables – leadership trust, clarity of task, and leadership power/authority – that match the style to the situation. Fiedler identifies two basic styles of leadership – task oriented and relationship-oriented (participative). He suggests that by using a least-preferred coworker scale, workers can be assigned to task oriented or participative leaders to achieve maximum effectiveness. Fiedler re-conceptualized existing leadership studies, theories and research to determine that task oriented leaders perform best in situations that are very favorable or very unfavorable to the leader and that relationship-oriented leaders perform best in situations that are intermediate in favorableness. His significant contribution to leadership theory was his focus on situational variables as moderating influences.

House (1971) presents a path-goal theory based upon motivation theory. House's leadership effectiveness theory, part of the contingency school, suggests that the leader influences (motivates) the team to find the path to their goals by using an appropriate leadership behavior (directive, supportive, participative and achievement-oriented). The leader adapts leadership behaviors to environmental factors (such as task structure, authority system, and work team) and subordinate factors (locus of control, experience, ability) resulting in more effective and satisfying team performance. House's theory suggests that the leaders diagnose the situation before attempting a leadership intervention. During the 1970s, Hersey and Blanchard (1974) developed a contingency theory that suggested a situational leadership style where the leader is flexible in what type of leadership behavior is used dependent upon the needs of the team.

The common thread for these approaches is that the leader should be flexible and be able to adapt and apply the appropriate leadership style as necessary. Later, Vroom (2003) suggested a contingency theory model that relates leadership style to the task at hand or situation. The Vroom Decision Tree Approach (Vroom, 2000) prescribes leadership styles appropriate for the situation. It uses five leadership styles that are dependent upon the subordinate participation to determine the degrees of being autocratic, consultative, or group oriented when making leadership decisions. Situations shape how leaders behave and influence the consequences of leader behavior (Vroom & Jago, 2007).

Project Management Leadership Research

The seminal contributions of these scholars shaped subsequent research for leadership theory for work teams and project teams. In the body of knowledge for project management leadership, these theories identify leadership styles for traditional project management. Determining whether different leadership styles are appropriate at different stages of the project life cycle and with different team structures has been explored and research conducted in the project management context, with the general conclusion that leadership styles theory can be appropriately applied to project management leadership. Applying these theories and research, then, to virtual project management could be the next step in exploring how leadership styles for virtual project teams are different than traditional leadership styles and traditional project management leadership.

Traditional Project Management Research

Slevin and Pinto (1991) challenged the complexity and often-contradictory research on leadership and the perception that the process of project leadership is confusing. They attempted to describe a cognitive approach to leadership to help project managers consciously select the correct leadership style. They proposed a two-dimensional leadership model (information input and decision authority) on which leadership style can be plotted using percentile scores that it is practical, simple and recognizes three main leadership decision styles (participative, delegation, and pressured). Shenhar's (1998) research also explored a two-dimensional model for management and determined differences in management style based upon a classification system of project type. Results indicated that fit between project leadership style and type of project are important to the success of the project. Turner and Muller's (2006) study attempted to develop guidelines on selecting the appropriate project manager for projects dependent upon leadership style. They found that leadership style was positively correlated with project success and that different combinations of leadership competencies were positively correlated with project success.

Virtual Project Management Research

Lee-Kelley (2002) suggested in her study of virtual project teams that Fielder's (1967) identification of the key situational variables influence a leader's style, and her study included Fiedler's leadership instrument and least preferred co-worker (LPC) scale. The theory that a manager's ability to control and influence the team or situation impacts his or her management style was confirmed by the study, as was Fiedler's proposal that task-motivated managers perform best when situational control is high as well as in situations where control is low. Konradt & Hoch's (2007) work is important in establishing virtual managers' perceptions of roles. They also questioned if men used more directive leadership styles (indicating a control-related leadership role) than women leaders to manage virtual teams. Hambley, O'Neill and Kline (2007) explored virtual team leadership behaviors in six different experimental conditions and connected virtual team leadership to transformational and transactional leadership styles.

APPLICATION OF THEORETICAL CONCEPTS FOR LEADERSHIP STYLES TO VIRTUAL PROJECT MANAGEMENT

Application of Control-Related Leadership

Konradt and Hoch (2007) research results showed that control-related leadership roles correlated to virtual team success and performance, A field study of two large companies in Germany by Hertel, Konradt, and Orlikowski (2004) showed that effective virtual team management practices included setting clear goals, tasks, and outcome interdependencies. They found that the higher the quality of goal setting processes and task interdependence, the more effective the virtual team. Hertel, Konradt, and Orlikowski suggest that e-leaders focus on high quality goal setting, high task interdependence and use team-based rewards to produce the best results from virtual teams. Hooijberg and Choi (2000) found that the goal achievement role, (attainment of goals, setting clear goals, and coordinating work) had a strong relationship with the perception of leadership effectiveness. Lee-Kelley's (2002) study indicates that the task-motivated leadership style for shorter projects would appear to be effective. Implications for the organization are the need to know the tenure of their projects and ensure that the project leaders' styles are appropriately matched to the term of the projects.

Application of Transformational and Transactional Leadership Styles

Motivation can be enhanced by providing challenges, recognition, and rewarding responsibility and creativity (Project Management Institute, 2001). Communicating the vision can be achieved through a well-developed project charter, developing emotional buy-in and ownership of the vision within the team, and using the vision to guide and direct the work (Kliem, 2004). Inspiring followers to work and motivating followers to complete goals by clearly identifying roles and setting vision are skills that can be learned. Training on transformational and transactional leadership skills and when each style is appropriate can provide an opportunity to apply these skills in real work situations. Hambley, O'Neill and Kline (2007) suggest developing training programs for virtual leaders and virtual project team members to increase team performance. Leaders can be taught skills (Capella, 2005) and learn the leadership techniques that can be most effective in virtual team management.

Application of Leadership Through Empowerment

Bell and Kozlowski (2002) suggest that virtual team leaders need to be proactive in providing clear direction and specific goals to encourage each team member to monitor their own performance and self-regulate their work to be successful. To do this, they suggest the leader develop rules, guidelines and habitual routines for the team. Self-managing teams, usually 10-15 people, usually report higher levels of job satisfaction (Capella, 2005), but the team norms and organizational culture can be influences on the success for teams that self-manage. It is often necessary for a virtual leader to provide motivational incentives, set objectives and mission, and develop an appropriate climate or tone for the virtual team (Bell & Kozlowski, 2002). Day (1999) suggests that empowerment is dependent upon a company cultural attitude that includes education about the organization and what is really happening in the organization, operational consistency, a proven process, loyalty, and trust. Increasing these company cultural behaviors may increase the success of leadership through empowerment. Wickham and Walther (2007) imply that the emergence of more than one leader may be the result of the situation or environment of the virtual team, and project managers must recognize this fact.

Application of Situational and Contingency Leadership Styles

The situational leadership style assumes that effective leaders can develop and adopt certain styles or behaviors dependent upon the needs of the project and team, analogous to the contingency school of leadership that emphasizes matching leadership style to the leadership situation. Tannebaum and Schmidt's (1958) situational leadership theory would provide the opportunity for the project manager to analyze the different patterns of leadership behavior, and how this range of

behaviors could determine the type of leadership needed to affect short- and long-range objectives. Determining the degree of authority used by the project manager and the degree of freedom experienced by the virtual team members, the continuum could help determine the behaviors needed. Hersey and Blanchard's (1969) life-cycle theory of leadership would assist the project manager in adjusting to the maturity of the team member, and become more flexible in what type of leadership behavior is needed dependent upon the needs of the individual. Adopting this model would help control any loss of mature, experienced virtual team members from the team.

The Vroom Decision Tree Approach (Vroom, 2000) could help the project manager understand the team members' level of participation to determine the degree of autocratic, consultative, or group oriented leadership necessary. An overview of this theory would be valuable to the project manager in understanding the relationship between the need for participation and the need for leadership with both the on-site and virtual team members and assist in balancing the team relationships and work. Slevin and Pinto's (1991) model plots four extremes of leadership style with the level of participation by project team members and could be used as a day-to-day working framework for project managers. Turner and Muller (2006) conclude that the project manager's leadership style and competencies contribute to project success and make suggestions for appointment and deployment of project managers based upon their findings.

Moving toward Multiple E-Leadership Styles

Benefits of Multiple Leadership Styles in Virtual Projects

By understanding control-related leadership roles (Konradt & Hoch, 2007), using transformational and transactional leadership styles

Table 1. Effective leadership concepts for virtual teams

Leadership Concept	Description	Application
Control-related	Leads by tasks Motivates Provides role clarity Sets clear goals and priorities Gives good directions	Use a high quality goal setting processes Encourage task inter-dependence Lead by task for shorter projects
Transformational	Inspires followers to work	Clearly identify roles Set the project vision
Transactional	Motivates followers to complete goals Clearly identifies roles Reinforces the vision	Use a well-developed project charter Develop emotional buy-in and ownership of the vision Use the vision to guide and direct the work
Empowerment	Leads self-managed work teams Distributes leadership functions	Develop rules, guidelines and habitual routines Provide motivational incentives Set strong objectives and mission Develop an appropriate climate or tone
Situational	Adopts certain styles or behaviors Adjusts to the maturity of the subordinate	Be skilled in multiple leadership styles Adopt the appropriate style dependent upon the experience and needs of the team member
Contingency	Matches leadership style to the activity/work Assigns workers to task oriented or participative leaders Adapts to environmental factors Leads dependent upon the needs of the team	Be trained on multiple leadership styles Remain flexible Adapt and apply the appropriate leadership style as necessary

(Hambley, O'Neill, & Kline, 2007), empowering virtual project teams to self-manage (Bell & Kozlowski, 2002), and incorporating situational and contingency leadership styles, those managing virtual teams will be able to offer benefits to the organization by providing positive, successful leadership, resulting in better project deliverables (see Table 1).

Virtual project management has become increasingly important and a necessity as the trend in virtual work teams continues. Leadership styles for managing virtual project teams are different from leadership roles for managing traditional, co-located teams. Understanding emerging e-leadership styles for virtual project teams and their application is an important part of our evolving virtual organizational behavior.

FUTURE RESEARCH DIRECTIONS

The literature reviewed may provide scholar-practitioners research topics related to the relationship between leadership orientation and adaptability for virtual project managers. Shenhar (1998) indicates that more research is needed to explore the role of contingencies in project management. Lee-Kelley and Loong (2003) recommend that there needs to be more evidence that the project manager can change leadership styles in response to altered circumstances.

Little research has been done to determine if situational and contingency theories of leadership can be applied to e-leadership of virtual project teams. The goal of future quantitative or qualitative research could be to determine if situational and contingency leadership style theories are applicable and increase the effectiveness of virtual project manager leadership. How leadership functions in virtual project teams evolve throughout the project and the best way(s) the project manager can adapt to these changes to lead the team to a successful deliverable - on time, in scope, with quality, and on budget – is vital to the future of e-leadership.

CONCLUSION

This paper provides a review that could be used as a starting point for defining successful management styles for virtual project team leaders. For each style, there are leadership skills that managers can use to ensure success. As we move toward virtual organizations, we need to understand more clearly leadership roles in the virtual environment.

The general conclusion, also supported by Turner & Muller (2005), is that multiple leadership styles can be appropriately applied to project management leadership. Applying these theories and research to virtual project management provides an improved approach for managing human resources. The application to human resource management is that this flexibility in leadership style can provide the key to profitable project work, satisfied team members, and continued organizational growth through successful virtual project deliverables.

REFERENCES

Ariss, S., Nykodym, N., & Cole-Laramore, A. A. (2002). Trust and technology in the virtual organization. *S.A.M. Advanced Management Journal*, *67*(4), 22–25.

Bell, B. S., & Kozlowski, S. W. (2002). A typology of virtual teams: Implications for effective leadership. *Group & Organization Management*, *27*(1), 14–49. doi:10.1177/1059601102027001003

Blake, R. R., & Mouton, J. S. (1964). *The managerial grid*. Houston, TX: Gulf Publishing Company.

Capella University. (2005). *Managing and organizing people*. Boston: Prentice Hall Custom Publishing.

Day, J. (1999). Getting the edge: The attitude of ownership. *Super Vision*, *60*(6), 3–6.

Duarte, D., & Snyder, N. (1999). *Mastering virtual teams*. San Francisco: Jossey-Bass.

Fiedler, F. E. (1967). *A theory of leadership effectiveness*. New York: McGraw Hill.

Goman, C. K. (2004). *This isn't the company I joined: How to lead in business turned upside down*. Berkley, CA: KCS Publishing.

Hambley, L., O'Neill, T., & Kline, T. (2007). Virtual team leadership: Perspectives from the field. *International Journal of e-Collaboration*, *3*(1), 40–63.

Hersey, P., & Blanchard, K. (1969). Life cycle theory of leadership. *Training and Development Journal*, *23*(5), 26–34.

Hersey, P., & Blanchard, K. (1974). So you want to know your leadership style? *Training and Development Journal*, *28*(2), 22–37.

Hersey, P., Blanchard, K., & Johnson, D. (2001). *Management of organizational behavior: Leading human resources*. Upper Saddle River, NJ: Prentice Hall.

Hertel, G., Konradt, U., & Orlikowski, B. (2004). Managing distance by interdependence: Goal setting, task interdependence and teambased rewards in virtual teams. *European Journal of Work and Organizational Psychology*, *13*(1), 1–28. doi:10.1080/13594320344000228

Hooijberg, R., & Choi, J. (2000). Which leadership roles matter to whom? An examination of rater effects on perceptions of effectiveness. *The Leadership Quarterly*, *11*(3), 341–364. doi:10.1016/S1048-9843(00)00044-8

House, R. J. (1971). A path-goal theory of leader effectiveness. *Administrative Science Quarterly, 16*(3), 321–339. doi:10.2307/2391905

Kliem, R. L. (2004). *Leading high performance projects*. Boca Raton, FL: J. Ross Publishing.

Konradt, U., & Hoch, J. E. (2007). A work roles and leadership functions of managers in virtual teams. *International Journal of e-Collaboration, 3*(2), 16–34.

Lee, M. R. (2009). E-ethical leadership for virtual project teams. *International Journal of Project Management, 27*(5), 456–463. doi:10.1016/j.ijproman.2008.05.012

Lee-Kelley, L. (2002). Situational leadership: Managing the virtual project team. *Journal of Management Development, 21*(5/6), 461–476. doi:10.1108/02621710210430623

Lee-Kelley, L., & Loong, K. L. (2003). Turner's five functions of project-based management and situational leadership in IT services projects. *International Journal of Project Management, 21*(8), 583–591. doi:10.1016/S0263-7863(02)00100-X

Martins, L. L., Gilson, L. L., & Maynard, M. T. (2004). Virtual teams: What do we know and where do we go from here? *Journal of Management, 30*(6), 805–835. doi:10.1016/j.jm.2004.05.002

Pearce, C., & Conger, J. (2002). *Shared leadership: Reframing the hows and whys of leadership*. Thousand Oaks, CA: Sage Publications.

Project Management Institute. (2001). *People in projects*. Newton Square, PA: Project Management Institute.

Shenhar, A. (1998). From theory to practice: Toward a typology of project-management styles. *IEEE Transactions on Engineering Management, 45*(1), 33–48. doi:10.1109/17.658659

Slevin, D. P., & Pinto, J. K. (1991). Project leadership: Understanding and consciously choosing your style. *Project Management Journal, 12*(1), 39–47.

Tannebaum, R., & Schmidt, W. H. (1958). How to choose a leadership pattern. *Harvard Business Review, 36*(2), 95–101.

Turner, J. R., & Muller, R. (2005). The project manager's leadership style as a success factor on projects: A literature review. *Project Management Journal, 36*(2), 49–61.

Turner, J. R., & Muller, R. (2006). *Choosing appropriate project managers: Matching their leadership styles to the type of project*. Newton Square, PA: Project Management Institute.

Vroom, V. (2000). Leadership and the decision-making process. *Organizational Dynamics, 28*(4), 82–94. doi:10.1016/S0090-2616(00)00003-6

Vroom, V. (2003). Educating managers for decision making and leadership. *Management Decision, 41*(10), 968–978. doi:10.1108/00251740310509490

Vroom, V. H., & Jago, A. G. (2007). The role of the situation in leadership. *The American Psychologist, 62*(1), 17–24. doi:10.1037/0003-066X.62.1.17

Wickham, K. R., & Walther, J. B. (2007). Perceived behaviors of emergent and assigned leaders in virtual groups. *International Journal of e-Collaboration, 3*(1), 1–17.

KEY TERMS AND DEFINITIONS

Contingency Style Leadership: Leading by matching the leadership style to the situation

Control-Related Leadership: Leading motivating, providing role clarity, setting clear goals and priorities, and by giving good directions to complete tasks

E-Leadership: The term e-leadership describes leadership in today's non-traditional virtual business environment.

Empowerment Leadership: Leading by allowing self-managed work teams to take on the responsibilities of traditional management

Situational Leadership: Leading by developing and adopting different styles or behaviors as necessary

Transactional Leadership: Leading by motivating followers to complete goals by clearly identifying roles and setting vision

Transformational Leadership: Leading by inspiring followers to work

Virtual Team: Virtual teams are groups of skilled individuals collaborating from geographically distant locations and linked by technology that communicate electronically to achieve the goals of a project or work together on solving problems.

Chapter 45
On-Line Credit Card Payment Processing and Fraud Prevention for E-Business

James G. Williams
University of Pittsburgh, USA

Wichian Premchaiswadi
Siam University, Thailand

ABSTRACT

As the volume of purchases for products and services on the Internet has increased and the chosen method of payment is a credit or debit card, e-commerce merchants must be capable of accepting such payment methods. Unfortunately, cyber-criminals have found ways to steal personal information found on credit cards and debit cards and fraudulently use this information to purchase products and services which costs merchants lost revenue and fees for chargebacks. This article discusses the process by which credit card payments are processed beginning with the e-commerce merchant's web site to a credit card processor or service gateway to the credit card company's network to the issuing bank's network with an accept or decline response being returned to the merchant's shopping cart system via the same networks. The article addresses the issue of credit card fraud in terms of how the cyber-criminals function and the potential solutions used to deter these attempts by the cybercriminals. A list of preventive measures that should be used by e-commerce merchants is provided.

INTRODUCTION

Consumers in the United States spend nearly 1 trillion dollars each year using a credit card over the internet (Woolsey and Schulz, 2009). Accepting credit cards is essential for any e-commerce Web site. Processing credit cards over the Internet is one of the fastest growing segments of business transactions today. This type of transaction or "card-not-present" transaction requires a special type of merchant account. In the early days of credit card usage, to accept credit cards, a merchant needed a merchant account through a bank. But today there are a number of services, generally referred to as credit card processors or merchant account services, which will permit a merchant to accept credit card payments online without their own merchant account. There are actually three different methods for

DOI: 10.4018/978-1-61520-611-7.ch045

processing credit card payments using a merchant account service. These are:

1. **Real-Time Processing:** Real-time processing allows e-commerce merchants to link their e-commerce shopping cart with a gateway merchant service which will automatically process credit card payments.
2. **Virtual Terminal (Online Interface):** An e-commerce merchant can also process credit card transactions, manually, 24 hours a day by logging in online and submitting a secure form through a merchant account interface. A merchant can use this to process credit card payments while taking the customer's information over the phone if the merchant is able to access the Internet at high speed while talking to the customer.
3. **Automated Recurring Billing (ARB):** Some e-commerce merchant services need to charge customers on a monthly or account threshold basis. Some merchant account services allow the merchant to set the time interval or account threshold level and some services allow a merchant to upload multiple subscriptions using a batch file like Microsoft Excel.

PayPal is generally accepted as the most widely used online merchant account service with more than 150 million users across the world. VeriSign operates a competing service called Payflow that is typically used by merchants with a high volume of transactions each month. Although the number of merchant account service providers continues to increase, some of the more popular one are listed below (TopTenReviews, 2009):

- Flagship Merchant Services
- Gomerchant Merchant Accounts
- Merchant Accounts Express
- MerchantWarehouse
- Electronic Transfer Inc.
- E-Commerce Exchange

- NorthAmericanBancard
- Total Merchant Services
- Charge
- Merchant Credit Card
- Free AuthNet
- Merchant Credit Card

Companies that sell merchandise and services over the Internet are referred to as e-tailers or e-commerce merchants. These credit card processing services make it easy for e-tailers to start accepting credit cards for purchases of their products and services.

BACKGROUND

Who are the Participants in On-Line Credit Card Purchases?

Consumers and Merchants

The consumer is an individual or organization that has the intent of making a purchase. They have money or credit and they desire goods and services. The merchant is the one with the goods and services and is looking to sell them to consumers. Consumers are motivated to select a particular merchant by things such as price, service, selection or preference. But the merchant's primary motivation is to make money by selling the goods or services for more money than they paid for them. This money between what they bought it for and what they sold it for is called their margin. There are several different methods to exchange money for products and services such as bartering, cash, checks, debit cards, installment payments or credit cards. When credit cards are used, the consumer and the merchant both have banks that they are working with that process the credit card payment transactions.

Issuing Bank

Consumers get their credit cards from a bank or credit union, called the "issuing bank." Sometimes an issuing bank is simply called an "issuer." An issuing bank may not just be associated with major credit card brands such as American Express, MasterCard and Visa, but also with credit cards called "private label credit cards." These are the ones that department stores or shops offer, such as Sears and Target credit cards. Issuing banks are lending institutions that support these credit cards by granting and managing extended credit. Some examples of these are Bank of America, Citibank, MBNA, Household Financial, GE and Wells Fargo. The purpose of the issuing bank is to grant credit directly to a consumer. They, typically, have a consumer fill out an application, check the applicant's credit history and maintain their account. The issuing bank is the one that decides what a consumer's credit limit is, based on credit history and current debt load. There are thousands of issuing banks in the United States. In Canada and the United Kingdom as well as most other countries in the world there are far fewer banks, so the number of issuing banks is much smaller. Issuing banks make money on the interest the consumer pays on outstanding balances from previous purchases, and they get a portion of every purchase a consumer makes with the credit card from a merchant.

Acquiring Bank

The acquiring bank represents the e-commerce merchant. The acquiring bank processes all of the merchant's credit card payments with the associations (American Express, MasterCard, Visa, etc.), and provide the merchant with reconciliation data and other financial tools. The acquiring bank also makes money on every transaction a merchant processes. There are many acquiring banks in the United States and abroad, and merchants are free to move from one acquirer to another. Merchants typically select their acquiring bank based on the amount of money, called basis points, they charge per transaction.

Payment Processors and Gateway Services

In theory, e-commerce merchants can connect directly to their acquiring bank, but there are a number of reasons why they may not want, or be able, to do so. There are technical and business requirements for conducting the payment process for credit cards and most merchants don't want to deal with these requirements. As an alternative, they use a third party to process credit card payments for them and their acquiring bank. These third parties are called credit card payment processors and gateway services. Credit card payment processors offer the physical infrastructure for the merchant to communicate with the acquiring banks and the credit card associations. They connect all the credit card payment participants together. This permits even very small banks to offer merchant services that they could not provide otherwise. Credit card payment processors make their money by charging a flat transaction fee or by charging basis points to the e-commerce merchant. Some credit card payment processors also provide acquiring bank services directly to the merchant.

Gateway services provide merchants physical infrastructure as well. They generally offer technology and integration services among all the participants. The gateway service providers charge the merchant a transaction fee or basis points for their services. These fees are in addition to the credit card payment processor fees the merchant is already paying. If a merchant decides to use a gateway service provider they have to set up accounts with an acquirer. The acquirer can be an acquiring bank or a credit card payment processor that offers acquiring bank services.

Credit Card Associations

The credit card associations such as Visa, Master-Card International, American Express, Discover, etc. are responsible for establishing the procedures and policies for how credit card transactions, services and disputes are handled. They are bound by national banking laws and provide the money that covers some of the fraud that occurs within their membership. Each of the credit card associations operate somewhat differently and even within the same association they may operate differently in different parts of the world.

For example, Visa has regions that operate somewhat autonomously. There is Visa U.S.A., Visa Europe, Visa Asia, etc. Each of these regions has slightly different rules, tools and services. Visa does not actually issue credit cards to consumers; they use issuing banks to issue credit cards that are branded as "Visa." MasterCard International is somewhat different from Visa in that there is one association for the entire world with all regions using the same basic structure, policies, and management procedures. MasterCard International also uses issuing banks to issue credit cards to consumers that are branded as "MasterCard." American Express differs by acting as the issuer for all American Express branded credit cards. American Express is one global organization with regional coverage. American Express also differs from Visa and MasterCard in permitting merchants to set up direct connections for performing the acquiring functions. Each of these credit card associations has their own network of systems, policies for use and payment processing. Each of these associations also develops fraud-prevention tools and attempt to get merchants to utilize them.

HOW THE ON-LINE CREDIT CARD PAYMENT PROCESS WORKS

When a merchant makes a sale over the internet; the card number, the amount of the sale, and the merchant identification (ID) are transmitted from the merchant's establishment or the internet Web site over the credit card processor's computer network. The credit card processor can either be a bank or a merchant account service company called a credit card processor that does nothing but provide credit card processing services as discussed above (Quick Start GA Dept. of Technical and Adult Education, 1996).

From the credit card processor's network the transaction is transmitted to the credit card company's computer network. If the customer is using MasterCard, for example, the transaction will go to MasterCard's computer network. Then, the electronic transaction is sent to the bank that issued the credit card to the customer. The bank's computer system checks the account and verifies that the customer has adequate credit to cover the purchase. The bank's computer system then sends the merchant an authorization over these same networks. Although the sale is complete, the transaction is not complete since no actual money has been exchanged.

At the end of the business day the merchant account service (credit card processor) sends that day's charges to the credit card network, e.g. MasterCard, for processing. The transactions are transmitted via the merchant's credit card processor service to the credit card network, e.g. MasterCard. Individual transactions are then extracted and sent back to the individual cardholders' banks. The issuing banks then debit the cardholders' accounts and make appropriate payments to the merchant's credit card processor through the Federal Reserve Bank's Automated Clearing House.

The credit card processor then credits the merchant's bank account for the transaction amount, minus its fees for the transaction. Those fees are also used for paying transaction fees to the issuing bank and the credit card network. Despite the use of computers, it can take two business days before the merchant's account is credited (Bank of America, 2009).

Opening a Merchant Account

In order to accept credit cards, a merchant can open a merchant account with a bank. However, many banks have gotten out of the credit card processing business, and those that remain are often reluctant to service small businesses, particularly ones with limited operating histories. Many small businesses must therefore go through a specialized credit card processor or an independent sales organization, commonly referred to as an "ISO." Whether a merchant uses a bans, ISO or a credit card processor, they need a merchant account before they can accept credit card payments.

An ISO or an Independent Sales Organization is an entity that acts more or less as a middle man, helping formulate a Bank or Bank/Credit Card Processor alliance. Within such an arrangement, an ISO has an agreement to sell the services of the Bank or Bank/Credit Card Processor alliance, and is allowed to mark up the Fees and sign up merchants. ISOs are also known as Member Service Providers (MSP). ISOs solicit new merchant relationships for a specific bank. Most merchants buy their processing services from an ISO and the ISOs buy their processing services from a backend credit card processor. However, depending on the situation there can be significant differences between the responsibilities of the ISO and the backend processor. Each ISO is classified depending on how much of the responsibility they take for covering risk:

Tier I - ISO: Also known as a Super ISO, Wholesale ISO, Full Liability ISO, and a Full Service ISO, a Tier I - ISO always does their own underwriting and risk-assessment and assumes full chargeback liability for their merchants and provide full technical support.

Tier II - ISO: These are shared liability ISOs. Usually, they do not do their own underwriting, or require underwriting approval from the ISO or credit card processor with which they are contracted. They provide technical support capabilities and they also have the support from the ISO or credit card processor with which they are contracted. They are referred to as a shared-risk ISO because they usually are responsible for a portion of the chargeback risk of their merchants.

Tier III - ISO: These are usually comprised of a few salespeople with no technical support to provide to their merchants, Tier III - ISOs also do take any responsibility for any chargeback risk. Since they do not assume any chargeback risk, they are subject to the underwriting guidelines of the ISO or credit card processor with which they have contracted

Although businesses can contact credit card processors directly for a merchant account, banks unable or unwilling to process credit card transactions often refer customers to an ISO to help them find a credit card processor and get the necessary equipment and training to begin accepting credit cards

Typical Information Required for a Merchant Account

Getting the required information together before applying for a merchant account can save time during the application process. Although different merchant account providers have different requirements typically what follows are required in order to obtain a merchant account:

1. Business checking account (some providers will create one for the merchant)
2. A copy of a voided check (if merchants use their own business checking account for funds to be deposited in)
3. A copy of the company's Articles of incorporation, business license or reseller license. (A 'Certificate of Assumed Name' from the county's Register of Deeds office may be all that is required and are relatively inexpensive, e.g. under $10.00) The purpose of this is to prove the applicant is a legitimate business.

4. Pictures of business office and location (this may save the merchant money in credit card processing costs)
5. Have a web site and URL (for real-time processing)
6. Photocopy of the merchant's return policy
7. Provide business references
8. Photocopy of recent tax returns (depends on monthly sales volume expected through the merchant account)
9. Site inspection (pictures of your inventory). Only a few providers require this.
10. A photocopy of the applicant's drivers license (Secondary verification of ID)

TECHNOLOGY REQUIREMENTS FOR PROCESSING CREDIT CARDS ON WEB SITES

The following are considered to be the technology requirements and best practices for e-commerce Web Sites that accept credit card payments (Authorize.com, 2009).

Create a Secure Payment Web Site. This is needed to protect credit card data and other sensitive information from hackers during the credit card transaction process. Identity theft and credit card fraud are occurring more frequently on the Internet, and merchants must ensure that their customers are protected from internet criminals. Many consumers will not buy from a site that does not provide secure transactions. Merchants can help secure their site by having a secure socket layer certificate, or SSL. SSL encrypts information being entered on the merchant site as it is sent across the Internet. Merchants can purchase their own SSL certificate, or the merchant's Web host may allow a merchant to use their SSL certificate as a part of its service.

Utilize a compatible shopping cart application. This is required to make sure the merchant's shopping cart application can communicate with the merchant's credit card payment-processing gateway. There are several different types of credit card payment gateways, and each has a set of standards that must be followed. Many of the free shopping cart application software packages do not support all of the available credit card payment gateways. A merchant should check with their merchant account provider or their shopping cart documentation to make sure that all the components will work together. Shopping cart applications fall into two basic categories namely: Local shopping carts that merchants can install on their own Web servers, and third-party shopping carts that run on a provider's site. If a merchant decides to install his own shopping cart software, he will have a variety of software packages from which to choose. Three of the more popular ones are Miva Merchant, OSCommerce, and Agoracart.

Miva Merchant is a shopping cart that many Web hosting companies include with their hosting packages. If a merchant's host doesn't offer it, the merchant will be required to pay a licensing fee before the package can be installed. Miva offers a variety of different options for small businesses, and the application is considered highly user-friendly.

OSCommerce is a free, open source shopping cart program that contains many features and a reputable development community. It is considered relatively easy to install and customize. Because OSCommerce is open source, support and improvements are readily available.

Agoracart is a simple, free, and basic functionality shopping cart application. If a merchant doesn't require a lot of features, this is a useful package to be utilized on a merchant's shopping cart site.

If a merchant would rather not install shopping cart software on his own web site, there are a number of third-party options available. When a merchant utilizes third-party shopping cart software, the merchant must place a link on his web site to the third party's web site where the application exists. This link takes customers to the merchant's offsite shopping cart software. Microsoft's BCentral is one of the more popular third-party shopping cart software. Yahoo! offers a similar third-party shopping cart software package. Storefront.net and 1shoppingcart.com both offer services that include shopping carts as well as advanced tools like email list management, affiliate program integration, etc.

Provide E-mail Message Encryptions. If a merchant plans on accepting orders and sending or receiving credit card information via email, the merchant will need to encrypt the information that is transmitted. PGP, which stands for "Pretty Good Privacy," is the most common form of email encryption. PGP encrypts an email when it is sent and decrypts the email when it has reached the intended recipient. If e-commerce merchants plan to use PGP, they will also need to make sure that their email clients support it. Merchants must keep the PGP security key in a location where it cannot be accessed by others.

Utilize a Firewall. If a merchant stores customer credit card numbers or other personal information on his server, it is necessary to have a site-wide firewall to protect this information. Many merchants expose their customers to hackers by neglecting to implement a proper firewall.

Use Anti-Virus Software and Update it Frequently. Anti-virus software will prevent most of the hacker's attempts to invade the merchant's Web site and steal personal information such as credit card numbers. This software should be updated on a regular basis.

Regularly Download and Install Security Updates. Software performance and security can be optimized by installing all service and security updates when they become available.

After merchants have implemented these basic technology requirements, they are ready to offer their customers an easy way to purchase their merchandise or services. Merchants can also give their customers comfort in knowing that they are providing a safe and secure environment for making credit card payments and providing other personal information.

HOW CREDIT CARDS PAYMENTS ARE ACCEPTED AND PROCESSED ONLINE

If most of a merchant's business is conducted on the Internet, Real-Time processing is the appropriate solution. When a customer who is using a merchant's Web site is finished shopping and is ready to pay, typically the customer simply clicks on a "Check Out" button which is a link to a secure page where customers type in their credit card information. After a few seconds, a message will then appear showing whether the credit card has been accept or declined. Two days later the money will be transferred into the merchant's business checking account. Real-Time credit card processor or merchant account service providers will have an online database containing all of the credit card transactions for a merchant which makes month-end accounting and balancing simple. Real-Time processing is the best solution for those who plan on having a high volume of daily transactions. Real-Time processing helps to automate the payment acceptance process, unlike in retail establishments where entering credit card information must be done manually. Most Real-Time solutions are coupled with a "Virtual Terminal" that allows a merchant to process Mail Order/Telephone Order (MOTO) orders manually via a web browser from any location that has access to the Internet.

The process a credit card transaction goes through is fairly complicated; however it generally only takes a few seconds. The steps below illustrate how credit card transactions are typically processed using a Real-Time credit card processing service (Smith, 2009; Murdock, 2006).

1. Using the merchant's shopping cart Web interface, customers select "check out" with the items they placed into their shopping cart or selected from an order form on a merchant's Website.

2. Customer then selects "credit card" as their method of payment.

3. The customer's Web browser then connects to the Merchant's website host's secure server, and brings up the secure payment form.

4. Customer enter their credit card information on the secure payment form, and authorize the transaction by clicking a "Complete Order" or "Continue" type of button.

5. The credit card transaction information is transmitted to the Website host's secure server using SSL encryption.

6. The merchant's secure server connects to the merchant's processing bank either via a secure payment gateway (a third party which provides the connection to the processing bank), or directly (some credit card processors have their own proprietary secure payment gateway and therefore do not require a third party to provide this service).

7. The credit card processor service sends the transaction to the credit card association network, such as Visa or MasterCard, directly, and the validity of the card and availability of funds is confirmed.

8. If the credit card transaction is approved, an authorization code is returned to the credit card processor service, or to the Secure Payment Gateway from the credit card association network.

9. The authorization is encrypted by the Payment Gateway or credit card processor and transmitted in encrypted form to the secure Web server of the merchant, which permits fulfillment of the order.

10. The merchant's secure Web server then sends the customer's Web browser a confirmation receipt.

11. The amount due for the credit card transaction is moved from the card holder's bank to the merchant's credit card processing bank. The merchant's credit card processing bank transfers the money to the merchant's local bank within 2 to 3 business days.

Figure 1 illustrates the technological components of a typical credit card processing system.

MINIMIZING INTERNET CREDIT CARD FRAUD

Although there are no verifiable global figures on losses from credit card fraud, an FBI report issued in 2005 indicated that credit cards represented the majority of the total $315 billion U.S. financial fraud loss for that year. A recent European study found that more than 22 million adults were victims of credit card fraud in 2006. Figures from the Banque de France, the country's central bank, showed a credit card fraud loss of $319 million, for 2005 (Conlin, (2007). For US buyers, credit card fraud does not pose a significant problem, as their loss is limited to $50. But, for merchants who shoulder the burden of the losses that is not the situation. Between November 1999 and February 2000, travel site Expedia.com lost 12% to 18% of sales through fraudulent card purchases. Visa and MasterCard claim a fraud rate of 0.08% to 0.09%, and have stated that there is little difference between Internet sales fraud and other type of credit card sales fraud, but they have invoked serious penalties for excessive chargebacks for on-line credit card fraud. When a consumer reports an instance of fraud, the disputed amount is removed from the merchant's account and credited back to the customer. This "chargeback" typically comes with a standard fee of $15 per instance. The Internet Fraud Prevention Advisory Council has established online transaction fraud rates at 2% to 40%, depending upon the product category. At highest risk are downloadable software and

Figure 1. Typical credit card processing system

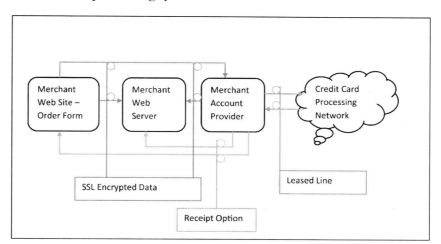

entertainment, and high ticket items such as airline tickets, computers, and diamonds.

Payment gateways in the US have developed sophisticated fraud checking techniques, but it has not halted credit card fraud. To protect themselves, merchants can capture the IP address of purchasers, carefully examine purchases made from free e-mail addresses, those with different shipping and billing addresses, bounced e-mail order confirmations, no-existent telephone numbers, and large middle-of-the-night transactions. Merchants must also be cautious about shipping to Eastern European and other countries with a history of fraudulent transactions and telephone the buyer before shipping high ticket items (Faughnan, 2007).

Sophisticated Security Required to Prevent Credit Card Fraud

Online merchants have been forced to develop sophisticated security protections that far exceed the normal security approval process by the credit card companies (Wilson, 2008). In 2005, an estimated 13.5 percent of U.S. adults (30.2 million consumers) were victims of one or more cases of identity fraud in the previous year. There were an estimated 48.7 million incidents of fraud during this one year period (Woolsey & Schulz, (2009). Currently, credit card companies only verify whether a credit card number is correct and then match the number against the customer's billing address but cyber-criminals can make sure the address is correct and that the addresses match. Cybercrime, in all forms, shows no signs of decreasing in the near future. For example, MSNBC reported that Visa quietly informed select merchants that 485,000 credit card numbers were stolen from a major e-tailer in January 1999 and in 2008 the Bank of America notified thousand of card holders that their MasterCard information had been compromised. E-tailers (Web Merchants) find themselves in a difficult position regarding credit card fraud (MasterCard Worldwide, 2009; Montague, 2004).

Credit Card Fraud Solution Approaches

While there does not appear to be any simple solutions, experts believe that potential cyber-criminals will soon begin to reconsider committing credit card fraud. This type of criminal activity has, for a long time, been considered too small to bother with, but using credit cards fraudulently is quickly becoming "identity theft"; which has been defined as a serious federal felony. Cyber-criminals do leave digital fingerprints and can get caught. There are a number of approaches used by criminals to commit credit card fraud and there are a number of procedures implemented to deter their attempts at credit card fraud. These are discussed below.

Security Codes

An important Internet security feature that now appears on the back of most Visa/MasterCard and Discover cards, and on the front of American Express cards is a security code. This code is generally a three or four-digit number which provides a cryptographic check of the information embossed on the card. The security code helps validate that the customer placing an online order actually has the credit card in his/her possession, and that the credit/debit card account is legitimate. The security code is only printed on the card and it is not contained in the magnetic stripe information nor does it appear on sales receipts or billing statements. The goal is to make certain that the customer must have the card in his/her possession in order to use this code. Since Card Security Codes are not scanned into standard credit card readers, in theory, these numbers are only visible to the customer. When customers give their Card Security Code to merchants, they assist merchants in verifying that the orders being placed are being placed by the credit card holder. Visa, MasterCard, Discover and American Express now require Internet commerce sites to obtain the security code for all cards that have a code printed on them. In order for a credit card transaction to be accepted and processed, this code is required as part of the transaction data.

Unfortunately, the cyber-thieves are also using advanced techniques to ascertain critical information about stolen card numbers. They have developed software that can determine which bank issued a card, harvest the three-digit card verification number and determine the available credit-card limit. They can check a card number's validity and personal information such as address and telephone number about the owner as well.

Credit Card "Skimming"

Criminal gangs recruit individuals who work within restaurants, hotels and retail outlets. The recruits are given battery powered electronic devices known as "skimmers" that read and capture all of the credit or debit cards details in the few seconds that it takes to swipe the card through the credit card reader machine. When customers pay their bill, their card is first swiped through the legitimate credit card machine, but then it is also swiped through the "skimmer" reader. The recruits then pass the "skimmer" machines onto counterfeiters, who pay the recruits for their part in the crime. Once the "skimmer" machines have been given to the counterfeiters, they download the information onto a computer and produce a fake clone of the credit card. The "cloned" card is embossed with the details of the victim's credit card and passed on to gang members who may sell it for between $400 and $700, depending on the perceived credit limit. The buyer then uses the "cloned" credit card to illegally purchase products and services. Skimming is costing credit card users worldwide millions of dollars in phony charges, as stolen clones are sold and used in the United States and elsewhere around the world. Often skimming is done at gas stations or restaurants, since those are the places that hire people who work for minimum wage and are businesses that don't bother with background checks, especially since many employees are part-time workers (Fraud Guides, 2009).

Skimming Prevention

The following are measures merchants can use to avoid credit card fraud by skimmers:

1. Subscribe to stolen credit card checking systems
2. Verify the address
3. Verify the telephone number
4. Call the credit card issuing bank
5. Examine the email address - hotmail and yahoo mail can be easily faked
6. Call the cardholder
7. Be cautious of bulk orders
8. Shipping and billing address should match
9. Single-use credit card numbers
10. Smart Cards

Single Use Credit Card Numbers

Some credit card companies have a new security and privacy offering which utilizes the concept of disposable credit card numbers. With this system, customers can get unique credit card numbers linked to their credit card account each time they make a purchase online. This allows the customer to avoid transmitting their "real" credit card numbers. The single-use numbers don't work for recurring charges but they also don't work for cyber-thieves who try to make multiple purchases. The utilization of single-use credit card numbers can help reduce the risk posed by hackers who steal and reuse numbers

Smart Card Technology for On-Line Purchasing

Newer "smart cards" are embedded with a computer chip containing a digital certificate. A digital certificate consists of basic information about the cardholder's digital identity. It contains elementary personal information such as the cardholder's name, e-mail address and digital signature. The digital signature is nothing more than a series of numbers called a public key which forms the basis of encryption algorithms. Unlike a written signature, a digital signature has two purposes. It authenticates who the cardholder is legally

and it also allows the cardholder's messages to be encrypted.

Because the smart card chips are programmable, "smart chip technology" is flexible, and designed for multiple applications. These cards are inserted into a, typically free, smart card reader plugged into the user's computer. The card, together with a PIN number, allows consumers to buy on the Internet using their digital certificate. The card allows access to an online wallet, which contains information such as shipping and ordering information. This information is automatically transmitted to the merchant's online order forms.

The current problem with digital certificates is a lack of standardization. Almost anyone can establish themselves as a digital certificate issuing authority (CA). Currently, the major players include retail-oriented certificate authorities such as Entrust, VeriSign, Thawte and Cybertrust although there are many others. Consumers are becoming increasingly aware of the role played by digital certificates. Many consumers will only buy from a merchant who displays a digital certificate issued by one of these certificate authorities. Secure communications generally requires five key elements to work correctly, namely: Confidentiality, authorization, authentication, integrity and non-repudiation. Confidentiality and authorization are supplied by encryption systems. The others, namely: authentication, integrity and non-repudiation depend on a digital signature.

Address Verification System (AVS)

E-commerce merchants can utilize an Address Verification System (AVS) for consumers from the United States. An AVS takes the consumer's ZIP code and the numbers in the street address, and compares them with the numbers in the credit card billing address. If they agree, the transaction is authorized; if they do not agree, the transaction is flagged as suspicious or in some cases not allowed, depending upon the merchant's preference. Using AVS lowers the merchant's discount rate, and can protect against stolen credit cards where the thief has the credit card number, but not a correct address.

Telephone Number Authentication

A Telephone authentication service can provide a decrease in the number of fraudulent transactions that pass through an on-line ecommerce web site. Most cyber-criminals are not willing to provide their real telephone number to complete a transaction and many, if asked for a telephone number will simply exit the transaction. There are a number of services that will provide real time telephone number authentication. These services can determine whether a telephone number is real, no longer in service, stolen or a legitimate working number at the address given by the user.

Telephone Verification

Telephone Verification works by automatically calling an online end-user's telephone number at the same time the end-user is making a transaction on a website. The user while on the website answers the phone and is provided a one-time personal identification number (PIN) presented via the web interface; an otherwise anonymous online end-user will be able to confirm that the person who received the phone call and the person who is interacting on the website are the same person. If the consumer, or end user, cannot verify through the phone, they should asked to try again with another phone number. If they cannot pass on the second attempt; assume the consumer or end user is high risk and do not allow the transaction.

Customer Transaction and IP History Databases Checks

Another approach for detecting online fraud is to compare a transaction with previous transactions made for a given credit card number and make sure it fits the pattern of use. There are companies that provide real time checks of credit cards with databases of millions and, in some cases billions, of records to detect anomalies (Wilson, 2008). This type of service will score a credit card transaction based on all the intelligence it has gathered both about the transaction and former purchases. In addition, online fraud detection solutions based on a combination of IP reputation analysis and a mutual collaboration network has proved successful. IP reputation uses geolocation and proxy detection by providing relevant information about the IP's historic behavior, both legitimate and suspicious (MaxMind Inc., 2008).

Intelligent Credit Card Fraud Detection

An intelligent credit card detection system monitors card transactions as they occur by gathering data from the current and previous transactions and uses this data to compute a transaction score for the current transaction. The algorithms used to compute such a score are called classifiers. Typically, high scores for transactions are more likely to be fraudulent than low scores thus transaction scores are compared to a threshold and the score is classified as normal or fraudulent. Credit card fraud detection is a complicated problem involving many input variables such as time, transaction amount, merchant, merchant category code, country, etc) acquired from multiple transactions in a sequence. A classifier computes a fraud score based on a number of these variables.

Two basic approaches have been used in developing classifiers, namely, neural networks and Bayesian decision methods. A neural network is a nonlinear function which takes multiple input variables and computes a score from them. A neural network consists of a series of interconnected neurons similar to the structure of the brain. The interconnections have weights assigned to them and the input neurons (input nodes) to a network represent each continuous variable and every value that a categorical variable can take. Since the weights in a neural network need to be optimized, a learning or training process iteratively passes through a database of card transactions containing both fraudulent and legitimate transactions and systematically adjusts the weights so that the resulting scores discriminates between fraudulent and legitimate transactions.

The Bayesian approach to card fraud detection is based on probability theory. Research has identified a number of characteristics derived from credit card transactions which tend to be predictive of fraud. A Bayesian approach computes the probability distributions for each of these credit card transaction characteristics using a process called evidence integration to compute a fraud probability from the individual characteristic probabilities. Therefore, in a Bayesian approach the classifier consists of credit card transactions characteristics, their probability distributions and an evidence integrator (Alaric Inc., 2008).

REGULATORY & LEGISLATIVE ISSUES

Management of information risk is now tied to regulatory mandates. Since 1999, laws enacted at the federal and state levels have forced companies to be extremely careful in protecting the confidentiality and reliability of medical, financial and other sensitive information stored on their computer systems. Failure to comply with these mandates can lead to civil and criminal penalties, lawsuits and related litigation costs and, of course, damage to reputations.

Although the earlier laws focused on financial and healthcare companies, two of the most recent laws, namely, the 2002 Sarbanes-Oxley Act and the California Data Protection Law (SB 1386), broadened the scope of companies that are required to comply. The Gramm-Leach-Bliley Act (GLB), also known as the Gramm-Leach-Bliley

Financial Services Modernization Act, is an Act of the United States Congress that stipulates that every financial institution must protect the security and confidentiality of its customers' personal information. The Federal Trade Commission in conjunction with several other federal and state agencies along with the Federal Bureau of Investigation (FBI) is the federal agency responsible for enforcement of these laws and mandates (United States Department of Justice, 2009).

FEDERAL TRADE COMMISSION (FTC)

The FTC deals with issues that are related to the economic life of every American citizen and business. It is the only federal agency with both consumer protection and competition jurisdiction across all sectors of the economy including e-commerce. The FTC is charged with law enforcement and protecting consumers' as well as business' interests by sharing its expertise with federal and state legislatures and U.S. and international government agencies; developing policy and research tools through hearings, workshops, and conferences; and creating practical educational programs for consumers and businesses in a global marketplace with constantly changing technologies. The FTC has also been directed to administer a wide variety of other consumer protection laws, including the Telemarketing Sales Rule, the Pay-Per-Call Rule and the Equal Credit Opportunity Act. In 1975, Congress gave the FTC the authority to adopt industry-wide trade regulation rules. The FTC's work is performed by the Bureaus of Consumer Protection, Competition and Economics. That work is aided by the Office of General Counsel and seven regional offices. Credit card fraud is within the FTC's domain of responsibility and this responsibility is shared with the Federal Bureau of Investigation (FBI) (Federal Trade Commission, 2009).

MANAGING INFORMATION RISK

Managing information risk must be integrated with a merchant's overall risk management strategy. The technology infrastructure; including servers, network monitors, and firewalls, needs to be assessed and managed in terms of its relation to people, operations, supply chains and other business drivers. Some of the steps involved with information technology (IT) risk management include paying attention to human factors, putting proper security policies in place, identifying critical assets and fostering better communication and an enterprise-wide perspective among IT managers and risk managers. Bringing together IT, risk management, internal audit, legal and human resources to address information management risk issues produce a consensus to the identification of threats, the areas of operation (ranked in order of most critical and sensitive) that could be affected by a threat, potential financial or reputational loss, and the most cost-effective way to reduce the risk (Stoneburner; Goguen; Feringa; Alexis, 2009).

An Information Risk Assessment

A risk assessment should be performed by any merchant accepting credit card payments and this assessment should examine the following risk factors (Cooney, 2007; Frank, 2004):

- **System Characteristics:** Assess and identify the resources and information that constitute the systems used for financial purposes and identify the business systems jointly with management personnel, IT personnel and users.
- **Threat Identification:** Conduct interviews and utilize work-group sessions with key management team members, technology administrators and system users to uncover potential threat agents that may impact the confidentiality, integrity and availability of information stored in databases and files.
- **Vulnerability Identification:** Conduct a technical assessment to detect vulnerabilities and to assess how effective the controls are for preventing unauthorized access,
- **Control Analysis:** Assess countermeasures regarding items such as firewalls, encryption, web server access policies, password policies, backup and recovery procedures, change-management procedures, currency of software, hardware maintenance and the physical environment.
- **Insurance Gap Analysis:** Assess current insurance policies in terms of coverage for financial loss arising out of unauthorized access or use of confidential information, damage to third-party software or data as well as damage to the business network or databases and files.

The risk assessment can not only help identify the critical areas of risk to be addressed, but can also be used to recommend best practices to remedy the risk. Creating a more secure environment can help produce and maintain consumer confidence and deter financial loss, which could, in turn, give a merchant a competitive edge (United States General Accounting Office- Accounting and Information Management Division, 1988).

CREDIT CARD FRAUD PREVENTIVE STEPS FOR ONLINE BUSINESS OWNERS

When a merchant physically accepts a credit card, and the charge is authorized, and the merchant has conformed to credit card regulation, the merchant will get paid, even if a stolen card is used. But, the liability for fraud shifts from the card issuer to the merchant for 'Card Not Present' sales (Internet sales, mail order, and telephone/fax order). After a credit card processor or registration service approves a credit card transaction, the merchant should perform additional checks, as fraudulent orders are sometimes approved.

The following methods and techniques can be utilized to protect an e-commerce merchant against credit card fraud (Wilson, 2000; Jepson, 2009; Authorize.com, 2009; Federal Trade Commission, 2009). Typically, a combination of methods is the best approach.

- **Follow the procedures** recommended by your credit card processor and the credit card companies.
- **Authorization approval** - make sure you get it from the issuing bank.
- **Address Verification System (AVS)** - AVS is only available for the U.S. and partially available in four European countries to verify the address matches.
- **Card Verification Methods (CVM)** - Security Codes: VISA = CVV2, MasterCard = CVC2, and American Express = CID use a security code of 3 or 4 extra digits.
- **Payer Authentification Programs** - Authentification programs (Verified by Visa and MasterCard's SecureCode) use personal passwords to ensure the identity of the online card user.
- **Real-Time Authorization** - Credit card information is sent to the processor for immediate approval.
- **Bin Check** - The first 6 digits of the credit card are called the Bank Identification Number (BIN).
- **Calling The Card-Issuing Bank** - Call the card-issuing bank, to verify the charge.
- **Different Bill And Ship To Addresses** - Use a search engine such as Google to search for the street address number, street name, and zip code.
- **Negative Historical File** - Keep a database or other electronic record of prior fraud attempts, problem customers, charge back records, and customers receiving refunds.
- **Shared Negative Historical File** - Combine negative historical databases/files from several e-commerce merchants.
- **Positive Database File** - Maintain a file that contains a list of good customers
- **Credit Service Database** - Use a credit database service, such as Equifax (www.equfax.com), Experian (www.experian.com), and Trans Union (www.tuc.com) for high-dollar value items.
- **Customizable Merchant Rules** - A merchant should establish rules to stop or flag specific orders for review.
- **Fraud Scoring Systems** - **Assign** weights, points or probabilities to different components of a transaction (IP Address, free-email account, time of day, AVS results, amount of sale, type of products ordered, shipment method, different shipping/billing addresses, certain zip codes, etc) to generate a fraud score to indicate the likelihood of fraud.
- **Pattern Detection** - Check if multiple orders are placed shipping to the same address, but different credit cards were used. Check orders for an unusually high quantity of a single item.
- **Alternate Thank You Page** - If an order is being shipped to a non-English speaking country, display an alternate thank you page. Require the customer to fax either a photo of the credit card or a scanned copy of his/her credit card bill.
- **Preventative Data Checking Measures** - Check the data fields entered by the buyer to determine if the buyer actually exists based on data entered on the order. Check to see if the ZIP Code the customer listed actually exists. Make sure the customer's e-mail address is formatted properly. Check for incomplete names or an address like 100 Elm Street.
- **Free Email Accounts** - There is a much higher incidence of fraud from free email

services. Many fraudsters use free email addresses to remain anonymous.

- **Reverse IP Address Checks** – Make sure the user's IP address matches the email address and physical billing address of the customer. The IP address identifies the location of the server where the order was placed. Numerical IP addresses can be checked through programs such as WsPing32.

- **Anonymous And Open Proxy IP Addresses** - IP addresses can be falsified thus hiding the falsified IP addresses true location of the criminal. Organized credit card fraud rings often use anonymous proxies.

- **Checking Telephone Numbers** - The web sites at http://www.freeality.com/finde.htm, http://www.theultimates.com/, http://www.anywho.com, http://nt.jcsm.com/ziproundacx.asp, and http://nt.jcsm.com/ziproundacx.asp provide tools to match a telephone area code to a postal zip code, reverse telephone directories, search for email addresses, maps, directions, etc. A merchant can call directory assistance to determine if the phone number on the order matches the customer's phone number based on their name and address.

- **Fax Orders** - When a credit card order is received by fax, require the customer to also fax copies of both sides of their credit card and a copy of their state-issued ID, or driver's license

- **International Orders** - Some countries have a bad reputation as a source of fraud transactions. Banks or credit card processors can provide a list of high-risk countries. High risk countries include developing nations like Indonesia, Malaysia, Benin, Nigeria, Pakistan, Israel, Egypt, and Eastern European countries. Placing an international phone call to the issuing bank may be worth the cost for large orders and/ or ask the customer to contact the merchant by phone or email for shipping costs. A cyber-criminal may consider this too much contact, and decide to go elsewhere.

- **Calling The Customer** - Calling customers is not only an excellent way to detect fraud, but it can also be a valuable part of your customer service

- **Web Site Information** – Make sure the order form includes fields to enter the CVV2 verification code imprinted on the credit card, the name of the card-issuing bank, and the bank's toll-free telephone number, the customer's telephone number and email address.

- **Processing Orders** – Do not ship any order until the charge can be verified by additional checks.

- **Use Temporary Activation Codes** - If the merchant wants to process orders immediately, issue thirty-day temporary validation keys for downloaded software

- **Anti-Fraud Groups** – Become educated about fraud prevention by attending seminars offered by credit card companies and card processors. Organizations such as www.antifraud.com and www.wiscocomputing.com offer help. These groups also offer tips, databases of stolen credit cards, and web lookup tools.

- **File a Complaint with the FTC and the FBI** – If you detect fraud or have been a victim of fraud, file a complaint with the FTC at https://www.ftccomplaintassistant.gov/ and the FBI's Internet Crime Complaint Center or IC3, a partnership of the FBI and the National White Collar Crime Center at http://www.fbi.gov/majcases/fraud/internetschemes.htm (Internet Crime Complaint Center (IC3), 2009).

CONCLUSION

Based on past performance and predictions for the future, it seems safe to say that purchasing goods and services over the internet will continue to increase. This is because it is more efficient for the merchants and they can reach a much larger audience than using the face-to-face, in-store methods of the past. But like most uses of technology, there are individuals who find ways to use the technology for criminal purposes. This has been the case when utilizing credit or debit cards for purchasing goods and services over the internet. Thus, a sort of battleground has evolved between the e-commerce merchants along with their customers and the cyber-criminals. As new technological security methods are implemented by merchants to protect themselves and their customers, the cyber-criminals attempt to find ways through or around these technological barriers. If past events are any indication of the future, this battle is not over and merchants and their customers must continue to find secure methods to combat the criminals attempting to fraudulently steal financial and other personal information for their own financial gain.

REFERENCES

Alaric, Inc. (2008). *Card fraud detection - Comparison of Detection Technologies*. Retrieved December 28, 2008 from http://www.alaric.com/public/products/fractals?gclid=CI20ofLAnZgCFQpxHgodKmPDmg

Authorize.com. (2009). *Security Best Practices (2009)*. Retrieved January 21, 2009 from http://www.authorize.net/upload/images/Files/White%20Papers/Security_0604.pdf

Bank of America. (2009). *Card Processing Basics (2009)*. Retrieved January 21, 2009 from http://www.bankofamerica.com/small_business/merchant_card_processing/index.cfm?template=card_processing_basics

Conlin, J. (2007, May 11). *Credit card fraud keeps growing on the Net*. Retrieved December 28, 2008 from http://www.iht.com/articles/2007/05/11/news/mcredit.php

Cooney, M. (2007, November 11). *Credit card transaction security fortified by new risk assessment system*. Retrieved from http://www.networkworld.com/community/node/21731

Dept, G. A. of Technical and Adult Education (Ed.). (1996). *Credit Card Processing Overview*. GA Dept of Tech & Adult Education, Quick Start.

Faughnan, J. G. (2007, November 23). *International Net-Based Credit Card/Check Card Fraud with Small Charges*. Retrieved from http://www.faughnan.com/ccfraud.html

Federal Trade Commission. (2009a). *Avoiding Credit and Charge Card Fraud*. Retrieved April 24, 2009, from http://www.ftc.gov/bcp/edu/pubs/consumer/credit/cre07.shtm

Federal Trade Commission. (2009b). *About the Federal Trade Commission (2009)*. Retrieved January 22, 2009 from http://www.ftc.gov/ftc/about.shtm

Frank, J. (2004). *Fraud risk assessments: audits focused on identifying fraud-related exposures can serve as the cornerstone of an effective antifraud program*. Retrieved from http://findarticles.com/p/articles/mi_m4153/is_2_61/ai_n6152654/

Fraud Guides. (2009). *Credit Card Skimming*. Retrieved from http://www.fraudguides.com/business-credit-card-skimming.asp

Internet Crime Complaint Center (IC3). (2009). Retrieved January 21, 2009 from http://www.ic3.gov/default.aspx

Jepson, T. (2009). *Merchant Credit Card Fraud: 31 Ways to Minimize Credit Card Fraud.* Retrieved from January 17, 2009 from http://www.wisco-computing.com/articles/ccfraud.htm

MasterCard Worldwide. (2009). *Site Data Reflections The top five Web intrusions.* Retrieved January 21, 2009, from http://www.northamericanbancard.com/google/smart_templates/default/web/MC_SECURITY.pdf

MaxMind, Inc. (2008). *IP Address Reputation and a Mutual Collaboration Network.* Retrieved December 28, 2008, from http://www.maxmind.com/minFraudWhitePaper.pdf

Montague, D. A. (2004). *Fraud Prevention Techniques for Credit Card Fraud.* Victoria, Canada: Trafford Publishing.

Murdock, K. (2006). *Credit Card Processing: How It All Works.* Retrieved January 21, 2009, from http://www.practicalecommerce.com/articles/168-Credit-Card-Processing-How-It-All-Works

Smith, R. (2009). *How Credit Card Processing Works. Review.* Retrieved January 21, 2009 from http://www.smithfam.com/news/nov99d.html

Stoneburner, G., Goguen, A., & Feringa, A. (2009). *Risk Management Guide for Information Technology Systems Recommendations of the National Institute of Standards and Technology.* Retrieved January 22, 2009, from http://csrc.nist.gov/publications/nistpubs/800-30/sp800-30.pdf

TopTenReviews. (2009). *Credit Card Processing Services Review.* Retrieved January 21, 2009 from http://credit-card-processing-review.toptenreviews.com/

United States Department of Justice. (2009). *Internet and Telemarketing Fraud.* Retrieved April 28, 2009, from http://www.usdoj.gov/criminal/fraud/internet/

United States General Accounting Office- Accounting and Information Management Division. (1988). *Information Security Risk Assessment, Practices of Leading Organizations.* GAO, May, 1988.

Wilson, R. F. (2000, March 15a). Sophisticated Fraud Protection Systems. *Web Commerce Today,* 32. Retrieved January 12, 2008 from http://www.wilsonweb.com/wct3/fraud-systems.cfm

Wilson, R. F. (2000, March 15b). Inexpensive Techniques to Protect Merchants against Credit Card Fraud. *Web Commerce Today,* 32. Retrieved from January 15, 2009 from http://www.wilsonweb.com/wct3/fraud-lowcost.cfm

Woolsey, B., & Schulz, M. (2009). *Credit Card Industry Facts, Debt Statistics 2006-2009.* Retrieved January 12, 2009 from http://www.creditcards.com/credit-card-news/credit-card-industry-facts-personal-debt-statistics-1276.php

KEY TERMS AND DEFINITIONS

Acquiring Bank: The bank that represents the e-commerce merchant and processes all of the merchant's credit card payments with the credit card associations

Credit Card Processor: A third party utilized to process credit card payments for merchants and their acquiring bank

Credit Card: A card issued by banks, savings and loans, retail stores, and other businesses that can be used to borrow money or buy products and services on credit.

Cyber-Criminal: An individual who commits a crime using a computer and the internet to steal a person's identity such as credit card information.

E-Commerce: The buying and selling of goods and services on the Internet.

Fraud: An act of deception for the purpose of unlawful financial gain using stolen credit card information.

Issuing Bank: The bank that issues consumers their credit cards.

Merchant Account: A legally binding contract wherein an acquiring bank extends a line of credit to a merchant who desires to accept payment using credit cards.

service gateway: This is another name for a credit card processor.

Skimming: This is a type of fraud wherein the numbers on a credit card are recorded and transferred to a duplicate card.

SSL: SSL is an abbreviation for Secure Sockets Layer, a protocol developed for transmitting documents over the Internet using a cryptographic system that uses two keys to encrypt data; namely a public key known to everyone and a private or secret key known only to the recipient of the document.

Chapter 46

Virtual Stock Markets as a Research Tool in Marketing and Management

Lorenz Zimmermann
Ludwig-Maximilians-University Munich, Germany

ABSTRACT

Virtual Stock Markets (VSM) are a young, powerful and still evolving research tool. VSM were developed around 20 years ago as forecasting instrument of election outcomes, having delivered very precise results ever since. In recent years, various business applications of the given concept have been presented, namely forecast generation, decision support, product concept evaluation and the identification of lead users. This article explains the basic concept of VSM, describes the potential areas of application and shows examples of successful implementations in business practice. Directions for further research are identified.

INTRODUCTION

Virtual Stock Markets[1] (VSM) are still relatively unknown as a research tool in marketing and management (Surowiecki, 2005). Yet, the concept of VSM has received increased attention in recent years. The number of scientific publications, dealing with the given concept, has grown substantially over the last years (Tziralis & Tatsiopoulos, 2007). Most notably, the year of 2007 saw the introduction of the *Journal of Prediction Markets*, an academic journal dedicated to this topic exclusively.

VSM can fulfill a number of purposes in marketing and management, ranging from relatively simple business forecasts to more complex tests of product concepts, decision support and the identification of lead users among traders. VSM are especially relevant in e-Business as they provide a means for companies to aggregate the knowledge and opinions of a very large number of participants from distant locations using electronic communication devices.

DOI: 10.4018/978-1-61520-611-7.ch046

BACKGROUND

VSM work similar to regular stock markets. However, the listed stocks do not represent the shares of companies but are tied to the outcomes of future events. Every stock has a fixed lifetime after which the actual outcome of the predicted event can be observed. The final value of the stock is determined accordingly. During the lifetime of the stock market, traders compare the current market prices with their individual expectations of the outcome and make trades accordingly. Supply and demand determine the prices of stocks.[2]

Following the logic of *Hayek hypothesis* (Hayek, 1945) and *information efficiency hypothesis* (Fama, 1970), the resulting market prices reflect the traders' aggregate expectations of the future events, which the stocks are tied to. According to Hayek (1945), this mechanism to aggregate information works efficiently even in the extreme case of all market participants holding diverging information.

The first application of VSM was the *Iowa Presidential Stock Market* (Forsythe et al., 1992). In this example, virtual stocks were traded representing the vote shares of the different candidates in the 1988 Presidential elections. Actual outcomes could be predicted very precisely. Forecasts based on VSM outperformed every pollster's forecast in terms of prediction accuracy and low fluctuation levels in forecasts prior to the election date. VSM have been able to repeat this remarkable performance in the subsequent implementations (e.g., Berg et al., 2008), sparking academics' interest and laying the basis for different applications in related fields, most importantly in business research and practice.

AREAS OF VSM DEPLOYMENT IN MARKETING AND MANAGEMENT

Forecast Generation

Companies can use VSM to predict a wide range of relevant problems. Market participants can either be company insiders (e. g., sales employees predicting futures price levels in the market) or outsiders (e. g., customers predicting market shares for specific products).

VSM are especially useful when other forecasting techniques cannot be used, e.g. when data are inaccessible or influencing factors are complex (Berg et al., 2003; Hanson, 2006a). Also, VSM bypass the flaws of traditional research instruments in business. VSM results are not dependent on a representative sample. Traders usually enjoy participating and do not have to be offered large monetary incentives. Furthermore, the results are unbiased by social desirable behavior or researcher´s influences because market participants act anonymously (Hanson, 2006b). VSM are a dynamic system, being able to incorporate new information quickly (Snowberg et al., 2007) and therefore make it possible to observe developments over time. Also, fluctuations in stock prices allow for the estimation of forecast precision and predictions of standard forecast errors (Berg et al., 2003).

VSM minimize the danger of *groupthink,* which can be a problem with traditional forecasting techniques like the Delphi method. VSM are immune to groupthink as traders are constantly in competition and profits can be made when deviating from the estimation of the majority of actors in the market (Hopman, 2007). Finally, VSM implementation and operation are very cost-efficient and VSM are perfectly scalable to integrating large numbers of participants (Spann et al., 2009).

Various companies have already successfully implemented VSM as a forecasting tool: *Google* uses VSM to continuously predict a wide number of developments relevant to the company, ranging from the future number of *Gmail* users to opening dates for new office locations around the world (Sunstein, 2006). *Hewlett Packard* uses VSM to estimate future sales volumes (Chen & Plott, 2002), *Intel's* VSM forecasts customer demand (Hopman, 2007). Probably, the best known example of VSM forecasts is the *Hollywood Stock Exchange (HSX)*:

Established in 1996, it brings together over 1.6 million participants trading movies' box office results (Hollywood Stock Exchange, 2009). HSX has received comprehensive attention by the general public (e.g., Alster, 2003) as well as by the scientific community (Elberse, 2007).

Decision Support

Besides these simple forecasts, VSM can be designed to serve as a decision support system. The underlying idea is to measure the interdependency of two events and to improve decision making. Like the basic concept of VSM, the concept of decision support stems from election forecasting. Berg and Rietz (2003) construct stocks that generate payoffs according to the vote share of a political party provided that the candidate of the other party is predicted correctly. This way, VSM deliver election forecasts, which depend on the parties' nominees.

Transfers into business applications are obvious. VSM can be used to evaluate the consequences of various business decisions for the overall company performance or the company's real stock price. Such a decision support makes VSM even more useful than simple forecasts because recommendations for action become easily available from market results. At the same time, such VSM implementations can be a means of making decisions more democratic as the estimations of large crowds can be taken into consideration (Hanson, 2006b).

To date, very few implementations have been documented in business practice. Kiviat (2004) presents the example of *Intel* using VSM to make allocation decisions and determine which factory should be chosen to produce computer chips and when.

Evaluation of Product Concepts

VSM can help to identify promising product concepts long before their market launch. For this purpose, participants trade stocks, representing future market shares or expected ratings by consumers (Spann & Skiera, 2004).

Unlike the above mentioned VSM variants, evaluations of product concepts are not an adoption from political research but rather an original concept from business research. Dahan et al. (2007) first demonstrate the applicability of VSM for these product concept tests. They show that VSM are able to deliver results even with very limited runtime of the markets. As the stock prices converge quickly, market durations of a few minutes to up to an hour are fairly sufficient. Product concept tests via VSM are very flexible, which allows comparing product concepts with products already being marketed. Also, full concepts can be studied and compared with single components of a product or concept. VSM generate unbiased estimations, allowing analyses for willingness to pay. The market mechanism also allows traders to learn from each other's estimations which is useful for evaluating fashion goods or products with network effects where one consumer's utility is co-determined by the other users' behavior.

The first large scale implementation of such product concept test is *Yahoo's Tech Buzz Game,* which was active between 2005 and 2008 (20082008Yahoo!, 2008!!). Its aim was to identify emerging technology trends by predicting the future number of search requests for a specific term in the *Yahoo!* search engine. The Tech Buzz Game comprised around 50 markets and attracted as many as 20,000 participants.

Identification of Lead Users

Very active and successful VSM participants show characteristics of lead users (Spann et al., 2009): They qualify by an excellent understanding of the relevant product category and develop needs prior to other users.[3] Therefore, companies can use VSM specifically to identify lead users and, subsequently, recruit them for more in-depth market research and e.g. set up focus groups.

Lead user identification through VSM can be very valuable for businesses as a large number of participants can join the market at low cost for a company. VSM are especially useful on consumer goods markets where companies face a large number of customers and do not interact with them in person. Also, VSM help to detect those users that are able to transfer their expertise in the relevant product category into predictions of future market success. VSM, detecting lead users, can easily be integrated into a company´s existing online community where users converge who qualify by their high product involvement. Such online communities will, therefore, contain a number of potential lead users.

To date, only one implementation of such lead user identification via VSM has been documented: Spann et al. (2009) have identified lead users among traders of a VSM predicting movies´ box office results. The authors are able to show that there is a significantly higher portion of lead users among the top 20% of traders than among the rest of the participants.

FUTURE RESEARCH DIRECTIONS

In recent years, there has been a lot of effort dedicated to the demonstration of the practical efficacy of VSM. The majority of publications have been focused on developing and describing applications of the concept (Tziralis & Tatsiopoulos, 2007). Future work also has to address the development of a theoretical basis for the concept and answer the questions outlined below. The newly established *Journal of Prediction Markets* can be an adequate outlet for this work.

The theoretical explanation of the excellent forecasting results is not yet complete. At the moment, not a single model is able to explain the exact way VSM work aggregating the information. Also, there is no coherent explanation for why people trade in the first place. Every trader potentially has to fear that other participants hold superior information, which certainly increases the risk of losing one´s money (Milgrom & Stokey, 1982). Also, there is no theoretical explanation for the individual trading behavior, which significantly varies among individual traders. Especially, characteristics of *marginal traders* have to be researched who qualify by their expertise and active trading behavior and are of great importance for the generation of precise forecasts (Forsythe et al., 1999). Besides, the exact factors have to be identified that influence the quality of the obtained results. The influence of different reward structures on forecast precision has to be especially analyzed. The question whether real money or play money should be used has not yet been resolved. Also, the optimal time horizon for making precise forecasts has yet to be identified.

To win a better understanding of the quality of VSM results, the effects of possible bias in VSM results need to be researched in more detail. Various authors observe *favorite-longshot bias* with traders systematically overestimating the likelihood of very improbable events and underestimating the likelihood of highly probable events making market prices slightly biased towards the center (e. g. Berg & Rietz, 2002; Tetlock, 2004; Wolfers & Zitzewitz, 2004). Even though it does not seem to affect market prices, there is evidence for individual trading behavior being biased towards outcomes more desirable for the company that runs the market (Cowgill et al., 2009) or for individual traders themselves (Forsythe et al., 1999).

From a manager´s point a view, clear guidelines are desirable on how VSM should be used in business practice. At present, no general rule exists for when VSM are the first choice over other research instruments. Even though VSM will always yield some results, they might not offer meaningful insights and have very little predictive power if important information is unavailable to traders. Sunstein (2006) documents cases in which relevant information is out of reach for market participants and subsequent VSM predictions are wrong. Also, diffusion of power can be a problem: When VSM are used for corporate decision making, neither a single person nor a group of people can be held responsible for decisions that turn out to be wrong. Instead, decisions are made based on the estimations of a pool of anonymous traders. In within-company applications, market participants can be tempted to withhold important information from their colleagues or influence actual outcomes negatively in order to benefit from their superior level of information (Hanson, 2006). Also, anonymous trading can run counter to a corporate culture encouraging openness (Hopman, 2007).

When VSM are used to evaluate product concepts based on the estimations of company outsiders, transparency of results can be disadvantageous. Market prices are open to all participants who might then draw conclusions from VSM results about future company policies. Hence, confidentiality of research results cannot be guaranteed. Also, legal concerns have to be clarified that still remain for VSM operating on the basis of real money. At present, VSM either use play money, operate from off shore locations where legal rules are less strict, or fulfill tight regulations so as to comply with online gambling laws[4] (Hahn & Tetlock, 2006). Finally, in order to win general acceptance as a standard research tool in business practice, the monetary benefits of VSM use need to be quantified, so that they can be compared with traditional instruments of business research.

CONCLUSION

VSM have the great potential to become a very powerful research tool in marketing and management. Their advantages have been identified over other research techniques, and companies clearly seem to be aware of the concept's potential. If the remaining questions can be resolved in the near future, VSM will further gain in importance and the number of implementations in business practice will most likely grow.

REFERENCES

Alster, N. (2003, November 23). It´s just a game, but Hollywood is paying attention. *The New York Times*, 4.

Berg, J., Forsythe, R., & Rietz, T. (1996). What makes markets predict well? Evidence from the Iowa Electronic Markets. In W. Albers, W. Güth, & P. Hammerstein (Eds.), *Understanding strategic interaction: Essays in honor of Reinhard Selten* (pp. 444-463). Berlin: Springer.

Berg, J., Nelson, F., & Rietz, T. (2003). *Accuracy and forecast standard error of prediction markets*. Retrieved January 27, 2009, from http://www.biz.uiowa.edu/iem/archive/forecasting.pdf

Berg, J., Nelson, F., & Rietz, T. (2008). Prediction market accuracy in the long run. *International Journal of Forecasting, 24*(2), 283–298. doi:10.1016/j.ijforecast.2008.03.007

Berg, J., & Rietz, T. (2002). *Longshots, overconfidence and efficiency on the Iowa Electronic Market*. Retrieved May 6, 2009, from http://www.biz.uiowa.edu/iem/archive/Longshots_2002January.pdf

Berg, J., & Rietz, T. (2003). Prediction markets as decision support systems. *Information Systems Frontiers, 5*(1), 79–93. doi:10.1023/A:1022002107255

Chen, K.-Y., & Plott, C. R. (2002). *Information aggregation mechanisms: Concept, design and implementation for a sales forecasting problem*. Retrieved February 10, 2008, from http://www.hss.caltech.edu/SSPapers/wp1131.pdf

Cowgill, B., Wolfers, J., & Zitzewitz, E. (2009). *Using prediction markets to track information flows: Evidence from Google.* Retrieved May 6, 2009, from http://www.bocowgill.com/GooglePredictionMarketPaper.pdf

Dahan, E., Lo, A. W., Poggio, T., Chan, N., & Kim, A. (2007). *Securities trading of concepts (STOC).* Retrieved January 27, 2009, from http://ssrn.com/abstract=1163442

Elberse, A. (2007). The power of stars: Do star actors drive the success of movies? *Journal of Marketing, 71*(4), 102–120. doi:10.1509/jmkg.71.4.102

Fama, E. (1970). Efficient capital markets: A review of theory and empirical work. *The Journal of Finance, 25*(2), 383–417. doi:10.2307/2325486

Forsythe, R., Nelson, F., Neumann, G. R., & Wright, J. (1992). Anatomy of an experimental political stock market. *The American Economic Review, 80*(5), 1142–1161.

Forsythe, R., Rietz, T., & Ross, T. (1999). Wishes, expectations and actions: a survey on price formation in election stock markets. *Journal of Economic Behavior & Organization, 39*(1), 83–110. doi:10.1016/S0167-2681(99)00027-X

Hahn, R., & Tetlock, P. (2006). A new approach for regulating information markets. *Journal of Regulatory Economics, 29*(3), 265–281. doi:10.1007/s11149-006-7399-z

Hanson, R. (2006a). Decision markets for policy advice. In A. S. Gerber & E. M. Patashnik (Eds.), *Promoting the general welfare: New perspectives on government performance* (pp. 151-173). Washington, DC: Brookings Institution Press.

Hanson, R. (2006b). Foul play in information markets. In B. Hahn & P. Tetlock (Eds.), *Information markets: A new way of making decisions* (pp. 126-141). Washington, DC: American Enterprise Institute Publishing.

Hollywood Stock Exchange. (2009). *Corporate Overview.* Retrieved January 26, 2009, from http://www.hsxresearch.com/corporate_overview.htm

Hopman, J. W. (2007). Using forecasting markets to manage demand risk. *Intel Technology Journal, 11*(2), 127–135.

Kiviat, B. (2004, July 12). The end of management? *Time,* Inside Business, A4.

Milgrom, P., & Stokey, N. (1982). Information, trade and common knowledge. *Journal of Economic Theory, 26*(1), 17–27. doi:10.1016/0022-0531(82)90046-1

Moore, W. L. (1982). Concept Testing. *Journal of Business Research, 10,* 279–294. doi:10.1016/0148-2963(82)90034-0

Snowberg, E., Wolfers, J., & Zitzewitz, E. (2007). Partisan impacts on the economy: Evidence from prediction markets and close elections. *The Quarterly Journal of Economics, 122*(2), 807–829. doi:10.1162/qjec.122.2.807

Spann, M., Ernst, H., Skiera, B., & Soll, J. H. (2009). Identification of lead users for consumer products via virtual stock markets. *Journal of Product Innovation Management, 26*(3), 322–335. doi:10.1111/j.1540-5885.2009.00661.x

Spann, M., & Skiera, B. (2003). Internet-based virtual stock markets for business forecasting. *Management Science, 49*(10), 1310–1326. doi:10.1287/mnsc.49.10.1310.17314

Spann, M., & Skiera, B. (2004). Opportunities of virtual stock markets to support new product development. In S. Albers (Ed.), *Cross-functional innovation management* (pp. 227-242). Wiesbaden, Germany: Gabler.

Sunstein, C. (2006). *Infotopia – how many minds produce knowledge.* Oxford, UK: Oxford University Press.

Surowiecki, J. (2005). *The Wisdom of Crowds.* New York: Anchor Books.

Tetlock, P. C. (2004). *How efficient are information markets? Evidence from an online exchange.* Retrieved May 6, 2009, from http://www.mccombs.utexas.edu/faculty/paul.tetlock/papers/Tetlock-Efficient_Info_Markets-01_02.pdf

Tziralis, G., & Tatsiopoulos, I. (2007). Prediction markets: An extended literature review. *Journal of Prediction Markets, 1*(1), 75–91.

von Hayek, F. A. (1945). The use of knowledge in society. *The American Economic Review, 35*(4), 519–530.

von Hippel, E. (1986). Lead users: A source of novel product concepts. *Management Science, 32*(7), 791–805. doi:10.1287/mnsc.32.7.791

Wolfers, J., & Zitzewitz, E. (2004). Prediction markets. *The Journal of Economic Perspectives, 18*(2), 107–126. doi:10.1257/0895330041371321

Yahoo! (2008). *Tech Buzz Game.* Retrieved January 29, 2008, from http://buzz.research.yahoo.com

KEY TERMS AND DEFINITIONS

Decision Support Systems: a computer information systems that support decision-making activities.

Groupthink: a pattern of decision making by a group characterized by reaching consensus without sufficient discussion and consideration of alternative solutions to the problem at hand.

Hayek Hypothesis: Market prices work as a quick and efficient means to aggregate information that are diversely held by individual market participants (Hayek, 1945).

Information Efficiency Hypothesis: A capital market is called "efficient" if its prices always fully reflect all available information (Fama, 1970).

Lead User: a user who faces needs months or years prior to the majority of users in a market and who benefits significantly from obtaining a solution to those needs (von Hippel, 1986).

Marginal Trader: a very active and well informed market participant. Marginal traders do not suffer from any bias when evaluating stock prices. They frequently make trades close to the current market price, thereby adjusting it to the information they hold.

Products Concept Testing: the process of estimating consumer responses to a product idea prior to its market launch. Product concepts are tested in order to improve the rate of successful new product introductions (Moore, 1982).

Virtual Stock Market (VSM): a market that allows trading of stocks representing the outcomes of future events. Market prices reflect the aggregate expectations of participants and can be used as a forecasting tool.

ENDNOTES

[1] Currently, there is no universally accepted terminology for the concept of Virtual Stock Markets (VSM). Alternative terms can be found, such as *Prediction Markets, Information Markets* or *Idea Futures.* For an overview of the different terms employed and their frequency of use, see Figure 1 in Tziralis and Tatsiopoulos (2007).

[2] More detailed descriptions of the functionality and theoretical foundation of VSM are offered in Spann and Skiera (2003).

[3] For the concept of lead users see von Hippel (1986).

[4] The operators of the IEM agreed to maintain the market's academic focus, not to seek any profit and limit maximum stakes to USD 500. In return, the *Commodities Futures Trading Commission (CFTC)* issued a no-action-letter extending no-action relief to the market (Berg et al., 1996).

Chapter 47
Potential Benefits of Analyzing Website Analytic Data

Elizabeth Votta
Roosevelt University, USA

INTRODUCTION

This article presents an overview of the potential benefits of analyzing website analytic data. During the last several years I have gained first-hand knowledge of Internet marketing programs of a variety of companies ranging from national name brands to small businesses. In addition, I have been active in the local chapter of the American Marketing Association. During this time, it has become clear to me that many small business owners and marketing managers at various size companies lack a basic understanding of the potential benefits of analyzing website analytic data. This article introduces the basics of website analytics and the potential benefits derived from analyzing that data.

The objectives of this article include:

- Define the following terms: website analytics, Internet marketing, bounce rate,

information architecture, Web 1.0, Web 2.0, and search engine spider.
- This article presents potential benefits of analyzing website analytic data, including: discovering traffic trends, target market segmentation, developing best practices, optimizing landing pages, and improving conversion rates.

BACKGROUND

Currently there is great interest in Internet marketing as Internet usage continues to increase. According to Internetworldstats.com (2009) world Internet usage has grown 338.10% from 2000 to 2008. Internet marketing offers both Business to Consumer (B to C) and Business to Business (B to B) companies a way to drive high-quality, low-cost traffic to their website(s). Internet marketing can include a mix of paid and unpaid media along with website adjustments and strategies to drive quality traffic

DOI: 10.4018/978-1-61520-611-7.ch047

to a website and improve conversion rates. The Internet marketing mix may include but is not limited to: Pay Per Click (PPC), Search Engine Optimization (SEO), banner advertising, landing pages, link building, and email campaigns.

Internet marketing is continuously evolving and offers substantial website statistical data to develop an understanding of return on investment (ROI) of Internet marketing strategies. It is crucial for companies to monitor their website analytic data and develop a baseline report to continually monitor and have the website evolve based on consumer usage of the site. While a percentage of businesses have embraced Web 2.0 trends, a larger percentage of businesses have not yet successfully harnessed the power of or comprehended Web 1.0. Web 1.0 refers to the first versions of websites that were and are basically online brochures. Web 2.0 refers to a website that has evolved past Web 1.0 and includes consumer-generated-content and/or user reviews that allow website visitors to interact with the site.

Website analytics are programs that capture website user data that can be analyzed to develop an understanding of website trends and website strategy ROI. The information varies depending on the analytic program being used but generally includes the total number of visitors to a site along with other data that can be analyzed for trends. Many analytic programs are available and each has its own list of advantages and disadvantages. The two analytic programs that are used for the purpose of this article are Google Analytics and AW Stats.

Google Analytics (2009) website states: "Use Google Analytics to learn which online marketing initiatives are cost effective and see how visitors actually interact with your site. Make informed site design improvements, drive targeted traffic, and increase your conversions and profits." An advantage of using Google Analytics is that it is continuously updated to include advanced reporting tools. A disadvantage is that by offer-ing the product for free, Google also has access to the data.

AW Stats (2009) website states: "AW stats is a free powerful and feature full tool that generates advanced web, streaming, ftp or mail server statistics, graphically. This log analyzer works as a CGI or from command line and shows you all possible information your log contains, in few graphical web pages." An advantage of using AW stats is that it captures the search engine spider visits. A disadvantage is that it is lacks in-depth reporting tools. Search engine spiders are bots (search engine robots) sent from the various search engines to crawl the pages of a website and index the pages based on what they find. It is important to note that search engines do not index a whole website but rather individual pages of a website.

Developing a routine analysis of a website will most likely lead to new ideas for improving the overall user site experience and improving conversion rates. The analysis can easily identify problem areas of the website that might otherwise be overlooked.

WEBSITE ANALYTICS DATA ANALYSIS

By professionally analyzing the marketing data available via an analytics program on a regular basis, new ideas for improved graphics, copy, and calls to action are likely to be developed. Generally the goal of Internet marketing options such as PPC, SEO, link building, banner advertising, and email campaigns is to drive low-cost, high-quality traffic to a website. Upon entry to the site, their job is done. It is up to the website to convert the consumer. Now that the consumer is on the site, it is up to an analytics program to offer insights into what the consumer is actually doing on the site.

It is crucial for companies to monitor their website analytic data and develop a baseline report. The recommended report will serve as a benchmark to develop best practices and have the website evolve based on consumer usage of the site. A baseline report is recommended to be pulled and analyzed monthly from the following Google Analytics data: visitors and new visitors, page views, time, bounce rate, landing pages, and conversion rates. Details and possible benefits of each are listed below. Initially it is recommended to pull and analyze the reports monthly until enough data is collected or testing is being conducted to justify daily or weekly reports. The more visitors that come to your website, the more accurate your analysis of trends will become. The overall goal of the monthly reports is to determine how successful or unsuccessful your website is for consumers.

Visitors and New Visitors

First, the monthly report should start tracking the total number of visitors and new visitors. By monitoring total visitor stats each month, it is possible to discover traffic patterns. A visitor is the total number of visits to the site. A new visitor will most likely be a smaller number as a new visitor is only counted the first time the program captures the Internet Protocol (IP) address used. For example, if a visitor uses her work computer for visits on a daily basis Monday through Friday she will only be counted once. However, if on Saturday she visits the site from home, she will now be counted as a new visitor for a second time due to the system capturing a new IP address. It is also possible that twenty different employees at work visiting the same website are only counted as one new visitor if they share one IP address.

Page Views

Overall total page views should be monitored on a month to month basis to watch for varying levels of interest in the overall site. Individual page views are also important to monitor as this can offer in-

sights into what parts of the website consumers are most interested in. For example, if one section of a website is receiving a disproportionate amount of website traffic, it may make sense to further develop this area of the site. Further, if a single website has several different target markets but one of the target markets website pages or areas of the website are receiving a higher total number of page views compared to other pages or areas of the site, it may make sense to develop more pages or run tests specifically aimed at this target market segment.

Time

Overall time spent on the site should be monitored month to month to determine if usage increases or decreases over time. This can give insights into overall interest of the site and overall site health. If the total time spent on the site is brief, this may indicate that consumers are not finding the copy or website materials relevant to their needs. Total time spent on the website may or may not be important to the overall website marketing goals. However, time spent on individual pages could be monitored for trends and for special marketing programs to develop best practices if appropriate. Google Analytics times out after thirty minutes if a website is idle and a new session is counted if the visitor is active again.

Bounce Rate

A bounce rate of a website page refers to a visitor that landed on the page and did not click through to any other pages on that website and hence "bounced" out. A high bounce rate is generally not relevant to blogs, as a consumer may read a post that is relevant to her search and not need to click through to any other pages. However, for many websites a high bounce rate may indicate that the information presented on the page is not relevant to the user, the page is not organized well, or that the page lacks a clear call to action.

Each website's statistics are unique and should be treated as such but in same cases benchmarking may be appropriate. A rule of thumb is that a page bounce rate over 50% may indicate that the page needs to be revisited and tested with improved design, calls to action, and/or copy.

Landing Pages

Landing pages are often used in PPC campaigns to offer the consumer a clear call to action or the most relevant copy determined by the keyword clicked. Particular website pages of a site may be well indexed by a search engine and act as a landing page for the website. If this is the case, the page will want to be optimized with relevant calls to action, design, and/or copy to improve the bounce rate of the page or improve conversions if appropriate.

Exit Pages

For an e-commerce site or a Web 2.0 site, the ideal exit page would be the thank you page for a purchase or a submission. Most likely, the website will have multiple pages that rank high as exit pages. These pages should be reviewed to determine if the calls to action, design, and/or copy can be improved to keep the consumer moving through the site.

Referrals

Referrals are keywords searched for on a search engine or other websites that link to a website to drive traffic to the site. These should be monitored for relevancy and popularity. It is important that over time the best converting keywords are used in a SEO campaign to drive more relevant traffic to the website.

Conversion Rates

Finally, are conversion rates. The majority of Web 1.0 websites end goal is for the consumer to contact the company or to complete a sales transaction online. Analyzing conversion rates can offer insights into possible ways to test or improve the site to continually fine-tune and improve the conversion rates.

Web 2.0 conversion rates may include calls to actions that may not be easily captured by an analytics program. However, measurable metrics should try to be monitored to determine overall effectiveness of reaching Web 2.0 goals. Overall conversion rates will reveal vital information about the effectiveness of the website converting the consumer. Conversion rates are essential information to analyze to monitor and gauge Internet marketing campaign's ROI.

Issues, Controversies, Problems

It is important to note that website analytics programs are not 100% accurate. This becomes very clear if you view a website analytics report for the same website using AW Stats and Google Analytics. Most likely they will show very different traffic statistics. This is due to the way the data is collected and is a good reminder that neither program is 100% accurate.

Although Google Analytics is a powerful program that is currently offered for free, sensitive website data is shared with Google in exchange for the free use of the program. Some companies will prefer to pay for a website analytics program that allows their website data to remain private. In addition, some companies will prefer a paid website analytics program that can be customized and offer reporting based specifically on their own reporting needs.

Solutions and Recommendations

Using readily available and free website analytics programs such as AW Stats and Google Analytics together offers the average marketer insights into website trends, and allows for benchmarking and gaining insights into return on investment of various Internet marketing campaigns.

However, using free website analytics programs may not be the ideal solution for all websites. It is recommended that the advantages and disadvantages of several website analytics programs are weighed by the company before a selection is made. In some cases, it may make sense to start with free programs such as AW Stats and Google Analytics and as analytics reporting becomes more advanced then upgrade to a paid program or invest in an executive becoming certified by Google via Conversion University to fully utilize Google analytics.

FUTURE RESEARCH DIRECTIONS

Website analytics programs continue to evolve at a fast pace as users become more savvy. I expect that the programs offered will continue to offer more advanced and in-depth analysis as this marketing segment grows. This article offers an introduction to website analytics and the potential benefits derived from analysis. Future research opportunities include building upon the foundation of this article, by delving deeper into the statistics provided by Google Analytics and giving insights into some of the more advanced features currently available.

CONCLUSION

If you build it, they will not come. Launching a website does not guarantee traffic, let alone quality traffic, to a website. A comprehensive Internet marketing strategy should be developed, and in its most basic form, it should include a comprehensive website analytics report. The report should include the basic information detailed in this article as a baseline to start. A well-written and analyzed report will naturally guide future website growth and evolution.

A website needs to evolve – it must evolve to stay relevant. A website can not afford to stay static because the technology and expectations of the consumer will pass the business by. By developing a website analytics program that continually monitors and reports on trends, a business is able to develop an understanding of consumers' usage and adapt the website and Internet marketing strategies accordingly to reach marketing goals.

REFERENCES

Analytics, G. (2009). *Google Analytics: Improve your website and increase marketing ROI*. Retrieved February 4, 2009, from https://www.google.com/analytics/reporting/login?ctu=https%3A%2F%2Fwww.google.com%2Fanalytics%2Fsettings%2F%3F

Internetworldstats.com. (2009). *Internet Usage Statistics*. Retrieved February 4, 2009, from http://www.internetworldstats.com/stats.htm

Stats, A. W. (2009). *AW Stats Official Website*. Retrieved February 4, 2009, from http://awstats.sourceforge.net/

ADDITIONAL READING

Burby, J., Atchison, S., & Sterne, J. (2007). *Actionable Web Analytics: Using Data to Make Smart Business Decisions*. Hoboken, NJ: Sybex.

Clifton, B. (2008). *Advanced Web Metrics with Google Analytics*. Hoboken, NJ: Sybex.

Eisenberg, B., Eisenberg, J., & Davis, L. T. (2006). *Call to Action: Secret Formulas to Improve Online Results*. Nashville, TN: Thomas Nelson.

Inan, H. (2001). *The Need for Web Site Traffic Analysis*, Retrieved February 4, 2009, from http://www.clickz.com/840921

Inan, H. (2001). *Web Site Traffic Analysis Untangled*. Retrieved February 4, 2009, from http://www.clickz.com/841671

Inan, H. (2001). *Two Limitations of Web Site Traffic Analysis Tools*. Retrieved February 4, 2009, from http://www.clickz.com/ 842331

Jackson, S. (2004). Case Study: www.healthylifepharmacy.com 1300% Increase in Sales. *The Conversion Chronicles*. Retrieved March 28, 2009, from http://www.conversionchronicles.com/Refer_us_and_receive_a_free_report.html

Jones, K. B. (2008). *Search Engine Optimization: Your Visual Blueprint for Effective Internet marketing*. Hoboken, NJ: John Wiley and Sons.

Kaushik, A. (2007). *Web Analytics: An Hour a Day*. Hoboken, NJ: Sybex.

Krug, S. (2005). Don't *Make Me Think: A Common Sense Apadvantageach to Web Usability, 2nd Edition*. Upper Saddle River, NJ: New Riders Press.

Ledford, J., & Tyler, M. E. (2007). *Google Analytics 2.0*. Hoboken, NJ: Wiley.

Lovegrove, C. (2005). *A Comprehensive Strategy for Using Web Site Statistics Track The Effectiveness Of Your Marketing Effort*. Retrieved January 15, 2009 from http://www.searchengineadvantagemotionhelp.com/m/articles/site-disadvantagetent-design/site-statistics-strategy-1.php

Perez, J. C. (2005). Google Dumps Fees For Analytics Tools. *IDG News Service*. Retrieved February 4, 2009, from http://www.pcworld.com/article/123519/google_dumps_fees_for_analytics_tools.html

Perez, J. C. (2005). Google Suspends Analytics Sign-Ups. *IDG News Service*. Retrieved February 4, 2009, from http://www.pcworld.com/article/123665/google_suspends_analytics_signups.html

Peterson, E. (2004). *Web Analytics Demystified: A Marketer's Guide to Understanding How Your Web Site Affects Your Business*. Portland, OR: Celilo Group Media.

Phippen, A., Sheppard, L., & Furnell, S. (2004). A practical evaluation of Web analytics. *Internet Research*, *14*(4), 284–293. doi:10.1108/10662240410555306

Sen, A., Dacin, P. A., & Pattichis, C. (2006). Current Trends in Web Data Analysis. *Communications of the ACM*, *49*(11), 85–91. doi:10.1145/1167838.1167842

Terdiman, D. (2004). *Website Analysis Isn't a Game*. Retrieved December 28, 2008 from http://www.wired.com/science/discoveries/news/2004/06/63767

Viney, D. (2008). *Get to the Top on Google: Tips and Techniques to Get Your Site to the Top of the Search Engine Rankings -- and Stay There*. Boston, MA: Nicholas Brealey Publishing.

KEY TERMS AND DEFINITIONS

Bounce: A bounce rate of a website page refers to a visitor that landed on the page and did not click through to any other pages on that website and hence "bounced" out. A high bounce rate is generally not relevant to blogs, but for other websites may indicate that the information presented on the page is not relevant to the user, the page is not organized well, or that the page lacks a clear call to action.

Information Architecture: Information architecture refers to the way information is organized on a website. Successful Information Architecture includes information that is easy to find and is arranged in a way that is intuitive to the website visitor.

Internet Marketing: Internet marketing can include a mix of paid and unpaid Internet media along with website adjustments and strategies to drive quality traffic to a website and/or improve conversion rates. The Internet marketing mix may include but is not limited to: Pay Per Click (PPC), Search Engine Optimization (SEO), banner advertising, landing pages, link building, and email campaigns.

Search Engine Spider: Search engine spiders are bots sent from the various search engines to crawl the pages of a website and index the pages based on what they find.

Web 1.0: Web 1.0 refers to the first versions of websites that were and are basically online brochures.

Web 2.0: Web 2.0 refers to a website that has evolved past Web 1.0 and includes consumer generated content and/or user reviews that allow website visitors to interact with the site.

Website Analytics: Website Analytics are programs that capture website user data that can be analyzed to develop an understanding of website trends and website strategy ROI.

Chapter 48
Teams of Leaders Concept (ToL) and E-Business Operations

Dag von Lubitz
MedSMART Inc., USA & Bieda Poco Dargante Inst., Denmark

GLOBALIZATION 3.0

Information Technology (IT), and the subsequent broad acceptance of Information and Knowledge Management (IM/KM) methods revolutionized the way business is thought of and practiced. With e-business facilitating the ability to do more, more, faster, at a wider range, and to influence ever larger and more diverse consumer groups, the impact of technology on commerce, finance, and global economy has been frequently compared to the "paradigm shift" that Kuhn (1970) proposed as the essence of scientific revolution. Yet, despite the transformational influence of modernity on the ancient art, the fundamental principles of business have not changed: overreliance on the *facilitation* of business operations as the substitution for the adherence to the *soundness* of their conduct fuelled

DOI: 10.4018/978-1-61520-611-7.ch048

rampant growth of corporate *laisse faire,* and already twice brought the world to the brink of economic disaster (Stiglitz, 2003; Steingart, 2008).

Ultimately, a new realization begins to emerge: e-business makes cut-throat competition, winning at any price, and "devil take the hindmost" philosophy (Chancellor, 1999) not only obsolete but perceived by the increasing number of business leaders as harmful if not even dangerous (e.g., Greenwald and Kahn, 2005; Mittlestaedt, 2005; Prahalad and Ramaswalmy, 2004). Instead, the notion that "we are in this boat together" is gaining an ever wider acceptance: under the influence of technology the world has, indeed, changed (e.g., Canton, 2006). It started to converge, and now some even conceive it as "flat" (Friedman, 2005.) In reality, the world is probably not "flat" but far more three-dimensional and textured than it has ever been before. Technology converted point to point interactions into a complex set of relations that, based on networks where knowledge is the most sought commodity (Wickramasinghe and von Lubitz, 2008), and we now live embedded in a rapidly evolving, globe-spanning mesh of a "network of networks" (von Lubitz, 2009; see fig.1). Simultaneously with the development of new technology-based transaction platforms, another major technology-facilitated transformation began to occur: subtly, but with an ever increasing force, business interactions begun to move away from the traditional concept of ownership and its transfer as the basis of transaction between firms, firms and their customers, and even among customers themselves. Instead, *access* to goods and services among organizations became the increasingly prominent form, and Friedman's era of Globalization 3.0 (Friedman, 2005) became synonymous with Rifkin's "Age of Access" (Rifkin, 2003). Individuals rather than state and corporate bureaucracies acquired unprecedented power, and started to actively shape the world. In contrast to the first and second stage of Globalization, the process of change altered its direction, the flow now moving upward, from the bottom up, instead of hierarchically sanctified top-down descent of orders, commands, and directives. The boost for the change was provided by the intensification of horizontal exchanges conducted across boundaries of time, space, and specialization among individuals and groups of increasingly diverse character. Technology not only altered the way we do business but caused a fundamental transformation in the way we think about business. While Globalization 2.0 (Friedman, 2005) had the characteristics of Kuhnian "paradigm shift" (Kuhn, 1970), the forces that induced Globalization 3.0 induced *business mutagenesis* – a permanent alteration in the hitherto immutable "genetic" structure of the organism.

THE CONSEQUENCES OF CHANGE

While transformation in global relations that Friedman (2005) termed as Globalization 1.0 and

2.0 took place over approximately 200 years, the second stage – Globalization 3.0 – occurred within less than ten, at a pace unprecedented in the history of humanity. The new political and economic realities of the "global world" (Haas, 2005; Sachs, 2005) provided fertile ground for the development of new customer- and knowledge-driven concepts of doing business (Wickramasinghe and von Lubitz, 2008) conducted by the growing number of learning organizations (Senge, 1990) able to both understand better and respond with a much greater agility to the shifting demands of markets. The concomitant intensification of consumer-generated pressures altered the nature of competition: "the hunter became the hunted" (Prahalad and Ramaswamy, 2004; Greenwald and Kahn, 2005). Size and power-based quest for market dominance that characterized earlier stages of globalization transformed into customer-driven need for innovation, adaptability, and highly innovative approaches to product development, marketing, and sales. Ultimately, business strategies based on collaboration, knowledge sharing, and increasing level of organizational transparency became increasingly the norm rather than exception (Christensen et al., 2004; Kim and Mauborgne, 2005; Evans and Wurster, 2000). Increasingly, and in a curious similarity to political confrontation and conflict (Smith, 2007), modern business operations became increasingly conducted "amongst the people."

Technology shrunk the world in both physical and temporal sense (Friedman, 2005.) It simplified processes, reduced bureaucratically-imposed loads on business, and increased efficiency. Yet, because it also increased the range of operational permutations, escalated the number of direct and indirect actors, intensified their mutual relationships, and introduced technology-specific complexities, technology also led to the emergence of a tightly coupled, highly intricate global system of mutual dependencies and vulnerabilities. With the chances of failure depending exponentially on system's complexity, and with the resulting

Figure 1. The network mesh consists of several network layers (e.g., financial, reporting, logistics, etc.) each associated with its data/information/knowledge storage facilities, analytic centers, and entry portals). Within each layer activities are conducted using a wide variety of computing and analytic platforms (grid and cloud computing, network-centric operations). All layers are interconnected, and data/information/knowledge flows are omnidirectional, i.e., the output of one entity (or network layer) may provide input to another one. User-oriented outputs consist predominantly of actionable information and actionable knowledge

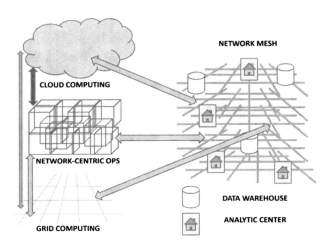

failures often having catastrophic proportions (Ebenhart, 2003; Mandelbrot, 2004; Taleb, 2007), globalization created the environment in which potential for such catastrophic events became increasingly greater.

The complexity characteristic of closely coupled systems is also the source of elevated "random noise", i.e., normal and quite harmless performance variation. However, that very same random noise may mask critically destabilizing events that hide below the level of detection based on casual observation (Mandelbrot, 2004; von Lubitz and Wickramasinghe, 2006; Taleb, 2007). Information technology is now used very extensively as the means to detect such events through gathering of business intelligence, operational performance monitoring and control, and alert generation. Increasingly more ubiquitous "smart portals" (Wickramasinghe and von Lubitz, 2007) provide access to web-based analytic tools, and grid- and cloud computing, and network-centric

approaches (von Lubitz, 2009; Chang, 2008) enhance the speed and the range of the data/information/knowledge retrieval, manipulation, and analysis. In turn, their outputs facilitate generation of pertinent knowledge and evidence-based practices (von Lubitz and Wickramasinghe, 2006a).

Under ideal circumstances, all participating actors, whether within the same entity or across collaborating entities would have equal status and equal access to all inputs and outputs involved in these processes. In reality, however, while inputs may be shared among collaborators, most of the outputs are generated within narrowly defined, discipline-oriented sectors of action. Furthermore, the products of analyses are distributed hierarchically in a bottom-up flow. Individual streams of knowledge are subsequently converted at the executive level of the organizational pyramids into *actionable knowledge*, then distributed in form of standard operational practices, doctrines, rules, and regulations in the top-bottom direction. More importantly, the generated actionable knowledge has also a very limited lateral spread: it is domain related and affects predominantly only those at whom it is directly aimed, i.e., intra-domain specialists and experts. Consequently, many actors for whom such knowledge would be *pertinent and germane* (von Lubitz and Wickramasinghe, 2006b) remain entirely unaware of its existence. Despite all advantages offered by information technology and increasingly ubiquitous information/knowledge management techniques, their current employment in business operations does not engender creation of the cardinal transforming catalyst – the *actionable understanding*. Yet, it is the latter which transforms the wealth of pre-existing actionable knowledge into a clear strategy and links it to cohesive operations conducted in the precise alignment with the strategy-defined objectives.

THE CONCEPT OF 'TEAMS OF LEADERS" (TOL)

The concept of *"actionable understanding"* has been introduced several years ago by the US Army general Frederic Brown (Brown, 2002; see also Bradford and Brown, 2008) to denote the final "product" of all actions and activities performed within the broad realm of the "Teams of Leaders" (ToL) environment. ToL is the direct outcome of the requirements faced by the US Army following the end of the Cold War, where decisions made by the "man on the spot" have the potential to influence national interests, the fate of alliances, and the difference between rebuilding broken societies and perpetuation of armed conflict. The new demand necessitated a new breed of soldier-leaders: flexible, adaptable, versatile, and comfortable in operating within the complex setting of Joint Interagency, Inter-government, Multinational (JIIM) operations in which military and civilian concepts intertwined into a tightly woven mesh (Brown, 2002; Brown,

2008a,b; Bradford and Brown, 2008). In several aspects, the issues affecting the US Army were and are nearly identical to those seen in the conduct of global-scale business activities: increasing organizational complexity and spectrum of operations, the need for mission-centered cooperation of others, be it corporate partners, regulatory agencies, or customers themselves, and the need to adapt in order to address increasingly larger host of rapidly diversifying issues. The process of this far ranging transformation is complicated by the fact that it must be enacted while continuing simultaneous engagement in routine activities (Brown, 2008a).

WHAT IS TOL?

Conceptually, ToL centers on the active, platform independent fusion of advanced IM, KM and High Performing Leader Teams (HPLT; see Bradford and Brown, 2008; also von Lubitz, 2009; Fig. 2). What distinguishes ToL from a specialized social network is the essential prerequisite for the development and functions of HPLT: the shared foundation of *skills, knowledge, and attitudes* based on the previously acquired appropriate and universally high-quality professional preparation of individual team members. The preparation demands intensive training to *task, condition, and standard*, and the ability to demonstrate complete, practical mastery of performance. To be efficient, the rigorous professional training must satisfy strictly defined metrics-based performance standards. Consequently, general uniformity of education/training outcomes is attained, assuring not only the high professional capability of the participants, but also shared confidence in mutual professionalism and ability to act appropriately under a very wide range of conditions both as individuals and teams of individuals. Mutual trust and sharing are the cornerstones of successful performance, and their development and strengthening a contiguous process.

Figure 2. A high performing leader team (HPLTs) may consist of individuals (I), teams of individuals (TI), organizations (O), and virtual organizations (VO). The latter may be created ad hoc by the team members as the means of addressing specialized aspects of the mission, or enter HPLT as already formed entities. The foundations of an HPLT are shared Skills, Knowledge, and Attitudes (SKA) whose team-based application promotes development of shared trust, vision, competence, and confidence. All intensely collaborative, purpose-oriented, and meaningful interactions among Team members are based on/facilitated by the extensive, platform independent use of all available IT/IM/KM resources. Interactions result in a rapid development of shared vision, empowering sense of mutual trust, and confidence, and the conversion of actionable knowledge possessed by individual team members into mission-oriented actionable understanding shared by all members of the team. In the process of that conversion, new knowledge is generated which is fed back (bottom-up generation) into the world of computing clouds, grids, nets, and Web, where it is converted into tacit and/or explicit knowledge, then distributed (top-bottom) either as such or as actionable information back into the HPLT "universe" (von Lubitz, 2009). The entire process is made possible through the intense use of all available IT/IM/KM tools and resources. The wide variety of high-level expertise characterizing HPLTs serves as the principal facilitator in access to, acquisition, and transformation of multi-domain information and knowledge into a unified, mission-relevant body of knowledge supported by mission-oriented actionable understanding. The latter constitutes the culminating output of the team (von Lubitz, 2009)

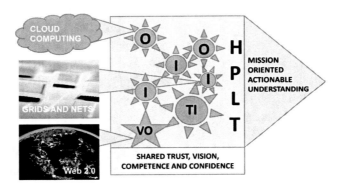

Training alone is not sufficient: it must have roots in active learning which, in the context of leader team development, requires collaborative learning shown to significantly improve critical thinking and task performance (Bradford and Brown, 2008, von Lubitz, 2009). To assure task performance to a predetermined standard, the learning process is experiential rather than didactic, and involves routine exposure to sudden, unpredictable scenario changes ("confounders"). The latter develops the required mental flexibility and adaptability of individuals within the team as well as the entire team (Brown 2002; Bradford and Brown, 2008). This type of training has been used with the great success in medicine, nursing, and in advanced business education, and assures the mastery of skills, knowledge, and also emergence of the related mental and physical attributes employed with equal ease under routine circumstances and in the environments of maximum stress, uncertainty, and tempo.

Performance assessment under rigorous and highly demanding conditions constitutes the essential part of High Performing Leader Team development: the process becomes a chain of objective self-evaluation which promotes further training leading to pitch efficiency of the teams. Due to the standardized approach used in HPLT development, teams can be inserted as "modular elements" whenever and wherever required, and the standardized training/testing regimen assures that organizations, whether real or virtual, which co-opt HPLTs as part of their operational profile will have full confidence and trust in their capabilities. The latter is of possibly the greatest significance in the development of efficiency and cohesion that, in turn, serve as the critical lubricant in multi-organizational efforts (Smith, 2007). Conversely, it has been demonstrated on several occasions that absence of such trust and acceptance are among the primary reasons for several failures (see von Lubitz, 2009 for further references).

THE IMPACT OF TOL ON GENERATION OF NEW KNOWLEDGE AND EVIDENCE-BASED, BEST PRACTICES

Continuing limitations in the use of sophisticated, technology-based methods in the process of generating actionable knowledge (see above, and von Lubitz, 2009) may lead to inadvertent "stove-piping." Implementation of ToL avoids this issue through the "horizontal spread" (Fig. 3) attained by means of platform-independent, peer-to-peer exchanges, social and professional networks, text- and visual blogs, avatars, etc., whose increasing functionality, reach, and practicality of use are supported and expanded by the rapidly growing impact of Web 2.0. Combined with the enterprise-wide access to the internal and external primary information and knowledge sources, the resulting pervasive, system-wide use of IT promotes generation of *ad hoc* collaborative entities (teams) needed to address common problems or develop "just-in-time" solutions. In the process of such interactions, and by fusing expertise of team members and teams with all

available e-based resources and analytic tools, both new knowledge and best practices are created.

Extensive use of a wide range of technology platforms and technology implementation concepts frees individual team members and teams themselves from the constraints of time, space, organizational/inter-organizational cultures, and – most importantly – the destructive influence of organizational status and rank (Bradford and Brown, 2008). For this reason ToL and its inherent processes of action and interaction have been employed with a great success by the US Army in a wide range of pilot projects involving both military and civilian affairs ((Brown, 2008a,b; Bradford and Brown, 2008). Moreover, with the already well proven methods and techniques ToL is now vigorously implemented on the national and international/multinational scale by the organization of great complexity, involved in a wide range of support and nation building missions which demand the closest possible cooperation with other, equally complex organizations of national, international, multi-national, or even global level (Brown 2008a; Bradford and Brown. 2008).

TOL AND "ACTION SWARMS"

The extensive use of IT, IM, and KM as the means of sharing information and knowledge serves as a powerful promoter of rapid development of shared vision, competence, confidence, and trust (Bradford and Brown, 2008) that constitute the critical attribute of High Performing Leader Teams. The close relationship of team members to each other, and to members of other teams is the chief mechanism which transforms previously top-down bureaucratic and organizational structures into a bottom-up/lateral knowledge and "best practices" generator. Due to the pervasive nature of the exchanges within the lattice of the rapidly forming relationships, the process of transformation helps to demolish the existing organizational barriers. Instead, close socialization ensues, and

Figure 3. Information and knowledge generation and distribution in ToL environment consisting of formal and informal teams. While informal teams provide supporting roles (background functionality), formal teams generate actionable knowledge, best practice definitions, and define the framework of actionable understanding. Individual HPLTs and Teams of Leaders share information and knowledge both horizontally among themselves (indicated by the overlap of individual teams) and vertically, along hierarchical chains of command. Horizontal spread results in the generation of new knowledge and formulation of "best practices." Vertical flows provide inputs to the executive layer of the organization where strategies are formulated and modified on the basis of bottom-up inputs. All flows are bi-directional (arrows). ToL-based interactions prevent both vertical and intra-specialty/domain information/knowledge distribution. Because of this characteristic, ToL environment provides the ideal setting for both broad-spectrum and specific intelligence gathering, analysis, and dissemination across organizational/institutional boundaries. At present, no other approach is equally powerful in these tasks (after von Lubitz, 2009)

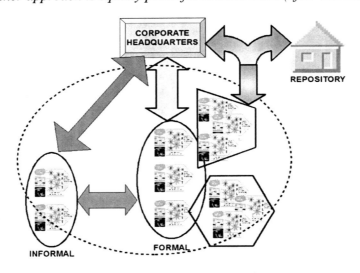

fosters further growth of mutual confidence and trust among members of leader teams.

The transforming process has chain-reaction characteristics: professional and social relationships based on universal trust and confidence expand rapidly and freely, and lead to the emergence of Teams of Leaders (Bradford and Brown, 2008; see also Lipnack et al., in press). Individuals and groups who have been physically and/or organizationally isolated convert into "swarms" and converge whenever needed based on the exact match to the requirements of the task and mission at hand (Fig. 4). Such swarms are essential when addressing problems affecting performance at the "Domain of Domains" complexity level, and the activities of Teams of Leaders have been

shown to restore coherence to disorganized multi-organizational efforts (Brown 2008a; Bradford and Brown, 2008), and help in aligning them with the underlying strategies. Indeed, ToL reached the level of maturity and broad utility that its implementation and applications manual has been developed and disseminated by the US Army (Lipnack et al., 2009).

TOL AND THE SYNTHESIS OF ACTIONABLE INTELLIGENCE AND ACTIONABLE KNOWLEDGE

Throughout the course of transition from HPLT to ToL a less tangible but critical advantage emerges:

Figure 4. Among the principal attributes of ToL interactions is task/mission-centered swarming. Simple, intra-domain tasks can be addressed by relatively small swarms representing relatively narrow range of often highly specialized expertise and knowledge (A). Very complex missions performed in domain of domain" environments (B) may require several HPLT "swarms" addressing individual sub-components or component-aggregates of the overall mission. Nonetheless, individual swarms cooperate very closely, coordinate their actions, and share information, knowledge, and results (bidirectional arrows). This type of interactions, possible only in ToL environments maximizes efficiency, maximizes strength and utility of effort, and increases operational OODA Loop revolution speed. Overall, strategic goals are attained through collaborative rather than confrontational means, and the entire process is both faster and less resource demanding

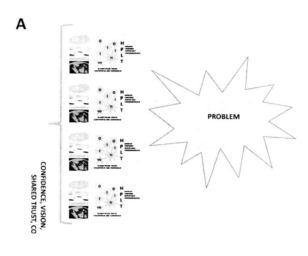

people who previously had no knowledge of each other, who might have been separated by distance, institutional or specialty barriers begin to rapidly form a network of close social relationships.

Consequently, the development of collaborative spirit that often characterizes interactions be-tween local actors can now emerge among groups of actors residing on different continents. The collaboration-building attribute of ToL is further strengthened by the fact that teams can change their status from informal to formal depending on circumstances. Also, because of the intensity of the existing interactions, team members co-operate as readily and effectively in distributed environments as when the contact is based either on the mix of physical and distributed, or direct interactions.

ToL based activities enhance both the external reach and tempo of action. It is important to stress that the enhancement is made possible due to significantly improved intelligence gathering which, in ToL environments transcend classical concepts of business intelligence. The largely multidisciplinary nature of HPLT permits gathering of intelligence data in a wide variety of forms and from a wide variety of sources (Brown, 2009a,b; Bradford and Brown, 2008), while close collaboration among HPLT members converts individual, domain-centered data streams into *intelligence-based operational picture*. The latter has two major functions: it helps in selecting the elements constituting *actionable intelligence* that leads to immediate organizational response, and as the predictor of the forthcoming needs to modify the accepted strategy to better suit and respond to the forthcoming changes within the operational environment. During the latter process action-able knowledge is rapidly generated. Altogether, the outcomes of network-centric activities that might have been shared between two isolated but professionally related groups (von Lubitz, 2009) are transformed through ToL-based interaction into a broad based *"actionable understanding"* which unifies several groups (Bradford and Brown, 2008).

Actionable understanding constitutes the most essential prerogative for operational efficiency in the environments of uncertainty and rapid, un-predictable change (Bradford and Brown, 2008) seen in complex, multi-entity business operations conducted in the environment of uncertain po-litical and economical influences. Circumstantial evidence clearly indicates that the lack of such understanding may be among the chief sources of errors (Mittelstaedt, 2005).

TOL AND SYNTHESIS AND DISSEMINATION OF MULTIDISCIPLINARY KNOWLEDGE

The process of globalization transformed rela-tively straightforward business operations into the new realm of "domain of domains." It is intensely complex, involves disciplines that, until recently, seemed to be entirely alien to commercial activities (e.g., military operations, nation building, global healthcare, etc.). Modern business conducted on the worldwide scale represents probably the only arena outside military operations where success of missions (particularly when conducted on a national, international, or global scale) *demands* extraordinarily close cooperation of vast numbers of individuals, agencies, and nations.

Implementation of ToL practices in business will unquestionably have major impact (Table 1) due to the nature in which information and knowl-edge are gathered, handled, and disseminated. At peer-to-peer level, ToL promotes lateral spread and sharing of information and knowledge to the audiences greatly extending beyond one's own professional specialty. Likewise, ToL supports *downward* migration of knowledge from more experienced/senior professionals within teams to the more junior ones. The direct advantage of such spread is the enhancement of *distributed* so-cialization *across unrelated but mutually relevant intra and inter-domain professional specialties.* In similarity to *within-profession* trends, on-line communities of practice will form. However, ToL promotes and consolidates from the outset the *interdisciplinary and trans-domain communities* of practice rather than narrow, domain-restricted ones. Cumulatively, ToL offers the most fertile ground for innovation, lateral and vertical dis-semination of knowledge, and the dissemination and development of evidence-based practices. All of these are of utmost importance for busi-ness in Globalization 3.0 environment: changed relationships that this stage introduced demands major change of practices and substitution of the

Table 1. Impact of tol-based activities (after von Lubitz, 2009)

TYPE	IMPACT
OPERATIONS	Generates actionable understanding Supports strategy development Promotes mission definition Promotes actor cooperation and collaboration across disciplines and domains Speeds OODA Loop cycles Increases OODA Loop operational space and reach Promotes extraction and analysis of mission-relevant intelligence Promotes generation of alternative approaches ("workarounds") Serves as force multiplier Maximizes mission support through the employment of shared skills, knowledge and attitudes
RESOURCES	Promotes strategy-relevant resource assembly Promotes mission-centered, parallel use of intellectual and material resources Maximizes optimal resource exploitation Utilizes legacy and future IT/IM/KM platforms Maximizes resource deployment speed Promotes mission-relevant resource concentration Maximizes utilization of platform-independent CT/IT/IM/KM resources
ORGANIZATION	Promotes creation of collaborative actor grids Promotes ad hoc creation of collaborative virtual organizations and communities pf practice Maximizes mission-centered utilization of actionable information and actionable knowledge Supports hierarchical and peer-to-peer interaction Maximizes information and knowledge sharing among all actors of the mission grid Generates bottom-up actionable knowledge generation and top-bottom actionable information flows Promotes interdisiciplinary and interdomain information and knowledge distribution and use
SOCIAL	Maximizes generation of trust and understanding among all actors Enhances mentoring Maximizes personal contacts Enhances personal knowledge and competence beyond boundaries of own discipline/specialization (promotes "generalist" education) Maximizes development of shared skills, knowledge, and attitudes

rigid top-down methods by the ultra-agile and dynamic bottom-up generated advances.

"FORCE MULTIPLIER" ROLE OF TOL

At present, there is a clearly perceptible absence of a clearly defined "global strategy" and foresight among the Western nations mirrored in the failure to incorporate into the future plans anything beyond the most obvious. The inability of the West to detect, analyze, and counteract the growing dissatisfaction with its policies is among the principal causes underlying the explosive emergence of anti-Western sentiment, religious extremism, and – ultimately – international terrorism as the sole means available to the populations of the "gap" to attain emotional if not economical "parity" with the developed countries.

In turn, the political destabilization that typically accompanies these extreme forms of protest weakens the economies in the underdeveloped regions, promotes escalation of poverty, and leads to an even greater decline of their already meager (or practically nonexistent) economies. Consequently, despite substantial funds provided by the multinational Western sources, most attempts to establish comprehensive solutions to the problems of the developing and underdeveloped world continue to fail.

ToL may change all that. It brings to the forefront the fact that technology, no matter how powerful it might be, serves nothing but the solution of "tactical" tasks whether simple or unimaginably complex. Processes (such as IM and KM) or their combination (network-centric operations) lead to the formulation and operational implementation of actionable knowledge, in typically very task specific (i.e., narrow) context. By bringing together people able to maximally exploit their mutual talents and expertise, able to efficiently implement technology and technology-based processes, and by rooting their activities in the *maximum, platform-independent use of all tools and methods and processes offered by ITC*, ToL permits to develop the *strategy* which serves as the guide and rationale of all subsequent operations (Fig. 5).

Such strategy cannot be devised by even the most intense application of either technology or processes alone. ToL provides the needed catalyst and *force multiplier*. It is in that context that ToL, contrary to "within the profession" approaches, supports the development of both evidence-based methods and of best practices among a much wider range of professionals, disciplines and agencies at a scale that has not been possible previously. The new "rules of engagement" that the jointly created best practices represent are among the major beneficial "side effects" of ToL implementation (Bradford and Brown, 2008).

Most importantly, however, ToL brings people to the forefront: it facilitates generation of locally appropriate solutions by the "people on the ground." It transforms grand but unrealistic international schemes into a coordinated

"bottom-up" effort whose ground effect becomes measurable, lasting, and aligned with the overall strategy devised on the basis of vertical inputs generated within the realm of ToL operations. All that relates directly to the manner in which e-tools, methods, and processes are used in the operational environment of ToL-based business operations: ToL transforms advanced technology from a Ferrari accessible only to a few into a hammer available to all.

TOL AS THE PLATFORM FOR THE DEVELOPMENT OF FLEXIBLE STRATEGIES

In the ToL environment, results are generated *at the practitioner level* rather than at the level of executive policies (von Lubitz and Beakley, 2009). What emerges is the *bottom-up* spread of knowledge developed through *consensus of practitioners supported by joint practical experience* and acceptable by the business communities, consumers, and regulatory bodies far more willingly than directives descending from the executive level of corporate headquarters or the governmental and international bureaucracies. Once thoroughly analyzed and tested within "communities of actors" (i.e., producers of goods and services, their distributors, and the consumers), the generated best practices can be converted via hierarchical process into a flexible and practical strategies with clear and attainable objectives. Endowed with these attributes, such strategies are readily acceptable and understandable to all involved actors at the horizontal and hierarchical levels of administration and operations. Moreover, the continuous up-down-lateral interactions keep will keep the strategy attuned to changes in the operational environment; knowledge ceases to be confined to the vertical and often entirely separated channels of profession and bureaucracy but spreads laterally and the strategy becomes actionable rather than bureaucratic (von Lubitz, 2009).

Figure 5. Operations of teams of leaders. Individual, multi-, inter-, and trans-disciplinary HPLTs join into mission-oriented "swarms." Their intense interactions both within and among individual HPLTs generate mutually shared actionable understanding. Through vertical bottom-up spread, actionable understanding assists in formulating a coherent strategy. The latter is then implemented as precise, focused ("effect-oriented"), and simultaneous operations. Actionable understanding is critical for the development of strategy-based, coherent operations conducted in "domain of domains" environments such as global range business activities. While for some of these operations actionable knowledge may be sufficient, increasing environmental complexity and the number of the participating actors shifts the balance toward ToL-based solutions and enhances the demand for actionable understanding prior to operational execution of the intended missions (after von Lubitz, 2009)

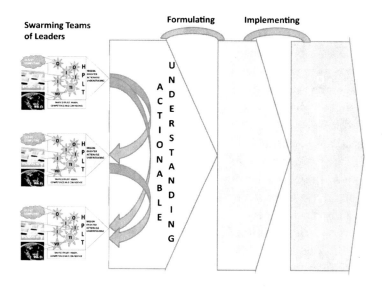

By promoting mutual trust, ToL furthers rapid development and coalescence of shared attitudes among all actors. It is a process of critical significance in international and multinational operations in any arena, be it civilian or military (Bradfford and Brown, 2008, Brown, 2008a, Smith, 2007). It has been said that, in the context of globalization, mutual trust has eroded since the policies of the developed nations are rooted within their mono-cultural, ethno-centric concepts, and the remedies proposed by the rich may therefore be both beyond the reach and without any relevance to the present and future problems of the poor (e.g., Sachs, 2005). ToL not only allows for fully empowered inclusion and interaction of all affected groups – in order to be effective, the concept of ToL *demands*

such inclusion since only then can problems be addressed effectively and efficiently. By its very nature, ToL makes global business into the business of the people of the globe.

WHY TOL?

It would be exceedingly naïve to expect that consequent implementation ToL practices will offer a dilemma-solving panacea for the global business. Nonetheless, in the realm of complex, modern business operations it may provide the launch-pad for the needed remedies. ToL is endowed with a number of distinct and unique advantages. First of all, the essential physical constituents already exist: computational methods based on grid- and cloud computing begin to impact the realm of near-real time data analysis, high-speed Internet access rapidly transforms from a Western luxury to high-speed Internet the popularly available global tool, wireless communications networks increase their reach and presence, while Web 2.0 offers increasingly wider range of tools and platforms. Intuitively applied, the ToL concept serves as the foundation of modern practice in national and global medicine and biomedical sciences (von Lubitz, 2009a,b). It is also a pre-eminently suitable tool in the development of disaster preparedness centered on mitigation of catastrophic incidents in which close collaboration among national and international agencies is required (von Lubitz et al., 2008). Most importantly, however, ToL is implemented with a remarkable success in solving extremely difficult challenges of international cooperation and collaboration by the US European Command (EUCOM) as part of its extensive interaction with the civilian authorities of several European and non-European countries (Bradford and Brown, 2008). Thus, the "lessons learned" can be readily adopted into a broad range of purely civilian environments and activities and in order to facilitate rapid dissemination of the concept into the widest practical implementation, EUCOM published recently a "rapid implementation manual" of ToL which allows users operating in practically any field to rapidly implement ToL-based operations at essentially no cost, and based on the already existing IT and personnel resources (EUCOM, 2008).

In conclusion, one aspect of ToL must be forcefully underlined: ToL unifies continuously disconnected fields of business, social responsibility, environmental protection, and global security and stability, and, for the first time, a concept has been crated that fosters rapid development of actionable understanding rather than actionable knowledge. As argued in the preceding sections, it is actionable understanding rather than actionable knowledge which serves as the prerequisite and the *essential* prelude to creating a solid foundation for the development of the very badly needed collaboration and cooperation among all involved actors on the global business stage. Without such understanding, all efforts to relieve the mounting pressures of conflicting demands, inequities, and deficiencies will ultimately fail. The signs of the approaching collapse are clearly visible already, and the currently favored erratic application of ever larger amounts of money or increasingly complex, technology-based solutions to avert the inevitable is, has been condemned by many leading businessmen and economists of the world as utterly inadequate. ToL does not represent a "paradigm shift" but a conceptual mutagenesis necessary if the increasingly more difficult and polarizing problems of the contemporary world are to be addressed successfully.

REFERENCES

Bradford, Z. B., & Brown, F. J. (2008). *America's Army: A Model for Interagency Effectiveness*. Westport, CN: Praeger Security International.

Brown, F. J. (2002, September-October). Imperatives for tomorrow. *Military Review*, 81–91.

Brown, F.J. (2008a). *Institutionalizing EUR ToL*. Unpublished working document.

Brown, F.J. (2008b). *Designing of ToL pilots*. Unpublished working document.

Canton, J. (2006). *The Extreme Future*. New York: Dutton/Penguin.

Chancellor, E. (2000). *Devil Take the Hindmost: A History of Financial Speculation*. New York: Plume Books.

Chang, W. (2008). *Network-centric Service Oriented Enterprise*. Dordrecht, Netherlands: Springer.

Ebenhart, M. (2003). *Why Things Fail*. New York: Three Rivers Press.

EUCOM (US Army European Command). (2009). *EUCOM Teams of Leaders Coaching Guide, Vs. 1.0*. Stuttgart, Germany: European Command.

Evans, P., & Wurster, T. S. (2000). *Blown to Bits*. Cambridge, MA: Harvard Business School Press.

Greenwald, B., & Kahn, J. (2005). *Competition Demystified*. New York: Portfolio/Penguin.

Haas, R. N. (2005). *The Opportunity*. New York: Public Affairs.

Holm, H. H., & Sorensen, G. (Eds.). (1995). *Whose World Order? Uneven Globalization and the End of the Cold War*. Boulder, CO: Westview Press.

Kim, W. C., & Mauborgne, R. (2005). *Blue Ocean Strategy*. Cambridge, MA: Harvard Business School Press.

Kuhn, T. S. (1970). *The Structure of Scientific Revolutions*. Chicago, IL: University of Chicago Press.

Lipnack, J., Stamps, J., Prevou, M., & Hannah, M. (2009). *Teams of Leaders Handbook*. Battle Command Knowledge System Combined Arms Center – Knowledge, Fort Leavenworth, KS.

Mandelbrot, B., & Hudson, R. L. (2004). *The (Mis) Behavior of Markets*. New York: Basic Books.

Mittlestaedt, R. E., Jr. (2005). *Will Your Next Mistake Be Fatal?* Upper Saddle River, NJ: Wharton School Publishing.

Prahalad, C. K., & Ramaswamy, V. (2004). *The Future of Competition*. Boston, MA: Harvard Business School Press.

Rifkin, J. (2001). *The Age of Access*. New York: Tarcher/Putnam.

Sachs, J. D. (2005). *The End of Poverty*. New York: Penguin.

Senge, P. M. (1994). *The Fifth Discipline*. New York: Currency (Doubleday).

Smith, P. (2007). *The Utility of Force: The Art of War in the Modern World*. New York: Knopf.

Steingart, G. (2008). *The War for Wealth*. New York: McGraw-Hill.

Stiglitz, J. E. (2003). *The Roaring Nineties*. New York: Norton & Co.

Taleb, N. N. (2007). *The Black Swan*. New York: Random House.

von Lubitz, D. K. J. E. (2009a). The Teams of Leaders (ToL) concept: the grid, the mesh, and the people in the world of information and knowledge-based global healthcare. In E. Kladiashvili (Ed.), *Grid Technologies for e-Health: Applications for Telemedicine Services and Delivery*. Hershey, PA: IGI Press.

von Lubitz, D. K. J. E. (2009b). Healthcare among the people: Teams of Leaders concept (ToL) and the world of technology-oriented global healthcare. In S. Kabene (Ed.), *Healthcare and the Effect of Technology: Developments, Challenges and Advancements*. Hershey, PA: IGI Press.

von Lubitz, D. K. J. E. (2009c). "Teams of Leaders" concept in homeland security and disaster management operations. *J. Homeland Sec. Disaster Manag., 1466*.

von Lubitz, D. K. J. E., Beakley, E., & Patricelli, F. (2008). Disaster Management: The Structure, Function, and Significance of Network-Centric Operations. *Journal of Homeland Security and Emergency Management, 1/1*(5). Retrieved from http://www.bepress.com/jhsem/vol5/iss1/1

von Lubitz, D. K. J. E., & Wickramasinghe, N. (2006a). Networkcentric healthcare: outline of entry portal concept. *Intl. J. Electronic Business Management, 4*(1), 16–28.

von Lubitz, D. K. J. E., & Wickramasinghe, N. (2006b). Networkcentric healthcare and bioinformatics: unified operations within three domains of knowledge. *Expert Systems with Applications, 30*, 11–23. doi:10.1016/j.eswa.2005.09.069

Wickramasinghe, N., & von Lubitz, D. K. J. E. (2007). *Knowledge-Based Enterprise: Theories and Fundamentals*. Hershey, PA: IDEA Group Publishing.

KEY TERMS AND DEFINITIONS

Actionable Knowledge: knowledge which is necessary for and required to initiate immediate response to changes in the operational environment. Hence, Actionable Knowledge includes in its fullest form both pertinent and germane forms of knowledge, the latter two providing only the supportive background. Actionable Knowledge is typically domain-restricted even if its application may affect several related domains.

Actionable Understanding: the state of uniform understanding of and agreement about the purpose, goal, strategy, and operational intent developed among all actors about to participate in a complex, often multidisciplinary operation performed on a very large scale within a domain-of-domains (national, international, or multinational/global) environment. Actionable Understanding is the most critical and fundamental prerequisite necessary in the development of strategy, formulation of "commander's intent" necessary for the translation of strategy into a set of actions to be executed (theater activities) in order to reach strategy-determined objective. Actionable Understanding assures maximum flexibility in the execution of strategy-determined actions, and frees individual subcomponents of the organization from command-control influences into share-collaborate-coordinate pattern of activities.

Domain-of-Domains (Environment): environment characterized by extreme complexity of interactions among individual often seemingly unrelated subcomponents, the latter existing as individual domains in their own right. In contrast to closely coupled systems, events in one domain may or may not affect events taking place within another constituent domain. Therefore, detection of critical events cap able of producing wide-ranging perturbations and crises is significantly more difficult, requires a much broader range of expertise and knowledge, and most often remains undetected by domain-centered human experts or automated monitoring systems (e.g., ERPs)

High Power Leader Team: (HPLT) a group of individuals, organizations, virtual organizations, or teams of individuals centered on devising solutions to a complex task or complex task aggregate. Members of the team can be either distributed (even globally) or partially co-located. All members posses demonstrable advanced professional skills, knowledge, and abilities (SKAs) and have been thoroughly trained in their practical use. All interactions within the team are built on mutual trust, competence, and shared vision, and most are conducted using the entire range of the available IT platforms and means of data/information/knowledge exchange. Rapidly developing trust promotes intensification of sharing necessary to develop broad-based solutions to the task at hand. HPLTs can be formal (created within the organization to address a specific task), informal (devoted to addressing general issues affecting the field or domain), permanent or ad hoc.

Network-Centric Operations: operations based on the maximum use of multi-layered data/information/knowledge networks (mesh of networks) that facilitate command and control of all activities. Originally devised as the means to decentralize the two latter functions, it evolved into a hierarchical up-down command approach that allows the executive levels full and instantaneous access to ground level information. Consequently, in current implementation, network-centric activities serve as a "peek over the shoulder" approach.

Teams of Leaders (ToL): HPLT groups united on addressing a common task within a domain-of domains environment. ToL interactions are based on the foundation of shared actionable understanding, trust, and vision. HPLTs within ToL environment can either act in full concert or aggregate as "just-in-time" swarms devoted to the solution of specific, suddenly emerging and mission-critical tasks, then disperse to participate in other strategy-dictated activities. ToL-based exchanges are both horizontal and vertical, and are also based on the maximum platform-independent utilization of all capabilities and advantages offered by IT/IM/KM Horizontal exchanges promote development of best practices and evidence-based methods. They also provide real-time upgrades to the state of actionable knowledge and significantly elevate the range and pertinence of intelligence gathering processes. Vertical interactions channel best practices, evidence-based methods, and newly generated actionable knowledge and high quality intelligence information needed to retain organizational agility, and strategic adaptability to sudden and unpredicted changes within the operational environment. ToL interactions are free from influences of organizational hierarchies, influence of rank or status of participants, and assure maximum freedom of content exchange and analysis.

Theater of Operations: The entire complex of people, processes, technologies, and methods involved in specific set(-s) of activities within a specific geographic/political realm and including both own resources, resources of allied organizations and entities, and those of the opposition. In order to have full utility, all actions executed within the theatre of operations need to have roots in a coherent strategy, be executed in a manner that promotes reaching strategy-determined objective(-s), and the execution of such actions must be characterized by coherence and cohesion. Actions performed within the theater of operations have strategic impact but are often executed as tactical events, i.e., activities affecting only a small segment of the major activity (e.g., construction of a new air/sea container terminals at strategic locations represents coherently conducted tactical action in the strategic effort to simplify transoceanic supply chain linking several collaborating and closely coupled entities).

Chapter 49

Customer Relationship Management (CRM):
A Dichotomy of Online and Offline Activities

Kelley O'Reilly
Utah State University, USA

David Paper
Utah State University, USA

ABSTRACT

By establishing the position that electronic customer relationship management (eCRM) is a form of CRM, this chapter sets out to aid the reader in understanding why CRM and eCRM initiatives are both promising and challenging. By exposing the reader to common CRM literature, the chapter documents how companies can determine the best blended approach to CRM initiatives that balance both online and offline marketing initiatives. Additionally, by considering that each unique customer touch point represents a key market strategy decision, companies can thoughtfully, and with strategic intent, design, develop, and ultimately deploy systems that effectively balance human and computer interaction. By following the suggested guidelines provided for optimizing strategic marketing decisions, companies are more likely to avoid the common pitfalls and barriers to success that have been experienced by others as documented in the literature.

INTRODUCTION

This chapter centers on the dichotomy (online v. offline) of customer relationship management (CRM). Specifically, we explore the challenges and opportunities that a CRM strategy can have for an organization. This article addresses (1) the importance of CRM and electronic CRM initiatives for enhancing customer relationships with the firm, (2) the challenges of CRM and eCRM, (3) how each key customer 'touch point' represents a marketing strategy decision for companies, and (4) how a blended approach to CRM will yield the best results in most cases.

DOI: 10.4018/978-1-61520-611-7.ch049

BACKGROUND

The practice of marketing to new as well as existing customers to enhance the relationship between company and consumer has become commonplace. This phenomenon, called relationship marketing (RM), is particularly salient for services marketing because of "the maturing of services marketing with the emphasis on quality, increased recognition of potential benefits for the firm and the customer, and technological advances" (Berry, 1995, p. 236). This RM practice is commonly referred to as customer relationship management (CRM). Today, CRM is rarely discussed without the additive construct of an Internet-oriented business model relying on e-business technologies with which to interact, communicate, and exchange information with customers and/or suppliers.

The Importance of CRM and eCRM Initiatives

In 2004, The American Marketing Association (AMA) changed its definition of marketing to "Marketing is an organizational function and a set of processes for creating, communicating, and delivering value to customers and for managing customer *relationships* in ways that benefit the organization and its stakeholders" (AMA, 2008). Since that time, the concept of RM has become accepted as a more modern view of marketing (Harker & Egan, 2006). Many marketing researchers proclaim that customers can no longer be viewed as being in endless supply and passive in regard to decision making – no longer can we take a 'one size fits all' approach to the simple manipulation of McCarthy's (1960) 4Ps: Product, Price, Place and Promotion, as has been the case for decades using a transactional approach to marketing.

Issues, Controversies, and Problems

While electronic customer relationship management (eCRM) is considered by many to hold even greater promise for business due to its digital foundation that enables greater data mining potential, it has yet to consistently deliver on its promise of facilitating better understanding of customer behavior (Adamson, Jones & Tapp, 2005; Bentum & Stone, 2005; Chen & Chen, 2004; Fjermestad & Romano, 2003; Jang, Hu & Bai, 2006; Li, Browne & Wetherbe, 2007; Lin & Huang, 2007). However, even with challenges, eCRM continues to be viewed as a "core element of enterprise competitive strategy" (Forrester Research, Inc., 2008, p. 5). According to Forrester Research, Inc. (2008) worldwide spending on CRM is expected to exceed $11 billion by 2010; almost double the spending level of 2003.

The eCRM challenge, as well as the promise, is interesting and perplexing. Many pundits cite an historic optimism and hope for the marketing 'silver bullet' as a key reason for the many eCRM failures. Meaning, many companies embraced eCRM without diligent and thoughtful strategic intent and planning. From these failures came a natural and cautious view of eCRM by many that had either previously dallied in the technology or considered doing so.

Although eCRM research is prolific, there appears to be a lack of consistent understanding and agreement as to the operationalization of the term eCRM. To complicate matters, in some instances, eCRM is differentiated as either analytical or operational (Fjermestad & Romano, 2003; Swift, 2002). Analytical eCRM focuses on the collection and analysis of customer data, while operational eCRM focuses on all customer touch points throughout a transaction. With CRM defined as the orientation of the company that involves direct customer interaction as well as the data and its uses for enhancing customer relations, it is appropriate to define eCRM as *the e-Business initiatives of a firm concerned with attracting, maintaining, and enhancing the relationship between the firm and the customers it serves.*

BEST PRACTICES FOR MAXIMIZING CRM IMPLEMENTATIONS

While there is a great body of research on both CRM and eCRM, the literature can generally be classified into a few strands focusing on strategies for success including, (1) the need to develop and nurture trust and loyalty, (2) the importance of leadership and strategy, and (3) systems integration and data issues. Each of these will be discussed in more detail below.

The Need to Develop and Nurture Trust and Loyalty

The value of nurturing and developing a relationship between a firm and its customers is well understood in the business world. At the center of such a relationship is trust. Specifically, in an effort to encourage repeat purchases, capture a greater share of 'wallet' (customer wealth) and improve the likelihood of referrals, many have recognized the role that trust must play (Bart, Shankar, Sultan & Urban, 2005; Chau, Hu, Lee, & Au, 2006; Kim & Tadisina, 2007; Porter & Donthu, 2008; Walczuch & Lundgren, 2004; Wang & Emurian, 2005). Fostering a relationship that will ultimately create trust between parties is both intuitive and logical. However, the direct links from *relationship → trust → repeat purchase intention → loyalty* have been difficult to demonstrate empirically. As a relevant example, while it is generally recognized that a relationship of trust (versus a relationship without trust) is more likely to result in a customer recommending a firm to their friends and family and to encourage repeat purchases, some findings show that recommendation intention alone is not a good predictor of a customers' future loyalty (Keiningham, Cooil, Aksoy, Andreassen & Weiner, 2007).

Leadership and Strategy

From the literature, leadership is identified as a critical success factor for successful CRM implementation. In a study by Chen and Chen (2004), the researchers identify the need for initial management support as well as ongoing management leadership as demonstrated by consistent organizational commitment. Additional research considers the use of incentives and training as key factors for combating resistance from associates and managers who will be users of the CRM system or tool (Fjermestad and Romano, 2003).

Strategic planning is also critical for CRM success. Without a sound business strategy that links directly to the expected outcomes of CRM, CRM systems and tools are unlikely to succeed. Strategic elements such as customer related benefits, the consolidation of customer information, and improved response times are examples that must be carefully planned and designed (Lin and Huang, 2007). Likewise, organizations with an existing culture of excellent customer care as demonstrated by service consciousness, a customer-centric organization, and customer-focused strategies are more likely to experience CRM success.

Systems Integration and Data

Systems integration and the alignment between business and information technology (IT) is another success factor prevalent in the literature. The failure to achieve this alignment is one of the most cited reasons for CRM failure. For instance, consideration for where data resides, the number of systems required for integration, the usability of, and resistance to, the system by users, and the expected outcomes and system functionality are commonly overlooked (Chen and Chen, 2004; Fjermestad and Romano, 2003; Lin and Huang; Padmanabhan and Tuzhilin, 2003).

While 'tight' system integration is important, a technology's ability to be flexible (Szmigin, Canning & Reppel, 2005) is also needed. Such flexibility allows the system to adapt to customer data and trends, and ultimately delivers the ability to personalize marketing information to customers. However, developing fully integrated systems is difficult. Understanding this, it is important to "continually measure and model customer sales, satisfaction, and value, both in terms of absolute figures and trends" (Cuthbertson and Bridson, 2006, p. 293) to ensure the system integrates with as well as improves the business.

The power of CRM tools lies in the application of data *and* knowledge. For instance, the power is not found in the simple collection or mining of data, but rather in the means and methods by which the data is analyzed and applied to improve customer relationships. Therefore, knowing what to collect, how to collect it, and subsequently understanding how to use data is critical. This power is often created through a balance between human and computer interaction (Chen, Chen & Kazman, 2007).

Customer 'Touch Points' as Determinants of Marketing Strategy

What is clear in the literature is that often, eCRM and CRM are viewed as two separate initiatives within companies. That is, IT often leads eCRM innovation, while Marketing leads CRM innovation. However, such a silo-based approach is sub-optimal and fails to consider that eCRM is simply a *form* of CRM, and as such, all elements related to CRM (whether electronic or not) should be contemplated holistically and inclusively.

Since the goal of CRM is to add value, CRM innovation should be a priority. However, adding value to a business should be process-based rather than silo-based so it is interesting that IT and Marketing tend to work in isolation when innovating in this realm. The determining factor of CRM and eCRM is after all always how we can better serve the customer, not whether the customer is served on or offline. Meaning, customer 'touch points' can be managed either online or offline and each determination for what is and is not online,

represents a distinct decision related to a firm's marketing strategy. For example, in the case of a carpet cleaning company, a customer could schedule the varying services online, over the phone, or face-to-face from an in-home service technician. Therefore, the idea of eCRM being anything other than complementary to CRM initiatives (versus a replacement) is not warranted. To provide a better understanding of this idea, we introduce Table One. This table illustrates the common 'stages' of customer interaction with a firm and some of the typical 'touch points' that companies can utilize as part of their strategic decision making.

For instance, when contemplating how the firm can interact during the 'follow-up & ongoing communications' stage with a customer, the firm can consider the various on and offline means with which to interact. Choosing the 'right' balance is best determined by seeking guidance from customers and then measuring the outcomes of those decisions.

For many organizations, these choices create a battle of the 'old offline ways' vs. the 'new online ways' and represent the struggle organizations face to find the appropriate balance between offline and online activities. Keep in mind that the struggle is internal. That is, the customer just wants to receive excellent service and believes that he/she should be able to choose at will whether such service is online or offline. Balancing a company's traditional offline RM strategies with the emerging, complementary, and inclusive strategy of e-enabled CRM should provide a reasonable *blended* approach (Chen et al., 2007). By blending both offline and online CRM activities, organizations are more likely to resonate with more customers simply by being flexible and responsive to a customer's preferred channel for interaction and communication.

A Blended Model of Success

The balance between offline and online activities must be navigated carefully. Consistent with Chen

Table 1. Key customer touch points and the dichotomy of online v. offline

Typical Firm/Customer 'Touch Points'	Common Examples of Online (eCRM)	Common Examples of Offline (CRM)
ATTRACTING The initial interactions between customer and firm to attract the customer to a specific product or firm.	• Company website adequately optimized for search engines. • e-marketing such as banner ads online.	• Multi-media and broadcast such as TV, radio, direct mail advertising, etc. • Personal selling such as outbound "cold calling" or door-to-door selling. • Neighborhood activities such as school contests and sponsorships. • Tradeshows & Fairs • Customer incentives for referring additional customers to company.
BROWSING The interactions between customer and firm during browsing when a customer is evaluating the degree to which a firm's product or service offerings meet customer needs.	• Company website • Robust search engine on company website for customer use. • Personalized web preferences offered on company website for customers after they have "registered" and defined their profile. • Instant messaging "live chat" with service reps via company website. • Product recommendations on company website via Recommendation Agents (RAs), product popularity based on "best sellers", etc.	• Brick and mortar traditional retail store formats. • Direct marketing such as direct mail catalogs. • Product and service displays, merchandising, and signage in store.
ORDERING The interactions between customer and firm after a customer has selected product and wants to place order.	• Via company website • Shopping cart functionality on company website. • Online booking for services and appointments.	• Customer service phone rep for ordering over the phone. • Retail Store clerk. • Door-to-door salesperson.
PAYING The interactions between customer and firm to execute the actual transaction.	• Online payment and confirmation via the company website.	• In-store • In-person (in home service) • By phone • By fax • By mail
SHIPPING/DELIVERY The interactions between customer and firm that occur after payment and up to point of customer taking possession of goods or services.	• Online tracking and integration between website and delivery agent. • Email confirmation of purchase and shipping details.	• In-store pick-up (typically at time of payment). • Service performed in home (e.g. carpet cleaning).
RETURNS The interactions between customer and firm to execute a product return, exchange, or request for service to be re-done due to customer satisfaction reasons.	• Online return authorization via the company website. • Online tracking and integration between website and delivery agent via the company website.	• Return via mail service. • Return initiated over the phone via company representative. • In-store returns, exchanges, or re-service. • Call-back for service re-do at customer's home.
FOLLOW-UP & ONGOING COMMUNICATIONS The interaction between customer and firm after transaction is complete to encourage next purchase or other customer referrals.	• Email marketing messages • Customer-Company Blogs • Social networks • Twitters • Mobile texting • Website promos and offers	• Personal visit • Follow-up phone call • Thank you letter • Direct mail marketing • Phone solicitation

et al. (2007), we adopt the view that eCRM value is gained through a *blended* approach to global CRM activities. Therefore, it is recommended to

consider the first contact with customers as the 'signal' for future contacts. That is, customers who initiate the relationship via the phone or face-to-face remain offline customers, and those who initiate the relationship via online means, remain as online customers. Of course, companies should remain flexible in offering offline customers online access, and online customers offline access - fundamentally, customer preference must be honored to balance the need for human and computer interaction (Sheth and Parvatiyar, 1995).

Guidelines for Determining a CRM Marketing Strategy

To aid companies in determining how to navigate their own unique 'blend' of online and offline CRM initiatives, we offer the following strategic questions and guidelines for management consideration:

Understand Your Own Bias for Online v. Offline Programs.

Commonly senior management determines strategic corporate direction. While this is not inherently problematic, consideration must be given to the decision-makers own characteristics and biases. For instance, managers in their 40s or 50s may not appreciate the value of mobile marketing or new social networking e-marketing developments. Therefore, leaders should understand their own biases and invite the views of customers and/or employees so that a wide range of consumer types provide feedback regarding how best to interact with customers.

Can Company Systems Fully Integrate Online and Offline Activities?

If the computer systems of a firm are unable to effectively integrate with all customer-facing initiatives (whether online or offline), priority should be to upgrade the system to make integration possible. Without a fully-integrated system, CRM and eCRM will be silo-based and unlikely

to optimally deliver new and compelling value to customers.

Is the Organizational Culture Open?

While no one culture has been identified as superior for CRM, it has been suggested that an open corporate culture will yield best results (Bentum & Stone, 2005). In closed cultures, internal employee opinions, ideas, and suggestions are stifled. As a result, creating customer-facing initiatives and optimizing customer touch points may not be considered a priority.

What Benefits Does the Company Expect to Derive from CRM Innovation?

Unmanaged, CRM can alter the balance between building relationships with customers and creating cost savings through streamlined transactions and automated e-marketing. In essence, the power of the one-to-one relationship can easily be converted into an efficient and effective exchange between customer and the company's computer. While customers do in fact value the benefits of electronic exchange (Porter & Donthu, 2008), we believe the benefits of combining human interaction and accessibility with electronic systems outweigh a purely electronic exchange. Therefore, if the only desire for CRM rests with minimizing overhead or automating customer touch points, CRM is unlikely to deliver optimally.

How Will the Company Measure CRM Success?

By understanding upfront how CRM innovation success will be measured, managers can thoughtfully consider if the benefits are likely to outweigh the costs. If the measure of success is simply a decrease in traditional (offline) marketing spending, how are changes in consumer interaction, response rates, referrals, or loyalty considered in a cost/benefit analysis? Reduced costs are only of value with concurrent value-added increases in customer behavior like repeat purchases, referrals, or increased job averages.

FUTURE RESEARCH DIRECTIONS

The nature of e-Business applications, of which CRM and eCRM are a part, will continue to hold great promise as well as challenge for practitioners. Understanding the role that people, business processes, and technology play as a conduit between firm and customer is key. Therefore, we suggest that future research on CRM should be viewed from a cross-disciplinary lens that considers research from information systems, marketing, management, and psychology to name but a few. To effectively bridge this research divide requires a holistic look at the combination of people, processes, and technology as key drivers of CRM innovation and change.

CONCLUSION

This chapter set out to provide an understanding of CRM and how eCRM is merely a *form* of CRM. By understanding this concept, companies are more likely to optimally deploy CRM programs that resonate with their customers. Additionally, by considering that each unique customer touch point represents a key market strategy decision, companies can thoughtfully, and with strategic intent, design, develop, and ultimately deploy systems that effectively balance human and computer interaction meaningfully with their customers. By following the suggested guidelines for making these strategic marketing decisions regarding the balance of online and offline CRM initiatives, companies are more likely to avoid the common pitfalls and barriers to success that have been experienced by others.

REFERENCES

Adamson, G., Jones, W., & Tapp, A. (2005). From CRM to FRM: Applying CRM in the football industry. *Database Marketing & Customer Strategy Management, 13*, 156–172. doi:10.1057/palgrave.dbm.3240292

AMA. (2008). *American Marketing Association Web site*. Retrieved October 23, 2008 from http://www.marketingpower.com/_layouts/Dictionary.aspx?dLetter=M

Bart, Y., Shankar, V., Sultan, F., & Urban, G. L. (2005). Are the drivers and role of online trust the same for all web sites and consumers? A large-scale exploratory empirical study. *Journal of Marketing, 69*, 133–152. doi:10.1509/jmkg.2005.69.4.133

Bentum, R. V., & Stone, M. (2005). Customer relationship management and the impact of corporate culture – A European study. *Database Marketing & Customer Strategy Management, 13*, 28–54. doi:10.1057/palgrave.dbm.3240277

Berry, L. L. (1995). Relationship marketing of services: Growing interest, emerging perspectives. *Journal of the Academy of Marketing Science, 23*, 236–245. doi:10.1177/009207039502300402

Berry, L. L., & Parasuraman, A. (1991). Marketing services: Competing through quality. *The Free Press.*

Chau, P. Y. K., Hu, P. J., Lee, B. L. P., & Au, A. K. K. (2006). Examining customers trust in online vendors and their dropout decisions: An empirical study. *Electronic Commerce Research and Applications, 6*, 171–182. doi:10.1016/j.elerap.2006.11.008

Chen, H. M., Chen, Q., & Kazman, R. (2007). The affective and cognitive impacts of perceived touch on online customers' intention to return in the Web-based eCRM environment. *Journal of Electronic Commerce in Organizations, 5*, 69–91.

Chen, Q., & Chen, H. M. (2004). Exploring the success factors of eCRM strategies in practice. *Database Marketing & Customer Strategy Management, 11*, 333–343. doi:10.1057/palgrave.dbm.3240232

Cuthbertson, R. W., & Bridson, K. (2006). Online retail loyalty strategies. *International Journal of Information Technology and Management, 5*, 279–294. doi:10.1504/IJITM.2006.012042

Fjermestad, J., & Romano, N. C. Jr. (2003). Electronic customer relationship management. Revisiting the general principles of usability and resistance – an integrative implementation framework. *Business Process Management Journal, 9*, 572–591. doi:10.1108/14637150310496695

Forrester Research, Inc. (2008). *Topic Overview: Customer Relationship Management 2008* (PDF document). Retrieved November 11, 2008, from http://www.forrester.com

Harker, M. J., & Egan, J. (2006). The past, present and future of relationship marketing. *Journal of Marketing Management, 22*, 215–242. doi:10.1362/026725706776022326

Jang, S., Hu, C., & Bai, B. (2006). A canonical correlation analysis of e-relationship marketing and hotel financial performance. *Tourism and Hospitality Research, 6*, 241–250. doi:10.1057/palgrave.thr.6050024

Keiningham, T. L., Cooil, B., Aksoy, L., Andreassen, T. W., & Weiner, J. (2007). The value of different customer satisfaction and loyalty metrics in predicting customer retention, recommendation, and share-of-wallet. *Managing Service Quality, 17*, 361–384. doi:10.1108/09604520710760526

Kim, E., & Tadisina, S. (2007). A model of customers trust in e-businesses: micro-level inter-party trust formation. *Journal of Computer Information Systems*, (Fall): 88–104.

Li, D., Browne, G. J., & Wetherbe, J. C. (2007). Online consumers switching behavior: A buyer-seller relationship perspective. *Journal of Electronic Commerce in Organizations, 5*, 30–42.

Lin, C., & Huang, Y. (2007). An integrated framework for managing eCRM evaluation process. *International Journal of Electronic Business, 5*, 340–359. doi:10.1504/IJEB.2007.014782

McCarthy, E. J. (1960). *Basic Marketing*. Homewood, IL: Irwin.

Padmanabhan, B., & Tuzhilin, A. (2003). On the use of optimization for data mining: theoretical interactions and eCRM opportunities. *Management Science, 49*, 1327–1343. doi:10.1287/mnsc.49.10.1327.17310

Porter, C. E., & Donthu, N. (2008). Cultivating trust and harvesting value in virtual communities. *Management Science, 54*, 113–128. doi:10.1287/mnsc.1070.0765

Sheth, J. N., & Parvatiyar, A. (1995). Relationship marketing in consumer markets: Antecedents and consequences. *Journal of the Academy of Marketing Science, 23*, 255–271. doi:10.1177/009207039502300405

Swift, R. (2002 February). Analytical CRM powers profitable relationships: Creating success by letting customers guide you. *Data Mining Review*.

Szmigin, I., Canning, L., & Reppel, A. E. (2005). Online community: enhancing the relationship marketing concept through customer bonding. *International Journal of Service Industry Management, 16*, 180–196. doi:10.1108/09564230510625778

Walczuch, R., & Lundgren, H. (2004). Psychological antecedents of institution-based consumer trust in e-tailing. *Information & Management, 42*, 159–177.

Wang, Y. D., & Emurian, H. H. (2005). An overview of online trust: Concepts, elements, and implications. *Computers in Human Behavior, 21,* 105–125. doi:10.1016/j.chb.2003.11.008

ADDITIONAL READING

Berry, L. L. (1983). Relationship marketing. In L. L. Berry, G. Shostack, & G. Upah (Eds.), *Emerging Perspectives on Services Marketing* (pp. 25-8). Chicago, IL: American Marketing Association.

Fink, L., Zeevi, A., & Te'eni, D. (2008). The effectiveness of online customer relations tools: Comparing the perspectives of organizations and customers. *Internet Research, 18,* 211–228. doi:10.1108/10662240810883281

Foss, B., Stone, M., & Ekinci, Y. (2008). What makes for CRM system success – or failure? *Database Marketing & Customer Strategy Management, 15,* 68–78. doi:10.1057/dbm.2008.5

Grönoos, C. (1994). From Marketing Mix to Relationship Marketing: Towards a paradigm shift in marketing. *Management Decision, 32,* 4–20. doi:10.1108/00251749410054774

Jain, R., Jain, S., & Dhar, U. (2003). Measuring customer relationship management. *Journal of Service Research, 2,* 97–109.

Kennedy, A. (2006). Electronic customer relationship management (eCRM): opportunities and challenges in a digital world. *Irish Marketing Review, 18,* 58–68.

Kim, C., Zhao, W., & Yan, K. H. (2008). An empirical study on the integrated framework of e-CRM in online shopping: Evaluating the relationships among perceived value, satisfaction, and trust based on customers' perspectives. *Journal of Electronic Commerce in Organizations, 6,* 1–19.

Palmatier, R. W., Dant, R. P., Grewal, D., & Evans, K. R. (2006). Factors influencing the effectiveness of relationship marketing: A meta-analysis . *Journal of Marketing, 70,* 136–153. doi:10.1509/jmkg.70.4.136

Pitta, D., Franzak, F., & Fowler, D. (2006). A strategic approach to building online customer loyalty: integrating customer profitability tiers. *Journal of Consumer Marketing, 23,* 421–429. doi:10.1108/07363760610712966

Ratnasingam, P. (2008). The impact of e-commerce customer relationship management in business-to-consumer e-commerce (Report). *Journal of Electronic Commerce in Organizations, 30*(17).

Scullin, S. S., Fjermestad, J., & Romano, N. C. Jr. (2004). E-relationship marketing: changes in traditional marketing as an outcome of electronic customer relationship management. *The Journal of Enterprise Information Management, 17,* 410–415. doi:10.1108/17410390410566698

KEY TERMS AND DEFINITIONS

Customer-Facing: An orientation that relates to the proximity and strength of customer-firm interactions. A customer-facing employee is one who regularly interacts with, speaks with, or services customers.

Customer Relationship Management (CRM): The orientation of the company that involves direct customer interaction as well as the data and its uses for enhancing customer relations. Effective CRM is integrated across the organization and throughout functional areas of the firm.

Customer Touch Points: All of the various points in time that the firm and customer interact throughout the initial stages of attracting a customer to a product or service through post-sale follow-up.

e-Business: All aspects of the firm that can be systematized in an electronic manner to improve operations inside the firm, outside the firm with customers, and with the firm's business partners.

Electronic Customer Relationship Management (eCRM): The e-Business initiatives of a firm concerned with attracting, maintaining, and enhancing the relationship between the firm and the customers it serves.

Marketing Strategy: The overarching operational and functional programs that determine a firms' market position, communication platform, and tactical marketing initiatives with the goal of optimizing customer interactions with the firm's product and services.

Relationship Marketing: The practice of marketing to new as well as existing customers to enhance the relationship between company and consumer.

Chapter 50

Understanding E-Payment Services in Traditionally Cash-Based Economies:
The Case of China

Xiaolin Li
Towson University, USA

Dong-Qing Yao
Towson University, USA

Yanhua Liu
Wuhan College of Economics and Management, China

INTRODUCTION

Electronic payment or e-payment refers to any payment transactions conducted electronically. In narrow terms, it usually refers only to online payment. E-payment is a crucial part of e-commerce. It increases transaction speed, improves merchants' liquidity, and enhances buyers' online shopping satisfaction. E-payment also reduces transport costs, robbery, and counterfeiting of fiat cash (Panurach, 1996).

However, e-payment development in emerging economies—most of which rely heavily on cash for e-commerce transactions—has not kept up with advances in e-commerce. As a result, inefficient payment methods have become a bottleneck of further e-commerce growth.

Over the past few years, China has witnessed phenomenal growth in e-payment. A variety of e-payment services have emerged in China. E-Payment penetration has also started to increase. As of June 2008, approximately 57 million (22.5% of) online shoppers have used e-payment services in China (CNNIC, 2008).

China's rapid e-payment development may provide ideas and lessons for the formulation of e-payment paradigms in similar economies. Despite numerous studies (Bin, Chen, & Sun, 2003; Daily & Cui, 2003; Davison, Vogel, & Harris, 2005; Hailey, 2002; Press, Foster, Wolcott, & McHenry, 2003) on China's e-commerce in general, little endeavor has been made on e-payment in China. This paper intends to fill the gap by examining a series of issues pertaining to China's e-payment services, which include China's e-payment growth, mechanisms, characteristics, opportunities and challenges.

DOI: 10.4018/978-1-61520-611-7.ch050

Table 1. E-Commerce payment methods (Source: Ciweekly, 2006)

E-Commerce Payment Methods	Percentage of Merchants
E-Payment	60.2%
Cash upon Receipt of Goods	39.4%
Postal Payment	12.3%
Bank Transfer	6%
Others	2.1%

The remainder of the paper is arranged as follows: Section 2 discusses e-payment development in China. Section 3 reports the major e-payment methods for online purchases in China. Section 4 focuses on the discussion of China's e-payment services. Section 5 analyzes the characteristics of e-payment in China. Section 6 and 7 discusses the opportunities and challenges of e-payment in China. Section 8 concludes the paper with major contribution of this study.

E-PAYMENT DEVELOPMENT IN CHINA

China's e-payment services started in 1997 when China Merchants Bank initiated an online payment service for B2B transactions. In 1998, the bank allied with a few major stores in Beijing and Shenzhen and launched its first B2C payment service. In 1999, China Construction Bank established online banking services in Beijing, Guangzhou, Shenzhen, Chongqing, and Qingdao. Other banks soon followed by establishing their own online banking services. The development of online banking built a foundation for e-payment growth in China.

China's e-payment growth was steady but slow in the first few years. In 2001, the total annual online transaction was only 900 million Chinese Yuan. In 2004, it grew to 7.5 billion Chinese Yuan. 2005 witnessed the fastest growth—China's annual online payment transactions reached 16.1 billion Chinese Yuan, a more than 100%

growth over the previous year. 2005 has thus been known as "The First Year of E-Payment" in China. (Heading-Century, 2008). Today, nearly a quarter (57 million) of shoppers use some forms of e-payment services in China.

MAJOR PAYMENT METHODS FOR ONLINE PURCHASES

Payment mechanisms for e-commerce transactions are more diversified in China than in countries with high credit card penetration. A variety of E-commerce payment methods are concurrently used in China. The most common ones include e-payment, cash upon receipt of goods, postal payment, and bank transfer (Table 1).

The majority (over 60%) of online merchants use e-payment. But a considerately large proportion of online businesses are still using traditional payment methods. In particular, nearly 40% of merchants are using "cash upon receipt of goods paradigm" — the buyer orders online, the seller physically delivers the goods to the buyer, and the buyer pays cash upon receipt of the goods.

E-PAYMENT SERVICES

In broad sense, there are three major e-payment methods in China: online payment, mobile payment, and telephone payment (Table 2). Our discussion focuses only on the most common method—online payment, which represents over

Table 2. Major e-payment services in China (Source: Ciweekly, 2006)

E-Payment Services	Percentage of Transactions
Online Payment	80.6%
Mobile Payment	9.5%
Telephone Payment	7.4%
Others	3.5%

80% of China's e-payment.

Bankcards: ChinaPay, sponsored by China Banking Association, is a pioneer of China's bankcard-driven e-payment services. It incorporates fourteen major commercial banks and is capable of both B2B and B2C payment transactions in most cities in China. By the end of 2006, all regional cities and 865 county-level cities had joined ChinaPay network, which included 152 member banks (issuing 900 million bankcards) and 570,000 online merchants. ChinaPay's annual transactions reached 255 trillion Chinese Yuan in 2008 (ChinaPay, 2009). In addition to its services in China, ChinaPay offers services in other countries including Singapore, Thailand, and South Korea.

Direct Online Payment: An online payment transaction that involves only a buyer, a merchant, and a bank is referred to as "direct online payment." Figure 1 describes the following operational procedures of direct online payment:

1. The buyer and merchant open accounts with the bank.

2. The buyer places an order for goods/services and sends his/her bank account information to the merchant

3. The merchant forwards to the bank information about the buyer's bank account and charged amount.

4. The bank verifies the buyer's account information and then transfers the charged amount from the buyer's to the merchant's account.

Indirect Online Payment: An online payment transaction that involves a third party as well as a buyer, a merchant, and a bank is described as "third- party online payment." Figure 2 delineates the following procedures of third-party online payment:

1. The buyer and merchant register accounts with the third party.

2. The buyer places order for products/services from the merchant's website.

3. The merchant provides payment information to the third party.

Figure 1. Direct payment procedures

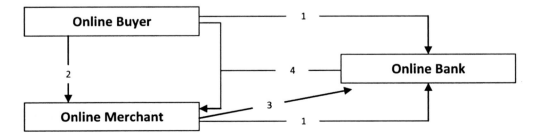

Figure 2. Third-Party online payment

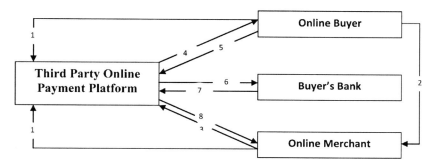

4. The third party issues payment request to the buyer.

5. The buyer provides bank account information.

6. The third party connects to buyer's bank to request for payment.

7. Buyer's bank transfers charged amount from buyer's to the third party's bank account

8. The third party releases the money to the merchant after the buyer acknowledges receipt of purchased products/services.

Alipay, launched by Alibaba, is one of China's biggest and most successful independent third-party Internet payment platforms. It has nearly 80 million users, with a daily transaction amount of over 1.5 million and total trading volume of over 350 million Chinese Yuan (China Tech News, July 10, 2008). The latest report on China's online shopping reveals that Alipay has gained a 76.2% market share in the e-payment sector (CNNIC, 2008).

CHARACTERISTICS OF E-PAYMENT IN CHINA

The dominant use of debit cards: The use of credit cards in China is believed to be riskier than in western countries. Therefore, unlike in those countries, a password is often required in China when using a credit card online. For instance, VISA and MasterCard, which have been in business in China since 2002, require online shoppers to have password-secured online shopping accounts with their banks. To avoid the risks and inconveniences of credit cards, merchants and buyers tend to prefer bankcards for their online purchases.

Increasing role of the third-party: Relying on creditability and a large user base, third-party online payment platforms are playing an increasing role in e-payment. Alipay, for instance, has not only played an important role in the fast growth of Alibaba's own e-commerce websites (Taobao.com and Alibaba.com), but also provided effective online payment services to other online merchants. Recently, Alipay has even started to offer online payment services for Amazon.com, a key competitor of Taobao (China Tech News, 2008).

Alliance among banks, major merchants, and the third party: Alliances among major banks, merchants, and the third party has been a key strategy for an e-payment service to gain credibility and user base. Alipay has established a strategic alliance with Giant Interactive, a major online gaming operator, to enhance Giant's online payment system. "Zhi Fu Bao" (Payment Treasure), a very successful third-party online payment platform, is the result of a strategic cooperation between Alibaba.com and the Industrial and Commercial Bank of China (ICBC).

OPPORTUNITIES

China has one of the largest Internet user populations and it is still growing rapidly. Over the past three years, China's Internet users have increased from 103 million in 2005 to 253 million in 2008 (CCNIC, 2008). The increase of Internet usage has fueled the growth of e-commerce, which in turn, increases the demand for online payment. By June 2008, 22.5% of online shoppers had used some form of online payment services, which represented a 71.7% growth rate compared with December 2007 (CNNIC, 2008).

Furthermore, online bank users have increased. More than 40 million people are using online banking today (CCNIC, 2008). China also has one of the largest bankcard infrastructures with 1.4 billion bankcards, which somehow overcomes the country's lower credit card penetration problem.

The Chinese government has not merely helped improve the legal and regulatory environment for online banking and e-payment growth, but also passed laws, such as the Electronic Signature Law (Yan, 2005), to safeguard e-commerce and e-payment transactions.

CHALLENGES

China's online payment penetration rate is still lower than western countries and the payment issue is still the single biggest bottleneck for the country's further growth of e-commerce. The following are among the major challenges China faces in e-payment development.

Low Credit Card Penetration: The primary reason why e-payment becomes such a big hassle in China while it is not as serious problem in western countries lies in China's lack of a reliable credit system and low credit card penetration. With a population of 1.3 billion, China has only about 40 million credit card users (Chinadaily, 2007); many of those credit cards are actually prepaid debit cards. Without a sizable and reliable credit

system, China has to be more innovative in creating online payment mechanisms. The development and diffusion of such mechanisms take more time and efforts as compared with using an existing functional credit card system.

Deficient Banking and Legacy Payment Systems: Despite China's recent reforms in its banking systems to cater to the needs of online monetary transactions, online banking in China is still immature. By June 2008, for instance, the penetration rate of online banking in China is only about 23%, much lower than the rate of western countries like the U.S., which has a penetration rate of 53% (CNNIC, 2008). China is also deficient in legacy payment systems. Traditional monetary transaction systems such as Electronic Data Interchange (EDI) and Electronic Funds Transfer (EFT) barely exist.

Heavy Reliance on Fiat Cash: Despite the introduction of various online payment services, buyers' reliance on fiat cash for online purchases is still prevalent. Cash upon delivery of goods, an order online and pay cash offline paradigm is still a common payment method, constituting nearly 40% of e-payment transactions in China (figure 1). Users' trust in and reliance on fiat cash is cultural and cannot be easily changed.

Geographical Imbalance: Development in e-payment services across different geographical regions in China is very imbalanced. In major cities and coastal regions where Internet penetration is high, a variety of e-payment services are available, but there may be no online payment services available at all in small cities and remote areas. Many e-payment services are provided only within specific cities, or even only at specific stores.

CONCLUSION

E-payment is one of the most critical components of e-commerce. But the development of e-payment services in most cash-based countries has not kept up with e-commerce advances, and as a result, has become a bottleneck for the further growth of e-commerce. Some innovative and practical e-payment mechanisms discussed in this study are widely accepted in China, mostly because they have successfully coped with the challenges and difficulties in online payment within China, including the country's low credit card penetration, deficient banking infrastructure, and traditional business transaction norms. Findings of this study may serve as a knowledge base and strategic foundation for e-payment services in similar economies.

REFERENCES

Bin, Q., Chen, S., & Sun, S. Q. (2003). Cultural differences in e-commerce: a comparison between the U.S. and China. *Journal of Global Information Management, 11*(2), 48–55.

China Tech News. (2005, March 4). Alibaba and ICBC promote online payment service. *China Tech News*. Retrieved January 11, 2009, from http://www.chinatechnews.com/2005/03/04/2555-alibaba-and-icbc-promote-online-payment-service/

China Tech News. (2008a, June 30). Rival cooperation: Alipay formally begins working with Amazon.com in China. *China Tech News*. Retrieved January 13, 2009, from http://www.chinatechnews.com/2008/06/30/6936-rival-cooperation-alipay-formally-begins-working-with-amazoncn-in-china/

China Tech News. (2008b, July 10). Alipay cooperates with Giant Interactive Group. *China Tech News*. Retrieved January 9, 2009, from http://www.chinatechnews.com/2008/07/10/6984-alipay-cooperates-with-giant-interactive-group/

Chinadaily. (2007, September 14). Credit card more popular in China. *China Daily.* Retrieved January 13, 2009, from http://www.chinadaily.com.cn/bizchina/2007-09/14/content_6107546.htm

Chinapay. (2009). *The development of ChinaPay*. Retrieved January 12, 2009, from http://www.chinapay.com/cpportal/about_us/unionpay.jsp

Ciweekly. (2006). Statistics on China's e-payment industry in 2006. *China Internet Weekly*. Retrieved January 13, 2009, from http://ebanking.ciweekly.com/

CNNIC. (2008). *Statistical Report on China Internet Development, July 2008*. Retrieved January 10, 2009, from http://cnnic.net.cn/uploadfiles/pdf/2008/7/23/170516.pdf

Daly, S. P., & Cui, L. X. (2003). E-logistics in China: basic problems, manageable concerns and intractable solutions. *Industrial Marketing Management, 32,* 235–242. doi:10.1016/S0019-8501(02)00267-5

Davison, R. M., Vogel, D. R., & Harris, R. W. (2005). The e-transformation of western China. *Communications of the ACM, 48*(4), 62–66. doi:10.1145/1053291.1053320

Hailey, G. T. (2002). E-commerce in China changing business as we know it. *Industrial Marketing Management, 31,* 119–124. doi:10.1016/S0019-8501(01)00183-3

Heading-Century. (2008). *Analytical Report of China's E-payment Industry*. Retrieved January 13, 2009, from http://my.icxo.com/?uid-338548-action-viewspace-itemid-111531

Panurach, P. (1996). Money in electronic commerce: digital cash, electronic fund transfer, and Ecash. *Communications of the ACM, 39*(6), 45–50. doi:10.1145/228503.228512

Press, L., Foster, P. W., & McHenry, W. (2003). The Internet in India and China. *Information Technologies and International Development, 1*(1), 41–60. doi:10.1162/itid.2003.1.1.41

Yan, W. (2005). The electronic signatures law: China's first national e-commerce legislation. *Intellectual Property & Technology Law Journal*, *17*(6), 6–10.

KEY TERMS AND DEFINITIONS

Bank Transfer: a payment mechanism in which payment transactions are made by transferring fund between bank accounts of the seller and buyer.

Cash Upon Receipt of Goods: a payment paradigm in which the buyer orders online, the seller physically delivers the goods to the buyer, and the buyer pays cash upon receipt of the goods.

ChinaPay: sponsored by China Banking Association, is a pioneer of China's bankcard-driven e-payment services.

Direct Online Payment: An online payment transaction that involves only a buyer, a merchant, and a bank.

Electronic Payment: refers to any payment transaction conducted electronically.

Postal Payment: a payment method where payment transactions are made via the postal services.

Third-Party Online Payment: An online payment transaction that involves a third party as well as a buyer, a merchant, and a bank.

Chapter 51
Scenario Driven Decision Support

M. Daud Ahmed
Manukau Institute of Technology, New Zealand

David Sundaram
University of Auckland, New Zealand

INTRODUCTION

Though traditional DSS provide strong data management, modelling and visualisation capabilities for the decision maker, they do not explicitly support scenario management appropriately. Systems that purport to support **scenario planning** are complex and difficult to use and do not fully support all phases of **scenario management**. This research presents a life cycle approach for scenario management. The proposed process helps the decision maker with idea generation, scenario planning, development, organization, analysis, execution, and the use of **scenarios for decision making**. This research introduces scenario as a DSS component and develops a domain independent, component-based, modular framework that supports the proposed **scenario management process**.

DOI: 10.4018/978-1-61520-611-7.ch051

BACKGROUND

Herman Kahn, a military strategist at Rand Corporation, first applied the term scenario to planning in the 1950s (Schoemaker, 1993). **Scenario analysis** was initially an extension of traditional planning for forecasting or predicting future events. Currently, scenarios are constructed for discovering possibilities, leading to a projection of the most likely alternative. **Scenarios** explore the joint impact of various uncertainties, which stand side by side as equals. Usually sensitivity analysis examines the effect of a change in one variable, keeping all other variables constant. Moving one variable at a time makes sense for small changes. However, if the change is much larger, other variables do not stay constant. Schoemaker (1995) argues that **scenario**, on the other hand, changes several variables at a time, without keeping others constant. Decision makers have been using the concepts of scenarios for a long time, but due to its complexity, its use is still limited to strategic decision making tasks. **Scenario planning** varies widely from one decision maker to another mainly because of lack of generally accepted principles for **scenario management**. Albert (1983) proposes three approaches for scenario planning, namely, Expert scenario approach, Morphological approach and Cross-Impact approach. Ringland (1998) identifies three-step scenario planning – namely brainstorming, building scenarios, and decisions and action planning. Schoemaker (1995) outlines a ten-step scenario analysis process. Huss and Honton (1987) describe three categories of scenario planning.

SCENARIO MANAGEMENT AND SUPPORT

Issues, Controversies, Problems

The literature still lacks a suitable approach for planning, developing, analyzing, organizing and evaluating the scenario using model-driven **decision support systems**. Currently available **scenario management processes** are cumbersome and not properly supported by the available tools and technologies. Therefore, we introduce a life cycle approach based scenario management guideline. Generation of multiple scenarios and sensitivity analysis exacerbate the decision makers problem. The available **scenario planning tools** are not suitable for assessing the quality of the scenarios and do not support the evaluation of scenarios properly through comparison processes. We introduce an evaluation process for comparison of instances of homogeneous and heterogeneous scenarios that will enable the user to identify the most suitable and plausible scenario for the organization. Considering the significance of scenarios in the decision-making process, this research includes scenario as a decision-support component of the DSS and defines **Scenario-driven DSS** as an interactive computer-based system, which integrates diverse data, models and solvers to explore decision scenarios for supporting the decision makers in solving problems.

Traditional **DSS** have been for the most part data-driven, model-driven and/or knowledge-driven but have not given due importance to scenario planning and analysis. Some of the DSS have partial support for sensitivity analysis and goal-seek analysis but this does not fulfil the needs of the decision maker. In most cases, the available **scenario analysis tools** deal with a single scenario at a time and are not suitable for development of multiple scenarios simultaneously. A scenario impacts on related scenarios but currently available tools are not suitable for developing a scenario based on another scenario.

To address the problems and issues raised above we followed an iterative process of observation/evaluation, theory building, and systems development (Nunamaker, Chen and Purdin, 1991), wherein we proposed and implemented a flexible framework and architecture for a scenario driven decision support systems generator (SDSSG). It includes scenario as a DSS component, extends the model-driven DSS, and incorporates knowledge- and document-driven DSS (Power, 2001). A prototype was developed, tested and evaluated using the evaluation criteria for quality and appropriateness of scenarios (Schoemaker, 1995) and principles of DSSG frameworks and architectures (Collier, Carey, Sautter and Marjaniemi, 1999; Geoffrion, 1987; Ramirez, Ching, and Louis, 1990).

Solutions and Recommendations

Scenario Management: A Life Cycle Approach

The scenario can be different for different problems and domains but a single management approach should support the model-driven scenario analysis process. Therefore, this research introduces a **scenario management process** using life cycle approach that synthesizes and extends ideas from

Figure 1. Scenario management: a life cycle approach

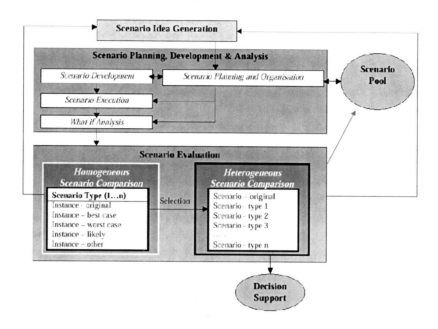

Ringland (1998, 2002), Schoemaker (1995), Albert (1983), Huss and Honton (1987), van der Heijden, (1996), and Wright, (2000). The proposed life cycle approach for scenario management process addresses a variety of problem scenarios. The life cycle process starts with scenario idea generation and finishes with the usage of scenario for decision support as illustrated in Figure 1. The following sections present all the phases of the life cycle approach for scenario management.

Idea Generation

The scenario planner foresees the key issues that exist within the scenario and analyses the concerns for identifying the influential driving forces and parameters for the scenarios. In addition the planner may also use the existing scenarios from the scenario pool. The leading factors, which could be either internal and/or external, could lead to various changes to the system. The decision maker as a domain expert predicts the possible changes to the indicators that would guide to the development of ideas for **scenario planning**.

Scenario Planning, Development and Analysis

In this phase, the decision maker will carry out the tasks of scenario planning and organization, scenario development, scenario execution, and what-if analysis. Existing scenarios could also act as inputs to this phase apart from the ideas generated from the previous phase.

Scenario Planning and Organization

The **scenario planning** step mainly focuses on decomposing the whole big scenario into multiple inter-related scenarios that are suitable for development, execution, analysis and evaluation. It also includes scenario structuring and identification of the scenario components.

A Mechanism for Structuring Scenarios

Scenarios are complex and dynamically related to other scenarios. In view of addressing the complexity and inter-relatedness of scenarios, we propose to divide larger scenarios into multiple simple scenarios having independent meaning and existence. In this context we identify three types of scenarios, namely:

- **Simple Scenarios** – The simple scenario is not dependent on other scenarios but completely meaningful and usable.
- **Aggregate Scenarios** – This scenario is comprised of several other scenarios. Top level scenario can be broken down to low level scenarios or several low level scenarios can be added together to develop a top level scenario. The structures of different scenarios or results from multiple scenarios are combined together to develop an aggregate scenario.
- **Pipelining Scenarios** – One scenario is an input to another scenario in a hierarchical scenario structure. In this type of scenario, each constituent scenario will have independent existence but the lower-level scenarios may be tightly or loosely integrated with the higher-level scenario.

The decision maker may combine simple as well as complex scenarios together using pipelining and aggregation to develop more complex scenarios.

Scenario Organization

Scenario organization activities include making available already developed scenarios, storing, retrieving, deleting, and updating scenarios to and from a scenario pool. This scenario pool should support both temporary and permanent storage systems. The temporary storage, termed as a runtime pool, is used for managing scenarios during development, analysis and evaluation. The newly developed and retrieved scenarios are cached in the runtime pool for developing aggregate and/or pipelined scenarios. The scenario pool also permanently stores scenarios for

future use or reference. Both the temporary and permanent storage systems are capable of storing the scenario structure, scenario instance and executed scenarios.

Scenario Development

Scenario planning and scenario development stages are inter-dependent and iterative. **Scenario development** is the process of conversion and representation of planned scenarios into fully computer based scenarios. Chermack (2003) argues that scenarios have rarely been applied to develop alternative processes. The proposed life cycle approach supports development of alternative process models and scenarios. In this stage, the decision maker organizes the related data, model, solver, and dependent scenarios for constituting the relationships among them to develop scenario(s). The decision maker could potentially use pre-customized and/or loosely coupled scenarios and may skip this step if they use previously developed scenarios. The scenarios are developed in mainly two steps. In step 1, the basic scenarios of the domain are developed, and in step 2, scenarios related to what-if (goal seek and sensitivity) analysis are developed.

Scenario Execution

The proposed scenario development process ensures that the scenario can be executed and analyzed for determining quality and plausibility. In this step, the models are instantiated with the data, and then the model instance is executed using the appropriate solver(s). Model selection is completely independent while one or more solvers may be used for a model execution. A flexible mapping process bridges the state attributes of the model and solver to engage in a relationship and to participate in the execution process. For a complex scenario, the decision maker may need to apply several models and solvers to analyze various aspects of the scenario. If a scenario contains other scenario instances, execution of the containing scenario will depend on the execution of the contained scenarios. But if the containing scenario contains the structure of the contained scenarios, the execution of the containing scenario depends on a series of model instantiation and model execution. This process may be pre-customized during the scenario development step or customized during the execution step. The decision maker can skip this step if they use only the previously stored scenario instances and executed scenarios from the scenario pool.

What-if Analysis

What-if analysis can be divided into two categories, namely sensitivity analysis and goal-seek analysis. **Sensitivity analysis** allows changing one or more parametric value(s) at a time and analyses the outcome of the change. It reveals the impact itself as well as the impact on other related scenarios. Because a scenario contains other scenarios, each and every change dynamically propagates to all the related scenarios. **Goal-seek analysis** accomplishes a particular task rather than analyzing the changing future. This goal seek analysis is just a reverse or feedback evaluation where the decision maker supplies the target output and gets the required input.

Scenario Evaluation Process

Scenario evaluation is a challenging task (Chermack, 2002) but some end-states are pre-determined dependent upon the presence of an interaction of identified events (Wright, 2000) which can be used to devise an evaluation process. The decision maker could potentially develop many scenarios. The question is – do all these scenarios represent a unique situation? Each scenario might appropriately draw the strategic question; represent fundamentally different issues; present a plausible future; and challenge conventional wisdom. Schwartz (1991) and Tucker (1999)

discourage too many scenarios and advocate the use of best-case scenario, worst-case scenario and most-likely scenario. The evaluation is done through scenario execution and comparison of the executed results. A visualisation object displays results of all the executed scenario instances either as a table or as a graph. This presentation helps comparing the computed inputs and outputs including other attributes. The comparison may take place among homogeneous scenarios or heterogeneous scenarios.

Decision Support

The above described scenario planning, development, and evaluation through comparative analysis results in improved participant learning (de Geus, 1988; Shoemaker, 1995; Godet, 2001) and helps decision makers re-perceive reality from several points of view (van der Heijden et al., 2002) and thereby provides better support for decision making. The following section proposes a framework that realizes the proposed scenario management process.

SCENARIO DRIVEN FLEXIBLE DECISION SUPPORT SYSTEMS FRAMEWORK

Few of the DSS frameworks emphasize fully featured scenario planning, development, analysis, execution, evaluation and their usage for decision support. DSS components such as data, model, solver, and visualization have been extensively used in many DSS framework designs but they do not consider scenarios as a component of DSS. Scenario plays such an important role in the decision-making process that it is almost impractical to develop a good **decision modelling** environment while leaving out this component. While scenarios resemble model-driven DSS they are more complex than models and need to be considered as independent entities in an explicit fashion. Therefore, we propose that **scenario-driven DSS** should add the scenario as an independent component in addition to existing decision-support components. The scenario does not have a separate existence without its base components. Every scenario is built up from a unique problem (model) that can have a number of alternative unique instances (data) and each instance can be interpreted, executed or implemented using one or more alternative methods (solvers).

To overcome the problems and address the issues mentioned above we propose a scenario-driven decision support systems generator (**SDSSG**) framework as illustrated in Figure 2. The SDSSG components are separated into the following three categories:

- Decision-support components (DSC) that include the data, model, solver, scenario and visualization.
- Integration Components (IC) that include Kernel, Component Set, Mapping, and Validation Component.
- Component Pools that include data pool, model pool, solver pool, scenario pool, and visualization pool. Each component of the DSC has a direct relationship with a component pool.

In this framework, the DSCs, ICs and Component pools are independent of each other. The DSCs communicate via the kernel component. Mapping component develops the correct path of communication between data and model, and model and solver, while the validation component tests the correct matching of the component interface and the proper communication between the components.

The data, model, solver, scenario, and visualization can be stored in different component pools as shown in Figure 2 and the framework allows retrieving these components from the component pools. The related model, data and solver can be combined together to develop a scenario. This scenario can be saved to the scenario pool for future use. This also allows using the scenario(s) as an input for developing a number of simple, aggregate, and pipelined scenarios. Every instance of the scenario can be termed as a specific decision support system. Therefore, the framework is a generator of scenarios as well as decision support systems.

Scenario information can be saved and retrieved to and from the scenario pool and the same can again be customized using models and solvers. The scenario instances can be used as complex data for input to the next level model for further analysis. Different scenarios can be computed simultaneously and **sensitivity** and **goal-seek analysis** can be done using different scenarios. The framework is suitable for analyzing internally coherent scenarios or scenario bundles, and examining the joint consequences of changes in the environment for supporting the decision maker's strategy.

FURTHER RESEARCH DIRECTIONS

The generalisability of these concepts, frameworks, and architectures has been proved in other domains and other paradigms. For instance, Ahmed and Sundaram (2007) have applied these principles for developing a generic DSS framework and architecture for sustainability modelling and reporting. The concept of this framework, architecture and scenario management processes can be applied to the decision making components of existing enterprise systems such as SAP and Oracle. Future research could explore the applicability of our concepts, frameworks, and architectures to other domains and paradigms as well as their use in conjunction with existing transaction processing, analytical, and strategic information systems.

Figure 2. Scenario-driven decision support systems generator (SDSSG) framework

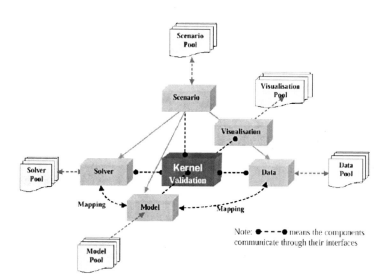

CONCLUSION

Current **scenario planning** and analysis systems are very complex, not user friendly, and do not support modelling and evaluation of multiple scenarios simultaneously. To overcome these problems we propose a scenario management life cycle, and a framework and architecture that support the lifecycle. The lifecycle as well as the framework and architecture are validated through a concrete implementation of a prototype. The implementation has been described in detail and fleshed out with examples in Ahmed and Sundaram (2008).

This research introduces the concepts of **scenario structure** and their development strategy. It decomposes large complex scenarios into multiple small and executable scenarios and uses the decomposition and re-composition methodology for defining the scenario structure. The research also proposes a life cycle approach for **scenario management** that supports a range of activities from conceptualizing and understanding the scenario to final use of the scenario for decision making. Key phases of the life cycle are idea generation, scenario planning, organization, development, execution, analysis, evaluation, and finally decision support. The process hides external factors and complexities of the scenario and allows the seamless combination of decision parameters for appropriate scenario generation. We also propose a generalized scenario evaluation process to enable the decision maker in finding appropriate and plausible scenarios through homogeneous and heterogeneous scenario comparisons among the multiple instances of similar and dissimilar scenarios respectively.

The research further realizes the scenario-driven decision-making processes through extending model-driven decision support systems. We develop a generic scenario driven flexible decision support systems generator framework and architecture that supports the above-mentioned scenario management processes as well as sensitivity and **goal-seek analysis**. Scenarios are introduced as a new **DSS component** alongside the traditional data, model, solver, and visualization components.

REFERENCES

Ahmed, M. D., & Sundaram, D. (2007). A Framework for Sustainability Decision Making System: A Proposal and an Implementation. In *eProceedings of the 9th International Conference on Decision Support Systems (ICDSS 2007)*, Kolkata, India. Retrieved from http://www.cba.uni.edu/ICDSS2007/PDFs/29.pdf

Ahmed, M. D., & Sundaram, D. (2008). A framework for scenario driven decision support systems generator. *International Journal of Information Technology and Web Engineering*, 3(2), 45–62.

Albert, K. J. (1983). *The Strategic Management Handbook*. New York: McGraw-Hill.

Chermack, T. J. (2002). The mandate for theory in scenario planning. *Futures Research Quarterly*, 18(2), 25–28.

Chermack, T. J. (2003). A Methodology for Assessing Performance-Based Scenario Planning. *Journal of Leadership & Organizational Studies*, 10(2), 55. doi:10.1177/107179190301000206

Collier, K., Carey, B., Sautter, D., & Marjaniemi, C. (1999). A Methodology for Evaluating and Selection Data Mining Software. In *Proceedings of the 32nd Hawaii International Conference on System Sciences*.

De Geus, A. (1988). Planning as learning. *Harvard Business Review*, 66(2), 70–74.

Geoffrion, A. (1987). An Introduction to Structured Modelling . *Management Science*, 33(5), 547. doi:10.1287/mnsc.33.5.547

Godet, M. (2001). *Creating futures: Scenario planning as a strategic management tool*. London: Economical Publishing.

Huss, W.R., & Honton, E. J. (1987 April). Scenario Planning: What Style Should You Use? *Long Range Planning*.

Nunamaker, J. F. Jr, Chen, M., & Purdin, T. D. M. (1991). Systems Development in Information Systems Research . *Journal of Management Information Systems*, 7(3), 89–106.

Power, D. J. (2001). Supporting Decision Makers: An Expanded Framework. In *Informing Science Conference*, Poland.

Ramirez, R. G., Ching, C., & St Louis, R. D. (1990). Model-Data and Model-Solver Mappings: A Basis for an Extended DSS Framework. In *ISDSS Conference Proceedings* (pp. 283-312).

Ringland, G. (1998). *Scenario Planning- Managing for the Future*. Hoboken, NJ: John Wiley & Sons.

Ringland, G. (2002). *Scenarios in business*. New York: John Wiley & Sons.

Schoemaker, P. J. H. (1993). Multiple Scenario Development: Its Conceptual and Behavioural Foundation. *Strategic Management Journal*, 14(3), 193–213. doi:10.1002/smj.4250140304

Schoemaker, P. J. H. (1995). Scenario Planning: A Tool for Strategic Thinking . *Sloan Management Review*, 36(2), 25–40.

Schwartz, P. (1991). *The Art of the Long View*. New York: Doubleday.

Tucker, K. (1999, April). Scenario Planning . *Association Management*, 51(4), 70–75.

van der Heijden, K. (1996). *Scenarios, The Art of Strategic Conversation*. Hoboken, NJ: Wiley.

van der Heijden, K., Bradfield, R., Burt, G., Cairns, G., & Wright, G. (2002). The Sixth Sense: Accelerating organizational learning with scenarios. New York: John Wiley.

Wright, A. D. (2000). Scenario planning: A continuous improvement approach to strategy. *Total Quality Management*, 11(4-6), S433–S438. doi:10.1080/09544120050007742

ADDITIONAL READING

Ahmed, M. D. (2002). *Design and implementation of Scenario driven flexible decision support systems generator.* Unpublished Masters Thesis, University of Auckland, Auckland, New Zealand.

Fahey, L., & Randall, R. M. (Eds.). (1998). *Learning from the future: competitive foresight scenarios.* New York: Wiley.

Georgantzas, N. C., & Acar, W. (1995). *Scenario-driven planning: learning to manage strategic uncertainty.* Westport, CT: Quorum Books.

Lindgren, M., & Bandhold, H. (2003). *Scenario planning: the link between future and strategy.* New York: Palgrave Macmillan

Ralston, B., & Wilson, I. (2006). *The scenario-planning handbook: a practitioner's guide to developing and using scenarios to direct strategy in today's uncertain times.* Mason, OH: Thomson South-Western.

Ringland, G. (1998). Scenario planning: managing for the future. New York: John Wiley.

Ringland, G., & Young, L. (Eds.). (2006). *Scenarios in marketing: from vision to decision.* Hoboken, NJ: Wiley

van der Heijden, K. (2005). *Scenarios: the art of strategic conversation* (2nd Ed.). Hoboken, NJ: John Wiley & Sons.

KEY TERMS AND DEFINITIONS

Aggregate Scenarios: The structure of different scenarios or results from multiple scenarios are combined / aggregated together to develop a more complex scenario.

Decision Support Systems/Tools: in a wider sense can be defined as systems/tools that affect the way people make decisions. But in our present context it is defined as systems that increase the intelligence density of data and supports interactive decision analysis.

Goal-Seek analysis: accomplishes a particular task rather than analyzing the changing future. This goal seek analysis is just a reverse or feedback evaluation where the decision maker supplies the target output and gets the required input.

Intelligence Density: is the useful 'decision support information' that a decision maker gets from using a system for a certain amount of time or alternately the amount of time taken to get the essence of the underlying data from the output.

Pipelining Scenarios: One scenario is an input to another scenario in a hierarchical scenario structure. In this type of scenario, lower-level scenario can be tightly or loosely integrated with the higher-level scenario.

Scenario: is a complex problem situation analogous to a model that is instantiated by data and tied to solver(s). A scenario can be presented dynamically using different visualizations. A scenario may contain other scenarios.

Scenario Life Cycle: is an iterative process of scenario idea generation, planning, organization, development, execution, what-if analysis, evaluation and decision support.

Scenario-Driven DSS: is an interactive computer-based system, which integrates diverse data, models and solvers to explore decision scenarios for supporting the decision makers in solving problems.

Sensitivity Analysis: allows changing one or more parametric value(s) at a time and analyses the outcome for the change. It reveals the impact on itself as well as the impact on other related scenarios.

Simple Scenarios: The simple scenario is not dependent on other scenarios but completely meaningful and usable.

Chapter 52
E–HRM in Turkey:
A Case Study

Yonca Gürol
Yildiz Technical University, Turkey

R. Ayşen Wolff
Haliç University, Turkey

Esin Ertemsir Berki
Yildiz Technical University, Turkey

ABSTRACT

This chapter is about the role of electronic Human Resource Management (E-HRM) in Turkey. E-HRM can be briefly defined as the planning, implementation and application of information technology for both networking and supporting at least two individuals or collective actors in their shared performing of HR activities. New knowledge economy increased competition throughout the world and living in an age of massive technological evolution is changing the nature of business; especially e-business. E-business is challenging current HRM policies and functions as it uses internet technology to drive organizational performance. This study attempts to investigate several specific and critical points that will contribute to a better understanding of E-HRM by illustrating how it is used by a Turkish firm in the health sector. In this sense, the authors' findings will try to exemplify how an E-HRM policy is realized. Our aim is to provide a model for the implementation of E-HRM in other companies.

INTRODUCTION

During the past ten years, emerging factors such as globalization, rapid technological developments and limited resources have created a new competitive landscape for all businesses. These developments forced companies to adopt several strategies to survive and to excel in their environment. Obviously, competition and attempts to increase market share between organizations play an important role in the business world. Today information is such an important competitive tool for businesses that a new era has begun known as "The Information Age" or "The New Economy".

Turkey is adapting economically and culturally to a web-based economy, seeing this as essential to its candidacy for the European Union. Although it has been observed that the human factor is among the leading strategic advantages of successful firms' in Turkey, "traditional personnel management" is still

DOI: 10.4018/978-1-61520-611-7.ch052

resisting change. Therefore, issues pertaining to human resources are under increasing investigation by academics, as well as by business people. In Turkey the beginning of academic research into human resource management dates back to the 1970s, to early studies of personnel management. In the 1980s, the transition from personnel management to human resource management has influenced academic study in Turkey in all relevant areas of the subject. The changes observed in these years were not limited to a change from personnel management to HRM. Rather, there is the much more important issue of change within the above mentioned transition stemming from the strategic role ascribed to HRM (Gurol *et al*, 2003). Following this evolutionary process, at present, academic interest in E-HRM has increased. This interest stems from E-HRM's role in cost reduction development of HR services helping to improve strategic planning. Furthermore E-HRM is seen as a driving force for companies growing both regionally and in labor force. It is becoming a prerequisite for the competitive success of any firm. Using the internet theoretically makes your labor pool global rather than local. You can use information technology to do all the routine HR administrative work automatically at any time, at anywhere.

BACKGROUND

As mentioned in the introduction part, living in age of massive technological evolution is changing the nature of business. This new business structure is named as electronic business(e-business) and can be defined as the overall business strategy that redefines the old business models and uses digital media and network technology to optimize customer value delivery (Karakanian, 2000, 1) which causes certain innovative changes in business life. These computer based innovative changes are especially found in customer relations, marketing, inventory control, and/or human resource

management and are clearly affecting the way in which business is conducted.

The new mechanism introduced by e-business utilizes Internet-based computing, which supports the open flow of information between systems. For this purpose, e-business uses business portals (established over the Internet) to interact with customers (Mitchell, 2001).

Information systems have also been applied to HRM for decades. However, the way of using information systems and the way of processing information for HRM have evolved and dramatically improved over the last decade. As a result human resource management has also gone through a change process, especially in terms of HRM policies and functions.

Moving from this point on, Strohmeier (2007) has defined electronic human resource management (E-HRM) as "the planning, implementation and application of information technology for both networking and supporting at least two individual or collective actors in their shared performing of HR activities." (p.20)

According to Ulrich (2007; 2009) human resource managers take place in the strategy designation process with the top managers. As one of the strategic partners, the HR manager derives benefit from Electronic Human Resource Management Systems (EHRMS), which is an important tool in E-HRM, to disseminate and execute the strategy within the organization. E-HRM has gained use of technology as it enables employees to manage much of their own HR administrative work. They can take care of many routine transactions whenever they wish, because automated systems don't keep office hours. In addition to their former operational role, HR professionals can also act as a competency manager by arranging the right people to the right positions in the right time with their new strategic architecture role.

With the use of IT for HRM purposes there will be more time left for strategic decision-making, as a result of a decrease in manually performed administrative tasks. Also as a result of the improvement of overall HRM system, there will be parallel decrease in HR related questions from employees and line management (Ruël, Bondarouk& Velde, 2007).

In light of all these, this study attempts to investigate several specific and critical points that will contribute to a better understanding of E-HRM. In the following sections, we will first briefly describe HR functions in E-HRM, following this; we will go over our findings of a case-study conducted to show how E-HRM and its certain functions are being used today by a Turkish firm in health sector.

HR FUNCTIONS IN E-HRM

Job Analysis and HR Planning

E-HRM offers online job descriptions which are the most important output of the job analysis process. The HR specialist can easily establish the competencies of the required applicant in a way that matches the applicant to the job descriptions and rapidly recruit the labor whenever and wherever needed. In the HR planning process it is easier to follow workforce gaps, the quantity and quality of the labor force and to plan future workforce requirements with the help of HR knowledge systems such as Oracle, SAP, People-Soft, Excel etc.

E-Recruitment and Selection

HR managers more often use the Internet for recruiting and the selection of new personnel (Stone, 2005). Internal and external labor pool and the job openings can be pursued by HR knowledge systems. It also creates advantage for internal staffing of open positions. Computerized testing for selection is increasingly replacing conventional paper-and-pencil manual tests (Dessler, 2005).

E-Learning / Training / Education / Knowledge Management

Setting the training needs, driving web-based courses, evaluating the success of training programs, keeping the results for the future use in the performance and career management functions and storing the organization's intellectual capital are the most prominent advantages of the E-HRM. The most frequently used education technologies are tele-training, video conferencing and training via internet. E-learning, gives the opportunity to learn online rather than face-to-face. Although it is a very flexible learning opportunity, many people may find it difficult to devote the necessary time.

Performance Management and Appraisal

Targeting the performance results and online evaluating the performance provide effectiveness and rapidness for the performance management process. Electronic performance monitoring (EPM) is the ultimate point in computerized appraising in which supervisors electronically monitor the work force and rate them (Dessler, 2005). Having the feedbacks online can diminish wasted time and keep records confidential.

Career Development

Knowing the competencies and educational background of the labor is important to make career targets and construct career paths online. The organization can offer on-site or online career centers, encourage role reversal, establish a "corporate campus"; computerized on and offline programs which are available for improving the organizational career planning process.

Compensation

HR managers prefer using knowledge management systems also for compensation and benefit systems, for accessing electronic databases and undertaking corporate promotion (Stone, 2005). Computers play an important role in benefits administration. PC-based systems let employees interactively update and manipulate their benefits packages. Inter and intranet systems enable employees to get medical information about hospitals and doctors and to do interactive financial planning and investment modeling. Additionally, online award programs can also be used to recognize employees on anniversary dates or give their success awards (Dessler, 2005).

Employee Safety and Health

Risk and security management is crucial to HR-related information because it involves private and highly sensitive individual data. It follows that data and multiplatform security aspects which are perhaps the most serious factors that need to be taken into consideration during the formulation of an organization's E-HRM strategy (Karakanian, 2000, p.3).

The workplace access through the carding system makes it possible to know where your worker is at the moment. As a result, HR department can easily search the work place for workers during job accidents and keep up with the workers' rotation.

Employee Relationships / Communication

Intranet systems, allow better interaction between the workforce and their managers and between colleagues as well. HR specialists can use online communication channels efficiently and share internal and external information with the organization as a whole. E-mail groups, discussion meetings, synchronized conferences via the internet keep the organization updated.

It is also possible to use the internet to manage union relations by mass e-mail announcements to collective bargaining unit members, supporters and government officials (Dessler, 2005).

THE RESEARCH METHOD AND RESULTS ON TURKISH E-HRM PRACTICE

Method

The method adopted in this research is the case study, since with this method it is possible to gain in-depth understanding of the factors that led to electronic use in HR functions and the way in which the process was realized. It will thus be possible to develop a basis upon which a theoretical framework could be attained for explaining the E-HRM system.

Researchers have conducted interviews with top managers and line managers in key positions related to HR and also with IT support system specialists. The semi-structured interview questions explored HR functions in general and the technical adaptation problems in the transformation process of E-HRM.

The data was collected through a variety of means including in-depth interviews, document analysis and the individual participation of the HR manager. Researchers tape-recorded as well as took notes of the answers during the interviews, and each interview took approximately 30 minutes.

Currently there are 10 workers in the HR unit and also a couple of interns who update the data of the workforce. On-site observations and small talks with the personnel have also been possible during the interview period. Researchers also examined and analyzed the firm's official web site, in addition to other written materials provided by the firm.

Electronic Human Resources Management System (EHRMS) and its Difference from the Other Softwares

Since Human Resources Department works differently from other departments, its software application is also unlike other departments. For example, in an accounting program, only data is used without any human contact. There is no face to face connection, it's all electronic!

Or the program that the purchasing department uses can be an institutional resource planning system, concerning only that department. The purchasing manager may or may not see an order, but the data will be shared electronically.

However, Human Resources Department is not like other departments. It is not related to only one or two people or departments. It gives support and service to all company employees; its' work is hard and the logic that it uses in its' software is pragmatic.

It is better to analyze Human Resources Software in two parts. The first part is the application that the Human Resources Department uses; the second is the application that the company workers use.

The Application used by Human Resources Department (Back Office)

This application organizes the HR Department's own operations by informing the front office, and in turn by being informed by them. Other departments besides HR do not use it. For example, it prepares payroll or calculates the budget by entering payment information. It defines the necessary competencies for certain positions which are used in evaluating performance and according to these competencies, mathematical grading is instituted and the right questions are asked. We will call this application **"HRMS"** (Human Resources Management System). Also it is called **"HRIS"** (Human Resource Information Systems). There

is a fundamental difference between HRIS and E-HRM in that basically HRIS are directed towards the HR department itself. Users of these systems are mainly HR staff. With e-HR, the target group is not the HR staff but people outside this department: employees and management (Ruël *et al.*, 2007).

The Application Used by the Company Workers (Front Office)

The employees of the company use this application. This application allows examining payrolls during the evaluation process. Data registration improves the back office feedback system between workers and management and defines performance. Data is screened and it is fed by the back office. We call this application **"EHRMS"** (Electronic Human Resources Management System).

CASE STUDY: APPLIED E-HRM AT THE HR DEPARTMENT OF THE AMERICAN HOSPITAL IN TURKEY

Human Resources in the Electronic Environment of Turkey

As Turkey has improved in the Human Resources field, use of related technology has grown and a variety of software applications have become integral to daily operations.

In the past, modules such as number of employees, paid leaves and over-time working hours were used for building payroll programs and payroll accounts. Although these modules made Human Resource work easier by storing data, preparing reports and various other reasons in terms of data access, it caused an extra work load.

Nowadays, as the value of Human Resources Department is more appreciated, its functionality has also increased in a parallel way and taken on much of the workload. In the past, Human Resources was seen as a department that registered workers, organized paid leave and prepared the payroll. It has now turned into a department that improves the performance of its employees, prepares training programs for them, specifies work definitions to clarify their career planning and finds the appropriate niche for each employee. At this point, it cannot be neglected to state that, Human Resources managed to adopt itself to such a big workload by taking advantage of the new technology seen especially by the growth of web software.

Interview Questions and Answers

Please Give Us Some Information about the Historical Background of your Organization.

Turkey's first, general, not -for profit hospital, American Hospital and School of Nursing, was established by Admiral L. Bristol in 1920. With its 300 bed capacity, American Hospital continues to develop and give the best quality of service to each specialty of modern medicine. Each year VKF American Hospital serves 131,000 patients. Seeking care, they come from all over Turkey and various parts of the world.

The VKF American Hospital offers diagnostic, inpatient and outpatient care in 38 medical specialties. Its 24 hour service meets international standards and has 500 physician specialists and a health care and support service staff of 1,150 people. World standard service is provided with the support of the most modern medical equipment and systems.

In 1995 the management of the American Hospital was transferred to Koç Holding. In 1996-1997, Koç Holding's managers (Arcelik, Otosan etc.) were invited to join the hospital administration and were introduced to health-care management. The first HR professionals were educated among them and the HR department was founded in 1997. There are 10 workers in the HR

unit at the moment and there are also interns who update the data of the workforce.

Can you Describe the Role of HR Department in your Organization? Is it Seen as a Strategic Partner? Is it a Support Unit?

Human Resources Management is a strategic partner; we undertake operational and managerial roles in our daily planning.

Can you Give Us Information about your Strategic Plans?

Our strategic plan is: to open a new hospital of radiology and oncology and to establish a medical faculty in the mid-term. These plans allow for progress.

Which HR Functions do you Outsource?

The HR department has no outsourcing activities but we do have IT support from the Koç Systems within the Koç Holding group.

Which HR Functions are Carried Out in your Organization?

Human Resources functions include job analyzing, planning, salary, employment, career development, employee satisfaction, and training topics. These are carried out in the hospital.

We Know that E-HRM is Successfully Implemented in your Hospital. How did you Manage the Transformation of the Related Process?

We first improved the IT infrastructure of the hospital. At the beginning of 2002, we started using Electronic Human Resource Management System and preferred Oracles' HR module for E-HRM activities. We chose it as an alternative to the SAP software. We use software like PYXIS and PAX in material management. Besides, pneumatic tube systems are supported by personal communication systems and are used in the flow of information and in sending blood and reports, etc.

Which HR Functions were Transferred to Electronic Environment?

All Functions transferred into the e-environment;

We first transferred job analyses, job definitions and completed their updates. Later on we continued with HR planning.

For Which Purposes did you Transfer These Functions to an Electronic Environment?

- With the e-environment we are now able to calculate easily in our integration system: HR Planning; work force loss analyses, follow-up of absenteeism and over-time. Hospital access is done through a carding system so there is the advantage of predicting change and knowing where the worker is. As a result, information is made available on both where the work place of the worker is during work accidents and keeping up with the workers' rotation. Through the e-system, the emergency nurse logs on so one can know the location of the nurse and where to call in case of an emergency. Through the intranet, doctors can fill out their absence forms. Both the work of the appointment center and the call center got easier, as our doctors made their weekly schedules within the system.
- Staffing; it is possible to predict the loss of workforce before it occurs through the e-system. For example, the assignment of 70 people to government jobs was known

before hand. We were able to plan, make evaluation of career potential in the candidate pool and were able to fill out positions without any trouble. By the help of EHRMS, we are able to calculate every detail of yearly absences, save them in the system and also plan leaving and replacement. Open positions are visible to everyone in the system and their registration is approved by the managers and HR.
- Training: In-house training is done through the intranet. The worker gets training whenever he/she wants it. There is no cost for physical space and the time factor can be used efficiently both by the trainer and the trainee.
- Performance Appraisal; every semester employees are transferred into the system and are tracked in the e-environment. An employees' development can be followed. Most importantly the "360-degree feedback" performance appraisal is done in this system.
- Career Planning: the career planning of workers can be tracked.
- Wage and Salary System: we use the HEY grading system to enable us to calculate the salaries.

What are the Advantages and Disadvantages of E-HRM?

Even though at the beginning of an E-HRM application it is necessary to stick to budget, in the long term there is an increase in the productivity of the workforce and a decrease in cost.

In the beginning the system increases workload due to the entering data, but when the system is used actively, the workload decreases. Through this system, data is kept orderly and reports are fully prepared. All statistical information such as; paid leave, performance evaluations and the candidate pool can be obtained easily in the data base. When the system is busy like in the performance appraisal period or career target defining process, the system may slow down as the access to the system increases.

As in every department, there is also an adaptation period in the HR department with the transfer to electronic systems. The help of IT professionals is necessary during this period.

Thank you very much for your contributions to our academic work and for sharing confidential information with us.

FUTURE RESEARCH DIRECTIONS

The geographically separated branches of the multinational company can easily handle recruitment and selection, staffing, performance appraisal, training functions via E-HRM applications. In the future, the number of studies in International Human Resource Management field regarding this issue will likely increase.

Also, another research trend that will gain importance will probably be based on the software and programs on HR. As mentioned before E-HRM is using web-based-technology channels for implementing HR practices. Setting the s-m-a-r-t targets, performance criteria, encouraging e-training, receiving the training results online and using these results as an input for the human performance system will provide further integration of HR functions. As long as the technology changes, electronic human resource management systems will be improved. Moreover, as HR software becomes easier to use and to afford, the number of organizations which prefer E-HRM will continue to increase day by day. It is expected that the HR knowledge systems such as Oracle, SAP, PeopleSoft, etc. will propose new and more functional software and the technology related issues of E-HRM will constitute an emerging trend within the field.

CONCLUSION

At the end of this case study, we concluded that the work of HR employees in the Human Resources Information System got easier and the cost of intra-organizational processes decreased. It was also concluded that better access to data in the e-environment decreased the need for decision-making at higher levels of management. For our research, we had information from the HR department managers and their team, and also from the users of the system. As expected, the selection and placement process got easier and through e-training, workers were better informed, better coordinated and were better prepared to improve their performance.

REFERENCES

Allard, S., & Holsapple, C. W. (2002). Knowledge Management as a Key for e-Business Competitiveness: From the Knowledge Chain to KM Audits. *Journal of Computer Information Systems, 42*(5), 19–25.

Biesalski, E. (2003). Knowledge Management and e-Human Resource Management. In *Workshop Lehren-Lernen-Wissen-Adaptivität*. Retrieved March 20, 2009, from http://km.aifb.uni-karlsruhe.de/ws/LLWA/fgwm/Resources/FGWM03_08_Ernst_Biesalski

Dessler, G. (2005). *Human Resource Management* (10th Ed.). Upper Saddle River, NJ: Prentice Hall.

Gürol, Y., Aşık, Ö., & Doğrusoy, G. (2003). An Examination of Areas of Interest in Turkish Academic Studies of Human Resource Management on the Dimensions of Past, Present and Future. In *Workshop on Management Knowledge on Time and Space*, Bilgi University, Istanbul.

Karakanian, M. (2000). Are Human Resources Departments Ready for E-HR*? Information Systems Management, 17*(4), 1–5. doi:10.1201/107 8/43193.17.4.20000901/31250.6

Lepak, D., & Snell, S. A. (1998). Virtual HR: Strategic Human Resource Management In The 21st Century. *Human Resource Management Review, 8*(3), 215–234. doi:10.1016/S1053-4822(98)90003-1

Miller, J. S., & Cardy, R. L. (2000). Technology and Managing People: Keeping the Human in Human Resources. *Journal of Labor Research, 21*(3), 447–461. doi:10.1007/s12122-000-1020-5

Mitchell, M.E. (2001). Human Resource Issues and Challenges for E-Business. *American International College Journal of Business,* 1-14.

Olivas-Lujan, M. R., Ramirez, J., & Zapata-Cantu, L. (2007). E-HRM in Mexico: Adapting Innovations for Global Competitiveness. *International Journal of Manpower, 28*(5), 418–430. doi:10.1108/01437720710778402

Ruël, H., Bondarouk, T., & Looise, J. K. (2004). E-HRM: Innovation or Irritation. An Explorative Empirical Study in Five Large Companies on Web-based HRM. *Management Review, 15*(3), 364–381.

Ruël, H., Bondarouk, T., & Velde, M. V. D. (2007). The Contribution of E-HRM to HRM Effectiveness. *Employee Relations, 29*(3), 280–291. doi:10.1108/01425450710741757

Stone, R. J. (2005). *Human Resource Management* (5th ed). Australia: John Wiley & Sons.

Strohmeier, S. (2007). Research in E-HRM: Review and Implications. *Human Resource Management Review, 17*(1), 19–37. doi:10.1016/j.hrmr.2006.11.002

Ulrich, D. (2007). The New HR Organization. *Workforce Management, 86*(21), 40–44.

Ulrich, D., Brockbank, W., Johnson, D., Sandholtz, K., & Younger, J. (2009). *IK Yetkinlikleri.* (Nazlı Şahinbaş Köksal, Trans.). Turkey/Istanbul: Hümanist Press.

Uyargil, C. (2008). *İşletmelerde Performans Yönetimi Sistemi.* Istanbul, Turkey: Arıkan Press.

Uyargil, C., Sadullah, O., Acar, A. C., Ozcelik, A. O., Dundar, G., & Tuzuner, L. (2006). *Cranfield International Strategic Human Resource Management Research Report of Turkey.* Istanbul: Donence Publishing

Voermans, M., & Veldhoven, M. (2007). Attitude Towards E-HRM: An Empirical Study at Philips. *Personnel Review, 36*(6), 887–902. doi:10.1108/00483480710822418

Walker, A. J., & Perrin, T. (2001). *Web-Based Human Resources.* New York: McGraw-Hill.

Yin, R. K. (1994). Application *of Case Study Research.* Thousand Oaks, CA: Sage Publications.

Zhang, L., & Wang, H. (2006). Intelligent Information Processing In Human Resource Management: An Implementation Case in China. *Expert Systems: International Journal of Knowledge Engineering and Neural Networks, 23*(5), 356–369. doi:10.1111/j.1468-0394.2006.00416.x

ADDITIONAL READING

Bondarouk, T., Ruël, H., & Heijden, B. V. D. (2009). E-HRM Effectiveness in a Public Sector Organization: a Multi-Stakeholder Perspective. *International Journal of Human Resource Management, 20*(3), 578–590. doi:10.1080/09585190802707359

Ceriello, V. R., & Freeman, C. (1998) *Human Resource Management Systems: Strategies, Tactics, and Techniques.* USA: John Wiley & Sons.

Chapman, D. S., & Webster, J. (2003). The Use of Technologies in the Recruiting, Screening, and Selection Processes for Job Candidates. *International Journal of Selection and Assessment, 11*(2/3), 113–120. doi:10.1111/1468-2389.00234

Collins, C. J., & Smith, K. G. (2006). Knowledge Exchange and Combination: The Role of Human Resource Practices in The Performance of High-Technology Firms. *Academy of Management Journal, 49*(3), 544–560.

Davenport, T. H. (1994). Saving IT's Soul: Human-Centered Information Management. *Harvard Business Review, 72*, 119–131.

Debowski, S. (2006). *Knowledge Management.* Singapore: John Wiley&Sons.

Dewett, T., & Jones, G. R. (2001). The Role of Information Technology in the Organization: A Review, Model and Assessment. *Journal of Management, 27*, 313–346. doi:10.1016/S0149-2063(01)00094-0

Farazmand, Ali (2004) Innovation in Strategic Human Resource Management: Building Capacity in the Age of Globalization. *Public Organization Review: A Global Journal, 4*, 3-24.

Gasco, J. L., Llopis, J., & Gonzales, M. R. (2004). The Use of Information Technology in Training Human Resources: An E-learning Case Study. *Journal of European Industrial Training, 28*(5), 370–382. doi:10.1108/03090590410533062

Gueutal, H., & Stone, D. L. (Eds.). (2005). *The Brave New World of e-HR: Human Resources in the Digital Age.* San Francisco: Pfeiffer.

Holsapple, C. W., & Lee-Post, A. (2006). Defining, assessing, and promoting e-learning success: An information systems perspective. *Decision Sciences Journal of Innovative Education, 4*(1), 67–85.

Hooi, L. W. (2006). Implementing E-HRM: The Readiness of Small and Medium Sized Manufacturing Companies in Malaysia. *Asia Pacific Business Review, 12*(4), 465–485. doi:10.1080/13602380600570874

Hopkins, B., & Markham, J. (2003). *e-HR: Using Intranets to Improve the Effectiveness of Your People.* Hampshire, UK: Gower Publishing.

Jennex, M. E. (Ed.). (2005). *Case Studies in Knowledge Management.* Hershey, PA: Idea Group Publishing.

Kulik, C. T., & Perry, E. L. (2008). When Less is More: The Effect of Devolution on HR's Strategic Role and Construed Image. *Human Resource Management, 47*(3), 541–558. doi:10.1002/hrm.20231

Lippert, S. K., & Swiercz, P. M. (2005). Human Resource Information Systems (HRIS) and Technology Trust. *Journal of Information Science, 31*(5), 340–353. doi:10.1177/0165551505055399

Martinez-Fierro, S., Mesina-Garrido, J. A., & Ruiz-Navarro, J. (2006) *Utilizing Information Technology in Developing Strategic Alliances Among Organizations.* Hershey, PA: Idea Group Publishing.

Pershing, J. A. (2006). *Handbook of Human Performance Technology.* San Francisco: Pfeiffer.

Rampton, G. M., Turnbull, I. J., & Doran, J. A. (1999). *Human Resource Management Systems: A Practical Approach.* New York: Carswell.

Steinbuch, P. I. (2005). e-HR: Using Intranets to Improve the Effectiveness of Your People. *Leadership and Organization Development Journal, 26*(1).

Strohmeier, S. (2009). Concepts of E-HRM Consequences: a Categorisation, Review and Suggestion. *International Journal of Human Resource Management, 20*(3), 528–543. doi:10.1080/09585190802707292

Torres-Coronas, T., & Arias-Oliva, M. (Eds.). (2004). *E-Human Resources Management: Managing Knowledge People*. Hershey, PA, USA: Idea Group Publishing.

Ulrich, D. (1997). *Human Resource Champions*. Boston: Harvard Business School Press.

Ulrich, D., & Brockbank, W. (2005). *The HR Value Proposition*. Cambridge, MA: Harvard Business School Press.

Wang, Z. (2005). Organizational Effectiveness Through Technology Innovation and HRM Strategies. *International Journal of Manpower, 26*(6), 481–487. doi:10.1108/01437720510625403

Wolff, A., Gümüş, S., Çalışkan, S., & Ürü, O. The Impact of The Knowledge-Based Economy on the Universities In Turkey, *International Research Conference*, 13-15 June 2008, Burgas Free University, Burgas, Bulgaria, proceedings pp. 30-36.

KEY TERMS AND DEFINITIONS

E-Business: e-business may be defined as the new business strategy that redesigns the old business models and differentiates with the use of information and communication technologies (ICT) in support of all the activities of business. E-business software requires special technical standards and provides the integration of intra and inter firm business processes as well as external relationships with customers and partners.

E-HRM: E-HRM is the planning and application of web-based-technology channels for implementing HR strategies, policies and practices in organizations.

EHRMS: Electronic human resource management systems refers to the systems and processes at the intersection between human resource management (HRM) and information technology(IT).

HRMS: Human Resource Management system or also called Human Resource Information System(HRIS) consists of software, hardware and systematic procedures used to acquire, store, analyze, report and distribute relevant demographic and performance information about an organization's human resources.

Human Resource Management: HRM is the process of managing the most valued assets of the organization; the employees. HRM include functions as job analyzing, recruitment and selection, staffing, training, performance management, career development, compensation, security and health issues of the workforce, and coordinates them in tune with the job and organizational requirements.

Information System: Information system or information technology refers to the specific software platforms and databases that are used to store data records in a computer system and manages all major functions of the organization provided by the softwares such as SAP, PeopleSoft etc.

Software Program: It may be defined as the instructions for computers to perform specific tasks.

Chapter 53
ARIBA:
A Successful Story in E-Commerce

Zhongxian Wang
Montclair State University, USA

Ruiliang Yan
Indiana University Northwest, USA

James Yao
Montclair State University, USA

ABSTRACT

Ariba services major corporations, and provides services to smaller companies as well. In this chapter, the authors will examine how Ariba, a small startup company during the Internet boom of the 90's was able to overcome hardships, survive market and industry downturns, and continue to thrive and survive in such a competitive industry. The authors will also review major events and innovations that helped the company to grow and succeed rather than to fail.

INTRODUCTION

Ariba, Inc. was born during the dot-com bubble, a star amid countless other e-commerce companies. In the universe of corporations, many bright meteors, like Commerce One, didn't shine too long. However, the interesting evolution of Ariba, from a pioneer to a sufferer to a survivor, has taught us much about survival in the competitive business to business (B2B) software industry. Ariba's software would help many companies save money on their procurements, and control expenses besides payroll. Ariba promised to help companies improve their bottom line. Many of Ariba's clients today hold positions on the coveted Fortune 100 list. Going public in 1999, Ariba's stock price at one time reached $259 per share. At the time, Ariba was still getting their feet wet; they had not yet made a profit. The next year their stock reached $168.75, but a negative turn in the economy lay ahead. Many companies began to cut back on investments and in just 9 months Ariba lost 95% of their value. This would be disastrous to any company, and would be the downfall of most, but Ariba made some critical key decisions that helped continue its leadership in the B2B world. They are one of the few companies to not only survive the burst of the dot-com bubble, and to this day to remain a successful company.

DOI: 10.4018/978-1-61520-611-7.ch053

BACKGROUND

E-commerce was in many ways revolutionized by Ariba Inc, a leading independent company in the sphere of B2B commerce network providers. The company has been evolving constantly, in cooperation with leading companies in the industry, in order to deliver E-commerce platform products to its customers/clients. Its value chain model has been able to develop business relationships further than anticipated, the results of which made it a top 40 Fortune 500 company.

Ariba has overcome many obstacles, including lawsuits, changing customer requirements, and organizational restructuring, however still managed to remain a leader in its specific niche area. They have done so by delivering solutions and services that meet customers' expectations, and have been able to cope with intense competition by keeping up with today's technologies as well as developing solutions for tomorrow. Ariba was founded in Sunnyvale CA, in September 1996, by seven men, the most influential individual being Steven Krach. Krach's early career accomplishments included being one of the youngest vice presidents General Motors (Ariba, 2008). Having struggled with the procurement process in his time there; it became a precursor and impetus for the birth of Ariba. Krach and his associates brainstormed and came up with the idea of automating the purchasing of common supplies and services. This is a seemingly simple idea, but one with a huge demand and potential.

After three months of intensive research, which included meeting with 60 Fortune 500 companies, Ariba had a prototype developed and ready for their initial marketing campaign. Having signed software licensing deals with Cisco Systems, Advanced Micro Devices and Octel Communications, prior to software completion, the pieces were put into place for the launch of their product. Among the early competitors to Ariba were Commerce One, Oracle, I2, and PeopleSoft, Inc.

The objective was to become a powerhouse company with the means and resources to provide procurement software and network consulting services, enabling corporations to manage their spending more effectively. This included essentially all non payroll expenses associated with running a business. Ariba offered their clients real-time data by providing information over the Internet. These applications were used in conjunction with the *Ariba Supplier Network* to purchase goods and services. Ariba is customer driven, and offered full support, including technical support, implementation, training, and consulting. E-payment and service agreements were made with American Express and Bank of America. All of these were considered large and bold undertakings for a young startup company at that time. In June of 1999, Ariba went public at a modest $23 per share, however traded as high as $259 per share at times later that year (Schneider, C. M Bruton, 2008; Haksoz and Seshadri, 2007). A stunning success for a three year old company which had yet to turn a profit, it benefited from being a "first mover" in the business. However, other Internet start-up companies were beginning to offer similar software and services. Over time, smaller companies began emerging with websites that provided a place to manage procurement, some with lower costs and fees. Facing challenges in the market, Ariba began to be faced with difficult challenges and had to make major decisions in order to stay in business.

Ariba finally saw a profit of $10 million in December of 2000, which also included the completion of three *acquisitions*. Soon after, in 2001, the economy began to weaken in a downward spiral and Ariba's stock plummeted 95%, making a business overhaul necessary. Ariba decided to take drastic cost-cutting measures, cutting about a third of their staff. Because of their specialized and niche product line, their business was able to continue and survive the setbacks faced by other Internet software companies. Krach resigned as CEO in 2001, but stayed on chairman and appointed a CEO that would later cost the company much money and negative publicity. The bursting of the dot-com "bubble" marked the beginning of a relatively mild yet rather lengthy early 2000s recession (Marshall, 2001; Sahay, 2007). In time, Ariba, along with the rest of the B2B business community ran into two big problems. First, the brick-and-mortar Old Economy was stable and could adjust more readily to economic downturns. Secondly, companies were interested in saving transaction fees by using alternate means of such as word processors instead of using costly B2B networks. However, they were less interested in cutting their savings in terms of transaction fees (Cerquides, López-Sánchez, Reyes-Moro, & Rodríguez-Aguilar, 2007).

Still, Ariba persisted and would once again regain its position as a leader in the B2B procurement industry. The firm made adjustments where necessary to still deliver the goods to their clients, without sacrificing their own bottom line. According to the current CEO, Bob Calderoni, Ariba is well positioned in the spend management market and will continue to grow in the current tough global economy.

The following sections explore the internal (*adaptations to a competitive environment, acquire to advance, consulting adds value, emphasis on the customer*) and external (*severe competition, high-priced software, regulator's investigation, unhappy customers*) factors that affect the company's struggles and challenges.

INTERNAL FACTORS

Adaptations to a Competitive Environment

At the height of the e-procurement frenzy, two companies dominated the B2B space: Commerce One and Ariba. With the near-collapse of the original B2B procurement model, both companies sought new niches. Commerce One moved towards web services in an attempt to

seek viable markets. Ariba, meanwhile, emphasized enterprise spending management (Kinsey, 2004). Ariba strongly believed that a software firm's role is to be a software tool provider. As the B2B world divided into industry sponsored exchanges and independent marketplaces, Ariba avoided involvement in managing its customers' exchanges. Conversely, Commerce One believed that software makers had to do more than simply provide software tools. They had formed strategic partnerships with its customers and helped manage their online marketplaces (Anderson, Opie, & Watton, 2003; Bannan, 2008). It also directed its customers towards an international trading network in order to build critical mass and facilitate e-commerce between them.

As a new CEO, Calderoni monitored the external environment, where a fundamental shift in the marketplace existed, and responded promptly to adjust the company's product offering. He believed that B2B e-business had a direct and indirect impact on all functional areas, and those linkages with a company's supply chain system was critical. In effect, Ariba was changing its focus from e-procurement, to offering products that can increase customer satisfaction by solving a variety of "spend-related" problems faced by corporations (Tadeschi, 2008).

With the concept of division of labor as a microeconomic view, Calderoni added a purchasing system, general ledger, and field system into Ariba's line of products. The added features in the company's products were favored by Ariba's existing customers in the auto, chemical, and manufacturing industries due to the ease of system comparability. The need to transfer data from legacy systems enabled these customers to remove outdated and inaccurate data from their systems and which also helped to improve relationships with their customers.

Acquire to Advance

According to Krach, a major component of Ariba's business model is partnering followed by organic growth and acquisition, and so the company continues to follow this basic approach to help ensure the firm's success. Ariba acquired companies that had the technology and resources they needed to survive, instead of taking the time to develop them in-house. By acquiring Agile Software, a leading provider of Internet-based B2B communication technology, Ariba was able to add collaboration capability to its services, allowing its customers to communicate and coordinate product supply, design, and other specialized electronic-commerce functions. Mr. Calderoni implemented an aggressive acquisition strategy that significantly expanded Ariba's technology offerings and service capabilities, and positioned the company as a recognized leader in its market. One goal was to secure top Fortune 10 companies and Global 500 companies as customers.

In 2004, Ariba acquired Alliente Inc. and FreeMarkets Inc. to link their spend management software with its existing capacities as a B2B procurement hub. The acquisition of FreeMarkets increased Ariba's offerings by providing global supply management software and services. This acquisition also positioned Ariba as a serious contender in the automotive industry, adding General Motors Corp., Daimler-Chrysler AG and Ford Motor Co. to their customer base. By acquiring Alliente, Ariba expanded its spend management and procurement capabilities to include a procurement out-sourcing provider (Hosford, 2007).

In December 2007, Ariba announced that it had completed the acquisition of Procuri, Inc. a privately held provider of on-demand supply management solutions, rounding out Ariba's offerings that help companies automate the procurement process. According to Ariba CEO Bob Calderoni, more than 70% of Procuri's 300 customers have under $5 billion in revenues. As a result, this deal also gave Ariba greater access to midmarket customers (Anonymous, 2007).

Consulting Adds Value

Calderoni believed that Ariba has survived by expanding beyond software that focused mainly on transactions, to encompassing additional facets of the buying process. Calderoni hired hundreds of consultants to advise companies on how to buy goods and services cheaply, using Ariba's software. Although consulting is less profitable than selling software, Calderoni predicted he can successfully combine the two as an integrated set of offerings. While consultants coach Ariba's clients on how to use the software effectively, Ariba's clients can also reply on Internet-based purchasing systems to help them buy direct materials that are core to their company's manufacturing processes.

In order to extend Ariba's consulting services, which in 2004 accounted for nearly half of the company's $323 million in sales, Ariba made consultants available via email and phone for a fraction of the price that is charged to the larger companies who require dedicated consultants through in site visits.

Emphasis on the Customer

In 2001, investors were looking for a change in leadership at Ariba after the firm missed revenue and earnings projections by a wide margin. Ariba moved Keith Krach out of the CEO position, filling the post with the company's President and COO, Larry Mueller. Mueller entered the position with a new strategy: to halt the company's current plans to enter new markets, and instead opting to add new features, including electronic payment and invoicing, to its existing e-procurement and auction applications. Mueller heightened the focus on improving e-procurement applications by making heavy investments in existing e-procurement and sourcing platforms; and building technology around the key interactions that enterprises have with trading partners.

Mueller remained focused on bolstering Ariba's role as a traditional B2B transaction platform. Ariba announced plans to invest heavily in its Ariba *Commerce Services Network* and its network-centric applications, including *Network Connect*, which allowed non-Ariba customers to come into the Ariba services network and conduct business or procure services. The company also organized its development, sales, and marketing staff to focus on specific industries. According to Mueller, "Customer ROI is the focus." A focus on international expansion has boosted revenue from outside the US from 10% in the third quarter 2000 to 25% in the same period for 2001 (Purdum, 2007). Ariba is trying to rebuild its fortunes as public marketplaces that use its technology are struggling - some economists feel this is due to the fact the industry just isn't ready for e-commerce.

Since joining the company in 2000, new (and current) chairman and CEO of Ariba, Mr. Calderoni has successfully transformed Ariba from a narrowly focused e-procurement vendor to a comprehensive spend management solutions provider that companies of all sizes rely on to transform the way they do business globally. Under Mr. Calderoni's leadership, Ariba has led the way in developing and delivering innovative solutions that combine technology, commodity expertise and services to help companies streamline the procurement process and drive bottom-line results.

EXTERNAL FACTORS

Severe Competition

Simply being a dot-com business survivor, however, would not ensure its continued existence and profitability, and Ariba was at risk of losing business to the likes of other competitors such as SAP and Oracle. SAP, a German enterprise resource planning software maker, joined this market and signed on with Hewlett-Packard for a product called mySAP.com e-business solutions. In addition, it built a marketplace for chemical and pharmaceutical firms by educating them on mySAP.com, and with the result of installing a large SAP user base among Fortune 500 companies.

Nevertheless, Oracle had already anticipated a shift in the market and made plans to capitalize on it. Right now, the procurement sector is dominated by leading software companies Ariba and Commerce One. But as the slowdown in the U.S economy continues, Oracle is hoping the opportunity for companies like Ariba will start to shrink as users look to more established ones, like Oracle, for an all around e-commerce package (Arora, Greenwald, Kannan, Karthik, & Krishnan, 2007). Ariba had in fact provided Oracle with an opportunity to gain market share when it cut a third of its workforce and announced reduced earnings during economic recent downturns.

Ariba recognized that to remain competitive, it had to address the problem of hidden costs associated with the products they sell, in addition to the price they charge for the software itself within the supply chain, especially when the product was in the later stage of its cycle. When a company does not paying attention to the hidden costs of new software implementation, it can creep up and well-intentioned efforts can be result in the form of financial penalties (Angeles & Nath, 2007; Brown, 2008).

By August 2008, the market for supply chain management (SCM) software market has grown. Worldwide spending on SCM solutions reached $6 billion in 2007, which was up 17.6% from 2006. SCM Technologies are well-positioned to address the economic realities facing worldwide markets where costs are skyrocketing while competition and customer demands are intensifying (Eschinger, 2008). A number of the SCM solution vendors are merging, and expanding their capabilities within the realm of supply chain technologies. In comparison, Ariba's 2007 revenue was $160.3 million, which significantly trailed behind Oracle and SAP, who reported $955.2 million and $1,334.4 million in revenue, respectively, showing that the threat of these products cutting into Ariba's bottom line is a real one (Orme & Etzkorn, 2007).

High-Priced Software

Without a doubt, e-procurement is rising substantially among the nation's largest 500 companies. Well-financed corporations are willing to invest in Internet software and technology that can reduce the inefficiency associated with the purchasing and buying processes. The use of this software can help companies to track spending and make sure they purchase products in accordance with contracts they have negotiated with suppliers. In fact, businesses that spend billions each year on supplies can often save tens of millions in costs by implementing such technology. However, it's only the large firms that can devote the time and money to installing such systems, which frequently required that suppliers link to such systems as well. Since the software is generally expensive and can be complicated to install on the customer's system, for small- and medium-sized businesses facing an uncertain economy, investments of this magnitude are can be difficult to justify.

Ariba took advantage of this situation, and in 2005 announced a strategy to sell its software and services to smaller companies on an on-demand basis, so they can buy supplies more efficiently online, as well. Ariba reshaped its software system so its customers can plug into Ariba's software through the Internet instead of installing it on their own systems. One major benefit of this approach, Mr. Calderoni said, is that Ariba can sell software to procurement managers and others in charge of spending, without involving the company's information technology staff.

Regulator's Investigation

In early 2003, Ariba became under investigation by the Security and Exchange Commissions (SEC). The reason for the investigation was linked to Ariba's accounting errors, doubtful partner deals, and questionable e-payments items including chartered airplanes. Among the specific allegations were that Ariba failed to record a $10 million payment from chairman Keith Krach to former chief executive Larry Mueller as an expense. The restatements are unusual because the chairman -- not the company -- covered the expense (Lau and Wang, 2007). Then three weeks later, Ariba had decided to do the same for $1.2 million in chartered jet services that was considered as Krach's compensation to Mueller, who subsequently left Ariba in July 2001. The problem is that United States laws and regulations require that payments by a principal holder to executives be treated as expenses paid on behalf of the company.

In addition, Ariba reported an additional $7.5 million to its expenses. In 2000, Ariba acquired TradingDynamic Inc., Tradex Technologies Inc., and SupplierMarket.com, and it reclassified stock options, or goodwill, that it gave to employees of these accompanies as a compensation expense. So by combining all of these expenses, the results were 18.7 million of added expenses. Ariba was aware that the regulator had begun an informal inquiry into its accounting practices after the firm said it would restate its earnings for 10 quarters.

Unhappy Customers

Ariba was subject to bad publicity after sending out automated emails to mid-size suppliers announcing their accounts had been upgraded to Premier level status. The email listed premier supplier benefits as well. However, the email also informed them that as a Premier Member, they were now required to pay associated annual fees. Many of the small and mid-size companies viewed this as a marketing ploy and felt they should not all of a sudden pay fees associated with their membership (Eschinger, 2008).

FUTURE RESEARCH DIRECTIONS

A number of the challenges Ariba faced from its start to the present time allowed them to evolve over time. Ariba has been able to face these challenges head on and continue to be the leading B2B software provider for the past 11 years. During the collapse of the dot-com era Ariba suffered a blow economically, as did others in the industry, and in effect had reduced the company's size by half (Lau and Wang, 2007), as did everyone else. However, they were able to build upon their core competencies and maintain key personnel, managing knowledge that formed the basis of their competitive advantage.

They were also able to stay ahead of the competition through strategic mergers which enhanced their products and services. These mergers should be credited to its CEOs, Presidents, and Board of Directors. Ariba would continue to enhance its products with the availability of constant upgrades and varieties of new products.

With incredible technology growth and its global demand, came the opportunity for Ariba to expand and acquire a more precise goal and target. Ariba has painted a vision of a world in which spend management would be affordable and available to all types of companies, and released an initial set of integrated, on-demand solutions designed to make this happen (Purdum, 2007). In keeping this promise, Ariba would make on-demand products and subscription-based purchasing software and services available to meet the needs of those mid-market customers not wanting to make huge upfront investments. This strategy of meeting the needs of various types of clients was in some way risky, but Ariba has thrived on making strategic, yet controversial decisions throughout the years. Having gone through ups and downs during the years, they still managed to

regain a leadership position even though markets and needs have evolved and changed. Overall, they have been able to provide customers with superb services and innovative products, and reliability is what keeps old customers, and helps to bring in new customers.

There is never a guarantee of success in business. Successful companies also must be surrounded by a committed and devoted management team, supported by well-trained employees. Are these together a recipe for success? We may never know for sure, but taking advice from a company which has been successful since its start, weathered some very tough times, and was able to survive and stay above the rest before seeking out the next realm of opportunity, is certainly an approach that appears to be sound.

CONCLUSION

Ariba achieved recognition for its *Supplier Network*, an e-business center where millions of buyers and suppliers can electronically transact business online, with the goal of more efficient procurement. In addition, Ariba developed spend management software, and is taking the network mainstream. Ariba's application-driven strategy of an open platform, hosted and implemented by partners with vertical-market domain expertise, has helped to secure them a dominant position in the B2B e-commerce application marketplace.

It is interesting to note that while many firms who came up around the time of Ariba and offered competing solutions, Ariba is one of the few that has survived and thrived, using continually new strategies to stay in business, providing a better customer experience, and utilizing advances in technology and ideas that no other companies dared to try. Ariba has been, and remained a pioneer and a leader in an exceedingly competitive and changing marketplace. Due to increased globalization and deregulation, for a company to succeed, it must have leverage over the impact of competitive forces. Ariba has done a great job in setting themselves apart from their competitors by strategically aligning themselves with their partners, and also expanding its service offerings to a wider range of customers. Ariba's software offerings help companies focus on profitability, and together with its wide array of service options, are customizable for both larger and smaller companies. The firm's products are concrete and customizable, depending on a client's needs. In addition, the product offerings are offered on a common platform, allowing information to travel accurately and quickly through the supply chain.

REFERENCES

Anderson, J., Opie, G., & Watton, J. (2003). The corporate spend agenda preview. *Business Strategy Review, 14*(2), 5–7. doi:10.1111/1467-8616.00252

Angeles, R., & Nath, R. (2007). Business-to-business e-procurement: success factors and challenges to implementation. *Supply Chain Management, 12*(2), 104–115. doi:10.1108/13598540710737299

Anonymous, . (2007). Moving forward by working backwards. *Preview Healthcare Purchasing News, 31*(7), 64–66.

Ariba, Inc. (2008). Preview contract management. *Resource Guide*, (Supplement), 62.

Arora, A., Greenwald, K., Karthik, R., & Krishnan, R. (2007). Effects of information-revelation policies under market-structure uncertainty. *Management Science, 53*(8), 1234–1248. doi:10.1287/mnsc.1060.0688

Bannan, K.J. (2008). Ariba creates controls for who sends marketing e-mails when. *B to B Chicago, 93*(10), 22.

Brown, D. (2008). It is good to be green, Environmentally friendly credentials are influencing business outsourcing decisions. *Strategic Outsourcing: an International Journal, 1*(1), 87. doi:10.1108/17538290810857493

Cerquides, J., López-Sánchez, M., Reyes-Moro, A., & Rodríguez-Aguilar, J. A. (2007). Enabling assisted strategic negotiations in actual-world procurement scenarios. *Electronic Commerce Research, 7*(3-4), 189–220. doi:10.1007/s10660-007-9007-4

Eschinger, C. (2008, August). No recession in the supply chain arena. *Industry Week, 257*(8), 56.

Haksoz, C., & Seshadri, S. (2007). Supply chain operations in the presence of a spot market: a review with discussion. *The Journal of the Operational Research Society, 58*(11), 1412–1429. doi:10.1057/palgrave.jors.2602401

Hosford, C. (2007). Ariba pins turnaround hopes on keeping in touch with customers. *B to B Chicago, 92*(1), 18.

Kinsey, E. P. (2004, Fall). Where has AU the common sense gone? *Mid-American Journal of Business, 19*(2), 7–11.

Lau, K.-K., & Wang, Z. (2007). Software component models. *IEEE Transactions on Software Engineering, 33*(10), 709. doi:10.1109/TSE.2007.70726

Marshall, J. (2001, May). A foundation to build on. *Preview By Financial Executive, 17*(3), 7–13.

Orme, A. M., & Etzkorn, L. H. (2007). A parallel methodology for reduction of coupling in distributed business-to-business e-commerce transactions. *Journal of Electronic Commerce in Organizations, 5*(3), 52–67.

Purdum, T. (2007). Online marketplace evolution: In their infancy, many online marketplaces kept their focus too narrow. Those that saw the big picture survived. *Industry Week, 356*(1), 18–19.

Sahay, A. (2007). How dynamic pricing leads to higher profits. *MIT Sloan Management Review, 48*(4), 53.

Schneider, G. P., & Bruton, C. M. (2008). Using portal web sites in the purchasing function. In *Proceedings of Allied Academies International Conference. Academy of Information and Management Sciences, 12*(2), 42-45.

Tadeschi, B. (2008, November 14). A software strategy helps the little guy buy smarter. *The New York Times*, C9(L).

ADDITIONAL READING

Angeles, R., & Nath, R. (2007). Business-to-business e-procurement: success factors and challenges to implementation. *Supply Chain Management, 12*(2), 104. doi:10.1108/13598540710737299

Brown, D. (2008). It is good to be green, environmentally friendly credentials are influencing business outsourcing decisions. *Strategic Outsourcing: an International Journal, 1*(1), 87. doi:10.1108/17538290810857493

Cerquides, J. (2007). Enabling assisted strategic negotiations in actual-world procurement scenarios. *Electronic Commerce Research, 7*(3-4), 189–221. doi:10.1007/s10660-007-9007-4

Dai, Q. Z., & Kauffman, R. (2006). To be or not to B2B: Evaluating managerial choices for e-procurement channel adoption. *Information Technology and Management, 7*(2), 109. doi:10.1007/s10799-006-8103-9

Degwekar, S. (2007). Constraint-based brokering (CBB) for publishing and discovery of web services. *Electronic Commerce Research, 7*(1), 45–57. doi:10.1007/s10660-006-0062-z

Elmaghraby, W. (2007). Auctions within E-Sourcing events. *Production and Operations Management, 16*(4), 409–422.

Gayton, C. (2006). Alexandria burned - securing knowledge access in the age of Google. *Vine, 36*(2), 155. doi:10.1108/03055720610682960

Giampetro, C., & Emiliani, M. (2007). Coercion and reverse auctions. *Supply Chain Management, 12*(2), 75. doi:10.1108/13598540710737253

Haksoz, C., & Seshadri, S. (2007). Supply chain operations in the presence of a spot market: A review with discussion. *The Journal of the Operational Research Society, 58*(11), 1412–1429. doi:10.1057/palgrave.jors.2602401

Hartley, J. (2006). Exploring the barriers to the adoption of e-auctions for sourcing. *International Journal of Operations & Production Management, 26*(1/ 2), 202–221. doi:10.1108/01443570610641675

Henry, C. (2007). Strategy in the media. *Strategy and Leadership, 35*(4), 52. doi:10.1108/10878570710761417

Holmqvist, M., & Pessi, K. (2006). Agility through scenario development and continuous implementation: a global aftermarket logistics case. *European Journal of Information Systems, 15*(2), 146. doi:10.1057/palgrave.ejis.3000602

Howard, M. (2005). Collaboration and the '3DayCar': a study of automotive ICT adoption. *Journal of Information Technology, 20*(4), 245. doi:10.1057/palgrave.jit.2000050

Huang, G. (2007). Do It Yourself (DIY) Portales for developing e-business solutions for small and medium enterprises. *Journal of Manufacturing Technology Management, 18*(1), 72. doi:10.1108/17410380710717652

Kim, M., & Ahn, J. (2006). Comparison of trust sources of an online market-maker in the e-marketplace: buyer's and seller's perspective. *Journal of Computer Information Systems, 47*(1), 84–95.

Kulp, S. L. (2006). Using organizational control mechanisms to enhance procurement efficiency: How GlaxoSmithKline improved the effectiveness of e-procurement. *Interfaces, 36*(3), 209–221. doi:10.1287/inte.1060.0209

Kwasnica, A., & Katok, E. (2007). The Effect of Timing on Jump Bidding in Ascending Auctions. *Production and Operations Management, 16*(4), 483–494.

Lau, K., & Wang, Z. (2007). Software component models. *IEEE Transactions on Software Engineering, 33*(10), 709. doi:10.1109/TSE.2007.70726

Orme, A., & Etzkorn, L. (2007). A parallel methodology for reduction of coupling in distributed business-to-business e-commerce transactions. *Journal of Electronic Commerce in Organizations, 5*(3), 52–67.

Raja, J., & Velmurgan, S. (2008). E-payments: Problems and prospects. *Journal of Internet Banking and Commerce, 13*(1), 1–18.

Ratnasingam, P. (2007). A risk-control framework for e-marketplace participation: the findings of seven cases. *Information Management & Computer Security, 15*(2), 149. doi:10.1108/09685220710748029

Rothkopf, M., & Whinston, A. (2007). On e-auctions for procurement operations. *Production and Operations Management, 16*(4), 404–408.

Sahay, A. (2007). How dynamic pricing leads to higher profits. *MIT Sloan Management Review, 48*(4), 53.

Sandholm, T. (2006). Changing the game in strategic sourcing at Procter & Gamble: expressive competition enabled by optimization. *Interfaces, 36*(1), 55–71. doi:10.1287/inte.1050.0185

Schneider, G., & Bruton, C. (2008). Using portal web sites in the purchasing function allied. *Academies International Conference. Academy of Information and Management Sciences, 12*(2), 42-46.

Sia, S., & Soh, C. (2007). An assessment of package-organisation misalignment: Institutional and ontological structures. *European Journal of Information Systems, 16*(5), 568–583. doi:10.1057/palgrave.ejis.3000700

Sledgianowski, D. (2006). Decisions in IT infrastructure integration: A case study in a global chemical company research note. *Journal of Information Technology Case and Application Research, 8*(1), 67–72.

Smart, A. (2008). E-business and supply chain integration. *Journal of Enterprise Information Management, 21*(3), 227. doi:10.1108/17410390810866619

Vaidya, K. (2006). Critical factors that influence e-procurement implementation success in the public sector. *Journal of Public Procurement, 6*(1/2), 70–99.

KEY TERMS AND DEFINITIONS

Acquisitions: Acquiring control of a corporation, called a target, by stock purchase or exchange, either hostile or friendly.

Business to Business (B2B): The exchange of products, services, or information between businesses.

E-Commerce (electronic commerce or EC): The buying and selling of goods and services on the Internet.

E-Payments (online payments, Electronic Payments, Internet Payments, Web Payments, and e Payment): An electronic payment made via a web browser for goods and services using credit or debit cards.

E-Procurement: A system utilizing Internet technology to streamline the purchases of goods and products to reduce costs.

Supplier Network: It works with a network of screened and qualified small-scale producers and committed medium-sized suppliers.

Supply Chain Management (SCM): The process of strategically managing flows of goods, services and knowledge, along with relationships within and among organizations, to realize greater economic value.

Chapter 54
Integrated Optimal Procedure of Internet Marketing

Lan Zhao

Chongqing University, China & SUNY/College at Old Westbury, USA

ABSTRACT

The article focuses on how to integrate all the phases of Internet marketing process into a seamless pipeline. The current techniques used in three main phases: (1) customer targeting; (2) ads piece designing; and (3) marketing budget allocation, are described in detail to reveal the cohering inside of searching optimal marketing strategies.

INTRODUCTION

The internet marketing is a comprehensive process that requires the coordination and efficiency of all the marketing departments. The functionalities of the marketing departments include, but are not limited to, identification of consumers, production of ads pieces, and selection of ad strategies.

Internet medium offers a great advantage in data collection. Abundant data allows us to measure the effectiveness of marketing efforts, and further, to model the advertise response as a function of advertising efforts for optimal strategy. Thus, internet marketing is special from the traditional one in the sense that it is data driven; it is able to take advantage

of mathematical methods and information technology. In this article, we pinpoint at main phases of the internet advertising process – customer targeting, internet ads production, and optimal budget allocation in internet media and based on them to show the production process of internet marketing which employs data mining, statistic and mathematical modeling, and mathematical algorithms.

The article is organized as follow: (1) Introduction section describes the general perspective of the article; (2) Background section briefs the industrial and academic efforts by others that are related to my position on the topic; (3) Operation Procedure and the Quantitative Method for Each of the Subroutines section describes in detail the mathematical

DOI: 10.4018/978-1-61520-611-7.ch054

models, theorems, and the methods to achieve the goals of internet marketing; (4) Future Research Direction section outlines the trend and remain issues of the topic in this article; and finally (5) is the Conclusion section.

BACKGROUND

Internet marketing technique consists of database marketing, information depository, statistical modeling, mathematical programming, and search and match techniques.

Database marketing started in 1990s. With the development of computer information science and internet, it is now a well developed technique that is used in all kind of marketing. (Jackson & Wang, 1994) The database marketing procedure starts with customer database, and then uses statistical method such as regression, clustering, tree, or neural networking to segment and profile customers according to their demographic, behavioral, and geographic attributes. As result, the targeted customers are identified. Since internet marketing is also data rich, customer targeting functionality of database marketing is adapted in the internet marketing procedure.

After the customers are segmented, next issue is how to communicate with them. On July 2, 2007 Yahoo launched its patent-pending tool, Yahoo! SmartAds (2007) to enhance its online advertising effectiveness. SmartAds takes advertisers' creative campaign elements, automatically converts the elements and offerings into highly customized and relevant display ads by delivering banner ads according to the web surfer's age, gender, location and online activities. Although the methodology behind SmartAds is not fully known by the public and the academic community, people believe that it uses behavioral, demographic and geographic segmentation capabilities for targeting (Story, 2007). SmartAds is currently in its pioneer stage where only Yahoo's travel portal is using it. On other hand, Google's Adsense is a

tool to display relevant ads on a webpage. With this tool, the content of a webpage is analyzed to determine a list of one or more topics associated with that webpage. An advertisement, submitted by advertisers, is considered to be relevant to that webpage if it is associated with keywords belonging to the list of one or more topics. One or more of these relevant advertisements may be provided for rendering in conjunction with the webpage or related web pages. The dominant industrial perspective is how to take advantage of searching technologies employed by Search Engines (Langville and Meyer (2006)).

In the academic community, there have been efforts devoted to studying internet marketing via mathematical programming, game theory, statistic predicting, and variational inequalities. In Chickering and Heckerman (2003), to maximize the click-through rate, given inventory-management constraints in the form of advertisement quotas, a system using predictive segments, in conjunction with a linear program to perform the constrained optimization, is developed. Kazienko and Adamski (2007) created the AdROSA system for automatic web ads personalization, which integrates web usage and content mining techniques to better target customers. Zhao and Nagurney (2006, 2008) used variational inequalities in conjunction with mathematical programming for the optimal allocation of marketing budget to variety of market places.

All the above efforts certainly have advanced internet marketing theory and practice. However, since each of them focuses on a specific issue, they failed to demonstrate the cohesive inside of all the aspects. Internet marketing is an integrated process that requires not only the efficiency of each of the phases but also the smoothness of the transition from one phase to another. Thus, this article is to connect all the pieces together for creating the seamless marketing pipeline.

Figure 1. Internet marketing flow chart

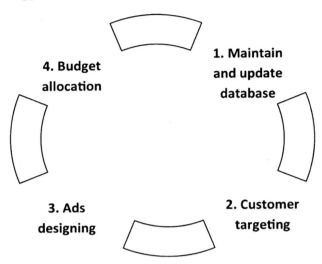

OPERATION PROCEDURE AND THE QUANTITATIVE METHOD FOR EACH OF THE PHASES

Internet marketing flow chart is shown as follow:

The database must contain at least three pieces of data: (1) customer attributes data, denoted by variables $x_1, x_2, \ldots, x_N$; (2) marketing elements data denoted by variables $u_1, u_2, \ldots, u_M$ which represent firms marketing offer and efforts such as investments, sale discounts, components of ads pieces, and attributes of web portals, etc.; (3) marketing performance data denoted by variables $y_1, y_2, \ldots, y_K$ which usually represent customer response rate, ROI, or revenue, etc.

Let's explain each phase of the flow chart in details as below.

Customer Targeting

Targeting refers to address the issue of who will a firm advertise to. In order to target efficiently, firm needs knowledge of its current/potential customers as much as possible, Data mining and statistic methods play an important role here. Once a consumer responses (click / purchase) to

ads in internet, his/her attributes and response are recorded in the web log. Based on the web data, statistical models can be used to segment customers. (Jackson & Wang, 1994) The typical methods are clustering and regression methods.

Clustering method segments consumers into clusters. Within each cluster, their attributes $v = (x_{l_1}, x_{l_2}, \ldots, x_{l_j}, y_{m_1}, \ldots y_{m_k})$, where the components of v forms a subset of consumers total attributes and marketing performance data, are similar. Upon Choice of components of v and number of clusters, both governed by business rule, is determined, the algorithm can be applied to consumers in the database to segment them:

Step 1: Choose arbitrarily clusters seeds v^{01}, v^{02}, ..., v^{0L}, where L is the number of clusters. Let $t = 0$.

Step 2: Label each point v (consumer) by r as v^r where

$$r = \{r \mid \| v - v^{tr} \| = \min_{k=1,2,\ldots L}(\| v - v^{tk} \|)\} \quad (1)$$

There will be L distinct r values, $r = 1, 2, \ldots, L$; and suppose that n_r points are label r.

Step 3: for each value of label r, find the center of the points v^r

$$v^{(t+1)r} = \frac{1}{n_r} \sum v^r \qquad (2)$$

Step 4: If $\|v^{(t+1)r} - v^r\| \leq \varepsilon \forall r = 1,2,\ldots,L$, then stop, consumers have been segmented into L clusters and go to phase of ads designing.

Otherwise, let $t = t+1$ and go back to Step 2.

The regression method is used to build a response model. The model predicts the probability that individual consumer will respond to the firm's marketing efforts so that the firm can differentiate consumers by their different probability values. Let p be the response probability, then its value is usually predicted by logistic regression: (Walpole et al 2007)

$$\log \frac{p}{1-p} = a_0 + a_1 x_{l_1} + a_2 x_{l_2} + \ldots + a_j x_{l_j} \qquad (3)$$

or equivalently,

$$P = \frac{1}{1 + e^{-(a_0 + a_1 x_{l_1} + a_2 x_{l_2} + \ldots + a_j x_{l_j})}} \qquad (4)$$

Then, consumers are segmented according to their response probabilities. In industrial practice, they are usually segmented into 10 groups. When the segmentation is completed, go to next phase that is the ads designing.

Internet Ads Designing

How to design web ads to attract most response within a firm's budget is now a heated issue in internet ad industry due to internet ads high price and declining response rate. This traditionally artistic territory is now explored by mathematicians and computer scientists. They found that, by combination of statistical modeling, mathematical programming, information depository, search and match techniques, the best choice of ads elements such as color, key words, size, position, discount, and launching date, etc., which are denoted by variables $(u_1, u_2, \ldots, u_M)$ in the database, can be obtained to form an optimal ads piece. (Anderson et al. 2006; Hai, Zhao & Nagurney 2009).

The method is described below:

Step 1: Let A_k^{tl} be the initial internet ads pieces for consumer cluster k, composed by $(u_{l_1}^t, u_{l_2}^t, \ldots, u_{l_k}^t)$ which is a subset of a firm's total marketing efforts $(u_1, u_2, \ldots, u_M)$. Suppose that there are $l = 1,2,\ldots,C_k$ ad pieces for cluster k. Optimal ads design starts with initial ads and their components that are inherited from the firm's previous ads elements.

Step 2: establish mathematical model that quantifies the marketing response

$$y_i^k = f(u_{l_1}, u_{l_2}, \ldots, u_{l_k}) \qquad (5)$$

where y_i^k is one of marketing performance variable $(y_1, y_2, \ldots, y_K)$. Choice of y_i^k is determined by goal of marketing. Model (5) can be obtained by mathematical methods including, but not limited to, statistical regression, interpolation, or simulation methods by analyzing web data that is related to A_k^{tl}, $l=1,2,\ldots,C_k$.

Step 3: to solve the optimization problem below:

$$\max y_i^k = f(u_{l_1}, u_{l_2}, \ldots, u_{l_k})$$
$$s.t. \quad g(u_{l_1}, u_{l_2}, \ldots, u_{l_k}) \leq 0 \qquad (6)$$

where function $g(\cdot)$ is the vector function that defined the constraint of variables. Problem (6) can be solved by mathematical programming method (Bazaraa 2006).

Suppose the solution is $(u_{l_1}^{t+1}, u_{l_2}^{t+1}, ..., u_{l_k}^{t+1})$, then optimal ad $A_k^{(t+1)l_o}$ for cluster k is composed by the optimal solution. Create trial ads $A_k^{(t+1)l}$ $l \neq l_o$ for data collecting purpose. Let $t = t+1$, update database and go to phase of optimal budget allocation.

When the optimal marketing elements are identified, a firm can provide them to portals like Yahoo to form ads on the fly (20072007Yahoo!, 2007!!), or a firm can compose the optimal ads and provide them to portals like Google to display according to web browsers' attributes.

Budget Allocation

After identified target and created optimal ad pieces, a firm needs to consider where (websites) and how to deliver the marketing efforts which is measured as amount of investment to realize the marketing objective. The issue of optimal allocation of web ads budget is a convex mathematical programming problem that can be easily modeled and solved by existing statistical and mathematical theory and methods. (Park & Fader 2004; Zhao & Nagurney 2006) Further, there are many firms compete in the internet market. A firm's ads response is affected by competitors marketing efforts as well. Every firm has to maximize its own ads response to win in the competition. As a result, Nash-equilibrium will be reached, at which every firm is at optimal status in the sense that any unilateral change of firm's total ads spending as well as its allocation only makes the firm worse-off. (Zhao & Nagurney 2008)

Let $u = (u_{m_1}, u_{m_2}, ..., u_{m_p})$ be a vector variable that denotes the allocation of the total budget to the internet market places. The total consumers' response y_r (the click-through rate, or purchase, whatever the marketing objective is.) is a concave function of u:

$$y_r = f(u_{m_1}, u_{m_2}, ..., u_{m_p}) \tag{7}$$

and the marginal increment of response per additional internet investment λ is an increasing function of total internet investment:

$$\lambda = \lambda(b) \tag{8}$$

where $b = u_{m_1} + u_{m_2} +, ..., + u_{m_p}$.

A firm's goal is to maximize y_r subject to budget constraint. It is well known in the optimization theory (Bazaraa 2006) that, at the optimum, all marginal responses per addition investment to individual internet market place are equal; those markets with smaller marginal responses will not be invested. When all the firms are competing for the same consumers through the optimization scheme, the equilibrium will be reached that no firm can unilaterally alter its strategy to be better off.

Marginal response is the partial derivatives of y_r defined by (7). If the marginal response is denoted by the vector function

$$g = (\frac{\partial y_r}{\partial u_{m_1}}, \frac{\partial y_r}{\partial u_{m_2}}, ..., \frac{\partial y_r}{\partial u_{m_q}}) \tag{9}$$

Then the procedure that searches for optimal budget and its allocation is described as follow:

Step 1: Let $(u_{m_1}^t, u_{m_2}^t, ..., u_{m_p}^t)$ are initial budget allocation to internet market places.

Step 2: build mathematical model based on the historical data including $(u_{m_1}^t, u_{m_2}^t, ..., u_{m_p}^t)$ that quantifies y_r as a function of budget allocation as described in (7), and take partial derivatives to obtain g that is a function of $(u_{m_1}, u_{m_2}, ..., u_{m_p})$.

Step 3: solve variational inequality

$$\langle g(u^*), u - u^* \rangle - \langle \lambda(b^*), b - b^* \rangle \leq 0$$
$$\forall (u, b) \in \{(u, b) \mid u_{m_1} + u_{m_2} + ... + u_{m_q} = b\} \tag{10}$$

solution of (10) is (u^*, b^*). Let $(u^{t+1}, b^{t+1}) = (u^*, b^*)$ and $t = t+1$.

Note that the procedure calculates the size of budget b as well as its allocation. Problem (10) can be solved by iteratively calling mathematical programming methods.

In summary, the procedure starts at data uploading; based on the data, consumers are segmented; for each cluster of consumers, ads elements are selected and ads are composed; then marketing investment strategy are determined. Ads, or the elements, are delivered to portals to attract consumers. When consumers' response data are collected and uploaded to database, next cycle of marketing begins. Thus, marketing becomes a self-learning, self-improving, and cyclical procedure that catches the dynamics of consumers.

FUTURE RESEARCH DIRECTION

There are issues in the above procedure that remain to be addressed. As described above, to increase the efficiency, a firm needs to model market response as function of marketing elements (offers, investments, etc). However, marketing is a competition, in which all the participating firms efforts impact interactively on consumers. As noted by Reibstein and Wittink (2005), the marketing literatures contain many articles on market response based on both aggregate and disaggregate data. However, there are few papers that deal with competitive reactions. Indeed, as Reibstein and Wittink (2005) further emphasize, "the marketing mix models offered by leading data suppliers often gloss over competitive spending and never include reaction functions." Zhao and Nagurney (2008) tried to address the issue by establishing a variational inequality model that includes competitors' efforts as independent variables, but the difficulty is that competitors' data is usually not accessible; therefore to build such a model seems not practical.

However, the data of consumers' response carries competitors' information since it is the result of the combined impact of all marketers' efforts. Can we use the data to build the estimated response function that contains only the firm's own variables to approximate the true response function that depends on all marketers' efforts? If we do so, are the error of the approximation and its consequences, i.e. the resulted decision based on the estimation, controllable?

The answer for these questions may be found in other fields such as Statistics, Economics, and Operations Research (Zhao & Zhu 2009).

CONCLUSION

Due to the richness of data, internet marketing can be done as an automatic procedure, within which, each of the phases is carried out quantitatively to ensure the measurability of the efficiency, optimality of decision making, and adjustability to the dynamics of the market places.

Both scholars and marketing practitioners have developed methods for some phases of marketing such as customer targeting, optimal ads design, and optimal budget size and allocation, etc. that take advantage of data depository, statistic and mathematical techniques. This article combines these methods to form an integrated marketing procedure. We demonstrate in detail how each phase is done and how to move from one phase to the next phase. Now it is clear that, to build marketing production pipeline, a firm needs to have database, statistical software, mathematical programming software, and professionals with expertise to guarantee to smoothness and efficiency of the pipeline.

Although this article is about internet marketing, the prospective described here can be applied to marketing in other media as long as the amount of data are able to support the models in each of the phases.

REFERENCES

Anderson, D., Buchheit, P., Carobus, A. P., Cui, Y., Dean, J. A., Harik, G. R., et al. (2006). *Serving Advertisements Based on Content*. Patent # 7,136,875, US Patent & Trademark Office, Patent Application Full Text and Image Database.

Bazaraa, M. (2006). *Nonlinear Programming: Theory and Algorithms* (3rd ed.). Hoboken, NJ: Wiley.

Chickering, D., & Heckerman, D. (2003). Targeted Advertising with Inventory Management. *Interfaces*, *33*, 71–77. doi:10.1287/inte.33.5.71.19248

Hai, L., Nagurney, A., & Zhao, L. (in press). An Integrated Framework for the Design of Optimal Web Banners. *NETNOMICS: Economic Research and Electronic Networking*.

Jackson, P., & Wang, P. (1994). *Strategic Database Marketing*. New York: McGraw-Hill Professional.

Kazienko, P., & Adamski, M. (2007). AdROSA-Adaptive Personalization of Web Advertising. *Information Sciences*, *177*, 2269–2295. doi:10.1016/j.ins.2007.01.002

Park, Y., & Fader, P. (2004). Modeling Brows Behavior at Multiple Websites. *Marketing Science*, *23*, 280–303. doi:10.1287/mksc.1040.0050

Reibstein, D., & Wittink, D. (2005). Competitive responsiveness. *Marketing Science, 23*, 280–303.

Story, L. (2007, July 2). Online Customized Ads Move a Step Closer. *New York Times*.

Walpole, R. E., Myers, R. H., Myers, S. L., & Ye, K. (2007). *Probability & Statistics for Engineers & Scientists*. Upper Saddle River, NJ: Prentice Hall.

Zhao, L., & Nagurney, A. (2006). A Network Modeling Approach for the Optimization of Internet-Based Advertising Strategies and Pricing with a Quantitative Explanation of Two Paradoxes. *NETNOMICS: Economic Research and Electronic Networking*, *7*, 97–114. doi:10.1007/s11066-006-9006-y

Zhao, L., & Nagurney, A. (2008). A Network Equilibrium Framework for Internet Advertising: Models, Qualitative Analysis, and Algorithms. *European Journal of Operational Research*, *187*, 456–472. doi:10.1016/j.ejor.2007.03.038

Zhao, L., & Zhu, J. (in press). Modeling Internet Marketing Budget Allocation Strategy: from Practitioner's Perspective. *Annals of Operations Research*.

KEY TERMS AND DEFINITIONS

An Internet Marketing Strategy: is a process that can allow an organization to optimize its internet marketing objective within its limited resources and competitive internet market place.

Customer Targeting: refers to going through the steps specifically and clearly profiling the types of customers who will likely to respond the marketing efforts.

Internet Advertisement Design: refers to identifying and combining ad elements to form an ad piece that generates internet browsers' response

Internet Advertisement Elements: are constituents of an internet advertisement piece. The examples of elements in an advertisement piece include, but not limited to: key words, position, imbedded URL, offer, launching time, duration of display, image, size, and color.

Internet Advertisement: is an announcement published in internet media. It may take form of email message, web page, web banner, web link, or web buttons.

Internet Marketing Budget Allocation: refers to determining amount of investment on internet marketing as well as allocating the total amount to internet publishers.

Internet Marketing: is the marketing of products or services over the Internet.

Internet Marketing Objective: is the achievement toward which marketing efforts are directed, it can be the sale of products or services, brand awareness, or return of investment. It can be measured as dollar amount made, number of items sold, number of clicks obtained per unit amount of impressions.

Internet Marketing Procedure: is used by marketing managers to control, organize, coordinate, and improve sales and marketing processes.

Internet Marketing Process: is a series of actions that involves web and customer data collection and processing, customer segmentation and profiling, internet ads design, internet ads budgeting, and internet publisher selection.

ENDNOTE

* This article is done while author is visiting Chongqing University as adjunct professor with her sabbatical leaves.

Chapter 55
Managerial Succession and E-Business

Anthonia Adenike Adeniji
Covenant University, Nigeria

INTRODUCTION

There have been several studies on managerial succession otherwise known as **succession planning** but greater percentage of them focused on succession planning as related to family owned small to medium sized enterprises (SME's), government establishments, effects of succession planning on **performance** and **profitability** of a business organization, CEOs perspectives on planning for succession, family business and **succession planning** to mention just a few (Motwani,et al 2006,Brown 2007, Dunemann & Barreff, 2004).

There is a dearth of research about managerial succession and e-business, in this world of globalization where organizations are clamoring for survival in the globally competitive environment

therefore; this chapter will focus on why **succession planning** is crucial in e-business and in the global economy. To do this effectively, available literature will be explored on the key aspects of an effective succession management system, the continuum of succession processes in e-business and in the global world. Also varieties of views and notions of individuals and groups in respect of the key issues to clarify and the key question impacting the design of succession management system in organizations and the **succession planning grid** will be considered.

The views of the academicians and professionals on the succession management process, obstacles to effective succession management in an e-business environment and the key recommendations for succession management to remain competitive and survive in a globally competitive environment will be traced.

DOI: 10.4018/978-1-61520-611-7.ch055

BACKGROUND

Succession planning in e-business is an issue of growing importance. **Businesses** generate a significant proportion of the economic activity in our countries, and a majority of these businesses are approaching the point where they will be transacting businesses on-line and will most likely by making serious decisions regarding their long time future .The manner in which such large number of potential business successions is managed will impact not only upon these individual businesses and society in which they operate but also upon the global economy .

As a result there is wide spread interest in various aspects of business succession planning and particularly, the central question of, how to do it.

However, some common themes emerge from a study of the succession management literature and the suggested models on offer .The required successor attributes needs to be identified and appropriate processes for selecting and nurturing a suitable successor determined .The timing and the manner of any handover needs to be matched to existing circumstances in the e- business environment .The roles and needs of all important participants should be acknowledged, e- business vision shared by all participants, maintaining good relationships and open communication processes is vital. Finally, the future of the incumbent in relation to the requirements of e-business must be clearly determined and managed.

Succession is the plan an organization employs to fill its most vital leadership and professions positions (Huang,2001).It is the ongoing, purposeful and systematic identification of qualified and appropriate successors to leadership, with a commitment to assessing, developing and investing in organizational leadership to enhance **performance**, development and preparedness (Kim2003; McDonald 2006).According to Michelson(2006),succession planning requires putting the right people on the business, getting the wrong people off the business and positioning the right people in the right seats .Others have argued that **succession planning** is simply having the right people in the right place at the right time(Conger and Fulmer,2003; Rothwell,2005). Succession planning reinforces the desired perceptions of the organization, fosters **employee legitimacy**, builds on the strategic plan to manage the organization through future challenges, meets the demand of the public and addresses the strength and weakness of the organization (Cohn,Khurana and Reeves 2005).

Effective succession management happens when corporations adopt a talent –finding mindset and developing guideline for building a leadership pipeline among which include; focusing on development, identifying linchpin position, making it transparent and measuring progress regularly.

MAIN FOCUS OF THE ARTICLE

Reasons Why Succession Planning is Important In E-Business

Scholars and knowledge practitioners' maintain that administrators are ignoring the coming leadership crisis and/or rejecting the imminence of the predicament (Green, 2000; Michelson, 2006; Ospina, 1992).

Consequently, many leaders of organizations lack an **exit strategy**, offer little evidence of a formal transition and treat succession management as nothing more than lining up personnel for vacancies (Michelson, 2006). Four distinct areas of exploration include the development of a succession plan, selection and training of staff, sustainability of the program and its impact on the workforce, and measurement and evaluation of the process in practice.

Planning and Development of Succession Planning

Succession planning usually begins when an organization initiates a demand forecast to determine overall future workforce needs, as well as succession analysis to predict the number of the employees to staff specific positions (Pynes, 2004). There is no "one best way" of developing, implementing or supporting a succession plan [Karaevli and Hall, 2003]. Therefore, administrators should not rely on an off-the-shelf, one-size-fits-all approach [Cohn, et al 2005]. Succession plans need not be overly complex or difficult [Berchelmann, 2005] and may employ formal versus informal tactical versus strategic [Ospina 1992] or "just-in-time" versus "integrated" methods (Young, 2005). Rothwell, (2005) and Waltuck, (2005) opined that strategic planning results in the socialization, development and advancement of potential high-performing managers.

Selection and Training

Many organizations fail in succession planning because they get "lost in the tree of **succession planning forest**" [Dessler 2006]. The importance of the identification and development of potential leader is lost among demographic statistics and summary information resulting in a talent shortage [Dychtwald, Erickson & Morrison 2006, Gandossy & Verma, [2006]. Succession planning seeks to resolve this disconnect by creating strong talent pools prepared to become future leaders of the organization. [Dessler 2006].

Organizations globally in an e- business environment are becoming more innovative in recruiting, developing and retaining talent (Patton and Pratt, 2002). Some of the creative ideas implemented include the increased usage of job rotation, establishment of co- managers in critical function to ease older leader into retirement and prepare new leaders for new role, and outsourcing hard- to fill functions and diverting existing

managers more strategic role [Green,2000]. In addition, organizations are offering to train their staff on job skills trend will make them relevant and better relate in the competitive global environment (Green, 2000). Thus, the organization offer resources and connections to the global world as well as provide the perfect venue to pursue learning objectives which serve as an excellent strategy for hiring and retaining top talent. (Green, 2000). This is because learning agility is needed in an e-business ever-changing, competitive, chaotic work environment where the differences in defining high-potential employees are as diverse as the organization involved (Karaevli & Hall, 2003).

Sustainability

Many organizations offer 'employment deals' promoting self-development over management-driven succession with an added emphasis on developing a talent pool that matches preferred competencies necessary for effective future business **performance** in an e-business environment (Waltuck, 2005). The main goal, whether high performances are identified or empowered is to find those employees who have a high sense of job satisfaction, encourage proactive career development and provide growth opportunities to those who are willing or able (Berchelmann, 2005; Karaevli & Hall, 2005).

Evaluation

Succession plans should provide assessment and measurement over the long-term by establishing core competencies matching the strategic focus of the organization, as well as identifying any gaps that may exist (Conger & Fulmer 2003and McDade, 2004). Succession plans specifically examine the ability of the organization to fill vacancies and respond to the needs in the e-business environment (Conger & Fulmer, 2003) and encourages self determination (Kim, 2003). Succession planners develop a comprehensive, organization-

Table 1. The continuum of succession processes in e-business

Replacement planning Succession planning Succession management Identify successors. Identify successors. Identify successors. Develop successors. Develop successors. Include all organization levels. Basic Comprehensive
Source: Human Resource Management (8th Edition).

wide, competency-focused, manager-centric career development program relying upon multiple dimensions of feedback (Kim, 2003).

Reasons Why Succession Planning is Important in E-Business

1. Rapid, radical and discontinuous change.
2. Increasingly complex challenges.
3. Greater leadership responsibility at lower levels.
4. Recruitment and retention of the best talent.

Different succession processes can be placed on a continuum ranging from relatively simplistic end bounded to relatively complex and comprehensive. At the most simplistic end of the continuum is the replacement planning. Replacement planning denotes a minimal succession approach in which successors (i.e. replacements) are identified at the top managerial levels, but there is little or no development of those successors other than ad-hoc on the job experience. The focus is on forecasting with no attention to development issues. **Succession planning** falls near the middle of this continuum of succession planning. It is more systematic and extensive than replacement planning because it is linked with intentional development initiative targeted at successors. However, it is mainly for the top two or three management levels, like replacement planning. Succession management anchors the most comprehensive end of this continuum in that it identifies successors (replacement

planning), develops them (succession planning) and it is also directed at all managerial levels. The overarching goal of succession management is to have a pool of or pipeline of prepared leaders and not just a list of prospective candidates across all organizational levels to fill vacancies in key positions when needed.

Key Questions Impacting the Design of Succession Management System

The followings are the key questions impacting the design of succession management system in organizations operating in an e-business environment that is highly competitive and dynamic.

- What is a key or "corporate –critical" position?
- What constitutes a high potential manager?
- What are the common aspects of exemplary job performance?
- How should the organization fill key positions?
- What percentage of open positions should be filled from within the organization?
- What percentage of key positions should have at least one identified successors?
- How should high-potential manager be prepared for advancement?
- How desirable are international assignments for designated successors?
- How important are individual employee career goals and objectives in the succession management plan?

Table 2.

Potential	Performance		
	Low	Medium	High
High	Demonstrated high potential for advancement but is not meeting current performance expectations. Needs coaching and intervention: Wrong job or wrong boss?	Demonstrated high potential and consistently meet performance expectations. Valued talent who need additional challenge, rewards, recognition or opportunity to develop.	Highest potential for senior leadership position that usually always exceeds performance expectations. Star talent who should be targeted for accelerated development opportunities
Medium	Promoting potential one level or lateral move with greater challenge but presently under-performing. Consider coaching or corrective action	Promotion potential one level or lateral move with greater challenge: presently meeting but not exceeding performance expectations. Keep things running but might need additional motivation, greater engagement or additional rewards.	Promotion potential one level or lateral move with greater scope or challenge always meets and usually exceeds expectations. Strong contributor who could have additional developmental challenges to grow and possibly improve potential.
Low	Has reached career potential and is not delivering. Counsel or terminate.	Specialized technical talent or has reached career potential but consistently meet performance expectations. Motivate and focus.	Specialized technical talent or has reached career potential but consistently exceeds performance expectations Valuable in developing others; retain and reward.

Effective Succession Management Process

This is critical for a successful talent identification process. A climate of honesty, trust and transparency is an important factor in the systems ultimate success. The following are the features of succession management process;

- High level review of the talent pipeline by the CEO and his direct reports.
- Review of each business function and strategic area of focusing on what new capabilities will be needed to deliver this strategy and any new corporate critical roles that will be needed.
- Review of top 200 leaders using the "**nine-box" performance /potential grid**. This is shown in Table 2;
- Development and discussion of succession plans for high and medium risks corporate-

critical roles that exist now and are anticipated in the future.
- Development planning for this population.
- Link the plan design to the needs and vision of the CEO, senior management team and the requirements of e-business in the global environment.

However, succession management process includes preparation, planning and development.

Preparation; the goal is to understand the context.

Planning; the goal is to identify positions on talents.

Development; the goal is to prepare and develop talent. The key processes here are assessment, challenge, and support.

OBSTACLES TO EFFECTIVE SUCCESSION MANAGEMENT

Ultimately, an investment in succession management is an investment in individual and organizational learning, but like many things, this is easier said than done. There are many potential factors that can derail succession management process. Below is the list and brief discussion on some likely culprits:

- Event-based or **episodic thinking**. This implies succession planning as well as leadership development. Both of them are ongoing processes, yet the conventional thinking is that they are addressed episodically. **Succession planning** typically is conducted only once in a year and leadership development is treated as a series of 'loosely coupled' events or episodes, usually in the form of programmes. It is a mistake to try to completely de-couple development from work.
- No strategy for development. What is the organization philosophy of succession management and development? These are the key concerns in terms of presenting and defining the concepts and principles that will serve as the pillars of the conceptual framework for the initiative.
- Assuming it is solely a staff function. In most cases, the human resource function has the primary responsibility for succession management. A common mistake and typical obstacle to effective implementation is failing to engage line management from the onset.
- Over-embedding the initiative in a single champion. Having a champion, especially at top levels, is an important driver for success, however, if the initiative becomes too heavily associated with any one person no matter how high ranking this could lead to follow through problems if that champion derails or leaves the organization.

- Not connecting with strategic business imperatives.

Development for development's sake might be a generally good thing; however it might not be helpful for long-term support. It is easy to lose sight of what specifically needs to be developed and why.

To implement a formal system with lack of fit with the organizational culture.

Trying to implement a formal system with a lot of preparation and paperwork in an informal culture would likely be met with resistance, if not outright hostility introducing an informal system into a highly structured and formal organization may result in the in the initiative not being taken seriously.

RECOMMENDATION

Succession management can also aid in the recruitment and retention of the talent that is needed to be competitive in the global economic and Electronic business.

However, the followings are the key recommendations for succession management;

- Understand the unique context of your organization.
- Recognize that organization have special challenges and opportunities when it comes to succession management in an E Business environment
- Identify key positions and the talent potentials for these potentials (**Nine-Box Grid"** may be helpful).
- Establish succession plans for key positions that identify at least one and preferable more than one potential successor.
- Engage in detailed developmental planning for the targeted successor populated.
- Use leadership competency models with caution – the future is imperfectly predicted.

- Avoid the basic obstacles to an effective succession management system.
- Work towards continuous succession management system improvement.

FUTURE RESEARCH DIRECTIVE

It had been said that effective succession planning involves more than just a replacement planning process. It also includes a comprehensive **employee development system**, thus, future researches should focus on development strategies for both the SME'S in their local markets and for the global competition in the international market.

CONCLUSION

The chapter dwells richly on the succession planning in an e – business environment. It considers the reason why succession planning is important in the global economy, the key aspects of an effective succession management system, the continuum of succession processes in e- business, and the key questions impacting the design of succession management system. Also, the chapter looked at the succession planning grid, the obstacle to effective succession management in an e- business environment and the key recommendation for succession management were given.

REFERENCES

Berchelmann, D. K. (2005). Succession Planning. *Journal for Quality and Participation*, *28*(3), 11–12.

Brown, M. C. (2007). Administrative Succession and Organizational Performance: The Succession Effect. *Journal of the Social Sciences*, *27*(1), 1–16.

Cohn, J. M., Khurana, R., & Reeves, L. (2005). Growing Talent As If Your Business Depended On It. *Harvard Business Review*, *83*(10), 62–70.

Conger, J., & Fulmer, R. (2003). Developing Your Leadership Pipeline. *Harvard Business Review*, *82*(12), 76–84.

Dessler, G. (2006). *Human Resource Management* (8th Ed.). London: Prentice Hall.

Dunemann, M., & Barreff, R. (2004). Family Business and Succession Planning. *Administrative Science Quarterly*, *25*(1), 26–40.

Dychtwald, K., Erickson, T. J., & Morison, R. (2006). *Workforce Crisis: How to Beat. The Coming Shortage of Skills and Talent.* Boston: Harvard Business School Press.

Gandossy, R. P., & Verma, N. (2006). Passing the Torch of Leadership. *Journal of Leadership*, *40*(1), 37–47.

Green, M. E. (2000). Beware and Prepare: The Government Workforce of The Future. *Public Personnel Management Journal*, *29*(4), 435–447.

Huang, R. J. (2001). Marginal Mentoring, the Effects of Type of Mentor, Quality of Relationship and Program Design on Work and Career Attitudes. *Academy of Management Journal*, *43*, 1177–1194.

Karaevli, A., & Hall, D. T. (2003). Growing Leaders for Turbulent Times. Is Succession Planning Up to The Challenge? *Organizational Dynamics*, *32*, 62–79. doi:10.1016/S0090-2616(02)00138-9

Kim, S. (2003). Linking Employee Assessment to Succession Planning. *Public Personnel Management*, *32*(4), 533–547.

McDade, S. A. (2004). Evaluating Leadership, Development Programs, New Directions for Leadership. *Development. The Leadership Quarterly*, *16*(3), 297–317.

McDonald, R. D. (2006). *Succession Planning is Mission Critical to Achieving Organizational Goals.* Pawcatuck, CT: Pearson Performance Solutions.

Michelson, R. (2006). Preparing Future Leaders for Tomorrow. *The Police Chief, 73*(6), 16–21.

Motwani, J., Levenbury, N., Schwarz, V., & Blankson, C. (2006). Succession Planning in SMEs. *International Small Business Journal, 24*(5), 471–495. doi:10.1177/0266242606067270

Ospina, S. (1992). When Managers Don't Plan, Consequences of Nonstrategic Public Personnel Management. *Review of Public Personnel Management, 12*(2), 52–67. doi:10.1177/0734371X9201200205

Patton, W. D., & Pratt, C. (2002). Assessing the Training Needs of High. Potential Managers. *Public Personnel Management, 31*(4), 465–484.

Pynes, J. (2004). The Implementation of Workforce and Succession in the Public Sector. *Public Personnel Management, 33*(4), 389–404.

Rothwell, W. J. (2005). *Effective Succession Planning Ensuring Leadership Continuity and Building Talent Within* (3rd Ed.). New York: American Management Association.

Waltuck, B. (2005). What's the Point of Planning? *Journal for Quality and Participation, 28*(4), 37–40.

Young, M. B. (2005). Building the Leadership Pipeline in Local State and Federal Government. *Human Resource Services, 52*, 561–610.

ADDITIONAL READING

Cantor, P. (2005 January/February). Succession Planning: Often Requested, Rarely Delivered. *Ivey Business Journal*, 1-10.

Cardon, M. S., & Stevens, C. E. (2004). Managing Human Resources in Small Organizations: What Do We Know? *Human Resource Review, 14*, 294–323.

Church, A. H. (1997). Managerial Self-Awareness in High Performing Individuals and Organizations. *The Journal of Applied Psychology, 82*, 281–292. doi:10.1037/0021-9010.82.2.281

Cunningham, M. R., & Waker, M. D. (2006). *Succession Planning is Mission Critical to Achieving Organizational Goals.* Pawcatuck, CT: Pearson Performance Solutions.

Day, D. V. (2000). Leadership Development: A Review in Context. *The Leadership Quarterly, 11*, 581–613. doi:10.1016/S1048-9843(00)00061-8

Diamond, A. (2006). Finding Success Through Succession Planning. *Security Management, 50*(2), 36–39.

Drath, W. (2001). *The Deep Blue Sea: Rethinking the Source of Leadership.* San Francisco, CA: Jersey-Bass.

Dweck, C. S. (1986). Motivation Process Affecting Learning. *The American Psychologist, 41*, 1040–1048. doi:10.1037/0003-066X.41.10.1040

Fegley, S. (2006). *SHRM 2006 Succession Planning Survey Report.* Alexandria, VA: Society for Human Resource Management.

Hannum, K. M., Martineau, J. W., & Reinelt, C. (Eds.). (2007). *The Handbook of Leadership Development Evaluation,* San Francisco, CA: Jossey Bass.

Heifetz, R. (1994). *Leadership Without Easy Answers.* Cambridge, MA: Harvard University.

Hollenbeck, G. P., McCall, M. W. Jr, & Silzer, R. F. (2006). Leadership Competency Models. *The Leadership Quarterly, 17*, 398–413. doi:10.1016/j.leaqua.2006.04.003

Ibarra, P. (2005). Succession Planning: An Idea Whose Time Has Come. *Public Management Journal*, 2(1), 107–117.

Ip, B., & Jacobs, G. (2006). Business Succession Planning: A Review of the Evidence. *Journal of Small Business and Enterprise Development, 13*, 326–350. doi:10.1108/14626000610680235

Karaevli, A., & Hall, D. T. (2003). Growing Leaders for Turbulent Times: Is Succession Planning Up to the Challenge? *Organizational Dynamics, 32*, 62–79. doi:10.1016/S0090-2616(02)00138-9

Lawler, E. E., III, & Worley, C. G. (2006). *Built to Change: How to Achieve Sustained Organizational Effectiveness*. San Francisco, CA: Jossey-Bass.

Lewis, R. E., & Heckman, R. J. (2006). Talent Management: A Critical Review. *Human Resource Management Review, 16*, 139–154. doi:10.1016/j.hrmr.2006.03.001

McCall, M. W., Jr., Lombardo, M. M., & Marrison, A. M. (1988). *The Lessons of Experience: How Successful Executives Develop on the Job*. Lexington, MA: Lexington Books.

Meister, J. C. (1998). Ten Steps to Creating a Corporate University. *Training & Development, 52*, 38–43.

Morrow, C. C., Jarrett, M. O., & Rupinski, M. T. (1997). An Investigation of the Effect and Economic Utility of Corporate-Wide Training. *Personnel Psychology, 50*, 91–119. doi:10.1111/j.1744-6570.1997.tb00902.x

Peterson, D. B. (1996). Executive Coaching at Work: The Art of One-On-One Change. *Consulting Psychology Journal: Practice and Research, 48*, 78–86. doi:10.1037/1061-4087.48.2.78

Ragins, B. R., Cotton, J. L., & Miller, J. S. (2000). Marginal Mentoring: The Effects of Types of Mentor, Quality of Relationship and Program Design on Work and Career Attitudes. *Academy of Management Journal, 43*, 1177–1194. doi:10.2307/1556344

Sanders, P. (2007). Once and Again: After Son's Death a Casino Mogul Returns to Helm. *The Wall Street Journal*, 16-17.

Sharma, P., Jess, H., & James, J. (2003). Succession Planning as Planned Behaviour: Some Empirical Results. *Family Business Review, 16*(1), 1–15. doi:10.1111/j.1741-6248.2003.00001.x

Van Velsor, E., & McCauley, C. D. (2004). Over View of Leadership Development. In C.D. McCauley and E. Van Velsor (Eds.), *The Centre for Creative Leadership Handbook of Leadership Development* (pp. 1-22). San Francisco: Jossey-Bass.

Ward, S. (2007). *Succession Planning*. Retrieved from http://www.sbinfocanada.about.com/od/businessplanning/g/successplanning.htm

Weick, K. E. (1993). The Collapse of Sensemaking in Organization: The Mann Gulch Disaster. *Administrative Service Quarterly, 38*, 628–652. doi:10.2307/2393339

Weiss, D. S., & Molinaro, V. (2005). *The Leadership Gap: Building Leadership Capacity for Competitive Advantage*. New York: John Wiley and Sons.

KEY TERMS AND DEFINITIONS

Competitive Environment: this is an environment where companies and nations have the opportunity to compete effectively with one another considering the regulations in the environment.

E-Business: this is the transacting of business on-line or on the internet.

Globalization: this is the interconnectivity of business of nations all over the world. In other words, that all economies are connected to do business together where each will now gain competitive advantage over its products.

Leadership Pipeline: this is having a pool of prepared leaders and not just a list of prospective candidates across all organizational levels to fill vacancies in key positions when needed.

Linchpin Positions: these are positions between middle to senior management positions that are essential to organization's long term health.

Managerial Succession: this is the ongoing, purposeful and systematic identification of qualified and appropriate successors to leadership, with a commitment to assessing, developing and investing in organizational leadership to enhance performance, development and preparedness.

Replacement Planning: this is the minimal succession approach in which successors (i.e replacements) are identified at the top managerial levels, but there is little or no development of those successors other than ad-hoc on the job experience.

Successor: this is when a person comes after and takes the place of somebody.

Chapter 56
E–Business and Web Accessibility

Panayiotis Koutsabasis
University of the Aegean, Greece

INTRODUCTION

E-business has developed due to the fast penetration of the Web to human activities ranging from work and education to news and entertainment. The power of the Web is in its universality, and, in principle, everyone can access e-business websites and benefit from available information, products and services. However, in practice, universal access to the Web - and subsequently e-business websites - is not merely an issue of availability or technical development.

Web accessibility emphasizes the incorporation of requirements of people with special needs to the design of Internet applications. Notwithstanding these requirements, the spectrum of accessibility concerns is even larger, for example if we think about the changing form of the computer and how people work and communicate: access is not required only from a PC, but also users are on the move and use other access devices (in terms of both hardware and software).

Research on Web accessibility has produced a wide range of results that are also used in mainstream Web design to promoted good design practice. These can be briefly outlined in terms of related legislation that aims at encouraging the development of accessible Web applications, open recommendations for accessible Web design, various accessibility evaluation tools that check – to some extend - the conformance of websites to the aforementioned specifications and various related open standards that promote accessibility.

Despite the large amount of work on Web accessibility, the vast majority of e-business websites are still not accessible. A report of accessible Internet shopping (Shindler, 2003) which involved 17 major high-street companies concluded that after the companies attempt to make their online shopping facilities accessible to people with disabilities during the period between August 2000 and June 2003 only

DOI: 10.4018/978-1-61520-611-7.ch056

five companies out of the seventeen examined, managed to pass the Watchfire Bobby test. The study of Loiacono and McCoy (2006) on evaluating Web accessibility in a large number of websites indicates that a poor 23% of federal homepages are accessible, while this percentage falls down to 11% for non-profit organisations and a totally disappointing 6% for corporate homepages.

The goals of the article are to:

- Argue for the importance of Web accessibility in e-business websites by reviewing related work and its impact at the technical, social, economic and legislative level and identifies typical accessibility problems of e-business websites;
- Propose measures for reaching and maintaining a good level of Web accessibility in terms of the specifications, design and evaluation phases of a user-centred approach to systems development. The proposed measures provide practical guidance to e-business applications stakeholders including managers, designers and developers.

PERSPECTIVES ON WEB ACCESSIBILITY

Accessibility has received several interpretations in related work. The W3C Web Accessibility Initiative (http://w3c.org/wai) defines Web accessibility as a set of "*strategies, guidelines and resources that make the Web accessible to people with disabilities*", highlighting that accessibility is not simply a technical development issue. The Wikipedia definition on accessibility reveals another dimension of the same coin: "*Web accessibility refers to the practice of making Web pages accessible to people using a wide range of user agent devices, not just standard web browsers. This is especially important for people with disabilities which require such devices to access the Web*". This perspective provides the dimension of

good user-based design of the Web that supports different access contexts and multiple device operability with the Web. The Webaim initiative about Web accessibility (http://webaim.org) refers to accessibility noting that: "*(with the advent of the Web) ... at the click of a mouse, the world can be "at your fingertips"—that is, if you can use a mouse... and if you can see the screen... and if you can hear the audio.*" Many other definitions of Web accessibility can be found in related initiatives and literature, which fall under three diverse ends that are briefly outlined below:

- **Accessibility as technology and network effectiveness:** in its most basic sense, accessibility is considered as synonymous to the technical capability to access the Internet. Related metrics of accessibility in this respect are the characteristics of network connection and of the software applications used. This is obviously a limited interpretation of accessibility: the availability of technology does not guarantee that people will use it.
- **Accessibility as good Web content design and implementation practice:** accessibility promotes the syntactic understandability of Web content by multiple access devices (e.g. see Viorres et al, 2003), enables content transformation to other formats and media, and eases the task of customization of presentation to user needs and preferences.
- **Accessibility as advanced personalization of content and services:** this approach promotes the semantic understandability of information from users with varying profiles and cognitive requirements and allows for dynamic system responses to user actions.

A mainstream conception about designing for accessibility is that design projects usually result to constrained solutions addressing very specific requirements of people with special needs. Indeed, as Keates and Clarkson (2003) remark in the context of inclusive design, *"traditionally, design research tends to focus on accommodating single, primarily major, capability losses."* Despite that some design solutions may indeed have specialized characteristics, the awareness created about the requirements of people with disabilities is radically changing the overall approach to address accessibility. People with special needs are not interested in specialized solutions, for various reasons, ranging from social acceptance to aesthetics, but require access to mainstream designs that may be used by as many people as possible. As noted by Paddison and Engefield (2003) *"it is not enough to follow accessible guidelines and make the appropriate technical accessibility changes... people with special accessibility needs should be considered as a distinct user profile with their own requirements, within a user-centered design process."*

RE-THINKING ACCESSIBILITY FOR E-BUSINESS: ASSOCIATED BENEFITS

There are many arguments for incorporating the requirements of people with disabilities to product and systems design in general (for further analysis see for example Paddison and Engefield, 2003). The ethical stand that calls for providing equal opportunities to all has for long ceased to be the main argument, since that there are numerous examples of people with special needs that are contributing in a distinguished way to society. The need to incorporate the requirements of people with disabilities to design has been identified in many countries in terms of legal frameworks. Despite that e-business websites do not need yet to conform to this legislation, doing so will gain them a competitive advantage both in terms of social responsibility and technical excellence.

The business prospects of incorporating accessibility can be identified in various ways. To start with, people with special needs are not simply those that suffer from permanent disabilities but also other groups such as the aging population. The percentage of people with disabilities in most countries ranges between 10% and 20% of the population (United Nations Statistics on Disability: http://unstats.un.org). The age group over 60 is the most rapidly growing and there is a large overlap between the groups of elderly and disabled. Furthermore, the percentage of elderly people that will be using ICT (Information and Communication Technologies) by 2020 will increase considerably since current ICT users will have grown older by that date. This rise in the elderly population and the envisaged use of ICT by this group of people signify that if not now, in the near future the ICT companies should provide mainstream technology and Web-based services that address fully the requirements of people with special needs.

Further to these arguments, perhaps the most important misconception about accessibility is that it does refer only to people with special needs. Designing for accessibility addresses other user access issues as well, such as for example, performance for low network speed, usable access under constrained environmental conditions, and variable, personalised contexts of use. Thus, "special needs" may not simply denote irreparable physical constraints, but actually include many other, temporal or permanent, limitations of access that may be related to various factors, such as user mobility, access from alternate devices, the work environment conditions and the context of use. A few examples of contexts of use where accessible design can overcome include "handicapping" situations where customers may:

- Not be in a position to hear spoken information – e.g. noisy environment
- Not be in a position to see visual information – e.g. while driving a car

- Not be able to use the mouse (pointing device) or keyboard – e.g. a temporal injury, or a mobile device
- Not understand the language used – e.g. foreign customers
- Be using a text-only screen, or screens with small screen analysis and a few colours - e.g. a mobile or household device

Thus, from a technical point of view, designing for accessibility promotes good technical design and implementation that has obvious implications for maintenance and extensibility, which is a critical aspect of e-business websites that often need to update the content and look & feel with new products and styles respectively. Actually, accessibility concerns are relevant to the mainstream design process, rather than the design for specific groups of people only, emphasising the design of alternate, rather than specialised, means, modes and forms of access.

MEASURES TO MANAGE AND MAINTAIN A GOOD LEVEL OF WEB ACCESSIBILITY IN E-BUSINESS APPLICATIONS

A number of important steps for the management of accessibility include: identifying accessibility requirements and specifications; applying rigorous and frequent Web accessibility assessment and re-design, if needed; and forming a Web accessibility policy to be consistently followed. These steps are briefly discussed below.

Identifying Relevant Accessibility Requirements and Specifications

User accessibility requirements can be identified when accessibility is included into the goals of a user centred design approach. Web accessibility specifications include:

- The US Rehabilitation Act (http://www.section508.gov);
- Open recommendations for accessible Web design such as the W3C.WAI Web Content Accessibility Guidelines (http://www.w3.org/WAI/intro/wcag) that are of particular interest to B2C (Business to Consumer) e-business websites;
- Various accessibility evaluation tools that check – to some extend - the conformance of websites to the aforementioned specifications (for a good overview of these tools see: http://www.w3.org/WAI/ER/tools/complete);
- Various related open W3C standards that promote accessibility including, among others: CSS (Cascading Style Sheets), XSLT (eXtended Stylesheet Language Transformations), SVG (scaleable Vector Graphics), SMIL (Synchronized Multimedia Integration Language) and the Device Independence Activity that builds on previous CC/PP recommendation.

Currently, there are many accessibility (and usability) evaluation groups that offer consultancy on accessibility as well as conduct fast assessments of an e-business website at a reasonable cost of a few hundred dollars. Keeping in mind the social and economic benefits of accessibility, this cost should not be considerable even for small in size online enterprises.

Web Accessibility Assessment and Re-Design Process

A fast assessment of Web accessibility is possible by using free accessibility tools (technical accessibility conformance to guidelines) and applying simple heuristics (manual, expert-based accessibility inspection). However, a thorough approach on accessibility assessment and redesign mainly requires another important element in the process: that of user involvement through user testing.

Tool-Based Accessibility Conformance to Guidelines

Accessibility evaluation tools scan the source code of a web page using interpretations of either WCAG or the United States Rehabilitation Act Section 508 standard. The use of these tools is the first step for accessibility evaluation since that they can quickly identify accessibility problems that can be identified at the level of the source code of a web page and produce reports with accessibility errors and warnings. These tools save the designer from the task to inspect source code for the evaluation of accessibility and provide a first account of accessibility problems. However they cannot provide a complete account of accessibility problems mainly because accessibility is not a solely technical issue, but primarily requires human judgement. According to Webaim (http://www.webaim.org) of the combined 65 checkpoints in WCAG 1.0 Priority 1 through Priority 3, only nineteen can be partially evaluated automatically.

Currently there are many accessibility evaluation tools available, both free and commercial (for a review see: http://www.webaim.org/articles/freetools) to the degree that methods that enable their comparison have been proposed (Brajnik, 2004). A major problem for accessibility tools is that their vast majority are designed for fast evaluations of single web pages. Currently, research on the design of new generation accessibility tools attempts to address these concerns such as the MAGENTA tool (Leporini et al, 2006) and the BenToWeb benchmarking tools that will include the aforementioned capabilities (Herramhof et al, 2006). Also, some proprietary solutions have appeared like Oracle's e-business suite accessibility (2008). Both types of works need also to be tested in practice though.

Expert (Manual) Accessibility Inspection

Manual evaluation includes a number of steps that must be followed by a designer to check the accessibility of web pages according to guidelines. These steps are another essential task of accessibility evaluation that can assess the accessibility in terms of the aspects that require human judgement. Such aspects include for example that alternative text for images substantially describes the meaning of an image in textual form, in case this is needed (i.e. when the image conveys information and is not used for other purposes such as decoration) and that the use of colours promotes accessibility of text and images if viewed in a constrained context of use (e.g. when printed by a black and white printer).

Expert inspections of accessibility can identify a considerable number of problems that are not possible to find by using accessibility tools alone. Typical inspections of Web accessibility include:

- Inspection of human checks for accessibility according to the WCAG guidelines: WCAG explicitly refers to accessibility issues that require human check and provides techniques that can assist expert evaluators
- Inspection of accessibility following simple heuristics: there is a number of empirical heuristics that complements the list provided by WeC.WAI, such as: turning frames off; turning sound off; navigating without a pointing device; accessing the website via multiple browsers; accessing the website via text browsers; accessing the website via a voice browser; test with different screen resolution; and others.

The expertise required to conduct accessibility evaluation is wide-ranging, including both organisational and technical skills. According to the W3C.WAI (http://w3c.org/wai) an accessibility evaluator should have "*an understanding of Web technologies, evaluation tools, barriers that people with disabilities experience, assistive technologies and approaches that people with disabilities use, and accessibility guidelines and techniques.*"

User Testing Of Accessibility

The involvement of users with disabilities is an important aspect of accessibility evaluation. Explicit user involvement is usually neglected in software development and maintenance practice mainly due to arguments related to the increase of costs and delivery times; some practitioners even doubt the usefulness of user involvement and instead promote training programmes instead. However careful user involvement has various advantages such as: increasing the amount of knowledge gained about a software development and maintenance project; identifying the advisability of target system components, which saves the project team from unneeded effort; contributing to system acceptability; reducing training costs; and assisting the identification of a wide range of usability problems. These advantages are particularly important for e-business websites that are interested to provide information and services to the widest range of potential users.

In the context of Web accessibility, user testing with people with disabilities contributes to a better understanding of accessibility issues by all people involved, and especially Web developers. For example, having Web developers see people with disabilities accessing a Web page with a voice browser makes them immediately identify related accessibility problems that their website may have such as the inappropriateness or absence of alternative text, the ordering of controls in a form, and others. Certainly, a user-centred accessibility evaluation will not be effective unless the site is already at a minimum level of accessibility. Furthermore, including users into the accessibility evaluation process can also identify various us-

ability problems. Analytic methods and guidelines for involving users in accessibility evaluation include the work of Gappa and Nordbrock (2004) and Petrie et al (2006).

Web Accessibility Policy

In order to reach and maintain a good level of Web accessibility, e-business websites need to establish a Web accessibility policy that will be applied during the design, development and up-date of their website. Currently, web accessibility policies have been established for a number of, mainly academic and governmental, websites and in a few e-business systems that are designed with the participation of organisations of people with disabilities, such as the RNIB (e.g. Gladstone et al, 2002).

An important issue for the design of the Web accessibility policy is what standards, guidelines, methods and processes to identify from related work. Indeed, there is ongoing work in all these respects (for a review see Gulliksen et al, 2004). However, the common basis for the standardisation aspects of the work related to Web accessibility is the W3C.WAI guidelines for the accessibility of Web content, authoring tools and user agents. W3C is the leading open standards (they are not called standards, but recommendations) organisation for Web technologies and their recommendations are the outcome of an open international process with participation from industry and academia.

SUMMARY AND CONCLUSION

The article argued for the need to include accessibility concerns into the lifecycle of e-business websites and proposed several measures to need to be taken up in order to ensure that Web accessibility is incorporated to the daily operation of e-business applications. There are many reasons for e-business websites to become accessible. The social responsibility of e-business companies requires that they provide accessible Web-based information and services. The market segment of people with disabilities including the elderly is too large to be ignored; these people want to autonomously access and use e-business. The robustness of the technical design when accessibility is taken into account is another major argument for taking up this approach. Last but not least, there are already legal frameworks for governmental organizations to apply accessibility to their design; e-business websites may need to follow up in order to ensure that there are equal obligations for all in terms of their legal responsibilities.

REFERENCES

Brajnik, G. (2004). Comparing accessibility evaluation tools: a method for tool effectiveness. *Universal Access in the Information Society, 3*(3), 252–263. doi:10.1007/s10209-004-0105-y

Darzentas, J. S., & Darzentas, J. (2004) Socially responsible design or just good sense? The role of education and research in getting the message across. In *ETHICOMP 2004*, 14-16 April, Syros, Greece (pp. 237-249).

E-Business Suite Accessibility. (2008 July). An Oracle White Paper. Retrieved December 12, 2008, from http://www.oracle.com/accessibility/collateral/ebs-accessibility-white-paper.pdf

Gappa, H., & Nordbrock, G. (2004). Applying Web accessibility to Internet portals. *Universal Access in the Information Society, 3*(1), 80–87. doi:10.1007/s10209-003-0070-x

Gladstone, K., Rundle, C., & Alexander, T. (2002). Accessibility and Usability of eCommerce Systems. In K. Miesenberger, J. Klaus, & W. Zagler (Eds.), *ICCHP 2002* (LNCS 2398, pp. 11–18). Berlin: Springer-Verlag.

Gulliksen, J., Harker, S., & Vanderheiden, G. (2004). Guidelines, standards, methods and processes for software accessibility (Special issue editorial). *Universal Access in the Information Society, 3*(3-4), 1–5. doi:10.1007/s10209-003-0068-4

Herramhof, S., Petrie, H., Strobbe, C., Vlachogiannis, E., Weimann, K., Weber, G., & Velasco, C. A. (2006). Test Case Management Tools for Accessibility Testing. In J. Klaus, K. Miesenberger, D. Burger & W. Zagler (Eds.), *Computers Helping People with Special Needs. Proceedings of 10th International Conference, ICCHP 2006*, Linz, Austria, 12-14 July 2006.

Keates, S., & Clarkson, P. J. (2003). Countering Design Exclusion Through Inclusive Design. In *CUU'03*, November 10-11, 2003, Vancouver, British Columbia, Canada. Retrieved from http://www.acm.org

Leporini, B., Paterno, F., & Scorcia, A. (2006). Flexible tool support for accessibility evaluation. *Interacting with Computers, 18*(5). doi:10.1016/j.intcom.2006.03.001

Loiacono, E. T., & McCoy, S. (2006). Website accessibility: a cross-sector comparison. *Universal Access in the Information Society, 6*(4), 393–399. doi:10.1007/s10209-005-0003-y

Paddison, C., & Englefield, P. (2003). Applying Heuristics to Perform a Rigorous Accessibility Inspection in a Commercial Context. In *CUU'03*, Nov. 10-11, 2003, Vancouver, Canada.

Petrie, H., Hamilton, F., King, N., & Pavan, P. (2006). Remote Usability Evaluations with Disabled People. In *CHI'2006*, Montréal, Quebec, Canada, April 22–27, 2006.

Shindler, J. (2004). *The Accessibility of Online Internet Shopping: An analysis and evaluation of the policies of seventeen major high street companies*. University of Salford.

Viorres, N., Koutsabasis, P., Arnellos, A., Darzentas, J. S., Velasco, C., Mohamad, Y., et al. (2003). An Approach for Personalisation and Content Adaptation of Internet Applications based on User and Device Profiles. In *Proceedings of HCI International 2003*, 24-26 June 2003, Heraklion, Crete.

KEY TERMS AND DEFINITIONS

Accessibility Specifications: an organised, validated and testable set of (among others) principles, guidelines, techniques, examples that have to be followed by design practitioners to ensure accessibility.

Accessibility: the property of a designed artifact to be usable, manipulable and undestandable by all people regardless temporal or permanent injuries or disabilities.

Expert (Manual) Web Accessibility Inspection: a generic category of accessibility evaluations that mainly includes experts that review a website for accessibility flaws on the basis of their knoweldge fo accessibility and with reference to accessibility specifications.

Inclusive Design: or Design for all: the practice of designing for all people as potential users, thus including the requirements of people with disabilities.

People in Handicapping Situations: people that face temporal disabilities mainly due to factors related to temporal injuries, the access context or the environment in which they are situated in.

User Testing of Web Accessibility: a generic category of accessibility evaluations that mainly includes user interaction with the web site and recording of accessibility flaws.

Web Accessibility Evaluation Tool: a software tool that checks the conformance of a web page to a set of Web accessibility specifications (that can be tested automatically)

Web Accessibility Policy: a set of practices for the design, development and update of a website that ensure that Web accessibility is maintained through time.

Web Accessibility: accessibility of (any type of) a website.

Chapter 57
Understanding the Use of Business–to–Employee (B2E) Portals in an Australian University though the Management Lens:
A Qualitative Approach

Md Mahbubur Rahim
Monash University, Australia

Mohammad Quaddus
Curtin University, Australia

Mohini Singh
RMIT University, Australia

INTRODUCTION

The application of the Internet for commercial purposes has led to different types of e-business initiatives, which have been widely discussed in the scholarly literature and trade magazines. However, it is the Business-to-Consumers (B2C) and Business-to-Business (B2B) e-businesses that have so far dominated discussion in the contemporary literature. These two types of e-business initiatives collectively are believed to have enormous impact on business practices, industry structure and our society at large. On the other hand, Business-to-Employee (B2E), which represents an employee

centric e-business initiative (Turban et al., 2008), is relatively less recognized in extant literature. Despite little attention given to B2E e-business, it represents an emerging area which has the potential to benefit businesses and IT vendors alike (Rahim and Singh, 2007). For businesses, B2E e-business solutions can act as a source of competitive advantage through retention of satisfied workforce (Hansen and Deimler, 2001). The IT vendors are currently competing to capture market share by offering various types of innovative web-based B2E solutions (e.g. employee portals, e-HR systems and ESS). According to several industry sources, an increased growth has been observed in the demand for various types of B2E products (Killen Associates Report, 2006; Merrill Lynch Capital Markets cited

DOI: 10.4018/978-1-61520-611-7.ch057

in Brooks, 2004; and Banks, 2004). Yet, despite industry forecasts, the use of B2E e-business solutions by employees has largely been ignored in the current scholarly IT/e-business literature. This lack of attention is possibly due to the implicit assumption made in the literature (due to media hype) that employees would happily embrace and use B2E systems once these technologies are introduced in organisations. We however disagree with this view and argue that evaluation of the use of B2E solutions by employees represents a key research concern because the benefits arising from the introduction of such solutions are unlikely to be realised when they are not satisfactorily diffused among employee community. Therefore, managers need to be aware of the factors that may potentially affect the use of B2E e-business systems in organisational settings.

We acknowledge that existing literature has reported the attempts made by several scholars (e.g. KieBling and Kostler, 2002; Gounaris and Dimitriadis, 2003; Holsapple and Sasidharan, 2005) who have studied such aspects as portal usability and portal design challenges associated with various types of online B2C interactive portals (e.g. tourist portals, citizen portals) which have some degree of similarity with B2E systems. Despite this similarity, clear differences still exist because unlike B2C portals the users are employees not external customers who need to be provided with access to organisational internal controls, and many different types of services, and more in-depth information of B2E systems. Therefore, as the motivations and purposes of B2E systems are different (although many of the underlying technical issues are similar), we can expect that the usage behaviour of B2E systems by employees is different from that of users of online B2C service portals. Consequently, although the findings of these scholars are useful they are not directly applicable to B2E systems context without further empirical confirmation. Recognising this difference is important because

little (if any) research attention has been given to understand use of B2E systems.

In this article, we thus report the experience of a large Australian university in introducing an employee portal. In particular, we analyse the views of the portal steering committee (who represent the interests of the university senior management) relating to the portal usage behaviour of university staff and identify the key factors which they believe to have contributed to employees' low usage practices of portals. Identifying factors from the perspective of senior management is important because unlike other employees (who act as ordinary users) they have better understanding of the strategic rationale for the introduction of portal initiatives in organisational settings. We argue that it is this focus of trying to understand B2E systems use from the viewpoint of senior management that sets our study apart from other existing adoption studies on online B2C service oriented systems which primarily adopt the viewpoint of actual users rather than the strategic management of the organisation which introduces their online systems. Hence, we contribute to literature by highlighting the views from a major stakeholder (i.e. senior management) in relation to B2E systems adoption.

Our article is organised as follows. First, we review e-business and human resources literature in which the notion of employee oriented e-business systems has been discussed. Consistent with our objectives, we however restrict our literature review attention to those studies which adopted the perspective of organisational management and then identify the research gaps and broad research concerns. Next, our research approach is described. Following that, the background of the participating tertiary educational institution is presented. Next, empirical evidence collected from the institution is described and discussed in light of the existing literature. Finally, the contributions of our research are highlighted and areas of possible further investigations are mentioned.

BACKGROUND LITERATURE: AN ANALYSIS

E-Business Literature

A review of literature on B2E e-business systems identifies two specific research aspects: *organisational adoption decisions of B2E e-business systems, and business impact from the adoption of B2E e-business systems*. We now summarise the key findings about these aspects below:

- **Organisational adoption decisions of B2E e-business systems:** In general, factor-based studies were undertaken to address these issues. In their studies, Sugianto et al. (2005) and Rahim (2007) identified several critical success factors that influence an organisation's decision to introduce a B2E system. These factors include perceived organisational need, cost, management support, IT expertise of organisations and portal complexity. In general, these factors were drawn from the diffusion of innovation and IT/IS implementation literature sources. Although the factor-based research is useful the findings of these authors are based on a single case study, they are quite difficult to generalise for organisations operating in other industry settings.

- **Business impact from the adoption of B2E e-business systems:** Business impact is generally expressed in terms of benefits for employees and organisational perspective. In general, benefits resulting from B2E e-business systems usage have traditionally been the key focus of practitioner oriented literature. Many short business articles have been published explaining how such systems can provide benefits to organisations. The commonly cited benefits in these articles include: cost savings, greater employee productivity,

and satisfied workforce among others (HP Report, 2001), BioSensors International (Sun Microsystems, 2001) and Bank Indonesia (Praweda, 2001).

Some of the claims made in the business articles have been substantiated to an extent by e-business scholars who analysed the perceptions of the senior management on the benefits from B2E systems adoption. For instance, Rahim (2006) and Rahim & Singh (2007) reported the benefits of traditional web-enabled B2E systems for both employees and their organisations. In their study, Scornvacca et al. (2006) examined the organisational impact of a mobile B2E application in a New Zealand restaurant. In another study, Rangone (2006) looked at the characteristics and benefits offered by mobile B2E applications in some Italian companies. It is interesting to note that the empirical evidence from these studies suggests a reduction in cost cutting but mixed findings were found with regard to benefits experienced by individuals using B2E systems.

Human Resource Literature

The adoption of various forms of employee related information systems (e.g. HRIS, e-ESS, online recruitment systems, e-HR systems) has been widely discussed in the HR literature. This stream attempts to understand the context necessary for the successful adoption of employee oriented systems and their potential impact on organisational effectiveness. Typical works representing this group include those of Kavanagh et al. (1990), Kinnei & Arthurs (1993), Jones & Arnett (1994), Pitman (1994), Lin (1997), Ball (2001) and Teo et al. (2001). This list is by no means exhaustive. Drawing on the findings of these studies, we identify top management support, employee training, support from the IT department, support for the HR staff, e-HR system characteristics, and total number of people employed by organisations to be important factors in the existing literature.

Gaps in the Literature

It is implicitly assumed in the above-mentioned streams of literature that adoption decisions made by senior management is likely to lead to wide spread diffusion of portal technologies among workforce. Hence, scholars have stopped short of measuring the B2E portal usage pattern of employees in organisations. As a result, factors affecting B2E portals use is not clearly known. In response to this gap, we have initiated this research to identify how various factors have influenced use of B2E portals by employees within a large Australian university. In doing so, we adopt an exploratory research approach, use the factors (identified above) as a template to guide our research, and analyse the importance of these factors from the viewpoint of senior management who are responsible for implementing B2E systems in the participating organisation.

RESEARCH APPROACH

Selection of Case Study Approach

As our research is exploratory in nature, and we wanted to discover insightful explanations regarding the influence of factors affecting B2E portals usage, we have adopted a single case study approach. Our choice is consistent with the views expressed by Zikmund (1997) and Yin (2003) and who argued that case study approach is suitable to explore a problem situation where little is known.

Choice of Case Organisation

The participating case organisation is a large Australian university; its selection is guided by the illustrative strategy principle (Veal, 2005) because of our intention to illustrate the effects of factors which could be observed in an organisation that

has made a serious attempt to introduce a B2E e-business system. Moreover, B2E portals are reported to have recently been initiated by some leading Australian universities (Tojib et al., 2005), and hence a case organisation from the tertiary industry is quite suitable as they tend to have distributed workforce in many campuses.

Case Study Participants

The development of the employee portal at the participating institution was monitored by Portal steering committee which includes senior members drawn from various functional areas. These members have in-depth knowledge of the strategic vision behind introducing the portal. As these members were intimately involved with how the portal project was conceived and eventually developed, we have conducted in-depth interviews with those members to identify their views about portal usage by employees in the university. A total of five members from the portal steering committee participated including CIO, three senior IT managers, and a senior university official who served as the chair of the portal steering committee. Based on our in-depth interviews with these members, a set of factors which they believed to have contributed to the low usage of employee portal were identified and later discussed in light of the existing literature.

Data Analysis

Each interview with portal steering committee members lasted for about an hour, was tape recorded, and subsequently transcribed. Interview transcripts were later sent to the interviewees for review and were revised based on their responses. The revised interview transcripts were analysed using a coding scheme which was prepared based on interview protocol. Using this coding scheme, each interview script was examined by two members of the research team. Any differences were resolved through mutual discussion.

Established methodological guidelines suggested by Pare (2004) and Yin (2003) were applied to generate reliable findings. Data collected through interviews were analysed using the pattern matching logic (Yin, 2003) which enabled us to compare the pattern of outcomes of portal usage factors reported in the existing literature with the pattern of outcomes deduced from the case data collected through verbal interviews and other documentary sources of the university.

EMPIRICAL FINDINGS

Our discussions with the interviewees and review of the university portal evaluation report indicate the presence of a low level of portal use by university employees. Employees are reported to access portals infrequently and a section of the employees even do not use it at all. The chair of the portal steering committee acknowledged this situation and remarked:

At the moment, our staff haven't got the buy-in to the portal. I think that probably less than 20% of staff use it as daily log on basis.

The CIO of the university also recognised the low use of the portal by the university employees and commented:

I must admit that our staff are not too big in the portal usage, they do not consider it to be very useful.

The view about low usage of the portal by various types of university staff is also highlighted in the usability report which describes low inclination prevailing among the university employees for using the portal. In-depth discussions with the key informants indicate the presence of two major factors which they believe to have contributed to the limited use of the portal by employees. These include: *low portal value perceived by employees*

and *declined management support for the portal project*. Each factor is explained below.

Low portal value perceived by employees: Rich insights were obtained from the key informants about why they think university employees may have perceived the portal to have low value for their work. In particular, deficiencies in three areas of the portal were identified: absence of killer applications, lack of relevant information, and multiple sources for employees to access relevant information.

The portal does not contain enough attractive applications for encouraging staff to use it more frequently. At present, the portal contains only four major applications (i.e. e-mail, library access, HR applications, and an online application to support flexible learning and teaching of units) for which employees use the portal. Apart from these, no major applications addressing employee benefits (e.g. superannuation, online training courses, online purchase from university utility and book shops) were included to attract greater usage of the portal by employees. The influence of the lack of killer applications into the portal on employees' low usage is explained by a senior It manager as follows:

Only about 20% of staff use portals. So the pick-up among our staff is much lower, and large part of that because the killer functions (e.g. HR) that we would like to have there are not there.

Furthermore, the portal does not contain adequate relevant information for three major categories of university staff (i.e. research staff, administrative staff and academics). For example, the research staff of the university need to know who else is involved in the research activities they are involved with and what latest research findings are available and where they are available. The portal provides little assistance to address these concerns which are of significance to research staff. According to the chair of the portal steering committee:

Our research staff has got a huge area of need of finding out what other people are doing for research. But inadequate research contents were included in the portal for them.

The deficiency of the portal to provide support for the research staff is also acknowledged by another senior IT manager who commented:

We did very little for the research portfolio at the moment and that's something is seen as a big failing of the portal.

For teaching staff, although the portal provides them with an access to online student learning system to organise the contents of the units they teach, however it does not provide online resources (e.g. electronic databases) required to facilitate their teaching needs. In other words, enough relevant contents were not made available within the portal to make it more appealing to teaching staff. This limitation is recognised by the director of the IT applications services who made the following remarks:

Relevant contents are not there for teaching staff. Our IT staff need to make the content available which takes time....At the moment, the contents are not very interesting to them.

Another observation is that a large portion of information relevant to university employees that can be accessed through the portal is also available in the websites of their respective faculties or administrative units. For example, a large pool of information needed by the library staff is available in the library website and hence there is no motivation for the library staff to find that information through the portal. The multiple sources of content availability is thus a barrier for the portal to attract high portal usage. According to the chair of the portal steering committee:

Many staff say that they have no motivations to use the portal because all the necessary information can be found in their faculty intranet-based web-pages. Why would they use a portal when they have got a perfectly good faculty website that contains necessary information?

This concern is shared by a senior IT manager who commented:

I must admit that our staff do not consider portal as very useful. The contents are not very interesting to them and our problem is we have got multiple intranets but not a single one which would converge everything.

These views are also highlighted in the usability report which explains that general staff in particular prefer to use the university website to find out information related to their work rather than rely on the portal to locate that information. This is because they are more familiar with their departmental web sites and hence consider it to be the quickest way to identify relevant information. Therefore, the presence of multiple intranet systems within the university means that there are usually multiple ways to find information and services which in turn discourage employees to use the portal.

Declined management support for the portal project: According to the steering committee members, management support was initially quite high for the introduction of the portal but gradually diminished as a change in senior management took place. Two members of the university's senior management team who were involved at the portal initiation stage, were strong supporters for implementing the portal. However, they had left the university while the portal was in the implementation stage. The attitude of the new senior management team members towards the portal was not as aggressive as it was at the outset of the portal project. Consequently, even though the portal project began with considerable momentum and strategic vision to support the flexible learning and teaching environment of the university; that enthusiasm soon waned and the focus had shifted to matters relating to operations and maintenance of the portal. This sentiment is expressed by the CIO as follows:

Main driving force for this portal project came from the office of the Deputy Vice Chancellor which provided the portal project with academic credibility. They could see the academic value of what we were doing and their involvement was critical to this project. However, the DVC and his associates have left this university and there has been a decrease in the enthusiasm of the high level management for the portal project.

Hence, adequate funding to include attractive contents and services in the portal could not be secured from the senior management. The budget allocated for the portal is currently being consumed by maintenance work, leaving very little for developing new features that would enhance the value of the portal to employees. This sentiment is expressed by the chair of the portal steering committee as follows:

"We need millions. We need funding to replace the in-house built portal. We probably need to buy commercial package or at least step-up the resources for the portal to grow. So, this is another stick in the mud, we are waiting for this to happen."

DISCUSSION

There is a general consensus among the portal committee members about the limited use of the portal by university staff. It is clear from this research that value of the system plays an important role in wining users. The case study evidence indicates that the limited perceived usefulness of the portal can be satisfactorily explained by:

the lack of adequate killer applications, absence of relevant information in the portal, and the continued availability of employee task related information from non-portal sources. This finding is consistent with the views expressed in the IS/IT implementation literature. According to Davis (1989) and Adams et al. (1992), perceived system usefulness is a dominant determinant of technology acceptance by individuals. Thus, for the B2E portal context, we argue that the lack of necessary core services and the absence of relevant information have created a negative perception among employees about the merits of the portal; this in turn has led to the low use of the portal. In addition, the availability of useful information for employees from multiple sources further reduced the value contribution of portals. This particular aspect has not been highlighted in the existing literature and represents a genuine contribution of our study as it has implications for university-wide policy formulation with regard to control and storage of information.

We have also found that management support (to make the portal truly useful) which was initially quite high for the portal project had later declined during the course of the project as a result of the change in senior level management team. The new management withdrew the patronage needed to include relevant contents and applications into the portal. Consequently, adequate funding which was initially committed for the portal project was not eventually assigned to the project. The shift in the level of financial support given to the portal project due to a change of management patronage is an interesting observation which is not always explicitly reported in the existing literature. We however acknowledge that many scholars such as Ewusi-Mensah (2003), Karimi et al. (2001) and Sauer (1993) have identified inadequate allocation of funding by senior management to be a critical factor that slows the uptake of innovative IT applications in organisational settings as those applications lack attractive functionalities.

We further argue that inadequate management support for the portal initiative has enabled employees to access relevant information from non-portal sources (i.e. web sites of individual functional units). This has been possible due to the lack of management recognition of the need for a single web strategy for the entire university within which the portal development should be conducted. At present, the university does not have a clearly documented strategy for the portal. According to the chair of the portal steering committee:

We need a clear strategy about how portal and many fragmented faculty initiated intranets can interact. We need a strategy in place in support of which we should put information into the portal so that the employees use that.

According to the key informants, even though the initial motivation of the portal was to support the flexible learning and teaching program, the actual development of the portal was hardly directed by this strategic goal. Without a clear direction, each individual faculty and administrative units thus have developed their own internal intranet websites incorporating contents which they believed to be relevant for their own staff. The absence of a clear web strategy has created an environment in which portals are often considered by employees to be redundant, and hence employees use their own faculty or administrative units' websites for related contents and services bypassing the portal. This finding too is consistent with the broad observations made in the IS/IT adoption literature in which scholars (e.g. Nidumolou, 1995; King and Teo, 2000; Salmela and Turunen, 2003) argue that senior management should take responsibility for ensuring IT applications acceptance (thus success) by setting a clear vision, communicating that vision with employees and participating in the organisational IT strategy process. In this particular university, we have observed evidence suggesting the lack

of top management's intention to engage in portal strategy process and their lack of support and commitment to roll out fully functional portal for employees by authorising necessary funding for training and relevant content access.

CONCLUSION

Unlike other popular types of e-business initiatives, B2E represents an under-researched (but important) initiative in which many organisations worldwide have made considerable investment. As such, despite its potential impact on organisations and their workforces, inadequate attention has been paid by e-business scholars to fully understand how the usage of B2E e-business systems is affected in organisational settings. Contrary to the scholarly literature, contemporary e-business trade literature has discussed the merits of commercially available B2E e-business products which promotes the view that employees would rush to using various types of B2E e-business solutions when they are introduced in organisations. We disagree with this view by critically analysing the experience of a large Australian university that has introduced an employee portal in recent years. We also offer rich explanations into how the employee portal usage in that particular university has been affected by a set of organisational factors and discuss those factors in light of the existing literature.

We report that despite maintaining a reasonable size IT department which developed an in-house portal solution for the use of the participating university, the uptake of the portal by various categories of employees within that particular university is less than satisfactory. We then identify the factors which the portal steering committee members think have contributed to the limited usage of the portal. In doing so, we provided rich insights into the factors that have slowed down acceptance and subsequent use of the portal by employees. We observe that these key factors are involved that negatively influenced the usage of the employee portal: perceived low value of the portal by employees, change in management support for the portal, and multiple sources of information availability for employees. These findings (although are not entirely new in the IT implementation literature), their relevance to the B2E portal context represents our major contribution to knowledge as an evaluation of the factors influencing portal usage is not readily available. However, the discovery of maintaining multiple sources of information and lack of developing an organisation wide policy for employee task related information storage and retrieval (which also contributes to the literature) represents a genuine contribution pf this study. We thus claim that our study will alert the e-business and IT managers of those organisations which are seriously contemplating the introduction of employee portals. Also, a discussion on the B2E portal presented in this chapter makes a contribution to a niche area of e-business theory.

There are several directions in which our study can be further improved. We do not claim generalisability of our findings as they are rooted in a single case study. Further effort needed to replicate this research across various private sectors. Likewise, we also argue that future studies should collect views from employees about the factors affecting their usage of portal and compare their views with those identified from the management.

REFERENCES

Adams, D. A., Nelson, R. R., & Todd, P. A. (1992). Perceived usefulness, ease of use, and usage of information technology: a replication. *MIS Quarterly*, 227–247. doi:10.2307/249577

Ball, K. S. (2001). The use of human resource information systems: a survey. *Personnel Review, 30*(6), 677–693. doi:10.1108/EUM0000000005979

Banks, J. (2004). Integrating people and content with business processes. In *2nd annual conference on Corporate Portal World Australia*, Sydney, Australia.

Brooks, M. (2001) Communications - General Productivity Gains with Employee Portals. *Communication & Benefits Management,* (Spring), 35-39.

Davis, F. D. (1989). Perceived usefulness, perceived ease of use, and user acceptance of information technology. *MIS Quarterly*, 319–340. doi:10.2307/249008

Ewusi-Mensah, K. (2003). *Software development failures.* Cambridge, MA: MIT Press.

Hansen, M., & Deimler, M. (2001). Cutting costs while improving morale with B2E management. *MIT Sloan Management Review, 43*(1), 96–100.

Jones, M. C., & Arnett, K. P. (1994). Linkages between the CEO and the IS environment: An empirical assessment. *Information Resources Management Journal, 7*(1), 20–33.

Karimi, J., Somers, T., & Gupta, Y. (2001). Impact of IT management practices on customer service. *Journal of Management Information Systems, 17*(4), 125–158.

Kavanagh, M. J., Gueutal, H. G., & Tannenbaum, S. (1990). *Human resource information systems: development and application.* Boston: PWS-Kent Publishing Co.

Killen & Associates Report. (2001). *Business-to-employees Communication: The competitive edge for tomorrow's global enterprises.* Killen & Associates, USA.

King, W., & Teo, T. (2000). Assessing the impact of proactive versus reactive modes of strategic information systems planning. *Omega, 28,* 667–679. doi:10.1016/S0305-0483(99)00079-1

Kinnei, N., & Arthurs, A. (1993). Will personnel people ever learn to love the computer? *Personnel Management, 25*(6), 46–51.

Lin, C. Y. Y. (1997). Human resource information systems: Implementation in Taiwan. *Human Resource Management, 5*(1), 57–72.

Pare, G. (2004). Investigating Information Systems with Positivist Case Study Research. *Communications of the AIS, 13*, 233–264.

Pitman, B. (1994). Critical success factors to organizational change . *Journal of Systems Management, 45*(9), 40.

Rahim, M. M. (2006). Understanding adoption and impact of b2e e-business systems: lessons learned from the experience of an Australian university. In *Proceedings of the sixth Collaborative Electronic Commerce Research (CollECTeR)*, Adelaide, Australia.

Rahim, M. M. (2007). Factors Affecting Adoption of B2E E-Business Systems: A Case of the Australian Higher Education Industry. In *Proceedings of the Pacific Asia Conference on Information Systems*, July 4-6, New Zealand.

Rahim, M. M., & Singh, M. (2007). Understanding benefits and impediments of B2E e-business systems adoption: Experiences of two large Australian universities. *Journal of Internet Commerce, 6*(2), 3–17. doi:10.1300/J179v06n02_02

Rangone, A. (2006). B2E mobile internet: An exploratory study of Italian companies. *Business Process Management Journal, 2*(3), 330–333. doi:10.1108/14637150610667999

Salmela, H., & Turunen, P. (2003). Competitive implications of information technology in the public sector. *International Journal of Public Sector Management, 16*(1), 8–26. doi:10.1108/09513550310456391

Sauer, C. (1993). *Why information systems fail: A case study approach.* Henley-on-Thames, UK: Alfred Waller.

Scornavacca, E., Prashad, M., & Lehmann, H. (2006). Exploring the organisational impact and perceived benefits of wireless personal digital assistants in restaurants. *International Journal of Mobile Communications, 4*(5), 558–567.

Sugianto, L., Rahim, M. M., & Alahakoon, D. (2005). B2E Portal Adoption: A conceptual model. In *Proceedings of the International Conference on Information and Automation* (ICIA2005), December 15-18, Colombo, Sri Lanka.

Teo, T. S. H., Lim, G. S., & Fedric, A. A. (2007). The adoption and diffusion of human resources information systems in Singapore. *Asia Pacific Journal of Human Resources, 45*(91), 44–62. doi:10.1177/1038411107075402

Teo, T. S. H., Soon, L. G., & Fedric, S. A. (2001). Adoption and impact of human resource information systems. *Research and Practice in Human Resource Management, 9*(1), 101–117.

Tojib, D. R., Sugianto, L. F., & Rahim, M. M. (2005). A New Framework for B2E Portal Development. In *IEEE International Conference on e-Technology, e-Commerce and e-Service*, Hong Kong.

Turban, E., King, D., Lee, J., & Viehland, D. (2008). *Electronic Commerce: A Managerial Perspective.* Upper Saddle River, NJ: Prentice Hall.

Veal, A. J. (2005). *Business Research Methods.* New South Wales, Australia: Pearson Education Australia.

Yin, R. K. (2003). *Case Study Research: Design and Methods* (3rd Ed.). Thousand Oaks, CA: Sage Publications, Inc.

Zikmund, W. G. (1997). *Business Research Methods* (5th Ed.). Orlando, FL: Dryden Press.

KEY TERMS AND DEFINITIONS

Business-to-Employee (B2E): It represents an employee centric e-business initiative. Typical examples include various types of innovative web-based B2E products including employee portals, e-HR systems and ESS.

Portal: It is defined as a web site or service that offers a broad array of resources and services (e.g. e-mails, search engines, online shopping malls) to individuals. The first web portals were online services, such as AOL, that provided access to the Web.

Usage Factors: They represent the conditions that influence the use of an IT application. These conditions can be related to technology (e.g. ease of use, complexity) and organisation (e.g. top management support).

Chapter 58
Understanding the Use of Business–to–Employee (B2E) Portals in an Australian University through the Employee Lens:
A Quantitative Approach

Md Mahbubur Rahim
Monash University, Australia

Mohammad Quaddus
Curtin University, Australia

Mohini Singh
RMIT University, Australia

INTRODUCTION

The focus of the existing body of e-business literature is primarily directed at Business-to-Consumers (B2C) and Business-to-Business (B2B) forms of e-business. In contrast, Business-to-Employee (B2E) is relatively less highlighted in the scholarly literature. Despite the lack of attention given to B2E systems, it represents an emerging area which has the potential to have a major impact on organisations. In general, B2E systems use intra-business networks allowing organisations to provide useful services, information, or products to their disperse employees (Turban et al., 2008). By providing easy access to

relevant information, services, and products, B2E systems help in creating satisfied workforce that is expected to be more loyal to organisations (Dube, 2005). These systems also help organisations in reducing their administrative costs by streamlining employee related process (Singh, 2005) and eliminating expenses related to paperwork, postage, printing and travel (Killen Associates Report, 2001). Adoption of B2E e-business systems can even assist organisations in outperforming competitors by connecting their employees together (Hansen and Deimler, 2001).

Recognising the above mentioned benefits, an increase in the demand for various types of B2E e-business solutions is noted by several industry reports (Killen Associates Report, 2006; Merrill Lynch

DOI: 10.4018/978-1-61520-611-7.ch058

Capital Markets cited in Brooks, 2004; and Banks, 2004). Regrettably, despite a growing demand for implementing B2E solutions, their usage in organisational settings has not been critically analysed and reported in the current scholarly literature. We argue that evaluation of the use of B2E solutions by employees represents a key research concern because the benefits arising from the introduction of such solutions are unlikely to be realised when they are not satisfactorily diffused among employee community. Therefore, managers need to be aware of the factors that may potentially affect the use of B2E e-business systems in their organisations. Against this background, we report the experience of a large Australian university in introducing an employee portal (a popular form of B2E e-business system) by analysing the perceptions of a segment of university staff about the influences of popularly discussed factors on their portal usage behaviour. Our findings provide interesting interpretations of the influence of several factors on the low usage of portal by employees. More specifically, we find that portal usefulness is a complex construct that fundamentally consists of two dominant dimensions (i.e. perceived collaboration usefulness and perceived information communication usefulness) – both of which are in turn influenced by management support. The discovery of these dimensions represents a major contribution of our work.

Our paper is organised as follows. First, we review various streams of literature related to B2E and similar other systems. Next, building on literature review and our prior research in this area, we identify a range of factors that may potentially affect use of B2E systems by employees. Then, our research approach is described. Next, background of the participating university is described. Then, the survey findings are presented and discussed in light of the existing e-business and IS/IT implementation literature. Finally, our contributions are highlighted and future directions of our research are indicated.

BACKGROUND LITERATURE: AN ANALYSIS

As the literature on B2E e-business systems is limited, we have consulted several related streams of literature to identify how various factors may influence the use of employee-oriented IT systems in organisational settings. These include: e-business literature, human resources (HR) literature, sales force automation (SSA) literature, diffusion of innovation and IS/IT implementation literature. In the following sub-sections, we provide a brief but insightful review of the key findings from each stream from the perspective of employees using some forms of B2E systems.

E-Business Literature

Existing e-Business literature cites the works of several scholars who have studied such aspects as usability and design challenges associated with various types of B2C interactive portals (e.g. Kiebling and Kostler, 2002; Gounaris and Dimitriadis, 2003; Holsapple and Sasidharan, 2005) tourist portals, citizen portals) which have some degree of similarity with employee portals. We acknowledge this similarity but argue that distinct differences exist between B2C portals and employee portals in such areas as type of users (external customers vs employees), degree of access given to organisational controls via portals (limited for customers vs high for internal employees), and type of services and information offered (e.g. superannuation is not relevant for customers but of importance to employees). Therefore, as the motivations and purposes of employee portals are different than B2C interactive portals (although many of the underlying technical issues are similar), we can expect that the usage behaviour of portals by employees is different from that of the users of B2C portals. Consequently, we have restricted our literature review attention to the B2E systems only.

A review of the B2E systems related studies reported identifies three specific research aspects that have received interest from scholars: *organisational adoption decisions of B2E systems, benefits arising from the adoption of B2E systems, and employee satisfaction with B2E systems.* The first two aspects are usually examined from management perspective. Typical works representing the first two aspects include those of Scornvacca et al. (2006), Rahim (2007), and Rahim and Singh (2007). The third aspect of this stream has adopted the viewpoint of individual employees about the success B2E systems. Several authors have measured success in terms of satisfaction and investigated employee satisfaction with various forms of B2E systems in terms of a model involving several factors. For example, Huang et al. (2004) analysed satisfaction of employees with a B2E benefit system at a Taiwanese company and found that such factors as convenience, interface, accuracy, price and security affected employee satisfaction with that application. In another study, Sugianto & Tojib (2006) proposed a conceptual model to measure user satisfaction with employee portal and identified nine factors that could affect employee satisfaction with portals. In a subsequent study, Tojib and Sugianto (2007) empirically tested that model in a large Australian university setting and found that five factors including usefulness, ease of use, portal design, confidentiality and convenience affected user satisfaction with employee portals.

Human Resource Literature

The adoption of various forms of employee related information systems (e.g. HRIS, e-ESS, online recruitment systems, e-HR systems) has been discussed in the HR literature. A group of HR scholars (e.g. Teo et al., 2007; Stone et al., 2007) have focused on the acceptance and usage of HR information systems from the perspective of individual employees. They found individual characteristics of employees and their attitudes to be the determinants of employees' acceptance and subsequent usage of HR related information systems.

Sales Automation Literature

A large portion of this stream addresses the factors that influence individual sales employee's decisions to use automated systems. Typical works include those of Parthasarathy and Sohi (1997), Speier and Venkatesh (2002) and Schillewaert et al. (2005) among others. In general, these studies acknowledge that perceived usefulness is a major factor to affect actual use of automation systems by sales employees. In addition, the importance of demographic profile of sales force on their acceptance and even use of sales automation technologies is also noted.

IS/IT Implementation Literature

Davis (1989) and Davis et al. (1989) proposed Technology Adoption Model (TAM) to address why users accept or reject information technologies. The model suggests that perceived ease of use and perceived usefulness are the two most important factors in explaining use of information technologies by individuals. More recently, a new version of TAM known as TAM2 is proposed by Venkatesh and Davis (2000) which includes subjective norms and was tested with longitudinal research designs. Many authors have applied TAM model in explaining use of various types of business IT applications. However, analysis of empirical research with TAM is not totally conclusive.

Diffusion of Innovation Literature

The adoption and diffusion of innovation literature examines how an innovation spreads through the market from the time of introduction. However, if an innovation meets resistance from consumers, the adoption process can be expected to begin only after this resistance has been overcome. If the resistance cannot be broken down, adoption slows down and the innovation is likely to fail. According to Rogers (2003), rejection to an innovation often takes place even after an innovation has been adopted by individuals. Two important reasons were identified for innovation rejection: a) an innovation is rejected as a result of dissatisfaction with its performance, and b) when an innovation which was initially found to be attractive was eventually observed to be incompatible with the beliefs of individuals. An early study by Rogers (2003) found acceptance and resistance to usage to innovation are related to an individual's innovativeness.

Gaps in the Existing Literature

These five streams of literature recognise that a number of factors influence an individual employee's decision to accept and use an IT application. They include demographic characteristics of employees, employee readiness, technological sophistication of employees, system usefulness as perceived by employees, perceived ease of use, attitudes of employees towards the IT system among others. We note that it is implicitly assumed in the e-business literature that adoption decisions made by senior management is likely to lead to wide spread diffusion of B2E technologies among workforce. Hence, scholars have stopped short of calling a measurement of B2E systems' usage pattern of employees in organisations. We acknowledge that the factors identified from various B2E related streams of literature are useful for understanding the usage of these systems by employees. However, as research into this area is virtually non-existent, it is necessary to dedicate further research effort examining the use of B2E portals. In keeping with this call, this research was undertaken to identify how various factors have influenced use of B2E portals by employees within a large Australian university. In doing so, we have adopted an exploratory research approach and

use the factors (identified above) and in our prior studies as a template to guide our research.

RESEARCH APPROACH

Choice of Case Organisation

The participating case organisation is a large Australian university; its selection is guided by the illustrative strategy principle (Veal, 2005) because of our intention to illustrate the effects of factors which could be observed in an organisation that has made a serious attempt to introduce a B2E system. Moreover, B2E portals are reported to have recently been initiated by some leading Australian universities (Tojib et al., 2005), and hence an organisation from the tertiary industry is quite suitable as they tend to have distributed workforce in many campuses.

Sample Size

A survey questionnaire was developed which included a set of items that operationalise several factors which were short-listed based on our prior qualitative research (Rahim et al., 2009) and literature review. This questionnaire was distributed among 500 staff of the participating university. A total of 161 responses were received yielding a response rate of 32.2%.

Scale Development

Drawing on our experience of a prior qualitative research (Rahim et al., 2009) in which several key informants from the portal steering committee were involved, a total of three factors (e.g. perceived portal usefulness, perceived management support, and perceived training) were included in a survey questionnaire (along with four other factors short listed from the literature review). The survey questionnaire included the items for measuring 7 factors. In this article, we however

Table 1. Sources of the items for measuring factors

Factors	No. of Items	Sources
Perceived portal usefulness	9	Yang et al. (2005) and developed by authors
Perceived management support	3	Developed by the authors
Perceived training	2	Developed by the authors
Use of portal	1	Hartwick and Barki (1994)

restrict our focus to only those 3 factors which were reported to be highly important by the key informants reported in our previous work (Rahim et al., 2009). A summary of how these three factors were measured is shown in Table 1 and a theoretical justification in support of the relationship between these factors and the employee use of B2E portals is given in Appendix-A. Each item was measured on a scale of 1 to 5, where 1 means strongly disagree, 2 means disagree, 3 means neutral, 4 means agree and 5 means strongly agree. The dependent variable (use of B2E portal) was measured on a five-point interval scale where 1 means never use, 2 means at least once in 3 months, 3 means at least once a month, 4 means at least once a fortnight, and 5 means at least once a week. The survey instrument was reviewed by three domain experts and several changes were incorporated.

To address validity of the instrument containing 14 items measuring 3 factors (listed in Table 1), an exploratory factor analysis was carried out. The results (shown in Appendix-B) are quite interesting

as a 4 factor solution was produced. A close look at the factor analysis results indicate that out of 14 items, 2 were removed as they loaded heavily on more than 2 factors (Hair et al., 2006). However, an interesting observation is that perceived portal usefulness can be considered to be of two types: *perceived collaboration usefulness* and *perceived information communication usefulness*.

Reliability of the items which were eventually retained after factor analysis were evaluated using Cronbach alpha (Nunnaly, 1978) and are found to be quite satisfactory as they had values over .70 and are shown in Table 2.

EMPIRICAL FINDINGS

The survey results report a low use of the employee portal as the mean use is found to be 3.29 (on a scale of 1 to 5). This means that employees do not regularly use the portal. In fact, they use portals at least once a fortnight. The mean use of the portal is found to vary depending on gender, role of

Table 2. Reliability results of the scales used for the factors

Factors	Items included	Reliability (Cronbach alpha)
Perceived collaboration usefulness	5 items PU1, PU3,PU4, PU7,PU9	.769
Perceived information communication usefulness	3 items PU2, PU5, PU6	.70
Perceived training	2 items PT1, PT2	.743
Perceived management support	2 items MS2, MS3	.816

Table 3. Mean use of employee portals by employees

Demographic Characteristics	Mean use	t-value	df	p-value
Gender Male Female	3.39 3.19	1.062	159	.290
Job Role Managerial Non-managerial	3.16 3.30	-.480	159	.632
Job Type Academic/research Administration	3.44 3.13	1.59	159	.112

employees (i.e. managerial and non-managerial), and type of employee (i.e. academic/research, administration). However, the differences are not statistically significant (as shown in Table 3). Moreover, the use of portal is not high across any of these demographic categories of employees as the mean portal use is far less than 4.0. We therefore suggest the presence of an overall low trend of portal use among university employees.

An interesting observation is that 9% of surveyed employees do not use the portal at all, and that another 19% employees use the portal once in a 3-month. In other words, 28% of employees have no or little interactions with the portal. In contrast, only 20% employees use the portal on a regular basis (at least once a week). Thus, these

findings collectively are indicative of the limited usage of the portal by university employees.

The mean values of the three independent factors (shown in Table 2) are shown in Table 4. The only benefits that employees experienced are their ability to access information and use that information in support of communication with others. In contrast, the portal is considered to have limited value from the perspective of exploring collaboration, acquiring work related items (via online ordering) and locating role specific information.

Table 4 further suggests that employees perceived a disappointingly low level of support by their senior management in terms of organising employee training (mean: 2.02) and workshops

Table 4. Mean rating of employee perceptions about portal

Item descriptionPerceived Portal Usefulness: Information Search & Communication Value	Mean Rating
PU1: The portal helps me efficiently carry out work related communication	3.53
PU2: The portal provides me with ready access to information sources	3.37
PU3: The portal reduces the time spent on HR related activities	3.51
PU4: The portal provides me with accurate information to fulfil my needs	3.71
PU5:The portal provides single point of access to work related information	3.16
Perceived Portal Usefulness: Collaboration Value	
PU6: The portal offers collaboration facility with other employees	2.75
PU7: The portal helps me quickly acquire work related items (e.g. online ordering)	2.34
PU8: The portal provides role-specific (e.g. managerial, academic, administrative) information	3.04
Perceived Portal Training	
PT1: I was provided with the necessary training to use the portal	2.02
PT2: I attended workshops to learn how to use the portal	1.80
Management Support	
MS1: My management supports regular updating of the portal features	2.88
MS2: My management supports regular updating of relevant information in the portal	3.07

Table 5. Results of regression analysis for portal usage

	Unstandardized Coefficients		Standardized Coefficients	t	Sig.
	B	Std. Error	Beta	B	Std. Error
(Constant)	.503	.427		1.178	.241
CollUsflns	.428	.110	.329	3.899	.000
InfoUsflns	.212	.104	.171	2.041	.043
Training	.019	.097	.016	.197	.844
MgmtSup	.043	.088	.042	.494	.622
Adjusted R Square = 16.4%, F = 7.882, p = .000					

(mean: 1.80) to help employees learn more about the potential merits of the portal. On the matter of management support for portal, the survey findings clearly indicate that employees were unhappy with the support they believed their management has offered to make the portal useful for employees. Employee responses indicate that university management was not seen to have supported regular updating of the relevant information in the portal (mean: 2.88) and inclusion of useful services through the portal (mean: 3.07).

We have conducted regression analysis (as shown in Table 5) and found that portal usage is significantly explained by both dimensions of portal usefulness. In contrast, perceived training support and management support were not found to have an effect on employees' portal usage. However, another two rounds of regression analysis was then conducted to find how perceived training and management support affect both dimensions of portal usefulness. The results (Tables 6 and 7)

indicate that management support is strongly related to both dimensions of regression analysis.

DISCUSSION

The limited usage of portal among university employees is surprising given the fact that portal is in use for about 5 years. The perceptions of employees about low portal value perceived by employees shed some light to understand the low usage of portals. Regression analysis confirms that both dimensions of portal usefulness are significantly related to the employees' portal usage. This observation is supportive of our previously reported qualitative investigation (Rahim et al., 2009) conducted at the same university from the perspective of the portal steering committee as well as is consistent with the views expressed in the IS/IT implementation literature. According to Davis (1989) and Adams et al. (1992), perceived

Table 6. Results of regression analysis for portal usefulness (information & communication value)

	Unstandardized Coefficients		Standardized Coefficients	t	Sig.
	B	Std. Error	Beta	B	Std. Error
(Constant)	2.814	.207		13.575	.000
training	-.062	.069	-.069	-.904	.368
management	.256	.059	.330	4.319	.000
Adjusted R Square = 9%, F = 9.34, p = .000					

Table 7. Results of regression analysis for portal usefulness (collaboration)

	Unstandardized Coefficients		Standardized Coefficients	t	Sig.
	B	Std. Error	Beta	B	Std. Error
(Constant)	1.806	.227		7.946	.000
training	.138	.075	.141	1.837	.068
management	.215	.065	.254	3.316	.001
Adjusted R Square = 9.6%, F = 8.43, p = .000					

system usefulness is a dominant determinant of technology acceptance by individuals. Likewise, many scholars who examined sales force automation systems adoption (e.g. Parthasarathy and Sohi; 1997; Speier and Venkatesh, 2002) have reported that employees were reluctant to use IT applications when those applications were not perceived useful by them in performing their tasks. Thus, for the B2E portal context, we argue that the lack of necessary core services for collaboration and the inability of portal to offer role specific information together have created a negative perception among employees about the usefulness of the portal; this in turn has led to the low use of the portal.

Although management support did not contribute directly to portal usage but it is significantly related to both dimensions of portal usefulness. This suggests that employees felt that management support for the portal was low as the portal contents and features were not only inadequate but were also infrequently updated. In other words, the lack of management's intention to understand how employees would like to use the portal in support of their work is seen to be a major barrier to enhance functionalities of the portal. Our argument is consistent with those of Ewusi-Mensah (2003), Karimi et al. (2001) and Sauer (1993) who identified inadequate involvement of senior management as a critical factor that slows the uptake of innovative IT applications in organisational settings.

According to the regression analysis, the training needs of employees were not adequately addressed by management (as the means score shown in Table 4 are very low), it had no significant effect on both their portal use and the perceived functionalities included in the portal. This is possibly because the portal is easy to use and understand and employees who have high computer literacy did not require much training support. We thus conclude that even though perceived low portal usefulness appear to be the immediate determinant of employees' low portal use, it is the absence of full commitment and involvement of the senior management that contributed to the perceived limited usefulness. The degree to which portal usefulness is perceived was influenced by the understanding of management about how employees would like to use portal to facilitate their work. We thus call for the greater participation of management in support of portal usage. We suggest that senior management should take responsibility for ensuring IT applications acceptance (thus success) by setting a clear vision, communicating that vision with employees and participating in the organisational IT strategy process. Our position is in agreement with the views of Yehon et al. (2000) and Kerans (2007) who strongly recommend top management support and participation in creating a positive internal environment to facilitate acceptance of IT projects in organisational settings.

CONCLUSION

Unlike other popular types of e-business initiatives, B2E represents an under-researched (but important) initiative in which many organisations worldwide have made considerable investment. As such, despite its potential impact on organisations and their workforces, inadequate attention has been paid by e-business scholars to fully understand how the usage of B2E e-business systems is affected in organisational settings. Contrary to the scholarly literature, contemporary e-business trade literature has discussed the merits of commercially available B2E e-business products. However, it is inappropriate to assume that employees would rush to using various types of B2E solutions when they are introduced in organisations. We thus critically analyse the experience of a large Australian university in which the uptake of the portal by employees was found to be less than satisfactory. We also identify the factors which have contributed to the limited usage of the portal. In doing so, we provide rich insights into the role of these factors for slowing down use of the portal by employees. Although these factors have been reported in various streams of related literature, their application to B2E portal context has not been explicitly discussed. Thus, a major contribution of our study is to reinforce the explanatory ability of the factors to satisfactorily describe the problematic situation of the portal used within the participating university. In addition, we have contributed to literature by discovering two specific dimensions of portal usefulness (i.e. perceived collaboration usefulness and perceived information communication usefulness) and interpreting their relationships with management support. This particular observation has not been reported in the literature. To sum up, we believe that our study will alert the e-business and IT managers of those organisations which are seriously contemplating the introduction of employee portals.

Our study however has some limitations. We have not examined the influence of employees' personal traits (e.g. innovativeness, techno-phobic or self-willed) in explaining their low use of the portal. Further studies are recommended to address how these aspects may affect employees' use of the portal. In addition, we have not considered the notion of *'customer activity life cycle'* in helping identify key services to be offered via the employee portal and its possible influence on portal usage. Further studies are recommended to examine this interesting aspect. Finally, there is a need to replicate this study in other industry sector to determine whether there is any influence of industry context on the factors affecting the uptake of portals by employees.

REFERENCES

Adams, D. A., Nelson, R. R., & Todd, P. A. (1992). Perceived usefulness, ease of use, and usage of information technology: a replication. *MIS Quarterly*, 227–247. doi:10.2307/249577

Banks, J. (2004). Integrating people and content with business processes. In *2nd annual conference on Corporate Portal World Australia*, Sydney, Australia.

Brooks, M. (2001). Communications - general productivity gains with employee portals. *Communication & Benefits Management*, Spring, 35-39.

Davis, F. D. (1989). Perceived usefulness, perceived ease of use, and user acceptance of information technology. *MIS Quarterly*, 319–340. doi:10.2307/249008

Davis, F. D., Bagozzi, R. P., & Warshaw, P. (1989). User acceptance of computer technology: a comparison of two theoretical models. *Management Science*, 985–989.

Dube, L., Bourhis, A., & Jacob, R. (2005). The impact of structuring characteristics on the launching of virtual communities of practice. *Journal of Organizational Change Management, 18*(2), 145–166. doi:10.1108/09534810510589570

Ewusi-Mensah, K. (2003). *Software Development Failures*. Cambridge, MA: MIT Press.

Gounaris, S., & Dimitriadis, S. (2003). Assessing service quality on the web: evidence from business-to-consumer portals. *Journal of Services Marketing, 17*(5), 529–548. doi:10.1108/08876040310486302

Hansen, M., & Deimler, M. (2001). Cutting costs while improving morale with B2E management. *MIT Sloan Management Review, 43*(1), 96–100.

Hartwick, J., & Barki, H. (1994). Explaining the role of user participation in information system use. *Management Science*.

Hawking, P., Foster, S., & Stein, A. (2004). E-HR and employee self service: a case study of a Victorian public sector organisation. *Journal of Issues in Informing Science and Information Technology, 1*, 017-1026.

Holsapple, C. W., & Sasisharan, S. (2005). The dynamics of trust in B2C e-commerce: a research model and agenda. *ISeB, 3*, 377–403. doi:10.1007/s10257-005-0022-5

Huang, J. H., Jin, B. H., & Yang, C. (2004). Satisfaction with business-to-employee benefit systems and organizational citizenship behaviour - an examination of gender differences. *International Journal of Manpower, 25*(2), 195–210. doi:10.1108/01437720410535990

Karimi, J., Somers, T., & Gupta, Y. (2001). Impact of IT management practices on customer service. *Journal of Management Information Systems, 17*(4), 125–158.

Kavanagh, M. J., Gueutal, H. G., & Tannenbaum, S. (1990). *Human Resource Information Systems: Development and Application*. Boston: PWS-Kent Publishing Co.

Kearns, G. S. (2007). How the internal environment impacts information systems project success: An investigation of exploitative and explorative firms. *Journal of Computer Information Systems*, 63–73.

KieBling. W., & Kostler, G. (2002). Preference SQL: design, implementation, experiences. In *Proceedings of the 28ᵗʰ VLDB Conference*, Hong Kong.

Killen Associates Report. (2001). *Business-to-employees Communication: The competitive edge for tomorrow's global enterprises*. Killen & Associate, USA..

King, W., & Teo, T. (2000). Assessing the impact of proactive versus reactive modes of strategic information systems planning. *Omega, 28*, 667–679. doi:10.1016/S0305-0483(99)00079-1

Lin, C. Y. Y. (1997). Human resource information systems: Implementation in Taiwan . *Human Resource Management, 5*(1), 57–72.

Mahmood, M. A., & Mann, G. J. (1993). Measuring the organizational impact of information technology investment: an exploratory study. *Journal of Management Information Systems, 10*(1), 97–122.

Moore, G. C., & Benbasat, I. (1991). Development of an instrument to measure the perceptions of adopting an information technology innovation. *Information Systems Research, 2*(3), 192–222. doi:10.1287/isre.2.3.192

Nunnaly, J. C. (1978) *Psychometric Theory.* New York: McGraw-Hill.

Parthasarathy, M., & Sohi, R. F. S. (1997). Sales force automation and the adoption of technological innovations by sales force: Theory and implications. *Journal of Business and Industrial Marketing, 12*(3/4), 96–208. doi:10.1108/08858629710188036

Pitman, B. (1994). Critical success factors to organizational change. *Journal of Systems Management, 45*(9), 40.

Rahim, M. M. (2006). Understanding adoption and impact of b2e e-business systems: lessons learned from the experience of an Australian university. In *Proceedings of the sixth Collaborative Electronic Commerce Research (CollECTeR)*, Adelaide, Australia.

Rahim, M. M. (2007). Factors affecting adoption of B2E e-Business systems: A case of the Australian higher education industry. In *Proceedings of the Pacific Asia Conference on Information Systems*, July 4-6, New Zealand.

Rahim, M. M., & Singh, M. (2007). Understanding benefits and impediments of B2E e-business systems adoption: Experiences of two large Australian universities. *Journal of Internet Commerce, 6*(2), 3–17. doi:10.1300/J179v06n02_02

Ram, S. (1989). Successful innovation using strategies to reduce consumer resistance: An empirical test. *Journal of Product Innovation Management, 6*, 20–34. doi:10.1016/0737-6782(89)90011-8

Rangone, A. (2006). B2E mobile internet: An exploratory study of Italian companies. *Business Process Management Journal, 2*(3), 330–333. doi:10.1108/14637150610667999

Rogers, E. M. (2003). *Diffusion of Innovations*, New York: Free Press.

Sauer, C. (1993). *Why Information Systems Fail: A Case Study Approach*. Henley-on-Thames, UK: Alfred Waller.

Schillewaert, N. (2005). The adoption of information technology in the sales force. *Industrial Marketing Management, 34*, 323–336. doi:10.1016/j.indmarman.2004.09.013

Scornavacca, E., Prashad, M., & Lehmann, H. (2006). Exploring the organisational impact and perceived benefits of wireless personal digital assistants in restaurants. *International Journal of Mobile Communications, 4*(5), 558–567.

Singh, M. (2005). Business to employee (B2E) e-management. Sixth International Working for E-Business Conference, Melbourne, Australia.

Speier, C., & Venkatesh, V. (2002, July). The hidden minefields in the adoption of sales force automation technologies. *Journal of Marketing, 66*, 98–111. doi:10.1509/jmkg.66.3.98.18510

Stone, D. L., Stone-Romero, E. D. F., & Lukaszewski, K. (2006). Factors affecting the acceptance and effectiveness of electronic human resources systems. *Human Resource Management Review, 16*, 229–244. doi:10.1016/j.hrmr.2006.03.010

Sugianto, L., Rahim, M. M., & Alahakoon, D. (2005). B2E portal adoption: A conceptual model. In *Proceedings of the International Conference on Information and Automation* (ICIA2005), December 15-18, Colombo, Sri Lanka.

Sugianto, L., & Tojib, D. (2006). Modeling user satisfaction with an employee portal. *International Journal of Business and Information, 1*(2), 239–255.

Teo, T. S. H., Lim, G. S., & Fedric, A. A. (2007). The adoption and diffusion of human resources information systems in Singapore. *Asia Pacific Journal of Human Resources, 45*(91), 44–62. doi:10.1177/1038411107075402

Teo, T. S. H., Soon, L. G., & Fedric, S. A. (2001). Adoption and impact of human resource information systems. *Research and Practice in Human Resource Management, 9*(1), 101–117.

Tojib, D., & Sugianto, L. (2007). The development and empirical validation of the B2E portal user satisfaction (B2EPUS) scale. *Journal of Organizational and End User Computing, 19*(3), 1–18.

Tojib, D. R., Sugianto, L. F., & Rahim, M. M. (2005). A new framework for B2E Portal development. In *IEEE International Conference on e-Technology, e-Commerce and e-Service*, Hong Kong.

Turban, E., King, D., Lee, J., & Viehland, D. (2008). *Electronic Commerce: A Managerial Perspective*. Upper Saddle River, NJ: Prentice Hall.

Veal, A. J. (2005). *Business Research Methods*. NSW: Pearson Education Australia.

Venkatesh, V., & Davis, F. D. (2000). A theoretical extension of the technology adoption model: Four longitudinal field studies. *Management Science, 46*(2), 86–204. doi:10.1287/mnsc.46.2.186.11926

Yetton, P. A., Martin, R., Sharma, R., & Johnston, K. (2000). A model of information systems development project performance. *Information Systems Journal, 10*, 263–289. doi:10.1046/j.1365-2575.2000.00088.x

KEY TERMS AND DEFINITIONS

Business-to-Employee (B2E): It represents an employee centric e-business initiative. Typical examples include various types of innovative web-based B2E products including employee portals, e-HR systems and ESS.

Portal: It is defined as a web site or service that offers a broad array of resources and services (e.g. e-mails, search engines, online shopping malls) to individuals. The first web portals were online services, such as AOL, that provided access to the Web.

Usage Factors: They represent the conditions that influence the use of an IT application. These conditions can be related to technology (e.g. ease of use, complexity) and organisation (e.g. top management support).

APPENDIX-A: DEVELOPMENT OF RESEARCH HYPOTHESES

Perceived system usefulness: According to the dictionary meaning, a system may be termed useful if it is valuable or productive. This interpretation is consistent with the views expressed by Davis (1989) and other leading scholars who describe perceived usefulness as an individual's belief that performing a specific behaviour will lead to favourable outcome. The outcome may involve tangible benefits such as some form of economic gains or work performance improvement and intangible benefits like greater work satisfaction. In the context of the B2E portal, customised services and easy access to relevant information would create a positive perception of employees about the merits of portal. This perception of the portal's quality would lead to greater use of the portal. When a portal provides relevant information to the employees for them to perform better by accomplishing tasks effectively and efficiently, the portal would be perceived as a tool for gaining work related benefits. As a result, the following proposition is put forward:

H1: Perceived system usefulness (PSU) has a positive influence on employee portal usage

Perceived Training: Although not mentioned in core theories, training is often considered to be a great facilitator of the use of IT-enabled applications. According to Mahmood & Mann (1993), training positively affects use of IT applications because it helps improve users understanding on how to use the application to their advantage. Thus, for the B2E portal, when employees think that they were provided with adequate training to use the system without "breaking" it, they would be more confident about using it to their advantage. Thus, the following proposition is developed:

H2: Provision of employee training is positively related with the portal usage by employees

Management support for portal: Senior management should authorise addition of new sources of information (both internal and external) and services, and encourage improving features of portals to meet employees' needs. This creates a positive impression on employees with respect to the management's interest is supporting the portal. By creating an evolving portal, management can ensure that employees' information demands are best met. Employee's perception of degree of support provided by their senior management to the portal would thus help ensure better use of the portal.

H3: Perceived management support for portal project will positively affect portal usage of employees

Appendix-B: Results of Factor Analysis

Table 8.

Item Code	Item description	Component			
		1	2	3	4
PU1	The portal helps me efficiently carry out work related communication	.633			
PU2	The portal offers collaboration facility with other employees		.774		
PU3	The portal provides me with ready access to information sources which enables me to find job related information quickly	.751			
PU4	The portal reduces the time spent on HR related activities (i.e. via employee self-service)	.703			
PU5	The portal helps me quickly acquire work related items (e.g. office stationery)		.841		
PU6	The portal provides role-specific (e.g. managerial, academic, administrative) information		.690		
PU7	The portal provides me with accurate information to fulfil my needs	.751			
PU9	The portal provides single point of access to work related information	.718			
PT1	I was provided with the necessary training to use the portal				.856
PT2	I attended workshops to learn how to use the portal				.910
MS2	My organization regularly updates the features of the portal			.879	
MS3	My organization updates relevant information on the portal regularly			.974	
	Eigenvalues	3.56	1.94	1.35	1.21
	% variance	29.7	16.1	11.30	10.14
	KMO measure of sampling adequacy	.709			
	Bartlett's Test of Sphericity	Approx. Chi-Square = 589.34 Df = 66, Sig = .000			

Chapter 59

An Exploratory Study on the User Adoption of Central Cyber Government Office of the Hong Kong Government

Kevin K.W. Ho
The University of Guam, Guam

Calvin Chun Yu
The Hong Kong University of Science and Technology, Hong Kong

Michael C.L. Lai
Hong Kong Police Force, Hong Kong

ABSTRACT

This chapter investigates those factors affecting the user adoption of the Intranet Portal of the Hong Kong Government, a.k.a., Central Cyber Government Office (CCGO). The authors conducted a survey study in 2004 and they interviewed some of the users to collect their feedbacks on the user adoption of CCGO based on the premises of the Technology Acceptance Model (TAM). Based on the results of their survey and interviews, the authors noted that civil servants of Hong Kong demonstrated strong reluctance to adopt CCGO.

INTRODUCTION

"**E-Government**" is a mission-critical visionary issue faced by the public sector as it pushed the delivery of public services to a new quality standard through a new set of delivery means. However, many of the stakeholders found it hard to fully embrace this new mode of service delivery. Through the

provision of e-services, stakeholders of government services expect that e-services can improve the efficiency of government departments (Gore, 1993; Information Technology and Broadcasting Bureau (ITBB), 1998). Indeed, information systems (IS) researchers have investigated the impact of information technology (IT) in public sector since the late 1970s, when personal computers were launched (Kraemer, 1977; Danziger et al., 1978). For recent research studies, their main

DOI: 10.4018/978-1-61520-611-7.ch059

focus is on the impact of Internet on the public sector, especially on the impact on the interaction among government departments and members of the public, i.e. citizens and business firms (or Government-to-Citizen, G2C, and Government-to-Business, G2B) (Devadoss, et al., 2002; Golden, et al., 2003). However, not too many studies are focused on the impact of Internet technology on the interaction among users within government departments (or Government-to-Employee, G2E, and Government-to-Government, G2G). Hence, the aim of this study is to analyze this impact of Internet technology on the interaction between the Government and its internal users.

The focus of this chapter is to examine the user adoption of the Intranet portal of the Hong Kong Government. We choose Hong Kong Government as our subject of study because it has been ranked amongst the top few countries in the Asia-Pacific Region and the seventh in the worldwide "Overall Maturity in e-Government" (Accenture, 2004). This indicates that Hong Kong is one of the pioneers in developing **e-Government** projects in the region. Hence, the result obtained will be very useful reference for policymakers and various stakeholders especially in the Asia-Pacific Region. We hope that our results can help policymakers to realign their internal IT strategies and fine-tune their **e-Government** policies.

BACKGROUND

To improve the internal communication within the government, the Hong Kong Government has developed an Intranet portal, i.e. the Central Cyber Government Office (CCGO), to facilitate internal communication and information flow. The CCGO used the Government Communication Network (GCN) to disseminate internal information, which had around 50,000 users when we conducted our study in 2003/2004, i.e. around 1/3 of the civil service workforce, and is now developed into a system, which provides a wide range of e-services

and disseminates information within the government (HKG, 2009). With more knowledge on the user acceptance of the CCGO, researchers, government officers, and the management of private sectors can gain insights on how to develop a more user-focused Intranet portal for their users. Our research was developed based on the **Technology Acceptance Model (TAM)**, which is the most common model used for analyzing user adoption of IT projects (Davis, 1989; Davis et al., 1989). In particular, we would like to address the following three research questions:-

(1) Does **perceived usefulness** (PU) affect the user adoption of Government Intranet portal?
(2) Does **perceived ease of use** (PE) affect the user adoption of Government Intranet portal?
(3) Does **subjective norm** (SN) affect the user adoption rate of Government Intranet portal?

Literature Review on Technology Acceptance Model (TAM)

In this study, we use the **Technology Acceptance Model (TAM)** (Davis, 1989; Davis et al., 1989; Venkatesh et al., 2003) to investigate the user adoption attitude of civil servants towards Government-to-Employee (G2E) Intranet portal. TAM is an information system theory derived from the **Theory of Reasoned Action** (TRA). The standard TAM has independent two constructs, i.e. **Perceived Usefulness** (PU) and **Perceived Ease of Use** (PE), and one dependent construct, i.e. Adoption Intention (A). PU is "the degree to which a person believes that using a particular system would enhance his/her job performance" whereas PE is "the degree to which a person believes that using a particular system would be free of effort" (Davis, 1989). In previous years, numerous studies have employed the TAM to investigate the user adoption studies on various

Figure 1. Research model on the TAM study on CCGO

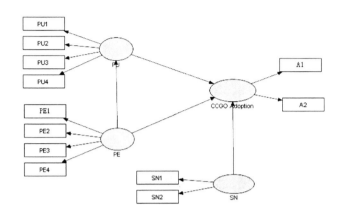

information systems (Adams et al., 1992; Davis, 1989; Davis, et al. 1989), such as ERP (Amoako-Gyampah & Salam, 2004), Internet banking (Tan & Teo, 2000), small business (Thong, 1999), etc. Based on the results of prior research studies on TAM, we develop our first set of hypotheses, which describe the relationships amongst these constructs for civil servants in using CCGO:

H1.1: When civil servants have a higher level of PU on CCGO, they will have a higher intention to adopt CCGO.

H1.2: When civil servants have a higher level of PE on CCGO, they will have a higher intention to adopt CCGO.

H1.3: When civil servants have a higher level of PE on CCGO, they will also have a higher level of PU on CCGO.

In our model, we also adapted the **Subjective Norm** (SN) from TRA and **Theory of Planned Behavior** (TPB) (Ajzen, 1991) as the third independent construct, which has positive impact on the adoption intention. SN is "the person's perception that most people who are important to him think he should or should not perform the behavior in question" (Fishbein & Ajzen, 1975). Thus, the second set of hypothesis is developed below:

H2: When civil servants have a higher level of SN on CCGO, they will have a higher intention to adopt CCGO.

Figure 1 summarizes our research model.

THE EMPIRICAL STUDY ON USER ADOPTION OF CCGO

Methodology

In this study, we collected the feedback of civil servants through a survey. It was conducted in several government departments, with an aim to investigate the adoption intention of CCGO. The survey last for 4 months from November 2003 to February 2004, and was conducted six months before the major upgrade of CCGO. The major system upgrade involved the launching of e-Leave (a leave application system) and departmental portals, and the extension of IT facilities from top management to the middle management, which increases the number of users from 1/10 of the workforce to around 1/3 of the workforce. Apart from conducting the survey, we also randomly interviewed ten civil servants and collected their feedbacks on the general impressions and expectations of G2E and G2G applications.

Table 1. Factor loading of the survey instrument

	A	PE	PU	SN	*t*-value	Composite Reliability
A1	**0.94**				63.66	0.91
A2	**0.88**				16.90	
PE1		**0.84**			28.61	0.88
PE2		**0.80**			14.75	
PE3		**0.86**			26.30	
PE4		**0.74**			10.89	
PU1			**0.87**		29.92	0.92
PU2			**0.83**		16.42	
PU3			**0.91**		36.71	
PU4			**0.82**		18.11	
SN1				**0.97**	6.41	0.92
SN2				**0.88**	5.16	

Design of the Survey Instrument

The questionnaire for the survey on CCGO was adapted from Davis (1989), and a pilot test was conducted which involved 12 doctoral students, of which two of them were part-time doctoral students who were civil servants. The composition of our pilot respondents enabled us to ensure that the views from both IS researchers and civil servants could be included. Pilot respondents took around 8 minutes to complete the questionnaire. Modifications in the wording and the general flow of the questionnaire were made. All questions in the finalized questionnaire were measured on a 5-point Likert scale.

After finalizing the questionnaire, we telephoned the office managers of various government departments and invited them to participate in the survey. Some departments, including the police department, post office and several public schools had agreed to participate in our survey. In total, we received 197 usable responses.

Data Analysis

As reported by Gefen et al. (2000), Partial Least Square (PLS) is a better structural equation model-ing (SEM) tools for exploratory study compared with LISREL. Hence, we used SmartPLS Version 2.0 (Ringle, et al., 2005) to analyze the survey data collected. Table 1 reports the loading of measurement items on their latent constructs, with *t*-values and composite reliability; and the correlation matrix is reported at Table 2. As *t*-values are significant, we can conclude that convergent validity is achieved for our survey. For discriminant validity, it is noted that all items are having loading higher than 0.7 on their associated factors, and are having a low loading on other factors. Hence, these factors are deemed reliable as suggested by Nunnally (1978). Also, the square root of each latent construct's Average Variance Extracted (AVE), i.e. the bolded figure on the correlation matrix, is much larger than the correlation of the construct concerned with other constructs, we can conclude that discriminant validity is also achieved.

The result of PLS is reported at Figure 2. It is shown that the first sets of hypotheses, which are derived from the TAM, are supported by our empirical data. However, it is shown that H2 is not supported by our data. In our model, we suggest that **subjective norm** will have a positive relationship with the adoption of CCGO. How-

Table 2. Correlation matrix of the contructs

	A	**PE**	**PU**	**SN**
A	**0.91**	0	0	0
PE	0.37	**0.81**	0	0
PU	0.34	0.43	**0.86**	0
SN	-0.22	-0.12	-0.02	**0.92**

ever, the result obtained is a significant negative relationship.

Interview with Civil Servants

After conducting the survey, we randomly interviewed 10 subjects (6 males and 4 females) and collected their feedbacks on CCGO. First, we noticed that quite a number of them thought that even though applications in CCGO helped them to obtain information faster, they had to adapt to an office environment, which required them to respond more quickly than before. They indicated that this increased their working pressure. Secondly, the frontline and junior management users suggested that the report format of these applications were standardized and with limited customization capacity. Hence, they needed to download the files and to customize them offline. Take the financial reporting module as an example, users could have limited rights to select the content to be included in the report online. However, they could not add any footnotes or highlight any important features there. If they wished to do so, they needed to download the file in CSV (comma separated value) format and add the notes offline. Hence, additional time would be required for such customization. However, as the management expected that these users could provide a faster service after the implementation of these **e-Government** systems, they had to complete their tasks under a very tight schedule.

Figure 2. Empirical result of the TAM study on CCGO

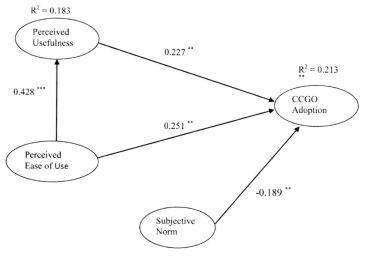

Note: * p < 0.1, ** p < 0.05, *** p < 0.01

Last but not least, some interviewees expressed the situation that as some senior colleagues still preferred to read reports and to communicate in a paper-based format, they were required to put in double-effort, i.e. to coordinate with some stakeholders electronically and to coordinate with others using a paper-based medium. Hence, in addition to handling paper channel only as in the past, they had to handle paper channel, electronic channel and to integrate the returns obtained from the two channels. This had more than doubled their efforts and had given them an impression that CCGO had worsened their working environment.

Discussion

In this study, we observe that the user adoption intention of CCGO was low. Originally, we expected that the user adoption rate for CCGO would be higher as it had been in place for 8 years and was designed to suit the general business needs of government departments. However, our result shows that civil servants did not like to use CCGO as much as we think. Based on our findings, it shows that PE has a significant positive impact on PU, and PE and PU both have significant positive impacts on CCGO adoption. Therefore, we have our first three hypotheses (i.e. H1.1 to H1.3) developed based on TAM supported empirically. However, we noted that SN has a significant negative impact on CCGO adoption, which is opposite to our expectation and hence, Hypothesis 2 is not supported.

According to our interviews with civil servants, we observed that even though the top management was eager to implement CCGO, most officers (and especially those from the frontline and in the middle management) had a general impression that CCGO would bring an additional workload and burden to them, instead of helping them to resolve their problems. Thus, their impression is just the opposite as predicted as the impact of SN on the user adoption of CCGO. This might explain why

we have observed a negative result for the impact of SN to the user adoption of CCGO.

There are some issues in this study. As an exploratory study, this research first focused on a metropolitan city, i.e. Hong Kong. The positive issue is that Hong Kong is one of the forerunners of **e-Government** and we are in the view that that the observations in Hong Kong are applicable and useful for other countries which are still developing the **e-Government** Strategy. However, as different countries are at different stages in the development of **e-Government** projects and have different kinds of information and reports published in the past few years, the result of this study may not be directly comparable to other countries.

IMPLICATION AND RECOMMENDATIONS

The negative impact of SN on the user adoption of CCGO implies that its design and implementation focused more on a top-down approach such that the priority has been accorded to satisfying the management vision of **e-Government** while paying insufficient attention to the user perceptions at the operation level. It is understandable that top-down approach is required to kick off those major **e-Government** initiatives to break the old procedures and operational bureaucracies. However, the formation of negative SN would unavoidably undermine the management effort in achieving their **e-Government** vision. In this connection, we have three recommendations for the relevant policy makers.

Firstly, while it is beneficial to deploy some sample applications in CCGO for demonstrating its benefits, CCGO should focus on implementing a flexible infrastructure to let user departments to customize for their own needs instead of implementing actual solutions. This strategy empowers the user departments to develop solutions that suit their own specific needs while providing a fundamental infrastructure as motivations. In addition, CCGO should also define the interoperability standard across departments so that further integration and interconnectivity among departments could be facilitated.

Secondly, pilot projects should be conducted in the largest government departments, e.g. Hong Kong Police, Housing Department, Education Department etc., as testing points for the new CCGO enhancements. These large departments are more sophisticated in terms of operation so it is more likely for them to encounter problems in the pilots. Given their sizable operation, they have more resources in tackling the relevant issues in the pilot projects. This should help improve the quality and relevance of the system in the early stage of development. In addition, with the largest department running pilot projects could give other smaller departments more confidence in adopting the final enhanced CCGO as the largest departments have setup role models and have gathered relevant experience for their reference.

The last but not the least, it is strongly recommended that the management involved the users at different levels of operations at a very early development stage when CCGO would be further enhanced or revamped. This would empower the end users to participate and to get involved so that project ownership could be established more easily. This should be helpful in alleviating the negative SN at the operation level.

FUTURE RESEARCH DIRECTIONS

For future research, it is suggested that a cross-country study should be conducted so that a cross-country analysis can be compiled to further validate the theoretical model.

CONCLUSION

In conclusion, this study brings some insight for IT policy makers when they develop their Intranet applications. Even though Hong Kong is one of the forerunners in **e-Government**, it is observed that it is unable to bring develop an Intranet systems, which has a high adoption rate by its internal users.

Therefore, it is suggested that policy makers should try to understand their internal customers more before implementing the system. This can help to improve user adoption of these internal applications and improve the efficiency and effectiveness of government through **e-Government** initiatives.

REFERENCES

Accenture. (2004). *E-Government leadership: Engaging the customer.* Retrieved March 31, 2009, from http://nstore.accenture.com/acn_com/PDF/Engaging_the_Customer.pdf

Adams, D. A., Nelson, R. R., & Todd, P. A. (1992). Perceives usefulness, ease of use and usage of information technology: A replication. *MIS Quarterly, 16*(2), 227–247. doi:10.2307/249577

Ajzen, I. (1991). The theory of planned behavior. *Organizational Behavior and Human Decision Processes, 50*(2), 179–211. doi:10.1016/0749-5978(91)90020-T

Amoako-Gyampah, K., & Salam, A. F. (2004). An extension of the Technology Acceptance Model in an ERP implementation environment. *Information & Management, 41*(6), 731–745. doi:10.1016/j.im.2003.08.010

Danziger, J. N., Kraemer, K. L., & King, J. L. (1978). An assessment of computer technology in U.S. local government. *Urban Systems, 3*(1), 21–37. doi:10.1016/0147-8001(78)90004-9

Davis, F. D. (1989). Perceived usefulness, perceived ease of use, and user acceptance of information technology. *MIS Quarterly, 13*(3), 318–339. doi:10.2307/249008

Davis, F. D., Bagozzi, R. P., & Warshaw, P. R. (1989). User acceptance of computer technology: A comparison of two theoretical models. *Management Science, 35*(8), 982–1003. doi:10.1287/mnsc.35.8.982

Devadoss, P. R., Pan, S. L., & Huang, J. C. (2002). Structural analysis of e-government initiatives: A case study of SCO. *Decision Support Systems, 34*(3), 253–269. doi:10.1016/S0167-9236(02)00120-3

Fishbein, M., & Ajzen, I. (1975). *Belief, attitude, intention, and behavior: An introduction to Theory and Research.* Reading, MA: Addison-Wesley.

Gefen, D., Straub, D., & Boudreau, M.-C. (2000). Structural equation modeling and regression: Guidelines for research practice. *Communications of the Association for Information Systems,* 4.

Golden, W., Hughes, M., & Scott, M. (2003). The role of process evolution in achieving citizen-centered e-government. In *Americas Conference on Information Systems 2003 Proceedings,* Tampa, Florida.

Gore, A. (1993). *Reengineering through information technology.* Accompanying Report of the National Performance Review. Washington, DC: Office of the Vice President.

Hong Kong Government (HKG). (2009). *IT infrastructure and standards – Infrastructure for e-government – Central Cyber Government Office.* Retrieved March 31, 2009, from http://www.ogcio.gov.hk/eng/infra/eccgo.htm

Information Technology and Broadcasting Bureau (ITBB). (1998). *Digital 21: Hong Kong Special Administrative Region Information Technology Strategy.* Retrieved March 31, 2009, from http://www.info.gov.hk/digital21/eng/related_documents/download/e-digital21.pdf

Kraemer, K. L. (1977). Local government, information systems, and technology transfer: Evaluating some common assertions about computer application transfer. *Public Administration Review, 37*(4), 368–382. doi:10.2307/974867

Nunnally, J. C. (1978). *Psychometric Theory* (2nd ed.). New York: McGraw-Hill.

Ringle, C. M., Wende, S., & Will, A. (2005*). SmartPLS 2.0 (beta).* Retrieved from www.smartpls.de

Tan, M., & Teo, S. H. (2000). Factors influencing the adoption of Internet banking. *Journal of the Association for Information Systems, 1.*

Thong, Y. L. (1999). An integrated model of information systems adoption in small businesses. *Journal of Management Information Systems, 15*(4), 187–214.

Venkatesh, V., Morris, M. G., Davis, G. B., & Davis, F. D. (2003). User acceptance of information technology: Toward a unified view. *MIS Quarterly, 27*(3), 425–478.

ADDITIONAL READING

Technology Acceptance Model (TAM), Theory of Reasoned Action (TRA) and Theory of Planned Behavior (TPB)

Adams, D. A., Nelson, R. R., & Todd, P. A. (1992). Perceives usefulness, ease of use and usage of information technology: A replication. *MIS Quarterly, 16*(2), 227–247. doi:10.2307/249577

Ajzen, I. (1991). The theory of planned behavior. *Organizational Behavior and Human Decision Processes, 50*(2), 179–211. doi:10.1016/0749-5978(91)90020-T

Amoako-Gyampah, K., & Salam, A. F. (2004). An extension of the Technology Acceptance Model in an ERP implementation environment. *Information & Management, 41*(6), 731–745. doi:10.1016/j.im.2003.08.010

Davis, F. D. (1989). Perceived usefulness, perceived ease of use, and user acceptance of information technology. *MIS Quarterly, 13*(3), 318–339. doi:10.2307/249008

Davis, F. D., Bagozzi, R. P., & Warshaw, P. R. (1989). User acceptance of computer technology: A comparison of two theoretical models. *Management Science, 35*(8), 982–1003. doi:10.1287/mnsc.35.8.982

Fishbein, M., & Ajzen, I. (1975). *Belief, attitude, intention, and behavior: An introduction to Theory and Research,* MA: Addison-Wesley.

Tan, M. & Teo, S. H. (2000). Factors influencing the adoption of Internet banking. *Journal of the Association for Information Systems, 1,* Article 5.

Thong, Y. L. (1999). An integrated model of information systems adoption in small businesses. *Journal of Management Information Systems, 15*(4), 187–214.

Venkatesh, V., Morris, M. G., Davis, G. B., & Davis, F. D. (2003). User acceptance of information technology: Toward a unified view. *MIS Quarterly, 27*(3), 425–478.

E-Government

Accenture (2004). E-Government leadership: Engaging the customer. Retrieved March 31, 2009, from http://nstore.accenture.com/acn_com/PDF/Engaging_the_Customer.pdf

Andersen, K. V., & Henriksen, H. Z. (2005). The first leg of e-government research: Domains and application areas 1998-2003. *International Journal of Electronic Government Research, 1*(4), 26–44.

Asgarkhani, M. (2005). Digital government and its effectiveness in public management reform. *Public Management Review, 7*(3), 465–487. doi:10.1080/14719030500181227

Danziger, J. N., Kraemer, K. L., & King, J. L. (1978). An assessment of computer technology in U.S. local government. *Urban Systems, 3*(1), 21–37. doi:10.1016/0147-8001(78)90004-9

Davison, R. M., Wagner, C., & Ma, L. C. K. (2005). From government to e-government: A transition model. *Information Technology & People, 18*(3), 280–299. doi:10.1108/09593840510615888

Devadoss, P. R., Pan, S. L., & Huang, J. C. (2002). Structural analysis of e-government initiatives: A case study of SCO. *Decision Support Systems, 34*(3), 253–269. doi:10.1016/S0167-9236(02)00120-3

Ebbers, W. E., & van Dijk, J. (2007). Resistance and support to electronic government, building a model of innovation. *Government Information Quarterly*, 24(1), 554–575. doi:10.1016/j.giq.2006.09.008

Evans, D., & Yen, D. C. (2005). E-Government: An analysis for implementation: Framework for understanding cultural and social impact. *Government Information Quarterly*, 22(3), 354–373. doi:10.1016/j.giq.2005.05.007

Flak, L. S., & Rose, J. (2005). Stakeholder governance: Adapting stakeholder theory to e-government. *Communications of the Association for Information Systems*, 16.

Golden, W., Hughes, M., & Scott, M. (2003). The role of process evolution in achieving citizen-centered e-government. In *Americas Conference on Information Systems 2003 Proceedings*, Tampa, Florida.

Gore, A. (1993). *Reengineering through information technology.* Accompanying Report of the National Performance Review. Washington, DC: Office of the Vice President.

Grant, G., & Chau, D. (2005). Developing a generic framework for e-government. *Journal of Global Information Management*, 13(1), 1–30.

Grönlund, Ä., & Horan, T. A. (2005). Introducing e-Gov: History, definition, and issues. *Communications of the Association for Information Systems*, 15(39), 713–729.

Heeks, R., & Bailur, S. (2006). Analysing eGovernment research: Perspectives, philosophies, theories, methods and practice. *iGovernment Working Paper Series*. Manchester, M13 9QH, UK, Institute for Development Policy and Management.

Ho, K. K. W. (2007). The e-Government development, IT strategies and Portals of Hong Kong SAR Government. *International Journal of Cases on Electronic Commerce*, 3(2), 71–89.

Ho, S. Y., & Ho, K. K. W. (2006). A study on the information quality satisfaction of communication portals in the Hong Kong Government, *Proceedings of 2006 IRMA International Conference*, in Washington D.C., U.S.A.

Kraemer, K. L. (1977). Local government, information systems, and technology transfer: Evaluating some common assertions about computer application transfer. *Public Administration Review*, 37(4), 368–382. doi:10.2307/974867

Singh, H., Amit, D., & Damien, J. (2007). Country-level determinants of e-government maturity. *Communications of the Association for Information Systems*, 20.

Yong, J. S. L. (Ed.). (2005). *Enabling public service innovation in the 21st Century: E-Government in Asia.* Singapore: Marshall Cavendish.

KEY TERMS AND DEFINITIONS

Electronic Government (e-Government): Electronic Government (e-Government) is referring to the use of information technology to provide government services online, which aims to provide faster and better services for stakeholders. It can be divided into four basic categories, viz. Government to Citizen (G2C), Government-to-Business (G2B), Government-to-Government (G2G), and Government-to-Employee (G2E).

Perceived Ease of Use (PE): Perceived Ease of Use (PE) is one of the independent constructs in the Technology Acceptance Model (TAM). It is "the degree to which a person believes that using a particular system would be free of effort" (Davis, 1989).

Perceived Usefulness (PU): Perceived Usefulness (PU) is one of the independent constructs in the Technology Acceptance Model (TAM). It is "the degree to which a person believes that using a particular system would enhance his/her job performance" (Davis, 1989).

Subjective Norm (SN): Subjective Norm (SN) is one of the independent constructs of the Theory of Reasoned Action (TRA). It is "the person's perception that most people who are important to him think he should or should not perform the behavior in question" (Fishbein & Ajzen, 1975).

Technology Adoption Model (TAM): Technology Acceptance Model (TAM) is an information systems (IS) research model, which is developed by Davis (1989). The original TAM has three constructs, viz., two independent contructs, Perceived Usefulness (PU), and Perceived Ease of Use (PE), and the dependent construct, User Acceptance (UA). While both independent constructs have positive impacts on the dependent construct, PE also has positive impact on PU.

Theory of Planned Behavior (TPB): Theory of Planned Behavior (TPB) reflects the relationship between Behavioral Intention (BI) and Behavior (as dependent constructs) with Attitude Towards Act or Behavior (AB), Subjective Norm (SN) and Perceived Behavioral Control (Ajzen, 1991).

Theory of Reasoned Action (TRA): Theory of Reasoned Action (TRA) reflects the relationship between Behavioral Intention (BI) (as dependent construct) with Attitude towards Act or Behavior (AB) and Subjective Norm (SN). Prior research has shown that that $BI = \beta_1 AB + \beta_2 SN$ (Fishbein & Ajzen, 1975).

APPENDIX: SAMPLE QUESTIONNAIRE

Perceived Usefulness of CCGO (PU)

PU1. Using CCGO improves my job performance.
PU2. Using CCGO in my job increases my productivity.
PU3. Using CCGO enhances my job effectiveness.
PU4. I find CCGO useful in my job.

Perceived Ease of Use of CCGO (PE)

PE1. My interaction with CCGO is clear and understandable.
PE2. Interacting with CCGO does not require lots of my mental effort.
PE3. I find CCGO easy to use.
PE4. I find it easy to get CCGO to do what I want to do.

Subjective Norms of CCGO (SN)

SN1. People who influence my behaviour think that I should use the system.
SN2. People who are important to me think that I should use the system.

Adoption Intention of CCGO (A)

A1. Assuming I have access to CCGO, I intend to use CCGO.
A2. Given that I have access to CCGO, I predict that I would use CCGO.
(1 = Disagree, 5 = Agree)

Chapter 60

An Exploratory Study on the Information Quality Satisfaction of Central Cyber Government Office of the Hong Kong Government

Kevin K.W. Ho
The University of Guam, Guam

ABSTRACT

Information quality is critical for a communication portal because there are myriad information types, including textual, audio, video and other complex information types, which an organization has to manage. In this chapter, the author examine the information quality satisfaction of the Central Cyber Government Office (CCGO), which is a communication portal developed by the Hong Kong Government. A survey study was conducted to investigate how users evaluate the information quality of CCGO. This portal case is interesting because: (1) Hong Kong Government has invested millions of US dollars in its implementation; and (2) the number of potential users is huge (over 140,000) in 2007.

INTRODUCTION

To keep governments operating smoothly, swift but careful fine-tuning of public policies and strategies are required. This situation creates a demand for establishing a seamless information flow between government agencies. To facilitate such information exchange, there is a global trend for governments to take advantages of information and Internet technologies for providing their services online. This

can improve both efficiency and service quality of business processes within governments. Therefore, in previous years, many governments have heavily invested in information technology infrastructures and software applications. Taking Hong Kong as an example, this Far Eastern metropolitan invested over US$100M per year in its **e-Government** projects since 2000. For the seven-year period between April 1999 and March 2006, Hong Kong Government invested US$1,094.4M in information technology (Ho, 2007). This huge investment helps Hong Kong to advance to one of the top countries/cities in the

DOI: 10.4018/978-1-61520-611-7.ch060

maturity of **e-Government** development (Accenture, 2004; Melitski et al., 2005).

Among these US$1,094.4M invested by the Hong Kong Government, 16% was invested in those projects related to the development of IT infrastructure and software applications, which aimed to support Government-to-Government (G2G) and Government-to-Employee (G2E) transactions (Ho, 2007). In this study, we investigate the impact of **information quality** on the **user satisfaction** of one of the key G2G and G2E applications in Hong Kong, i.e., the Intranet portal of the government, a.k.a. the Central Cyber Government Office (CCGO).

BACKGROUND

Central Cyber Government Office (CCGO)

In 2000, the Hong Kong Government launched its Intranet communication portal, the Central Cyber Government Office (CCGO), for its employees (HKG, 2009). This portal is designed for disseminating information within the government. It also acts as a hub for linking up services provided to internal customers from different government agencies. Its function is similar to GovHK, (http://www.gov.hk), the **e-Government** one-stop portal for members of the public developed by the Hong Kong Government. Users can access to CCGO via their network terminals, which are connected to the government Intranet. Apart from acting as a communication portal, CCGO also provides other add-on services, ranged from simple search functions, such as telephone directory and glossaries, to bulletin boards and discussion forums. Plus, CCGO acts as a platform for G2E and G2G applications. New applications, such as the electronic leave application system, electronic payroll system, and departmental portals were launched in the past few years (HKG, 2009).

In this study, we examine the **user satisfaction** on this Intranet portal. We choose CCGO as the focus of our study based on the following reasons. First, the Hong Kong Government is one of the pioneers in implementing **e-Government** projects in the world and ranked the seventh in the worldwide "Overall Maturity in **e-Government**" (Accenture, 2004). Thus, we conjuncture CCGO would be well designed. Second, the number of users of CCGO is huge. When we conducted our study in 2003/2004, the number of users of CCGO was around 50,000, i.e. 1/3 of the staff force. In the past few years, its user population has increased to 140,000 and it is now accessible by nearly all civil servants. With more knowledge on how **information quality** factors affecting **user satisfaction** on CCGO, business firms and governments can obtain insights on how to develop their own communication portals. Therefore, we aim at addressing the following research questions:

(1) How does **information accuracy** (Ac) affect the **user satisfaction** of Government Intranet portal?

(2) How does **presentation format** (P) affect the **user satisfaction** of Government Intranet portal?

(3) How does **information timeliness** (Ti) affect the **user satisfaction** of Government Intranet portal?

(4) How does **content relevancy** (C) affect the **user satisfaction** of Government Intranet portal?

Literature Review on Information Quality

Information Systems (IS) researchers study the relationship between **information quality** and **user satisfaction** for over 30 years (Melone, 1990). Bailey and Pearson (1983) studied **user satisfaction** and developed 39 factors for measuring computer **user satisfaction**. These factors include **information quality** constructs. Srinivasan (1985) examined the implementation of computerized modeling systems of 29 organizations. He noticed that system effectiveness can be measured by **information quality** constructs. In addition, DeLone and McLean (1992) noted that **information quality** is one of the six dimensions, which has a significant impact on the success of information systems.

IS researchers also develop theoretical models and methodologies to explain the impact of **information quality** on **user satisfaction** (Lee et al., 2002), systems development and implementation (Shim & Min, 2002; Mahmood, 1987), and data integrity (Lee et al., 2004). New methods, such as structural equation modeling (SEM) (Bharati, 2003; Khalil & Elkordy, 2005), elaboration-likelihood model (ELM) (Bhattacherjee & Sanford, 2006), and experiments (Aladwani, 2003), are used for analyzing this impact.

With the rapid development of e-commerce in recent years, IS researchers begin to investigate the impact of **information quality** on the user acceptance and satisfaction on e-commerce websites and portals. Negash et al. (2003) and Shih (2004) studied the impact of **information quality** on the effectiveness of web-based customer support system and the user acceptance of e-shopping respectively. Sullivan and Walstrom (2001) studied the impact of **information quality** on the consumer perception on the e-commerce website. Also, Park and Kim (2006) studied the impact of **information quality** on information satisfaction on e-commerce in Korea. Plus, Cheung and Lee (2005) studied the asymmetric effects of website attributes on **user satisfaction**.

IS researchers also investigate the impact of **information quality** on **e-Government** for more than 10 years. Cykana et al. (1996) discussed the data quality management guidelines used by the Department of Defense and reported that **information accuracy**, completeness, consistency, **information timeliness**, uniqueness and validity

are the core factors of data quality requirements. In addition, Aladwani (2002) studied the **user satisfaction** on the information systems in public organizations in Kuwait.

In this study, we include the four basic **information quality** constructs in our model, i.e. **information accuracy** (Ac), **presentation format** (P), **information timeliness** (Ti), and **content relevancy** (C). Table 1 reports the related prior studies. Based on the result of Doll and Torkzadeh (1998), we conjuncture the level of **user satisfaction** (S) is positively related to these four constructs. Thus, we have the following four hypotheses:

H1.1: When **information accuracy** is at a higher level on the Intranet portal, civil servants will have a higher level of **user satisfaction** on the Intranet portal.

H1.2: When **content relevancy** is at a higher level on the Intranet portal, civil servants will have a higher level of **user satisfaction** on the Intranet portal.

H1.3: When **presentation format** is at a higher level on the Intranet portal, civil servants will have a higher level of **user satisfaction** on the Intranet portal.

H1.4: When **information timeliness** is at a higher level on the Intranet portal, civil servants will have a higher level of **user satisfaction** on the Intranet portal.

We also conjuncture some of these information quality constructs are depended on other constructs. Thus, we developed the following six self-explanatory hypotheses:

H2.1: When **content relevancy** is at a higher level on the Intranet portal, **information accuracy** will also at a higher level.

H2.2: When **presentation format** is at a higher level on the Intranet portal, **information accuracy** will also at a higher level.

Table 1. Information quality constructs used in the study

Constructs	Prior Studies
Information Accuracy (A)	Bailey & Pearson (1983) Cykana et al. (1996) Doll & Torkzadeh (1998) Mahmood (1987) Miller & Doyle (1987) Srinivasan (1985)
Presentation Format (P)	Doll & Torkzadeh (1998) Cykana et al. (1986)
Information Timeliness (T)	Bailey & Pearson (1983) Cykana et al. (1996) Doll & Torkzadeh (1998) Mahmood (1987) Miller & Doyle (1987) Srinivasan (1985)
Content Relevancy (C)	Bailey & Pearson (1983) Doll & Torkzadeh (1998) Miller & Doyle (1987) Srinivasan (1985)

H2.3: When **presentation format** is at a higher level on the Intranet portal, **content relevancy** will also at a higher level.

H2.4: When **information timeliness** is at a higher level on the Intranet portal, **information accuracy** will also at a higher level.

H2.5: When **information timeliness** is at a higher level on the Intranet portal, **content relevancy** will also at a higher level.

H2.6: When **information timeliness** is at a higher level on the Intranet portal, **presentation format** will also at a higher level.

Figure 1 summarizes our research model.

THE EMPIRICAL STUDY ON USER SATISFACTION ON CCGO

Methodology and the Design of the Survey Instrument

The survey on the **user satisfaction** on CCGO was administered from late 2003 to early 2004, which was lasted for 12 weeks. The questionnaire is adapted from the scale developed by Doll and Torkzadeh (1988) and Lee et al. (2002), which measures **information quality** from the systems. A pilot test was conducted with a panel of 12 doctoral students. Two of the panelists were also government officers (i.e. part-time doctoral students). Hence, both the views of IS researchers and civil servants were considered when we refined the questionnaire. The respondents took approximately 10 minutes to complete the questionnaire, which consisted of 12 questions, on a 5-point Likert scale.

We invited various government agencies to participate in this study. Agencies from education sector, disciplined force, and post office took part in this study. We conducted the survey on site and distributed paper questionnaires. Each survey session was conducted on company time and a member of our research team explained the purpose of the survey and answered any questions raised by respondents on site. A total of 197 usable responses were collected.

Figure 1. Research model of the study

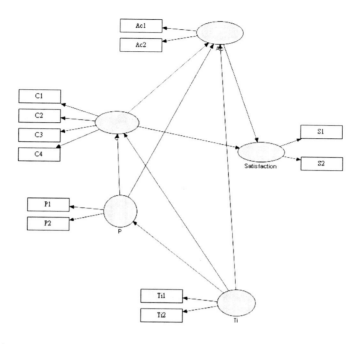

Data Analysis

To analysis our research model, we used Structural Equation Modeling (SEM) technique to analyze our data collected. As suggested by Gefen et al.

(2000), Partial Least Square (PLS) method is more suitable for exploratory study. Therefore, we used SmartPLS Version 2.0 (Ringle, et al., 2005) to conduct our analysis. Table 2 reports the loading of measurement items, and the correlation matrix

Table 2. Factor loading of the survey instrument

	S	Ac	C	P	Ti	*t*-value	Composite Reliability
Ac1		0.95				71.85	0.95
Ac2		0.95				69.70	
C1			0.85			25.21	0.89
C2			0.88			30.00	
C3			0.76			9.59	
C4			0.77			15.36	
P1				0.93		69.63	0.93
P2				0.93		62.77	
S1	0.91					51.50	0.89
S2	0.88					28.81	
Ti1					0.94	77.38	0.93
Ti2					0.93	50.40	

Table 3. Correlation matrix of the contructs

	Ac	C	P	S	Ti
A	**0.95**				
C	0.66	**0.82**			
P	0.74	0.72	**0.93**		
S	0.64	0.59	0.61	**0.90**	
Ti	0.57	0.63	0.63	0.50	**0.94**

is reported at Table 3. As shown in Table 2, as all *t*-values are significant, convergent validity is achieved. It is also noted that all items have high loadings (>0.70) on their associated factors, and have low loadings on other factors. Plus, the square root of each latent construct's Average Variance Extracted (AVE), i.e. the bolded figure on the correlation matrix, is much larger than the correlation of the construct concerned with other construct. Therefore, we can conclude that discriminant validity is also achieved (Nunnally, 1978).

The result of PLS is at Figure 2, with the results summarized at Table 4. The R^2(adj) values obtained for various paths are ranged from 0.395 to 0.591, which are acceptable. As shown in Table 4, we observe that **information accuracy** (H1.1) and **content relevancy** (H1.2) are the two significant factors, which have positive effects on **user satisfaction**. It is also observed that **information accuracy** is depended on **content relevancy** (H2.1) and **presentation format** (H2.2); **content relevancy** is depended on **presentation format** (H2.3) and **information timeliness** (H2.5); and **presentation format** is depended on **information timeliness** (H2.6).

Discussion

With plenty of in-house IT and development resources, the Hong Kong Government was one of the first municipal governments to implement an advanced communication portal. The benefits of CCGO include more secure creation of and access to information, versioning, information audit trails, approval paths, secured distribution, and workflow and collaboration automation. The major drawback of it is the high software and implementation costs, which costs millions of US dollars.

In our model, we conjuncture that all four information quality constructs would have significant impacts on **user satisfaction** on CCGO. However, our result shows that **information accuracy** and **content relevancy** are the two factors, which have direct impacts on the **user satisfaction** of CCGO. While the other two factors, viz. **presentation formats** and **information timeliness** do not have direct impact on the **user satisfaction** of CCGO, they have indirect impacts on the **user satisfaction** of CCGO as they are the factors affecting **information accuracy** (for **presentation format**) and **content relevancy** (for both **presentation format** and **information timeliness**). In brief, all the four **information quality** constructs are either having direct or indirect impacts on **user satisfaction**. Hence, it is suggested that the management of public and private sectors should take these four issues when they decide their Intranet portal.

To further collecting feedback from users of CCGO, 10 of the survey subjects, including six males and four females, were informally interviewed. They reckoned that as CCGO users, they had a concerned on **information accuracy** and **content relevancy** of the information presented in CCGO. It is because these information were essential for them in their daily work, and they might need to use these information to prepare reports for internal (i.e. other civil servants within

Figure 2. Empirical result of the information quality satisfaction study on CCGO

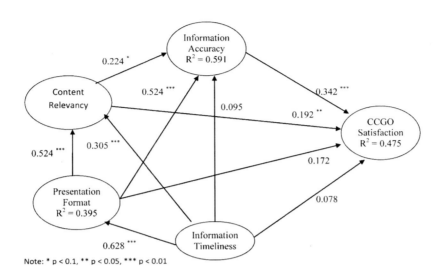

Note: * p < 0.1, ** p < 0.05, *** p < 0.01

the government) and external (i.e. members of the public) clients. However, they had less concerns on the **presentation format**. Concerning **information timeliness**, we observed a very interesting observation. We notice that government officers in Hong Kong felt that it was a burden to receive timely information. This is probably due to an adaptation problem as Hong Kong Government had just moved from paper-base information flow to paperless mode. As a result, civil servants were adjusting their mindset from a slow paper-based information flow to a fast Intranet-fuelled system. This brought a paradigm shift to the civil servants when we conducted our study. Therefore, it is also suggested that the management should take into account of the feeling of the users.

FUTURE RESEARCH DIRECTIONS

For further research directions, it is suggested that a comparative study could be conducted for

Table 4. Path coefficients

Path	Coefficient	t-value	R^2 (adj)	Supported?
Ac → S (H1.1)	0.342	3.75 ***	0.475	**Yes**
C → S (H1.2)	0.192	2.12 **		**Yes**
P → S (H1.3)	0.172	1.46		No
Ti → S (H1.4)	0.078	0.88		No
C → Ac (H2.1)	0.224	1.88 *	0.591	**Yes**
P → Ac (H2.2)	0.524	5.01 ***		**Yes**
Ti → Ac (H2.4)	0.095	1.22		No
P → C (H2.3)	0.524	6.34 ***	0.569	**Yes**
Ti → C (H2.5)	0.305	3.25 ***		**Yes**
Ti → P (H2.6)	0.628	10.28 ***	0.395	**Yes**

comparing the development of Intranet portal for business and government agencies. Also, it is also worthy to conduct multi-country studies on the **user satisfaction** on Intranet portal and investigate whether cultural difference would have a significant impact on this issue.

CONCLUSION

Our study conducted a survey in a number of government departments to examine the **information quality** satisfaction of an in-house developed communication portal by the Hong Kong Government. **Information quality** is critical for a communication portal because there are myriad information types, including textual, audio, video and other complex information types, which an organization has to manage. Results show that all four **information quality** constructs are important **information quality** factors, which have either direct or indirect impacts on **user satisfaction** on the Intranet portal. We suggest public and business organizations should take into account of the impact of **information quality** on the **user satisfaction** of their portals when they design their Intranet portals.

REFERENCES

Accenture (2004). E-Government leadership: Engaging the customer. Retrieved March 31, 2009, from http://nstore.accenture.com/acn_com/PDF/Engaging_the_Customer.pdf

Aladwani, A. M. (2002). Organizational actions, computer attitudes, and end-user satisfaction in public organizations: An empirical study. *Journal of End User Computing, 14*(1), 42–49.

Aladwani, A. M. (2003). A deeper look at the attitude-behavior consistency assumption in information systems satisfaction research. *Journal of Computer Information Systems, 44*(1), 57–63.

Bailey, J. E., & Pearson, S. W. (1983). Development of a tool for measuring and analyzing computer user satisfaction. *Management Science, 29*(5), 530–545. doi:10.1287/mnsc.29.5.530

Bharati, P. (2003). People and information matter: Task support satisfaction from the other side. *Journal of Computer Information Systems, 43*(2), 93–102.

Bhattacherjee, A., & Sanford, C. (2006). Influence process for information technology acceptance: An elaboration likelihood model. *MIS Quarterly, 30*(4), 805–825.

Cykana, P., Paul, A., & Stern, M. (1996). DoD guidelines on data quality management. *Proceedings of the Conference on Information Quality*, Cambridge, MA, 154-171.

DeLone, W. H., & McLean, E. R. (1992). Information systems success: The quest for the dependent variable. *Information Systems Research, 3*(1), 60–95. doi:10.1287/isre.3.1.60

Doll, W. J., & Torkzadeh, G. (1988). The measurement of end-user computing satisfaction. *MIS Quarterly, 12*(2), 259–274. doi:10.2307/248851

Gefen, D., Straub, D., & Boudreau, M.-C. (2000). Structural equation modeling and regression: Guidelines for research practice. *Communications of the Association for Information Systems*: Vol. 4, Article 7. from http://aisel.aisnet.org/cais/vol4/iss1/7

Ho, K. K. W. (2007). The e-Government development, IT strategies and portals of Hong Kong SAR Government . *International Journal of Cases on Electronic Commerce, 3*(2), 71–89.

Hong Kong Government (HKG). (2009). *IT infrastructure and standards – Infrastructure for e-government – Central Cyber Government Office.* Retrieved: March 31, 2009, from http://www.ogcio.gov.hk/eng/infra/eccgo.htm

Khalil, O. E. M., & Elkordy, M. M. (2005). EIS information: Use and quality determinants. *Information Resources Management Journal, 18*(2), 68–93.

Lee, Y. W., Pipino, L., Strong, D. M., & Wang, R. Y. (2004). Process embedded data integrity. *Journal of Database Management, 15*(1), 87–103.

Lee, Y. W., Strong, D. M., Kahn, B. K., & Wang, R. Y. (2002). AIMQ: A methodology for information quality assessment. *Information & Management, 40*(2), 133–146. doi:10.1016/S0378-7206(02)00043-5

Mahmood, A. (1987). Systems development methods – A comparative investigation. *MIS Quarterly, 11*(3), 293–311. doi:10.2307/248674

Melitski, J., Holzer, M., Kim, S.-T., Kim, C. G., & Rho, S. Y. (2005). An e-Government assessment of municipal web sites. *International Journal of Electronic Government Research, 1*(1), 1–19.

Melone, N. P. (1990). A theoretical assessment of the user-satisfaction construct in information systems research. *Management Science, 36*(1), 76–91. doi:10.1287/mnsc.36.1.76

Miller, J., & Doyle, B. A. (1987). Measuring effectiveness of computer-based information systems in the financial services sector. *MIS Quarterly, 11*(1), 107–124. doi:10.2307/248832

Negash, S., Ryan, T., & Igbaria, M. (2003). Quality and effectiveness on Web-based customer support systems. *Information & Management, 40*(8), 757–768. doi:10.1016/S0378-7206(02)00101-5

Nunnally, J. C. (1978). *Psychometric theory* (2nd edition). New York: McGraw-Hill.

Park, C. H., & Kim, Y. G. (2006). The effect of information satisfaction and relational benefit on consumers' online shopping site commitments. *Journal of Electronic Commerce in Organizations, 4*(1), 70–90.

Ringle, C. M., Wende, S., & Will, A. (2005): SmartPLS 2.0 (beta), www.smartpls.de.

Shih, H. P. (2004). An empirical study on predicting user acceptance of e-shopping on the Web. *Information & Management, 41*(3), 351–368. doi:10.1016/S0378-7206(03)00079-X

Shim, S. J., & Min, B. K. (2002). Organizational factors associated with expert systems implementation. *Journal of Computer Information Systems, 42*(4), 71–76.

Srinivasan, A. (1985). Alternative measures of system effectiveness: Associations and implications. *MIS Quarterly, 9*(3), 243–253. doi:10.2307/248951

Sullivan, J. R., & Walstrom, K. A. (2001). Consumer perspectives on service quality of electronic commerce web sites. *Journal of Computer Information Systems, 41*(3), 8–14.

ADDITIONAL READING

E-Government

Accenture. (2004). *E-Government leadership: Engaging the customer*. Retrieved March 31, 2009, from http://nstore.accenture.com/acn_com/PDF/Engaging_the_Customer.pdf

Andersen, K. V., & Henriksen, H. Z. (2005). The first leg of e-government research: Domains and application areas 1998-2003. *International Journal of Electronic Government Research, 1*(4), 26–44.

Danziger, J. N., Kraemer, K. L., & King, J. L. (1978). An assessment of computer technology in U.S. local government. *Urban Systems, 3*(1), 21–37. doi:10.1016/0147-8001(78)90004-9

Davison, R. M., Wagner, C., & Ma, L. C. K. (2005). From government to e-government: A transition model. *Information Technology & People, 18*(3), 280–299. doi:10.1108/09593840510615888

Devadoss, P. R., Pan, S. L., & Huang, J. C. (2002). Structural analysis of e-government initiatives: A case study of SCO. *Decision Support Systems, 34*(3), 253–269. doi:10.1016/S0167-9236(02)00120-3

Ebbers, W. E., & van Dijk, J. (2007). Resistance and support to electronic government, building a model of innovation. *Government Information Quarterly, 24*(1), 554–575. doi:10.1016/j.giq.2006.09.008

Evans, D., & Yen, D. C. (2005). E-Government: An analysis for implementation: Framework for understanding cultural and social impact. *Government Information Quarterly, 22*(3), 354–373. doi:10.1016/j.giq.2005.05.007

Flak, L. S., & Rose, J. (2005). Stakeholder governance: Adapting stakeholder theory to e-government. *Communications of the Association for Information Systems*, 16.

Golden, W., Hughes, M., & Scott, M. (2003). The role of process evolution in achieving citizen-centered e-government. In *Americas Conference on Information Systems 2003 Proceedings*, Tampa, Florida. Retrieved March 31, 2009, from http://aisel.aisnet.org/amcis2003/100

Gore, A. (1993). *Reengineering through information technology*. Accompanying Report of the National Performance Review. Washington, DC: Office of the Vice President.

Grant, G., & Chau, D. (2005). Developing a generic framework for e-government. *Journal of Global Information Management, 13*(1), 1–30.

Grönlund, Ä., & Horan, T. A. (2005). Introducing e-Gov: History, definition, and issues. *Communications of the Association for Information Systems, 15*(39), 713–729.

Heeks, R., & Bailur, S. (2006). Analysing eGovernment research: Perspectives, philosophies, theories, methods and practice. *iGovernment Working Paper Series*. Manchester, M13 9QH, UK, Institute for Development Policy and Management.

Ho, K. K. W. (2007). The e-Government development, IT strategies and Portals of Hong Kong SAR Government. *International Journal of Cases on Electronic Commerce, 3*(2), 71–89.

Ho, S. Y., & Ho, K. K. W. (2006). A study on the information quality satisfaction of communication portals in the Hong Kong Government. In *Proceedings of 2006 IRMA International Conference*, Washington, DC.

Kraemer, K. L. (1977). Local government, information systems, and technology transfer: Evaluating some common assertions about computer application transfer. *Public Administration Review, 37*(4), 368–382. doi:10.2307/974867

Melitski, J., Holzer, M., Kim, S.-T., Kim, C. G., & Rho, S. Y. (2005). An e-Government assessment of municipal web sites. *International Journal of Electronic Government Research, 1*(1), 1–19.

Melone, N. P. (1990). A theoretical assessment of the user-satisfaction construct in information systems research. *Management Science, 36*(1), 76–91. doi:10.1287/mnsc.36.1.76

Singh, H., Amit, Das, & Damien, Joseph. (2007). Country-level determinants of e-government maturity. *Communications of the Association for Information Systems*, 20.

Yong, J. S. L. (Ed.). (2005). *Enabling public service innovation in the 21st Century: E-Government in Asia*. Singapore: Marshall Cavendish.

User-Satisfaction and Information Quality

Aladwani, A. M. (2002). Organizational actions, computer attitudes, and end-user satisfaction in public organizations: An empirical study. *Journal of End User Computing, 14*(1), 42–49.

Aladwani, A. M. (2003). A deeper look at the attitude-behavior consistency assumption in information systems satisfaction research. *Journal of Computer Information Systems, 44*(1), 57–63.

Bailey, J. E., & Pearson, S. W. (1983). Development of a tool for measuring and analyzing computer user satisfaction. *Management Science, 29*(5), 530–545. doi:10.1287/mnsc.29.5.530

Bharati, P. (2003). People and information matter: Task support satisfaction from the other side. *Journal of Computer Information Systems, 43*(2), 93–102.

Bhattacherjee, A., & Sanford, C. (2006). Influence process for information technology acceptance: An elaboration likelihood model. *MIS Quarterly, 30*(4), 805–825.

Cheung, C. M. K., & Lee, M. K. O. (2005). The Asymmetric Effect of Website Attribute Performance on Satisfaction: An Empirical Study. In *Proceedings of the 38th Annual Hawaii International Conference on System Sciences*, Waikoloa, Hawaii.

Cykana, P., Paul, A., & Stern, M. (1996). DoD guidelines on data quality management. *Proceedings of the Conference on Information Quality*, Cambridge, MA, 154-171.

DeLone, W. H., & McLean, E. R. (1992). Information systems success: The quest for the dependent variable. *Information Systems Research, 3*(1), 60–95. doi:10.1287/isre.3.1.60

Doll, W. J., & Torkzadeh, G. (1988). The measurement of end-user computing satisfaction. *MIS Quarterly, 12*(2), 259–274. doi:10.2307/248851

Fisher, C., Lauría, E., Chengalur-Smith, S., & Wang, R. (2008). *Introduction to Information Quality*. Cambridge, MA: M.I.T. Information Quality Program Press.

Jin, X.-L., Cheung, C. M. K., Lee, M. K. O., & Chen, H. (2008). User Information Satisfaction with a Knowledge-Based Virtual Community: An Empirical Investigation. *In Emerging Technologies and Information Systems for the Knowledge Society*. Berlin: Springer.

Khalil, O. E. M., & Elkordy, M. M. (2005). EIS information: Use and quality determinants. *Information Resources Management Journal, 18*(2), 68–93.

Lee, Y. W., Pipino, L., Strong, D. M., & Wang, R. Y. (2004). Process embedded data integrity. *Journal of Database Management, 15*(1), 87–103.

Lee, Y. W., Strong, D. M., Kahn, B. K., & Wang, R. Y. (2002). AIMQ: A methodology for information quality assessment. *Information & Management, 40*(2), 133–146. doi:10.1016/S0378-7206(02)00043-5

Mahmood, A. (1987). Systems development methods–A comparative investigation. *MIS Quarterly, 11*(3), 293–311. doi:10.2307/248674

Miller, J., & Doyle, B. A. (1987). Measuring effectiveness of computer-based information systems in the financial services sector. *MIS Quarterly, 11*(1), 107–124. doi:10.2307/248832

Negash, S., Ryan, T., & Igbaria, M. (2003). Quality and effectiveness on Web-based customer support systems. *Information & Management, 40*(8), 757–768. doi:10.1016/S0378-7206(02)00101-5

Park, C. H., & Kim, Y. G. (2006). The effect of information satisfaction and relational benefit on consumers' online shopping site commitments. *Journal of Electronic Commerce in Organizations, 4*(1), 70–90.

Shih, H. P. (2004). An empirical study on predicting user acceptance of e-shopping on the Web. *Information & Management, 41*(3), 351–368. doi:10.1016/S0378-7206(03)00079-X

Shim, S. J., & Min, B. K. (2002). Organizational factors associated with expert systems implementation. *Journal of Computer Information Systems, 42*(4), 71–76.

Srinivasan, A. (1985). Alternative measures of system effectiveness: Associations and implications. *MIS Quarterly, 9*(3), 243–253. doi:10.2307/248951

Sullivan, J. R., & Walstrom, K. A. (2001). Consumer perspectives on service quality of electronic commerce web sites. *Journal of Computer Information Systems, 41*(3), 8–14.

Wang, R., & Strong, D. (1996). Beyond accuracy: What data quality means to data consumers. *Journal of Management Information Systems, 12*(4), 5–34.

Wang, R. Y., Pierce, M. E., Stuart, E., & Madnick, E. S. (2005). *Information Quality*. Armonk, NY: M.E. Sharpe.

KEY TERMS AND DEFINITIONS

Content Relevancy: Content Relevancy is "the degree of congruence between what the user wants or requires and what is provided by the information products and services" (Bailey & Pearson, 1983). It is one of the elements of Contextual data quality (Wang & Strong, 1996).

Electronic Government (e-Government): Electronic Government (e-Government) is referring to the use of information technology to provide government services online, which aims to provide faster and better services for stakeholders. It can be divided into four basic categories, viz. Government to Citizen (G2C), Government-to-Business (G2B), Government-to-Government (G2G), and Government-to-Employee (G2E).

Information Accuracy: Information Accuracy relates to "the correctness of the output information" (Bailey & Pearson, 1983). It is one of the elements of intrinsic data quality (Wang & Strong, 1996).

Information Quality: Information quality is "the quality of the information that the systems produces" (DeLone & McLean, 1992). It can further divided into four data quality (DQ) categories, viz. Intrinsic DQ, Contextual DQ, Representational DQ, and Accessibility DQ (Wang & Strong, 1996).

Information Timeliness: Information Timeliness relates to "the availability of the output information at a time suitable for its use" (Bailey & Pearson, 1983). It is one of the elements of Contextual data quality (Wang & Strong, 1996).

Intranet Portal: Intranet Portal is a gateway on the Intranet developed by an organization, which unifies access to all information and applications related to the daily operation of the organization.

Presentation Format: Presentation Format is the measure of how "the output is presented in a useful format and whether the information is clear" (Doll and Torkzadeh, 1998)

APPENDIX: SAMPLE QUESTIONNAIRE

User Satisfaction of CCGO (S)

S1. The system is successful.
S2. I am satisfied with the system.

Information Accuracy (Ac)

Ac1. The system is accurate.
Ac2. I am satisfied with the accuracy of the system.

Presentation Format (P)

P1. The output is presented in a useful format.
P2. The information is clear.

Information Timeliness (Ti)

Ti1. I get the information you need in time.
Ti2. The system provides up-to-date information.

Content Relevancy (C)

C1. The system provides the precise information you need.
C2. The information content meets your needs.
C3. The system provides reports that seem to be just about exactly what I need.
C4. The system provides sufficient information.
(1 = Disagree, 5 = Agree)

Chapter 61

Visual Merchandising in Online Retailing Based on Physical Retailing Design Principles

Tony Pittarese
East Tennessee State University, USA

ABSTRACT

Effective design guidelines aid in the creation of successful online stores. One possible resource to aid in formulating effective online store design guidelines is found in principles and practices of physical retailers. In particular, physical store merchandising techniques provide a significant body of research from which online store guidelines may be constructed. By examining the research literature and common practices of physical retailers, online retailers may glean new and interesting ideas upon which to base guidelines for online store design.

INTRODUCTION

While retailing on the World Wide Web began in the United States in the mid-1990's (Netscape Communications Corporation, 1997; Petrak, 2000; Zakon, 2002), traditional store-based retailing has been practiced for centuries. Although some have argued for starting with a "blank slate" strategy when building online retailing research (Childers, Carr, Peck, & Carseon, 2001), it would be unwise for those studying online retailing to disregard the decades of research that exists in traditional retailing (Chen, Gillenson, & Sherrell, 2002; Hübscher,

DOI: 10.4018/978-1-61520-611-7.ch061

Pittarese, & Lanford, 2002; Pittarese, 2003). Research focusing particularly on the use of physical retail merchandising techniques in e-Commerce is currently underdeveloped.

Early research in physical store merchandising can be traced to the 1960's. During this time researchers first began to focus on how the display and presentation of products in the selling environment could be used to enhance sales (K. Cox, 1964, 1970; Kotzan & Evanson, 1969). **Merchandising**, defined as "the activities required in the attempt to make a product interesting to buyers" (Rosenberg, 1995), encompasses areas such as store organization (Hart & Davies, 1996), product display and presentation (Bryan & Gershman, 1999), and overall design and maintenance of the entire retailing environment (Kotler, 1974). It is well established that success in merchandising results in increased sales and enhanced customer satisfaction (Berman & Evans, 1998; Levy & Weitz, 1998).

BACKGROUND

Study has shown that customer satisfaction in online shopping is based upon the customer's assessment of various critical factors including **site design**, convenience (Szymanski & Hise, 2000), and perceptions of usefulness and ease of use (Chen, et al., 2002; Qiu & Li, 2008). One challenge an online store faces is organizing and presenting their products in a way that the customer will find enticing. One potential advantage an online retailer has is its ability to offer customers more products than would be possible in a physical environment, however for this benefit to be fully realized the products must be presented in a manner that enhances the retailer's overall site design and shopper convenience. There is a direct relationship between a customer's assessment of the aesthetic quality of an online store, and their assessment of the quality and organization of the product information provided on the site (S. Y. Kim & Lim, 2001; Park & Stoel, 2002).

While Kotler coined the term "**atmospherics**" to describe use of the physical shopping environment to influence customer shopping (Kotler, 1974), Childers originated the term "**webmospherics**" to describe the same concept in online stores (Childers, et al., 2001) and others have built on that work (Hausman & Siekpe, 2009; Richard, 2005). Presenting large numbers of products tends to create confusion and a feeling of being overwhelmed (Huffman & Kahn, 1998). Forcing customers to scroll through long product lists or pages of information is tedious and reflects poor store design (Tilson, Dong, Martin, & Kieke, 1998). The grouping of products into smaller collections and the use of **product selection cues**

such as recommendation systems can reduce confusion and motivate additional product sales (Lee, Kim, & Moon, 2000; Senecal, Kalczynski, & Nantel, 2005). Removing potential confusion and enhancing the enjoyment of shopping is a key element in online retail success (Cai & Xu, 2006; A. D. Cox, Cox, & Anderson, 2005).

The key in this process is to recognize that although online retailers do not face the same physical constraints as store-based retailers, they do face practical constraints in managing a shopper's attention and motivation. For this reason visual merchandising in the online environment is an important concern. How can products best be presented to facilitate a shopper's navigation among the products and positively influence his purchase decision?

VISUAL MERCHANDISING ONLINE

Research was conducted by the author to test the viability of extracting merchandising principles from physical retailing for use as the foundation of design guidelines for online retailing. A set of candidate merchandising principles was selected, an online store guideline based on each principle was formulated, a prototype store was constructed for each guideline, and the stores were usability tested by users.

Store Variation One: Unsought Products

In physical stores shoppers are immersed in an environment where they see many products not specifically related to a conscious shopping goal. Frequently these **unsought products** will attract the shopper's attention and will be purchased. In many online stores only products within a selected category or matching a product search term are displayed. This provides little opportunity for the shopper to be influenced by something outside of their explicit focus.

The following design guideline was applied in a test store: As customers navigate through the online store, other randomly selected products are placed in their view. These interjected products are not the focal point of product presentation, but rather they are displayed as small pictures along the bottom of the screen. These unsought products are swapped out every 30 seconds, independent of other screen content.

Store Variation Two: Affinity Positioning

In physical stores products are often arranged using affinity positioning: placing products that are likely to be purchased together in close physical proximity to one another (Blischok, 1995), often on the same display rack (Buchanan, Simmons, & Bickart, 1999). **Affinity positioning** recognizes that products frequently are bought in groups, and their joint display permits the customer to view related products at the same time, often with one eye fixation. This grouping suggests items that can (and should) be purchased together, thus enhancing the retailer's revenue.

The following design guideline was applied in a test store: Every product category is displayed in conjunction with a related product category to facilitate joint product selection. When a customer chooses a product category for viewing, selected products from a complementary product category are displayed at the bottom of the screen. Complementary products can attract customer attention while the overall focus is the selected product category.

Store Variation Three: Visual Dominated Shopping

In physical stores shoppers do not receive detailed product information as they begin **browsing**. Initial product selection is done visually. Although a customer may be able to take in several hundred products in one eye fixation, it is easy and natural for a customer to be able to quickly find and focus on a single product of interest. Once a shopper focuses on a particular item of interest, they then receive detailed information by further examination of the merchandise, related tags, and/or signage. Customers never seek, nor are given, this information for products in which they are not interested.

The following design guideline was applied in a test store: products are initially displayed to customers in picture form only. More products can be presented to the shopper at one time, since text and other elements which might cause distraction have been removed. Once a customer selects an item of interest additional information is displayed. The store is purposely designed to use minimal text until product information is requested by the shopper.

Store Variation Four: Visual Shopping Cart

In physical stores shoppers accumulate products in shopping carts or similar devices to which they have ready, continuous visual access. Ongoing shopping activities are often related to items already selected for purchase. Customers desiring to make product comparisons can easily glance at merchandise in their shopping cart for assistance. As they travel through the store, their cart provides a frequent visual reminder of their shopping task.

The following design guideline was applied in a test store: Rather than hide the contents of a shopper's cart on another display screen, the customer is presented with an always-visible shopping cart. The shopping cart displays small pictures of the cart contents on the right side of every page. These product pictures make it easier for a customer to keep track of exactly what he has selected for purchase and may influence a customer's later product selection.

Testing Protocol

Undergraduate college students were selected as the target audience for this study, partially because of convenience, but primarily because of their level of experience with both physical and online shopping. The current generation of undergraduate college students represents the first generation to achieve buying power during an era when both physical and online shopping alternatives existed.

The testing framework was based upon **usability** testing practices and guidelines suggested by Barnum, Rubin, and Nielsen (Barnum, 2002; Nielsen, 1999; Nielsen & Mack, 1994; Rubin, 1994). A baseline store was created similar in appearance to store design templates used in Yahoo Shopping's online mall. A variation store was created for each of the previously stated guidelines. These variations were the same as the baseline store except they featured a different store name and color scheme, and employed one of the previously stated guidelines. Each store featured the same selection of fashion products. Fashion items were chosen as the product line to be featured because of the interesting inter-product relationships fashion items possess. A set of shopping tasks was created, giving test participants an overall goal to accomplish while evaluating the stores.

Each test participant interacted with two online stores, typically the baseline store and a variation store (although other testing combinations were recorded as well). A Store Evaluation Worksheet was developed asking test participants a variety of questions about their shopping session. The primary focus of the instrument was the participant's perceptions and preferences for each of the stores they interacted with during testing. Each participant was asked which of the two stores they liked better. They were then presented with seven categories for rating their experience with each store on a 10 point scale—attractive/unattractive, easy to use/hard to use, well organized/poorly organized, easy to find things/hard to find

things, exciting/boring, easy to understand/hard to understand, and efficient/inefficient. These categories were drawn from characteristics of successful stores as suggested by the literature (Jarvenpaa & Ouellete, 1994; Lohse & Spiller, 1998; Nielsen & Norman, 2000; Smith & Whitlark, 2001; Wexelblat & Maes, 1999). This set of questions was followed by additional closed and open-ended questions.

184 undergraduate students participated in the testing, generating 368 store visitation sessions. Several alternative store designs other than those presented here were also considered. In addition to the data collected from above described worksheet, log files maintained by the web server were available for analysis. The evaluation worksheet recorded information allowing each shopper's responses to be paired with their entries in the log.

Testing Results

When examining the store preference question and the seven subjective rating factors for store quality, the results were mixed. No clear indication of preference was present. Several stores scored higher in various categories, but overall the baseline store and the revised stores were very similar in their effect. None of the proposed guidelines outlined here demonstrated *statistically significant* superiority in testing overall.

The variation stores did exhibit clear differences in factors such as time spent in accomplishing tasks and the number of products viewed when completing a task. Both of these measures are significant, as over time they should contribute to additional product sales for a retailer (J. Kim, Fiore, & Lee, 2007). However, given the overall test results, this raises an obvious question about the study goal of extracting online design guidelines from the merchandising literature and practices of physical retailers.

Reflecting on the testing protocol and process, although care was taken in determining an appropriate evaluation protocol, several unavoidable test characteristics eroded the quality of the results. The number of test participants, although large overall, was reduced in statistical power by having their testing spread out over eight variation stores. Focusing the testing on a smaller number of stores may have improved the statistical power of the results.

Perhaps most significantly, participants in the testing process realized that they were not patronizing actual online stores and they were not really choosing products that they would be purchasing. The tasks they were given to complete, although typical and appropriate, were not tasks of their own choosing which they were really interested in accomplishing. Perhaps most importantly, they were not spending real money in the expectation of acquiring real merchandise. Given all of these factors, test participants were not really interacting with the test stores in the same manner as if they were actually shopping for their own benefit.

FUTURE RESEARCH DIRECTIONS

Given that the outcomes of this research were mixed, additional research in this area seems warranted. While partnering with an actual online retailer was not possible for the sake of this research, the possibility of doing that in future research does exist. A more complete picture of the viability of the design variation can be determined by comparing the current practices of a retailer with other design variations under consideration for that retailer. Such a partnering with an actual online retailer would provide extremely valuable data to the researcher, but it would also require extensive trust, cooperation, and, in all likelihood, confidentiality between the online retailer and the researcher.

Although four design guidelines have been proposed here, and a total of eight were tested overall, many more principles can certainly be extracted from store-based retailing literature and practice.

The author continues to believe that by mining the literature of physical retailing store design and merchandising, online retailers may gain valuable insights for future design guidelines.

CONCLUSION

To ignore store-based merchandising principles and practices when creating online stores is believed by this author to be a mistake. This practice robs online store designers of a valuable input to the store creation process. By creating stores that reflect the design principles and practices of physical stores, online retailers can create stores that seem familiar to shoppers and increase sales revenue. By focusing on established best practices in retail merchandising, new insights for online merchandise display may results. Although the research work presented here does not establish statistically significant outcomes, the overall goal of continuing to explore this path seems valid. A wide array of literature exists in store-based merchandising. Online store designers may find great benefit in mining that literature for new design techniques and guidelines.

REFERENCES

Barnum, C. (2002). *Usability Testing and Research*. New York: Longman.

Berman, B., & Evans, J. R. (1998). *Retail Management: A Strategic Approach* (7th ed.). Upper Saddle River, NJ: Prentice Hall.

Blischok, T. J. (1995). Every Transaction Tells a Story. *Chain Store Age Executive, 71*(3), 50–57.

Bryan, D., & Gershman, A. (1999). *Opportunistic Exploration of Large Consumer Product Spaces*. Paper presented at the First ACM Conference on Electronic Commerce, Denver, Colorado.

Buchanan, C., Simmons, C. J., & Bickart, B. A. (1999). Brand Equity Dilution: Retailer Display and Context Brand Effects. *JMR, Journal of Marketing Research, 36*(3), 345. doi:10.2307/3152081

Cai, S., & Xu, Y. (2006). Effects of outcome, process and shopping enjoyment on online consumer behaviour. *Electronic Commerce Research and Applications, 5*(4), 272–281. doi:10.1016/j.elerap.2006.04.004

Chen, L.-d., Gillenson, M. L., & Sherrell, D. L. (2002). Enticing online consumers: an extended technology acceptance perspective. *Information & Management, 39*(8), 705–719. doi:10.1016/S0378-7206(01)00127-6

Childers, T. L., Carr, C. L., Peck, J., & Carseon, S. (2001). Hedonic and Utilitarian Motivations for Online Retail Shopping Behavior. *Journal of Retailing, 77*(4), 511–535. doi:10.1016/S0022-4359(01)00056-2

Cox, A. D., Cox, D., & Anderson, R. D. (2005). Reassessing the pleasures of store shopping. *Journal of Business Research, 58*(3), 250–259. doi:10.1016/S0148-2963(03)00160-7

Cox, K. (1964). The Responsiveness of Food Sales to Shelf Space Changes in Supermarkets. *JMR, Journal of Marketing Research, 1*, 63–67. doi:10.2307/3149924

Cox, K. (1970). The Effect of Shelf Space Upon Sales of Branded Products. *JMR, Journal of Marketing Research, 7*, 55–58. doi:10.2307/3149507

Hart, C., & Davies, M. (1996). The Location and Merchandising of Non-food in Supermarkets. *International Journal of Retail & Distribution Management, 24*(3), 17. doi:10.1108/09590559610147892

Hausman, A. V., & Siekpe, J. S. (2009). The effect of web interface features on consumer online purchase intentions. *Journal of Business Research, 62*(1), 5–13. doi:10.1016/j.jbusres.2008.01.018

Hübscher, R., Pittarese, T., & Lanford, P. (2002). Navigation in e-Business Web Sites. In S. Nansi (Ed.), *Architectural Issues of Web-Enabled Electronic Business*: Idea Group.

Huffman, C., & Kahn, B. E. (1998). Variety for Sale: Mass Customization or Mass Confusion? *Journal of Retailing, 74*(4), 492–514. doi:10.1016/S0022-4359(99)80105-5

Jarvenpaa, S. L., & Ouellete, S. J. (1994). Consumers' Perception of Risk and the Purchase of Apparel from Catalogs. *Journal of Direct Marketing, 8*, 23–36. doi:10.1002/dir.4000080205

Kim, J., Fiore, A. M., & Lee, H.-H. (2007). Influences of online store perception, shopping enjoyment, and shopping involvement on consumer patronage behavior towards an online retailer. *Journal of Retailing and Consumer Services, 14*(2), 95–107. doi:10.1016/j.jretconser.2006.05.001

Kim, S. Y., & Lim, Y. J. (2001). Consumers' Perceived Importance of and Satisfaction with Internet Shopping. *Electronic Markets, 11*(3), 148–154. doi:10.1080/101967801681007988

Kotler, P. (1974). Atmospherics as a Marketing Tool. *Journal of Retailing*, (3): 48–64.

Kotzan, J. A., & Evanson, R. V. (1969). Responsiveness of Drug Store Sales to Shelf Space Allocations. *JMR, Journal of Marketing Research, 1*(6), 465–469. doi:10.2307/3150084

Lee, J., Kim, J., & Moon, J. Y. (2000, April 2000). *What Makes Internet Users Visit Cyber Stores Again? Key Design Factors for Customer Loyalty.* Paper presented at the Conference on Human Factors and Computing Systems, The Hague, The Netherlands.

Levy, M., & Weitz, B. (1998). *Retailing Management* (3rd ed.). New York: Irwin/McGraw-Hill.

Lohse, G. L., & Spiller, P. (1998). Electronic Shopping: Designing Online Stores with Effective Customer Interfaces. *Communications of the ACM, 41*(7), 81–87. doi:10.1145/278476.278491

Netscape Communications Corporation. (1997). *Internet Shopping Network Uses KIVA Server Software from Netscape for Online Retailing Service.* Retrieved July 2, 2003, 2003, from http://wp.netscape.com/newsref/pr/newsrelease550.html

Nielsen, J. (1999). *Designing Web Usability.* Indianapolis, IN: New Riders Publishing.

Nielsen, J., & Mack, R. L. (1994). *Usability Inspection Methods.* New York: Wiley.

Nielsen, J., & Norman, D. (2000). Usability on the Web Isn't a Luxury. *Information Week, 773,* 65–73.

Park, J. H., & Stoel, L. (2002). Apparel Shopping on the Internet: Information Availability on U.S. Apparel Merchant Web Sites. *Journal of Fashion Marketing and Management, 6*(2), 158–176. doi:10.1108/13612020210429908

Petrak, L. (2000). Staking Claim in Cyberspace. *National Provisioner, 214*(9), 47–54.

Pittarese, T. (2003). *Creating Effective Online Fashion Stores: Merchandising in an Online Retail Environment Based on Design Principles from Physical Stores.* Unpublished Doctoral Dissertation, Auburn University.

Qiu, L., & Li, D. (2008). Applying TAM in B2C E-Commerce Research: An Extended Model. *Tsinghua Science and Technology, 13*(3), 265–272. doi:10.1016/S1007-0214(08)70043-9

Richard, M.-O. (2005). Modeling the impact of internet atmospherics on surfer behavior. *Journal of Business Research, 58*(12), 1632–1642. doi:10.1016/j.jbusres.2004.07.009

Rosenberg, J. M. (1995). *Dictionary of Retailing and Merchandising.* New York: Wiley.

Rubin, J. (1994). *Handbook of Usability Testing.* New York: Wiley.

Senecal, S., Kalczynski, P. J., & Nantel, J. (2005). Consumers' decision-making process and their online shopping behavior: a clickstream analysis. *Journal of Business Research, 58*(11), 1599–1608. doi:10.1016/j.jbusres.2004.06.003

Smith, S. M., & Whitlark, D. B. (2001). Men and Women Online: What Makes Them Click? *Marketing Research, 13*(2), 20–26.

Szymanski, D. M., & Hise, R. T. (2000). e-Satisfaction: An Initial Examination. *Journal of Retailing, 76*(3), 309–323. doi:10.1016/S0022-4359(00)00035-X

Tilson, R., Dong, J., Martin, S., & Kieke, E. (1998). *Factors and Principles Affecting the Usability of Four e-Commerce Sites.* Paper presented at the Fourth Conference on Human Factors and the Web, AT&T Labs USA.

Wexelblat, A., & Maes, P. (1999). *Footprints: History-Rich Tools for Information Foraging.* Paper presented at the Conference on Human Factors and Computing Systems.

Zakon, R. H. (2002, November 1, 2006). *Hobbes' Internet Timeline 8.2.* Retrieved March 27, 2009, from http://www.zakon.org/robert/internet/timeline/

KEY TERMS AND DEFINITIONS

Affinity Positioning: physical placement and combined visual merchandising of products frequently purchased together

Atmospherics: recognition that the entire physical retail experience influences the purchase process; an attempt to positively control the entire retail environment to motivate purchasing

Browsing: a shopper's opportunistic exploration of a retail environment; unfocused navigation and viewing of products

Merchandising: activities employed by a retailer to entice consumers to make a purchase

Shopping: a shopper's focused exploration of a retail environment in search of a particular product or type of product; distinct from browsing based on the shopper's thought process and intent

Unsought Products: products selected by consumers on the spur of the moment without prior intent and often without full evaluation of the purchase decision; often referred to as impulse purchases

Visual Merchandising: merchandising activities that particularly focus on the presentation and display of merchandise in a retail setting

Webmospherics: application of the concept of atmospherics to web-based shopping; an attempt to control the entire web-shopping experience to motivate online purchasing

Section 7
Online Consumer Behavior

Chapter 62
Internet Consumer Behavior:
Flow and Emotions

Marie-Odile Richard
University of Montreal, Canada

Michel Laroche
Concordia University, Canada

INTRODUCTION

As the internet is a new medium and a new distribution channel, it is important to understand the behavior of site visitors. This requires the development of a new model of Internet consumer behavior. The model in Figure 1-1 is an original model based on Mehrabian and Russell's (1974) *SOR* paradigm (i.e., *s*timulus, *o*rganism, *r*esponse) which is explicated in this chapter and the next three ones. In this chapter we will explain the shaded areas of Figure 1

BACKGROUND

The key concepts which are part of the stimulus dimension of *SOR*, i.e., inputs to the organism and response variables are flow, emotions and web atmospherics. This chapter develops the flow construct, composed of skills, challenge and interactivity, and the emotions construct, composed of pleasure, arousal and dominance. The next chapter will develop the web atmospherics variables.

Flow

Flow is defined as a state occurring during internet navigation which: *1)* is characterized by a seamless sequence of responses facilitated by machine interactivity; *2)* is intrinsically enjoyable; *3)* is accompanied by a loss of self-consciousness; and *4)* is self-reinforcing and *5)* leads to a sense of playfulness (Hoffman & Novak, 1996). Flow is related to skills, challenges and interactivity.

DOI: 10.4018/978-1-61520-611-7.ch062

Figure 1. Model of consumer navigation behavior: flow and emotions **(***Source: Adapted from Richard, M.O. (2009). Modeling the internet behavior of visitors by the study of cognitive variables and moderators, unpublished doctoral dissertation, HEC-Montreal Business School.***)**

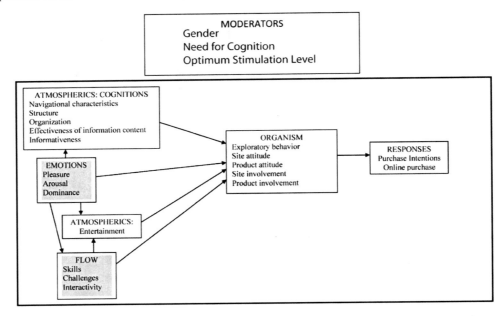

Skills

Novak, Hoffman and Yung (2000) define *skills* as the consumer's capacity for action during the online navigation process. Ghani and Deshpande (1994) report that skills directly affect the flow: they show that the level of perceived skills, as well as perceived challenges, is positively associated with the achievement of flow which, in turn, predicts exploratory behavior. Ghani (1991) discovers that flow is related to exploratory use behavior (considered as the consequences of flow; Hoffman & Novak, 1996). Ghani and Deshpande (1994) state that flow is present when skills and challenges are both high, since they independently contribute to the flow (Novak, Hoffman, & Yung, 2000). Although they operate independently, studies demonstrate that high skill and high challenge levels lead to satisfying consumer experiences on the Internet (Csikszentmihalyi, 2000; Richard & Chandra, 2005). Although marginally significant, skills are a predictor of perceived interactivity and

people with high skills levels perceive the website as having greater interactivity (Jee & Lee, 2002; Wu, 2000).

Challenge

Another predictor of flow is challenge in internet activities. Novak, Hoffman, and Yung (2000) define challenges as the opportunities for action on the internet. Skills at navigating the web do not affect the surfing experiences and behavior of site visitors, since those planning to make online purchases have already developed basic navigational skills. But, positive challenges have an important influence on web experiences, since visitors must use their skills and abilities in navigating the site, learning how to interact with it, process information and make decisions on the purchase of needed products. On the other hand, negative challenges lead to slow downloading times, frustration and aborted buying processes. Positive challenges lead to positive site and product attitudes, as well as purchase intentions and behavior (Koufaris, Kambil, & LaBarbera, 2001).

The level of challenges may have an impact on attitudes toward the website. Websites that are not challenging are considered boring sites (Anand & Sternthal, 1990). If a website offers enough challenges, a positive attitude is attainable by surfers (Luna, Peracchio, & de Juan, 2002). Challenges are positively related to attitudes towards the site only if the level is not excessive. Flow can occur if surfers are challenged enough, that is neither are they bored nor do they reach the point of anxiety (Csikszentmihalyi, 2000).

Balance Between Skills and Challenge

To obtain an autotelic experience, flow arises from a balance between challenges (i.e., action opportunities) and skills (i.e., action capabilities; Csikszentmihalyi, 2000). For Massimini and Carli (1988), flow begins when skills and challenges are balanced and are above individual means. However, there are limitations on creation of flow as it does not depend entirely on either the objective nature of the challenges or the objective skills level (Csikszentmihalyi, 2000). The presence of flow depends on perceptions of skills and challenge. With the same level of challenge, people can feel anxious, then bored, and in flow immediately afterward and thus, it is impossible to predict in which state people will be (Csikszentmihalyi, 2000).

People skilled at using the web and finding it challenging more likely search for and purchase online a wide range of products; hence, skills and challenges predict online consumers search and purchase behavior (Novak, Hoffman, & Yung, 2000). There is a positive relationship between the difference between skills and challenges and online search and purchase of computer-related products, but a negative one with search and purchase of non-computers related products in traditional media (Novak, Hoffman, & Yung,

2000). If skills are greater than challenge, search for entertainment online and purchase in retail stores will ensue. If challenges are greater than skills, search and purchase in traditional media will occur (Novak, Hoffman, & Yung, 2000). Challenges positively affect information search and perceived interactivity. They may create arousal and lead to more site activities (Jee & Lee, 2002).

Interactivity

The Internet incorporates higher vividness and *interactivity* than traditional media (Coyle & Thorson, 2001). It is characterized by the following: interactivity, irrelevance of distance and time, low set-up costs, wide coverage, and ease of entry (Berthon, Pitt, & Watson, 1996). Among these, interactivity is a key advantage (Rafaeli & Sudweeks, 1997).

Classified as interactivity on the Internet are: clicking, providing feedback, or information search (Gallagher, Foster, & Parsons, 2001). Interactive sites give opportunities to engage customers in exchanges with the website or its sponsor. There are several interactive functions: online problem diagnostics, games, virtual reality displays, and user groups. Other interactive functions used in other media are: coupons, dealer locators, surveys, and contact information (Gallagher, Foster, & Parsons, 2001).

Conceptualization of Interactivity

There is little agreement on how interactivity should be conceptualized (Heeter, 2000).

Initially, interactivity was considered as communication through a medium, and later defined as a property of the medium (Ha & James, 1998). Interactivity has been operationalized as a part of the communication process (Kirsch, 1997), a medium characteristic (Hoffman and Novak 1996), an individual trait (Chen, 1984), a psychological state (Newhagen, Corders, & Levy, 1995), and a variable characteristic of communication settings (Rafaeli, 1988).

Definitions of Interactivity

Several definitions of interactivity are:

- The extent of sequencing of messages, especially whether later messages relate to earlier messages (Rafaeli & Sudweeks. 1997);
- The ability of users to modify in real time the form and the content of a mediated environment (Steuer, 1992);
- The ability of two or more communication parties to act on each other, on the communication medium, and on the messages and their degree of synchronization (Liu & Shrum, 2002).
- The surfers' perceptions that the site provides effective and personalized methods to search and retrieve information, and permits surfers to build the information to which they would be exposed (Luna, Peracchio, & de Juan, 2002).

Dimensions of Interactivity

- Liu and Shrum (2002) propose *three* dimensions: (1) active control, as users' ability to voluntarily participate in and instrumentally influence a communication; (2) two-way communication, as the bi-directional flow of information; and (3) synchronicity, as the speed of the interaction. Active control is a voluntary and instrumental action that directly influences the surfer's experience; two-way communication is the ability for reciprocal communication between companies and users; and synchronicity is the degree to which users' input and the response they receive from the communication are simultaneous.

- Ha and James (1998) use interpersonal and mechanical perspectives. Their *five* dimensions of interactivity are: playfulness, choice, connectedness, information collection, and reciprocal communication. Applied to websites, an interactive site has good mapping, quick transitions between input and resulting actions, and several ways to manipulate its contents.

Influences of Interactivity

Interactivity impacts *loyalty* for multiple reasons. For Alba et al. (1997), interactivity enables search to quickly locate a desired product, thereby replacing dependence on memory. Another is that interactivity increases the amount of information presented to consumers to help them choose desired products. Finally, the navigational process facilitated by interactivity increases freedom of choice and the level of surfer control (Hoffman & Novak, 1996).

Interactivity reflects the perception that the *information is relevant* to consumer needs (Fortin & Dholakia, 2000), leading to positive attitude formation (MacInnis & Jaworski, 1989). For Bucy (2003) interactivity gives sites their "stickiness," or continuing appeal beyond expected content. Sundar, Kalyanaraman and Brown (2003) show that interactivity helps in customization, i.e., surfers receive unique combinations of messages. They find strong correlations between perceived interactivity and perceived relevance of, and involvement with, information content, which predicts website attitudes.

Although interactivity and vividness are attributes of computer-mediated environments and not similar to involvement, site involvement hides effects due to increasing levels of vividness and interactivity. The more site attitudes are positive, the more interactive and vivid they are (Richard & Chandra, 2005). Others show that increased interactivity contributes to higher *site involvement* (Bucy, 2003) and more positive attitudes toward the portal (Sundar, Kalyanaraman, & Brown, 2003). Also, interactivity relates to *exploratory behavior*, and greater interactions between surfers and the web when their search for information leads to greater exploratory behavior.

There are *disagreements* regarding the influence of interactivity on purchase intentions and other behavioral changes. Some find it has a direct influence on purchase intention (Wu, 2000; Yoo & Stout, 2001), whereas for others interactivity influences decision making through perceived website quality (Ghose & Dou, 1998). Perceived interactivity has a direct impact on intentions to revisit a website and on consumer purchases from it (Luna, Peracchio, & de Juan, 2002).

Emotions

Studies using emotions focus on emotional responses to ads, and the mediating role of emotions on satisfaction (Phillips & Baumgartner, 2002).

Basic PAD Model

The basic model used in marketing is Mehrabian and Russell's (1974) *PAD* model, consisting of three dimensions: *arousal* relates to feelings of being stimulated, excited and aroused; *pleasure* relates to feelings of happiness, satisfaction or contentment; *dominance* relates to feelings of being in control, important and autonomous. It is useful for studying emotions in retail environments (Sherman, Mathur, & Smith, 1997) and capturing emotional components of consumption experiences (Havlena & Holbrook, 1986). By extension, it is useful for web navigation behavior. The role of dominance in approach-avoidance behavior remains unclear and has received little research attention. Foxall and Greenley (1999) find that *PAD* explains approach-avoidance behavior over several situations. Biggers and Rankis (1983) find more approach behavior toward situations with high dominance and more avoidance behavior toward situation with low dominance. This ap-

proach is capable of characterizing emotional responses in internet navigation (Mehrabian & Russell, 1974).

Hierarchy of Emotions and Cognitions

In the past, researchers used "liking an advertisement" (A_{ad}) to measure affect and claimed a direct link between affect and cognition, that cognition precedes affect, or that affective reactions are mediated by cognition (Greenwald & Leavitt, 1984). Others suggest that cognition and affect are separate and distinct in persuasion (Petty et al., 1993).

Two Schools of Thought Contribute to Understanding These Relationships

- The *emotion-cognition model* (Zajonc & Markus, 1982). In the servicescapes model, the emotional process begins when some message, object, or event triggers a cognitive appraisal resulting in evaluations mediated by beliefs and shaped by personal values (Bitner, 1992). Izard, Kagan, & Zajonc (1984) and Zajonc and Markus (1982) posit that emotions take place without antecedent cognitive processes, and can be generated by biological, sensory or cognitive events. Arousal and motor activities are hard representations of emotions. The cognitive experience is not part of the emotional process, and the experience of emotion is uniquely the cognition of having one. Izard, Kagan, & Zajonc (1984) do not deny that cognition is a sufficient condition to produce emotions, the question is whether it is a necessary cause.

- The *cognition-emotion model* (Lazarus, 1991) posits the role of cognition as a necessary but not sufficient condition to elicit emotions. External and internal cues are appraised in terms of one's own experience and goals. Appraisal of the significance of the person-environment relationship is necessary and sufficient; without personal appraisal there is no emotion; with an appraisal an emotion is generated. Chebat and Michon (2003) find support for this hierarchy in studying the effects of ambient scent on emotions and cognitions.

Empirical Evidence

In studies of website quality, few combine emotions and cognitions. There is a need to further understand the interplay and the hierarchy of cognitions and emotions in website navigation. Studies of emotions as mediator of responses to advertising show that cognition can drive affect (Edell & Burke, 1987), while others posit that affect can directly influence attitudes (Brown & Stayman, 1992) and that cognitive-based models fail to measure emotions associated with information sources (Edell & Burke, 1987). Support for the influence of affect has been found in studies of mood (Petty et al. 1993), judgment (Pham et al., 2001), susceptibility (Fabrigar & Petty, 1999), and those linking affect and behavioral prediction (Smith, Haugtvedt, & Petty, 1994). Advertising researchers struggle with two questions: what is more predictive of consumer response-thoughts or feelings? In the paradigm of cognitive, affective and conative attitudes do cognitions dominate and do they mediate the relationship between affect and conation? These issues have yet to be resolved (Morris et al., 2002) and the question of whether evaluation is preceded by low-level affective processes, low-level cognitive processes, or both represents a fertile area for research (Ajzen, 2001).

Relationship between Arousal and Pleasure

Only two studies look at the relationship between arousal and pleasure. Kaltcheva and Weitz (2006) find that arousal mediates the relationship between retail physical environment and pleasure. Wang et al. (2007) also find a direct positive relationship between arousal and pleasure.

Emotions and Site Attitudes

When consumers feel pleasure, it influences attitudes, and affective responses play an important role in perceptions (Isen, 1984). Affective conditioning theory predicts that a pleasant experience transfers to attitudes (Madden, Allen, & Twible, 1988). The applicability of classical conditioning to websites seems likely, as consumers transfer positive (or negative) feelings from interaction with the website to their attitudes toward it. In addition, because control is desirable, if consumers perceive the website as enhancing their control, their site attitude is more favorable (Peterman, Rohem, & Haugtvedt, 1999). Thus, when users experience high levels of pleasure and dominance, they have a more favorable site attitude.

FUTURE RESEARCH DIRECTIONS

- Clarify the structure and operationalization of the flow experience.
- Clarify the structure and operationalization of site interactivity.
- Determine whether site evaluation is preceded by low-level affective processes, low-level cognitive processes, or both.

CONCLUSION

Flow and emotions are two major inputs to the evaluations of websites. Their important role in the model has been explicated. The next chapter covers the other major input, i.e., web atmospherics.

REFERENCES

Ajzen, I. (2001). Nature and operation of attitudes. *Annual Review of Psychology, 52*(1), 27–58. doi:10.1146/annurev.psych.52.1.27

Alba, J., Lynch, J., Weitz, B., Janiszevski, C., Lutz, R., Sawyer, A., & Wood, S. (1997). Interactive home shopping: Consumer, retailer and manufacturer incentives to participate in electronic marketplaces. *Journal of Marketing, 61*(July), 38–53. doi:10.2307/1251788

Anand, P., & Sternthal, B. (1990). Ease of message processing as a moderator of repetition effects in advertising. *JMR, Journal of Marketing Research, 27*(August), 345–353. doi:10.2307/3172591

Berthon, P., Pitt, L., & Watson, R. T. (1996). The world wide web as an advertising medium: Toward an understanding of conversion efficiency. *Journal of Advertising Research, 36*(Jan-Feb), 43–54.

Biggers, T., & Rankis, O. E. (1983). Dominance-submissiveness as an affective response to situations and as a predictor of approach-avoidance. *Social Behavior and Personality, 11*(2), 61–69. doi:10.2224/sbp.1983.11.2.61

Bitner, M. J. (1992). Servicescapes: The impact of physical surroundings on customers and employees. *Journal of Marketing, 56*(2), 57–71. doi:10.2307/1252042

Brown, S. P., & Stayman, D. M. (1992). Antecedents and consequences of attitudes toward the ad: A meta analysis. *The Journal of Consumer Research, 19*(June), 4–51.

Bucy, E. P. (2003). The interactivity paradox: Closer to the news but confused. In E.P. Bucy & J.E. Newhagen (eds.), *Media access: Social and psychological dimensions of new technology use* (pp. 47-72). Mahwah, NJ: Erlbaum.

Chebat, J. C., & Michon, R. (2003). Impact of ambient odors on mall shoppers' emotions, cognition, and spending: A test of competitive causal theories. *Journal of Business Research, 56*, 529–539. doi:10.1016/S0148-2963(01)00247-8

Chen, M. (1984). Computers in the lives of our children: Looking back on a generation of television research. In R. Rice, et al, (eds.), *The New Media: Communication, Research and Technology,* (pp. 269-286). Beverly Hills, CA: Sage.

Coyle, J. R., & Thorson, E. (2001). The effects of progressive levels of interactivity and vividness in web marketing sites. *Journal of Advertising, 30*(3), 65–77.

Csikszentmihalyi, M. (2000). *Beyond boredom and anxiety: Experiencing flow in work and play.* San Francisco, CA: Jossey-Bass.

Edell, J. A., & Burke, M. C. (1984). The moderating effects of attitude toward an ad on ad effectiveness under different processing conditions. In T.C. Kinnear (ed.), *Advances in Consumer Research,* (pp. 644-649). Ann Arbor, MI: Association for Consumer Research.

Fabrigar, L. R., & Petty, R. E. (1999). The role of the affective and cognitive bases of attitudes in susceptibility to affective and cognitively based persuasion. *Personality and Social Psychology Bulletin, 25*(3), 363–381. doi:10.1177/0146167299025003008

Fortin, D. R., & Dholakia, R. R. (2000). The impact of interactivity and vividness on involvement: An empirical test of the Hoffman-Novak model. *INFORMS Conference on Understanding consumer behavior on the Internet.*

Foxall, G. R., & Greenley, G. E. (1999). Consumers' emotional responses to service environments. *Journal of Business Research, 46*, 149–158. doi:10.1016/S0148-2963(98)00018-6

Gallagher, K., Foster, K. D., & Parsons, J. (2001). The medium is not the message: Advertising effectiveness and content evaluation in print and on the web. *Journal of Advertising Research, 41*(4), 57–70.

Ghani, J. A. (1991). Flow in human-computer interactions: Test of a model. In J. Carey (ed.), *Human factors in management information systems: An organizational perspective* 3. Norwood, NJ: Ablex.

Ghani, J. A., & Deshpande, S. P. (1994). Task characteristics and the experience of optimal flow in human-computer interaction. *The Journal of Psychology, 128*(4), 381–391.

Ghose, S., & Dou, W. (1998). Interactive functions and their impacts on the appeal of Internet presence sites. *Journal of Advertising Research, 38*(2), 29–43.

Greenwald, A. G., & Leavitt, C. (1984). Audience involvement in advertising: Four levels. *The Journal of Consumer Research, 11*(June), 581–592. doi:10.1086/208994

Ha, L., & James, E. L. (1998). Interactivity reexamined: A baseline analysis of early business web sites. *Journal of Broadcasting & Electronic Media, 42*(4), 457–469.

Havlena, W. J., & Holbrook, M. B. (1986). The varieties of consumption experience: Comparing two typologies of emotions in consumer behavior. *The Journal of Consumer Research, 13*, 394–404. doi:10.1086/209078

Heeter, C. (2000). Interactivity in the context of designed experience. *Journal of Interactive Advertising, 1*(1). Retrieved from www.jiad.org/vol1/no1/heeter/index.html

Hoffman, D. L., & Novak, T. P. (1996). Marketing in hypermedia computer-mediated environments: Conceptual foundations. *Journal of Marketing, 60*(3), 50–68. doi:10.2307/1251841

Isen, A. M. (1984). Toward understanding the role of affect in cognition. In R.S. Wyer & T.K. Srull (eds). *Handbook of Social Cognition*, 3 (pp. 179-236). Mahwah, NJ: Erlbaum

Izard, C. E., Kagan, J., & Zajonc, R. B. (1984). *Emotions, cognitions, and behaviour.* Cambridge, MA: Cambridge Press.

Jee, J., & Lee, W. N. (2002). Antecedents and consequences of perceived interactivity: An exploratory study. *Journal of Interactive Advertising, 3*(1), 1–16.

Kaltcheva, V. D., & Weitz, B. A. (2006). When should a retailer create an exciting store environment? *Journal of Marketing, 70*(January), 107–118. doi:10.1509/jmkg.2006.70.1.107

Kirsch, D. (1997). Interactivity and multimedia interfaces. *Instructional Science, 25*, 79–96. doi:10.1023/A:1002915430871

Koufaris, M., Kambil, A., & Labarbera, P. A. (2001). Consumer behavior in Web-based commerce: An empirical study. *International Journal of Electronic Commerce, 6*(2), 115–138.

Lazarus, R. S. (1991). *Emotion and adaptation.* New York: Oxford Press.

Liu, Y., & Shrum, L. J. (2002). What is interactivity and is it always such a good thing? Implications of definition, person, and situation for the influence of interactivity on advertising effectiveness. *Journal of Advertising, 31*(4), 53–64.

Luna, D., Peracchio, L. A., & de Juan, M. D. (2002). Cross-cultural and cognitive aspects of website navigation. *Journal of the Academy of Marketing Science, 30*(4), 397–410. doi:10.1177/009207002236913

MacInnis, D. J., & Jaworski, B. J. (1989). Information processing from advertisements: Toward an integrative framework. *Journal of Marketing, 53*(Oct), 1–23. doi:10.2307/1251376

Madden, T. J., Allen, C. T., & Twible, J. L. (1988). Attitude toward the ad: An assessment of diverse measurement indices under different processing sets. *JMR, Journal of Marketing Research, 25*(Aug), 242–252. doi:10.2307/3172527

Massimini, F., & Carli, M. (1988). The systematic assessment of flow in daily experience. In M. Csikszentmihalyi & I. Csikszentmihalyi, (eds.), *Optimal experience: Psychological studies of flow in consciousness* (pp. 288-306). New York: Cambridge.

Mehrabian, A., & Russell, J. A. (1974). The basic emotional impact of environments. *Perceptual and Motor Skills, 38*, 283–301.

Morris, J. D., Woo, C., Geason, J., & Kim, J. (2002). The power of affect: Predicting intention. *Journal of Advertising Research, 42*(3), 7–17.

Newhagen, J. E., Corders, J. W., & Levy, M. R. (1995). Audience scope and the perception of interactivity in viewer mail on the internet. *The Journal of Communication, 45*(3), 164–175. doi:10.1111/j.1460-2466.1995.tb00748.x

Novak, T. P., Hoffman, D. L., & Yung, Y. F. (2000). Modeling the flow construct in online environments: A structural modeling approach. *Marketing Science, 19*(1), 22–42. doi:10.1287/mksc.19.1.22.15184

Peterman, M. L., Rohem, H. A. J., & Haugtvedt, C. P. (1999). An exploratory attribution analysis of attitudes toward the WWW as a product information source. *Advances in Consumer Research. Association for Consumer Research (U. S.), 26*, 75–79.

Petty, R. E., Schumann, D. W., Richman, S. A., & Strathman, A. J. (1993). Positive mood and persuasion: Different roles for affect under high- and low-elaboration conditions. *Journal of Personality and Social Psychology, 64*, 5–20. doi:10.1037/0022-3514.64.1.5

Pham, M., Cohen, J. B., Pracejus, J., & Hughes, G. (2001). Affect Monitoring and the Primacy of Feelings in Judgment. *The Journal of Consumer Research, 28*(September), 167–188. doi:10.1086/322896

Phillips, D. M., & Baumgartner, H. (2002). The role of consumption emotions in the satisfaction response. *Journal of Consumer Psychology, 12*(3), 243–252. doi:10.1207/S15327663JCP1203_06

Rafaeli, S. (1988). Interactivity from new media to communication. In R.P. Hawkins, J.M. Wiermann, & S. Pingree, (eds.), *Advancing communication science: Merging mass and interpersonal processes,* (pp. 110-134). Beverly Hills, CA: Sage.

Rafaeli, S., & Sudweeks, F. (1997). Networked interactivity. *Journal of Computer Mediated Communication*. Retrieved from www.207.201.161.120/jcmc/vol2/issue4/rafaeli.sudweeks.html

Richard, M. O. (2009). *Modeling the internet behavior of visitors by the study of cognitive variables and moderators.* Unpublished doctoral dissertation, HEC-Montreal, Canada.

Richard, M. O., & Chandra, R. (2005). A model of consumer web navigational behavior: Conceptual development and application. *Journal of Business Research, 58*(8), 1019–1029. doi:10.1016/j.jbusres.2004.04.001

Sherman, E., Mathur, A., & Smith, R. B. (1997). Store environment and consumer purchase behavior: Mediating role of cognitions. *Psychology and Marketing, 14*, 361–378. doi:10.1002/(SICI)1520-6793(199707)14:4<361::AID-MAR4>3.0.CO;2-7

Smith, S. M., Haugtvedt, C. P., & Petty, R. E. (1994). Attitudes and recycling: Does the measurement of affect enhance behavioral prediction? *Psychology and Marketing, 11*(4), 359–374. doi:10.1002/mar.4220110405

Steuer, J. (1992). Defining virtual reality: Dimensions determining telepresence. *The Journal of Communication, 42*(4), 73–93. doi:10.1111/j.1460-2466.1992.tb00812.x

Sundar, S. S., Kalyanaraman, S., & Brown, J. (2003). Explicating Web site interactivity: Impression formation effects in political campaign sites. *Communication Research, 30*(1), 30–59. doi:10.1177/0093650202239025

Wang, L. C., Baker, J., Wagner, J. A., & Wakefield, K. (2007). Can a retail web site be social? *Journal of Marketing, 71*(July), 143–157. doi:10.1509/jmkg.71.3.143

Wu, G. (2000). *The role of perceived interactivity in interactive ad processing.* Unpublished dissertation, Texas at Austin.

Yoo, C. Y., & Stout, P. A. (2001). Factors affecting users' interactivity with the web site and the consequences of users' interactivity. In C.R. Taylor (ed.), *Proceedings,* (pp. 53-61). Villanova, PA: American Academy of Advertising.

Zajonc, R. B., & Markus, H. (1982). Affective and Cognitive Factors in Preferences. *The Journal of Consumer Research, 9,* 123–131. doi:10.1086/208905

ADDITIONAL READING

Richard, M. O. (2005). Modeling the Impact of Internet Atmospherics on Surfer Behavior. *Journal of Business Research, 58*(12), 1632–1642. doi:10.1016/j.jbusres.2004.07.009

KEY TERMS AND DEFINITIONS

Active Control: ability to voluntarily participate in and instrumentally influence a communication.

Arousal: feelings of being stimulated, excited and aroused.

Challenge: opportunities for action on the Internet.

Dominance: feelings of being in control, important and autonomous.

Flow: state occurring during internet navigation which is intrinsically enjoyable, accompanied by loss of self-consciousness, self-reinforcing and leads to a sense of playfulness.

Interactivity: degree several communication parties act on each other, the communication medium, and the messages and their synchronization.

Pleasure: feelings of happiness, satisfaction or contentment.

Skills: capacity for action during the online navigation process.

Synchronicity: degree to which users' input and the response they receive from the communication are simultaneous.

Two-Way Communication: ability for reciprocal communication between companies and users.

Chapter 63
Internet Consumer Behavior:
Web Atmospherics

Marie-Odile Richard
University of Montreal, Canada

Michel Laroche
Concordia University, Canada

INTRODUCTION

This chapter develops the major components of web atmospherics (Richard, 2005). In retailing research, retail atmospherics (e.g., scents, color, design) are very important to the success of retailers. Similarly, Richard (2005) demonstrates that web atmospherics are important to the development of positive attitudes toward the website and the products it describes. In Figure 1, these are the shaded areas.

BACKGROUND

Web atmospherics are the conscious development of website environment to induce a positive response by visitors. These are critical to the effectiveness of a site since they determine consumer online brows-

ing and purchase behavior. Six variables are part of web atmospherics: navigational characteristics, website structure, website organization, effectiveness of its content, website informativeness, and website entertainment.

Navigational Characteristics

Characteristics of the products and websites encountered early in online browsing can influence the level of arousal and pleasure (emotions) that consumers experience, and thus can influence their shopping behavior. Two manipulations by Menon and Kahn (2002) show that if the starting experiences encountered by consumers in a simulated internet shopping trip are high in pleasure, then there is a positive influence on approach behavior (attitudes) and shoppers engage in more arousing activities such as more exploration and tendencies

DOI: 10.4018/978-1-61520-611-7.ch063

Figure 1. Model of consumer navigation behavior: web atmospherics(Source: Adapted from Richard, M.O. (2009). Modeling the internet behavior of visitors by the study of cognitive variables and moderators, unpublished doctoral dissertation, HEC-Montreal Business School.)

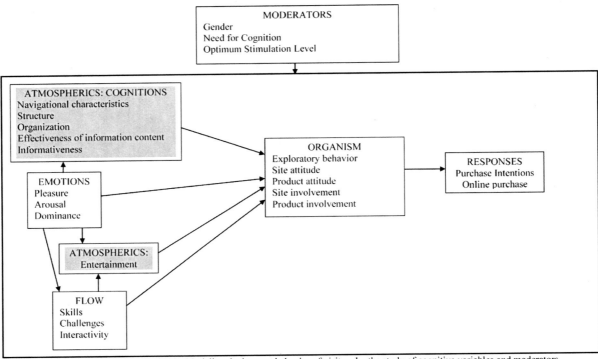

Source: Adapted from Richard, M.O. (2009). Modeling the internet behavior of visitors by the study of cognitive variables and moderators, unpublished doctoral dissertation, HEC-Montreal Business School.

to examine new products and stores (Menon & Kahn, 2002).

Lynch, Kent and Srinivasan (2001) identify three characteristics of a website (i.e., site quality, affect and trust) that affect purchase behavior. *Site quality* is represented by ease of use, provision of helpful graphics, usefulness of search engines, and completeness of information (Lynch, Kent, & Srinivasan, 2001). Online sellers believe that site quality influences surfers' probability of buying during the visit and returning to visit the website (Lynch, Kent, & Srinivasan, 2001). The impact of site quality on purchase intentions depends on the selected product category and the world region examined (Lynch, Kent, & Srinivasan, 2001).

Wayfinding

In brick-and-mortar shops, physical maneuvering of a store's environment (i.e., social, visual and design factors) by consumers is called *wayfinding* (Passini, 1984). It is also possible to apply the wayfinding concept to the Internet, but the physical maneuvering process is replaced with maneuvering through scrolling and linking on the Web. Wayfinding on the web is labeled *navigation*. Hoffman and Novak (1996) define navigation as the process of self-directed movement through a computer-mediated environment. Navigational cues are important in brick-and-mortar stores as well as on the web. Text and icon links are cues that help consumers in navigation (Hoffman & Novak, 1996).

High- and Low-Task Relevant Cues

There are two categories of cues: *high-task* relevant cues and *low-task*-relevant or design cues (Eroglu, Machleit, & Davis 2001). Among navigational cues, there are 'next', 'previous links', navigation bars, and site indexes with navigation bars. If surfers' navigational control is hindered by navigational cues, they may indirectly develop avoidance behavior (i.e., negative attitudes) toward the site, such as stopping exploratory site navigation, leaving the site, locating and browsing similar websites. The attitude-behavior literature suggests that attitudes lead to behavioral intentions and behavior (Eagly & Chaiken, 1993). If surfers experience negative attitudes toward a website, they likely develop negative behavior toward it.

Intentions to *revisit* websites, one of the variables explaining attitudes toward a website, are stimulated by good information on the website, frequent change and newness in its content, personalized services, and contests (Ellsworth & Ellsworth 1997). According to Chaffey et al. (2000), other determinants of customers' intentions to return to the website are high-quality content, ease of use, fast downloading, and frequent updating.

In the same vein, Ducoffe (1996) states that both informative elements (via the central route) and creative and entertaining elements (via the peripheral route) in Internet ads have positive effects on perceptions of the value of these ads. Both creative or entertaining and informative elements of a site affect attitudes towards the site, which affects behavioral intentions to revisit (Supphellen & Nysveen 2001).

Evaluation of Websites

Sandvig and Bajwa (2004) analyze the qualitative evaluation of websites. Among most liked attributes are simple layouts, useful and well organized information, simple and comprehensive menus, ease in following menu options, ease in transitions between pages, ease in navigating (browse), good use of graphics and color, visually appealing, and user friendly. Among least liked attributes are outdated links, incomplete and outdated information, information overload on pages, inability to find needed information, cluttered and disorganized information, difficult search options, confusing menus, slow download-times, and small fonts.

Structure of the Website

Store layouts, which improve consumer's wayfinding, are important to the success of retailers. This is also true with the Internet, as it is easy to leave a site in order to surf other competitive sites. Among all design elements of a store layout, signage is an important one. In an online retailing context, layout refers to the *structure* of a site.

The structure of websites influences online information search. Huizingh (2000) reports four navigational types of structure: a tree, a tree with a return-to-home page button, a tree with some horizontal links and an extensive network. Most websites have a simple structure: over 60% had a tree structure or a tree structure with a back to home page button. For Poruban (2002), a tree structure helps consumers to move and access information easily. Consumers must learn the navigational cues of the site. The easier it is to use, the more cognitive capacities are available to process information in this site, and goal achievement results in a higher product-brand recall, attitude toward the retailer, site attitude and/or product purchase intentions.

An efficient online site structure increases the motivation and ability of consumers to search for information (Celsi & Olson, 1988). Similarly, the more efficient and effective is the structure, the better is the ability to process product information, diminishing the cost of search, permitting a faster search, increasing the probability of success, and enhancing attitudes toward the website (Elliott & Speck, 2005). Thus, the consumer surfing the site more likely acquires the information needed to develop not only purchase intentions but also positive attitudes toward the retailers and the websites they developed (Griffith, 2005).

Organization of the Website

Early in the adoption of the Internet by marketing researchers, the organization of the information in websites was not a major concern of website designers. Over time, they developed good website designs. Early on, they found that a great deal of information on a site may be interesting to visitors if they find the presentation of information logical and easy to understand.

Organization is defined as the ability of a website to arrange content, information, images, and graphics in order to increase the clarity of the information provided and to make it easier for visitors to find the information they need (Chen & Wells, 1999). Thus, a well-organized website is less complex, more user friendly, and increases the quality of a visitor's experience at the site, improving the effectiveness of the website.

Organization of a website is evaluated by elements such as effective arrangement of content, hyperlinks, and graphics, its e-comprehension, its readability, the chunking of its information and its complexity (Bauer, Grether, & Leach, 2002; Leong, Ewing, & Pitt, 2002). According to the Elaboration Likelihood Model (ELM), organization of a website is a high relevant cue inducing surfers to follow the central route, and for marketers to evaluate how well a website presents itself and for designers how it tour-guides its surfers. Poor organization is caused by too many links, layers or animations, leading surfers to develop lower site attitudes and involvement (Chen & Wells, 1999).

Effectiveness of the Information Content of the Website

Effectiveness of information content is defined as the currency of the information content of a website and to the degree that the information

on a website is convenient, accurate, up-to-date, complete and relevant to visitors (Richard 2005). Even though most studies show that perception of site content can be measured by its level of information and detailed and specific information levels on its products or other relevant topics, Dolakia and Rego (1998) find the information content of Web pages, per se, does not attract visitors. It may be that sometimes the information is not easy to find on a website. Online purchasers frequently complain that sites they would like to patronize have inadequate navigation and search engine capabilities. Thus, it is important to reduce irrelevant information, improve information organization and offer better information processing aids (Wolfinbarger & Gilly, 2001).

Information is important to consumers who use websites in a *goal-directed* fashion; the availability of information is one reason that many surfers view search and purchase on the Internet as a utilitarian activity (Wolfinbarger & Gilly, 2001). Product information includes the amount, accuracy, and form of information about products (i.e., goods and/or services) offered on a website. Since e-consumers cannot physically examine a product, they depend on information to identify, compare, and select products. Online information includes text, tables, graphs, photos, audio, and video. Better product information helps online shoppers make better decisions, feel more confident about their decisions, increase their satisfaction with the shopping experience, and improve their attitudes toward the site.

Several studies report a positive association between product information and attitude toward a website (Donthu, 2001; Kwon, Kim, & Lee, 2002). Product information increases attitude toward online shopping (Vijayasarathy & Jones, 2000), the amount of online shopping (Kwak, Fox, & Zinkhan, 2002), online spending (Korgaonkar & Wolin, 1999), and satisfaction with online purchases (Szymanski & Hise, 2000).

Johnson and Misic (1999) report that both the content and the site are evaluated for currency and presentation. Currency is important as it implies that all the information on a site is updated (Yang, Peterson, & Huang, 2001). Currency is more than updated data as it includes news, special promotions, and announcements of upcoming events, anything that refreshes the content or appearance of the website, with new page designs, photos and headlines (Elliott & Speck, 2005).

Informativeness of the Website

Hoffman and Novak (1996) define *informativeness* as the ability of a website to make information available. It is viewed as static information available on a website. A site may be high on informativeness irrespective of manner of presentation. Concerns about information overload or formatting are not related to the ability of the website to provide useful information. Thus, informativeness is a perceptual construct, and it is not the same as the actual amount of information available on a website, even though it may be correlated with it.

Informativeness focuses on the site as an interactive provider. Intelligent, resourceful, and knowledgeable are adjectives often used (Maddox, 1999). Information often available in a website is product information and the perception of the site content may be measured by the degree it is considered to be informative (Huizingh, 2000). An informative site provides detailed specific information on products, the company or other relevant topics. It includes texts, tables, graphs, photos, audio and video. A website concentrates on functions such as information, transactions or entertainment. With better search engines/browsers, faster downloading, sites are becoming more advanced, with elements such as information on the company, products, non-commercial information; transactions; and entertainment (Huizingh, 2000).

Eighmey (1997) finds that effective websites have productive combinations of information and entertainment. Chen and Wells (1999) find that informativeness of a website is the second most important factor in explaining variance in attitudes toward the website. Lohse, Bellman and Johnson (2000) find that search for product information is the most important predictor of online purchases. Finally, for Chen, Clifford, and Wells (2002), informativeness is closely related to attitudes toward a website.

Entertainment of the Website

Even though *entertainment* is viewed as a peripheral cue and may be an attractive source (Cho, 1999), it is important for visitors to determine whether or not the site is worth revisiting and it develops purchase intentions for the products it describes. For Katerattanakul (2002), many surf online just for information search or pure enjoyment. The effectiveness of a website depends on whether visitors feel that it is capable of attracting their attention by being fun, exciting, pleasurable, enjoyable, or entertaining (Bruner & Kumar, 2000; Chen & Wells, 1999). Uses of interesting themes, good graphics, or appealing designs contribute to a website being perceived as entertaining (Chakraborty, Lala, & Warren, 2002). Entertainment involves sensory and hedonic stimuli (e.g., color, music, action, and interactivity) that promote enjoyment while using a site.

Like brick-and mortar shoppers, e-shoppers prefer experiences that create positive feelings. Past research suggests that vividness, aesthetically pleasing elements, and engaging material are positively related to website attitudes (Coyle & Thorson, 2001; Kwon, Kim, & Lee, 2002; McMillan, Hwang, & Lee, 2003). Entertainment increases attitude toward online shopping (Vijayasarathy and Jones, 2000), intention to shop online (Lynch, Kent, & Srinivasan, 2001), and frequency of online purchases (Korgaonkar & Wolin 1999).

For McQuail (1983), the value of entertainment is in its ability to fulfill needs for escapism, diversion, aesthetic enjoyment or emotional release. People scoring web ads high in entertainment value develop favorable attitudes and high involvement with the information content of the site (De Pelsmacker, Dedock, & Gueuns, 1998).

For Ducoffe (1996), both 'informativeness' and 'entertainment' are important for evaluating an ad, and by extension a website. Surfers rating web ads high develop favorable site attitudes and involvement with information content. Entertainment developed during site visits is due to sensory and hedonic stimuli (e.g., color, music, action, pictures, graphs, videos, and interactivity). Chen and Wells (1999) find that those with greater perceptions of a site's entertainment value have more positive attitudes toward websites (McMillan, Hwang, & Lee 2003), and develop more positive attitudes toward the brand and stronger purchase intentions.

FUTURE RESEARCH DIRECTIONS

The study of other forms of web atmospherics is needed such as the use of colors, different fonts, music, movement, illustrations, etc. Findings will help web designers provide more effective websites

CONCLUSION

Understanding web atmospherics is important for firms who need effective websites to generate traffic and sales. The more important variables identified by research are effectiveness of information content, informativeness and entertainment.

REFERENCES

Bauer, H. H., Grether, M., & Leach, M. (2002). Building customer relations over the Internet. *Industrial Marketing Management, 31*(2), 155–163. doi:10.1016/S0019-8501(01)00186-9

Bruner, G. C. II, & Kumar, A. (2000). Web commercials and advertising hierarchy-of-effects. *Journal of Advertising Research, 40*(1-2), 35–42.

Celsi, R. L., & Olson, J. C. (1988). The role of involvement in attention and in comprehension processes. *The Journal of Consumer Research, 15*(2), 210–224. doi:10.1086/209158

Chaffey, D., & Mayer, R. Johnstone, K., & Ellis-Chadwick, F. (2000). *Internet marketing.* Harlow, UK: Pearson.

Chakraborty, G., Lala, V., & Warren, D. (2003). What do customers consider important in B2B websites? *Journal of Advertising Research, 43,* 50–61.

Chen, Q., Clifford, S. J., & Wells, W. D. (2002). Attitude toward the site II: New information. *Journal of Advertising Research, 42*(2), 33–45.

Chen, Q., & Wells, W. D. (1999). Attitude toward the site. *Journal of Advertising Research, 39*(5), 27–37.

Cho, C. H. (1999). How advertising works on the world wide web: Modified elaboration likelihood model. *Journal of Current Issues and Research in Advertising, 21*(1), 33–49.

Coyle, J. R., & Thorson, E. (2001). The effects of progressive levels of interactivity and vividness in web marketing sites. *Journal of Advertising, 30*(3), 65–77.

De Pelsmacker, P., Dedock, B., & Geuens, M. (1998). A study of 100 likeable TV commercials: Advertising characteristics and the attitude towards the ad. *Marketing Research Today, 27*(4), 166–179.

Dholakia, U. M., & Rego, L. L. (1998). What makes commercial web pages popular? *European Journal of Marketing, 32*(7/8), 724–736. doi:10.1108/03090569810224119

Donthu, N. (2001). Does your website measure up? *Marketing Management, 10*(4), 29–32.

Ducoffe, R. H. (1996). Advertising value and advertising on the web. *Journal of Advertising Research, 36*(5), 21–35.

Eagly, A. H., & Chaiken, S. (1993). *The psychology of attitudes*. Fort Worth, TX: Harcourt Brace Jovanovich.

Eighmey, J. (1997). Profiling user responses to commercial web sites. *Journal of Advertising Research, 37*(3), 59–66.

Elliott, M. T., & Speck, P. S. (2005). Factors that affect attitude toward a retail website. *Journal of Marketing Theory and Practice, 13*(1), 40–51.

Ellsworth, J. H., & Ellsworth, M. V. (1997). *Marketing on the Internet*. New York: Wiley.

Eroglu, S. A., Machleit, K. A., & Davis, L. M. (2001). Atmospherics qualities of online retailing: A conceptual model and implications. *Journal of Business Research, 54*(2), 177–184. doi:10.1016/S0148-2963(99)00087-9

Griffith, D. A. (2005). An examination of the influences of store layout in online retailing. *Journal of Business Research, 58*(10), 1391–1396. doi:10.1016/j.jbusres.2002.08.001

Hoffman, D. L., & Novak, T. P. (1996). Marketing in hypermedia computer-mediated environments: Conceptual foundations. *Journal of Marketing, 60*(3), 50–68. doi:10.2307/1251841

Huizingh, E. (2000). The content and design of websites: An empirical study. *Information & Management, 7*, 123–134. doi:10.1016/S0378-7206(99)00044-0

Johnson, K. L., & Misic, M. M. (1999). Benchmarking: A tool for website evaluation and improvement. *Internet Research, 9*(5), 383–392. doi:10.1108/10662249910297787

Katerattanakul, P. (2002). Framework of effective website design for business-to-consumer internet commerce. *INFOR, 40*(1), 57–70.

Korgaonkar, P. K., & Wolin, L. D. (1999). A multivariate analysis of web usage. *Journal of Advertising Research, 39*(2), 53–68.

Kwak, H., Fox, R. J., & Zinkhan, G. M. (2001). Factors influencing consumers' internet purchases: attitudes, internet experiences, demographics, and personality traits. In *Proceedings,* (pp. 106-107), Chicago, IL: American Marketing Association.

Kwon, O. B., Kim, C. R., & Lee, E. J. (2002). Impact of website information design factors on consumer ratings of web-based auction sites. *Behaviour & Information Technology, 21*(6), 387–402. doi:10.1080/0144929021000050256

Leong, E. K. F., Ewing, M. T., & Pitt, L. F. (2002). E-comprehension: Evaluating B2B websites using readability formulae. *Industrial Marketing Management, 31*(2), 125–131. doi:10.1016/S0019-8501(01)00184-5

Lohse, G. L., Bellman, S., & Johnson, E. J. (2000). Consumer buying behavior on the Internet: Findings from panel data. *Journal of Interactive Marketing, 14*(1), 15–29. doi:10.1002/(SICI)1520-6653(200024)14:1<15::AID-DIR2>3.0.CO;2-C

Lynch, P. D., Kent, R. J., & Srinivasan, S. S. (2001). The global internet shopper: Evidence from shopping tasks in twelve countries. *Journal of Advertising Research, 41*(3), 15–23.

Maddox, L. M. (1999). The use of pharmaceutical website for prescription drug information and product requests. *Journal of Product and Brand Management, 8*(6), 488–496. doi:10.1108/10610429910299728

McMillan, S. J., Hwang, J. S., & Lee, G. (2003). Effects of structural and perceptual factors on attitude toward the website. *Journal of Advertising Research, 43*(4), 400–409.

McQuail, D. (1993). *Mass communication theory: An introduction*. London: Sage.

Menon, S., & Kahn, B. (2002). Cross-category effects of induced arousal and pleasure on the internet shopping experience. *Journal of Retailing, 78*(1), 31–40. doi:10.1016/S0022-4359(01)00064-1

Passini, R. E. (1984). Spatial representations: A way-finding perspective . *Journal of Environmental Psychology, 4*(2), 153–164. doi:10.1016/S0272-4944(84)80031-6

Poruban, S. (2002). Effective use of the web. *Oil & Gas Journal, 100*(12), 19.

Richard, M. O. (2005). Modeling the Impact of Internet Atmospherics on Surfer Behavior. *Journal of Business Research, 58*(12), 1632–1642. doi:10.1016/j.jbusres.2004.07.009

Richard, M. O. (2009). *Modeling the internet behavior of visitors by the study of cognitive variables and moderators*. Unpublished doctoral dissertation, HEC-Montreal Business School.

Sandvig, J. C., & Bajwa, D. (2004). Information seeking on university web sites: An exploratory study. *Journal of Computer Information Systems, 45*(1), 13–22.

Supphellen, J. S., & Nysveen, H. (2001). Drivers of intention to revisit the websites of well-known companies. *International Journal of Market Research, 43*(3), 341–352.

Szymanski, D. M., & Hise, R. T. (2000). E-satisfaction: An initial examination. *Journal of Retailing, 76*(3), 309–322. doi:10.1016/S0022-4359(00)00035-X

Vijayasarathy, L. R., & Jones, J. M. (2000). Print and internet catalog shopping: Assessing attitudes and intentions. *Internet Research, 10*(3), 191–202. doi:10.1108/10662240010331948

Wolfinbarger, M., & Gilly, M. C. (2001). Shopping online for freedom, control and fun. *California Management Review, 43*(2), 34–55.

Yang, Z., Peterson, R. T., & Huang, L. (2001). Taking the pulse of internet pharmacies. *Marketing Health Services, 21*(2), 4–10.

ADDITIONAL READING

Richard, M. O., & Chandra, R. (2005). A model of consumer web navigational behavior: conceptual development and application. *Journal of Business Research, 58*(8), 1019–1029. doi:10.1016/j.jbusres.2004.04.001

KEY TERMS AND DEFINITIONS

Effectiveness of Information Content: currency of the information content of a website and degree that the information is convenient, accurate, up-to-date, complete and relevant.

Entertainment: ability to attract attention by being fun, exciting, pleasurable, enjoyable, or entertaining

Informativeness: amount and richness of the information contained in a website.

Navigation: the process of self-directed movement through a computer-mediated environment.

Organization: ability of a website to arrange content, information, images, and graphics to increase the clarity of provided information and make it easier to find need information.

Site Quality: represented by ease of use, provision of helpful graphics, usefulness of search engines, and completeness of information.

Structure: the layout of a site such as a tree, a tree with a return-to-home page button, a tree with some horizontal links and an extensive network.

Wayfinding: physical maneuvering of a store's environment (i.e., social, visual and design factors)

Web Atmospherics: conscious development of website environment to induce a positive response.

Chapter 64

Internet Consumer Behavior:
Behavioral Variables

Marie-Odile Richard
University of Montreal, Canada

Michel Laroche
Concordia University, Canada

INTRODUCTION

In the previously, the authors covered the major stimulus variables, i.e., flow, emotions and web atmospherics, which impact the organism and response variables of the model. This chapter now covers some behavioral variables as indicated in the shaded areas of Figure 1.

BACKGROUND

The key behavioral variables identified by the literature are: exploratory behavior, site attitude, product attitude, site involvement and product involvement. This chapter will define them and explain their roles in the model.

DOI: 10.4018/978-1-61520-611-7.ch064

Exploratory Behavior

Exploratory behavior is defined as a behavior with the unique function of changing the stimulus field (Berlyne, 1963). Raju (1980) lists risk taking, innovativeness, brand switching, repetitive behavior proneness, information seeking, exploration through shopping and interpersonal communication as aspects of exploratory consumer behavior. There are several specific types of exploratory behavior: innovative behavior (Foxall, 1986), cognitive responses to ads (Faison, 1977), and curiosity-motivated search for product information (Hirschman, 1980).

Studies suggest a two-factor conceptualization of exploratory consumer buying behavior: exploratory acquisition of products and exploratory information seeking (Baumgartner & Steenkamp, 1996). Browsing, one form of exploratory behavior, is performed when surfers do not have knowledge of

Figure 1. Model of consumer navigation behavior: behavioral variables (Source: Adapted from Richard, M.O. (2009). Modeling the internet behavior of visitors by the study of cognitive variables and moderators. Unpublished doctoral dissertation, HEC-Montreal Business School.)

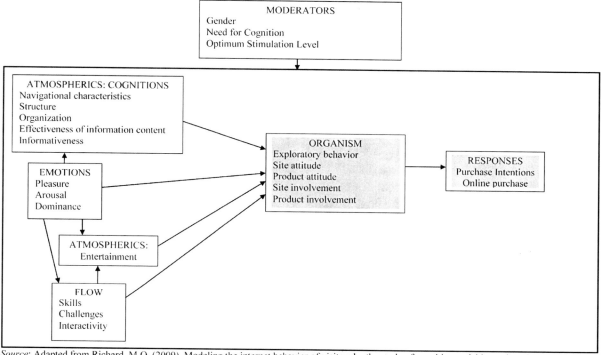

Source: Adapted from Richard, M.O. (2009). Modeling the internet behavior of visitors by the study of cognitive variables and moderators. Unpublished doctoral dissertation, HEC-Montreal Business School.

available information, are not sure whether their requirements can be met or how these requirements may be achieved. Browsing is either general or purposeful. *Purposive* browsing occurs when surfers have specific requirements, whereas general browsing is an opportunity for surfers to fine-tune the perceptions of their requirements or simply keep themselves up-to-date on the latest changes in a field or product type (Rowley, 2000).

Exploratory behavior by site visitors influences their site attitudes. The more they explore the possibilities offered by the site, the more they fine-tune their requirements and have a positive idea of the site they visit, triggering approach behavior.

Site Attitudes and Product Attitudes

As there are few studies on site attitudes, the literature on ad attitudes can be used for websites. Ad attitude consists of feelings of favorability/ unfavorability toward the ad and mediates the influence of brand attitudes on purchase intentions (Shimp, 1981). Laczniak and Muehling (1990) define ad attitude as the predisposition of individuals to answer favorably or not to an ad exposure; product/brand attitudes as the predisposition of individuals to answer favorably or not to a product or a brand.

Findings from Ad Attitude Research

Ad attitude is unidimensional, purely affective without any cognitive or behavioral components

(MacKenzie & Lutz, 1989). For Gardner (1983), it is predominantly affective. Most authors perceive it as a situationally-bound construct. However, Shimp (1981) describes it as multidimensional, composed of a cognitive dimension (i.e., conscious responses to executional elements) and an affective (i.e., emotional responses without any conscious processing) dimension. He hypothesizes that these dimensions likely have an unequal impact on consumers. Zinkhan and Zinkhan (1985) position the cognitive dimension as high involvement (i.e., central processing), and the affective dimension as low involvement (i.e., peripheral processing).

Lutz (1975) defines five antecedents of attitudes toward the ad: *1)* ad credibility, *2)* ad perceptions, *3)* attitude toward the advertiser, *4)* attitudes toward advertising in general, and *5)* mood. According to the *Elaboration Likelihood Model* (ELM), attitude toward an object is based on central and peripheral processes (Petty et al., 1993). *Peripheral* processes use simple decision rules, conditioning processes, mere-exposure processes, and others not involving scrutiny of central merits of the object (Petty & Cacioppo, 1986). Many peripheral cues have a greater impact when motivation and/or ability to investigate the central merits of the products are low (Maheswaran, 1994). Motivation moderates the effect of peripheral cues by focusing on the central merits of the products, then decreasing the impact of peripheral cues (Haugtvedt & Petty, 1992). Even though ELM theory explains attitude change, neither the central nor the peripheral approaches alone account for the results (Petty, Cacioppo, & Schumann, 1983). According to dual process models of attitude change, when the motivation or the ability to investigate relevant information is lacking, one or more peripheral processes likely determine persuasion results.

Application to Site Attitudes

Stevenson, Bruner, and Kumar (2000) show that site attitude is worth including in research on websites, their content, and the ads they include. Luna, Peracchio, and de Juan (2002) consider site attitudes as an antecedent of flow mediating three effects: two site characteristics (interactivity and challenges) and focused attention. Brown and Stayman (1992) find that attitudes toward the ad influence brand attitudes and purchase intentions. By analogy, attitudes toward the website is an indicator of site value. A website can be estimated according to three dimensions (entertainment, informativeness and organization) which relate to site attitudes (Chen, Clifford, & Wells, 2002). For Kwak, Fox, and Zinkhan (2002) online ad attitudes are not related to Internet purchase process and is weaker Internet involvement in explaining web buying in specific categories, whereas researchers measure attitude toward Internet ads in general.

Effects on Product Attitudes

If websites reflect the characteristics of traditional ads, site attitudes lead to consequences identical to those found in attitude research (Jee & Lee, 2002). Flow mediates the effects of site attitudes on intentions to revisit and to purchase the product, but it is not needed to predict purchase intentions (Luna, Peracchio, & de Juan, 2002). Also, site attitudes have a positive and strong impact on ad attitudes, product/brand attitudes and purchase intentions (Bruner & Kumar 2000). Finally, it is important to evaluate attitudes toward the company behind the site, which may be related to site attitudes (Supphellen & Nysveen 2001).

Product Involvement and Website Involvement

Involvement is important in audience processing of both traditional advertising (Petty & Cacioppo, 1986) and web advertising (Cho, 1999). Involvement is a motivational state influenced by perceptions of the object's relevance based on inherent needs, values and interests (Zaichkowsky, 1985). Its main antecedents are the characteristics of the person, the stimulus/object, and the situation. For Zaichkowsky (1985) involvement is unidimensional. Her PII scale consists of two groups of adjectives: the first one contains items as indicators of involvement (states), whereas the second is associated with the measure of attitudes. Both represent conceptually different constructs, but there is a caution that the involvement scale suffers from attitudinal contamination. On the other hand, for Laurent and Kapferer (1985) involvement is multifaceted: importance of the product and consequences of making a wrong choice, probability of making a wrong purchase, and symbolic and emotional values of the product.

Two Types of Involvement

There are two types of involvement: enduring and situational involvement. *Enduring* involvement predicts behavior such as information search (Higie & Feick, 1989). There is enduring involvement for a product category when there are intrinsic rewards (Schmidt & Spreng, 1996). Enduring involvement directly predicts skills and challenges, two antecedents of flow (Novak, Hoffman, & Yung, 1998). *Situational* involvement links a product or a situation and outcomes or consequences of that situation (Schmidt & Spreng, 1996). It leads to an increase in attention and information processing because of the belief that these efforts produce favorable outcomes (Schmidt & Spreng, 1996). However, its role had not been explored as well as goal-directed and experiential navigation behaviors (Novak, Hoffman, & Yung, 1998). Based on involvement and search behavior, researchers differentiate flow states from these behaviors. Among the opposite characteristics are: extrinsic vs. intrinsic motivation, situational vs. enduring involvement, directed vs. non-directed research, goal-directed vs. navigational choice (Hoffman & Novak, 1996). In internet contexts, a distinction is made between product (enduring) involvement and website (situational) involvement.

Goal-Directed and Experiential Search

There are motivations that are both *goal-directed* (i.e., to obtain information) and *experiential* (i.e., to be entertained). Goal-directed Internet use suggests an intentional selective manner, reflecting a deliberate exposure to specific content (Rubin & Perse, 1987). When users log on, they have a specific objective in mind. For example, an online session spent searching for information about a specific product suggests goal-directed motivation. In contrast, when people use the Internet for diversion, escape, and/or relaxation (i.e., experiential use), there is no specific outcome-oriented goal. The Internet is used primarily for the experience. The focus is more directed on the medium than on special content and focuses on the satisfactions offered by the medium itself (Perse & Greenberg-Dunn, 1998). However, as online surfers are active and involved, researchers look for factors influencing motivation. Eighmey (1997) studies perceptions of the use of commercial websites and finds that visitors liked information placed in an enjoyable milieu. Thus, both goal-directed and experiential gratifications can be obtained from the Internet.

MacInnis and Jaworski (1989) studies processing and evaluation of the information by the consumers' motivation, their ability and opportunity to process information. Information relevance (i.e., involvement) impacts both motivation to process information (MacInnis & Jaworski, 1989) and the way it is processed (Johnson & Eagly, 1990). Ability to process (i.e., skills and challenges) is related to the amount and type of knowledge acquired through experience. Opportunity to process depends on the facets of the immediate environment such as situational distractions (e.g., noise, crowding), information overload, information board (i.e., organized by brand or by attribute), and modality (i.e., print or broadcasting) (Celsi & Olson, 1988). However, with the Internet, there is some restriction on information processing ability due to inexperience, but not knowledge.

Elaboration Likelihood Model (ELM)

For *ELM* involvement affects motivation to process information (Petty & Cacioppo, 1986). Does involvement affect motivation to process the content of a website and, if so, could it moderate the relationship between website factors and site attitude? According to ELM, high involvement individuals more likely access a product-specific site, explore product-specific information, and generate thoughts about products. If these product-related arguments are strong, involved shoppers more likely form positive attitudes toward these products. On the other hand, low involvement visitors less likely look for product-related information and likely attend to peripheral content. Entertainment elements are more peripheral than central, and entertainment should be more important for low involved visitors. Two studies find that involvement has a positive effect on site attitude (Coyle & Thorson, 2001; McMillan, Hwang, & Lee, 2003). Two others consider whether it has a moderating effect: one finds evidence that it does (Cho, 1999); the other that it does not (McMillan, Hwang, & Lee, 2003). Entertainment is also significant in explaining site attitude, especially for low involved surfers (Elliott & Speck, 2005). The differences between low and high involved visitors reflects a difference between peripheral and central processing. Peripheral processors (low involved surfers) are less purposeful, more easily attracted to extraneous design elements, and more satisfied by them. Currency is a determinant of site attitude, especially for high involved visitors. Those more interested in and familiar with a product category more likely appreciate new information about the category. Fogg et al. (2002) find that frequency of updates is strongly related to website credibility. This suggests that e-tailers must not merely update website information; they must signal it. Every time customers visit the site, they should find something new; otherwise they would have fewer reasons to return.

Highly-involved individuals search for information before purchase, process relevant information in depth, and use more criteria in their decisions than others (Leong, 1993). Internet-involved customers more likely purchase online than low-involved ones (Kwak, Fox, & Zinkhan, 2002). In general, visitors acquire high involvement levels related to overall Internet purchases and for most personal products (except for entertainment and music) (Kwak, Fox & Zinkhan, 2002). Balabanis and Reynolds (2001) posit that aspects related to the product attract the interest of highly-involved consumers, whereas low-involved ones focus more on the peripheral stimuli of the site or its design characteristics. The relationship between involvement and website attitudes is partially dependent on the characteristics of the site (Balabanis & Reynolds, 2001). Harvin (2000) indicates that consumers are more comfortable with strong offline brands they already know and trust. For Yoo and Stout (2001), consumers with a high level of product involvement have more intentions to interact with a website, leading to more extensive search and more trials of interactive functions.

Involvement varies according to the optimum stimulation level of site visitors (covered in Chapter 4). Involved surfers are more prone to search for information when surfing the websites and in doing that, explore new stimuli and situations because of a higher need for environmental stimulation.

Purchase Behavior

Online purchasing is the most rapidly growing form of shopping, with sales growth rates that surpass buying through traditional retailing. Forrester Research (2007) reports that in 2007 Internet sales to consumers amounted to $259 billion, an annual growth rate of 18% over 2006. This is increasingly recognized in the literature.

Among reasons cited for abortion of information search processes and shopping trials, researchers include: lack of enthusiasm to supply personal and credit card information, technical problems with websites, and problems in locating products. Consumer search experiences at retailers' websites are determinants of their online purchasing behaviors (Shim et al., 2001). More precisely, information search is the most important element leading to online purchases. If search intentions play a central role in predicting future purchasing intentions, search attitudes are a valuable tool for purchasing on the Web. Consequently, no-purchase decisions on the Web are consequence of unfavorable reactions to a site rather than a broader lack of interest in this channel (Shim et al., 2001). Search intentions mediate the relationships between purchase intentions and key antecedents of purchase intentions, chiefly when shopping online. Visitors' perceptions that the Internet's role in consumer information search is one of its most pronounced features indicates that information search online continues to progress as a major vehicle for comparison shopping (Dickson, 2000).

Intentions consist of motivational components of behavior and are characterized by the degree of efforts a person exerts to perform this behavior (Shim et al., 2001). Donovan and Rossiter (1982) demonstrate that store-induced pleasure and arousal are positively linked to willingness to buy. Arousal is due to the level of challenges. Pleasure in atmospherics is similar playfulness in the theory of the flow. Playfulness is an important indicator of flow and is predicted by the antecedents of skills (through control), challenges (through arousal), and focused attention during the interaction. It leads to consequences of flow such as positive effect, more exploratory behavior, and greater web use. Also, a short intense flow state can move consumers to buy in an expedient manner by providing feelings of pleasure of control that result from flow, while reducing deliberation time necessary before buying (Smith & Sivakumar, 2002).

Shim et al. (2001) show that intention to use the Internet to search for information for search goods is not only the strongest predictor of Internet purchase intentions but also mediates the relationships between purchase intentions and predictors such as attitudes toward online shopping, perceived control and online purchase experience. Sansgiry, Cady, and Sansgiry (2001) evaluate simulated over-the-counter (OTC) product labels for two product categories in random order and find that when consumers are involved in their purchases, they significantly more likely understand information from the label and evaluate it appropriately. However, involvement neither affects attitudes toward the product label nor enhances purchase intentions.

FUTURE RESEARCH DIRECTIONS

- Identify additional behavioral variables.
- Further explore the nature and structure of site attitude and site involvement.
- Clarify the distinction between site attitudes, product attitudes, and brand attitudes in the same website.
- Develop new measures of website effectiveness.

CONCLUSION

This chapter showed the important role of the key variables of site attitude and site involvement within the overall model of internet consumer behavior, and their relationship to product involvement, product attitudes and online purchase intentions.

REFERENCES

Balabanis, G., & Reynolds, N. L. (2001). Consumer attitudes towards multi-channel retailers' web sites: The role of involvement, brand attitude, internet knowledge and visit duration. *The Journal of Business Strategy, 18*(2), 105–131.

Baumgartner, H., & Steenkamp, J. B. E. M. (1996). Exploratory consumer behavior: Conceptualization and measurement. *International Journal of Research in Marketing, 13*(2), 121–137. doi:10.1016/0167-8116(95)00037-2

Berlyne, D. E. (1963). Motivational problems raised by exploratory and epistemic behavior. In S. Koch (ed). *Psychology: A study of science,* (p. 284-364). New York: McGraw-Hill.

Brown, S. P., & Stayman, D. M. (1992). Antecedents and consequences of attitudes toward the ad: A meta analysis. *The Journal of Consumer Research, 19*(June), 4–51.

Bruner, G. C. II, & Kumar, A. (2000). Web commercials and advertising hierarchy-of-effects. *Journal of Advertising Research, 40*(1-2), 35–42.

Celsi, R. L., & Olson, J. C. (1988). The role of involvement in attention and in comprehension processes. *The Journal of Consumer Research, 15*(2), 210–224. doi:10.1086/209158

Chen, Q., Clifford, S. J., & Wells, W. D. (2002). Attitude toward the site II: New information. *Journal of Advertising Research, 42*(2), 33–45.

Cho, C. H. (1999). How advertising works on the world wide web: Modified elaboration likelihood model. *Journal of Current Issues and Research in Advertising, 21*(1), 33–49.

Coyle, J. R., & Thorson, E. (2001). The effects of progressive levels of interactivity and vividness in web marketing sites. *Journal of Advertising, 30*(3), 65–77.

Dickson, P. R. (2000). Understanding the trade winds: The global evolution of production, consumption and the internet. *The Journal of Consumer Research, 27*(June), 115–122. doi:10.1086/314313

Donovan, R. J., & Rossiter, J. R. (1982). Store atmosphere: an environmental psychology approach. *Journal of Retailing, 58*(1), 34–57.

Eighmey, J. (1997). Profiling user responses to commercial web sites. *Journal of Advertising Research, 37*(3), 59–66.

Elliott, M. T., & Speck, P. S. (2005). Factors that affect attitude toward a retail website. *Journal of Marketing Theory and Practice, 13*(1), 40–51.

Faison, E. W. J. (1977). The neglected variety drive: A useful concept for consumer behavior. *The Journal of Consumer Research, 4,* 172–175. doi:10.1086/208693

Fogg, B. J., Soohoo, C., Danielsen, D., Marable, L., Stanford, J., & Tauber, E. (2002). How do people evaluate a web site's credibility? Results from a large study. *Consumer WebWatch.* Available at http://credibility.stanford.edu/mostcredible.html

Forrester Research. (2007). Retrieved from www.forrester.com/ER/Press/Release/0,1769,1145,00.html.

Foxall, G. R. (1986). Consumer innovativeness: Novelty seeking, creativity and cognitive style. In E.C. Hirschman & J.N. Sheth (eds). *Research in Consumer Behavior* 3 (pp. 79-113). Greenwich, CT: JAI.

Gardner, M. P. (1983). Advertising effects on attributes recalled and criteria used for brand evaluations. *The Journal of Consumer Research, 10*(Dec), 310–318. doi:10.1086/208970

Harvin, R. (2000). In internet branding the offlines have it. *Brandweek, 41*(4), 30–31.

Haugtvedt, C. P., & Petty, R. E. (1992). Personality and persuasion: Need for cognition moderates the persistence and resistance of attitude changes. *Journal of Personality and Social Psychology, 63,* 308–319. doi:10.1037/0022-3514.63.2.308

Higie, R. A., & Feick, L. F. (1989). Enduring involvement: Conceptual and measurement issues. [Ann Arbor, MI: Association for Consumer Research.]. *Advances in Consumer Research. Association for Consumer Research (U. S.)*, *16*, 690–696.

Hirschman, E. C. (1980). Innovativeness, novelty seeking, and consumer creativity. *The Journal of Consumer Research*, *7*(Dec), 283–295. doi:10.1086/208816

Hoffman, D. L., & Novak, T. P. (1996). Marketing in hypermedia computer-mediated environments: Conceptual foundations. *Journal of Marketing*, *60*(3), 50. doi:10.2307/1251841

Jee, J., & Lee, W. N. (2002). Antecedents and consequences of perceived interactivity: An exploratory study. *Journal of Interactive Advertising*, *3*(1), 1–16.

Johnson, B. T., & Eagly, A. H. (1990). Involvement and persuasion: Types, traditions and the evidence. *Psychological Bulletin*, *107*, 375–384. doi:10.1037/0033-2909.107.3.375

Kwak, H., Fox, R. J., & Zinkhan, G. M. (2001). Factors influencing consumers' internet purchases: attitudes, internet experiences, demographics, and personality traits. In *Proceedings, 12* (pp. 106-107). Chicago: American Marketing Association.

Laczniak, R. N., & Muehling, D. D. (1990). Delay effects of advertising moderated by involvement. *Journal of Business Research*, *20*, 263–277. doi:10.1016/0148-2963(90)90017-8

Laurent, G., & Kapferer, J. N. (1985). Measuring consumer involvement profiles. *JMR, Journal of Marketing Research*, *22*(Feb), 41–53. doi:10.2307/3151549

Leong, S. M. (1993). Consumer decision making for common, repeat-purchase products: a dual replication. *Journal of Consumer Psychology*, *2*(2), 193–208. doi:10.1016/S1057-7408(08)80024-1

Luna, D., Peracchio, L. A., & de Juan, M. D. (2002). Cross-cultural and cognitive aspects of website navigation. *Journal of the Academy of Marketing Science*, *30*(4), 397–410. doi:10.1177/009207002236913

Lutz, R. J. (1975). Changing brand attitudes through modification of cognitive structure. *The Journal of Consumer Research*, *1*(4), 49–59. doi:10.1086/208607

MacInnis, D. J., & Jaworski, B. J. (1989). Information processing from advertisements: Toward an integrative framework. *Journal of Marketing*, *53*(Oct), 1–23. doi:10.2307/1251376

MacKenzie, S. B., & Lutz, R. J. (1989). An empirical examination of the structural antecedents of attitude toward the ad in an advertising pretesting context. *Journal of Marketing*, *53*(Apr), 48–65. doi:10.2307/1251413

Maheswaran, D. (1994). Country of origin as a stereotype: Consumer expertise and attribute strength on product evaluations. *The Journal of Consumer Research*, *21*, 354–365. doi:10.1086/209403

McMillan, S. J., Hwang, J. S., & Lee, G. (2003). Effects of structural and perceptual factors on attitude toward the website. *Journal of Advertising Research*, *43*(4), 400–409.

Novak, T. P., Hoffman, D. L., & Yung, Y. F. (2000). Modeling the flow construct in online environments: a structural modeling approach. *Marketing Science*, *19*(1), 22–42. doi:10.1287/mksc.19.1.22.15184

Perse, E., & Greenberg-Dunn, D. (1998). The utility of home computers and media use: Implications of multimedia and connectivity. *Journal of Broadcasting & Electronic Media*, *42*(4), 435.

Petty, R. E., & Cacioppo, J. T. (1986). *Communication and Persuasion: Central and Peripheral Routes to Attitudes Change*. New York: Springer-Verlag.

Petty, R. E., Cacioppo, J. T., & Schumann, D. (1983). Central and peripheral routes to advertising effectiveness: The moderating role of involvement. *The Journal of Consumer Research, 10*(2), 135–146. doi:10.1086/208954

Petty, R. E., Schumann, D. W., Richman, S. A., & Strathman, A. J. (1993). Positive mood and persuasion: Different roles for affect under high- and low-elaboration conditions. *Journal of Personality and Social Psychology, 64*, 5–20. doi:10.1037/0022-3514.64.1.5

Raju, P. S. (1980). Optimum stimulation level: It's relationship to personality, demographics and exploratory behavior. *The Journal of Consumer Research, 7*(Dec), 272–282. doi:10.1086/208815

Richard, M. O. (2009). *Modeling the Internet Behavior of Visitors by the Study of Cognitive Variables and Moderators, unpublished doctoral dissertation*, HEC-Montreal Business School.

Rowley, J. (2000). Product search in e-shopping: A review and research propositions. *Journal of Consumer Marketing, 17*(1), 20–35. doi:10.1108/07363760010309528

Rubin, A. M., & Perse, E. M. (1987). Audience activity and television news gratifications. *Communication Research, 14*(1), 58–84. doi:10.1177/009365087014001004

Sansgiry, S. S., Cady, P. S., & Sansgiry, S. (2001). Consumer involvement: Effects on information processing from over-the-counter medication labels. *Health Marketing Quarterly, 19*(1), 61–78. doi:10.1300/J026v19n01_05

Schmidt, J. B., & Spreng, R. A. (1996). A proposed model of external consumer information search. *Journal of the Academy of Marketing Science, 24*(3), 246–256. doi:10.1177/0092070396243005

Shim, S., Eastlick, M. A., Lotz, S. L., & Warrington, P. (2001). An online prepurchase intentions model: The role of intention to search. *Journal of Retailing, 77*(3), 397–416. doi:10.1016/S0022-4359(01)00051-3

Shimp, T. A. (1981). Attitude toward the ad as a mediator of consumer brand choice. *Journal of Advertising, 10*(2), 9–15.

Smith, D. N., & Sivakumar, K. (2004). Flow and internet shopping behavior: A conceptual model and research propositions. *Journal of Business Research, 57*(10), 1199–1208. doi:10.1016/S0148-2963(02)00330-2

Stevenson, J. S., Bruner, G. C. II, & Kumar, A. (2000). Web page background and viewer attitudes. *Journal of Advertising Research, 40*(1/2), 29–34.

Supphellen, J. S., & Nysveen, H. (2001). Drivers of intention to revisit the websites of well-known companies. *International Journal of Market Research, 43*(3), 341–352.

Yoo, C. Y., & Stout, P. A. (2001). Factors affecting users' interactivity with the web site and the consequences of users' interactivity. In C.R. Taylor (ed.), *Proceedings* (pp. 53-61). Villanova, PA: American Academy of Advertising.

Zaichkowsky, J. L. (1985). Measuring the involvement construct. *The Journal of Consumer Research, 12*(4), 341–352. doi:10.1086/208520

Zinkhan, G. M., & Zinkhan, F. C. (1985). Response profile and choice behavior: An application to financial services advertising. *Journal of Advertising, 14*(3), 39–66.

ADDITIONAL READING

Richard, M. O. (2005). Modeling the Impact of Internet Atmospherics on Surfer Behavior. *Journal of Business Research, 58*(12), 1632–1642. doi:10.1016/j.jbusres.2004.07.009

KEY TERMS AND DEFINITIONS

Enduring Involvement: degree of interest in a product on an ongoing basis.

Exploratory Behavior: behavior with the sole function of changing the stimulus field.

Involvement: a motivational state influenced by perceptions of the object's relevance based on inherent needs, values and interests.

Peripheral Cues: Peripheral processes use simple decision rules, conditioning processes, mere-exposure processes, and others not involving scrutiny of central merits of the object.

Product Attitude: predisposition to answer favorably or not to a product in a consistent manner.

Product Involvement: degree of interest in a product on an ongoing basis.

Site Attitude: predisposition to answer favorably or not to a particular website in a consistent manner.

Site Involvement: degree of interest in a specific website.

Situational Involvement: degree of interest in a specific situation or occasion.

Chapter 65

Internet Consumer Behavior:
Major Moderating Variables

Marie-Odile Richard
University of Montreal, Canada

Michel Laroche
Concordia University, Canada

INTRODUCTION

This chapter concludes the model of internet consumer behavior by describing some key moderating variables such as gender, need for cognition (NFC) and optimum stimulation level (OSL)(Figure 1).

BACKGROUND

The selection of each moderating variable (i.e., gender, NFC and OSL) is justified with appropriate background and its moderating effects on the model of Internet consumer behavior are explained.

Gender

As shopping online becomes more common, the number of women shopping online shows a cor-

DOI: 10.4018/978-1-61520-611-7.ch065

responding increase although male consumers are considered to be early adopters of Internet shopping (Asch, 2001). By 2005, men and women are equally likely to be online, including 68% of men and 66% of women (Pew, 2005). There has been an increase of 3% for men versus 12% of women (2000-2005) for information search on products and services, and by 2005, 82% of men vs. 75% of women conducted searches on products.

Despite the growing importance of the Internet, little research has investigated web browsing behavior. Some investigated differences between males and females in their perceptions of web advertising (Schlosser, Shavitt, & Kanfer, 1999), use patterns (Weiser, 2000), and online privacy concerns (Sheehan, 1999). However, little is known about how Internet experience and web atmospherics impact navigational behavior and about the moderating effects of gender on the relationship between Internet experience and web atmospherics, on one hand, and browsing behavior, on the other.

Figure 1. Model of consumer navigation behavior: selected moderators (Source: Adapted from Richard, M.O. (2009). Modeling the internet behavior of visitors by the study of cognitive variables and moderators. Unpublished doctoral dissertation, HEC-Montreal Business School.)

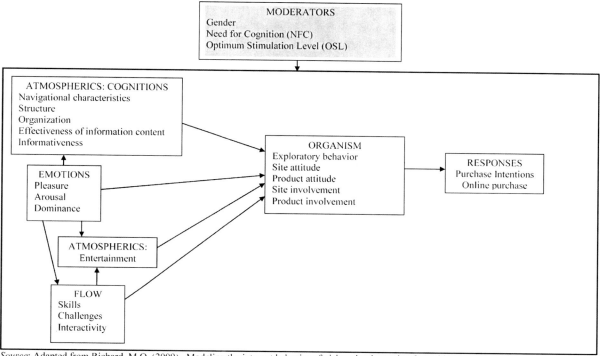

Source: Adapted from Richard, M.O. (2009). Modeling the internet behavior of visitors by the study of cognitive variables and moderators. Unpublished doctoral dissertation, HEC-Montreal Business School.

Males have more internet experience and higher skills than females, except with emailing; but over time, this gender gap in experience and skills has narrowed (Schumacher & Morahan-Martin, 2001). Since males engage in less detailed elaboration of commercial messages than females and less likely to engage in detailed and thorough examinations of messages which involve extended decisions based on product attributes (Putrevu, 2004), the effects of *both* skills and challenge on exploratory behavior are stronger for females compared to males. In addition, no gender differences are expected on the effect of challenge on attitude toward the website (Luna, Peracchio, & de Juan, 2002). Finally, since males buy more online than females (Rodgers & Harris, 2002), and are less likely to fully explore the website,

their challenge is more focused on developing pre-purchase evaluations (Putrevu, 2004).

Explanations from Psychology

According to the *selectivity hypothesis*, females are comprehensive processors, i.e., they give equal weight to self- and other-generated information; males are heuristic processors, i.e., they do not process all the information, but rather a subset of it, and are driven by overall message themes or schemas (Meyers-Levy & Maheswaran, 1991). An alternative explanation comes from Putrevu (2004): females are *relational* processors, i.e., they value category-based messages that focus on common themes; males are *item-specific* processors, i.e., they value attributes-based messages that bring out distinctive or unique features of the site. The difference between these theories is that the first one looks at the *depth* of processing, while the second at the *style* of processing. Thus, both predict that the more structured a site is, the more males find it easy to navigate, acquire specific information, find the experience enjoyable, and like the website more. Conversely, females are not affected by site structure and gather needed information pieces and decipher the interrelationships among them.

For Smith and Whitlark (2001) men and women have different needs and motivations in using the Internet: men use it for computer interest and hobbies, for personal productivity, and to connect with the world; women use it to make friends, nurture children, role play and for job productivity. For Wolin and Korgaonkar (2003), functional sites are designed for users to review, extract, and reference information, but are not designed for shopping. Moreover, in traditional markets, females spend more time shopping than men, enjoy it more, make more comparison shopping and bargain hunt (Wood, 1998). Since females more likely use websites for enjoyment and information gathering, effectiveness of information content has a stronger influence on both exploratory behavior and site involvement for females compared to males. Further, since women are more interested in information-rich sites processed in a relational way, while men consider only nonverbal reinforcements such as pictures, women react in a stronger exploratory fashion to increased site informativeness (Putrevu 2004).

Based on the *elaboration likelihood model* (Petty & Cacioppo, 1986), males use the peripheral route rather than the central route to persuasion, i.e., they focus more attention on peripheral cues, such as color, and behavior flows from entertainment. Women follow the central route by thoroughly analyzing site contents to find out what they want and search for, generate enjoyment in the 'online shopping experience', which stimulates *more* exploratory behavior (Putrevu,

2004). For Wolin and Korgaonkar (2003) males prefer functional sites, while women prefer shopping sites; but both groups like entertaining sites; thus, there is no gender difference on how entertainment affects both site involvement and site attitude.

Females have higher exploratory behavior when they visit a website compared to males, as they more likely engage in detailed elaboration of information content (Meyers-Levy & Maheswaran, 1991), browsing more to get all the information required, and understanding the interrelationships among them (Putrevu, 2004). Thus, women develop stronger site attitudes relative to their exploratory behavior. Since males do not process all information, but a selected subset of it, their relationship between exploratory behavior and site attitude is weaker than for females (Putrevu, 2004).

Explanations from Neurology

Neuro-anatomical studies with technologies such as MRI (Magnetic Resonance Imaging) point to gender differences concerning verbal and visual-spatial abilities. Men perform better than women on visuo-spatial tasks, i.e., those requiring mental rotation of 3-D images (Weiss, Kemmler, & Deisenhammer, 2004). Mental rotation is a complex cognitive ability. As both genders show very high and similar levels of activation, differences in activation patterns are attributed to gender-specific strategies in solving the mental rotation task (Weiss, Kemmler, & Deisenhammer 2003). Men use a gestalt strategy (object rotation-recognition), whereas women use a more analytic-serial strategy. The former is reflected by activation in parietal areas, whereas the latter activates right frontal areas (Cabeza & Nyberg, 2000). Results suggest gender differences in the right temporal gyrus in mental rotation. Gender differences arise at different processing levels (including perception, encoding, and rotation-matching). Strong neural connections between the posterior parietal cortex and the hippocampus as well as the parahippocampal region suggest functional interactions during spatial-cognition tasks such as orienting, navigating and forming visuo-spatial memory traces (Seltzer & Pandya, 1994). Also, right prefrontal areas are activated by visuo-spatial working memory tasks and play a role in complex navigation (Salmon et al., 1996).

There is a link between these neurological findings and the browsing of consumers when they visit a site with few or many specific landmarks. During navigation, there is an activation of parahippocampal and an activity of right hippocampal areas related to the allocentric (i.e., world-centered representation of the environment) aspects of route finding (Grön et al., 2000). The hippocampus is activated for processing spatial arrangements to serve navigation per se, meanwhile the parahippocampus is involved in processing specific places and routes (Epstein et al., 1999). Concerning navigational performance between genders, for spatial cognition, women engage right parietal and right prefrontal areas whereas men activate the left hippocampal region (Grön et al., 2000). They process spatial information differently. These explanations suggest interesting avenues for research with the use of new mapping techniques.

Need for Cognition (NFC)

NFC is conceptualized by Cohen, Stotland, and Wolfe (1955) as a need to understand and make reasonable the experiential world. NFC is defined as a stable individual difference in people's tendency to engage in and enjoy effortful cognitive activity. Low NFC is the relative absence of motivation for effortful cognitive activities that defines high NFC.

Findings from Advertising Research

From findings in *advertising*, high NFC individuals process and evaluate information more

thoroughly than low NFC individuals. High-NFC people are intrinsically motivated intellectually, tend to exhibit curiosity, and are tolerant of different ideas (Sadowski & Cogburn, 1997). High-NFC individuals enjoy thinking and doing complex tasks, less likely diminish their efforts on cognitive tasks in situations where reduction of efforts occurs (Cacioppo & Petty, 1989) and derive their attitudes based on the merits of the arguments presented (Haugtvedt & Petty, 1992). NFC operationalizes the motivational component of the ELM (Petty & Cacioppo, 1986): people high in NFC more likely think about and elaborate cognitive processes on relevant information when they are forming attitudes than people low in NFC. For, Haugtvedt and Petty (1992), even though attitudes and beliefs of high and low NFC people may seem identical after a persuasive communication, they differ in their persistence over time and resistance to counter-persuasion attempts. According to ELM, persuasion uses one of two routes, central or peripheral, to change attitudes. Individuals develop both the motivation and the ability to evaluate message arguments thoughtfully via the central route. However, by the peripheral route, customers lack the motivation or ability to "scrutinize" message arguments and use some heuristics or cues for their judgment (Petty & Cacioppo, 1986). Situational factors such as personal relevance influence the extent of message processing and the type of routes to persuasion (Petty & Cacioppo, 1986).

NFC and the Internet Medium

NFC has an impact in the internet medium. High-NFC visitors engage in more search activities that lead to greater perceived interactivity. For Jee and Lee (2002), NFC is a predictor of perceived interactivity. Mantel and Kardes (1999) find that high-NFC people more likely search for a website before making a purchase decision compared to low-NFC ones. To find information, high-NFC visitors favor information-orientated media, with a verbal instead of a visual processing style (Heckler, Childers, & Houston, 1993). High-NFC individuals are more interested in the quality of verbal information, than in executional characteristics such as graphics (Cacioppo et al., 1986). Low-NFC individuals are more prone to the influence of symbolic cues, as they avoid elaborative processing. Thus, low-NFC individuals base their attitudes not on the actual informational content of the website, but on the attractiveness of the executional characteristics.

Compared to low-NFC visitors, high-NFC ones are more favorable toward a website that combines complex verbal with simple visual elements. Low-NFC visitors do not evaluate a website with high visual and low verbal complexity more favorably than high-NFC ones, suggesting that high-NFC visitors find this condition equally persuasive. From a resource-matching perspective, less relevant peripheral visual cues influence high NFC evaluations. Specifically, cognitive resources available to high-NFC visitors for website processing are greater than those needed to process the verbal information (Peracchio & Meyers-Levy, 1997). Although they are predisposed toward verbal information (Cacioppo & Petty, 1989), high NFC people utilize visual stimuli as central cues to help in their evaluations, instead of disregarding them in favor of verbal information (Meyers-Levy & Peracchio 1995). However, in low complexity sites, low NFC visitors express more positive attitudes than high NFC ones.

The extent to which visitors are motivated to think about information when they are exposed to persuasive situations, including advertisements or websites, influences the formation of attitudes (Haugtvedt & Petty, 1992), is important to understand the information provided on the internet (Macias, 2003; Shon, Chen, & Chang, 2003) and it influences how advertising information is evaluated (Mantel and Kardes, 1999; Zhang & Buda, 1999).

Dual Mediation versus Affect Transfer Models

Sicilia, Ruiz, and Manuera (2005) study how levels of NFC affect the relationship between site attitudes and brand attitudes. They find that greater cognitive demands allow high-NFC visitors to make an informed decision, and the higher the NFC, the greater the access to product information and the motivation to think about it (Putrevu & Lord, 2003). Thus, thinking about the brand motivated visitors to spend time and effort for processing information, and that thinking is influenced by their evaluation of the website. This suggests the *dual mediation model*. However, low-NFC visitors, less motivated to think, adopt a simple approach in their evaluations (Tuten & Bosnjak, 2001). They find it less necessary to think about product information provided on the website, and more likely use the characteristics of the website to form their product attitudes (Chatterjee, Heath, & Mishra, 2002). Their opinion towards the website is directly transferred to the product. With visitors motivated to think about the information and who interact with the website (i.e., high NFC), the model that best explains the relationship is the dual mediation model. This suggests attitude formation via the central route, with firmly held opinions. In contrast, with low NFC surfers, site attitude directly influences brand attitudes through the peripheral route. This process of attitude formation is the *affect transfer model*. The difference in how the two groups form attitudes means that those in the low NFC group hold their opinions less firmly than those in the high NFC group.

Optimum Stimulation Level (OSL)

OSL refers to the amount of stimulation people prefer in life (McReynolds, 1971). For Mehrabian and Russell (1974), preference for an environment is linked to preferred arousal level: some prefer quiet settings, whereas others actively search to increase arousal levels by selecting novel, complex, or unpredictable settings.

Findings from Psychology

High OSL people explore more new stimuli and situations, while low OSL people are more comfortable with familiar situations and stimuli and avoid new or unusual situations or stimuli (Raju, 1980). OSL determines the degree of exploratory tendencies across many situations (Raju, 1980). Researchers suggest a link between OSL and exploratory tendencies (Steenkamp & Baumgartner, 1992). For Mittelstaedt et al. (1976) OSL is correlated with various exploratory tendencies, such as seeking information out of curiosity. Exploratory tendencies are categorized as curiosity-motivated behaviors, variety seeking, and risk taking (Raju, 1980). Even if there are studies done on that subject, some gaps remain in understanding the relationship between OSL and exploratory consumer behavior (Steenkamp & Baumgartner, 1992).

As Raju (1980) suggests, exploratory behavior (EXPB) and OSL are useful in studying individual differences. Links exist between personality traits, OSL and consumer exploratory behavior. Specifically, relationships exist between OSL and personality traits and between OSL and EXPB (Raju, 1980). Unfortunately, there is scant research on the relationship between OSL and personality traits, as the only personality traits studied are intolerance for ambiguity, rigidity, and dogmatism. Thus, it is difficult to generalize this relationship. OSL mediates the relationship between personality traits and EXPB. However, no data are collected on personality, OSL and EXPB simultaneously. Apparent links may be present between personality traits including OSL and consumer EXPB.

OSL and the Internet Medium

High OSL people more likely possess autotelic personality traits and develop flow; low OSL ones more likely experience anxiety in their interactions with computer-mediated environments: there is no link between OSL and playfulness, but OSL leads to a greater exploratory behavior on the web (Hoffman & Novak, 1996).

OSL is related to curiosity-motivated behavior, variety seeking, and risk taking. Study of curiosity-motivated behavior has not looked at consumer reactions to specific stimuli (specific curiosity). Acquisition of information to purchase a product and information seeking out of curiosity (exploratory behavior) are two motives that lead to information seeking behavior (Steenkamp & Baumgartner, 1992). High OSL people search for more information than low OSL ones when information acquisition is motivated by curiosity. There is no reason to assume that OSL has an effect on purposeful information search behavior, but is only weakly related to information seeking (Raju, 1980; Steenkamp & Baumgartner, 1992). High OSL people generate more cognitive responses while they are visiting a site than low OSL ones. However, it is difficult to separate true exploratory information seeking from a goal-directed one.

OSL is related to exploratory purchase behavior. Precisely, OSL is an antecedent of exploratory purchasing behavior tendencies (Baumgartner & Steenkamp 1996). High levels of OSL decrease the persistence of the same purchase response over time. OSL is positively related to tendency to buy new products and brands (Venkatraman & Price 1990).

FUTURE RESEARCH DIRECTIONS

- Use of medical imaging technology to study gender differences in website navigation.
- Conduct more research on the role of OSL in website navigation

- Identify other important moderators, such as culture or the nature of websites.
- Develop a typology of website visitors based on individual variables.

CONCLUSION

This chapter explains the role of important moderators such as gender, NFC and OSL and their impacts on the model of internet consumer behavior. Better understanding of the effects of these moderators will lead to more effective use of websites by online companies.

REFERENCES

Asch, D. (2001). Competing in the new economy. *European Business Journal, 13*(3), 119–126.

Baumgartner, H., & Steenkamp, J. B. E. M. (1996). Exploratory consumer behavior: Conceptualization and measurement. *International Journal of Research in Marketing, 13*(2), 121–137. doi:10.1016/0167-8116(95)00037-2

Cabeza, R., & Nyberg, L. (2000). Imaging cognition II: An empirical review of 275 PET and f-MRI studies. *Journal of Cognitive Neuroscience, 12*, 1–47. doi:10.1162/08989290051137585

Cacioppo, J. T., & Petty, R. E. (1989). Effects of message repetition on argument processing, recall, and persuasion. *Basic and Applied Social Psychology, 10*, 3–12. doi:10.1207/s15324834basp1001_2

Cacioppo, J. T., Petty, R. E., Kao, C. F., & Rodriguez, R. (1986). Central and peripheral routes to persuasion: An individual difference perspective. *Journal of Personality and Social Psychology, 51*, 1032–1043. doi:10.1037/0022-3514.51.5.1032

Chatterjee, S., Heath, T. B., & Mishra, D. B. (2002). Communicating quality through signals and substantive messages: The effects of supporting information and need for cognition. In S.M. Broniarczyk & K. Nakamoto (eds.), *Advances in Consumer Research,* (Vol. 29, pp. 228-229). Valdosta, GA: Association for Consumer Research.

Cohen, A., Stotland, E., & Wolfe, D. (1955). An experimental investigation of need for cognition. *Journal of Abnormal and Social Psychology, 51*, 291–294. doi:10.1037/h0042761

Epstein, R., Harris, A., Stanley, D., & Kanwisher, N. (1999). The parahippocampal place area: Recognition, navigation or encoding? *Neuron, 23*, 115–125. doi:10.1016/S0896-6273(00)80758-8

Grön, G., Wunderlich, A. P., Spitzer, M., Tomczak, R., & Riepe, M. W. (2000). Brain activation during human navigation: Gender-different neural networks as substrate of performance. *Nature Neuroscience, 3*, 404–408. doi:10.1038/73980

Haugtvedt, C. P., & Petty, R. E. (1992). Personality and persuasion: Need for cognition moderates the persistence and resistance of attitude changes. *Journal of Personality and Social Psychology, 63*, 308–319. doi:10.1037/0022-3514.63.2.308

Heckler, S. E., Childers, T. L., & Houston, M. J. (1993). On the construct validity of the SOP scale. *Journal of Mental Imagery, 17*(3&4), 119–132.

Hoffman, D. L., & Novak, T. P. (1996). Marketing in hypermedia computer-mediated environments: Conceptual foundations. *Journal of Marketing, 60*(3), 50. doi:10.2307/1251841

Jee, J., & Lee, W. N. (2002). Antecedents and consequences of perceived interactivity: An exploratory study. *Journal of Interactive Advertising, 3*(1), 1–16.

Luna, D., Peracchio, L. A., & de Juan, M. D. (2002). Cross-cultural and cognitive aspects of web site navigation. *Journal of the Academy of Marketing Science, 30*(4), 397–410. doi:10.1177/009207002236913

Macias, W. (2003). A preliminary structural equation model of comprehension and persuasion of interactive advertising brand web sites. *Journal of Interactive Advertising, 3*(2).

Mantel, S. P., & Kardes, F. R. (1999). The role of direction of comparison, attribute-based processing, and attitude-based processing in consumer preference. *The Journal of Consumer Research, 25*(4), 335–352. doi:10.1086/209543

McReynolds, P. (1971). The nature and assessment of intrinsic motivation. In P. McReynolds (ed). *Advances in Psychological Assessment,* (Vol. 2, pp. 157-177). Palo Alto, CA: Science and Behavior.

Mehrabian, A., & Russell, J. A. (1974). The basic emotional impact of environments. *Perceptual and Motor Skills, 38,* 283–301.

Meyers-Levy, J., & Maheswaran, D. (1991). Exploring differences in males' and females' processing strategies. *The Journal of Consumer Research, 18*(1), 63–70. doi:10.1086/209241

Meyers-Levy, J., & Peracchio, L. A. (1995). Understanding the effects of color: How the correspondence between available and required resources affects attitudes. *The Journal of Consumer Research, 22*(2), 121–138. doi:10.1086/209440

Mittelstaedt, R. A., Grossbart, S. L., Curtis, W. W., & Deverre, S. P. (1976). Optimum stimulation level and the adoption decision process. *The Journal of Consumer Research, 3*(3), 84–94. doi:10.1086/208655

Peracchio, L. A., & Meyers-Levy, J. (1997). Evaluating persuasion-enhancing techniques from a resource-matching perspective. *The Journal of Consumer Research, 24*(3), 178–191. doi:10.1086/209503

Petty, R. E., & Cacioppo, J. T. (1986). *Communication and persuasion: Central and peripheral routes to attitudes change.* New York: Springer-Verlag.

Pew. (2005, December 28). *Internet and American Life Project Survey: How women and men use the internet.*

Putrevu, S. (2004). Communicating with the sexes: Male and female responses to print advertising. *Journal of Advertising, 33*(3), 51–62.

Putrevu, S., & Lord, K. R. (2003). Processing internet communications: A motivation, opportunity and ability framework. *Journal of Current Issues and Research in Advertising, 25,* 45–59.

Raju, P. S. (1980). Optimum stimulation level: It's relationship to personality, demographics and exploratory behavior. *The Journal of Consumer Research, 7*(4), 272–282. doi:10.1086/208815

Richard, M. O. (2009). *Modeling the internet behavior of visitors by the study of cognitive variables and moderators.* Unpublished doctoral dissertation, HEC-Montreal Business School.

Rodgers, S., & Harris, M. A. (2003). Gender and e-commerce: An exploratory study. *Journal of Advertising Research, 43*(3), 322–329.

Sadowski, C. J., & Cogburn, H. E. (1997). Need for cognition in the big five factor structure. *The Journal of Psychology, 131*(3), 307–312. doi:10.1080/00223989709603517

Salmon, E., Van der Linden, M., Collette, F., & Delfiore, G. (1996). Regional brain activity during working memory tasks. *Brain, 119,* 1617–1625. doi:10.1093/brain/119.5.1617

Schlosser, A. E., Shavitt, S., & Kanfer, A. (1999). Survey of internet users' attitudes toward internet advertising. *Journal of Interactive Marketing*, *13*(3), 34–54. doi:10.1002/(SICI)1520-6653(199922)13:3<34::AID-DIR3>3.0.CO;2-R

Schumacher, P., & Morahan-Martin, J. (2001). Gender, internet and computer attitudes and experiences. *Computers in Human Behavior*, *17*(January), 95–110. doi:10.1016/S0747-5632(00)00032-7

Seltzer, B., & Pandya, D. N. (1994). Further observations on parieto-temporal connections in the rhesus monkey. *Experimental Brain Research*, *55*, 301–312.

Sheehan, K. B. (1999). An investigation of gender differences in online privacy concerns and resultant behaviors. *Journal of Interactive Marketing*, *13*(4), 24–38. doi:10.1002/(SICI)1520-6653(199923)13:4<24::AID-DIR3>3.0.CO;2-O

Shon, Z. Y., Chen, F. Y., & Chang, Y. H. (2003). Airline e-commerce: The revolution in ticketing channels. *Journal of Air Transport Management*, *9*(5), 325–331. doi:10.1016/S0969-6997(03)00040-1

Sicilia, M., Ruiz, S., & Munuera, J. L. (2005). Effects of interactivity in a web site. *Journal of Advertising*, *34*(3), 31–45.

Smith, S. M., & Whitlark, D. B. (2001). Men and women online: What makes them click? *Marketing Research*, *13*(2), 20–25.

Steenkamp, J. B. E. M., & Baumgartner, H. (1992). The role of optimum stimulation level in exploratory consumer behavior. *The Journal of Consumer Research*, *19*(3), 434–448. doi:10.1086/209313

Tuten, T. L., & Bisnjak, M. (2001). Understanding differences in web usage: The role of need for cognition and the five factor model of personality. *Social Behavior and Personality*, *29*(4), 391–398. doi:10.2224/sbp.2001.29.4.391

Venkatraman, M. P., & Price, L. (1990). Differentiating between cognitive and sensory innovativeness. *Journal of Business Research*, *20*(4), 293–315. doi:10.1016/0148-2963(90)90008-2

Weiser, E. B. (2000). Gender differences in internet use patterns and internet application preferences: A two-sample comparison. *Cyberpsychology & Behavior*, *3*(2), 167–178. doi:10.1089/109493100316012

Weiss, E., Kemmler, G., & Deisenhammer, E. A. (2004). Sex differences in cognitive functions. *Personality and Individual Differences*, *35*(4), 863–875. doi:10.1016/S0191-8869(02)00288-X

Wolin, L. D., & Korgaonkar, P. (2003). Web advertising: Gender, differences in beliefs, attitudes and behavior. *Internet Research*, *13*(5), 375–385. doi:10.1108/10662240310501658

Wood, M. (1998). Socio-economic status, delay of gratification, and impulse buying. *Journal of Economic Psychology*, *19*(3), 295–320. doi:10.1016/S0167-4870(98)00009-9

Zhang, Y., & Buda, R. (1999). Moderating effects of need for cognition on responses to positively versus negatively framed advertising messages. *Journal of Advertising*, *28*(2), 1–15.

ADDITIONAL READING

Richard, M.O., Chebat, J.C., Yang, Z., & Putrevu, S. (in press, 2010). A proposed model of online consumer behavior: assessing the role of gender. *Journal of Business Research*.

KEY TERMS AND DEFINITIONS

Affect Transfer Model: process of attitude formation where site attitude directly influences brand attitudes through the peripheral route.

Dual Mediation Model: process of process of attitude formation via the central route; thinking about the brand motivates efforts for processing information, and is influenced by evaluation of the website.

Need for Cognition (NFC): stable individual difference in people's tendency to engage in and enjoy effortful cognitive activity.

Optimum Stimulation Level (OSL): amount of stimulation people prefer in life.

Relational Hypothesis: a theory whereby females are described as relational processors and males as males are item-specific processors. It relates to the style of processing.

Selectivity Hypothesis: a theory whereby females are described as comprehensive processors and males as heuristic processors. It relates to the depth of processing.

Chapter 66
Consumer Information Sharing

Jonathan Foster
University of Sheffield, UK

Angela Lin
University of Sheffield, UK

INTRODUCTION

One area of e-business that has visibly changed in the last few years is the capacity of the Internet for supporting consumer-to-consumer *information sharing*. By using a variety of *social media* software applications such as online reviews, blogs, social tagging, and wikis, consumers are increasingly able to generate and share content about the products and services that are available in the marketplace. Collectively the labor expended by consumers in generating such content is considerable, influencing other consumers' perceptions of these products and services and informing their purchasing decisions. It has been estimated for example that more than 5 million customers have reviewed products on the *Amazon.com* site, with many more making purchasing decisions informed by reading such reviews (Amazon, 2008). According to the findings of a recent *Pew Internet & American Life Project* survey, consumer generated information sources such as product reviews and blogs are also considered equally as important as commercial information, e.g. manufacturers' specifications, when making a purchasing decision (Horrigan, 2008). This article aims to provide an up-to-date review of the practice of consumer information sharing. First the different kinds of information sought by consumers are identified; second the social media software applications that consumers use to create, organize and share information with other consumers are discussed; and finally consideration is given to the marketing implications of consumer information sharing and how e-businesses can utilize social media for developing and managing relations with their customers.

DOI: 10.4018/978-1-61520-611-7.ch066

CONSUMER INFORMATION

Consumers seek information in order to reduce any uncertainties or risks associated with an intended purchase (Conchar, Zinkhan, Peters, and Olavarrieta, 2004). Consumers also seek information in order to make sense of a product or group of products. The kinds of information sought by consumers typically relate to product attributes (e.g. specification, price, quality standards), expert and consumer opinions, and vendor reputation. Identifying relevant information sources involves the consumer either in an internal search of their prior knowledge of the same or similar products, and/or an external search of new information sources. An internal search is said to occur when consumers rely on their personal knowledge and experience of a product, while an external search occurs when consumers look for information beyond their own personal knowledge and experience. The range of external consumer information sources includes: store representatives, salespersons, and company websites; commercial media (e.g. magazines, advertisements), expert reviews; social sources (e.g. word of mouth, family and friends) and recommendations; and an increasing range of social media (e.g. blogs, social bookmarking tools, social shopping sites, and wikis) that consumers use to generate, organize, and communicate information about products and services. In sum, consumers seek a range of different kinds of information in order to reduce the uncertainties and risks associated with making a purchasing decision and to make sense of the products. Information sources can be both internal and external to the consumer and span a spectrum that includes ratings, reviews and recommendations on the one hand, more interactive resources e.g. blogs, and opportunities for fuller participation in consumer wikis and customer communities.

CONSUMER INFORMATION AND SOCIAL MEDIA

Socially-owned media applications such as blogs, social tagging, and opinion sites have been enthusiastically adopted by consumers; with the resulting consumer generated content being widely used by consumers in the course of their purchasing activities. Reasons for this adoption include the relatively low costs associated with their implementation, and the dynamic and recent nature of the content. In contrast to traditional commercially-produced sources the use of social media enables consumers to access, produce, and share content generated by their peers. Rather than describe the different types of social media applications that have been developed, the review is organized in terms of the uses that such media have for consumers and for generating consumer content. Consumer uses of social media include reviewing and rating products and services, organizing content for subsequent access by other consumers, communicating with other consumers through weblogs, and collaborating and participating in the development of more substantive resources such as consumer wikis and customer communities. A description of each of these uses is provided here, along with illustrative examples. The review concludes with a short summary of some of the problems that can arise from consumers' use of social media.

Perhaps the most evident use of social media in the consumer domain is in enabling the publishing and reading of consumer reviews. Reviews written by consumers are perceived to be less biased than the information provided by advertisers and can provide additional information that enhances the credibility of what is already available from retailers and manufacturers. Different types of consumer review exist, depending on the purpose for which they are intended. These include product reviews, content reviews, and seller reviews. Product reviews normally focus on the functionalities of a product e.g. its usability, efficiency, quality, design, reliability, and so on e.g. *Epinions* (http://www.epinions.com/); content reviews focus and share opinions on the content of a product e.g. a book, music, or movie e.g. *Music Emissions* (http://www.musicemissions.com); seller reviews are often used as a mechanism to establish trust between buyers and sellers and to convey a sense of product and service quality e.g. *Froogle* (http://www.froogle.com), and *Ebay* (http://www.ebay.com). Consumer reviews have become a valued consumer information source and their use increases consumers' confidence when making a purchasing decision (Harrell, 2008). Therefore, a growing number of retailers incorporate customer reviews on their site in order to enrich their consumers' shopping experience. An interactive dimension can be added to these reviews by providing a facility for other consumers to rate the usefulness of particular reviews e.g. *Amazon* (http://www.amazon.com). Ratings are also used as a simple way of evaluating goods and services. These include dedicated ratings and reviews sites e.g. *Bizrate* (http://www.bizrate.com) as well as the embedding of ratings scales into reputation systems. Reputation systems enable a consumer to rate a vendor on a given scale. Displays of reputation information often include an aggregated statistical score for positive, negative and neutral ratings; along with the facility to read related limited free-text comments. Enhancements of reputation systems include an interactive facility enabling vendors to respond to consumers' comments, often in the interests of equity when the vendor perceives a comment to be unfair or partial. A further mechanism for aggregating consumer opinions are voting systems. *ILikeTotallyLoveIt. com* for example carries a facility enabling consumers to vote on their agreement with consumers product stories. Consumers' preferences can also aggregated and displayed via recommender systems. Recommender systems in e-commerce identify a similarity in the preferences or tastes of one consumer and others (e.g. goods purchased, products viewed); and make recommendations for

new purchases drawn from the set of other goods bought or viewed by each of the like-minded consumers (Foster, 2006).

Social media also provide an opportunity for users to describe and organize content though the use of descriptors called tags e.g. *Flickr* (http://www.flickr.com). In contrast to the hierarchical category systems developed by organizations and designers on the basis of a standardized vocabulary, social tagging systems enable users to generate and navigate meta-data that describe and organize content flexibly on the basis of users' rather than experts' terminology. If a critical mass of users use the social tagging system, a folksonomy (a blending of the words 'folk' and 'taxonomy') of terms is generated that displays the terms used and chosen by users to assign meaning to the site's content. Although dedicated social tagging sites exist that carry consumer generated content e.g. *Digg* (http://www.digg.com), the more popular use of social tags in a consumer context is for them to become embedded in other media and act as metadata for describing and organizing consumer-generated content. For example *Amazon* (http://www.amazon.com) provides facilities for customer to tag their products. Other consumers then have the opportunity to search for and retrieve relevant products by clicking on these tags. Emerging tags can also be displayed as an ordered alphabetical list, while it has also become popular for groups of user-generated tags to be displayed in the form of a tag cloud that utilizes typographic devices to visualize the frequency and recency with which the tags have been used. Further interactivity is provided by enabling other customers to vote on whether they agree or not that the selected tag is related to the product.

A further highly trusted source for influencing the customer decision process are consumer weblogs or blogs. These are a form of online journal with entries that record consumers' personal experiences and opinions of products and companies, as well comments on issues relevant to the consumer marketplace and consumer culture more generally. An important element of consumer blogs is the ability of other consumers to comment on the entries. Third party hosted and personal consumer blogs exist. *Gizmodo* (http://www.gizmodo.com) for example is currently a popular third party site hosting consumer-to-consumer communication around gadgets; while *Festival of Frugality* (http://www.festivaloffrugality.com) enables consumers to share cost saving tips. Consumers also use blogs to record their personal experience with a product and make comment on the product after its use. *Things I Bought That I Love* (http://thingsiboughtthatilove.com) is a personal consumer blog dedicated to describing and recommending products that a consumer has purchased to other consumers; while *A Suitable Wardrobe* (http://asuitablewardrobe.dynend.com) is a blog written by a men's clothing enthusiast to share his knowledge of men's dressing style. Video sharing websites e.g. *Youtube* (http://www.youtube.com) and *Expo* (http://www.expotv.com) also carry consumer video reviews; thus combining the benefits of trusted consumer reviews with an element of storefront demonstration. Finally, social media such as wikis allow consumers to edit and modify content and collaborate on the generation of consumer information resources (Foster, in press). *Wikitravel* (http://wikitravel.org) is a consumer-generated travel guide that aims to be a free, complete, up-to-date, and reliable guide to worldwide travel; while *Shopwiki* (http://www.shopwiki.com/wiki) carries consumer authored buying and gift guides.

Consumers' use of social media gives rise to a number of business and design challenges. Preeminent among these challenges is the quality and usefulness of the content generated. At its best, consumer information shares similar properties with those attributed to crowd wisdom that contributions are voluntary, diversified, independent, decentralized, and aggregated (Surowiecki, 2004). There is no guarantee however that opinions shared by consumers are free from bias and are those of individuals who are acting independently; and a

number of mechanisms have been put in place to safeguard against this e.g. ranking and voting mechanisms that judge review and reviewer helpfulness, more detailed breakdowns and explanations of ratings and reputation scores, and vendor feedback facilities that enable right of reply. In addition, while the quality of some amateur reviews and customer ratings can be questioned, if there is sufficient critical mass, statistical answers from groups of sufficiently large sizes tend to be accurate (Sunstein, 2006). Hence, aggregation in itself is often a sufficient safeguard against idiosyncratic or commercially-motivated contributions; while more collaboratively developed resources such as consumer wikis rely on the distributed knowledge of individuals as a guide to the accuracy and reliability of the content.

E-BUSINESS, CONSUMERS, AND SOCIAL MEDIA

The advent of consumer information sharing and their take up of social media is both an opportunity and a threat for conducting e-business. On the one hand, consumers willing participation in what is from an e-business perspective marketing and brand building is a boon to businesses and brings marketing benefits and increased exposure to branding and an enhanced reputation. On the other hand in a networked environment reputation is often fragile; and therefore one of the key lessons of this trend is for e-businesses to develop and manage relations with their customers in these same social media environments (Lin and Foster, forthcoming). Some of the strategies that businesses can use to engage with this new breed of active and participatory consumer include listening, talking, energizing, supporting, and embracing customers and their ideas (Li and Bernoff, 2008). One way to combine these strategies is to develop *customer communities*. *Starbucks* for example has developed *My Starbucks Idea* (http://mystarbucksidea.force.com/ideaHome) which combines crowdsourcing and relationship management in one application; while *Amazon* hosts a range of customer communities from Harry Potter to martial arts (http://amazon.com/communities) that aim to develop customer loyalty and that utilize all the social media applications described here. In sum, media convergence and the increasingly ubiquitous nature of networked communication have provided marketing opportunities for businesses that go beyond information access and exchange to meaning making and identity formation (Deighton and Kornfeld, 2007).

FUTURE RESEARCH DIRECTIONS

Although consumer information has increased in availability and accessibility, there remain many factors that can influence effective consumer information sharing and where further research is needed to understand more of the conditions that affect the take-up of consumer-generated content and its impact on purchasing decisions. These include individual differences among consumers, the quality of the information shared and perceptions of the value of such content. Consumers vary for example in their prior knowledge of a product or brand, their knowledge of appropriate information sources and channels, search skills, as well as external factors such as the time available to them within which to make a decision. The depth of an *information search*, i.e. the extent to which a consumer will search, will also depend on balancing the costs and benefits of doing the information search. That is, when the benefits of an information search are perceived to outweigh the costs, consumers are likely to continue searching; if not consumers are likely to stop searching and to engage in satisficing. Increasing the quality and authority of consumer-generated content will continue to present technical and business challenges; while knowing more about when during the purchasing process and why such content is valued

would be valuable for consumer information systems designers and marketing personnel.

CONCLUSION

The topic of consumer information sharing can be considered to incorporate study not only of the mechanisms available for the search, aggregation and sharing of information and opinions, but also of the facilities available for discussing these information and opinions once shared – an advance that may also have helped to counter bias in consumer judgments. Of the range of information sources available, non-commercial information sources are regarded by consumers as normally being more accurate, i.e. free from commercial interest and related to objective facts. Access to traditional social sources such as word of mouth and face-to-face communication can sometimes be limited by shared preconceptions of a product or brand; and recent developments in social media have created the reality of making purchasing decisions that are informed, even possibly optimally informed, not only by information and judgments that come from immediate social networks and strong ties but also from extended virtual networks and weak ties (Frenzen and Nakamoto, 1993). In sum, it is clear that engaging with and sharing social media has proven to be popular among consumers and that with certain safeguards as to the quality, authority, and usefulness of the contributions, also beneficial to businesses' marketing and branding operations.

REFERENCES

Amazon.com. Inc. (2008, November 24). *Investors relations: Press release*. Retrieved December 10, 2008 from http://phx.corporate-ir.net/phoenix.zhtml?c=97664&p=irol-newsArticle&ID=1229410&highlight=

Conchar, M. P., Zinkhan, G. M., Peters, C., & Olavarrieta, S. (2004). An integrated framework for the conceptualization of consumers' perceived-risk processing. *Journal of the Academy of Marketing Science*, *32*(4), 418–436. doi:10.1177/0092070304267551

Deighton, J., & Kornfeld, L. (1997). *Digital interactivity: Unanticipated consequences for markets, marketing, and consumers*. [Working Paper 08-017]. Retrieved from http://www.hbs.edu/research/pdf/08-017.pdf

Foster, J. (2006). Collaborative information seeking and retrieval. *Annual Review of Information Science & Technology*, *40*, 329–356. doi:10.1002/aris.1440400115

Foster, J. (Ed.). (in press). *Collaborative information behavior: User engagement and communication sharing*. Hershey, PA: IGI Global.

Frenzen, J., & Nakamoto, K. (1993). Structure, cooperation, and the flow of market information. *The Journal of Consumer Research*, *20*(3), 360–375. doi:10.1086/209355

Harrell, D. (2008). The influence of consumer generated content on customer experiences and consumer behavior. In P.C. Deans, (Ed.), *Social software and Web 2.0 technology trends*. Hershey, PA: IGI Global.

Horrigan, J. B. (2008). *The Internet and Consumer Choice: Online Americans Use Different Search and Purchase Strategies for Different Goods*. Pew Internet and American Life Project [Report]. Retrieved from http://www.pewinternet.org

Li, C., & Bernoff, J. (2008). *Groundswell: Winning in a world transformed by social technologies*. Boston: Harvard University Press.

Lin, A. & Foster, J. (forthcoming). *Consumer information systems and relationship management: Design, implementation, and use*. Hershey, PA: IGI Global.

Sunstein, C. R. (2006). *Infotopia: How many minds produce knowledge*. Oxford, UK: Oxford University Press.

Surowiecki, J. (2004). *The Wisdom of crowds: Why the many are smarter than the few*. London: Abacus.

KEY TERMS AND DEFINITIONS

Consumer Generated Content: content generated by consumers' use of social media. Examples include reviews, ratings, tags, and weblog or wiki entries.

Consumer Information: the information needed by consumers when researching, purchasing, and completing a purchase. Examples of consumer information needs include: product attributes (e.g. specification, price, quality standards), expert and consumer opinions, and vendor reputation.

Customer Decision Process: The set of stages that consumers pass through when deciding to purchase products or services. When purchasing products, consumers typically pass through a prepurchase stage that involves recognition of need, information gathering, and the evaluation of different product alternatives; a purchase stage in which a decision to purchase is taken; and a postpurchase stage during which customers evaluation the purchase, consider becoming a loyal customer; and finally, dispose of the product.

Information Sharing: an umbrella term for the processes involved in the creation, exchange and use of information. Information sharing includes the sharing of pre-defined information, and discussion of the information once shared.

Recommender System: Recommender systems in e-commerce identify a similarity in the preferences or tastes of one consumer and others (e.g. goods purchased, products viewed); and make recommendations for new purchases drawn from the set of other goods bought or viewed by each of the like-minded consumers.

Social Media: socially rather than commercially-owned media enabling its users to rapidly publish and distribute ideas and opinions, primarily although not exclusively, to a peer audience. Examples of social media include: weblogs, social tagging systems, and wikis.

Social Tagging: in contrast to the pre-defined categories and terms of a classification scheme, social tagging systems enable users to create and assign tags that meaningfully organize the content of a website. Aggregation of tags leads to the generation of a folksonomy, a socially-owned socially owned vocabulary, whose terms define and organize the content of a website from the perspective of members of the user community rather than that of experts.

Chapter 67

B2C E–Commerce Acceptance Models Based on Consumers' Attitudes and Beliefs:
Integrating Alternative Frameworks

Ángel Herrero-Crespo
Universidad de Cantabria, Spain

Ignacio Rodríguez-del-Bosque
Universidad de Cantabria, Spain

INTRODUCTION

The novelty and dynamism of Internet and e-commerce have lead to the revision of the classic paradigm of consumer behaviour and to the continuous study of individuals' conduct in virtual environments. In this context, the literature on Internet has placed special attention on the development and testing of theoretical models aimed to describe and explain e-commerce acceptance by final consumers. In this sense, two theoretical frameworks stand out as the most relevant and widely used approaches in e-commerce adoption literature: the Theory of Planned Behaviour (Schifter & Ajzen, 1985; Ajzen, 1991) and the Technology Acceptance Model (Davis, 1989; Davis et al., 1989). Both models are based on traditional theory of consumer behaviour and focus on individuals' attitudes and beliefs about e-commerce and virtual transactions. However, TPB and TAM differ in the variety of explanatory variables they include and in the identification of beliefs considered as determinants of individuals' attitudes towards a behaviour or technology.

Taking into account the theoretical basement shared by both models, Taylor & Todd (1995) propose the Decomposed Theory of Planned Behaviour which integrates the TAM and TPB, enjoying the strengths of both frameworks. Thus, the DTPB provides greater insight into the factors that influence behaviour or technology acceptance (Tayor & Todd, 1995; Rodríguez-del-Bosque & Herrero, 2005). Nevertheless, the relative trade off of the deeper understanding of IT usage provided by the Decomposed Theory of Planned Behaviour is the

DOI: 10.4018/978-1-61520-611-7.ch067

Figure 1. Theory of planned behavior

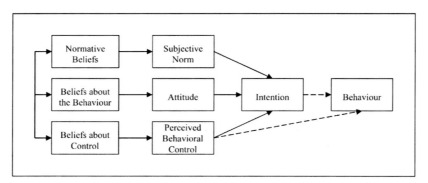

increased complexity and decreased parsimony of the model.

Given the widespread use of the TPB, the TAM and the DTPB in literature about IS and e-commerce adoption, this paper intends to describe their main principles and to examine their weaknesses and strengths for the research of e-commerce acceptance. Additionally, discussion about the integration and development of these models to study Internet shopping behaviour are presented. Finally, future research directions on this topic are proposed.

BACKGROUND: B2C E-COMMERCE ACCEPTANCE MODELS BASED ON CONSUMERS' ATTITUDES AND BELIEFS

The Theory of Planned Behaviour, the Technology Acceptance Model and the Decomposed Theory of Planned Behaviour are described next. In addition, the most important studies carried out in the field of e-commerce which are based on these theoretical frameworks are analysed.

Theory of Planned Behavior (TPB)

The Theory of Planned Behaviour (Schifter & Ajzen, 1985) focuses on those conducts in which the individual is influenced to a certain extent

by the availability of certain requirements and resources. The TPB considers intention as the best predictor of behaviour, as it expresses the effort that individuals are willing to make to develop a particular action (Ajzen, 1991). Likewise, the model identifies three types of determinants and explanatory variables of the intention of behaviour: attitude towards behaviour, subjective norm and perceived behavioural control (Figure 1).

The *attitude* towards behaviour refers to the overall disposition, favourable or unfavourable, towards the development of this conduct and it is the result of the individuals' beliefs with respect to the behaviour and its consequences. On the other hand, the *subjective norm* reflects the effect that other people's opinion –family or friends, among others– has on the consumer's behaviour. Finally, *perceived behavioural control* represents the individual's perceptions with regard to the presence or the absence of the necessary resources and opportunities to develop the conduct.

The Theory of Planned Behaviour has been extensively used and supported in research on the Internet and e-commerce (see Rodríguez-del-Bosque & Herrero, 2005). Particularly, this theoretical model has been taken as a reference to examine the acceptance of the Internet as a shopping channel (Limayem et al., 2000; Keen et al., 2002; Bosnjak et al., 2006; Herrero & Rodríguez-del-Bosque, 2008), the adoption of shopping through mobile telephone systems

Figure 2. Technology acceptance model (TAM)

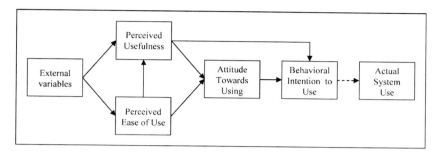

(Khalifa & Cheng, 2002) and the use of a shopping robot (Gentry & Calantone, 2002). On the whole, the empirical evidence obtained by these studies has supported the validity of the TPB to explain e-commerce acceptance.

Technology Acceptance Model (TAM)

Davis' (1989) Technology Acceptance Model focuses on the behaviour of new technologies' usage. Thus, the TAM identifies two specific beliefs that fundamentally affect the acceptance of computer innovations: perceived usefulness (PU) and perceived ease of use (PEOU). The first one is defined as "the user's subjective probability that using a specific system will increase his or her performance in a particular activity", while perceived ease of use refers to the "degree to which the user expects the target system to be free of effort".

The Technology Acceptance Model postulates that the use of a computer innovation is determined by behavioural intention. However, the TAM considers two direct determinants of intention: attitude towards technology and its perceived usefulness (Davis, 1989; Davis et al., 1989). Likewise, perceived usefulness also affects attitude. On the other hand, according to this model, the perceived ease of use in technology determines both attitude towards it and perceived usefulness in it. Figure 2 shows the basic structure of the Technology Acceptance Model.

The TAM represents the most significantly applied theoretical framework in research on information systems in general, and on the Internet in particular –see Lee et al. (2003)–. Regarding this subject, it is worth mentioning the studies supported by the TAM to analyze electronic shopping acceptance, whether considering this behaviour from a general perspective (Teo et al., 1999; Childers et al., 2001; Fenech & O'Cass, 2001; Salisbury et al., 2001; O'Cass & Fenech, 2003; Park et al., 2004; Shih, 2004; Bosnjak et al., 2006; Herrero & Rodríguez-del-Bosque, 2008; Rodríguez-del-Bosque & Herrero, 2008; Herrero et al., 2009) or studying the usage of a specific virtual store or service (Gefen & Straub, 2000; Chen et al., 2002; Gefen, 2003; Pavlou, 2003; Van-der-Heijden et al., 2003). On the whole, the different studies that have analyzed Internet behaviour based on the Technology Acceptance Model support the main relationships postulated in it.

Decomposed Theory of Planned Behavior (DTPB)

The Decomposed Theory of Planned Behaviour (Taylor & Todd, 1995) represents an effort to integrate the contributions of the TPB and the TAM in order to provide a more thoughtful explanation of the adoption of technology innovations. Hence, based on literature on innovation characteristics, the model develops the dimensions of attitude,

Figure 3. Decomposed theory of planned behavior

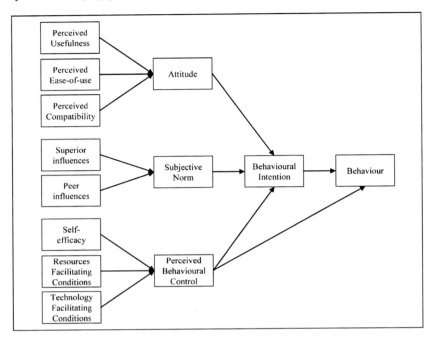

subjective norm and perceived behavioural control, decomposing them into specific beliefs groups (Figure 3).

Based on literature regarding innovation characteristics (Rogers, 1983; Moore & Benbasat, 1991), the model proposes three determinants of attitude towards a new technology: relative advantage, complexity and compatibility. Relative advantage refers to the degree to which an innovation is superior to other alternatives and it can incorporate aspects such as economic profits, image improvement, convenience and satisfaction (Rogers, 1983), making it comparable to the concept of "perceived usefulness" (Davis, 1989). On the other hand, complexity represents the degree to which an innovation is perceived as difficult to understand, learn or operate (Rogers, 1983), and it is an analogous dimension to "perceived ease of use". Finally, compatibility refers to the degree to which a new technology meets the habits, values and needs of the potential adopter (Rogers, 1983).

With reference to the subjective norm, different research supports its decomposition in diverse structures that represent the influence of different groups of reference (Oliver & Bearden, 1985; Burnkrant & Page, 1988). In particular, Taylor & Todd (1995) propound the inclusion of three groups in a business context: superiors, equals and subordinates. Finally, perceived behavioural control is decomposed into the dimensions of self–efficacy (Bandura, 1982) and facilitating conditions (Triandis, 1977).

Some authors have applied the Decomposed Theory of Planned Behaviour to the study of Internet use and e-commerce acceptance (Bhattacherjee, 2000; Lau et al., 2001; Lu et al., 2001; Hsu and Chiu, 2004a; Hsu and Chiu, 2004b; Pavlou and Fygenson, 2006). Overall, the results obtained in these papers have supported the causal structure proposed by the DTPB and their authors have pointed out the usefulness of this theoretical framework to provide a global explanation of the adoption of e-commerce and e-services.

STRENGHTS AND WEAKNESSES OF TPB, TAM AND DTPB TO EXPLAIN E-COMMERCE ACCEPTANCE: AN OPEN ISSUE

Although the theories examined have been extensively used in literature about IS and e-commerce adoption, none of these alternative models have achieved universal acceptance, as there are strong points and weak points in each one (see Ajzen, 1991; Mathieson, 1991; Gentry & Calantone, 2002; Venkatesh et al., 2003; Bosnjak et al., 2006). In this sense, the investigations focused on the comparison of the Theory of Planned Behaviour and the Technology Acceptance Model have found that the TAM may be more appropriate to analyse IS adoption, since it has been developed specifically to study this behaviour while the TPB is a general model (Davis et al., 1989; Gentry & Calantone, 2002). However, Mathieson (1991), Taylor & Todd (1995) and Herrero et al. (2006) point out the excessive simplicity of the TAM to explain IS adoption, as it only considers attitudes, perceived usefulness and ease of use as predictive variables. In contrast, these authors acknowledge that the TPB provides a deeper understanding of the factors that determine IS adoption, including social pressures and facilitating conditions. Taking into account the particular strengths of both theoretical models, Mathieson (1991) proposes the combined use of the TAM and the TPB, using the first model to identify dissatisfied IS users and discover the general nature of their complaints, and the TPB to obtain more specific information about the problem.

Following this approach, the Decomposed Theory of Planned Behaviour integrates both the TAM and TPB approaches, enjoying the strengths of both theoretical frameworks. Thus, this model is specifically designed to explain IS acceptance and also includes detailed attitudinal, social and control influences, by decomposing the beliefs structures. As a result, the DTPB provides greater insight into the factors that influence behaviour

or technology acceptance (Taylor & Todd, 1995; Rodríguez-del-Bosque & Herrero, 2005). Nevertheless, the relative trade off of the deeper understanding of IT usage provided by this theory is its higher complexity and lower parsimony. In this sense, Bagozzi (1992) points out that explanatory power being equivalent, the "best" model is the one which is the most parsimonious. Moreover, Mulaik et al. (1989) state that a model that leads to good prediction while using only a few predictors is preferable. Other researchers, however, have argued that parsimony is desirable only to the extent that it facilitates understanding (Browne & Cudeck, 1993). According to this approach, the DTPB seems to be especially appropriate for research aimed at providing a deeper understanding of IT usage (in this case, e-commerce acceptance).

FUTURE RESEARCH DIRECTIONS

Although different studies have supported the usefulness of the three models examined to explain e-commerce acceptance, the empirical evidence available regarding this issue is still limited, and somehow contradictory (Gentry & Calantone, 2002; Bosnjak et al., 2006; Herrero et al., 2006), and additional research is needed.

Firstly, the relationship between beliefs, attitude, intention and behaviour propounded in the TPB, the TAM and the DTPB should be re-examined. Regarding this subject, the TAM includes a direct influence of perceived usefulness on the intention to accept/use IS, an effect that has been supported by various studies in the scope of e-commerce (Gefen & Straub, 2000; Gentry & Calantone, 2002; Featherman & Pavlou, 2003). However, the DTPB does not incorporate this effect, and only consider the indirect influence of perceived usefulness on intention through its effect on attitudes towards the system. On the contrary, some authors have even propounded to eliminate attitudes from TAM, considering perceived usefulness and ease of use as direct determinants of IS acceptance intention (Chau, 1996; Szajna, 1996; Venkatesh and Davis, 2000). This approach implies significant limitations for the integration of TAM and TPB in a single model (DTPB) as the main connection between both frameworks would disappear. Therefore, more evidence is required to clarify the relationship between beliefs, attitudes and intention to accept e-commerce.

Likewise, more research is needed about the decomposed beliefs that influence attitudes, subjective norm and perceived behavioural control. In particular, the TAM and the DTPB only incorporate technological attributes of the system (perceived usefulness, ease of use, and compatibility) as determinants of attitudes. However, given the business nature of e-commerce, in this specific field the consideration of the commercial attributes of the channel may provide greater insight and explanatory power about online shopping behaviour. Thus, variables such as the price, variety and quality of the products available on the Internet, the playfulness of virtual shopping experience or the information offered on the web may be relevant determinants of attitudes towards e-commerce. Similarly, more evidence is required about the specific groups whose opinions determine the subjective norm with respect to Internet shopping. Thus, the collectives propounded for other information systems or for organizational environments may not be applicable to B2C e-commerce. Similarly, additional research about the structure of beliefs that give form to perceived control on Internet shopping is needed.

Finally, it would be necessary to analyze the effect of product category in the process of e-commerce adoption. In particular, the influence of attitudes, the subjective norm or the attributes perceived in the system could vary from one product to another. Thus, the effect of perceived ease of use on attitudes towards e-commerce could be particularly important for those products whose shopping process is habitually more difficult. On the other hand, subjective norm could have a greater influence for those products and services in which fashion and trends are especially relevant, such as exclusive clothing or art pieces.

CONCLUSION

According to the literature reviewed, the TPB, the TAM and the DTPB are models valid to explain e-commerce acceptance and use. However each of these theoretical frameworks present strong and weak points, so their use in research must be conditioned by the objective of the investigation (predictive or explanatory), and the parsimony desired in the study. Thus, TAM may be more appropriate to analyse e-commerce acceptance from a technological perspective, while the TPB and DTPB provide a deeper understanding of the factors that determine online shopping, including social pressures and facilitating conditions. Moreover, the DTPB provides greater insight into the beliefs that influence e-commerce acceptance but it is a more complex and less parsimonious model. In fact, despite the widespread use of these theories in literature about IS and e-commerce adoption, none of them have achieved universal acceptance and much research is still needed on this topic.

REFERENCES

Ajzen, I. (1991). The Theory of Planned Behaviour. *Organizational Behavior and Human Decision Processes*, *50*, 179–511. doi:10.1016/0749-5978(91)90020-T

Bagozzi, R. P. (1992). The Self-Regulation of Attitudes, Intentions and Behaviour. *Social Psychology Quarterly*, *55*(2), 178–204. doi:10.2307/2786945

Bandura, A. (1982). Self-efficacy Mechanism in Human Agency. *The American Psychologist*, *37*, 122–147. doi:10.1037/0003-066X.37.2.122

Bhachatterjee, A. (2000). Acceptance of E-Commerce Services: The Case of Electronic Brokerages. *IEEE Transactions on Systems, Man, and Cybernetics. Part A, Systems and Humans, 30*(4), 411–420. doi:10.1109/3468.852435

Bosnjak, M., Obermier, D., & Tuten, T. L. (2006). Predicting and explaining the propensity to bid in online auctions: a comparison of two action-theoretical models. *Journal of Consumer Behaviour, 5*, 102–116. doi:10.1002/cb.38

Browne, M. W., & Cudeck, R. (1993). Alternative Ways of Assessing Model Fit. In K. Bollen & J.S. Long (Eds.) *Testing Structural Equation Models*. London: Sage Publications.

Burnkrant, R. E., & Page, T. J. (1988). The Structure and Antecedents of the Normative and Attitudinal Components of Fishbein's Theory of Reasoned Action. *Journal of Experimental Social Psychology, 24*, 66–87. doi:10.1016/0022-1031(88)90044-3

Chau, P. Y. K. (1996). An Empirical Assesment of a Modified Technology Acceptance Model. *Journal of Management Information Systems, 13*(2), 185–204.

Chen, L., Gilleson, M. L., & Sherrel, D. L. (2002). Enticing Online Consumers: An Extended Technology Acceptance Perspective. *Information & Management, 39*, 705–719. doi:10.1016/S0378-7206(01)00127-6

Childers, T. L., Carr, C. L., Peck, J., & Carson, S. (2001). Hedonic and Utilitarian Motivations for Online Retail Shopping Behaviour. *Journal of Retailing, 77*, 511–535. doi:10.1016/S0022-4359(01)00056-2

Davis, F. D. (1989). Perceived usefulness, perceived ease of use and user acceptance of information technology. *MIS Quarterly, 13*(3), 319–339. doi:10.2307/249008

Davis, F. D., Bagozzi, R. P., & Warshaw, P. R. (1989). User Acceptance of Computer Technology: A Comparison of Two Theoretical Models. *Management Science, 35*(8), 982–1003. doi:10.1287/mnsc.35.8.982

Featherman, M. S., & Pavlou, P. A. (2003). Predicting E-services Adoption: A Perceived Risk Facets Perspective. *International Journal of Human-Computer Studies, 59*, 451–474. doi:10.1016/S1071-5819(03)00111-3

Fenech, T., & O'Cass, A. (2001). Internet Users' Adoption of Web Retailing: User and Product Dimensions. *Journal of Product and Brand Management, 10*(6), 361–381. doi:10.1108/EUM0000000006207

Gefen, D. (2003). TAM of Just Plain Habit: A Look at Experienced Online Shoppers. *Journal of End User Computing, 15*(3), 1–13.

Gefen, D. & Straub, D. (2000). The Relative Importance of Perceived Ease of Use in IS Adoption: A Study of E-Commerce Adoption. *Journal of the Association for Information Systems, 1*.

Gentry, L., & Calantone, R. (2002). A Comparison of Three Models to Explain Shop-Bot Use on the Web. *Psychology and Marketing, 19*(11), 945–956. doi:10.1002/mar.10045

Herrero, A., García-de-los-Salmones, M. M., & Rodríguez-del-Bosque, I. (2009). The influence of perceived risk on Internet shopping behavior: A multidimensional perspective. *Journal of Risk Research, 12*(2), 259–277. doi:10.1080/13669870802497744

Herrero, A., & Rodríguez-del-Bosque, I. (2008). The effect of innovativeness on the adoption of B2C e-commerce: A model based on the Theory of Planned Behavior. *Computers in Human Behavior, 24*, 2830–2847. doi:10.1016/j.chb.2008.04.008

Herrero, A., Rodríguez-del-Bosque, I., & Trespalacios, J. A. (2006). La adopción del comercio electrónico B2C: Una comparación empírica de dos modelos alternativos. *Revista Española de Investigación de Marketing ESIC, 10*(1), 69–90.

Hsu, M. H., & Chiu, C. M. (2004a). Internet self-efficacy and electronic service acceptance. *Decision Support Systems, 38*(3), 369–381. doi:10.1016/j.dss.2003.08.001

Hsu, M. H., & Chiu, C. M. (2004b). Predicting electronic service continuance with a decomposed theory of planned behaviour. *Behaviour & Information Technology, 23*(5), 359–379. doi:10.1080/01449290410001669969

Keen, C., Wetzels, M., De Ruyter, K., & Feinberg, R. (2004). E-Tailers versus Retailers. Which Factors Determine Consumer Preferences. *Journal of Business Research, 57*(7), 685–695. doi:10.1016/S0148-2963(02)00360-0

Khalifa, M., & Cheng, S. (2002). Adoption of Mobile Commerce: Role of Exposure. In *Proceedings of the 35th Hawaii International Conference on System Science*.

Lau, A., Yen, J., & Chau, P. Y. K. (2001). Adoption of On-line Trading in the Hong Kong Financial Market. *Journal of Electronic Commerce Research, 2*(2), 58–65.

Lee, Y., Kozar, K. A., & Larsen, K. R. T. (2003). The Technology Acceptance Model: Past, Present, and Future. *Communications of the Association for Information Systems, 12*, 752–780.

Limayem, M., Khalifa, M., & Frini, A. (2000). What Makes Consumers Buy from Internet? A Longitudinal Study of Online Shopping. *IEEE Transactions on Systems, Man, and Cybernetics. Part A, Systems and Humans, 30*(4), 421–432. doi:10.1109/3468.852436

Lu, J., Liu, C., Yu, C.-S., & Yao, J. E. (2001). Exploring Factors Associated with Wireless Internet via Mobile Technology Acceptance in Mainland China. *Communications of the International Information Management Association, 3*(1), 101–119.

Mathieson, K. (1991). Predicting User Intentions: Comparing the Technology Acceptance Model with the Theory of Planned Behaviour. *Information Systems Research, 2*(3), 173–191. doi:10.1287/isre.2.3.173

Moore, G. C., & Benbasat, I. (1991). Development of an Instrument to Measure the Perceptions of Adopting an Information Technology Innovation. *Information Systems Research, 2*(3), 192–222. doi:10.1287/isre.2.3.192

Mulaik, S. A., James, L. R., Alstine, J. V., Bennett, N., Lind, S., & Stilwell, C. D. (1989). Evaluation of goodness of fit indices for structural equation models. *Psychological Bulletin, 105*(3), 430–445. doi:10.1037/0033-2909.105.3.430

O'Cass, A., & Fenech, T. (2003). Web Retailing Adoption: Exploring the Nature of Internet Users Web Retailing Behaviour. *Journal of Retailing and Consumer Services, 10*, 81–94. doi:10.1016/S0969-6989(02)00004-8

Oliver, R. L., & Bearden, W. O. (1985). Crossover Effects in the Theory of Reasoned Action. *The Journal of Consumer Research, 12*(3), 324–340. doi:10.1086/208519

Park, J., Lee, D., & Ahn, J. (2004). Risk-Focused e-Commerce Adoption Model: A Cross-Country Study. *Journal of Global Information Technology Management, 7*(2), 6–30.

Pavlou, P. A. (2003). Consumer Intentions to Adopt Electronic Commerce – Incorporating Trust and Risk in the Technology Acceptance Model. *International Journal of Electronic Commerce, 7*(3), 101–134.

Pavlou, P. A., & Fygenson, M. (2006). Understanding and Predicting Electronic Commerce Adoption: An Extension of the Theory of Planned Behaviour. *MIS Quarterly, 30*(1), 115.

Rodríguez-del-Bosque, I., & Herrero, A. (2005). La aceptación de Internet y el comercio electrónico basados en las actitudes. In A.M. Gutiérrez, & M.J. Sánchez-Franco, (Ed.), *Marketing en Internet, Estrategia y Empresa*, (pp. 371-412).

Rodríguez-del-Bosque, I., & Herrero, A. (2008). Antecedentes de la utilidad percibida en la adopción del comercio electrónico entre particulares y empresas. *Cuadernos de Economía y Dirección de la Empresa, 34*, 107–134.

Rogers, E. M. (1983). *Diffusion of Innovations*, (3rd Ed.). New York: The Free Press.

Salisbury, W. D., Pearson, R. A., Pearson, A. W., & Miller, D. W. (2001). Perceived security and World Wide Web Purchase Intention. *Industrial Management & Data Systems, 101*(4), 165–176. doi:10.1108/02635570110390071

Schifter, D. B., & Ajzen, I. (1985). Intention, perceived control, and weight loss: An application of the theory of planned behaviour. *Journal of Personality and Social Psychology, 49*, 842–851. doi:10.1037/0022-3514.49.3.843

Shih, H. P. (2004). An Empirical Study on Predicting User Acceptance of e-Shopping on the Web. *Information & Management, 41*, 351–368. doi:10.1016/S0378-7206(03)00079-X

Szajna, B. (1996). Empirical Evaluation of the Revised Technology Acceptance Model. *Management Science, 42*(1), 85–92. doi:10.1287/mnsc.42.1.85

Taylor, S., & Todd, P. A. (1995). Understanding Information Technology Usage: A Test of Competing Models. *Information Systems Research, 6*(2), 144–176. doi:10.1287/isre.6.2.144

Teo, T. S. H., Lim, V. K. G., & Lai, R. Y. C. (1999). Intrinsic and Extrinsic Motivation in Internet Usage. *Omega International Journal of Management Science, 27*, 25–37. doi:10.1016/S0305-0483(98)00028-0

Triandis, H. C. (1977). *Interpersonal behaviour*. New York: Brooks/Cole.

Van-der-Heijden, H., Verhagen, T., & Creemers, M. (2003). Understanding Online Purchase Intentions: Contributions from Technology and Trust Perspectives. *European Journal of Information Systems, 12*, 41–48. doi:10.1057/palgrave.ejis.3000445

Venkatesh, V., & Davis, F. D. (2000). A Theoretical Extension of the Technology Acceptance Model: Four Longitudinal Field Studies. *Management Science, 46*(2), 186–204. doi:10.1287/mnsc.46.2.186.11926

Venkatesh, V., Morris, M. G., Davis, G. B., & Davis, F. D. (2003). User Acceptance of Information Technology: Towards a Unified View. *MIS Quarterly, 27*(3), 425–478.

KEY TERMS AND DEFINITIONS

Acceptance Model: Theoretical structure that models and explains how users come to accept and use an innovation, technology or information system.

Attitude towards Behavior: Overall disposition, favorable or unfavorable, towards the development of a conduct, resulting from the individuals' beliefs with respect to the behavior and its consequences.

Facilitating Conditions: External resource constraints to develop a behavior (Triandis, 1977).

Perceived Behavioral Control: Individual's perceptions with regard to the presence or the absence of the necessary resources and opportunities to develop the conduct.

Perceived Compatibility: Degree to which a new technology meets the habits, values and needs of the potential adopter (Rogers, 1983).

Perceived Ease of Use: Degree to which the user expects an information system to be free of effort (Davis, 1989).

Perceived Usefulness: User's subjective probability that using a specific system will increase his or her performance in a particular activity (Davis, 1989).

Self–Efficacy: People's beliefs about their capabilities to produce designated levels of performance that exercise influence over events that affect their lives (Bandura, 1994).

Subjective Norm: Effect that other people's opinion –family or friends, among others– has on the consumer's behavior.

Chapter 68

Effect of Perceived Risk on e-Commerce Acceptance:
State of the Art and Future Research Directions

Ángel Herrero-Crespo
Universidad de Cantabria, Spain

Ignacio Rodríguez-del-Bosque
Universidad de Cantabria, Spain

INTRODUCTION

The risk or uncertainty perceived on a conduct (e.g. purchasing or consuming of a product, or using an information system) by the individuals has been traditionally identified as one of the main determinants of consumer behavior. In particular, the influence of perceived risk has been specially linked to high involvement products or conducts (Laurent & Kapferer, 1985) which imply a high value or concern for the individual, and that are usually purchased after long and careful consideration. In the specific context of e-commerce, perceived risk has been traditionally identified as one of the main barriers for Internet shopping acceptance and diffusion (Korgaonkar & Wolin, 1999; Goldsmith &

Lafferty, 2001; Miyazaki & Fernández, 2001; Wu & Wang, 2005). However, the empirical evidence available regarding this issue is contradictory, and some authors have found that the influence exerted by perceived risk on consumers' online shopping behavior may not be so relevant (Jarvenpaa & Todd, 1997; Herrero & Rodríguez del Bosque, 2008).

In this context, this paper examines the influence that perceived risk in online shopping has on the process of e-commerce adoption by end consumers. Therefore, first the concept of perceived risk is studied from a general perspective, examining the different theoretical approaches to this construct and how it is defined from each perspective. Moreover, the perceived risk is analyzed as a multidimensional concept, taking into consideration the different risk facets identified in literature. In each case, the empirical evidence available in the field of Inter-

DOI: 10.4018/978-1-61520-611-7.ch068

net and e-commerce is examined. Additionally, discussion about the influence of perceived risk on e-commerce adoption by end consumers is presented and future research directions on this topic are proposed.

BACKGROUND: CONCEPT OF PERCEIVED RISK IN E-COMMERCE

Since it was introduced in the marketing and consumer behavior literature (Bauer, 1960), the perceived risk concept has been analyzed from diverse perspectives. Thus, the classical theory of decision conceives this variable as a distribution that reflects the behavior possible results, probabilities and subjective values (Pratt, 1964; Arrow, 1965). From a similar perspective, first analyses of perceived risk in the context of consumer behavior agree in defining this variable as a combination of two factors: the probability of loss as a consequence of certain behavior and the importance attributed to that loss (Kogan & Wallach, 1964; Cunningham, 1967; Cox, 1967). Nevertheless, some authors such as Sjoberg (1980) criticize this conception of perceived risk as they consider it too rigid and specific to cover such an ambiguous variable. Following this approach, Stone & Winter (1987) break away from the expectation-value traditional normative orientation and consider the perceived risk exclusively as a subjective expectation of loss (Mitchell, 1999). Finally, perceived risk has been traditionally linked to the concept of uncertainty. Thus, diverse authors have suggested that both concepts are equivalent (Bauer, 1960; Taylor, 1974). On the contrary, other researchers consider that risk and uncertainty are different concepts (Peter & Ryan, 1976; Stone & Gronhaug, 1993), but acknowledge that the distinctions between both terms have become blurred in consumer research, and risk and uncertainty are used interchangeably.

According to this approach, diverse studies have supported the disincentive effect of perceived risk or uncertainty on e-commerce acceptance and Internet shopping behavior. Hence, several authors have observed that the perceived risk has a negative effect on e-commerce adoption (Korgaonkar & Wolin, 1999; Joines et al., 2003), intention to shop on the Internet in the future (Liang & Huang, 1998; Vijayasarathy & Jones, 2000; Liao & Cheung, 2001; Salisbury et al., 2001; Pavlou, 2003; Kim et al., 2008; Herrero et al., 2009), transactions frequency (Miyazaki & Fernández, 2001), attitudes toward e-commerce (Jarvenpaa & Todd, 1997; Vijayasarathy & Jones, 2000; Fenech & O'Cass, 2001; Van der Heijden et al., 2003; Hsu & Chiu, 2004a; Shih, 2004; Herrero et al., 2009) and e-service satisfaction (Hsu & Chiu, 2004b). However, other authors have not found a significant influence of perceived risk on e-commerce acceptance (Herrero & Rodríguez del Bosque, 2008) or have found contradictory evidence (Wu & Wang, 2005), raising reasonable doubts about this issue.

MULTIDIMENSIONAL APPROACH TO PERCEIVED RISK ON E-COMMERCE

A traditional research stream in perceived risk literature focuses on the identification and analyses of the risk facets that affect consumer behavior. In this sense, it is worth pointing out that, although very different classifications have emerged on this matter (Cunningham, 1967; Roselius, 1971; Jacoby & Kaplan, 1972; Peter & Ryan, 1976; Ingene & Hughes, 1985; Stone & Gronhaug, 1993), it is possible to identify five facets of perceived risk common to most of the approaches: economic, performance, social, time and psychological risks. Furthermore, with the development of information technologies, an additional dimension has been proposed: privacy risk (Jarvenpaa & Todd, 1997; Lim, 2003). Table 1 shows a definition for each one of these facets.

In the context of e-commerce research, few studies have analyzed the influence of perceived

Table 1. Definition of the main perceived risk facets proposed in marketing literature (Adapted from Featherman & Pavlou, 2003)

Dimension	Definition
Economic, monetary or financial risk	The potential monetary outlay associated with the initial purchase price as well as the subsequent maintenance cost of the product, and the potential financial loss due to fraud.
Functional or Performance risk	The possibility of the product malfunctioning and not performing as it was designed and advertised and therefore mailing to deliver the desired benefits.
Psychological risk	Potential loss of self-esteem (ego loss) from the frustration of not achieving a buying goal.
Social risk	Potential loss of status in one's social group as a result of adopting a product or service, looking foolish or untrendy.
Time risk	Potential loss of time associated with making a bad purchasing decision by wasting time researching and making the purchase, only to have to replace it if it does not perform to expectations.
Privacy risk	Potential loss of control over personal information, Such as when information about you is used without your knowledge or permission.

risk from a multidimensional perspective. On this matter, it is worth mentioning Jarvenpaa & Todd's (1997) contributions, which confirm the impact of economic, performance, social, physical and privacy risks facets on attitudes toward Internet shopping, but they do not observe their influence on future behavior intention. On the other hand, Forsythe & Shi (2003) analyze the effect that performance, financial, time and privacy risk facets have on e-commerce adoption and they observe that the first three facets affect the purchase frequency, while expenditure is only influenced by the economic component. More recently, Herrero et al. (2009) observe that financial, performance, social, time, psychological and privacy risk facets influence attitudes towards e-commerce and Internet shopping intention through overall risk perceived in e-commerce. With a more limited perspective, diverse studies have supported the influence of perceived risk specific facets on e-commerce adoption. Particularly, the empirical evidence available regarding this issue shows that shopping behavior on the Internet is negatively influenced by economic (Van den Poel & Leunis, 1999; Bhatnagar et al., 2000), performance (Dahlén, 1999; Bhatnagar et al., 2000), social (Eastlick & Lotz, 1999) and privacy (Swaminathan et al., 1999; Liu et al., 2005) risks. Nevertheless, there is not a consensus in the literature regarding

which are the main facets of perceived risk that influence Internet shopping behavior.

FUTURE RESEARCH DIRECTIONS

Although perceived risk has been traditionally identified as one of the main barriers for Internet shopping acceptance, the empirical evidence available regarding this issue is insufficient. Therefore, additional research is needed to clarify how perceived risk affects e-commerce acceptance and usage.

Firstly, the empirical evidence available about the influence of perceived risk dimensions in the scope of e-commerce and Internet shopping is limited and contradictory. Thus, although some authors have confirmed that shopping behavior on the Internet is negatively influenced by different risks facets, other studies have not obtained the same results (Forsythe & Shi, 2003; Lim, 2003). Moreover, the studies that have focused on the influence exerted by perceived risk facets on Internet shopping behaviour have considered a wide range of dependant variables as attitudes toward e-commerce (Jarvenpaa & Todd, 1997; Herrero et al., 2009), online shopping intention (Jarvenpaa & Todd, 1997; Eastlick & Lotz, 1999; Van den Poel & Leunis, 1999; Herrero et al., 2009), purchase

Table 2. Definition perceived risk sources (Adapted from Lim, 2003)

Source	Definition
Technology risk	Degree to which individuals believe that if the purchase products or services through the Internet they will suffer losses caused by the Internet and its related technologies.
Vendor risk	Degree to which individuals believe that if the purchase products or services through the Internet they will suffer losses caused by Internet vendors
Consumer risk	Degree to which individuals believe that if the purchase products or services through the Internet they will suffer losses caused by social pressure (received from their families, friends or colleagues).
Product risk	Degree to which individuals believe that if the purchase products or services through the Internet they will suffer losses caused by products.

frequency (Forsythe & Shi, 2003) or expenditure (Swaminathan et al., 1999; Forsythe & Shi, 2003). Therefore, the empirical evidence available does not provide a clear and consistent explanation of how the diverse dimensions of perceived risk influence Internet shopping behavior.

Likewise, it would be necessary to complement the study of perceived risk dimensions with the analyses of the sources of perceived uncertainty (Lim, 2003). Thus, while the traditional facets of perceived risk represent potential negative consequences of consumers' behaviour little attention has been paid to the study of the sources of such risk facets. The relevance of this issue is evident, as identifying the sources of perceived risk may allow Internet vendors to target their resources appropriately to reduce consumers' perceived uncertainty in online shopping. In this sense, Lim (2003) propounds four sources of risk perceived by consumers in B2C e-commerce (Table 2): technology risk, vendor risk, consumer risk, and product risk. The empirical evidence available regarding this topic is however very limited, and much research is needed to clarify which factors give place to consumer's risk perceptions about e-commerce and Internet shopping.

Finally, it would be necessary to analyze the influence of perceived risk on Internet shopping behaviour for different types of products and services. In this sense, it seems logical to think that the impact of perceived risk may vary notably between tangible goods and services, as well as between products of high and low implication. Moreover, the effect of diverse dimensions of perceived risk may be different depending of the product to purchase or its attributes. Thus, financial risk could have a more intensive influence for product categories characterized by higher prices while performance risk may be particularly relevant in the case of technological products. Similarly, social risk perceptions could have a greater influence for those products and services in which fashion and trends are especially relevant.

CONCLUSION

Although perceived risk in e-commerce has been traditionally identified as one of the main determinants of Internet shopping behavior, the empirical evidence available regarding this topic is still insufficient and new research is need. Firstly, some authors have pointed out that the disincentive effect of perceived risk on e-commerce acceptance and usage may not be as relevant as expected (Jarvenpaa & Todd, 1997; Herrero & Rodríguez del Bosque, 2008). Moreover, there is not a consensus in literature about how perceived risk influence Internet shopping behavior. In particular, some authors have studied the effect exerted by this variable from a global perspective (Liang & Huang, 1998; Vijayasarathy & Jones, 2000; Pavlou, 2003; Van der Heijden et al., 2003; Hsu & Chiu, 2004a; Hsu & Chiu,

2004a), while other researchers have applied a multidimensional approach, considering different facets of perceived risk in e-commerce (Jarvenpaa & Todd, 1997; Bhatnagar et al., 2000; Forsythe & Shi, 2003; Herrero et al., 2009). In addition, the empirical evidence available about the influence of perceived risk dimensions is contradictory, and more research is needed to confirm which are the main facets of perceived risk that influence e-commerce acceptance and use. Finally, little attention have been paid in the literature to the identification of the sources of consumer's risk perceptions, an issue that is particularly relevant to take the appropriate measures to reduce perceived uncertainty in e-commerce.

Therefore, despite the fact that perceived risk has been traditionally considered as one of the main barriers for e-commerce acceptance and use, much research is still needed to clarify how this influence is exerted and how Internet vendors can reduce the different dimensions of risk perceived by consumers.

REFERENCES

Arrow, K. (1965). *Aspects of the Theory of Risk Bearing*. Helsinki, Finland: Yrjö Hahnsson Foundation.

Bauer, R. A. (1960). Consumer Behavior as Risk Taking. In R.S. Hancock (Ed.), *Dynamic Marketing for a Changing World*, (pp. 389-398).

Bhatnagar, A., Misra, S., & Rao, H. R. (2000). On Risk, Convenience, and Internet Shopping behaviour. *Communications of the ACM, 43*(11), 98–105. doi:10.1145/353360.353371

Cox, D. F. (1967). *Risk Taking and Information Handling in Consumer Behavior*. Boston: Harvard University Press.

Cunningham, S. M. (1967). The Major Dimensions of Perceived Risk. In D.F. Cox (Ed.) *Risk Taking and Information Handling in Consumer Behavior*. Boston: Harvard University Press.

Dahlén, M. (1999). Closing in on the Web Consumer – A Study of Internet Shopping. In E. Bohlin, K. Brodin, A. Lundgren, & B. Thorngren (Eds.), *Convergence in Communications and Beyond*, (pp. 1-18).

Eastlick, M. A., & Lotz, S. (1999). Profiling Potential Adopters and Non-adopters of an Interactive Electronic Shopping Medium. *International Journal of Retail & Distribution Management, 27*(8), 209–223. doi:10.1108/09590559910278560

Featherman, M. S., & Pavlou, P. A. (2003). Predicting E-services Adoption: A Perceived Risk Facets Perspective. *International Journal of Human-Computer Studies, 59*, 451–474. doi:10.1016/S1071-5819(03)00111-3

Fenech, T., & O'Cass, A. (2001). Internet Users' Adoption of Web Retailing: User and Product Dimensions. *Journal of Product and Brand Management, 10*(6), 361–381. doi:10.1108/EUM0000000006207

Forsythe, S. M., & Shi, B. (2003). Consumer Patronage and Risk Perceptions in Internet Shopping. *Journal of Business Research, 56*(1), 867–875. doi:10.1016/S0148-2963(01)00273-9

Goldsmith, R. E., & Lafferty, B. A. (2001). Innovative Online Buyers. In *Proceedings of the Society for Marketing Advances.*

Herrero, A., García de los Salmones, M. M., & Rodríguez del Bosque, I. (2009). The influence of perceived risk on Internet shopping behavior: A multidimensional perspective. *Journal of Risk Research, 12*(2), 259–277. doi:10.1080/13669870802497744

Herrero, A., & Rodríguez del Bosque, I. (2008). Explaining B2C e-commerce acceptance: An integrative model based on the framework by Gatignon and Robertson. *Interacting with Computers, 20*(2), 212–224. doi:10.1016/j.intcom.2007.11.005

Hsu, M. H., & Chiu, C. M. (2004a). Internet self-efficacy and electronic service acceptance. *Decision Support Systems, 38*, 369–381. doi:10.1016/j.dss.2003.08.001

Hsu, M. H., & Chiu, C. M. (2004b). Predicting electronic service continuance with a decomposed theory of planned behaviour. *Behaviour & Information Technology, 23*(5), 359–379. doi:10.1080/01449290410001669969

Ingene, C. A., & Hughes, M. A. (1985). Risk Management by Consumers. In J. Sheth (Ed.), *Research in Consumer Behavior 1*, (pp. 103-158). Greenwich, UK: JAI Press Inc.

Jacoby, J., & Kaplan, B. (1972). The Components of Perceived Risk. In *Proceedings of the Third Annual Conference of the Association for Consumer Research*, (pp. 382-393).

Jarvenpaa, S. L., & Todd, P. A. (1997). Is There a Future for Retailing on the Internet. In R.A. Peterson (Ed.) *Electronic Marketing and the Consumer*, (pp. 139-154). Thousand Oaks, CA: Sage Publications.

Joines, J. L., Scherer, C. W., & Scheufele, D. A. (2003). Exploring Motivations for Consumer Web Use and their Implications for E-Commerce. *Journal of Consumer Marketing, 20*(2), 90–108. doi:10.1108/07363760310464578

Kim, D. J., Ferrin, D. L., & Rao, R. (2008). A trust-based consumer decision-making model in electronic commerce: The role of trust, perceived risk, and their antecedents. *Decision Support Systems, 44*, 544–564. doi:10.1016/j.dss.2007.07.001

Kogan, N., & Wallach, M. A. (1964). *Risk-taking: A Study in Cognition and Personality*. New York: Holt, Rhinehart & Winston.

Korgaonkar, P. K., & Wolin, L. D. (1999). A Multivariate Analysis of Web Usage. *Journal of Advertising Research, 39*(2), 53–68.

Laurent, G., & Kapferer, J. (1985). Measuring Consumer Involvement Profiles. *JMR, Journal of Marketing Research, 22*, 41–53. doi:10.2307/3151549

Liang, T.-P., & Huang, J.-S. (1998). An Empirical Study on Consumer Acceptance of Products in Electronic Markets: A Transaction Cost Model. *Decision Support Systems, 24*, 29–43. doi:10.1016/S0167-9236(98)00061-X

Liao, Z., & Cheung, M. T. (2001). Internet-based E-Shopping and Consumer Attitudes: An Empirical Study. *Information & Management, 38*(5), 299–306. doi:10.1016/S0378-7206(00)00072-0

Lim, N. (2003). Consumers' perceived risk: Sources versus consequences. *Electronic Commerce Research and Applications, 2*, 216–238. doi:10.1016/S1567-4223(03)00025-5

Liu, C., Marchewka, J. T., Lu, J., & Yu, C.-S. (2005). Beyond Concern – A Privacy-trust-behavioral Intention Model of Electronic Commerce. *Information & Management, 42*(3), 289–304. doi:10.1016/j.im.2004.01.003

Mitchell, V. W. (1999). Consumer Perceived Risk: Conceptualisations and Models. *European Journal of Marketing, 33*(1), 163–195. doi:10.1108/03090569910249229

Miyazaki, A. D., & Fernandez, A. (2001). Consumer Perceptions of Privacy and Security Risks for Online Shopping. *The Journal of Consumer Affairs, 35*(1), 27–44.

Pavlou, P. A. (2003). Consumer Intentions to Adopt Electronic Commerce – Incorporating Trust and Risk in the Technology Acceptance Model. *International Journal of Electronic Commerce, 7*(3), 101–134.

Peter, J. P., & Ryan, M. J. (1976). An Investigation of Perceived Risk at the Brand Level. *JMR, Journal of Marketing Research, 13*(2), 184–188. doi:10.2307/3150856

Pratt, J. W. (1964). Risk Aversion in the Small an in the Large Firm. *Econometrica, 32*, 122–136. doi:10.2307/1913738

Roselius, T. (1971). Consumer Rankings of Risk Reduction Methods. *Journal of Marketing, 35*(1), 56–61. doi:10.2307/1250565

Salisbury, W. D., Pearson, R. A., Pearson, A. W., & Miller, D. W. (2001). Perceived security and World Wide Web Purchase Intention. *Industrial Management & Data Systems, 101*(4), 165–176. doi:10.1108/02635570110390071

Shih, H. P. (2004). An Empirical Study on Predicting User Acceptance of e-Shopping on the Web. *Information & Management, 41*, 351–368. doi:10.1016/S0378-7206(03)00079-X

Sjoberg, L. (1980). The Risks of Risk Analysis. *Acta Psychologica, 45*(August), 301–321. doi:10.1016/0001-6918(80)90039-6

Stone, R. N., & Gronhaug, K. (1993). Perceived Risk: Further Considerations for Marketing Discipline. *European Journal of Marketing, 27*(3), 39–50. doi:10.1108/03090569310026637

Stone, R. N., & Winter, F. W. (1985). *Risk in Buyer Behavior Contexts: A Clarification.* Working Paper 1216 EWP 860505, College of Commerce and Business Administration, University of Illinois.

Swaminathan, V., Lepkowska-White, E., & Rao, B. P. (1999). Browsers of Buyers in Cyberspace? An Investigation of Factors Influencing Electronic Exchange. *Journal of Computer-Mediated Communication, 5*(2).

Taylor, J. W. (1974). The Role of Risk in Consumer Behavior. *Journal of Marketing, 38*(2), 54–60. doi:10.2307/1250198

Van den Poel, D., & Leunis, J. (1999). Consumer Acceptance of the Internet as a Channel of Distribution. *Journal of Business Research, 45*(3), 249–256. doi:10.1016/S0148-2963(97)00236-1

Van der Heijden, H., Verhagen, T., & Creemers, M. (2003). Understanding Online Purchase Intentions: Contributions from Technology and Trust Perspectives. *European Journal of Information Systems, 12*, 41–48. doi:10.1057/palgrave.ejis.3000445

Vijayasarathy, L. R., & Jones, J. M. (2000). Print and Internet Catalog Shopping: Assessing Attitudes and Intentions. *Internet Research: Electronic Networking Applications and Policy, 10*(3), 191–202. doi:10.1108/10662240010331948

Wu, J.-H., & Wang, S.-C. (2005). What drives mobile commerce? An empirical evaluation of the revised technology acceptance model. *Information & Management, 42*, 719–729. doi:10.1016/j.im.2004.07.001

KEY TERMS AND DEFINITIONS

Economic (Monetary or Financial) Risk: The potential monetary outlay associated with the initial purchase price as well as the subsequent maintenance cost of the product, and the potential financial loss due to fraud

Functional (or Performance Risk): The possibility of the product malfunctioning and not performing as it was designed and advertised and therefore mailing to deliver the desired benefits.

Perceived Risk: Consumers' subjective expectation of loss derived from a behavior.

Privacy Risk: Potential loss of control over personal information, Such as when information about you is used without your knowledge or permission.

Product Risk: Degree to which individuals believe that if the purchase products or services through the Internet they will suffer losses caused by products.

Psychological Risk: Potential loss of self-esteem (ego loss) from the frustration of not achieving a buying goal.

Social Risk: Potential loss of status in one's social group as a result of adopting a product or service, looking foolish or untrendy.

Technology Risk: Degree to which individuals believe that if the purchase products or services through the Internet they will suffer losses caused by the Internet and its related technologies.

Time Risk: Potential loss of time associated with making a bad purchasing decision by wasting time researching and making the purchase, only to have to replace it if it does not perform to expectations.

Vendor Risk: Degree to which individuals believe that if the purchase products or services through the Internet they will suffer losses caused by Internet vendors.

Chapter 69
Third Party Internet Seals:
Reviewing the Effects on Online Consumer Trust

Peter Kerkhof
VU University of Amsterdam, the Netherlands

Guda van Noort
University of Amsterdam, the Netherlands

ABSTRACT

Buying online is still perceived as risky. A key strategy of online marketers to increase consumer trust in online ordering is to display privacy and security seals on their web sites. Although research indicates that these Internet seals do not necessarily mean better safety for online consumers, findings of several other studies demonstrated that these safety cues do influence consumer responses. The goal of this chapter is to provide the reader with an overview of findings regarding the persuasiveness of Internet seals and to reflect upon possible explanatory mechanisms for these effects. Future research directions and managerial implications for e-business are provided.

INTRODUCTION

Consumers perceive buying in online stores as more risky than buying in conventional stores (e.g., Miyazaki & Fernandez, 2001). Third party verification and Internet seals are important means to convey a sense of safety to potential customers. For example, many online sites show their Verisign or Trustwave security seal to convince consumers that transactions can be done safely. Similarly, many online stores proudly show their Bizrate top-ranked store awards on their homepage, or display their membership of the CNET certified store program. All these safety cues serve to persuade customers that the online store is a safe environment to conduct a purchase. The questions at hand are whether these third party security seals are indeed effective in reducing perceived risk, what determines their effectiveness, and whether a lower sense of risk as a result of encountering a third party seal is substantiated by objectively lower risks for websites carrying such a seal.

DOI: 10.4018/978-1-61520-611-7.ch069

BACKGROUND

Many web stores display third party Internet seals on their homepage to inform consumers about their adherence to rules regarding privacy and security. Well-known examples include Verisign, Trustwave, BBBOnline, Trust.e, Validated Site, and Trust Guard. Third party Internet seals serve to promote a sense of safety among online consumers. A great body of research has shown that considerations regarding safety and risk are an impediment for shopping in an online environment (e.g., Jarvenpaa, Tractinsky, & Vitale, 2000; Miyazaki & Fernandez, 2001; Pavlou, 2003; Ranganathan & Ganapathy, 2002). Most of the risks that consumers experience on the Internet can be categorized as privacy risks and security risks. Privacy risks pertain to attempts of the online retailer to collect, use and distribute information about consumers without prior permission or even awareness of the consumer. Security risks refer to either the security of the Internet itself, or to concerns about the competence and integrity of the online retailer (Miyazaki & Fernandez, 2001).

Despite the inherent insecurity of online shopping, consumer spending on the Internet is rapidly growing. Apparently, consumers have established ways to find places that they consider safe. To establish whether a web store is safe, consumers typically do not study the privacy regulations or the conditions of use (Milne & Culnan, 2004). Instead, they rely on online cues that provide information about website privacy and security and that can be processed in a relatively effortless manner. In information economics, cues that inform the other party about characteristics such as quality or safety that cannot easily be observed, and that are relevant to a sale or an agreement are called signals (Spence, 1973). Signaling theory assumes a rational consumer that takes into account that for a firm it would be economically ill-advised to send signals that imply product or service qualities that cannot be substantiated.

Third party Internet seals are signals send to consumers to inform them that the firm adheres to certain standards regarding security and /or privacy, and that there would be adverse consequences of not adhering to these standards. Aiken and Boush (2006) note several problems in the use of third party Internet seals as signals: most consumers are unfamiliar with the (firms issuing the) seals, and the firms issuing the seals are paid by the firms carrying the seals. Others raise the question whether the most commonly used seals really denote different practices in dealing with Internet security and privacy. The evidence regarding this last question is mixed. Miyazaki and Krishnamurthy (2002) coded the privacy policy compliance of 60 major commercial websites that displayed either a third party privacy seal or no privacy seal. Their main finding was that the actual privacy policy did not differ between seal holders and non-seal holders. More recently, LaRose and Rifon (2006) compared 200 websites that either carried the Trust.e privacy seal, the BBBOnline seal or no privacy seal. The Trust.e and BBBOnline websites provided consumers with more information about their privacy regulations, deposited fewer cookies, reported more often a formal procedure for consumer complaints and provided more assurances for data security. Interestingly, websites displaying privacy seals asked for more personal information (last names, credit card number, email addresses) than websites without privacy seals. Thus, the question remains whether carrying a third party Internet seal is a reliable signal of web store safety and security.

ARE ONLINE SAFETY CUES PERSUASIVE?

Even though an Internet seal does not necessarily mean better safety for online consumers, it might still have the effect of lowering the perception of risk among consumers. Several studies have been published about the question whether consumers perceive websites that display third party Internet seals as safer than websites without such a seal. Most of these studies employ experimental designs. In a typical experimental study, half of the participants are exposed to a website carrying a third party privacy or security seal, the other participants visit a website without such a seal. Several such studies have shown effects, particularly for respondents who think that they are in risk when shopping online. Miyazaki and Krishnamurthy (2002) showed their participants websites with the BBBOnline seal, the Trust.e seal, or no seal at all. The presence of a seal led to more favorable attitudes towards the privacy policy of the web store, and made consumers more willing to disclose personal information. This effect only occurred for the participants who perceived Internet shopping as risky, however this interaction effect could not be replicated in a follow up study.

Using a similar kind of design, LaRose and Rifon (2007) found that people who had been exposed to a warning about their privacy expected more negative outcomes, but only when the warning was not accompanied by a privacy seal. Thus, again only those who perceived risk were affected by the third party seal. The intention to disclose information about oneself on the website was higher on the website carrying a privacy seal, regardless of the privacy warning. In a similar vein, but departing from a different theoretical framework, Van Noort, Kerkhof, and Fennis (2008) demonstrated that the effect of Internet seals depends on the consumer goal. Consumers whose aim is to prevent negative outcomes rather than obtain positive outcomes (as is the case for many online consumers, see Van Noort, Kerkhof, and Fennis, 2007) are affected more strongly by Internet seals and reported lower risk perception, more positive attitudes towards the site, and higher purchase intentions.

Internet seals are not the only signals firms can use to convince consumers that their web store is safe. Firms can also use objective-source ratings like those published in Consumer Reports to lower risk perceptions and enhance trust. Alternatively, firms may try and overcome the impression that a web store comes without the huge investments that a brick-and-mortar store demands. High investments in advertising signal to consumers that a firm is certain about future profits and communicating these investments has been shown to positively affect consumer attitudes towards a brand (Kirmani, 1990). Departing from signaling theory, Aiken and Boush (2006) tested which of these three types of signaling best predicted consumer attitudes, and found that third party seals have the greatest effects on the trustworthiness of the web store, on beliefs about privacy and security and on the willingness to disclose personal information. Peterson, Meinert, Criswell II, and Crossland (2007) compared the effect of seals to the effect of self-reported privacy statements. Compared to a control condition without seal or privacy statement, Internet seal did show a positive effect on the willingness to disclose information, but a strong privacy statement had a stronger effect.

Not all studies report positive effects and some report effects on some dependent variables but not on others. For example, Kim, Ferrin, and Rao (2008) found effects of the presence of a third party seal on perceived risk, but not on consumer trust. They explain the latter by the low level of awareness of the meaning of third party seals among their participants: almost 75% did not know that websites are sometimes endorsed by third parties. McKnight, Kacmar, and Choudhury (2004) studied the effects of privacy assurances and industry endorsement seals on consumer trust in the web store within the context of services (i.e., legal advice). They found no support for the trust enhancing effects of third party Internet seals. Several other studies did not find an effect of third part seals on consumer attitudes and intentions (e.g., Houston and Taylor, 1999; Kimery & McCord, 2002).

A few studies have delved into the question which mechanisms may explain when and why Internet seals are effective in persuading online customers. Yang, Hung, Sung, and Farn (2006) depart from the Elaboration Likelihood Model (ELM; Petty & Cacioppo, 1986). The ELM states that information may be processed in either a relatively unthinking and automatic way (the peripheral route) and in a more elaborative way (the central route). People tend to reserve elaborative processing for important matters, for matters which they are knowledgeable about, and for situations in which they have the time and knowledge to do so. These conditions are typically not met for consumers shopping online. Instead, these consumers rely on the signals (peripheral cues) sent by the web store. Following this reasoning, Yang et al. (2006) find that third party seals help to build trust especially among consumers who are low in product involvement or high in (trait) anxiety. Consumers high in product involvement rely more on (high quality) product information.

Another limiting condition for the persuasiveness of Internet seals may be that Internet seals work mainly for consumers who feel they are at risk. This may be a risk specific to the purchase they plan to conduct, but this may also be a more general feeling of vulnerability, as is shown in the effect of trait anxiety reported by Yang et al. (2006), and in the effect of being focused on preventing negative outcomes as reported by Van Noort, Kerkhof, and Fennis (2008). Thus, consumers need not necessarily consciously perceive a web store as unsafe, even when they are generally anxious or in a situation where they are geared towards not making a mistake, Internet seals are more likely to affect consumers' online trust and risk perception.

ISSUES, CONTROVERSIES, PROBLEMS

The literature so far has been quite unsystematic in the sense that there is a lot of variation in the materials used to test the effectiveness of third party Internet seals in lowering risk perceptions. This may explain why no explanations have been offered (or tested) as to why some studies do find effects of third party Internet seals on consumer attitudes, whereas others do not find such effects. Studies have been conducted among fictitious and real web stores, and among well-known or unknown web stores, Internet seals have been placed on the homepage versus the page where consumers actually make a purchase decision, and different types of products and services have been used to test the effects of Internet seals. A systematic (meta-)analysis of the influence of these differences on seal effectiveness would help to better understand the working of Internet seals and the conditions that mitigate their effects. Moreover, it may help to explain unexpected and contradictory findings.

More attention should be paid particularly to the different types of seals that were tested on their persuasiveness and to how consumers understand these seals. These seals all relate to different kinds of assurances, but it is still unclear how consumers perceive these seals. Houston and Taylor (1999) showed that seals sometimes are perceived incorrectly, and that consumers attribute more assurance to seals than they should. Also, among consumers the awareness of what Internet seals mean is very low (Kim, Steinfield, & Lai, 2008). Thus, consumers are not only unaware of the ins and outs of privacy and security regulations in general and the specific regulations of the stores they attend online, but they are also unaware of what it means to display a third party Internet seal. In fact, most consumers do not even recognize the seals that are used most often on the Internet (Kim, Ferrin, & Rao, 2008).

Aiken and Boush (2006) raise the question whether there is an optimum number of Internet seals on a web page and whether exceeding that number might lead to the perception of more risk and to less web store trust. In their own study, these authors find no effect of the number of signals on a web page, but in no experimental condition were the participants exposed to more than three signals. Yet, another study (Van Noort, 2009) examined a total of four seals commonly used in the context of online auctions and demonstrated a linear relationship between the number of signals and online spending. Future studies should look at the possibility that adding more Internet seals undermines the effectiveness of the Internet seals.

SOLUTIONS, RECOMMENDATIONS, AND FUTURE RESEARCH DIRECTIONS

Third party Internet seals are often not recognized by consumers and may not always reflect a better practice of dealing with privacy and security but have nonetheless been shown to be effective in lowering consumer risk perception in several studies. One can wonder about whether this reflects an ideal practice of consumer dealing with safety on the Internet. Many think it does not and plead for consumer education on these matters. However, one should not be too optimistic about the effects of consumer education. Kim et al. (2008) describe the effects of an educational intervention aimed at increasing consumers' awareness of security and privacy issues. They conclude that education does help to increase awareness and the perceived importance of Internet seals. However, a host of other measures (e.g., web store trustworthiness, perceived web site information quality) did not show a significant association with the presence of Internet seals. Consumer education is needed, but at the same time may require large and enduring efforts to be effective

Several managerial recommendations for enhancing the effectiveness of Internet seals are presented and discussed in academic research, for example by LaRose and Rifon (2006). The presentation of seals on the web site might be standardized and made more salient by banishing advertisements and distracting graphics from

places close to the seals. Privacy and security regulations may be standardized and presented in such a way that they are easily accessible and clearly understood by consumers. However, to our knowledge, no attempts are currently made to start a process of standardization. Another suggestion, made by Pollach (2006, 2007) regarding privacy statements, is that businesses could increase consumers' trust if they do not only address what they do with user data, but also what they do *not* do. Uncertainties about privacy risks may be reduced if consumers can learn about what practices a business does not engage in. Also, online privacy policies could reduce more uncertainties if the language used would be more exact and transparent.

Although many studies report positive effects of third party Internet seals, many questions remain unanswered. The empirical findings discussed show evidence for the persuasiveness of Internet seals, but sometimes are contradicting or rather incomparable since effects are studied on different consumer responses, and using different kinds of seals. Future research should focus on examining the relations between these responses (i.e., mediating processes between variables) and on the underlying mechanisms. Moreover, findings considering the persuasiveness of Internet seals are rather limited to self-report measures. Therefore, in studying mediating and moderating processes, persuasiveness should be studied to the full domain of consumer responses, also by using implicit measures.

In studying underlying processes, future research could focus on the information processing style of safety cues. On the one hand, Internet seals are symbols, visual elements of a web site that might serve as a heuristic. Furthermore, during online shopping, consumers are probably mostly involved with their shopping goals and less with informational symbols because they do not directly facilitate the actual product selection and its actual payment. This would imply a heuristic processing style and relatively low levels of elaboration (cf. the findings by Yang et al., 2006). On the other hand, it can also be assumed that consumers are motivated to prevent their online perceived risks and to reduce uncertainties regarding online shopping. Following the ELM (Petty & Cacioppo, 1986) this would then imply higher levels of elaboration. More research is needed to test these assumptions.

CONCLUSION

The goal of this chapter was to provide the reader with an overview of findings regarding the persuasiveness of Internet seals and to reflect upon possible explanatory mechanisms. To reach this goal, we have summarized the effects found in a great number of studies that have been conducted on this topic and looked at whether or not persuasive effects were found, and how these findings are explained. Based on this review, the evidence for possible effects of Internet seals on online consumer trust and risk perception is mixed. Several studies show that consumers perceive less risk and are more trusting web stores that display a third party Internet seal. Third party assurances through Internet seals thus do seem to convey to online consumers a sense of safety. However, other studies show no effect of third party seals and more research is needed to establish which factors determine whether an Internet seal is effective in persuading consumers that a web store is safe. To solve these inconsistencies, future research on Internet seals should focus on the conditions under which Internet seals are effective. An important step would be to conduct a meta-analysis on the studies that already have been conducted to test the effect of Internet seals on online trust.

Fortunately, for consumers there are alternative ways to distinguish between bad and good on the Internet. Social media, like online consumer forums, may be better understood than Internet seals by online consumers. Also, retailer reputation is a powerful signal of quality. Still, Internet seals could help to boost e-commerce. More systematic research on third party seal effectiveness, better consumer education and a better differentiation by Internet seals between good and bad practices regarding privacy and security on the Internet may all help to create effective Internet seals.

REFERENCES

Aiken, K. D., & Boush, D. M. (2006). Trustmarks, objective-source ratings, and implied investments in advertising: Investigating online trust and the context-specific nature of Internet signals. *Journal of the Academy of Marketing Science*, *34*(3), 308–323. doi:10.1177/0092070304271004

Houston, R. W., & Taylor, G. K. (1999). Consumer perceptions of CPA WebtrustSM assurances: Evidence of an expectation gap. *International Journal of Auditing*, *3*(2), 889–105. doi:10.1002/(SICI)1099-1123(199907)3:2<89::AID-IJA44>3.0.CO;2-5

Jarvenpaa, S., Tractinsky, N., & Vitale, M., M. (2000). Consumer trust in an Internet store. *Information Technology and Management Journal*, *1*, 45–71. doi:10.1023/A:1019104520776

Kim, D. J., Ferrin, D. L., & Rao, H. R. (2008). A trust-based consumer decision-making model in electronic commerce: The role of trust, perceived risk, and their antecedents. *Decision Support Systems*, *44*(2), 544–564. doi:10.1016/j.dss.2007.07.001

Kim, D. J., Steinfield, C., & Ying-Ju Lai, Y.-J. (2008). Revisiting the role of Web assurance seals in business-to-consumer electronic commerce. *Decision Support Systems*, *44*(4), 1000–1015. doi:10.1016/j.dss.2007.11.007

Kimery, K. M., & McCord, M. (2002). Third-party assurances: mapping the road to trust in e-retailing. [JITTA]. *Journal of Information Technology Theory and Application, 4*(2), 63–82.

Kirmani, A. (1990, September). The effect of perceived advertising costs on brand perceptions. *The Journal of Consumer Research, 17*, 160–171. doi:10.1086/208546

LaRose, R., & Rifon, N. J. (2006). Your privacy is assured - of being disturbed: websites with and without privacy seals. *New Media & Society, 8*(6), 1009–1029. doi:10.1177/1461444806069652

LaRose, R., & Rifon, N. J. (2007). Promoting i-safety: Effects of privacy warnings and privacy seals on risk assessment and online privacy behavior. *The Journal of Consumer Affairs, 41*(1), 127–149. doi:10.1111/j.1745-6606.2006.00071.x

McKnight, Kacmar, & Choudhury. (2004). Shifting factors and the ineffectiveness of third party assurance seals: A two-stage model of initial trust in a web business. *Electronic Markets, 14*(3), 252–266. doi:10.1080/1019678042000245263

Milne, G. R., & Culnan, M. J. (2004). Strategies for reducing online privacy risks: Why consumers read (or don't read) online privacy notices. *Journal of Interactive Marketing, 18*(3), 15–29. doi:10.1002/dir.20009

Miyazaki, A. D., & Fernandez, A. (2000). Internet privacy and security: An examination of online retailer disclosures. *Journal of Public Policy & Marketing, 19*(1), 54–61. doi:10.1509/jppm.19.1.54.16942

Miyazaki, A. D., & Fernandez, A. (2001). Consumer perceptions of privacy and security risks for online shopping. *The Journal of Consumer Affairs, 35*(1), 27–44.

Miyazaki, A. D., & Krishnamurthy, S. (2002). Internet seals of approval: Effects on online privacy policies and consumer perceptions. *The Journal of Consumer Affairs, 36*(1), 28–49.

Pavlou, P. A. (2003). Consumer acceptance of electronic commerce: Integrating trust and risk with the technology acceptance model. *International Journal of Electronic Commerce, 7*(3), 101–134.

Peterson, D., Meinert, D., Criswell, J. II, & Crossland, M. (2007). Consumer trust: privacy policies and third-party seals. *Journal of Small Business and Enterprise Development, 14*(4), 654–669. doi:10.1108/14626000710832758

Petty, R. E., & Cacioppo, J. T. (1986). *From Communication and Persuasion: Central and Peripheral Routes to Attitude Change.* New York: Springer-Verlag.

Pollach, I. (2006). Privacy statements as a means of uncertainty reduction in WWW interactions. *Journal of Organizational and End User Computing, 18*(1), 21–46.

Pollach, I. (2007). What's wrong with online privacy policies? *Communications of the ACM, 50*(9), 103–108. doi:10.1145/1284621.1284627

Ranganathan, C., & Ganapathy, S. (2002). Key dimensions of business-to-consumer web sites. *Information & Management, 39*, 457–465. doi:10.1016/S0378-7206(01)00112-4

Spence, M. (1973). Job market signaling. *The Quarterly Journal of Economics, 87*(3), 355–374. doi:10.2307/1882010

Van den Poel, D., & Leunis, J. (1999). Consumer acceptance of the Internet as a channel of distribution. *Journal of Business Research, 45*(3), 249–256. doi:10.1016/S0148-2963(97)00236-1

Van Noort, G. (2009). *Validating the persuasiveness of online safety cues: The effect of multiple cues on online spending* Paper presented at the 8th ICORIA Conference, Klagenfurt, Austria.

Van Noort, G., Kerkhof, P., & Fennis, B. M. (2007). Online versus conventional shopping: Consumers' risk perception and regulatory focus. *Cyberpsychology & Behavior*, *10*(5), 731–733. doi:10.1089/cpb.2007.9959

Van Noort, G., Kerkhof, P., & Fennis, B. M. (2008). The persuasiveness of online safety cues: the impact of prevention focus compatibility of web content on consumers' risk perceptions, attitudes, and intentions. *Journal of Interactive Marketing*, *22*(4), 58–72. doi:10.1002/dir.20121

Yang, S. C., Hung, W. C., Sung, K., & Farn, C. K. (2006). Investigating initial trust toward e-tailers from the elaboration likelihood model perspective. *Psychology and Marketing*, *23*(5), 429–445. doi:10.1002/mar.20120

ADDITIONAL READING

Biswas, D., & Biswas, A. (2004). The diagnostic role of signals in the context of perceived risks in online shopping: Do signals matter more on the web? *Journal of Interactive Marketing*, *18*(3), 30–45. doi:10.1002/dir.20010

Hu, X., Lin, Z., & Zhang, H. (2003). Myth or reality: effect of trust-promoting seals in electronic market. In Petrovic, O., Posch, R., Marhold, F. (Eds.), *Trust in Network Economy*, Idea Group, Hershey, PA, pp. 143-150.

Kim, D. J., Sivasailam, N., & Rao, H. R. (2004). Information assurance in B2C websites for information goods/services. *Electronic Markets*, *14*(4), 344–359. doi:10.1080/10196780412331311784

McKnight, D. H., & Chervany, N. L. (2002). What trust means in e-commerce customer relationships: An interdisciplinary conceptual typology. *International Journal of Electronic Commerce*, *6*(2), 35–59.

Tan, Y. H., & Thoen, W. (2001). Toward a generic model of trust for electronic commerce. *International Journal of Electronic Commerce*, *5*(2), 61–74.

KEY TERMS AND DEFINITIONS

Online Consumer Trust: The online consumer's general belief or expectancy that a specific online firm and/or third party can be relied upon.

Privacy Risk: The risk that information about online consumers collected for commercial purposes is not treated in a fair and responsible manner.

Security Risk: The risk deriving from either the competence or integrity of an online firm or from the Internet itself that the storage or transmission of information about online consumers is not secure.

Third Party Internet Seals: Signals sent to consumers to inform them that the online firm adheres to certain standards regarding security and /or privacy.

Chapter 70

The Importance of Gender, IT Experience, and Media-Rich Social Cues on Initial Trust in E-Commerce Websites

Khalid AlDiri
University of Bradford, UK

Dave Hobbs
University of Bradford, UK

Rami Qahwaji
University of Bradford, UK

INTRODUCTION

The rapid advance of the Internet and global information technology has changed the way many people view shopping and undertake daily transactions. Despite the Internet advantages, the rate of Internet shopping remains low; commonly explained by a lack of trust in the new shopping mode (Kim & Tadisina, 2005).

Consumer trust may be even more important in electronic transactions than in traditional forms, lacking the assurance provided in traditional settings through formal proceedings, receipts and face-to-face interactions. Since trust should play an essential role in online transactions, identifying the antecedents of a consumer's trust is important in the context of Internet transactions so that consumers can feel relaxed and confident.

However, heretofore gender differences and their impact in a technological environment were largely ignored in HCI research. In fact, there has been a general lack of investigative studies of gender in the context of information technology (IT). However, several recent studies have indicated that there may be interesting differences in how males and females perceive and use information technology. Female shopping online is gradually increasing, although relatively little is known about gender differences related to attitudes, behaviour, activities and design preferences when shopping on the web.

Also, research has yet to consider the impact of consumers' cumulative online knowledge and experiences regarding their reactions to e-vendors' trust. It is believed that as consumers gain more

DOI: 10.4018/978-1-61520-611-7.ch070

knowledge and experience with the online environment, their perceptions, attitudes and behaviours will evolve.

Research Objectives

This research believes it is essential to establish design guidelines for increasing website trustworthiness, and aims to investigate how to increase the perceived trustworthiness of vendor websites. Attractive people in media cues (photo, video clip, avatar and audio) have been frequently utilized by the marketing industry to stimulate affective responses from consumers, while in the field of Business-to-Consumer (B2C) e-commerce they have been rarely used, even in recent years (Riegelsberger, Sasse, & McCarthy, 2005). Research into the effects of social presence cues (or interpersonal cues) represented in media cues on B2C e-commerce trust is scarce and the findings contradictory (Corritore, Kracher, & Wiedenbeck, 2003). Hence, this study investigates this element. In addition, this study further tests the effects of multiple forms of media cues on trust, based on the perceptions of different groups of users in order to investigate the effects of media cues on males and females and between IT experts and novices; all with respect to vendor website trustworthiness.

THEORETICAL BACKGROUND AND HYPOTHESES

Trust

Trust is a highly complex and multi-dimensional phenomenon (AlDiri, Hobbs & Qahwaji, 2008) that has been widely studied but remaining difficult to describe because of its dynamic, evolving and multi-faceted nature (Ambrose & Johnson, 1998). Basically, the key concepts of trust, highlighted in the literature, are risk, vulnerability, expectation, confidence and exploitation (Gefen & Straub, 2004).

The perception of three characteristics – ability, benevolence and integrity (trust beliefs) (Mayer, Davis & Schoorman, 1995) – can lead to the willingness of the trusting party to rely upon the trustee (trust intention) (McKnight, Choudhury & Kacmar, 2002). These three specific factors are often not observable directly, but are inferable from signals in the website interface (McKnight et al., 2002).

Many researchers in human computer interaction (HCI) have studied trust in an online context. The following factors have all been discussed as influencing trust (For more information on trust see (AlDiri et al., 2008):

- Computer error.
- Appropriate content.
- Conveying of expertise.
- Adequate information.

However, the web contains enormous numbers of alternatives, in vendors, products and prices, making it trivial to switch to different online stores after an initial visit. Thus this study focuses on the initial trust that develops after a customer's first interaction with a website.

Online Trust and Media Cues

Various representations of social presence cues can be embedded in technology today in the form of media cues (e.g. photo, audio, video and avatar). However, research on media cue usage in websites is conflicting, with some studies finding them helpful while others finding them neutral or even negative (Corritore et al., 2003). Rich media representations may result in higher levels of trust in mediated interactions something supported by research that suggests richer representations give more interpersonal cues perhaps leading to increased trustworthiness (e.g. Nielsen, 2004).

The Effect of Consumer Gender and Media Cues on Initial Trust In B2C E-Commerce

Literature relevant to this topic is scattered across different areas that tend to stay separate and, therefore, not well-integrated. Many empirical studies have demonstrated significant gender differences across such diverse fields as information science, human-computer interaction, economics, library science, psychology, advertising and marketing studies (AlDiri, Hobbs, & Qahwaji, 2007).

Although the literature is extensive, only a modest amount of research exists on the role of gender in online trust and the interaction between gender and media cues with respect to e-vendor trust assessment. However, since media cues represent a source that can be used for emitting interpersonal (social presence) cues, several empirical studies have demonstrated significant gender differences across various tasks and traits. Men often do better on spatial direction tasks while females usually score better on decoding verbal and nonverbal tasks (Meyers-Levy, 1989). Females were more visually oriented, more intrinsically motivated, and more romantic (Holbrook, 1986). Jones, Stanaland, & Gelb (1998) found that men and women have significant differences in their reaction to visual images which affects their recognition. In psychology, research literature shows that women can be more easily persuaded than men by nonverbal communications (Becker, 1986).

This research also aims to investigate the relationship between online trust and the gender of the user. It takes an exploratory look at whether consumers with different genders (a) differ significantly in their trusting of the vendor website, and (b) differ in relying on media cues during assessment of their first impression of e-commerce vendor trustworthiness. Hence the following research hypotheses were proposed:

H1-a: *Across websites embedded with media cues there will be significant differences in trustworthiness between females and males.*

H1-b: *Richer media cue representations will have a higher positive trust toward an e-vendor website for females compared to males.*

The Interaction Between Consumer IT Experience and Media Cue on Initial Trust

Rieh has shown that user characteristics must be investigated for website usage to be properly understood (Rieh, 2003). IT experience may be yet another definable characteristic by which to examine subgroup differences, and cumulative Internet experience will impact both affective and cognitive components of online trust. However, many studies (e.g. Rieh, 2003) suggest that web novices tend to rely on the most basic and attractive features of the website interface they use, while web experts use their experience and can retrieve knowledge to facilitate their information processing and have sufficient knowledge to differentiate between relevant and irrelevant information.

Also, Fogg (2002) introduced a prominence-interpretation theory that describes how people assess the credibility of websites. This theory states that two things happen when people assess credibility online: 1) the user notices something, and 2) the user makes an interpretation. However, the experience and involvement of the user in regards to subject matter or website conventions represent major affective factors in this theory.

Another support of the proposition regarding this important point in recent online trust research can be found in persuasion research. Much persuasion literature (e.g. Chaiken & Maheswaran, 1994) suggests that people employ very different processing strategies when evaluating trust in different environments – and a number of two-process theories of judgment under different conditions of involvement issue have emerged: a heuristic strategy – where people base decisions on only the most apparent information. The second process is a systematic strategy that involves the detailed processing of message content. These studies describe experiments that show that People with low involvement adopted a heuristic approach to evaluating a message and were primarily influenced by the attractiveness, whereas those with high involvement adopted a systematic approach presenting more arguments to support their judgment.

Consumers with a high level of online experience are likely to have different perceptions and preferences for the attributes of the online features compared to consumers lacking such experience. Investigating this gap in knowledge in our research area has not been tackled before. However, as a result of the foregoing, the following research hypotheses were proposed:

H2-a: *Across websites embedded with media cues there will be significant differences in trustworthiness between IT experts and IT novices.*

H2-b: *Richer media cue representations will have a higher positive trust toward an e-vendor website for IT novices compared to IT experts.*

RESEARCH METHODOLOGY

The hypothesis-testing laboratory experimental approach was used for this study, allowing relatively easy control of intervening variables. While allowing a high level of experimental control for independent variables while keeping resource requirements relatively low, a greater emphasis to maximize validity of the laboratory situation was required. Additionally, it also allows inducement of experimental laboratory financial risk that represents an important factor when investigating a complex context like online trust (Keser, 2002,

Bohnet & Frey, 1999). However, it is acknowledged that financial risk in a laboratory situation does not fully model real-world complex risk, since laboratory experiments use sessions that take only a few hours and long term effects investigations generally cannot be undertaken.

This study combined two methods of collecting data by using behavioural measures, and questionnaires. In behavioural measures, rather than asking individuals for their own inferences regarding their behaviour, the researcher directly inferred it. This experiment controlled the trustworthiness of the e-commerce vendor (trustee) and the participants played the role of the trustor, having to make trust decisions based on the website interface (surface cues) they perceived. This approach observes trusting action (e.g. participant's assessment of an e-commerce vendor website) and investment of participation pay to make inferences about the participant's internal non-observable level of trust both under financial risk. As in a real situation, trusting a trustworthy vendor yielded a gain (increased participation pay), whereas trusting an untrustworthy one resulted in a loss (reduced participation pay) see Appendix.

Experiment Participants

The study subjects comprised faculty members in the colleges of computer and information sciences in two of Saudi Arabia's Universities, males and females as they represented IT experts, and also students studying at the foundation level of computer and information science, this group represented the novice group. The sampling frames targeted towards an equal distribution between sexes and the level of expertise in order to satisfy the study objectives.

Experiment Materials

This experiment used semi-functional copies of four existing e-commerce vendor websites whose trustworthiness was known to the researcher.

Vendor trustworthiness had been collated by independent agencies (e.g. BizRate.com). A usability test for the four experimental websites was made using the checklist developed by (Keevil, 1998). The results showed that the four websites had almost the same usability index.

However, this study investigated the effect of two media cues (media representations): video clip and avatar. Each of these media cues can be manipulated by the culture effects by using it either in a Saudi fashion or Western fashion. These media cue representations spoke in five seconds the same text (greeting), but in different languages (Arabic and English). The avatar was created with many features such as synchronized lip movements and cues of liveliness (e.g. face movement and eye blinks). However, the experiment websites display scenario was designed by a predefined method to make sure that all media cues were displayed in all websites and to avoid the participants learning effects.

Data Collection

The experiment was designed to involve four tasks; the first was a questionnaire eliciting socio-demographic data, the second and the third were the behavioural measures (assessment, and investment) that have been adapted from (Riegelsberger et al., 2005), while the fourth was a trust questionnaire that has been adapted from Kammerer (2000), for more detail see Appendix. To examine any prior familiarity with the vendors, participants were shown logos and names of all e-commerce vendors included in the study and were asked whether they had seen the vendors' sites or shopped from them before. This served as a screening procedure and satisfied our condition for investigating initial trust.

Data Analysis

The total number of participants was 32 of which 50% were male and 50% were female. The ages

ranged from 18 to 50 years; the majority of people who responded were between 18 and 25 years representing a proportion of 50%.

The data analysis for this experiment was based on the context that the data followed an approximately normal distribution. Subsequently, a one way ANOVA can be performed since it represents a powerful and common statistical procedure, and if the results indicate a statistically significant outcome then a Least Square Difference (LSD) post hoc test and contrast test, to indicate the nature of the significance, can be applied (Sheskin, 2004).

Identifying the Effects of Media Cues on Gender Factor With Respect To Vendor Trustworthiness

A one-way ANOVA was performed to assess the potential differences between the four websites for the following categories of participants:

- Male Experts vs. Female Experts.
- Male Novices vs. Female Novices.

Depending on the significance of the test statistic for the ANOVA, follow up comparisons were performed to assess the nature of the differences using contrast comparisons, where differences were observed, 95% confidence intervals for the average differences were calculated and specified. The analysis yielded that there were significant differences between the above groups with respect to vendor trustworthiness across all websites and throughout all study trust measures. The analysis yielded that the rating of female participants was significantly more than males throughout all study trust measures. Also, the analysis yielded that the greatest effectiveness or manipulation of media cues came from the Saudi video, the Saudi avatar, and then the Western video respectively, and the final one was a plain website without any media cues. These results appeared consistently in all key measures of vendor trustworthiness in the experiment. Thus related hypotheses are confirmed for all three keys of trust measures.

Since this study implemented three kinds of trust measures, used four e-vendors websites, and analyzed two different categories, the data analysis covered a huge range of data and due to the space limitation in this article we could not display it here.

Identifying the Effects of Media Cues on Experience Factor With Respect To Vendor Trustworthiness

The same previous analysis procedures were performed to assess the potential differences between the four websites for the following categories of participants:

- Male Experts vs. Male Novices.
- Female Experts vs. Female Novices.

However, the analysis yielded that there were significant differences between the above groups with respect to vendor trustworthiness across all websites, and throughout all study measures. The rating of novice participants was significantly more than the experts throughout all study measures. Nevertheless, the analysis also yielded that the greatest effectiveness of media cues came from the Saudi video clip, the avatar, and then the Western video clip respectively, and the final one was a plain website without any media cues. Also, these results appeared consistently in all key measures of vendor trustworthiness in the experiment.

The findings signify the importance of the media cues and how they can interact with IT experiences to yield significant improvements with respect to vendor trustworthiness. Thus hypotheses are confirmed for all three key measures.

DISCUSSION

Media Cues and Participants' Gender

One of the main questions addressed by this study was to investigate the effect of visual media cues on one of the most important user characteristics, gender, and considered how this interaction affected the trustworthiness of e-commerce vendor sites. The aim was to identify whether the strategy of adding a media cue holds when tested across several vendors' sites and different types of media cues – and when trust is measured by different kinds of tools and under financial risk.

There was a noteworthy difference between male and female subjects with respect to vendor website trustworthiness in all study measurements.

The findings of this study are in line with many empirical studies that have demonstrated significant gender differences across a variety of tasks and traits (e.g. Meyers-Levy, 1989). Females may be more accurate than men in decoding nonverbal cues, and more visually oriented, intrinsically motivated, and more subjective compared to males (Meyers-Levy, 1989). Men and women have significant differences in their reaction to visual images which in turn affect their recall and recognition (Jones et al. 1998). Visual cues can be seen as tools that have a higher impact on online choices, and gender may be a basis for visual discrimination used to attract online shoppers. Also, using the selectivity model by (Meyers-Levy & Maheswaran, 1991), males do not engage in comprehensive processing of all available information but instead are selective. In contrast, females tend to use a comprehensive strategy and attempt to assimilate all available cues.

However, in cognitive theories, the research literature contains evidence of dependable gender differences in persuasiveness, with women being more easily persuaded than men (e.g. Becker, 1986). Women respond to nonverbal stimuli by evoking more associative, imagery-laced interpretations, and more elaborate descriptions than male. Men have been depicted as more analytical and logical in processing orientation, whereas women are more subjective and intuitive (Becker, 1986).

Media Cues and Participants' IT Experience

The empirical findings provide interesting insights. Both media cues and IT experience of participants appear to play an important role in determining trust in an e-vendor. However, the finding of this study is consistent with what was hypothesized.

The interpretation of these results can be done through analyzing that, in an initial interaction; the assessment of whether a party can be trusted depends, generally speaking, on a pre experience of each party that develops through lifelong interaction. Once interaction with the trusted party takes place, this experience is mitigated. Likewise, a customer's perceived trustworthiness of an e-vendor change as he get acquainted with the Internet and learns more of its capabilities. Based on that, an expectation can be set forth regarding differences between novice and expert IT consumers. Novice and expert IT customers are likely to differ in their trust in the e-vendor. Additionally, novice customers who lack enough experience with IT are likely to depend heavily on the acquaintance of superficial antecedents that are presented in the website, while expert customers should be based on actual experience and knowledge.

However, the findings of this study are consistent with the findings of Fogg (2002) and his Prominence-Interpretation Theory, (Stanford, Tauber, Fogg & Marable, 2002), and with many persuasion studies (e.g. Albaracin & Kumkale, 2003) that been introduced in theoretical background section. This study found that experts (those having a high involvement with the website) were highly influenced by factors such as

information quality and source and perceived motive, while in contrast the ordinary consumers (having a low involvement with the website) were much more influenced by the attractiveness of website design.

CONCLUSION

This experiment first investigated gender effectiveness with respect to identifying the trustworthiness of e-commerce vendors based on surface cues. Secondly, this experiment tested the effectiveness of users' IT experience with respect to identifying the trustworthiness of e-commerce vendors based on surface cues. Thirdly, this experiment went deeper to investigate the effect of different forms of visual media cues, i.e. visual media cues (video clip and avatar) represented in an e-commerce vendor's homepage on user trust. This study found support for earlier claims that users' perceived trust for a vendor fluctuates based on the surface cues they perceive in the interface of the website with respect to their gender: female participants trusted vendors' websites on average more than the male participants. Also, the results support the earlier claims that users perceived trust for a vendor indeed differs based on the surface cues they perceive in the interface of the website with respect to their IT experience: novice participants trusted vendor websites on average more than the expert participants. A clear picture emerged regarding the effect of the media cues. Video clip was found to have a significantly more positive effect than avatar on vendor websites' trust as perceived by the experiment participants across all websites in the study and across all groups of participants, and across all trust measures.

Finally, the experiments in this research were conducted in the form of laboratory experiments. This approach had several benefits such as the possibility of controlling potential sources of error variance and experimentally manipulating the variables. However, it put limitations on the level and type of financial risk that could be observed. Furthermore, with the limited length of experiments, laboratory sessions made it difficult to study long-term effects. Further research suggests that it will indeed be important to investigate user trust over longer periods of time. Also, while the study samples provide us with a good understanding of the online behaviour of a different educated in computer and information systems consumer group, they may not provide insights into the behaviour of other consumers, as Internet use is exploding across all demographics. Finally, our research results are limited due to the sample size.

REFERENCES

Al-Diri, K., Hobbs, D., & Qahwaji, R. (2008). The Human Face of e-Business: Engendering Consumer Initial Trust Through the use of Images of Sales Personnel on e-Commerce Websites. *International Journal of E-Business Research*, *4*(4), 58–78.

Al-Diri, K., Hobbs, D. J., & Qahwaji, R. (2007) The effect of Consumer Gender and Media Cue on Initial Trust in B2C E-Commerce. In *Proceedings of the Eighth Informatics Workshop*, (pp. 35-36). University of Bradford, UK.

Albarracin, D., & Kumkale, G. (2003). Affect as information in persuasion: A model of affect identification and discounting. *Journal of Personality and Social Psychology*, *84*, 453–469. doi:10.1037/0022-3514.84.3.453

Ambrose, P. J., & Johnson, G. J. (1998). *A trust based model of buying behaviour in electronic retailing*. Paper presented at the Fourth Conference of the Association for Information Systems.

Becker, B. (1986). Influence again: An examination of reviews and studies of gender differences in social influence. In *The psychology of gender: Advances through meta-analysis*, (pp. 178–209).

Bohnet, I., & Frey, B. S. (1999). The sound of silence in prisoner's dilemma and dictator games. *Journal of Personality and Social Psychology*, *38*, 43–57.

Chaiken, S., & Maheswaran, D. (1994). Heuristic processing can bias systematic processing: Effects of source credibility, argument ambiguity, and task importance on attitude judgment. *Journal of Personality and Social Psychology*, *66*, 460–473. doi:10.1037/0022-3514.66.3.460

Corritore, C., Kracher, B., & Wiedenbeck, S. (2003). On-line trust: concepts, evolving themes, a model. *International Journal of Human-Computer Studies*, *58*(6), 737–758. doi:10.1016/S1071-5819(03)00041-7

Fogg, B. J. (2002). *Stanford Guidelines for Web Credibility A Research Summary from the Stanford Persuasive Technology Lab*. Retrieved October 29, 2005, from http://www.webcredibility.org/guidelines

Gefen, D., & Straub, D. (2004). Consumer trust in B2C e-Commerce and the importance of social presence: experiments in e-Products and e-Services. *Omega*, *32*(6), 407–424. doi:10.1016/j.omega.2004.01.006

Holbrook, M. (1986). Aims, Concepts, and Methods for the Representation of Individual Differences in Esthetic Responses to Design Features. *The Journal of Consumer Research*, *13*(3), 337. doi:10.1086/209073

Jones, M., Stanaland, A., & Gelb, B. (1998). Beefcake and Cheesecake: Insights for Advertisers. *Journal of Advertising*, *27*(2).

Kammerer, M. (2000). *Die Bestimmung von Vertrauen in Internetangebote*. Zurich: Lizenziatsarbeit der Philisophischen Fakultaet der Universitaet Zurich.

Keevil, B. (1998, September 24-26). *Measuring the Usability Index of Your Web Site*. Paper presented at the annual Special Interest Group on Systems Documentation conference SIGDOC98, Quebec City, Province of Quebec, Canada.

Keser, C. (2002). *Trust and Reputation Building in E-Commerce*. CIRANO Working Paper 2002-75. Montreal, Canada: Cirano.

Kim, E., & Tadisina, S. (2005). Factors Impacting Customers' Initial Trust in E-Businesses: An Empirical Study. In *Proceedings of the Hawaii International Conference on System Sciences*, Big Island, HI, (pp. 1-10).

Mayer, R. C., Davis, J. H., & Schoorman, F. D. (1995). An integrative model of organizational trust. *Academy of Management Review*, 3(20), 709–734. doi:10.2307/258792

McKnigh, D. H., Choudhury, V., & Kacmar, C. (2002). Developing and validating trust measures for e-commerce: An integrative typology. *Information Systems Research*, 13(3), 334. doi:10.1287/isre.13.3.334.81

Meyers-Levy, J. (1989). *Gender differences in information processing: A selectivity interpretation*. Lexington: Lexington Books.

Meyers-Levy, J., & Maheswaran, D. (1991). Exploring Differences in Males' and Females' Processing Strategy. *The Journal of Consumer Research*, 18(June), 63–70. doi:10.1086/209241

Nielsen, J. (2004). *Designing for Web Usability*. Indianapolis: New Riders Publications.

Riegelsberger, J., Sasse, M., & McCarthy, J. (2005). The mechanics of trust: A framework for research and design. *International Journal of Human-Computer Studies*, 62(3), 381–422. doi:10.1016/j.ijhcs.2005.01.001

Rieh, S. (2003). Investigating Web searching behavior in home environments. Paper presented at the *Proceedings of the American Society for Information Science and Technology*.

Sheskin, D. J. (2004). *Handbook of Parametric and Nonparametric Statistical Procedures*. Boca Raton, FL: CRC Press.

Stanford, J., Tauber, E., Fogg, B., & Marable, L. (2002). *Experts vs. Online Consumers: A Comparative Credibility Study of Health and Finance Web Sites*. Retrieved October 13, 2006, from http://www.consumerwebwatch.org/news/report3_credibilityresearch/slicedbread

KEY TERMS AND DEFINITIONS

Avatar: is a virtual representation of a human figure which is created and controlled by a computer programme.

Business-to-Customer (B2C): One of the most common models in e-commerce. In B2C e-commerce, the transactions are made between businesses and individual consumers.

Culture: is characterized as the degree to which people share attributes, values, beliefs and behaviors.

E-Commerce: describes the process of buying, selling, or exchanging products, services, and information via computer networks, including the Internet.

Gender: refers to the differences between men and women.

Social Presence Cues: are the Para-verbal and non-verbal signals that make a person aware of the presence of other people, it used to describe media effects on interpersonal perception.

Video Clip: A short video presentation.

APPENDIX

Assessment Measure

In this measure, participants were asked to imagine that they had enough money to buy a laptop that would serve their needs for the next two years assuming that all sites offered the product they were looking for at the same price with the same condition.

Then they were asked to rate vendors' trustworthiness on a scale from 1 for untrustworthy website to 10 for a fully trusted website. Participants deduced the trustworthiness of the vendor under research and tested their accuracy of estimation to find the trustworthiness of the e-commerce vendor from the website under a high stimuli financial risk, since their financial incentive gain was guaranteed but the amount depended on how close their assessment was. The participants' financial incentive was designed using certain mathematical formulas that satisfied this criterion.

Investment Measure

Participants had to infer from the vendor's website interface the observable trust-cues. Based on the level of trust that resulted from these inferences, they had to decide whether and to what extent they should make themselves vulnerable, in other words engage in trusting action. Participants could invest nothing or go up to the amount gained from the assessment measure in each website. As they could invest in four websites, participants' decisions for this measure could potentially impact their final pay. The amount risked on a particular vendor was taken as a measure of the level of trust a participant had in this vendor.

Chapter 71
Using the Internet to Study Human Universals

Gad Saad
Concordia University, Canada

INTRODUCTION & BACKGROUND

Many human preferences, choices, emotions, and actions occur in universally similar manners because they are rooted in our common biological heritage. As such, irrespective of whether individuals are Peruvian, French, or Togolese, they are likely to share commonalities as a result of their shared Darwinian histories. In the current article, I provide a brief overview of how the Internet is a powerful tool for investigating such human universals. Given my work at the nexus of evolutionary theory and consumption, I begin with an example from marketing.

Few marketing scholars are versed in evolutionary theory and related biological formalisms (Saad, 2007a; Saad, 2008a). As such, they generally view the environment as the key driver in shaping consumption patterns. This is part and parcel of

the blank slate view of the human mind (Pinker, 2002), which purports that humans are born with empty minds that are subsequently filled via a wide range of socialization forces (e.g., parents, advertising content, or movies). Given that marketing scholars rely heavily on the expansive shoulders of socialization in explaining consumption, they are strong proponents of cultural relativism namely the notion that cultures need to be investigated from an emic perspective. Hence, marketers spend much of their efforts cataloging endless cross-cultural differences, seldom recognizing that there are numerous commonalities shared by consumers around the world.

A long-standing and yet to be resolved debate in international marketing is whether it is best to standardize one's advertising message across cultural settings or tailor-make it to each local culture (Agrawal, 1995; Theodosiou & Leonidou, 2003). Saad (2007a, chapter 4) proposed that the key reason

DOI: 10.4018/978-1-61520-611-7.ch071

that this matter has yet to be satisfactorily resolved is that marketers have not used the appropriate meta-framework for deciding which phenomena are culture-specific versus those that are human universals. Evolutionary psychology is exactly such a framework as it permits scholars to catalog marketing phenomena into three distinct categories (see Saad, 2007b, for additional details): (1) Emic-based consumption patterns that are outside the purview of evolutionary psychology as they are rooted in historical and cultural specificity. For example, that the French consume more wine than Saudis (religious edict against drinking alcohol) has nothing to do with evolutionary theory; (2) Cross-cultural differences that are rooted in adaptive processes. For example, some culinary traditions utilize a greater amount of spices than others, as a means of protecting against food-borne pathogens. It turns out that a country's latitude (which correlates with its ambient temperature) is a predictor of the extent to which spices will be used (Sherman & Billing, 1999), and this effect is greater for meat dishes as compared to vegetable dishes, since the former are more likely to contain food pathogens (Sherman & Hash, 2001). In other words, these culinary cross-cultural differences are adaptations to local environments; and (3) Human universals that are manifestations of the common biological heritage that are shared by all humans. Examples here include the universal recognition that facially symmetric individuals are beautiful, and the universal penchant for highly caloric foods.

Given its global reach, the Internet affords scholars with the capacity to explore a wide range of evolutionary-based human universals, a topic that I address in the remainder of this article. Incidentally, not only can the Internet be used to study human universals but also the Internet's own evolution can be modeled as a Darwinian process (Dovrolis, 2008).

UNCOVERING HUMAN UNIVERSALS AND FOSSILS OF THE HUMAN MIND IN THE ONLINE MEDIUM

In their quest to understand the evolution of the human mind, evolutionary behavioral scientists including behavioral ecologists, Darwinian anthropologists, and evolutionary psychologists have cataloged a wide range of human universals (Brown, 1991; Norenzayan & Heine, 2005). The premise is that some universal phenomena transcend time and space and hence are manifestations of our evolved biology. As an example, Dr. David P. Schmitt founded the International Sexuality Description Project, which seeks to explore human universals dealing with sexuality. Surveys have been administered in 56 different nations spanning six continents, and 28 languages (cf. Schmitt et al., 2003). Such an extraordinarily laborious endeavor is greatly facilitated by the ability to use the Internet to collect cross-cultural data using online surveys. It is important to note that the reliability and validity of data collected via web-based surveys have been found to be no lesser than their offline counterparts (Gosling, Vazire, Srivastava, & John, 2004). Interested readers can refer to Birnbaum (2004) who provides a detailed discussion of the pros and cons of conducting Internet-based behavioral research, and Ilieva, Baron, and Healey (2002) who contrast several methods for collecting survey data, including the Web, when carrying out marketing research across national boundaries.

Saad (2007a) argued that since the human mind does not fossilize, one of the ways to understand its evolution is to explore cultural products that have been created by it, throughout vastly different time periods and cultural settings. Take songs as an example. Humans have been singing songs (or uttering poems) for thousands of years in wildly varying cultural traditions. Are there any universal similarities when it comes to this form of human expression? What, if any, are the similarities between King Solomon's Song of Songs, contemporary Bollywood movie love songs, hip hop songs, and the poetry of troubadours of the middle ages? For one, the great majority of songs deal with mating irrespective of the musical genre. This is perhaps not surprising given that humans are a sexually reproducing species. Secondly, the specific lyrical contents are highly indicative of evolved and hence universal mating preferences. For example, men are much more likely to sing about women's beauty whereas women are much more likely to discuss men's social status (see Saad, 2007a, chapter 5 for additional details). Given the number of websites that serve as repositories for song lyrics (in numerous languages), the Internet can be used to conduct content analyses of song lyrics across cultural settings. In the same way that paleontologists painstakingly excavate fossil and skeletal remains as a means of understanding the evolutionary history of a species, the Internet can be used to excavate fossils of the human mind (i.e., cultural products) in an attempt to understand the evolutionary forces that have shaped our human nature. Next, I turn to a study that I recently conducted along those lines.

Saad (2008b) investigated men's near-universal preference for women who possess waist-to-hip ratios of 0.70 (see Singh, 2002 for a review of the evolutionary reasons for such a preference). Using the Internet, 1,068 online profiles of female escorts were coded. Data were collected from 48 countries (25 countries in Europe; 13 in Asia; 6 in Latin America; and Canada, the United States, Australia, and New Zealand). The objective was to determine whether the WHRs that female escorts advertise online are congruent with men's evolved preference. Incidentally, the term "near-universal" recognizes the fact that men's WHR preferences are responsive to environmental contingencies. For example, in cultures where caloric scarcity and uncertainty are more likely to occur, men's WHR preferences tend to be slightly higher (see chapters in Swami & Furnham, 2008 for additional details regarding the malleability of men's WHR preferences). Saad obtained the following

WHR per regional breakdown: Europe = 0.703; Asia = 0.712; Oceania = 0.75; Latin America = 0.691; North America = 0.763. The global WHR was 0.72. Additionally, Saad conducted a content analysis of the WHRs of sex dolls as advertised on a firm's web site. As expected, given men's evolved preferences, the mean WHR for the ten advertised dolls was 0.68 (see Kock et al. 2008, p. 139, for additional details). Whereas this last study could conceivably have been conducted in an offline medium (e.g., by ordering a physical catalog of the sex dolls), the escort study would have been next-to-impossible to complete without the Internet. In other words, the online medium affords scholars with the opportunity to have access to global data at their fingertips.

FUTURE RESEARCH DIRECTIONS

Given the power of the Internet both in its ability to facilitate cross-cultural research as well as its capacity to serve as an endless repository of cultural materials, the future research opportunities at the nexus of evolutionary theory and the online medium are fertile. Possible research agendas might include:

1. Conduct content analyses on other cultural products of relevance to business as a means of demonstrating human universals. For example, assuming that advertising repositories exist on the Internet as originating from widely different countries, it becomes relatively easy to conduct content analyses of ads to explore factors that are either similar or different across cultures.

2. Establish whether an evolutionary-based finding in the offline world replicates in the online medium. For example, Dunbar (2003) summarizes research that demonstrates that evolutionarily speaking, humans evolved in bands of roughly 150 individuals. The psychologist Eliot R. Smith reported to me

during my visit to Indiana University in 2007 that in his research on online social networks (e.g., *Facebook* or *MySpace*) he found that the average number of e-friends that people had was 150. This is consistent with Golder, Wilkinson, and Huberman (2007) who found that the median number of friends for a set of 4.2 million *Facebook* users was 144. Hence, the same optimal size that is operative in the offline world replicates in the online medium. See Mahfouz, Philaretou, and Theocharous (2008), Kock (2008; 2005), and Stenstrom, Stenstrom, Saad, and Cheikhrouhou (2008), for works that have explored such correspondences between the offline and online worlds.

CONCLUSION

The proverbial global village has become a reality given the interconnectivity that is afforded by the Internet (Barabási, 2002). That said, the Internet bears to light a more fundamental connection linking all members of the global village namely our common and evolved biological-based human nature. Hence, rather than strictly focusing on identifying cross-cultural differences in the online world (cf. Cyr, 2008; Maynard & Tian, 2004; Robbins & Stylianou, 2003, each of whom explored how firms' web sites are designed and/ or evaluated differently across cultural settings), scholars can also develop a deeper understanding of our common and evolved human nature via the use of the Internet.

REFERENCES

Agrawal, M. (1995). Review of a 40-year debate in international advertising: Practitioner and academician perspectives to the standardization/adaptation issue. *International Marketing Review, 12*(1), 26–48. doi:10.1108/02651339510080089

Barabási, A.-L. (2002). *Linked: The new science of networks*. New York: Basic Books.

Birnbaum, M. H. (2004). Human research and data collection via the Internet. *Annual Review of Psychology, 55*, 803–832. doi:10.1146/annurev.psych.55.090902.141601

Brown, D. E. (1991). *Human Universals*. New York: McGraw Hill.

Cyr, D. (2008). Modeling web site design across cultures: Relationships to trust, satisfaction, and e-loyalty. *Journal of Management Information Systems, 24*(4), 47–72. doi:10.2753/MIS0742-1222240402

Dovrolis, C. (2008). What would Darwin think about clean-slate architectures? *Computer Communication Review, 38*(1), 29–34. doi:10.1145/1341431.1341436

Dunbar, R. I. M. (2003). The social brain: Mind, language, and society in evolutionary perspective. *Annual Review of Anthropology, 32*(1), 163–181. doi:10.1146/annurev.anthro.32.061002.093158

Golder, S., Wilkinson, D., & Huberman, B. (2007). Rhythms of social interaction: Messaging within a massive online network. *3rd International Conference on Communities and Technologies* (CT2007). East Lansing, MI. June 28-30, 2007.

Gosling, S. D., Vazire, S., Srivastava, S., & John, O. P. (2004). Should we trust web-based studies? A comparative analysis of six preconceptions about Internet questionnaires. *The American Psychologist, 59*(2), 93–104. doi:10.1037/0003-066X.59.2.93

Ilieva, J., Baron, S., & Healey, N. M. (2002). Online surveys in marketing: Pros and cons. *International Journal of Market Research, 44*(3), 361–376.

Kock, N. (2005). Media richness or media naturalness? The evolution of our biological communication apparatus and its influence on our behavior toward E-communication tools. *IEEE Transactions on Professional Communication, 48*(2), 117–130. doi:10.1109/TPC.2005.849649

Kock, N. (2008). E-collaboration and e-commerce in virtual worlds: The potential of Second Life and World of Warcraft. *International Journal of e-Collaboration, 4*(3), 1–13.

Kock, N., Hantula, D. A., Hayne, S., Saad, G., Todd, P. M., & Watson, R. T. (2008). Darwinian perspectives on electronic communication. *IEEE Transactions on Professional Communication, 51*(2), 133–146. doi:10.1109/TPC.2008.2000327

Mahfouz, A. Y., Philaretou, A. G., & Theocharous, A. (2008). Virtual social interactions: Evolutionary, social psychological and technological perspectives. *Computers in Human Behavior, 24*(6), 3014–3026. doi:10.1016/j.chb.2008.05.008

Maynard, M., & Tian, Y. (2004). Between global and glocal: Content analysis of the Chinese web sites of the 100 top global brands. *Public Relations Review, 30*(3), 285–291. doi:10.1016/j.pubrev.2004.04.003

Norenzayan, A., & Heine, S. J. (2005). Psychological universals: What are they and how can we know? *Psychological Bulletin, 131*(5), 763–784. doi:10.1037/0033-2909.131.5.763

Pinker, S. (2002). *The blank slate: The modern denial of human nature.* New York: Viking.

Robbins, S. S., & Stylianou, A. C. (2003). Global corporate web sites: An empirical investigation of content and design. *Information & Management, 40*(3), 205–212. doi:10.1016/S0378-7206(02)00002-2

Saad, G. (2007a). *The evolutionary bases of consumption.* Mahwah, NJ: Lawrence Erlbaum.

Saad, G. (2007b). *Homo consumericus: Consumption phenomena as universals, as cross-cultural adaptations, or as emic cultural instantiations.* Submitted manuscript.

Saad, G. (2008a). The collective amnesia of marketing scholars regarding consumers' biological and evolutionary roots. *Marketing Theory, 8*(4), 425–448. doi:10.1177/1470593108096544

Saad, G. (2008b). Advertised waist-to-hip ratios of online female escorts: An evolutionary perspective. *International Journal of e-Collaboration, 4*(3), 40–50.

Schmitt, D. P., & 118 Members of the International Sexuality Description Project. (2003). Universal sex differences in the desire for sexual variety: Tests from 52 nations, 6 continents, and 13 islands. *Journal of Personality and Social Psychology, 85*(1), 85–104. doi:10.1037/0022-3514.85.1.85

Sherman, P. W., & Billing, J. (1999). Darwinian gastronomy: Why we use spices. *Bioscience, 49*(6), 453–463. doi:10.2307/1313553

Sherman, P. W., & Hash, G. A. (2001). Why vegetable recipes are not very spicy. *Evolution and Human Behavior, 22*(3), 147–163. doi:10.1016/S1090-5138(00)00068-4

Singh, D. (2002). Female mate value at a glance: Relationship of waist-to-hip ratio to health, fecundity and attractiveness. *Neuroendocrinology Letters, 23*(suppl. 4), 81–91.

Stenstrom, E., Stenstrom, P., Saad, G., & Cheikhrouhou, S. (2008). Online hunting and gathering: An evolutionary perspective on sex differences in website preferences and navigation. *IEEE Transactions on Professional Communication, 51*(2), 155–168. doi:10.1109/TPC.2008.2000341

Swami, V., & Furnham, A. (Eds.). (2008). *The body beautiful: Evolutionary and sociocultural perspectives.* Basingstoke, UK: Palgrave Macmillan.

Theodosiou, M., & Leonidou, L. C. (2003). Standardization versus adaptation of international marketing strategy: An integrative assessment of the empirical research. *International Business Review, 12*(2), 141–171. doi:10.1016/S0969-5931(02)00094-X

KEY TERMS AND DEFINITIONS

Blank Slate/Tabula Rasa: The premise that humans are born with empty minds that are subsequently filled by a wide range of socialization forces. This has been the central dogma of the great majority of social scientists, many of whom are referred to as social constructivists.

Cultural Relativism: The tenet that all cultures are inherently different from one another and hence must be evaluated using their own idiosyncratic contexts. In this sense, it is antithetical to the existence of human universals.

Evolutionary Behavioral Science: The application of Darwinian approaches to study behavioral phenomena. Hence, behavioral ecology, Darwinian anthropology, and evolutionary psychology are sub-disciplines within the greater field of Evolutionary Behavioral Science.

Fossils of the Human Mind: Since the human mind does not fossilize, scientists can investigate cultural products across a wide range of cultural and temporal settings, as a means of understanding the evolution of the human mind.

Global versus Local Advertising: The strategic decision to either create one advertising copy that is transportable to all cultural settings (global) or tailor-make the message and associated semiotics to be in line with idiosyncratic cultural differences (local).

Human Universal: A phenomenon that is found in the same form irrespective of cultural setting and/or time period. Such universals are typically construed as rooted in a common biological and evolutionary-based heritage.

Waist-to-Hip Ratio: A morphological metric that is used by both men and women in evaluating the phenotypic quality of prospective mates.

Chapter 72

The Neurocognitive and Evolutionary Bases of Sex Differences in Website Design Preferences:
Recommendations for Marketing Managers

Eric Stenstrom
Concordia University, Canada

Gad Saad
Concordia University, Canada

INTRODUCTION

Marketing managers habitually use sex as a form of segmentation since it satisfies several requirements for efficient implementation including profitability, identifiability, accessibility, and measurability (Darley & Smith, 1995). Nevertheless, sex differences in marketing remain under-researched and continue to be a source of confusion for managers (Hupfer, 2002). Sex differences in cognitive processing are particularly relevant to e-business managers given that online consumers must process various types of spatial and perceptual information while navigating online. Despite the large body of evidence documenting consistent sex differences in cognition (Kimura, 2004), there is a paucity of research

DOI: 10.4018/978-1-61520-611-7.ch072

exploring how male and female consumers respond differently to various website design aspects (Cyr & Bonanni, 2005; Moss, Gunn, & Heller, 2006; Simon, 2001). Moreover, the few studies that have examined sex differences in online preferences were not grounded in any consilient theoretical framework.

The main objective of this paper is to examine how sex differences in the processing of spatial and perceptual information lead to differential preferences in website design for men and women. We argue that sex differences in website design preferences are best understood within a framework based on both recent findings in neurocognitive psychology and on evolutionary theory (as originally reported in Stenstrom, Stenstrom, Saad, & Cheikhrouhou, 2008). Such a framework would enable e-business managers to tailor the design of their websites according to the sex ratio of their clientele. In other words, depending on whether a website is equally visited by both sexes, or largely visited by only one of the two sexes, will determine the design features of the site in question. The structure of this chapter is as follows. First, the latest cognitive and neuropsychological evidence relating to sex differences in spatial and perceptual processing are explored, including a discussion of the particular selective pressures that have led to their emergence. This section also includes an examination of how these sex differences are likely to translate into the corresponding sex differences in the online processing of information. Next, website design recommendations for e-business managers are put forth, followed by a discussion of possible future research avenues.

BACKGROUND

Researchers have highlighted the importance of website design as an antecedent of e-satisfaction (Evanschitzkya, Iyer, Hessea, & Ahlerta, 2004; Szymanski & Hise, 2000) and trust (Cho, 2006). Yet, few papers have investigated how various website design aspects are differentially appreciated by men and women (Cyr & Bonanni, 2005; Simon, 2001), and have done so without any consilient theoretical grounding. Our framework is based on the evolutionary underpinnings of sex differences in cognition, these being founded on the differential roles assumed by men and women throughout our evolutionary history. Specifically, whereas men predominantly hunted, women primarily gathered. This division of labor exerted a sex-specific selective pressure on various aspects of human cognition, leading to male cognitive abilities specialized for hunting and female cognitive abilities specialized for gathering (Alexander, 2003; Geary 1995; New, Krasnow, Truxaw, & Gaulin, 2007; Silverman & Eals, 1992). In the ensuing section, sex differences in spatial and perceptual processing are reviewed in light of the

evolutionary forces that led to their development. In addition, the findings from the few studies that have investigated how men and women process online information differently are discussed within the context of our proposed framework.

SEX DIFFERENCES IN COGNITIVE PROCESSING AND WEBSITE DESIGN PREFERENCES

Spatial Processing

Sex differences in the processing of spatial information have been studied widely, particularly with regards to navigation, object location, and spatial rotation. It has been suggested that men evolved a large-scale, orientation-based (i.e., Euclidean) navigational style due to the fact that hunting required the tracking of animals over novel expansive terrain while maintaining one's spatial orientation in order to find a direct route back home. In contrast, women are believed to have evolved a short-scale, landmark-based (i.e., topological) navigational style given that gathering necessitated the collection of various fruits and plants in relatively close proximity to home (Choi & Silverman, 1996; Silverman & Eals, 1992). Numerous studies have demonstrated sex differences in navigational styles and abilities that are in line with the notion that males and females have inherited sexually dimorphic navigational propensities. When completing navigational tasks or when providing directions, women rely mainly on landmarks, whereas men focus more on Euclidean properties of the environment (Dabbs, Chang, Strong, & Milun, 1998; Galea & Kimura, 1993; Saucier et al., 2002). Men are more proficient than women in route-learning tasks in virtual three-dimensional mazes in terms of time efficiency and errors committed (Moffat, Hampson & Hatzipantelis, 1998), as well as accuracy in pointing in the direction of the maze's starting point (Lawton & Morrin, 1999). The male advantage in navigation is also evident in environments resembling those traveled by ancestral hunters. After being lead through a long, circuitous route through a wooded area, men performed better than women in pointing to the starting position and returning to it via the most direct route (Silverman et al., 2000).

In the online realm, navigating through websites seems to rely on similar cognitive processes to those operative in naturalistic environments. Websites are hierarchically structured and require navigation through various pages. When browsing online, clicking on links to go from one page to the next is likely processed cognitively in a similar manner as when navigating from one physical area to another. In line with this reasoning, Simon (2001) reported that women were more likely to favor websites with pull-down menus rather than those that require clicking through numerous levels of pages. Given that a pull-down menu can serve as a landmark, this finding suggests that women might also utilize a landmark navigational style in the online realm. In addition, this finding implies that women may disfavor deep navigational structures that necessitate browsing through multiple levels of pages void of a landmark. Cyr and Bonanni (2005) asked participants to select a digital camera on a major electronics website and measured the participants' reactions to the website task. Women rated the website as being more difficult to navigate than did men. However, the study was limited given that no website design elements were manipulated as a means of establishing a causal relationship between a website's navigational structure and ease of navigation. Stenstrom, Stenstrom, Saad, and Cheikhrouhou (2008) recently conducted a pilot study examining how efficiently men and women perform product search tasks in one of two book websites that vary in navigational structure. Whereas both sites had the exact same informational content, one site was wide but shallow with two levels of navigational depth, whereas the other was deep but narrow with five levels of depth. Compared to women, men reported taking less time performing the

search task in the website with a deeper structure that required navigation through various levels of web pages. In addition, men appeared to be more efficient in the deeper website compared to the wider website by reportedly spending less time conducting the tasks in the deeper structure than their male counterparts who navigated in the wider one. These results suggest that a website with a deeper navigational structure is better suited for the male orientation navigational style than the female landmark style.

Women have evolved the ability to outperform men in spatial tasks that gauge object-location memory. Ancestral foraging required the ability to remember the location of a wide variety of static food sources and the detection of subtle changes in the environment as the food sources ripened over time (Silverman & Eals, 1992). The female advantage in object-location memory has been demonstrated utilizing a variety of paper-and-pencil and computer-mediated tasks (Alexander, Packard, & Peterson, 2002; Eals & Silverman, 1994; Lejbak, Vrbancic, & Crossley, 2009; Voyer, Postma, Brake, & Imperato-McGinley, 2007). This female advantage has also been found in naturalistic environments. At a farmer's market, women pointed more accurately towards the location of various food products that had been previously seen (New et al., 2007).

Numerous studies have shown that men tend to outperform women in mental spatial rotation tasks. Geary (1995) proposed that this male advantage in spatial rotation tasks stems from the spatial requirements of hunting, namely throwing projectiles at moving targets. In both pencil-paper and computer-mediated tasks that require the mental rotation of complex shapes, males perform better in matching objects that are different only in their three-dimensional spatial orientation (Hubona & Shirah, 2006; Shepard & Metzler, 1971; Voyer, Voyer, & Bryden, 1995). Sex differences in spatial rotation processing are evident in the differential patterns of brain activation between men and women when engaged in such tasks.

Functional magnetic resonance imaging (fMRI) studies examining mental rotation have yielded sex differences in spatial task-related activation patterns (Jordan, Wustenberg, Heinze, Peters, & Jancke, 2002).

Males appear to utilize a more effective and automatic "bottom-up" spatial processing pattern whereas females use a more cognitively effortful "top-down" neural strategy during spatial rotation tasks (Butler et al., 2006). The manner in which men and women differentially process the rotation of objects is particularly relevant to web design. Advances in web design technologies have enabled consumers to visualize products in three-dimensions while allowing them to control their rotation. However, given its high production costs, the use of rotation technology is mainly used for relatively high-priced products (e.g., cars). The benefit of investing in the three-dimension portrayal of products likely depends on the sex of one's consumer base. In line with this reasoning, Cyr and Bonanni (2005) found that men perceived the three-dimensional portrayal of a digital camera, via a set of photos taken from several different angles, as being more meaningful than did women. In sum, the literature suggests that men and women have evolved dimorphic spatial cognitions that engender sex differences in online preferences. Next, sex differences in perceptual processing are explored.

Perceptual Processing

Men and women possess specialized perceptual systems also rooted in the ancestral sex-specific roles in food foraging and game hunting (Alexander, 2003). Sex differences in perceptual processing, which are particularly relevant to the online realm, include the processing of movement, form, and color. Neurologically speaking, the human visual system can be categorized into the parvocellular and magnocellular processing streams (Bullier, Schall, & Morel, 1996; Milner, Paulignan, Dijkerman, Michel, & Jeannerod,

1999). The female perceptual system is biased towards the parvocellular pathway, which deals primarily with the processing of colors. On the other hand, the male perceptual system is biased towards the magnocellular pathway, which is predominantly responsible for the processing of motion and spatial information. Given that foraging required the identification of edible plants and ripe fruits from large varieties of vegetation, a more developed parvocellular visual pathway would have provided ancestral women with a significant adaptive advantage. For men, a more developed magnocellular visual pathway was crucial for successfully detecting moving animals and throwing projectiles at them as accurately as possible (Alexander, 2003).

That men and women have inherited sexually differentiated perceptual systems is supported by numerous empirical findings. Men display faster reaction times (Silverman, 2006) and judge the relative velocity and trajectory of moving objects more accurately than do women (Law, Pellegrino, & Hunt, 1993; Poduska & Phillips, 1986). Males also have an accuracy advantage when throwing projectiles (Watson & Kimura, 1991). Furthermore, motion-related perceptual sex differences appear very early in development. For example, one-day-old boys have been found to exhibit stronger preferences for moving objects than one-day-old girls (Connellan, Baron-Cohen, Wheelwright, Batki, & Ahluwalia, 2000). Given that the male perceptual system is more sensitive to moving stimuli, males should pay more attention to, and make more efficient use of, moving web elements. In line with this reasoning, Simon (2001) reported that a greater number of surveyed males favored websites that had extensive animated objects and graphics as compared to females. Likewise, Cyr and Bonanni (2005) found that men conveyed a preference towards the animations and interactivity of a website more so than did women.

Although males tend to perform better in motion-related tests, females have an advantage in tasks involving the processing of colors and object features. For example, females outperform males both in object and form discrimination (Overman, Pate, Moore, & Peuster, 1996), as well as in color naming tasks (Bornstein, 1985). In addition, whereas only an estimated 0.4% of women have inherited color blindness or green-red perception deficiencies, their prevalence in men is estimated at 8% (Birch, 1993). In the online medium, Cyr and Bonanni (2005) reported that women were more attracted to the colors of a website than were men. It is also possible that the use of vibrant red and green hues might be particularly appreciated by women given that the ability to perceive these two colors is particularly dependent on the parvocellular pathway (Hendry & Reid, 2000). In addition, since women have an advantage in discriminating between objects and forms, it is likely that they will be less distracted by visual clutter and respond more favorably to a large number of product images located on a single web page. To sum up, men and women have inherited specialized cognitions that manifest themselves in the online world as sexually differentiated website preferences. Recommendations to e-business managers are proposed next.

Recommendations

Given the aforementioned literature on sex differences in spatial and perceptual processing, e-business managers should tailor their websites according to the sex of their target market. For websites intended for a primarily male market, we recommend a deep rather than wide navigational structure to suit the male navigational style. We also advise e-business managers to invest in dynamic web elements in order to capture and maintain the interest of male browsers. In addition, the use of web elements which are displayed three-dimensionally, and those that can be rotated by users are more likely to be worth the investment for a male clientele. Given the female advantage in object-location memory, women will likely be more proficient than men in remembering the

locations of products presented within a wide array of items on a single web page. Thus, men will likely benefit more from website programs that assist in finding a previously-viewed product for purchase. Finally, the use of colors to portray meaning should be used with greater caution for a male clientele given the relatively high prevalence of color-blindness in men. For websites designed for a primarily female market, we recommend having noticeably visible landmarks on every web page to clearly indicate their location within the site, in order to suit the female navigational style. Likewise, the use of pull-down menus that enable navigation while staying on the home page, as well as the emphasis on the choice of colors are more likely to be appreciated by the female clientele. Future research avenues are explored next followed by our concluding remarks.

FUTURE RESEARCH DIRECTIONS

The framework and recommendations proposed herein can be empirically tested in future studies. Additionally, to further investigate sex differences in online navigational style, clickstream analyses could shed light on the particular navigational paths taken by men and women (cf., Kalczynski, Sénécal, & Nantel, 2006). Research relating to the response to movement might be enriched via the use of eye tracking technology to test sex differences in attention to moving website elements (e.g., banner ads). Another worthy avenue of future research would be to consider within-subject variations in cognitive abilities. For instance, a woman's navigational and mental rotation abilities have been found to depend on which phase of her menstrual cycle that she is in (Hausmann, Slabbekoorn, Van Goozen, Cohen-Kettenis, & Güntürkün, 2000). Accordingly, might women's website preferences change across their menstrual cycles? Finally, our framework can be extended to other computer-mediated environments such as videos games, as well as other elements of a firm's marketing mix such as advertising and product design (for an evolutionary perspective on sex differences in brand design preferences, see Moss, Hamilton, & Neave, 2007).

CONCLUSION

E-business managers must make important decisions such as how to structure their websites, whether to use moving elements, which color schemes to use, and whether to invest in portrayals of rotating products. We posit that the optimal design will likely depend on whether the given consumer base is primarily male or female. By better understanding the cognitive and evolutionary bases of sex differences in website design preferences, e-business managers will be better able to meet the needs of their online clientele.

REFERENCES

Alexander, G. M. (2003). An evolutionary perspective of sex-typed toy preferences: Pink, blue, and the brain. *Archives of Sexual Behavior, 32*(1), 7–14. doi:10.1023/A:1021833110722

Alexander, G. M., Packard, M. G., & Peterson, B. S. (2002). Sex and spatial position effects on object location memory following intentional learning of object identities. *Neuropsychologia, 40*(8), 1516–1522. doi:10.1016/S0028-3932(01)00215-9

Birch, J. (1993). *Diagnosis of defective colour vision*. New York: Oxford University Press.

Bornstein, M. H. (1985). On the development of color naming in young children: Data and theory. *Brain and Language, 26*(1), 72–93. doi:10.1016/0093-934X(85)90029-X

Bullier, J., Schall, J. D., & Morel, A. (1996). Functional streams in occipito-frontal connections in the monkey. *Behavioural Brain Research, 76*(1-2), 89–97. doi:10.1016/0166-4328(95)00182-4

Butler, T., Imperato-McGinley, J., Pan, H., Voyer, D., Cordero, J., & Zhu, Y. S. (2006). Sex differences in mental rotation: Top-down versus bottom-up processing. *NeuroImage, 32*(1), 445–456. doi:10.1016/j.neuroimage.2006.03.030

Cho, J. (2006). The mechanism of trust and distrust formation and their relational outcomes. *Journal of Retailing, 82*(1), 25–35. doi:10.1016/j.jretai.2005.11.002

Choi, J., & Silverman, I. (1996). Sexual dimorphism in spatial behaviors: Applications to route-learning. *Evolution & Cognition, 2*(2), 165–171.

Connellan, J., Baron-Cohen, S., Wheelwright, S., Batki, A., & Ahluwalia, J. (2000). Sex differences in human neonatal social perception. *Infant Behavior and Development, 23*(1), 113–118. doi:10.1016/S0163-6383(00)00032-1

Cyr, D., & Bonanni, C. (2005). Gender and website design in e-business. *International Journal of Electronic Business, 3*(6), 565–582. doi:10.1504/IJEB.2005.008536

Dabbs, J. M. Jr, Chang, E. L., Strong, R. A., & Milun, R. (1998). Spatial ability, navigation strategy, and geographic knowledge among men and women. *Evolution and Human Behavior, 19*(2), 89–98. doi:10.1016/S1090-5138(97)00107-4

Darley, W. K., & Smith, R. E. (1995). Gender differences in information processing strategies: An empirical test of the selectivity model in advertising response. *Journal of Advertising, 24*(1), 41–56.

Eals, M., & Silverman, I. (1994). The hunter-gatherer theory of spatial sex differences: Proximate factors mediating the female advantage in recall of object arrays. *Ethology and Sociobiology, 15*(2), 95–105. doi:10.1016/0162-3095(94)90020-5

Evanschitzkya, H., Iyer, G. R., Hessea, J., & Ahlerta, D. (2004). E-satisfaction: A re-examination. *Journal of Retailing, 80*(3), 239–247. doi:10.1016/j.jretai.2004.08.002

Galea, L. A. M., & Kimura, D. (1993). Sex differences in route learning. *Personality and Individual Differences, 14*(1), 53–65. doi:10.1016/0191-8869(93)90174-2

Geary, D. C. (1995). Sexual selection and sex differences in spatial cognition. *Learning and Individual Differences, 7*(4), 289–301. doi:10.1016/1041-6080(95)90003-9

Hausmann, M., Slabbekoorn, D., Van Goozen, S. H. M., Cohen-Kettenis, P. T., & Güntürkün, O. (2000). Sex hormones affect spatial abilities during the menstrual cycle. *Behavioral Neuroscience, 114*(6), 1245–1250. doi:10.1037/0735-7044.114.6.1245

Hendry, S. H. C., & Reid, R. C. (2000). The koniocellular pathway in primate vision. *Annual Review of Neuroscience, 23*, 127–153. doi:10.1146/annurev.neuro.23.1.127

Hubona, G. S., & Shirah, G. W. (2006). The Paleolithic stone age effect? Gender differences performing specific computer-generated spatial tasks. *International Journal of Technology and Human Interaction, 2*(2), 24–48.

Hupfer, M. (2002). Communicating with the agentic woman and the communal man: Are stereotypic advertising appeals still relevant? *Academy of Marketing Science Review, 2002*(3). Retrieved from http://www.amsreview.org/articles/hupfer03-2002.pdf

Jordan, K., Wustenberg, T., Heinze, H. J., Peters, M., & Jancke, L. (2002). Women and men exhibit different cortical activation patterns during mental rotation tasks. *Neuropsychologia, 40*(13), 2397–2408. doi:10.1016/S0028-3932(02)00076-3

Kalczynski, P., Sénécal, S., & Nantel, J. (2006). Predicting online task completion with clickstream complexity measures: A graph-based approach. *International Journal of Electronic Commerce, 10*(3), 123–143. doi:10.2753/JEC1086-4415100305

Kimura, D. (2004). Human sex differences in cognition: Fact, not predicament. *Sexualities, Evolution & Gender, 6*(1), 45–53.

Law, D. J., Pellegrino, J. W., & Hunt, E. B. (1993). Comparing the tortoise and the hare: Gender differences and experience in dynamic spatial reasoning tasks. *Psychological Science, 4*(1), 35–40. doi:10.1111/j.1467-9280.1993.tb00553.x

Lawton, C. A., & Morrin, K. A. (1999). Gender differences in pointing accuracy in computer-simulated 3D mazes. *Sex Roles, 40*(1-2), 73–92. doi:10.1023/A:1018830401088

Lejbak, L., Vrbancic, M., & Crossley, M. (2009). The female advantage in object location memory is robust to verbalizability and mode of presentation of test stimuli. *Brain and Cognition, 69*(1), 148–153. doi:10.1016/j.bandc.2008.06.006

Milner, A. D., Paulignan, Y., Dijkerman, H. C., Michel, F., & Jeannerod, M. (1999). A paradoxical improvement of misreaching in optic ataxia: New evidence for two separate neural systems for visual localization. *Proceedings. Biological Sciences, 266*(1434), 2225–2229. doi:10.1098/rspb.1999.0912

Moffat, S. D., Hampson, E., & Hatzipantelis, M. (1998). Navigation in a "virtual" maze: Sex differences and correlation with psychometric measures of spatial ability in humans. *Evolution and Human Behavior, 19*(2), 73–87. doi:10.1016/S1090-5138(97)00104-9

Moss, G., Gunn, R., & Heller, J. (2006). Some men like it black, some women like it pink: Consumer implications of differences in male and female website design. *Journal of Consumer Behaviour, 5*(4), 328–341. doi:10.1002/cb.184

Moss, G., Hamilton, C., & Neave, N. (2007). Evolutionary factors in design preferences. *Journal of Brand Management, 14*(4), 313–323. doi:10.1057/palgrave.bm.2550073

New, J., Krasnow, M. M., Truxaw, D., & Gaulin, S. J. C. (2007). Spatial adaptations for plant foraging: Women excel and calories count. *Proceedings. Biological Sciences, 274*(1626), 2679–2684. doi:10.1098/rspb.2007.0826

Overman, W. H., Pate, B. J., Moore, K., & Peuster, A. (1996). Ontogeny of place learning in children as measured in the radial arm maze, Morris search task, and open field task. *Behavioral Neuroscience, 110*(6), 1205–1228. doi:10.1037/0735-7044.110.6.1205

Poduska, E., & Phillips, D. G. (1986). The performance of college students on Piaget-type tasks dealing with distance, time, and speed. *Journal of Research in Science Teaching, 23*(9), 845–848. doi:10.1002/tea.3660230908

Saucier, D. M., Green, S. M., Leason, J., MacFadden, A., Bell, S., & Elias, L. J. (2002). Are sex differences in navigation caused by sexually dimorphic strategies or by differences in the ability to use the strategies? *Behavioral Neuroscience, 116*(3), 403–410. doi:10.1037/0735-7044.116.3.403

Shepard, R. N., & Metzler, J. (1971). Mental rotation of three-dimensional objects. *Science, 171*(972), 701–703. doi:10.1126/science.171.3972.701

Silverman, I. (2006). Sex differences in simple visual reaction time: A historical meta-analysis. *Sex Roles, 54*(1-2), 57–69. doi:10.1007/s11199-006-8869-6

Silverman, I., Choi, J., MacKewn, A., Fisher, M., Moro, J., & Olshansky, E. (2000). Evolved mechanisms underlying wayfinding: Further studies on the hunter-gatherer theory of spatial sex differences. *Evolution and Human Behavior, 21*(3), 201–213. doi:10.1016/S1090-5138(00)00036-2

Silverman, I., & Eals, M. (1992). Sex differences in spatial abilities: Evolutionary theory and data. In J. H. Barkow, L. Cosmides, & J. Tooby (Eds.), *The adapted mind: Evolutionary psychology and the generation of culture,* (pp. 533-549). New York: Oxford University Press.

Simon, S. J. (2001). The impact of culture and gender on web sites: An empirical study. *The Data Base for Advances in Information Systems, 32*(1), 18–37.

Stenstrom, E., Stenstrom, P., Saad, G., & Cheikhrouhou, S. (2008). Online hunting and gathering: An evolutionary perspective on sex differences in website preferences and navigation. *IEEE Transactions on Professional Communication, 51*(2), 155–168. doi:10.1109/TPC.2008.2000341

Szymanski, D. M., & Hise, R. T. (2000). E-satisfaction: An initial examination. *Journal of Retailing, 76*(3), 309–322. doi:10.1016/S0022-4359(00)00035-X

Voyer, D., Postma, A., Brake, B., & Imperato-McGinley, J. (2007). Gender differences in object location memory: A meta-analysis. *Psychonomic Bulletin & Review, 14*(1), 23–38.

Voyer, D., Voyer, S., & Bryden, M. P. (1995). Magnitude of sex differences in spatial abilities: A meta-analysis and consideration of critical variables. *Psychological Bulletin, 117*(2), 250–270. doi:10.1037/0033-2909.117.2.250

Watson, N. V., & Kimura, D. (1991). Nontrivial sex differences in throwing and intercepting: Relation to psychometrically-defined spatial functions. *Personality and Individual Differences, 12*(5), 375–385. doi:10.1016/0191-8869(91)90053-E

ADDITIONAL READING

Buss, D. M. (1999). *Evolutionary psychology: The new science of the mind.* Boston, MA: Allyn and Bacon.

Dennis, C., & McCall, A. (2005). The savannah hypothesis of shopping. *Business Strategy Review, 16*(3), 12–16. doi:10.1111/j.0955-6419.2005.00368.x

Ecuyer-Dab, I., & Robert, M. (2004). Have sex differences in spatial ability evolved from male competition for mating and female concern for survival? *Cognition, 91*(3), 221–257. doi:10.1016/j.cognition.2003.09.007

Joseph, R. (2000). The evolution of sex differences in language, sexuality, and visual-spatial skills. *Archives of Sexual Behavior, 29*(1), 35–66. doi:10.1023/A:1001834404611

Pinker, S. (2002). *The blank slate: The modern denial of human nature.* New York: Penguin Putnam.

Saad, G. (2007). *The evolutionary bases of consumption.* Mahwah, NJ: Lawrence Erlbaum.

KEY TERMS AND DEFINITIONS

Euclidean Navigation: A navigational strategy that utilizes geometrical properties of the environment such as distances, angles, and cardinal directions.

Evolutionary Psychology: The study of the adaptive functions of the mind and how its cognitive structure was shaped by natural and sexual selection to solve recurrent problems that existed in human ancestral environments.

Functional Magnetic Resonance Imaging (fMRI): A neuroimaging technique that measures neural activity in the brain and allows the mapping of particular brain areas associated with various psychological phenomena.

Hunter-Gatherer Theory: The proposition that the sexual division of labor that existed throughout human evolution when men primarily hunted while women predominately gathered led to the evolution of sex-specific cognitive abilities.

Neurocognitive Psychology: The study of cognitive functions and their associations to particular brain areas and neural pathways.

Pull-Down Menu: A list of navigational options that appears only when the item is selected.

Topological Navigation: A navigational strategy that relies predominantly on landmarks and their relational properties.

Chapter 73
Exploring Video Games from an Evolutionary Psychological Perspective

Zack Mendenhall
Concordia University, Canada

Marcelo Vinhal Nepomuceno
Concordia University, Canada

Gad Saad
Concordia University, Canada

INTRODUCTION AND BACKGROUND

Video games are a relatively recent form of entertainment whose sales growth has been enormous (almost 700% from 1996 to 2007), with sales for 2007 reaching 9.5 billion dollars in the US (Entertainment Software Association, 2007). This figure does not include the sales of hardware components such as consoles and accessories, or subscriptions to high-speed Internet providers. To contextualize this sales figure, the US cinema industry garnered 9.6 billion dollars domestically in the same year (MPAA, 2007). The video game industry is so robust that it appears to be impervious to the current economic crisis (Economist, December 20, 2008).

Video game research typically follows one of two avenues. Authors either champion games for their positive effects on users (hand-eye coordination, problem solving, and teamwork, for instance) or lament them for promoting violence (see Mäyrä, 2008 for a broad overview of gaming studies). More recent work (Ducheneaut et al., 2006) has focused on descriptive statistics of online gamers, but all these streams of research tend to rely on "Blank Slate" reasoning (Pinker 2002), leading them to overlook robust explanations of video gaming phenomena. Of relevance to the current article, video games are seldom studied from an evolutionary psychological perspective (but see Cherney & Poss, 2008; Kock, 2008; Mazur, Susman, & Edelbrock, 1997). On a related note, Stenstrom et al. (2008) find evidence for sex-differentiated strategies in navigating websites, with these results being potentially applicable to the video gaming context. In the current paper we demonstrate how an evolutionary psychological (EP)

DOI: 10.4018/978-1-61520-611-7.ch073

approach could elucidate why this entertainment choice has increased in popularity, and how it is related to our evolved human nature. We begin by describing relevant video game genres, to illustrate the latest developments and trends in the industry. Subsequently we highlight links between some of these genres and EP principles.

Different game genres tend to attract players with highly heterogeneous demographics, personalities, and motivations to play. Whereas the industry has developed numerous genres, we restrict our discussion to two major genres that are highly distinguishable from one another: *Massively Multiplayer Online Role Playing Games (MMORPG)* and *First Person Shooters (FPS)*. *MMORPGs* are based on the classic pen-and-paper role-playing games. These games were originally played in a setting similar to that in which one might play a board game (i.e., around a kitchen table, with friends and family). The RPG was created during the 1970s and since then has quickly evolved. Traditionally the RPG is an interpretive game in which the participants create characters and role-play as their character in an imaginary world. Players aim to become powerful entities in that world, and typically cooperate in that pursuit. The objective of traditional RPGs is vague. There is no end-point (as in most games); one simply 'adventures' until one dies or gets bored. Killing monsters and saving princesses are common threads, however.

RPGs established a style of game play that MMORPGs inherited. Central to this style is the notion that an avatar grows in power over time. This concept was formalized by implementing 'experience points' and 'levels.' As characters slay monsters or complete quests, they are awarded 'experience points.' When they have accumulated a sufficient amount of experience points, they 'level up.' Characters begin at level 1, and each subsequent level up requires more experience points than the previous. By digitizing the rules of traditional RPGs, MMORPGs have obviated many of the problems native to the pen-and-paper

format. Players of MMORPGS do not have to keep tabs of their own experience points, levels, or calculate damage, for instance. Aspects of the game which required rote computation are now handled by the computer.

First Person Shooter games are the most frequently studied genre by scholars wishing to correlate video games to real-world violence. In these games, the avatar is controlled using the first person perspective. To succeed in the game, the player must use a variety of weapons (rifles, laser guns, chainsaws, etc.) to shoot, dismember, or subdue enemies. This genre of game often comes in two modes. In the story-driven mode, which can be played either alone or as part of a team, enemies are controlled by fairly advanced artificial intelligences. The second (and more popular) mode is "player versus player," which encourages direct competition between human players (and not against an artificial intelligence). In time, players become skilled tacticians and will form teams (often called clans) of compatible players and compete online and/or in official tournaments. A major selling point of FPSs is the competitiveness that is triggered amongst the relevant consumer base.

KEY EVOLUTIONARY PSYCHOLOGY CONCEPTS

The basic tenet of EP is that evolution does not only shape physical traits but also mental ones. Furthermore, EP posits that the human mind consists of domain-specific mechanisms that have evolved to solve specific evolutionarily relevant challenges. EP has developed into a field with immense explanatory power. Interested readers can refer to Barkow, Cosmides, and Tooby (1992) and Buss (2005a) for exhaustive overviews of areas in which EP has been applied. It is important to note that EP is most often employed to understand *ultimate* causes of phenomena, in contrast to *proximate* ones. For example, a proximate explanation of the subjective enjoyment of sex would involve detailed analyses of the neuronal mechanisms at work. An ultimate explanation attempts to clarify *why* (in the adaptive sense of the question) sex is pleasurable (to ensure the extension of one's genes).

Two core concepts from EP will be used herein to analyze video games. The first is the Savanna Principle, which posits that if a theory is discordant with the environmental realities in which *Homo sapiens* evolved, it will eventually be rejected (Kanazawa, 2004). However, a theory that is congruent with the ancestral environment in which humans have evolved will be more likely to withstand scientific scrutiny. For example, any theory that posits no innate sex differences is incongruent with the Savanna Principle, as it is clear that the two sexes have faced some adaptive problems that are sex-specific. For the current purposes, one can argue that successful video games are those that adhere most closely to central tenets of the Savanna Principle. Secondly, Saad (2007) highlighted the fact that mental traits (as compared to corporeal ones) do not leave a fossil record. Whereas osteologists and biological anthropologists have documented the phylogenetic history of *Homo sapiens* through their meticulous collection of fossil remains, no such fossil or skeletal record exists for the evolution of the human mind. As such, Saad suggests that cultural products can be understood as fossils of the human mind. One can apply this logic in analyzing the contents of video games.

VIDEO GAMES AS 'SAVANNA SIMULATORS'

Our minds possess features that are designed to optimize survival and reproduction in the African savanna, as it was during the Pleistocene era. Such an environment had predators, prey, mates, family, friends, enemies, and natural hazards. Contem-

porary humans enjoy many of the same pursuits as those tackled long ago by our ancestors. Since modern technological environments change faster than our genes do, the value propositions of modern day products can be thought of as appealing to our 'Savanna' psychology. Thus, successful products often cater to our survival and reproduction (e.g., fast food restaurants cater to our evolved liking for highly caloric food sources). The lack of engaging plotlines in hardcore pornography is driven by the recognition that men have an evolved penchant for 'no-strings-attached' sexual encounters. Accordingly, the themes in pornographic movies replicate contents that are congruent with evolved male psychology. With that in mind, what are the evolved proclivities that video games must indulge in order to satisfy consumer needs?

Video games provide consumers with a virtual experience. It only makes good sense then that the best-selling of these experience packages are ones which most effectively and efficiently tap into the psychological motives that were shaped by natural and sexual selection in the Pleistocene savanna. It follows that we should expect certain game features to necessarily accord with the rules of 'reality' as our minds have evolved to perceive it. For example, adhering to tenets of folk physics is rather important in a video game. Accordingly, this has accelerated technological advances that accurately recreate believable physical laws in virtual worlds. In any recently developed FPS game, if an avatar is shot from behind while standing on a balcony, he will properly fold over that balcony and tumble to his doom with 'satisfying' realism. That said, some game elements could be construed as forms of escapism including the ability to fly (which is hardly congruent with folk physics and/or folk biology). Interestingly, many of these "reality-busting" abilities are reserved for expert players. In other words, escapism from the constraints of our biological reality could be viewed as a reward (e.g., *World of Warcraft* allows only extremely high-level players to ride on flying mounts). In so doing, these violations of reality become badges of honor meant to signal one's proficiency and status to other players.

Knowing one's position within a hierarchy of social status is an enduring problem for social species, and thus, humans have evolved mechanisms for signaling and interpreting status (Cummins, 1996). In the MMORPG, this task is expedited. Every character's level is an honest signal of ability, and the information can be acquired by simply clicking on the appropriate button. No player can lie about their level as occurs in real life where people oftentimes misinform others regarding their achieved status. In most game genres, other evolutionarily important phenomena are artificially (conspicuously) present. Most character options are hyperbolically sex-typed (see the female characters in the recent *Age of Conan*, and the male characters in the *Gears of War* series). This sex-typing invariably exaggerates sexually attractive characteristics. For female characters, faces tend to have highly estrogenized features (large, narrow-set eyes, round faces, small noses, small chins, and full lips), as well as fertile-looking bodies (low waist-to-hip ratios, symmetric bosoms and bottoms, and a youthful gait). On the other hand, faces of male characters tend to be testosteronized (wide-set eyes, larger noses, square jaw, large cleft chins, and thin lips), and bodies tend to exude physical dominance (tall, exceedingly muscular, and far more agile than any real-life, comparably-sized body builder).

Games are designed at the level at which human beings have evolved to perceive reality. Richard Dawkins communicated this point eloquently when he stated: "...there is more to truth than meets the eye; or than meets the all too limited human mind, evolved as it was to cope with medium-sized objects moving at medium speeds through medium distances in Africa." (2003, p. 19). This is why game designers only bother to recreate environments at the medium scale. Games are not colorful recreations of a generic reality, but recreations of an adaptive (and thus, biased)

human reality, with certain psychologically salient (evolutionarily relevant) elements distilled down to their most compelling forms. Elucidating all of the different psychological mechanisms to which video games appeal would be a lengthy endeavor, so the present article focuses on one broad theme: the manner by which video games provide players with a forum to acquire and signal status, at a 'cost' (financially and biologically) that is far lower than any real-life equivalent.

DIGITAL 'PEACOCKING': GAMES AS CONDUITS FOR SIGNALING STATUS

Evolution by natural selection is a process whereby wasteful traits are typically selected out of the gene pool. If so, what might explain the evolution of the peacock's tail, which is large, colorful, and iridescent, implying that it requires a lot of energy and resources to grow and to preen, and it serves to make the peacock an *easier* meal for a Bengal tiger—natural predator of the peacock? Darwin suggested that ornaments could evolve through *sexual* (as opposed to *natural*) selection. If a trait yielded reproductive benefits, it could be selected notwithstanding the fact that its conspicuousness resulted in a shorter lifespan to the organism. However, in the case of the peacock's tail, the disadvantage of such a tail (via natural selection) appears to be so great that sexual selection would seem insufficient to yield its evolution.

In 1975, the Israeli biologist Amotz Zahavi solved the puzzle via "the handicap principle." Zahavi's discovery originated from work with a different avian species (Arabian babbler), but the principle generalizes to peacocks. It posits that peacocks with the largest, brightest, and most ornate tails probably possess the best genes. The reason that this signal is accurate is *precisely because* such tails are also the most encumbering. Therefore, any peacock surviving *despite* his tremendous tail is signaling that he has the necessary traits to survive. Signals are indicators of traits that are otherwise not directly observable including fertility, genetic quality, or dominance. For an excellent book on the evolution of the human mind as a signaling device, the reader is referred to Miller (2000).

Signaling is both ubiquitous and diverse in *Homo sapiens*. We signal with clothes, vocabulary, grades, degrees, mastery of trivia, cars, houses, etc. Within the video gaming context, status-signaling was originally accomplished in arcade games by having one's initials positioned on a scoreboard, which would scroll by while the machine idled. In order to get your initials on the screen, you had to be an elite player, and many rolls of quarters and endless hours were lost in the pursuit. Since the only way to achieve a high score is to play well, one's score serves as a credible signal of playing ability. For a telling example of status signaling (and cheating) among arcade gamers, see the documentary film *The King of Kong* (2007).

The primary mode of signaling in the player versus player mode of a FPS is via one's score. Points are accrued by defeating enemies, and lost by accidentally harming oneself or one's teammates. It is safe to conclude that the player with the highest score was not only more accurate with weapons but also was better at predicting enemy behavior, memorizing the locations of useful items and weapons in the arena, and had excellent hand-eye coordination and three-dimensional spatial rotation skills. More complex scoring schemes include partial credit for assistance in kills and in accomplishing group objectives when appropriate. In such a communal situation a high score can act as a signal of sportsmanship or of loyalty toward a team. Note that coalitional thinking with its requisite loyalty to in-group members is an adaptive mental mechanism (cf. Kurzban, Tooby, & Cosmides, 2001). At times, skilled players engage in self-handicapping by using only low-power weapons. In so doing they augment the credibility (honesty) of their achieved score (signal) by making it (the score) more difficult to acquire. Incidentally, all kills are broadcast in

real time to all of the players. As such, everyone knows who killed you and with which weapon you were killed. In attempting to elucidate the ultimate cause of these dominance-signaling behaviors, we must consider the adaptive payoffs that such competitive signaling might have had, an issue to which we turn to next.

For most animals, intra-sexual competition is usually resolved prior to the occurrence of serious injuries. This is accomplished via signaling. If one male detects that his rival has a reasonably better chance to defeat him, he will slink away, perhaps defeated but alive to fight another day. In social species, a sufficient number of these encounters between many different individuals will stratify them into dominance hierarchies. Sporting seasons (which involve repeated tests of skill and the determination of a 'champion team') are an excellent example of dominance stratification among humans (see De Block & Dewitte, 2009 for a Darwinian-based approach for studying sports). FPSs offer consumers the ability to vicariously slay rivals without risking death, time, money or the energy needed to master a sport. Daly and Wilson (1988) and Buss (2005b) have contributed vastly to our understanding of the evolutionary roots of violence among *Homo sapiens*. They uncovered startling evidence of sex-differentiation in the propensity for violence, and particularly so when reproductive success is at stake. Accordingly, evolutionary theory can explain the overrepresentation of males who play FPSs, as such virtual games trigger men's greater penchant for violence.

In MMORPGs, signaling is taken even further than in FPSs. As previously discussed, players accumulate publicly displayed levels. These serve to objectively differentiate characters in terms of how powerful they are. Additionally, players' accoutrements (such as swords, axes, boots, spaulders, and helmets) serve as signals of their accomplishments. Certain items can only be gained through highly intricate teamwork over an extended period of time with focused effort.

Characters are often seen in garish, intricate, matching sets of armor (like a peacock's tail). These armor sets can take months for a player to acquire, so they act as reliable signals of dedication, skill, and teamwork.

Since humans are a social species with highly altricial (dependent) offspring, perseverance through hard times and dedication to cooperative endeavors are desirable traits to possess. This is particularly true for women when evaluating prospective mates. In order to be selected by women, men will most often brag about their occupational accomplishments, their income, and their potential for career advancement. They will also derogate other men along these same dimensions (Schmitt & Buss, 1996). It is perhaps not surprising then that some of the attractive design features of MMORPGs are those that appeal to this universal desire for social status.

One might argue that dedicated gamers are wasting their time acquiring virtual status when they could be expending the same amount of effort into achieving "real-world" status. In the high-risk, high-reward pursuit of status in real life, the chance that one might exert substantial effort and not experience the expected bump in status is daunting. From an evolutionary perspective, organisms need not be concerned with maximizing the *accuracy* of their decisions, but in *minimizing* the cost of errors (Haselton & Buss, 2000). When we look at MMORPGs through this lens, it seems clear that players are receiving feedback that they are growing in status and prestige at a rate that is more rapid and more predictable than that which they can experience in the real world. Despite the dedication required to acquire status-imbuing items and levels, there is *certitude* to their availability. We propose that this is precisely the computational tradeoff that takes place in the mind of the MMORPG enthusiast: "I can put in the same amount of time and energy elsewhere and risk getting nothing back, or I can put it into my MMORPG and become a master of a virtual domain."

Ultimately, the MMORPG and the FPS are successful because they offer users a psychological experience that was, during the evolution of our species, a rare but honest signal of a fitness-promoting activity. The gaming industry has designed products that harness these evolved motives by tricking our brains to respond in universally predictable manners albeit in a novel online medium.

FUTURE RESEARCH DIRECTIONS

Given the paucity of research at the intersection of evolutionary psychology and gaming studies, the future research opportunities appear endless. In addition to the ideas that we have presented in this paper that have yet to be empirically tested, we provide below a list of possible topics worthy of investigation:

- Do economic rules in MMORPGs conform to evolved mechanisms meant to reduce cheating?
- Do the sizes of 'raid' groups in virtual war games approximate that of hunter-gatherer war bands?
- Does the sexually dimorphic 2D:4D finger ratio, which is shaped by an individual's in utero exposure to sex-specific hormones, correlate with gaming preferences? In other words, do masculinized (feminized) ratios map onto masculinized (feminized) gaming preferences? In some preliminary research conducted by our group, there appears to be some evidence for this effect.
- How does anonymity affect behavior? Since players are represented by their avatars, which fitness-related indulgences might they pursue without fearing any social repercussions?
- Players often belong to publicly announced groups called 'guilds.' How does game

design reflect evolved in-group and out-group dynamics?

- Do games that are more popular with each of the two sexes possess features that map onto sex-specific adaptive problems? For example, *The Sims* is the best-selling game of all time, and women constitute the majority of players. Many of the pursuits in this game (e.g., running a family and developing meaningful and intimate relationships) are stronger drivers of the female psyche.

- Do virtual landscapes correspond to evolutionary-based landscape preferences as postulated by prospect-refuge theory (Orians & Heerwagen, 1992)?

- Are there sex differences in games such as *Second Life* that replicate evolutionary-based sex differences in the offline world? For example, are women more likely to seek meaningful and intimate relationships in *Second Life* whereas men are more likely to desire short-term mating opportunities? In other words, are evolved behaviors in the offline world transferable to the virtual medium (Lucas & Sherry, 2004)?

CONCLUSION

Traditionally, videogames have been studied using non-evolutionary approaches. In the present paper, we discussed how the success of the videogame industry can be analyzed using an evolutionary psychological approach. EP is grounded in a parsimonious and consilient meta-framework, and thorough empirical research. Based on constructs derived from evolutionary science (the savanna principle and the handicap principle), we suggest that gamers' motives include strong desires both to compete in dominance hierarchies and to conspicuously signal social status. The future research opportunities at the nexus of evolutionary theory and gaming studies are highly promising.

REFERENCES

Barkow, J., Cosmides, L., & Tooby, J. (Eds.). (1992). *The adapted mind: Evolutionary psychology and the generation of culture*. New York: Oxford University Press.

Buss, D. M. (Ed.). (2005a). *The handbook of evolutionary psychology*. New York: Wiley.

Buss, D. M. (2005b). *The Murderer Next Door: Why the Mind is Designed to Kill*. New York: Penguin.

Cherney, I. D., & Poss, J. L. (2008). Sex differences in nintendo Wii™ performance as expected from hunter-gatherer selection. *Psychological Reports*, *102*, 745–754. doi:10.2466/PR0.102.3.745-754

Cummins, D. D. (1996). Dominance hierarchies and the evolution of human reasoning. *Minds and Machines*, *6*, 463–480.

Daly, M., & Wilson, M. (1988). *Homicide*. Piscataway, NJ: Aldine Transaction.

Dawkins, R. (2003). *A devil's chaplain*. Boston: Mariner Books.

De Block, A., & Dewitte, S. (2009). Darwinism and the cultural evolution of sports. *Perspectives in Biology and Medicine*, *52*(1), 1–16. doi:10.1353/pbm.0.0063

Ducheneaut, N., Yee, N., Nickell, E., & Moore, R. J. (2006). Building an MMO With Mass Appeal: A Look at Gameplay in World of Warcraft. *Games and Culture*, *1*(4), 281–317. doi:10.1177/1555412006292613

Economist, The. (2008). *Play On*. Retrieved January 15, 2009, from http://www.economist.com/business/displayStory.cfm?source=hptextfeature&story_id=12815694

Entertainment Software Association. (2007). *Industry Facts*. Retrieved January 15, 2009, from: http://www.theesa.com/facts/index.asp

Haselton, M. G., & Buss, D. M. (2000). Error management theory: A new perspective on biases in cross-sex mind reading. *Journal of Personality and Social Psychology, 78*, 81–91. doi:10.1037/0022-3514.78.1.81

Kanazawa, S. (2004). The savanna principle. *Managerial and Decision Economics, 2*, 41–54. doi:10.1002/mde.1130

Kock, N. (2008). E-collaboration and e-commerce in virtual worlds: The potential of Second Life and World of Warcraft. *International Journal of e-Collaboration, 4*(3), 1–13.

Kurzban, R., Tooby, J., & Cosmides, L. (2001). Can race be erased? Coalitional computation and social categorization. *Proceedings of the National Academy of Sciences of the United States of America, 98*(26), 15387–15392. doi:10.1073/pnas.251541498

Lucas, K., & Sherry, J. L. (2004). Sex differences in video game play: A communication-based explanation. *Communication Research, 31*(5), 499–523. doi:10.1177/0093650204267930

Mäyrä, F. (2008). *An introduction to game studies: Games in culture*. London: Sage.

Mazur, A., Susman, E. J., & Edelbrock, S. (1997). Sex difference in testosterone response to a video game contest. *Evolution and Human Behavior, 18*(5), 317–326. doi:10.1016/S1090-5138(97)00013-5

Miller, G. F. (2000). *The mating mind: How sexual choice shaped human nature*. New York: Doubleday.

Motion Picture Association of America. (2007). *Entertainment Industry Market Statistics*. Retrieved January 15, 2009, from: http://www.mpaa.org/USEntertainmentIndustryMarketStats.pdf

Orians, G. H., & Heerwagen, J. H. (1992). Evolved responses to landscapes. In J. H. Barkow, L. Cosmides, & J. Tooby (Eds.), *The adapted mind: Evolutionary psychology and the generation of culture* (pp. 555–580). New York: Oxford University Press.

Pinker, S. (2002). *The blank slate: The modern denial of human nature*. New York: Viking.

Saad, G. (2007). *The evolutionary bases of consumption*. Mahwah, NJ: Lawrence Erlbaum.

Schmitt, D. P., & Buss, D. M. (1996). Strategic self-promotion and competitor derogation: Sex and context effects on the perceived effectiveness of mate attraction tactics. *Journal of Personality and Social Psychology, 70*, 1185–1204. doi:10.1037/0022-3514.70.6.1185

Stenstrom, E., Stenstrom, P., Saad, G., & Cheikhrouhou, S. (2008). Online hunting and gathering: An evolutionary perspective on sex differences in website preferences and navigation. *IEEE Transactions on Professional Communication, 51*(2), 155–168. doi:10.1109/TPC.2008.2000341

Zahavi, A. (1975). Mate selection: A selection for a handicap. *Journal of Theoretical Biology, 53*, 205–221. doi:10.1016/0022-5193(75)90111-3

KEY TERMS AND DEFINITIONS

Evolutionary Psychology: The study of the human mind as consisting of domain-specific mental capacities, as forged by the dual forces of natural and sexual selection.

First Person Shooter (FPS): A video-game genre in which the player views the scenario from the eyes of the protagonist and wherein the challenge is based mostly on shooting a wide range of enemies.

Handicap Principle: A theory that explains the evolution of costly traits (e.g., peacock's tail) via sexual selection.

Massively Multiplayer Online Role-Playing Game (MMORPG): A video-game genre in which players assume the role of a fictional character through which they interact with an immense number of players through the Internet. In MMORPGs, the scenario (world) in which the game takes place continues to evolve even when the player is away from the game.

Savanna Principle: Hypotheses regarding human behavior that do not account for *Homo sapiens'* evolutionary history in African savannas will, in time, be falsified.

Sexual Selection: The evolution of morphological traits or behaviors as a result of intersexual wooing (e.g., plumage coloration in some male birds) or intra-sexual competition (e.g., moose antlers used for combat).

Signaling Theory: The study of how animals including humans typically communicate their value along unobservable traits (e.g., risk-taking proclivity or dominance).

Ultimate Causation: The adaptive reason behind a particular phenomenon of interest. For example, the greater proclivity for men to engage in violent forms of intra-sexual competition is rooted in the evolutionary force of sexual selection.

Virtual World: An online/digital environment such as *Second Life* wherein individuals simultaneously interact, typically through the use of self-chosen avatars.

Chapter 74

An Integrated Model for E–CRM in Internet Shopping:
Evaluating the Relationship between Perceived Value, Satisfaction and Trust

Changsu Kim
Yeongnam University, Korea

Weihong Zhao
Jiangxi Normal University, China

Kyung Hoon Yang
University of Wisconsin-La Crosse, USA

INTRODUCTION

Customer relationship management in electronic commerce (e-CRM) is one of the fastest growing management techniques adopted by online enterprises (Letaifa & Perrien, 2007). Much research has been done on topics such as e-CRM management (Romano & Fjermestad, 2003; Letaifa & Perrien, 2007), e-CRM marketing techniques (Jackson & Wang 1995; Pan & Lee, 2003), the adoption of e-CRM in organizations (Wu & Wu, 2005), and e-CRM applications that facilitate Internet business (Wang & Head 2001; Adebanjo, 2003; Joo & Sohn,

2008). Still, many online enterprises encounter difficulties implementing effective e-CRM because they tend to overlook customer's perspective on e-CRM issues (Woodcock & Starkey, 2001).

The objective of this study is to develop an integrated e-CRM model by investigating the psychological process that occurs when a customer maintains a long-term relationship with an Internet online retailer. By highlighting key factors, a series of dynamic linkages among these factors affecting customer long-term relationship orientation are empirically investigated. Finally, managerial implications and limitations are discussed in the conclusion.

DOI: 10.4018/978-1-61520-611-7.ch074

BACKGROUD

Overview of Web-Based Customer Relationship Management

E-CRM is a newly developed customer-oriented business philosophy that reorients online enterprise operations in order to improve customer satisfaction, loyalty, and retention (Adebanjo, 2003; Pan & Lee, 2003; Letaifa & Perrien, 2007). Many of the e-CRM facets that are analyzed in the literature correspond to the stages discussed in Oliver's cognitive-affective-cognitive-action model for loyalty (1980). In the next three sections, e-CRM is explained in terms of the cognitive, affective, and cognitive stages that lead to the final stage of "action loyalty."

Explanation of Cognitive Belief

Purchasing stages in Internet shopping can be classified into five phases: information research, placing an order, requesting post-purchase services, delivery options and online payment (Nour & Fadlalla, 2000). Through these experiences, customers have a cognitive response related to the perceived benefits and costs of a purchase from a specific retailer (Zeithaml 1988). Cognition can also be described as awareness, knowledge, or beliefs that may or may not have been derived from previous shopping experiences (Fishbein, 1967).

According to the Theory of Reasoned Action (TRA) (Fishbein & Ajzen, 1975; Ajzen & Fishbein, 1980), an individual's performance is determined by his or her behavioral intentions, which are jointly determined by cognitive factors such as attitudes and subjective norms. As an extended model of TRA, the Theory of Planned Behavior (TPB) was derived by adding the perceived behavioral control as a determinant of behavior (Ajzen, 1985). Davis (1989) proposed the Technology Acceptance Model (TAM), based on TRA and TPB, to explain and predict the user's

acceptance of information systems or information communication technology (ICT). In TAM, cognitive beliefs such as the perceived usefulness and perceived ease of use are counted as key factors for technology acceptance. The three theories (TRA, TPB, and TAM) have been widely validated and are widely used to predict or explain the cognitive behavior in social psychology.

Explanation of Affective Experience

The expectation-confirmation theory (ECT) has suggested that satisfaction is the primary motivation for the continued purchase of a product or service (Oliver, 1980). The majority of previous studies consider satisfaction to be an effective response to an expectancy confirmation involving a cognitive process (Pascoe 1983; Melone 1990; Taylor 1994; Oliver, 1997). Anderson and Srinivasan (2003) suggest that customer satisfaction should be evaluated as a positive, indifferent, or negative feeling following the customer's initial experience with the service. This affective evaluation is identical to the notion of attitude in the IS-use literature (Melone 1990), and the attitude-intention association validated in IS-use research provides additional support for the association between satisfaction and choice or continued usage (Davis, 1989; Mathieson 1991; Taylor & Todd 1995).

Explanation of Cognitive Behavior

Geyskens et al. (1996) describe commitment as a customer's long-term orientation toward a business relationship. Morgan and Hunt (1994), Kalafatis and Miller (1997), and Wu and Cavusgil (2006) consider commitment as the crucial factor in determining long-term customer retention. Morgan and Hunt's (1994) empirically validated and widely accepted commitment-trust theory (CTT) claims that long-term relationships are built on the foundation of mutual "trust-commitment," which is similar to the process of creating long-term traditional buyer-seller relationships (Wu & Cavusgil, 2006; Pan et al., 2006). Because of the connection between customer commitment and the buyer-seller relationship, inducing customer commitment is a crucial issue for the development and implementation of an e-CRM strategy.

On the basis of CTT, some researchers have analyzed the importance of trust in online relationships as a cognitive response to cognitive beliefs and affective experiences (Lee & Turban, 2001; McKnight & Chervany, 2002). Lack of trust has been regarded as one of the greatest factors inhibiting online business (Marti & Garcia-Molina, 2006). On the other hand, Business Week (2001) reported that customers are willing to frequently buy from the most trusted sites. Thus, online retailers rely on strong trust to build committed, cognitive customer behavior.

An Integrated Model for E-CRM in Internet Shopping

Based on the theoretical background, this study suggests that e-CRM should satisfy customers'

psychological needs and induce them to commit to long-term relationships.

Previous studies from manifold research areas such as technology and human factors have contributed to successful e-CRM. The majority of studies have focused on factors that affect customers' long-term relationship orientation (Cole et al. 1999; Sukpanich & Chen 1999; Liu & Arnett 2000; Phau & Poon 2000; Vellido et al. 2000). Less research has been centered on an integrated conceptual model to explain why customers commit to a long-term exchange relationship with a specific online retailer.

To address this gap in the research, this study concentrates on customers' cognitive beliefs, affective experiences and cognitive behaviors in order to propose an integrated model for e-CRM that identifies a series of linkages among the psychological variables of perceived value, satisfaction and trust. In addition, three key exogenous variables affecting shopping experiences are considered for the integrated model (see Figure 1).

As shown in Figure 1, trust is regarded as the key factor affecting customer relationship commitment

Figure 1. An integrated model for e-CRM in internet shopping

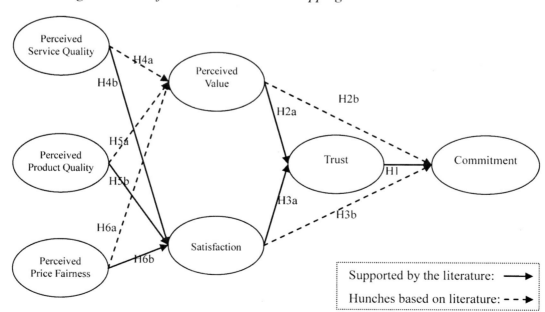

(Morgan and Hunt 1994; McKnight & Chervany, 2002; Flavian et al., 2006). Perceived value (as a cognitive belief) and satisfaction (as an affective experience) directly and indirectly influence trust (as conative behaviors) and commitment. According to related literature, however, this cognitive belief or affective experience alone is insufficient; both are critical antecedents to behavioral intention, which can be considered a cognitive behavior (Cronin et al., 2000; Parasuraman & Grewal, 2000; Sirdeshmukh et al., 2002).

In examinations of exogenous factors influencing customer commitment, most studies have focused on service quality (Sharma & Patterson, 1999; Zeithaml et al., 2000; Venetis & Ghauri, 2004; Joo & Sohn, 2008). Much attention has been given to the intangibility of service quality (Bebko, 2000; Elliot & Fowell, 2000; Crosby & Johnson, 2004; Joo & Sohn, 2008). These studies emphasize that service quality is a necessary but not sufficient factor leading to customer commitment to a long-term relationship. Perceived product quality is also regarded as an important exogenous factor related to customer commitment (Elliot & Fowell, 2000; Crosby & Johnson, 2004). Price, which has been investigated in previous studies (Voss et al., 1998; Crosby & Johnson, 2004; Homburg et al., 2005), is another important factor influencing customer commitment.

CONCLUSION

Based on customers' cognitive, affective and cognitive experiences in Internet shopping, this study, from a customer perspective, proposes an integrated e-CRM model identifying a series of linkages among the main psychological variables affecting customer commitment. Moreover, most of the linkages proposed in the integrated model are found to be significant (see Table 1).

There are managerial implications for these findings. First, the integrated model shows factors that explain why customers maintain long-term exchange relationships. The proposed integrated e-CRM model can provide an understanding about what brings customers back. For example, online customers commit to an e-store when the service quality, product quality, and price fairness are perceived as beneficial and satisfactory. Therefore, as presented in the model, successful e-CRM needs to effectively enhance customer value management, customer satisfaction management, and customer trust management through ICT in order to induce customer commitment.

Second, the integrated model suggests that perceived value and satisfaction, as cognitive and affective antecedents, influence online trust directly; however, they influence customer commitment through trust only indirectly. Trust is the core factor that directly affects relationship commitment. Thus, it is critically important for online retailers to build customer trust in the shopping context. Providing superior value and a satisfying shopping experience are two effective ways to build customer trust.

Third, the results clearly suggest that superior value and customer satisfaction originate from superior perceived service or product quality, and from perceived price fairness. Thus, for online retailers, a successful implementation of e-CRM should integrate business and ICT to work closely together to effectively offer superior customer value and satisfaction via customized services or products, and competitive pricing.

FUTRUE RESEARCH DIRECTIONS

First, the study of an e-CRM integrated model based on customers' perspectives is relatively new to e-commerce researchers. In future, additional research efforts are needed to evaluate the validity of the e-CRM integrated model. Second, the model's constructs need to be measured more completely, with multi-dimensional instruments. Finally, the research findings gathered from university students need greater generalization

Table 1. A summary of the model's hypotheses and results

Hypotheses	Estimate	C.R.	Results	Basis of hypothesis
H1: Trust ⇒ commitment	0.66	5.22***	Strongly Supported	Supported by the literature
H2a: Perceived value ⇒ trust	0.27	3.66**	Supported	Supported by the literature
H2b: Perceived value ⇒ commitment	-0.07	-0.78	Rejected	Hunches based on literature
H3a: Satisfaction ⇒ trust	0.58	8.24***	Strongly Supported	Supported well by the literature
H3b: Satisfaction ⇒ commitment	0.27	2.63*	Weakly Supported	Hunches based on literature
H4a: Perceived service quality ⇒ perceived value	0.25	2.21	Rejected	Hunches based on literature
H4b: Perceived service quality ⇒ satisfaction	0.44	3.32**	Supported	Supported by the literature
H5a: Perceived product quality ⇒ perceived value	0.17	2.72**	Supported	Hunches based on literature
H5b: Perceived product quality ⇒ satisfaction	0.50	6.64***	Strongly Supported	Supported by the literature
H6a: Perceived price fairness ⇒ perceived value	0.55	7.89***	Strongly Supported	Hunches based on literature
H6b: Perceived price fairness ⇒ satisfaction	0.20	2.88*	Weakly Supported	Supported by the literature

in B2C e-commerce. There may be limitations related to using university students in the survey. However, online access and purchasing power among students is high. As stated previously, the focus of the study is on the development of an integrated model. Thus, additional research efforts are needed to evaluate the validity of the proposed model and research findings.

REFERENCES

Adebanjo, D. (2003). Classifying and Selecting e-CRM Applications: an Analysis-Based Proposal. *Management Science*, *41*(6), 570–577.

Ajzen, I., & Fishbein, M. (1980). The Prediction of Behavior From Attitudinal and Normative Variables. *Journal of Experimental Social Psychology*, *6*(4), 466–487. doi:10.1016/0022-1031(70)90057-0

Anderson, R. E., & Srinivasan, S. S. (2003). E-satisfaction and E-loyalty: A Contingency Framework. *Psychology and Marketing*, *20*(February), 123–138. doi:10.1002/mar.10063

Bebko, C. P. (2000). Service Intangibility and Its Impact on Consumer Expectations of Service Quality. *Journal of Services Marketing*, *14*(1), 9–26. doi:10.1108/08876040010309185

Cole, M., O'Keefe, R. M., & Siala, H. (1999). From the User Interface to the Consumer Interface. *Information Systems Frontiers*, *1*(4), 349–361. doi:10.1023/A:1010009923913

Cronin, J., J., Brady, M. K. and Hult, G. T. (2000). Assessing the Effects of Quality, Value, and Customer Satisfaction on Consumer Behavioral Intentions in Service Environments. *Journal of Retailing*, *76*(2), 193–218. doi:10.1016/S0022-4359(00)00028-2

Crosby, L. A., & Johnson, S. L. (2004). Making the Intangible…Tangible. *Marketing Management, 13*(3, May/June), 12-13.

Davis, F. D. (1989). Perceived Usefulness, Perceived Ease of Use, and User Acceptance of Information Technology. *MIS Quarterly, 13*(3), 319–340. doi:10.2307/249008

Elliot, S., & Fowell, S. (2000). Expectations versus Reality: A Snapshot of Customer Experiences with Internet Retailing. *International Journal of Information Management,* (20): 323–336. doi:10.1016/S0268-4012(00)00026-8

Fishbein, M. (1967). *Readings in Attitude Theory and Measurement.* New York: Wiley.

Fishbein, M., & Ajzen, I. (1975). *Beliefs, Attitude, Intention and Behavior: An Introduction to Theory and Research.* Reading, MA: Addison-Wesley.

Flavian, C., Guinaliu, M., & Gurrea, R. (2006). The Role Played by Perceived Usability, Satisfaction and Consumer Trust on Website Loyalty. *Information & Management, 43,* 1–14. doi:10.1016/j.im.2005.01.002

Geyskens, I., Steenkamp, J., Steenkamp, E. M., Scheer, L. K., & Kumar, N. (1996). The Effects of Trust and Interdependence on Relationship Commitment: a Trans-Atlantic Study. *International Journal of Research in Marketing, 13,* 303–317. doi:10.1016/S0167-8116(96)00006-7

Jackson, R., & Wang, P. (1995). *The convergence of database marketing and interactive media networks.* In E. Forrest & R. Mizerski, (Eds.), *Interactive Marketing: The Future Present* (pp. 355-372). Lincolnwood, IL: NTC Publishing Group.

Joo, Y. G., & Sohn, S. Y. (2008). Structural Equation Model for Effective CRM of Digital Content Industry. *Expert Systems with Applications, 34,* 63–71. doi:10.1016/j.eswa.2006.08.016

Kalafatis, S. P., & Miller, H. (1997). A Re-examination of the Commitment-Trust Theory. In H. G. Gemünden, T. Ritter, & A. Walter, (eds.), *Relationships and Networks in International Markets* (pp. 213-27). Oxford, UK: Pergamon.

Lee, M., & Turban, E. (2001). Trust Model for Consumer Internet Shopping. *International Journal of Electronic Commerce, 6*(1), 75–91.

Letaifa, S. B., & Perrien, J. (2007). The Impact of E-CRM on Organizational and Individual Behavior: The Effect of the Remuneration and Reward System. *International Journal of E-Business Research, 3*(2), 13–23.

Liu, C., & Arnett, K. P. (2000). Exploring the Factors Associated with Web site Success in the Context of Electronic Commerce. *Information & Management, 38*(October), 23–34. doi:10.1016/S0378-7206(00)00049-5

Marti, S., & Garcia-Molina, H. (2006). Taxonomy of Trust: Categorizing P2P Reputation Systems. *Computer Networks, 50,* 472–484. doi:10.1016/j.comnet.2005.07.011

Mathieson, K. (1991). Predicting User Intentions: Comparing the Technology Acceptance Model with the Theory of Planned Behavior. *Information Systems Research, 2*(3), 173–191. doi:10.1287/isre.2.3.173

McKnight, D., & Chervany, N. (2002). What Trust Menas in e-Commerce Customer Relationship: an Interdisciplinary Conceptual Typology. *International Journal of Electronic Commerce, 6*(2), 35–59.

Melone, N. P. (1990). A Theoretical Assessment of the User-satisfaction Construct in Information Systems Research. *Management Science, 36*(1), 76–81. doi:10.1287/mnsc.36.1.76

Morgan, R. M., & Hunt, S. E. (1994). The Commitment-Trust Theory of Relationship Marketing. *Journal of Marketing, 58*(July), 20–38. doi:10.2307/1252308

Nour, M. A., & Fadlalla, A. (2000). A Framework for Web Marketing Strategies. *Information Systems Management*, 41–50.

Oliver, R. L. (1980). A Cognitive Model of the Antecedents and Consequences of Satisfaction Decisions. *JMR, Journal of Marketing Research, 17*(November), 460–469. doi:10.2307/3150499

Oliver, R. L. (1997). *Satisfaction: A Behavioral Perspective on the Consumer.* New York: McGraw-Hill.

Pan, G., Pan, S. L., Newman, M., & Flynn, D. (2006). Escalation and De-escalation of Commitment: a Commitment Transformation Analysis of an e-Government Project. *Information Systems Journal, 16*, 3–21. doi:10.1111/j.1365-2575.2006.00209.x

Pan, S. L., & Lee, J. (2003). Using e-CRM for a United View of the Customer. *Communications of the ACM, 46*(4), 95–99. doi:10.1145/641205.641212

Parasuraman, A., & Grewal, D. (2000). The Impact of Technology on the Quality-Value-Loyalty Chain: A Research Agenda. *Journal of the Academy of Marketing Science, 28*(1), 168–174. doi:10.1177/0092070300281015

Pascoe, G. C. (1983). Patient Satisfaction in Primary Health Care: A Literature Review and Analysins. *Evaluation and Program Planning, 6*, 185–197. doi:10.1016/0149-7189(83)90002-2

Phau, I., & Poon, S. M. (2000). Factors Influencing the types of Products and Services Purchased over the Internet. *Internet Research, 10*(2), 102–113. doi:10.1108/10662240010322894

Romano, N. C., & Fjermesad, J. (2003). Electronic Commerce Customer Relationship Management: A Research Agenda. *Information Technology and Management, 4*, 233–258. doi:10.1023/A:1022906513502

Sharma, N., & Patterson, P. G. (1999). The Impact of Communication Effectiveness and Service Quality on Relationship Commitment in Consumer Professional Services. *Journal of Services Marketing, 13*(2), 151–170. doi:10.1108/08876049910266059

Sirdeshmukh, D., Singh, J., & Sabol, B. (2002). Consumer Trust, Value, and Loyalty in Relational Exchanges. *Journal of Marketing, 66*, 15–37. doi:10.1509/jmkg.66.1.15.18449

Sukpanich & Chen. (1999). Antecedents of Desirable Consumer Behaviors in Electronic Commerce. In *Proceedings of 5th Americas Conference on Information Systems*, Omnipress, Milwaukee, WI.

Taylor, S. A. (1994). Distinguishing Service Quality from Patient Satisfaction in Developing Health care Marketing Strategies. *Hospital & Health Services Administration, 39*(2), 221–236.

Taylor, S. A., & Todd, P. A. (1995). Understanding Information Technology Usage: A Test of Competing Models. *Information Systems Research, 6*(2), 144–176. doi:10.1287/isre.6.2.144

Vellido, A., Lisboa, P. J. G., & Meehan, K. (2000). Quantitative Characterization and Prediction of Online Purchasing Behavior: A Latent Variable Approach. *International Journal of Electronic Commerce, 4*(4).

Venetis, K. A., & Ghauri, P. N. (2004). Service Quality and Customer Retention: Building Long-term Relationships. *European Journal of Marketing, 38*(11/12), 1577–1598. doi:10.1108/03090560410560254

Voss, G. B., Parasuraman, A., & Grewal, G. (1998). The Roles of Price, Performance, and Expectations in Determining Satisfaction in Service Exchanges. *Journal of Marketing, 62*(October), 46–61. doi:10.2307/1252286

Wang, F., & Head, M. (2001). Designing Web-based Information Systems for E-commerce. In *Proceedings of the 224 World Congress on the Management of Electronic Commerce*, Hamilton, Canada.

Woodcock, N., & Starkey, M. (2001). I wouldn't Start from Here' Finding a Way in CRM projects. *Journal of Database Marketing, 18*(1), 61–74. doi:10.1057/palgrave.jdm.3240059

Wu, F., & Cavusgil, S. T. (2006). Organizational Learning, Commitment, and Joint Value Creation in Interfirm Relationships. *Journal of Business Research, 59*, 81–89. doi:10.1016/j.jbusres.2005.03.005

Wu, I. L., & Wu, K. W. (2005). A Hybrid Technology Acceptance Approach for Exploring e-CRM Adoption in Organizations. *Behaviour & Information Technology, 24*(4), 303–316. doi:10.1080/0144929042000320027

Zeithaml, V. (1988). Consumer Perceptions of Price, Quality, and Value: A Means-End Model and Synthesis of Evidence. *Journal of Marketing, 52*(3), 2–22. doi:10.2307/1251446

Zeithaml, V., Parasuraman, A., & Malhotra, A. (2000). *e-Service Quality: Definition, Dimensions and Conceptual Model*. Working Paper, Marketing Science Institute, Cambridge, MA.

KEY TERMS AND DEFINITIONS

Commitment: is defined as customer's behavioral intention to continue a business relationship. It refers not only to a customer's future transactional intentions, but also to the purposefulness of these intentions, distinguishing a committed relationship from a mere transactional one. It reflects the affective and cognitive motivations that maintain a long-term relationship and the tendency to resist changing preferences.

e-CRM: is defined as customer relationship management techniques adopted by online enterprises in the electronic commerce. It is based on the belief that developing long-term relationships with customers is the best way to gain customer loyalty.

Perceived Price Fairness: is defined as an evaluation of the overall price fairness when considering both monetary and non-monetary costs of acquiring the product or service.

Perceived Product Quality: is defined as the customer's judgment about the superiority or excellence of a product.

Perceived Service Quality: is defined as customer's judgment about the extent to which a Web site facilitates efficient and effective shopping, purchase, and delivery of products and services.

Perceived Value: is defined as cognition about attributes and benefits directly related to perceived needs or wants in the shopping experience.

Satisfaction: is defined as the extent to which customers perceive their prior expectations of a product or service to be confirmed during actual use.

Trust: is defined as a set of specific relationship intentions dealing primarily with integrity, benevolence, competence, and predictability of a retailer.

Section 8
Mobile Commerce

Chapter 75
Mobile Communications / Mobile Marketing

Suzanne Altobello Nasco
Southern Illinois University Carbondale, USA

INTRODUCTION TO MOBILE COMMUNICATIONS

Mobile communications have become so widespread around the world that they are now ubiquitous, mostly due to the widespread availability, adoption, and affordability of mobile technologies. Today, there are almost 5 billion mobile phone subscriptions worldwide. Wireless services have grown at an annual rate of over 20% per annum over the past 8 years and mobile penetration has more than doubled every 4 years. Mobile penetration is now at over 60% worldwide (based on number of mobile subscriptions, not people); this growth is driven mostly by the Brazil, Russia, India, and China (BRIC) economies (Acharya, 2008). China is the largest wireless market, with over 600 million subscribers for mobile services. Reports by the mobile industry's trade association, Cellular Tele-

communications and Internet Association (CTIA), state that the U.S. mobile phone market accounted for over 276 million wireless subscriptions in June 2009 and over 89% of the U.S. population has at least one wireless phone subscription (CTIA, 2009). As of early 2009, worldwide, there are over 1 billion more mobile phones than there are computers (Mandel, 2008).

Technological advancements in mobile devices have created new opportunities for multimedia communications through audio, visual, and combined audio-visual modalities (Nasco and Bruner 2007). Most mobile communications take the form of audio-only (voice) formats, such as the telephone call itself or the use of voice-messaging. Communications via mobile phones can also take a visual-only form, most commonly in the form of text messages, or short message service (SMS). These messages are limited to text-only, 160-character communications. SMS or "texting" has become

DOI: 10.4018/978-1-61520-611-7.ch075

an essential part of mobile communications. It is a more economical form of communication, as sending text messages is cheaper than making phone calls. CTIA (2009) reports than an average of 135 billion text messages were sent in the U.S. in June 2009 alone, marking an increase of 300% over the 28.8 billion messages reported in June 2007. More than 77% of all mobile subscribers in the U.S. have signed up for or purchased text-messaging services, 53% out of 77% send or receive text messages on a regular basis and by early 2008, the number of text messages sent by U.S. mobile subscribers outpaced the number of phone calls placed at a 1.75: 1 ratio (Covey, 2008). SMS leads all non-voice data and communication services worldwide and texting is even more common in other countries than in the U.S. In a Nielsen Telecom Practice Group survey (cited in Covey, 2008), almost 90% of mobile subscribers in Russia and 85% in Switzerland have used text messaging in the past month (compared to 53% of U.S. mobile users). Finally, with the emergence of third generation (3G and 3.5G) mobile phone technology, it is now possible to also send full video messages via multimedia message service (MMS), however, not all mobile handsets used presently can accept such sophisticated messages. In addition, not all consumers have experience with using sophisticated devices to obtain multimedia messages. Another limitation to widespread use of MMS is the network speed, which affects the consumer's ability to download large files and a company's ability to present large images and videos to be viewed on mobile devices. Finally, screen size can be a limitation to mobile communications. But, as mobile devices and technology improve, more interactive and innovative mobile communication forms will become more common. In conjunction with broadband access, the mobile communications landscape is different from traditional marketing communication mediums because, as Mandel (2008) states, a person's mobile device is always on, always with the user, and knows the location of the user.

MOBILE MARKETING

Such widespread use of mobile communications presents opportunities for marketers to reach consumers through this alternative medium with a variety of marketing messages. Most of these types of communications have come in the form of text-only messaging. SMS has been used to market and promote everything from cars to toothpaste to university athletic events to President Obama's choice of Senator Joe Biden as his vice-presidential choice in the 2008 U.S. Presidential race. These messages can be in the form of a one-way communication, with a branded message being sent via SMS to consumers who have opted-in or signed up to receive such messages. These mobile marketing messages can take the form of text messages that inform the customer about the product/service, text messages that direct readers to a website, coupons sent to the mobile phone that can be exchanged for a rebate or financial discount, or a simple brand awareness message or new product launch message. These one-way mobile messages can also be in the form of audio advertisements that can take the form of a commercialized jingle that the user hears before proceeding to check voicemail messages or an audio recording played while the consumer interacts with a telephone-based service, such as when the mobile user calls directory assistance or a movie ticketing service and must listen to a paid advertisement before getting the information he/she desires.

Mobile marketing can also take the form of a two-way dialogue, encouraging the consumer to communicate back to the company. Examples of this type of mobile marketing include participation in company-sponsored mobile surveys, downloading branded content to mobile devices, and entering mobile contests or text-to-vote campaigns. Many popular television reality shows, such as *American Idol* and *Dancing with the Stars* (along with their international counterparts), encourage viewers to text in their vote for their favorite competitor and count those texts as votes in the tally to determine the winner of the show. In most cases, to initiate these two-way dialogues with a company, a customer is required to send an SMS message to a short code to participate in the contest or to retrieve an offer. Short codes are special telephone numbers that are significantly shorter than full telephone numbers that are used to address SMS and MMS messages from mobile phones. For example, instructions can be to "text YOUR NAME to 313131 to enter our mobile contest." Companies can buy their own short codes, contract with mobile marketing firms and use those firms' short codes, or mobile service providers can provide short codes to users for specific efforts. Each country has their own format for mobile short codes, but they usually range from three to eight digits, with five or six digits being a common length. In the U.S., short codes are administered by the CTIA.

Although most mobile marketing communications takes a "push" approach to advertising, whereby an identifiable corporate sponsor sends a branded message to consumers via the mobile device, the growth of smartphones, such as the Apple iPhone introduced in 2007, has created a new "pull" approach to mobile marketing efforts. Namely, via the use of "apps" (short for "applications"), customers can download branded applications that can help them to find nearby restaurants, check the status of an airline flight, or learn foreign language phrases. Large corporations are finding success by creating mobile applications that extend their brand presence into the (literal) hands of their customers, merging "pull" from customers who seek the application with "push" from the company regarding products or services. An excellent example of the future of branded smartphone applications is the Kraft Food iFood assistant. For a $.99 fee, users download the iFood application to their mobile smartphones and use the information to create shopping lists or find recipes based on ingredients or prep time. While using the application, consumers will see traditional advertisements for Kraft Food products and Kraft will collect valuable, target demographic and behavioral data from consumers who use the application (York, 2009).

Mobile video is still in its infancy stage, but also offers big potential for branded messages in the future. When users opt to watch video using their mobile devices, for instance, by logging onto a network website directly from the mobile browser, they may be presented with interstitial ads that are presented between content pages. For instance, before watching the newest episode of *Lost* by logging on to www.abc.com from their mobile phone, viewers must first watch a 30-second video advertisement prior to seeing the episode. Mandel (2008) highlights made-for-mobile videos on mobile TV, video-on-demand, or sponsorship of network mobisodes (mobile television episodes) as additional avenues for future mobile branding opportunities.

MOBILE ADVERTISING STRATEGY

Currently, the majority of mobile commercial messaging is coming directly from the mobile service providers, alerting mobile users to new services or upgrades available from the provider. However, many consumer goods and services companies are also exploring mobile advertising as a new medium to communicate directly with their consumers, especially as mobile users begin to use more sophisticated devices to access the internet using their mobile devices. Major brands are beginning to invest heavily in mobile marketing: marketing budgets devoted to mobile marketing are predicted to increase 150% by 2013 (Wissinger, 2008) and worldwide mobile advertising (including display ads shown on websites accessed by mobile devices, text messages sent to consumers, and mobile search ads presented to customers who use mobile devices to do an internet search) is expected to grow from $2.7 billion in 2007 to $19 billion by 2012 (eMarketer, 2008).

Regionally, the projected $19 billion is split fairly evenly between U.S., Asia-Pacific, and Western European countries.

The ability to use mobile advertising to target the customer via specific demographic and even behavioral attributes is especially appealing to companies who want a more direct, immediate, and personal relationship with customers. Nielsen (2008) states that "mobile advertising is present on less than two-thirds of website homepage page views across leading mobile websites, and roughly half of that is unpaid house advertising (p. 3). Yet, over 57 percent of mobile internet users recall seeing a mobile advertisement, suggesting that these mobile display ads are a great way to drive brand awareness.

In a survey of mobile phone subscribers across Western Europe (France, Germany, Italy, Spain, and the United Kingdom) and the United States, M:Metrics reports the steady increase in business-to-consumer text-based marketing. The number of mobile phone users who have received an ad via SMS grew at a rate of 27% in the U.S. and 15% in Western Europe from May 2007 to January 2008. In early 2008, 31% of U.S. mobile subscribers recalled seeing or hearing a mobile advertisement (Gfk/NOP Research, 2008). Nielsen (2008) reported that 58 percent of teen mobile data users recalled seeing a mobile advertisement in mid-2008, up from 46 percent in late 2007. Advertising via SMS also leads to high recall, with estimates at over 50 percent recall (Nielsen, 2008). Important for mobile advertisers, M:Metrics found that mobile subscribers who actually have responded to an SMS ad has grown as well; redemption rates for mobile commercial messages were 1.9% in Germany, 2.4% in the U.S., 3.6% in Spain, 3.7% in the UK, 4.6% in France and 8.1% in Italy. Similarly, other research reports that two-thirds of business owners believe that mobile advertising campaigns generate a higher response rate than traditional methods due to the highly targeted nature of a mobile campaign (Cellular-news, 2008).

Of all mobile marketing solutions, SMS marketing is proving to be the most popular with almost a third of businesses surveyed by Cellular-news (2008) reporting using text messages to reach their existing or potential customers. Mobile marketing efforts are a cost-effective and targeted way "for businesses to interact with exactly the people they want, from sending a text reminder to alert a customer to an overdrawn bank account to confirming a delivery via SMS" (Cellular-news, 2008). Real-world discounts or coupons are the most popular types of incentives that companies can send to consumers via SMS or MMS (Berliant, 2008). Juniper Research (2008) predicts that mobile coupon growth and use worldwide will increase fourfold from 50 million to almost 200 million by 2013. Several recent practitioner and academic articles have discussed customers' willingness to accept mobile coupons and the frequency and types of messages they want to receive (c.f., ABIResearch, 2008; Belic, 2008; Coker & Nasco, 2009; Ransford, 2007).

THE FUTURE OF MOBILE MARKETING

The future of mobile marketing (and mobile advertising, in particular) may lie in the ability of consumers to customize their ad experiences. When a customer has to opt-in to receive a branded mobile message, he/she is ultimately customizing the experience. However, companies can go further by allowing customers to limit when and how many mobile messages are received in a given time period. Often, this requires the need for a third-party mobile marketing internet-based solution provider (e.g., Clickatell.com, Air2web. com) that creates an interface for consumers to state their mobile preferences and designs computer-based programs that ensure the company's mobile messages are within the consumer's parameters. In addition, customers want customizability in their viewed ad experiences. For instance, most customers, mobile users included, understand that in order to provide viewers with free content, some websites sell advertising or obtain paid sponsors to subsidize the free content. Internet users have tolerated banner ads, pop-up ads, and website sponsorship advertising for years and there is no reason to expect that mobile users won't also tolerate branded communications on their mobile devices. Companies may do well, nonetheless, to consider that, because the mobile device is so personal, the consumer may also want to personalize the mobile ads that they receive. Hulu.com is an internet site that is allowing customers to choose which type of ads they would like to see. Before presenting free episodes of current and past television series, Hulu viewers can watch traditional 30-second ads aired during the longer video (like traditional TV advertising), but they can also choose to watch a 2 ½ minute branded-entertainment segment instead of normal commercial breaks before watching uninterrupted videos (Steinberg, 2009). It is this author's belief that companies and service providers integrating a mobile advertising strategy with their current marketing plan would do well to follow Hulu's example of allowing customers to choose ad experiences that "complement the viewing experience instead of taking away from it" (Steinberg, 2009, p. 8).

Another emerging trend in mobile marketing is the use of two dimensional (2D) barcodes, also called "Quick Response" (QR) codes. These codes store web addresses and URLs and companies can create unique barcodes that can be printed on outdoor or in-store signage, placed in magazine or newspaper print ads, or placed directly on product packaging. Viewers of the code who are interested in learning more about a product can "scan" the code by taking a picture of it with a web-enabled mobile phone with a camera and barcode reader software. The consumer's mobile internet browser is immediately launched and the user is taken directly to the product's website for more information on the product or to a mobile commerce website that will allow the user to buy the product directly. In the U.S., most mobile users have never seen QR barcodes, but in Japan, an estimated 70% of all mobile users take photos of 2D barcodes and currently, several large consumer goods manufacturers are joining together to promote the use of these codes in North America (Mobile Marketing Watch, 2009). Of course, consumers who are unfamiliar with the use of 2D barcodes will have to be educated on their use and value. Current models of consumer acceptance of technology (e.g., Nasco et al., 2008) can be used to inform organizations of the factors that lead to consumer intentions, use, and adoption of advanced mobile marketing tools, such as QR codes and MMS trends noted above.

Mobile advertising should no longer be considered a unique type of online advertising; rather, companies should start to consider how best to engage the mobile consumer and to enlarge or deepen the relationships between the consumer and the brand. Above all, a company should not integrate mobile marketing into their existing promotional strategy simply because they are able to; rather, companies should focus on delivering true value to their target market via mobile marketing. This effort requires more market research into the specific needs and desires of a company's target mobile audience regarding mobile communications. It is also necessary to examine how mobile marketing is used differently among large and small to medium-sized enterprises (SMEs). Large, global brands will have more marketing dollars to spend on mobile marketing activities, however, many SMEs may also benefit from the personal, two-way dialogue that can be achieved with mobile communications. These emerging mobile trends for large and small companies can complement, and in some cases may begin to supplant, other traditional modes of advertising in the 21st century.

REFERENCES

ABIresearch.com. (2008). *Putting coupons in mobile users' hands.* Retrieved March 31, 2009, from http://www.emarketer.com/Article.aspx?id=1006522

Acharya, S. (2008). *Worldwide mobile cellular subscribers to reach 4 billion mark late 2008.* Retrieved December 15, 2008, from http://www.itu.int/newsroom/press_releases/2008/29.html

Belic, D. (2008). *Nielsen Mobile: 58 million U.S. mobile subscribers have seen advertising on their phones.* Retrieved March 30, 2009, from http://www.intomobile.com/2008/03/08/nielsen-mobile-58-million-us-mobile-subscribers-have-seen-advertising-on-their-phones.html

Berliant, S. (2008). *Are US consumers ready for mobile marketing?* Retrieved January 6, 2009, from http://insight.eyetraffic.com/public/item/212657

Cellular-news. (2008). *Brands set to treble spend on mobile marketing by 2013.* Retrieved January 6, 2009, from http://www.cellular-news.com/story/34048.php

Coker, K., & Nasco, S. A. (2009). *Consumer likelihood of using mobile devices to obtain commercial messages.* Manuscript submitted for publication.

Covey, N. (2008). *Flying Fingers: Text-messaging overtakes monthly phone calls.* Retrieved November 3, 2008 from http://en-us.nielsen.com/main/insights/consumer_insight/issue_12/flying_fingers

CTIA. (2009). *Wireless quick facts.* Retrieved January 25, 2010, from http://www.ctia.org/advocacy/research/index.cfm/AID/10323

eMarketer (2008). *Mobile advertising spending worldwide by format 2007-2012.* Retrieved January 7, 2009, from http://totalaccess.emarketer.com/Chart.aspx?N=0&Nr=P_ID:73703&xsrc=chart_articlex

Gfk/NOP Research. (2008). *Three in ten US mobile users recall seeing mobile ads.* Retrieved January 7, 2009, from http://www.marketingcharts.com/interactive/three-in-ten-us-mobile-users-recall-seeing-mobile-ads-3016/limbo-mobile-ad-recall-by-service-typejpg/

Juniper Research. (2008). *Mobile advertising – Because I'm worth it.* Retrieved August 18, 2008, from http://www.juniperresearch.com/shop/view-whitepaper.php?whitepaper=62

Mandel, M. (2008). Mobile marketing: From simple to complex. *Marketing Science Institute,* 08-1204pmm.

Mobile Marketing Association. (2008). *Mobile marketing industry glossary.* Retrieved December 15, 2008, from http://www.mmaglobal.com/glossary.pdf

Mobile Marketing Watch. (2009). *Five companies joining together for 2D barcode push.* Retrieved July 15, 2009, from http://www.mobilemarketingwatch.com/category/mobile-partners/

Nasco, S. A., & Bruner, G. C. (2007). Perceptions and recall of advertising content presented on mobile handheld devices. *Journal of Interactive Advertising, 7*(2), 1–22.

Nasco, S. A., Kulviwat, S., Bruner, G. C., & Kumar, A. (2008). The CAT model: Extensions and moderators of dominance in technology acceptance. *Psychology and Marketing, 25*(10), 987–1005. doi:10.1002/mar.20249

Nielsen. (2008). *Realizing potential: Overcoming barriers to the U.S. mobile advertising market.*

Ransford, M. (2007). *Ball State study finds collegians more receptive to getting advertising via cell phones.* Retrieved November 8, 2008, from http://www.bsu.edu/news/article/0,1370,7273-850-53637,00.html

Reardon, M. (2008). *U.S. text usage hits record despite price increases.* Retrieved February 28, 2009, from http://reviews.cnet.com/8301-12261_7-10038634-51.html?tag=mncol;txt

Shankar, V., & Hollinger, M. (2007). Online and mobile advertising: Current scenario, emerging trends, and future directions. *Marketing Science Institute Report*, 07-206.

Steinberg, B. (2009). Top-notch content makes site a success. *Advertising Age, 80*(11), 8.

Wissinger, C. (2008). *Mobile advertising: 18-24 year olds lead the parade.* Retrieved November 7, 2008, from http://www.marketwire.com/press-release/Bigresearch-866741.html

York, E. B. (2009). Kraft hits on killer app for iPhone marketing. *Advertising Age.* Retrieved March 31, 2009, from http://adage.com/digital/article?article_id=133869.

KEY TERMS AND DEFINITIONS

MMS: Multimedia messaging; mobile messages that can incorporate text, audio, and streaming video.

Mobile Advertising: branded messages paid for by an identified sponsor sent or displayed via mobile devices.

Mobile Commerce: trade that occurs via the use of a web-enabled mobile phone; products/services can be bought or sold using the mobile device as an interface.

Mobile Coupons: SMS messages that are sent directly to consumers' mobile devices; consumers show the mobile message at the point of sale for redemption or the coupon contains a unique code that can be entered at the point of purchase for redemption.

QR Code: Quick response code; a two dimensional barcode that, when scanned with a mobile phone, take the mobile user to a specific website or URL embedded in the code.

Short Code (or Common Short Code (CSC) in the U.S.): special telephone numbers, significantly shorter than full telephone numbers, which can also be used to address SMS and MMS messages from mobile phones.

SMS: short messaging service; mobile messages that are limited to 160 characters (including spaces).

Chapter 76
C2C Mobile Commerce:
Acceptance Factors

Lori N. K. Leonard
University of Tulsa, USA

ABSTRACT

C2C e-commerce is being changed by the acceptance of mobile commerce devices. However, the extent of the use of mobile devices for C2C e-commerce is affected by many factors. A model of an individual's intention to make use of mobile devices for C2C e-commerce is presented. That model includes usefulness, ease of use, convenience, trust, and security. Propositions are developed for future research endeavors.

INTRODUCTION

Consumer-to-consumer (C2C) e-commerce has not been studied as much as other areas of e-commerce (Jones & Leonard, 2007), but C2C e-commerce is one of the fastest growing segments in e-commerce, heavily due to the increase in popularity of online auctions. However, C2C e-commerce includes more than the use of online auctions. C2C e-commerce can be seen in places such as web forums, chat rooms, and third party consumer listings. With this increase in C2C e-commerce popularity, there is still very little known about the acceptance of mobile devices for C2C e-commerce transactions.

DOI: 10.4018/978-1-61520-611-7.ch076

Mobile devices provide users the ability to conduct transactions anywhere, at anytime.

Mobile devices offer a unique opportunity to conduct C2C e-commerce. Many individuals are conducting C2C e-commerce as a means to acquire products at a more reasonable price, to acquire products that are considered scarce, or to sell items as another source of income, to name a few. However, these same individuals have jobs and other activities that may otherwise limit one's ability to utilize C2C e-commerce frequently, especially when online auctions end during the work day hours. Therefore, mobile devices offer the ability to monitor online items at any time. Mobile devices offer the opportunity for users to conduct transactions at their convenience, raising the question, "What factors impact the acceptance of mobile devices for conducting C2C e-commerce?"

This chapter addresses that question by exploring the mobile commerce research regarding intention to use. From that research, a model is proposed, utilizing previously studied factors, for an individual's intention to utilize mobile devices for C2C e-commerce. Propositions are provided for future research as well.

BACKGROUND

Mobile devices open a range of opportunities for conducting C2C e-commerce. However, determining the acceptance of mobile devices for C2C e-commerce transactions is yet to be determined. Many researchers have examined mobile commerce in terms of adoption, intent to use, and success. In this section, a few of those studies will be explored.

The intention to use and the acceptance of mobile devices has been examined. Wang, Lin, and Luarn (2006) explored the behavioral intention of users with regards to mobile commerce. Using the technology acceptance model (TAM), the theory of planned behavior (TPB), and the mobile banking acceptance model, they collected data from 258 users in Taiwan and found self efficacy, perceived financial resources, perceived usefulness, perceived ease of use, and perceived credibility to impact a users intent to use mobile services. Wu and Wang (2005) studied users' acceptance of mobile commerce in terms of behavioral intent. Surveying users who were invoked in online banking, shopping, investing and or online services, they found perceived risk, cost, compatibility, and perceived usefulness to impact a user's intent. Bhatti (2007) also studied mobile commerce's acceptance by looking at behavioral intent. Collecting data from a survey of mobile commerce users, he found perceived behavioral control, perceived ease of use, and subjective norms to impact intent.

Xu and Gutierrez (2006) examined critical success factors in mobile commerce. Utilizing a Delphi panel of experts in mobile commerce and wireless communications, they found four factors to be important in mobile commerce success – convenience, ease of use, trust, and ubiquity. Jih (2007) also found convenience to be vital in shopping intention via mobile commerce.

Finally, Fang, Chan, Brzezinski, and Xu (2005-6) examined acceptance of mobile commerce with regards to intended use. They took a different approach than the previous studies by looking at task type – general, gaming, and transactional. Therefore, they developed and tested a model for each. For general tasks, perceived usefulness and perceived ease of use influenced the user's intention to use mobile commerce. For gaming tasks, perceived playfulness influenced the user's intention to use mobile commerce. For transactional tasks, perceived usefulness and perceived security influenced the user's intention to use mobile commerce.

From these studies it is evident that many factors can play a role in influencing mobile commerce's use. The next section will take the results of the previously mentioned studies and apply them to C2C e-commerce, therefore, resulting in a model to determine mobile device use in C2C e-commerce.

MODEL FORMULATION

Given the above studies' findings, a model for the intent to use mobile devices for C2C e-commerce is presented. The model incorporates variables from the mobile commerce studies as they apply to C2C e-commerce. The model proposes that perceived ease of use, usefulness, convenience, trust, and security impact the intention for users to utilize mobile devices for C2C e-commerce. Figure 1 presents the proposed model.

Figure 1. Determinants of an individual's intent to use mobile devices for C2C e-commerce

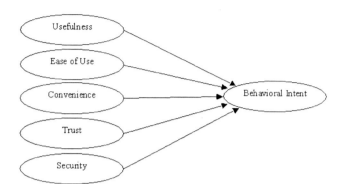

Usefulness and Ease of Use

Perceived usefulness is an individual's expectation that the information technology (i.e. mobile device) will result in improved performance (Davis, Bagozzi, & Warshaw, 1989, 1992). Usefulness has been found to determine system usage (Adams, Nelson, & Todd, 1992; Davis, Bagozzi, & Warshaw, 1989, 1992), to contribute to an individual's intent to reuse a Web site (Lin, Wu, & Tsai, 2005), to be important in forming consumer attitudes and satisfaction with an electronic commerce channel (Davis, 1993; Devaraj, Fan, & Kohli, 2002), and to predict frequency of Web usage (Page-Thomas, 2006).

Perceived ease of use is the degree to which an individual expects the information system (i.e. mobile device) to be free of effort (Davis, Bagozzi, & Warshaw, 1989). Ease of use has been found to determine Web usage (Atkinson & Kydd, 1997; Davis, Bagozzi, & Warshaw, 1989; Davis, 1993; Pearson & Pearson, 2008), predict Web use for entertainment purposes (Atkinson & Kydd, 1997), and predict frequency of Web usage (Page-Thomas, 2006).

Devaraj, Fan, & Kohli (2002) studied online shoppers by surveying undergraduate and graduate students. They found both perceived usefulness and perceived ease of use to be significantly related to satisfaction with the e-commerce channel.

Gefen, Karahanna, & Straub (2003) also found perceived usefulness of a given website to play an important role in determining a repeat customer's intention to purchase from that website. Pavlou (2003) conducted a study of perceived usefulness and perceived ease of use and an individual's intention to transact on a web site. The study found perceived usefulness and perceived ease of use to be significant predictors of intention to transact. Additionally, Vijayasarathy (2004) used perceived ease of use and perceived usefulness, among other constructs, to examine consumer intention to use online shopping. Using a mail survey, both factors were found to predict attitude towards online shopping. Grandon & Pearson (2004) studied small and medium-sized organizations in the U.S. to establish factors affecting the e-commerce adoption. They found perceived ease of use and perceived usefulness to be determinants of e-commerce adoption.

Therefore, we propose:

Proposition 1: The intention to utilize mobile devices for C2C e-commerce is influenced by usefulness.

Proposition 2: The intention to utilize mobile devices for C2C e-commerce is influenced by ease of use.

Convenience

It is obvious that e-commerce creates convenience. However, the extent of that convenience is perceived by the user. With a mobile device, C2C e-commerce transactions should become more convenient. Convenience is defined as the extent the individual believes the mobile device will improve the simplicity of C2C e-commerce. A significant relationship has been found between perceived convenience and shopping intention and a positive effect of perceived convenience on shopping intention (Jih, 2007). Convenience has also been identified as one of the most important factors in mobile commerce success (Xu & Gutierrez, 2006).

In a study of home Internet banking and mobile banking, Laukkanen (2007) studied efficiency, convenience, and safety. He found all three factors to be important in determining differences in use (Gefen, Karahanna, & Straub, 2003). Trust can influence the overall transaction outcome (Mayer et al., 1995) and a consumer's value perceptions between home Internet banking and mobile banking. More specifically, mobile banking was found to eliminate needless trips home to utilize the online banking service. Laukkanen also found a relationship between efficiency and convenience, with a time saving being equated with efficiency.

Therefore, we propose:

Proposition 3: The intention to utilize mobile devices for C2C e-commerce is influenced by convenience.

Trust

Trust is traditionally defined as the expectation that others, one chooses to trust, will not behave opportunistically by taking advantage of the situation (Gefen, Karahanna, & Straub, 2003); they will behave in a dependable, ethical, and socially appropriate manner. Trust helps online consumers in overcoming perceptions of uncertainty and risk

with online transactions (McKnight, Choudhury, & Kacmar, 2002). However, in mobile commerce, it is not only the trust in the other individual but it is the trust also in the medium of the transaction (i.e., the mobile device) (Siau & Shen, 2003). Gaining trust in mobile commerce is precarious given the unique nature of mobile devices. Mobile devices can be limited in their screen size and resolution displays, as well as computational power and memory (Siau & Shen, 2003). Wireless networks can also be limited in bandwidth, and connection speed and reliability (Siau & Shen, 2003). Therefore, trust must be established for the other consumer (given the C2C relationship) and for the mobile device.

Trust has been found to impact perceived usefulness, and trust and perceived usefulness to impact intent to purchase online (Gefen, Karahanna, & Straub, 2003). Siau and Shen (2003) also indicate that mobile devices can be more difficult to trust given that data transmission is more vulnerable to eavesdropping.

Therefore, we propose:

Proposition 4: The intention to utilize mobile devices for C2C e-commerce is influenced by trust.

Security

With any new technology, security is always a concern. The same applies to mobile commerce. Perceived security is defined as the extent an individual believes mobile commerce will be free of risk to conduct C2C e-commerce. Fang, Chan, Brzezinski, and Xu (2005-06) studied the acceptance of mobile commerce. They found perceived security to impact intended use for transactional tasks, but not for general or gaming tasks. Given that C2C e-commerce is a transactional task, perceived security will play a part. Security is also important given that mobile devices can be perceived to be less secure than traditional Internet connection devices (Siau & Shen, 2003).

Therefore, we propose:

Proposition 5: The intention to utilize mobile devices for C2C e-commerce is influenced by security.

FUTURE RESEARCH DIRECTIONS

Given the proposed model of the determinants of an individual's intent to use mobile devices in C2C e-commerce, future research should be aimed at testing the propositions set forth. The use of mobile devices is extensive with the rise in wireless technology. However, there has not been made a distinction between business-to-business (B2B) e-commerce transactions, business-to-consumer (B2C) e-commerce transactions, C2C e-commerce transactions, and so forth. There are clearly differences in these types of transactions. The nature of C2C e-commerce makes it a unique entity. C2C e-commerce has a distinctive user demographic, with younger individuals utilizing it more extensively than other demographic groups; the products being exchanged can be more scarce than in the other venues; and the communication mechanisms utilized go beyond web sites and email (such as discussion rooms). Also, mobile devices are often needed in C2C e-commerce transactions when the individuals decide a face-to-face meeting is needed. Therefore, testing the proposed model will determine the factors that affect the intention to use mobile devices for such transactions. This is a first step in examining the acceptance of mobile devices in C2C e-commerce transactions.

CONCLUSION

Mobile devices are changing every day. For example, cell phone capabilities are virtually limitless. Therefore, by understanding acceptance factors for using mobile devices in C2C e-commerce, cell phones can be designed with those factors in mind. This is clearly different than B2C e-commerce transactions and B2B e-commerce transactions. These types of transactions involve businesses, and in particular for B2B, mobile devices would be provided by the employer. In many cases, the employee would be expected to use the mobile device to conduct the B2B e-commerce transaction. There is still an acceptance factor but there is also the requirement to use the device which trumps the acceptance. For B2C, there is more freedom to make a choice to use the mobile device; however, there is also the choice to visit the physical store. This is definitely different from C2C.

Mobile devices and C2C e-commerce should go hand-in-hand. However, current research has not examined their combination. This chapter provides a model of one's intention to utilize mobile devices in C2C e-commerce. By determining the factors of importance when using a mobile device for C2C e-commerce, researchers will be able to ultimately determine how to make mobile devices more applicable for such types of transactions.

REFERENCES

Adams, D. A., Nelson, R. R., & Todd, P. A. (1992). Perceived usefulness, ease of use, and usage of information technology: a replication. *MIS Quarterly*, 227–247. doi:10.2307/249577

Atkinson, M., & Kydd, C. (1997). Individual characteristics associated with World Wide Web use: an empirical study of playfulness and motivation. *The Data Base for Advances in Information Systems*, *28*(2), 53–62.

Bhatti, T. (2007). Exploring factors influencing the adoption of mobile commerce. *Journal of Internet Banking & Commerce*, *12*(3), 1–13.

Davis, F. D. (1993). User acceptance of information technology: system characteristics, user perceptions and behavioral impacts. *International Journal of Man-Machine Studies, 38,* 475–487. doi:10.1006/imms.1993.1022

Davis, F. D., Bagozzi, R. P., & Warshaw, P. R. (1989). User acceptance of computer technology: a comparison of two theoretical models. *Management Science, 35*(8), 982–1003. doi:10.1287/mnsc.35.8.982

Davis, F. D., Bagozzi, R. P., & Warshaw, P. R. (1992). Extrinsic and intrinsic motivation to use computers in the workplace. *Journal of Applied Social Psychology, 22*(14), 1111–1132. doi:10.1111/j.1559-1816.1992.tb00945.x

Devaraj, S., Fan, M., & Kohli, R. (2002). Antecedents of B2C channel satisfaction and preference: validating e-commerce metrics. *Information Systems Research, 12*(3), 316–333. doi:10.1287/isre.13.3.316.77

Fang, X., Chan, S., Brzezinski, J., & Xu, S. (2005-6). Moderating effects of task type on wireless technology acceptance. *Journal of Management Information Systems, 22*(3), 123–157. doi:10.2753/MIS0742-1222220305

Gefen, D., Karahanna, E., & Straub, D. W. (2003). Trust and TAM in online shopping: An integrated model. *MIS Quarterly, 27,* 51–90.

Grandon, E. E., & Pearson, J. M. (2004). Electronic commerce adoption: an empirical study of small and medium US businesses. *Information & Management, 42*(1), 197–216.

Jih, W. (2007). Effects of consumer-perceived convenience on shopping intention in mobile commerce: an empirical study. *International Journal of E-Business Research, 3*(4), 33–46.

Jones, K., & Leonard, L. N. K. (2007). Consumer-to-consumer electronic commerce: a distinct research stream. *Journal of Electronic Commerce in Organizations, 5*(4), 39–54.

Laukkanen, T. (2007). Internet vs mobile banking: comparing customer value perceptions. *Business Process Management Journal, 13*(6), 788–797. doi:10.1108/14637150710834550

Lin, C. S., Wu, S., & Tsai, R. J. (2005). Integrating perceived playfulness into expectation-confirmation model for web portal context. *Information & Management, 42*(5), 683–693. doi:10.1016/j.im.2004.04.003

Mayer, R. C., Davis, J. H., & Schoorman, F. D. (1995). An integrative model of organizational trust. *Academy of Management Review, 20,* 709–734. doi:10.2307/258792

McKnight, D. H., Choudhury, V., & Kacmar, C. (2002). Developing and validating trust measures for e-commerce: an integrative typology. *Information Systems Research, 13,* 334–359. doi:10.1287/isre.13.3.334.81

Page-Thomas, K. (2006). Measuring task-specific perceptions of the world wide web. *Behaviour & Information Technology, 25,* 469–477. doi:10.1080/01449290500347962

Pavlou, P. A. (2003). Consumer acceptance of electronic commerce: integrating trust and risk with the technology acceptance model. *International Journal of Electronic Commerce, 7*(3), 101–134.

Pearson, J. M., & Pearson, A. M. (2008). An exploratory study into determining the relative importance of key criteria in web usability: a multi-criteria approach. *Journal of Computer Information Systems, 48*(4), 115–127.

Siau, K., & Shen, Z. (2003). Building customer trust in mobile commerce. *Communications of the ACM, 46*(4), 91–94. doi:10.1145/641205.641211

Vijayasarathy, L. R. (2004). Predicting consumer intentions to use on-line shopping: the case for an augmented technology acceptance model. *Information & Management, 41*(6), 747–762. doi:10.1016/j.im.2003.08.011

Wang, Y., Lin, H., & Luarn, P. (2006). Predicting consumer intention to use mobile service. *Information Systems Journal, 16*, 157–179. doi:10.1111/j.1365-2575.2006.00213.x

Wu, J., & Wang, S. (2005). What drives mobile commerce? An empirical evaluation of the revised technology acceptance model. *Information & Management, 42*, 719–729. doi:10.1016/j.im.2004.07.001

Xu, G., & Gutierrez, J. A. (2006). An exploratory study of killer applications and critical success factors in m-commerce. *Journal of Electronic Commerce in Organizations, 4*(3), 63–79.

ADDITIONAL READING

Ba, S., & Pavlou, P. A. (2002). Evidence of the effect of trust building technology in electronic markets: price premiums and buyer behavior. *MIS Quarterly, 26*, 243–268. doi:10.2307/4132332

Backhouse, J., Hsu, C., Tseng, J. C., & Baptista, J. (2005). A question of trust. *Communications of the ACM, 48*, 87–91. doi:10.1145/1081992.1081994

Barnes, S. J. (2002). The mobile commerce value chain: analysis and future developments. *International Journal of Information Management, 22*, 91–108. doi:10.1016/S0268-4012(01)00047-0

Bruner, G. C., & Kumar, A. (2005). Explaining consumer acceptance of handheld Internet devices. *Journal of Business Research, 58*, 553–558. doi:10.1016/j.jbusres.2003.08.002

Cheung, C. M. K., & Lee, M. K. O. (2006). Understanding consumer trust in internet shopping: a multidisciplinary approach. *Journal of the American Society for Information Science and Technology, 57*, 479–492. doi:10.1002/asi.20312

Choi, J., Seol, H., Lee, S., Cho, H., & Park, Y. (2008). Customer satisfaction factors of mobile commerce in Korea. *Internet Research, 18*(3), 313–335. doi:10.1108/10662240810883335

Dahlberg, T., Mallat, N., Ondrus, J., & Zmijewska, A. (2008). Past, present and future of mobile payments research: a literature review. *Electronic Commerce Research and Applications, 7*, 165–181. doi:10.1016/j.elerap.2007.02.001

DeLone, W. H., & McLean, E. R. (1992). Information systems success: the quest for the dependent variable. *Information Systems Research, 3*(1), 60–95. doi:10.1287/isre.3.1.60

DeLone, W. H., & McLean, E. R. (2003). The DeLone and McLean model of information systems success: a ten-year update. *Journal of Management Information Systems, 19*(4), 9–30.

DeLone, W. H., & McLean, E. R. (2004). Measuring e-commerce success: applying the DeLone & McLean information systems success model. *International Journal of Electronic Commerce, 9*(1), 31–47.

Everard, D. F., & Galletta, A. (2006). How presentation flaws affect perceived site quality, trust, and intention to purchase from an online store. *Journal of Management Information Systems, 22*, 55–95. doi:10.2753/MIS0742-1222220303

Gebauer, J., Tang, Y., & Baimai, C. (2008). User requirements of mobile technology: results from a content analysis of user reviews. *Information System E-Business Management, 6*, 361–384. doi:10.1007/s10257-007-0074-9

Gruen, T. W., Osmonbekov, T., & Czaplewski, A. J. (2006). eWOM: the impact of customer-to-customer online know-how exchange on customer value and loyalty. *Journal of Business Research, 59,* 449–456. doi:10.1016/j.jbusres.2005.10.004

Jarvenpaa, S. L., Lang, K. R., Takeda, Y., & Tuunainen, V. K. (2003). Mobile commerce at crossroads. *Communications of the ACM, 46*(12), 41–44. doi:10.1145/953460.953485

Jones, K., & Leonard, L. N. K. (2008). Trust in consumer-to-consumer electronic commerce. *Information & Management,* (45): 88–95. doi:10.1016/j.im.2007.12.002

Kim, H., Chan, H. C., & Gupta, S. (2007). Value-based adoption of mobile Internet: an empirical investigation. *Decision Support Systems, 43,* 111–126. doi:10.1016/j.dss.2005.05.009

Lax, G., & Sarne, G. M. L. (2008). CellTrust: a reputation model for C2C commerce. *Electronic Commerce Research, 8,* 193–216. doi:10.1007/s10660-008-9019-8

Leonard, L. N. K., & Jones, K. (2009). (forthcoming). The role of self-efficacy, trust, and experience and the mediating effects of satisfaction in the choice of C2C e-commerce among young adults. *Journal of Electronic Commerce in Organizations.*

Leonard, L. N. K., & Riemenschneider, C. K. (2008). What factors influence the individual impact of the web? An initial model. *Electronic Markets, 18*(1), 75–90. doi:10.1080/10196780701797698

McCloskey, D. W. (2006). The importance of ease of use, usefulness, and trust in online consumers: an examination of the technology acceptance model with older consumers. *Journal of Organizational and End User Computing, 18,* 47–65.

Molla, A., & Licker, P. S. (2001). E-commerce systems success: An attempt to extend and re-specify the DeLone and McLean model of IS success. *Journal of Electronic Commerce Research, 2,* 1–11.

Ramus, K., & Nielsen, N. A. (2005). Online grocery retailing: what do consumers think? *Internet Research, 15*(3), 335–352. doi:10.1108/10662240510602726

Riemenschneider, C. K., Jones, K., & Leonard, L. N. K. (2009). (forthcoming). Web trust – a moderator of the web's perceived individual impact. *Journal of Computer Information Systems.*

Salam, A., Rao, H., & Pegels, C. (2003). Consumer-perceived risk in e-commerce transactions. *Communications of the ACM, 46,* 325–331. doi:10.1145/953460.953517

Salam, A. F., Iyer, L., Palvia, P., & Singh, R. (2005). Trust in e-commerce. *Communications of the ACM, 48,* 73–77. doi:10.1145/1042091.1042093

Strader, T. J., & Ramaswami, S. N. (2002). The value of seller trustworthiness in C2C online markets. *Communications of the ACM, 45*(12), 45–49. doi:10.1145/585597.585600

Tan, Y., & Thoen, W. (2001). Toward a generic model of trust for electronic commerce . *International Journal of Electronic Commerce, 5,* 61–74.

Tan, Y., & Thoen, W. (2002). Formal aspects of a generic model of trust for electronic commerce . *Decision Support Systems, 33,* 233–246. doi:10.1016/S0167-9236(02)00014-3

Wareham, J., Zheng, J. G., & Straub, D. (2005). Critical themes in electronic commerce research: a meta-analysis. *Journal of Information Technology, 20,* 1–19. doi:10.1057/palgrave.jit.2000034

KEY TERMS AND DEFINITIONS

Consumer-to-Consumer (C2C): e-commerce includes the use of online auctions, web forums, chat rooms, and third party consumer listings to conduct commerce transactions.

Mobile Commerce: provides users the ability to conduct transactions anywhere, at anytime using a wireless technology device.

Perceived Convenience: is the extent the individual believes a mobile device will improve the simplicity of C2C e-commerce.

Perceived Ease of Use: is the degree to which an individual expects the information system (i.e. mobile device) to be free of effort.

Perceived Security: is the extent an individual believes a mobile device will be free of risk to conduct C2C e-commerce.

Perceived Trust: is defined as the confidence the user has in the mobile device being used to conduct the online transaction.

Perceived Usefulness: is an individual's expectation that the information technology (i.e. mobile device) will result in improved performance.

Chapter 77
Exploring the Mobile Consumer

Kaan Varnali
Bogazici University, Turkey

Cengiz Yilmaz
Bogazici University, Turkey

ABSTRACT

The article provides insights into consumers' experience with mobile marketing by presenting a review of the mobile consumer behavior literature in an organized framework. An important contribution of this study is that it compiles a list of prominent predictor variables that come into play in the process of consumer adoption and acceptance of mobile marketing. The resulting list is purported to be beneficial to both academics by providing a state-of-the-art and practitioners by providing a powerful item battery to be used in setting up effective mobile marketing campaigns.

INTRODUCTION

The use of personal mobile and wireless devices as a medium for communicating with and delivering value to consumers, a new marketing venue often labeled "mobile marketing," has recently become a rapidly growing practice. Many industry analysts agree that the notion of one-to-one marketing is now a more realistic vision due to the rise of mobile marketing (hereafter, m-marketing). Accordingly, several global brands including Coca-Cola, Disney, BMW, McDonald's, Adidas, Nestle, Visa, and MTV are currently implementing m-marketing programs

DOI: 10.4018/978-1-61520-611-7.ch077

in order to benefit from its unique features. M-advertising revenue has reached to US$4,957 million in 2008, and is projected to exceed US$16 billion within the next 3-4 years (eMarketer, 2007).

The present chapter focuses on consumer responses to m-marketing applications. Extant research on the consumer side of m-marketing appears to be highly scattered and fragmented. One of the purposes of the chapter is to present this literature in an organized framework. The consumer behavior discipline has a well established body of knowledge which includes a pool of cognitive and affective constructs that influence behavioral outcomes. Prior research about mobile consumers has focused primarily on these frameworks in exploring the behavioral and attitudinal responses to m-marketing practices. In reviewing this literature, we first focus on consumer perceptions of the value created through m-marketing. We then focus on the processes through which consumers adopt and accept m-marketing practices. Finally, we discuss post-usage constructs such as m-satisfaction and m-loyalty.

PERCEIVED VALUE IN THE MOBILE CONTEXT

Since customer value is what every business entity ultimately seeks, there is a need to understand which elements and unique features of mobile medium provides value from the consumers' perspective. The most frequently noted value proposition of m-marketing is "ubiquity," that is, the omnipresence of information and continual access to commerce (Clarke, 2001). Ubiquity creates value to consumers by fulfilling time-critical needs and arrangements regardless of time and place (Anckar and D'Incau, 2002). Indeed, a large proportion of mobile service value is derived from time savings (Kleijnen, Ruyter and Wetzels, 2007).

Next, "convenience," the agility and accessibility provided by mobile devices (Clarke, 2001), is another key advantage of mobile medium for consumers. Anckar and D'Incau (2002) suggest that "convenience" creates value to consumers by fulfilling efficiency needs and ambitions, such as the need to increase productivity during dead spots of the day as the consumer is unable to access PC-based Internet. In fact, mobile services are used primarily for convenience (Kim, Chan and Gupta, 2007). Spontaneity, flexibility, immediacy, accessibility, time-criticality and instant connectivity are other terms used to refer to forms of ubiquity and convenience. None of these value propositions are mutually exclusive, but each provides important insights into the drivers of m-marketing adoption.

A distinctive feature of m-marketing is that it allows precise identification of the location of the consumer through the use of GPS technology. Leveraging this technology, m-marketers are able to send location-specific messages capturing contextuality. Applications involving this "localization" value proposition include time- and location-sensitive discount offers, roadside assistance, services allowing identification of nearby buyers and sellers, route guidance, road pricing, weather or traffic updates, accessibility information for disabled users, and speech-based guidance for visually impaired.

Another value proposition of the mobile medium is "personalization." The fact that mobile devices are typically used individually makes it an ideal tool for one-to-one marketing. Indeed, personalization is one of the most important factors affecting consumer attitudes toward m-advertising. Personalization makes marketing messages increasingly relevant to the target consumer. People who find m-marketing campaigns relevant are more likely to take actions such as visiting a web site, visiting a shop, replying to the message, supplying email address, or buying the product (Rettie, Grandcolas and Deakins, 2005).

Finally, studies indicate that both utilitarian and hedonic value perceptions contribute to consumers' adoption of m-marketing. In fact, the influence of hedonic value perceptions in building attitudes towards m-marketing appears to be stronger than that of utilitarian value especially among users with limited internet experience and low trust of mobile technology (Park and SuJin, 2006). Utilitarian value assessments correlate positively with importance given to service costs and connection stability, whereas hedonic value appears to correlate negatively with importance of service costs and positively with use convenience and information quality (Park, 2006). In addition, a hedonic tendency is found to be associated positively with perceptions of service quality, whereas a utilitarian tendency relates negatively to perceptions of service quality (Kim and Hwang, 2006).

THE ROLE OF PERMISSION

The literature unanimously agrees on the significance of explicit consumer permission for the acceptance and success of m-marketing practices. Prior explicit permission is so critical that, without it, m-marketing messages could even reduce brand equity by causing resentment and irritation (Barwise and Strong, 2002). Empirical studies provide support that user control has a significant effect on consumers' attitudes toward m-marketing. Three types of user control are particularly important in the m-marketing domain: timing, frequency and content. Consumers should not only give permission to receive messages but also choose the timing they wish to receive them, the number of messages they shall receive, and the content of the messages (Carroll et al., 2007).

The concept of intrusiveness, which refers to feelings of resentment and irritation as a result of unexpected exposure to advertisements (Godin, 1999) is highly relevant to m-marketing due to the personal and "always on" nature of mobile devices. Factors that may mitigate intrusiveness include permission, message relevance, and monetary benefits (Krishnamurthy, 2000). The situational context, particularly time and location in which a mobile ad is received by a consumer, is of crucial importance to how he/she reacts to it (Barnes and Scornavacca, 2004). Therefore, the delivery of the message at the most appropriate time and location (role/situation congruence) is another factor that should mitigate intrusiveness. Supporting this view, Wehmeyer (2007) provide evidence that in high activity situations mobile ads are perceived more intrusive than during lower levels of activity.

THE ROLE OF TRUST

Trust in the context of mobile services refers to a set of specific beliefs dealing primarily with the integrity, benevolence, competence, and predict-ability of a particular service provider. Trust is usually regarded as a catalyst in consumer-marketer relationships because it provides expectations of successful transactions and facilitates willingness to become vulnerable to a mobile Internet site after having taken the Internet site's characteristics into consideration (Lee, 2005). Prior research provides empirical support for the positive influence of trust on attitudes toward m-advertising and intentions to receive messages (Karjaluoto et al., 2008). In addition to its direct effects, trust also seems to increase positive dispositions toward m-marketing indirectly through increasing perceived usefulness of m-advertising (Zhang and Mao, 2008). Trust and value perceptions are also found to improve customer loyalty through their positive impacts on satisfaction (Lin and Wang, 2006).

THE ROLE OF ATTITUDES AND PERSONAL VARIABLES

Attitudes are among the prime determinants of m-marketing adoption. Prior research seems to have focused primarily on message characteristics as antecedents of m-marketing attitudes. Findings indicate that informativeness, entertainment, credibility, and interactivity of the advertising message have the greatest impacts on consumer attitudes towards m-advertising (Haghirian and Inoue, 2007; Okazaki, 2004). The effects of prior knowledge and general attitude toward advertising, while being significant, seem to be of secondary importance (Bauer et al., 2005). Lee and Jun (2007) further reveal that the prime motivation for which an individual uses mobile media also relates to attitudes toward m-advertising. Consumers using mobile media for the purpose of mobility/convenience (functional benefits) have more favorable attitudes toward m-advertising in comparison to those who use mobile media for symbolic means. One of the few studies that focus on source characteristics indicate that promotional messages are perceived more positively if they come from another person rather than from a company (Wais and Clemons, 2008).

In their attempts to understand m-marketing acceptance and adoption, researchers have successfully validated extended versions of well established frameworks in marketing and consumer behavior literatures, including the Theory of Reasoned Action, the Theory of Planned Behavior, Technology Acceptance Model, Innovation Diffusion Theory, and uses and gratifications theories. These arch-theories were extended to include several innovation-based perceptions and personality traits as antecedents to consumer attitudes and intentions to accept m-marketing. A comprehensive list of these factors is provided in Table 1. Collectively, these works provide valuable insights into the adoption process of mobile services and the relative effects of predictor variables.

Consumer demographics such as gender, household income, age, education, social class, and student-status are generally posited as moderating the relationships between adoption determinants and attitudinal/behavioral responses. Likewise, several other individual characteristics such as average volume of advertising messages received, prior non-store shopping experience, prior usage of mobile services, and prior usage of the Internet are among the most commonly examined moderators describing differences among respondent groups in terms of adoption behavior. For instance, Nysveen, Pedersen and Thorbjørnsen (2005) reveal that social norms and intrinsic motives such as enjoyment are important determinants of intention to use mobile chat services among female users, whereas extrinsic motives such as usefulness and expressiveness are the key drivers among men. Karjaluoto et al. (2008) show that the strength of the relationship between intentions to receive messages and intentions to visit the advertised shop is greater for women than for men. It is also important to note that a few studies indicate nonsignificant effects of gender, education, and income on m-commerce frequency or future m-commerce intention (e.g., Bigné, Ruiz and Sanz, 2007).

Regarding the role of culture, cross-cultural investigations suggest that adoption and usage of mobile services and the process of attitude formation towards m-marketing are strongly influenced by cultural and structural factors. For example, Muk (2007) examine whether cultural differences have a significant impact on consumers' adoption of SMS advertising. Findings indicate that American consumers' decisions on accepting SMS ads are based solely on attitudinal considerations, whereas Taiwanese consumers are influenced by both social norms and attitudinal factors. Likewise, Harris, Rettie, and Kwan (2005) reveal significant differences between the UK and Hong Kong in usage of and attitudes to m-commerce services. They attribute these differences to disparities in levels of collectivism, power distance, and structural aspects of the two markets. Hence, the search for a single, global m-marketing strategy may be misguided.

A closer investigation of the aforementioned works indicates two critical issues. First, it appears that, due to the inherent characteristics of the mobile medium, a comprehensive understanding of mobile consumer behavior requires an integrative approach that views the end-user not only as a technology user but also as a service consumer and a network member (Pedersen, Methlie and Thorbjørnsen, 2002). Second, extant theories in the consumer behavior discipline should be adapted and utilized in the mobile context to capture a broader set of emotional, cognitive, social, and cultural influences. In fact, the list of elements and factors that are in interplay in shaping behaviors of mobile consumers is extremely long. A review of the accumulated literature on m-marketing adoption has revealed 70 determinants classified under 5 broader categories (see Table 1).

Table 1. M-marketing adoption determinants

Determinants	Definition
Consumer-based	
Demographics	
Age	
Gender	
Household income	
Education	
Occupation	
Social class	
Student-status	High school, college, and non-student adults
Average volume of ad messages received	
Prior non-store shopping experience	Mail, catalogue, television, mobile and Internet
Existing knowledge	Prior usage of the mobile medium
Prior usage of the Internet	Users of a technology are thought to gain the ability to predict outcomes of using a similar technology
Frequency of mobile use	
Length of mobile use	How long the user is subscribed?
Mobile affinity	Individual's relationship with mobile medium
Consumer Traits	
Innovativeness	Willingness to try out any new information technology
Opinion leadership	The extent to which a person is held in high esteem by those that accept his or her opinions
Concern for privacy	The anxious sense of interest that a person has because of various types of threats to the person's state of being free from intrusion
Optimum stimulation level	Individual's general response to environmental stimuli
Susceptibility to social influence	The degree to which an individual is influenced by personal recommendations, actions, and adoption of products by significant others
Optimism	Overall feeling toward technological development
General attitude towards advertising	Degree of like or dislike for advertising
General attitude towards mobile	Degree of like or dislike for the mobile medium
Critical mass	Minimum amount of people who have already adopted the innovation necessary for adoption
Mobile technology readiness	Individual's propensity to use or embrace new mobile technologies
Self efficacy	Beliefs in one's capabilities to mobilize the motivation, cognitive resources, and courses of action needed to meet given situational demands
Love of shopping	The degree to which an individual receives emotional gratification from shopping
Time consciousness	Proneness to recognize the scarcity of time as a resource
Personal attachment	The extent to which the mobile phone represents an integral part of a person's self-concept, and defines his/her role in a cultural sub-group
Playfulness	Tendency to interact spontaneously, inventively, and imaginatively with microcomputers

continued on the following page

Table 1. continued

Perceived financial resources	Subjective assessments of one's own economic resources
Information seeking behavior	Tendency for seeking external information
Price-consciousness	Being interested in getting the lowest price in shopping
Involvement level	Intensity of interest that a buyer shows for a certain service in a specific purchase decision
Cultural background	Culture-based values, beliefs and tendencies
Innovation-based (Perceived)	
Relative advantage	Relative benefits of using the service when compared to its alternatives
Complexity/Cognitive effort	The extent to which an innovation is perceived as difficult to understand or use
Trialability	The extent to which potential adopters can try out components, but decide to return to their prior conditions without great cost
Compatibility	The degree to which an innovation is perceived to be consistent with consumers' previous experiences, values and needs
Observability	The extent to which potential adopters can observe or find out about the properties and benefits of an innovation
Visibility/Communicability	The degree to which the use of innovation is visible to others
Enjoyment	The extent to which the activity of using a product is perceived to be enjoyable in its own right, apart from any performance consequences
Navigation ergonomics/Interaction quality	Perceived quality of interaction
Connection quality/reliability	The degree to which users perceive that the connection between the mobile device and the internet is satisfying in terms of speed and reliability
Cost	Perceived expensiveness of the service fee
Privacy	The extent to which users perceive having control over sharing personal information with others
Time convenience	Perceptions regarding the benefit of time convenience
Security	Perceptions regarding the safety of the exchanged information
Permission/User control	Perceived user control over message delivery and the timing, content, and frequency of message delivery
Content credibility/reliability	The extent to which a consumer perceives claims made about the brand in the ad to be truthful and believable
Trust	Belief that allows consumers to willingly become vulnerable to the mobile service
Risk	Subjective expectation of suffering a loss in pursuit of the desired outcome of using a mobile service
Usefulness	The degree to which a person believes that engaging with a mobile service would enhance his or her performance or satisfy a concrete need
Ease of use	The degree to which a person believes that engaging with a mobile service would be free of effort
Novelty	The degree to which the mobile service is perceived as novel
Relevance of the content/Content quality	Relevance of the content of the m-marketing message to the target consumer
Technicality	The degree to which the mobile service is perceived as being technically excellent in the process of providing services
Information value/utility	The extent to which the message is perceived as an opportunity to gratify consumer's need for information
Entertainment value/utility	The extent to which the message is perceived as an opportunity to gratify consumer's need for entertainment

continued on the following page

Table 1. continued

Social value/utility	The extent to which the message is perceived as an opportunity to gratify consumer's need for social acceptance
Intrusiveness	Utility and expectedness of an interruption
Design aesthetics	Balance, emotional appeal, or aesthetic of the user interface
Context-based	
Peer/Social influence	
Task type	The objective of the user when engaging in a mobile service
Contextual quality	Delivery of the message at the most appropriate time and location
Usage characteristics/Motivational uses	A variety of usage situations are characterized by changing levels of utilitarian and hedonic motives.
Strategy-based	
Incentives	Clarity and type of incentives (e.g., free offers, coupons, discounts, lottery)
Ease of opt-out	Ease of getting out of the service
Information communication source	Media, opinion leader, less active members of the society
Frequency of message sending	
Variety of payment options	Availability of more than one payment method

M-SATISFACTION AND M-LOYALTY

Satisfaction is traditionally defined as an overall affective and cognitive evaluation of the product or service experience (Oliver, 1980). As a direct outcome of a customer's perception of value received, satisfaction is a strong predictor of re-purchase intentions, complaining, product usage, word-of-mouth recommendations, and loyalty. Loyalty is defined as "a deeply held commitment to re-buy or re-patronize a preferred product/service consistently in the future" (Oliver, 1999, p.34), and is seen as the key factor in developing a sustainable competitive advantage in competitive markets.

Pura (2005) analyze the direct effects of four value dimensions (conditional, emotional, monetary, and social) on commitment to and behavioral intentions towards using location-based mobile services. Findings of this study indicate that behavioral intentions are most strongly influenced by conditional value, i.e., the extent to which a mobile service offers entertaining service experiences in the right context, commitment, and monetary value. Commitment is further found to relate positively to emotional value and conditional value. Social value perceptions are found to be unrelated to the outcome variables. In another study, Pihlström (2007) finds that intentions to re-use the same service provider are directly influenced by commitment to the provider and indirectly by emotional and social value perceptions of the MMS content. The equivocal nature of these findings calls for future research attention on m-loyalty.

Another study investigates the role of information quality in increasing m-satisfaction and m-loyalty (Chae et al., 2002). Dimensions of information quality are identified as connection quality, content quality, interaction quality, and contextual quality (see Table 1). All four constructs are found to have significant effects on user satisfaction, which, in turn, relates to customer loyalty. In terms of relative effects, interaction quality and connection quality appear to have stronger impacts on user satisfaction than content quality and contextual quality. Choi et al. (2008) find perceived credibility of the advertiser/advertising as the most important driver of m-satisfaction and m-loyalty, which was followed by perceived connection quality. These finding indicate that provision of content and contextual quality is insufficient if the information is not easily accessible because of connection failures or interaction difficulties.

Regarding the effects of design aesthetics of mobile services on consumer satisfaction or loyalty, Bruner and Kumar (2005) show that visually oriented consumers are more likely to adopt mobile handheld devices than other consumers. This finding implicitly suggests that visual design is an important factor, at least for a segment of mobile device users. Drawing upon research on visual aesthetics in a variety of situations, Cyr, Head and Ivanov (2006) show design aesthetics having significant effects on perceived usefulness, ease of use, and enjoyment from mobile services (all of which are further shown to affect consumer loyalty). Nonetheless, there exist contradictory findings as well. For instance, Magura (2003) finds that site design has little relevance to mobile commerce acceptance. Obviously, further research in this area would be of great value.

FUTURE RESEARCH DIRECTIONS

The current state of research in consumer responses to m-marketing seems to have approached the issue from an innovation-adoption perspective, focusing primarily on initial adoption requirements rather than on post-usage constructs such as satisfaction, repeat buying, loyalty, and switching behavior. This is to some extent reasonable, because mobile services are radical technological innovations and m-marketing is still in its initial phases. However, considering the fact that mobile devices have infiltrated almost every aspect of life, we now need excessive research effort to understand more about post-usage constructs.

Likewise, cross-cultural studies in the domain of m-marketing are still quite scarce.

Perhaps more important, the concept of mobile social networking, which involves making and sharing content through mobile Internet, is on the rise. Therefore, research should also focus on types of mobile social networks, drivers and inhibitors of mobile social networking, and consumer needs that drive this new trend.

Overall, although there has been substantial progress in the consumer side of m-marketing, the field still offers fertile research avenues.

CONCLUSION

As shown in Table 1, consumer intentions to receive and engage in m-marketing depends upon a multitude of antecedent factors, including personal variables such as personality traits, predispositions, demographics, and cultural background, as well as upon several perceptual variables. All these factors are important in terms of driving consumer attitudes and behavioral intentions, hence excessive focus on any group of factors in isolation is unlikely to result in desired responses.

REFERENCES

Anckar, B., & D'Incau, D. (2002). Value creation in mobile commerce: Findings from a consumer survey. *JITTA: Journal of Information Technology Theory & Application, 4*(1), 43–65.

Barnes, S. J., & Scornavacca, E. (2004). Mobile marketing: the role of permission and acceptance. *International Journal of Mobile Communications, 2*(2), 128–139. doi:10.1504/IJMC.2004.004663

Barwise, P., & Strong, C. (2002). Permission-based mobile advertising. *Journal of Interactive Marketing, 16*(1), 14. doi:10.1002/dir.10000

Bauer, H. H., Reichardt, T., Barnes, S. J., & Neumann, M. M. (2005). Driving consumer acceptance of mobile marketing: a theoretical framework and empirical study. *Journal of Electronic Commerce Research, 6*(3), 181–192.

Bigné, E., Ruiz, C., & Sanz, S. (2007). Key drivers of mobile commerce adoption: an exploratory study of Spanish mobile users. *Journal of Theoretical & Applied Electronic Commerce Research, 2*(2), 48–61.

Bruner, G. C., & Kumar, A. (2005). Explaining consumer acceptance of handheld Internet devices. *Journal of Business Research, 58*(5), 553–558. doi:10.1016/j.jbusres.2003.08.002

Carroll, A., Barnes, S. J., Scornavacca, E., & Fletcher, K. (2007). Consumer perceptions and attitudes towards SMS advertising: recent evidence from New Zealand. *International Journal of Advertising, 26*(1), 79–98.

Chae, M., Kim, J., Kim, H., & Ryu, H. (2002). Information quality for mobile Internet services: a theoretical model with empirical validation. *Electronic Markets, 12*(1), 38–46. doi:10.1080/101967802753433254

Choi, J., Seol, H., Lee, S., Cho, H., & Park, Y. (2008). Customer satisfaction factors of mobile commerce in Korea. *Internet Research, 18*(3), 313–335. doi:10.1108/10662240810883335

Clarke, I. (2001). Emerging value propositions for M-commerce. *The Journal of Business Strategy, 18*(2), 133–149.

Cyr, D., Head, M., & Ivanov, A. (2006). Design aesthetics leading to m-loyalty in mobile commerce. *Information & Management, 43*, 950–963. doi:10.1016/j.im.2006.08.009

eMarketer. (2007, October). *Mobile Brand Advertising*.

Godin, S. (1999). *Permission Marketing: Turning Strangers into Friends, and Friends into Customers*. New York: Simon & Schuster.

Haghirian, P., & Inoue, A. (2007). An advanced model of consumer attitudes toward advertising on the mobile Internet. *International Journal of Mobile Communications, 5*(1), 48–67. doi:10.1504/IJMC.2007.011489

Harris, P., Rettie, R., & Kwan, C. C. (2005). Adoption and usage of m-commerce: a cross-cultural comparison of Hong Kong and the United Kingdom. *Journal of Electronic Commerce Research, 6*(3), 210–225.

Karjaluoto, H., Standing, C., Becker, M., & Leppaniemi, M. (2008). Factors affecting Finnish consumers' intention to receive SMS marketing: a conceptual model and an empirical study. *International Journal of Electronic Business, 6*(3), 298–318. doi:10.1504/IJEB.2008.019109

Kim, D. J., & Hwang, Y. (2006). A study of mobile Internet usage from utilitarian and hedonic user tendency perspectives. In *Proceedings of the Twelfth Americas Conference on Information Systems*.

Kim, H., Chan, H. C., & Gupta, S. (2007). Value-based adoption of mobile Internet: an empirical investigation. *Decision Support Systems, 43*(1), 111–126. doi:10.1016/j.dss.2005.05.009

Kleijnen, M., Ruyter, K., & Wetzels, M. (2007). An assessment of value creation in mobile service delivery and the moderating role of time consciousness. *Journal of Retailing, 83*(1), 33–46. doi:10.1016/j.jretai.2006.10.004

Krishnamurthy, S. (2000). A comprehensive analysis of permission marketing. *Journal of Computer-Mediated Communication, 6*(2).

Lee, T. (2005). The impact of perceptions of interactivity on customer trust and transaction intentions in mobile commerce. *Journal of Electronic Commerce Research, 6*(3), 165–181.

Lee, T., & Jun, J. (2007). The role of contextual marketing offer in Mobile Commerce acceptance: comparison between Mobile Commerce users & nonusers. *International Journal of Mobile Communications, 5*(3), 339–356. doi:10.1504/IJMC.2007.012398

Lin, H.-H., & Wang, Y.-S. (2006). An examination of the determinants of customer loyalty in mobile commerce contexts. *Information & Management, 43*(3), 271–282. doi:10.1016/j.im.2005.08.001

Magura, B. (2003). What hooks m-commerce customers? *MIT Sloan Management Review, 44*(3), 9.

Muk, A. (2007). Cultural influences on adoption of SMS advertising: a study of American and Taiwanese consumers. *Journal of Targeting . Measurement & Analysis for Marketing, 16*, 39–47. doi:10.1057/palgrave.jt.5750062

Nysveen, H., Pedersen, P. E., & Thorbjørnsen, H. (2005). Explaining intention to use mobile chat services: moderating effects of gender. *Journal of Consumer Marketing, 22*(4/5), 247–257. doi:10.1108/07363760510611671

Okazaki, S. (2004). How do Japanese consumers perceive wireless ads? A multivariate analysis. *International Journal of Advertising, 23*(4), 429–454.

Oliver, R. L. (1980). A cognitive model of the antecedents and consequences of satisfaction decisions. *JMR, Journal of Marketing Research, 17*(4), 460–469. doi:10.2307/3150499

Oliver, R. L. (1999). Whence consumer loyalty. *Journal of Marketing, 63*, 33–44. doi:10.2307/1252099

Park, C. (2006). Hedonic and utilitarian values of mobile internet in Korea. *International Journal of Mobile Communications, 4*(5), 497–508.

Park, J. & SuJin Y. (2006). The moderating role of consumer trust and experiences: value driven usage of mobile technology. *International Journal of Mobile Marketing, 1*(2), 24–32.

Pedersen, P. E., Methlie, L. B., & Thorbjørnsen, H. (2002) Understanding mobile commerce end-user adoption: a triangulation perspective and suggestion for an exploratory service evaluation framework. *Proceedings of the 35th Hawaii International Conference on System Sciences.*

Pihlström, M. (2007). Committed to content provider or mobile channel? Determinants of continuous mobile multimedia service use. *JITTA: Journal of Information Technology Theory & Application, 9*(1), 1–24.

Pura, M. (2005). Linking perceived value and loyalty in location-based mobile services. *Managing Service Quality, 15*(6), 509–539. doi:10.1108/09604520510634005

Rettie, R., Grandcolas, U., & Deakins, B. (2005). Text message advertising: response rates and branding effects. *Journal of Targeting . Measurement & Analysis for Marketing, 13*(4), 304–313. doi:10.1057/palgrave.jt.5740158

Wais, J. S., & Clemons, E. K. (2008). Understanding and implementing mobile social advertising. *International Journal of Mobile Marketing, 3*(1), 12–18.

Wehmeyer, K. (2007) Mobile Ad Intrusiveness – The effects of message type and situation. In *Proceedings of the 20th Bled eConference.*

Zhang, J., & Mao, E. (2008). Understanding the acceptance of mobile SMS advertising among young Chinese consumers. *Psychology and Marketing, 25*(8), 787–805. doi:10.1002/mar.20239

ADDITIONAL READING

Balasubramanian, S., Peterson, R. A., & Jarvenpaa, S. L. (2002). Exploring the implications of m-commerce for markets and marketing. *Journal of the Academy of Marketing Science, 30*(4), 348–361. doi:10.1177/009207002236910

Michael, A., & Salter, B. (2006) *Mobile Marketing*, UK: Butterworth-Heineman.

Sugai, P. (2005). Mapping the mind of the mobile consumer across borders: an application of the Zaltman metaphor elicitation technique. *International Marketing Review, 22*(6), 641–657. doi:10.1108/02651330510630267

KEY TERMS AND DEFINITIONS

Customer Value: Overall assessment of the utility of a market offering based on what is received and what is given.

M-Loyalty: A deeply held commitment to re-use a preferred mobile service or service/network provider consistently in the future.

Mobile Marketing: The use of personal mobile and wireless devices as a medium for creation, communication and delivery of customer value.

M-Satisfaction: Overall affective and cognitive evaluation of the mobile service experience

Permission Marketing: Type of marketing campaign that requires consumers to 'opt in' before they receive marketing messages of any kind and have the option to 'opt out' at any stage.

Personalization: The degree to which a service/message is tailored to meet the needs and wants of the individual consumer.

Chapter 78
The Personalization Privacy Paradox:
Mobile Customers' Perceptions of Push–Based vs. Pull–Based Location Commerce

Heng Xu
Pennsylvania State University, USA

John M. Carroll
Pennsylvania State University, USA

Mary Beth Rosson
Pennsylvania State University, USA

INTRODUCTION

Recent advances in positioning technologies, such as global positioning systems and cellular triangulation techniques, have not only provided consumers with unprecedented accessibility to network services while on the move, but also enabled the localization of services (Bellavista, Kupper, & Helal, 2008). Locatability, that is, the ability of mobile hosts to determine the current physical location of wireless devices, is thus the key enabler of an alluring mobile business operation (Junglas & Watson, 2003). In the literature, commercial location-sensitive applications and services that utilize geographical positioning information to provide value-added services are generally termed location-based services (LBS),

marketed under terms like 'Location-Commerce' or 'L-Commerce' (Barnes, 2003).

Despite the growing attention given to LBS, little is understood about the differential effects of alternative protocols for locating client devices on the mobile consumer perceptions and behaviors. To offer personalized services that are tailored to mobile consumers' activity contexts, LBS providers deliver information content through mobile communication and positioning systems in two ways – push and pull mechanisms. In the pull mechanism (i.e., reactive LBS), individuals request information and services based on their locations, e.g., a user might request a list of nearby points of interest. In the push mechanism (i.e., proactive LBS), location-sensitive content is automatically sent to individuals based on tracking their locations. From the consumer perspective, the pull-based L-Commerce entails a higher

DOI: 10.4018/978-1-61520-611-7.ch078

level of control, but consequent time and cognitive investment to manage personal information are relatively high. The push-based L-Commerce, on the other hand, allows for the regular canvassing of information sources for updated information and automatic delivery (Edmunds & Morris, 2000): less control but also less effort. Although the push-based L-Commerce may reduce consumers' information processing and retrieval efforts, it increases the amount of potentially irrelevant information that consumers have to deal with as well as the amount of personal location information that they have to disclose to service providers (Eppler & Mengis, 2004).

Will the push-based L-Commerce be experienced as more intrusive to individual privacy and/or as interruptive to the mobile consumer's activity? How will mobile consumers make the tradeoff between privacy concerns and instrumental values of L-Commerce? In this chapter, we attempt to respond to these questions by discussing the differences between push and pull mechanisms and discussing how these differences may lead to different mobile consumers' perceptions of push-based and pull-based L-Commerce. In what follows, we present the conceptual analysis, describing the personalization privacy paradox, and discussing the different impacts of pull and push mechanisms on the privacy personalization paradox. This is followed by a discussion of the key results, directions for future research, and theoretical implications.

CONCEPTUAL ANALYSIS

The Personalization Privacy Paradox

Information privacy refers to the ability of the individual to control the terms under which personal information is acquired and used (Westin, 1967). Within the robust body of research that attempts to understand the nature of consumer privacy, it has been found that the *calculus* perspective of

privacy is "the most useful framework for analyzing contemporary consumer privacy concerns" (Culnan & Bies, 2003, p.326). This perspective reflects an implicit understanding that privacy is not absolute (Klopfer & Rubenstein, 1977); rather, the individual's privacy interests can be interpreted based on a "calculus of behavior" (Laufer & Wolfe, 1977, p.36). That is to say, individuals can be expected to behave as if they are performing a risk-benefit analysis (i.e., privacy calculus) in assessing the outcomes they will receive as a result of providing personal information to corporations (Culnan & Bies, 2003). Applying the notion of privacy calculus to the understanding of the tradeoff between personalization and privacy, we may interpret the usage of personalized information or service as an exchange where consumers disclose their personal information in return for the customized information or services. Prior studies have confirmed that users are more likely to provide personal information when they perceive higher value in the personalization services offered (White, 2004).

Labeled as one type of context-awareness applications, L-Commerce can provide a user with the value of contextualization by sending the user with relevant promotional information based on the user's location, identity, activity and time (Barnes, 2003). Personalization has been generally defined as "the ability to provide content and services that are tailored to individuals based on knowledge about their preferences and behaviors" (Adomavicius & Tuzhilin, 2005, p.84). In the context of L-Commerce, personalization with the emphasis on individualized utility has been acknowledged as one key value that adds to the user experiences and smoothness of interactions (Zimmermann, Specht, & Lorenz, 2005). Consumers may be motivated to disclose their personal information in exchange for personalized services and/or information access. L-Commerce can obviously be personalized as the services are invariably tied to a mobile device (e.g., a mobile phone). To the extent that a mobile device could be uniquely identified (e.g., via the SIM card in the case of a mobile phone) and is always handy and available, the device is ideal for marketers to channel their marketing and advertising opportunities into tailoring wireless content delivery for mobile consumers. Indeed, personalization, as one important antecedent of perceived benefits identified by prior studies (Junglas & Watson, 2003; Zimmermann et al., 2005), is gained when L-Commerce applications are tailored to individual customers' interests, locations, and the time of the day. Therefore, we propose that *the value of personalization increases consumers' perceived benefits of information disclosure in L-Commerce.*

It has been suggested by prior studies that personalized information and services have significant privacy implications because of large amounts of personal information collected for performing personalization (Kobsa, 2007). Consumers are vulnerable to at least two kinds of risks if their personal information is not used fairly or responsibly (Culnan and Armstrong 1999). First, a consumer may perceive that her privacy is invaded if unauthorized access is made to her personal information as a result of a security breach or in the absence of appropriate internal controls (Culnan and Armstrong 1999). Second, as computerized information may be readily duplicated and shared, a consumer is vulnerable to the risk that the personal information provided is being put to secondary use for unrelated purposes without prior knowledge or consent (Culnan and Armstrong 1999).

In the L-Commerce context, the concerns center on the confidentiality of the dynamic location data, accumulated location data and other personal information, and the potential risks that consumers experience over the possible breach of confidentiality (Shiels, 2008). Improper handling of personal information could result in the discovery of consumer identity and behavior, which may be used for unsolicited marketing, price discrimination or unauthorized access (Kobsa, 2007). In the

context of mobile commerce, it has been shown that consumers' privacy concerns were triggered when they were presented with a personalized shopping list that was derived from an analysis of their purchasing history (Kourouthanassis & Roussos, 2003; Roussos et al., 2002). Despite the benefits or added value provided by personalized information and services, consumers are concerned about their personal information collected and used to perform personalization (Awad & Krishnan, 2006). Therefore, we propose that *the value of personalization increases consumers' perceived risks of information disclosure in L-Commerce.*

Influences of Information Delivery Mechanisms – Push vs. Pull

To offer personalized services that are tailored to mobile consumers' activity contexts, marketers and advertisers deliver information content through mobile communication and positioning systems in two ways – push and pull mechanisms. In the push-based L-Commerce, service providers send relevant information or content to consumers by background observation of their behaviors through tracking physical locations of their mobile devices. With these data, personalization systems tailor the services based on the user's known proximity to a store or merchant. Haag et al. (2005) describes an application that pushes video rental information to customers: whenever appearing in the vicinity of a participating video store, the customer's mobile phone triggers a system within the video store that evaluates that customer's rental history against store inventory. If the system indicates an available video will be of interest, it sends a text message to the customer's mobile phone with the rental details on the film.

In contrast to the push-based mechanism, the pull-based mechanism only locates users' mobile devices when the users initiate specific requests. Such pull-based L-Commerce may be seen in some 'on demand' services where the user dials or signals a service provider for specific information / service such as the nearest Starbucks store. In this approach, location information is ephemeral and useful only to complete the transaction requested (e.g., informing the user of the Starbucks store). One of the first examples was a service launched by ZagMe in the United Kingdom (Buckley, 2007). By calling a number or sending a text message to activate location tracking, customers could receive promotional information and coupons through text messages based on their geographical location in a designated mall.

As discussed earlier, higher level of personalization leads to higher level of perceived benefits of information disclosure. However, this relationship is likely to be contingent on the type of information delivery mechanisms (push/pull). Comparing to pull mechanism, push-based L-Commerce should increase the level of timeliness and locatability of information access as push approach enables users to obtain their needed information as soon as it is available (Kendall & Kendall, 1999; 2000). Hence, the benefits of push system are that it allows for the regular canvassing of selected information sources for updated information and having that information sent to users seamlessly (Herther, 1998). Comparing to pull-based LBS, push may result in a substantial reduction in the amount of consumers' information search as the subscribed content is being delivered, rather than retrieved (Kendall & Kendall, 1999; 2000). Due to the limited information-processing capacity of the human mind (Alba et al., 1997), consumers tend to reduce the amount of efforts on information search and decision making through the push system (Kendall & Kendall, 1999; 2000). Hence, for push-based L-Commerce, a user may perceive higher level of personalization value when the service content adapts itself automatically based on the user's profile without the user's involvement. Therefore, we propose that *the positive association between personalization and perceived benefits of information disclosure will be stronger when*

the information delivery mechanism is push than when it is pull.

The negative effect of perceived privacy risks on intention to disclose personal information, however, is likely to be moderated by the level of *control* inherent in the type of information delivery mechanism (i.e., push/pull). Empirical evidence shows that the ability of the consumer to control the disclosure of personal information could offset the risk of possible negative consequences (Eddy, Stone, & Stone-Romero, 1999). L-Commerce applications in different information delivery mechanisms offer different levels of *control* over the disclosure of personal information (Gidari, 2000; Levijoki, 2001). In pull-based L-Commerce, the consumer exercises greater control over the interaction: the decision to initiate contact with the marketer is volitional, and location information is provided only to complete the transaction requested. In contrast, in push-based L-Commerce, the consumer's location is tracked all the time and location-based information / services are automatically sent to a consumer's mobile device based on that consumer's location and previously stated preferences. Although pushing selected information to users reduces their information processing and retrieval needs, it increases the amount of potentially irrelevant information that users have to deal with and the amount of location information that they have to disclose to service providers (Eppler & Mengis, 2004). Since consumers have less control over their interactions with service providers, push-based L-Commerce would be potentially more intrusive to individual privacy and tend to interrupt the consumer (Unni & Harmon, 2007). This would amplify the impacts of privacy risk perceptions. Therefore, we propose that *the predicted positive association between personalization and perceived risks of information disclosure will be stronger when the information delivery mechanism is push than when it is pull.*

Figure 1 depicts the conceptual framework.

Figure 1. The conceptual framework

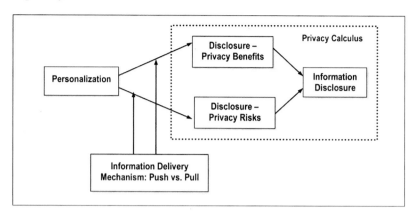

In addition, it seems reasonable to argue that the conceptual structure of personalization privacy paradox is context-dependent. For example, the usage of the location-based buddy-finder services such as tracking friends and sending restaurant coupons based on friends' locations may lead to a positive outcome of the privacy calculus and hence higher willingness to disclose location information. Thus it is important to explore the contextual nature of privacy theory—knowing what "more" or "less" privacy might mean for different individuals in the specific context. Thus, Waldo et al. (2007) called for more research on the contextual nature of privacy, as they believe that research along this direction will make it clear that questions about privacy necessarily imply specifying privacy "from whom," "about what," "for what reasons," and "under what conditions." Because of such context-specific nature of privacy calculus, we propose that *parameter estimates in the conceptual framework (e.g., factor mean levels, path coefficients) may not be the same among different contexts or applications.*

FUTURE RESEARCH DIRECTIONS

Research on L-Commerce is in the early stages and our exploratory efforts represent one of the first attempts to examine how the information delivery mechanism (push/pull) may influence the personalization privacy paradox. This chapter represents the early attempts at exploring the relative effectiveness of push and pull mechanisms with privacy considerations as a focal point. Further research should be directed to empirically test the conceptual framework (Figure 1). A field experiment in which participants can gain more realistic experiences of using LBS is recommended to test the framework because this approach allows us to manipulate key variables and exercise control over extraneous variables. This study could be designed as a one-factorial experiment manipulating information delivery mechanism (push and pull) with participants randomly assigned to one of the two groups. One specific push-based application and one pull-based application could be adapted from present applications described in Haag et al. (2005) and Buckley (2007) to have two balanced experiment scenarios. At the final stage of the experiment, participants will be asked to complete a questionnaire regarding the major research constructs – *perceived benefits of information disclosure* (Unni & Harmon, 2007), *perceived risks of information disclosure* (Dinev & Hart, 2006), *personalization* (Zeithaml, Parasuraman, & Malhotra, 2000), and *information disclosure* (Culnan & Armstrong, 1999). Upon collecting the data, the multi-group analyses (push and pull subgroups) through structural equation modeling techniques (e.g., Partial Least Squares) can be conducted to test the research model.

The challenge is to design the manipulations for both pull and push mechanisms in a balanced and realistic manner. Particularly, it would be challenging to mimic user behaviors for the pull-based LBS in an experimental setting. Because in pull-based LBS (e.g., "where is the nearest Japanese restaurant offering discounts right now?"), a consumer's decision to initiate contact with the service provider is volitional. Therefore, triggering consumers' natural motives of initiating the use of pull-based LBS in an experimental setting remains a challenge.

The notion of privacy calculus interprets the individual's privacy interests as an exchange where individuals disclose their personal information in return for certain benefits. Such calculus perspective of privacy has been found in many studies to be one of the major frameworks analyzing consumer privacy concerns (Culnan & Bies, 2003; Dinev & Hart, 2006). This chapter suggested that the conventional understanding of privacy as a calculus can be applied to explain to the personalization privacy paradox in the new L-Commerce context. Privacy concerns in such new context of surveillance-based technologies become particularly salient as merchants and service providers may have access to a large volume of potentially sensitive consumer information. This research is an initial examination of issues relating to the moderating roles of push versus pull information delivery mechanism in the personalization and privacy paradox.

CONCLUSION

Location-based technologies that are aware of the circumstances of users can deliver relevant services or information in a productive, personalized and context-relevant way, deepening customer relationships. The convergence between marketing, customer relationship management and mobile commerce represents a potentially powerful platform for L-Commerce. This chapter has provided preliminary analysis about how consumers strike a balance between value and risk. The current research contributed to existing literature by theoretically investigating the personalization privacy paradox through a privacy calculus lens, for information delivery mechanism (push vs. pull), in an understudied L-Commerce environment. Our initial analysis that the influence of personalization on the privacy calculus model depends on the type of information delivery mechanisms suggest the need for future studies to understand these effects more fully. Using the groundwork laid in this study, future research along various possible directions could contribute to extending our theoretical understanding and practical ability to foster the acceptance of L-Commerce.

REFERENCES

Adomavicius, G., & Tuzhilin, A. (2005). Personalization technologies: a process-oriented perspective. *Communications of the ACM, 48*(10), 83–90. doi:10.1145/1089107.1089109

Alba, J., Lynch, J. G., Weitz, B., Janiszewski, C., Lutz, R., Sawyer, A., & Wood, S. (1997). Interactive Home Shopping: Consumer, Retailer, and Manufacturer Incentives to Participate in Electronic Marketplaces. *Journal of Marketing, 61*(July), 38–53. doi:10.2307/1251788

Awad, N. F., & Krishnan, M. S. (2006). The personalization privacy paradox: An empirical evaluation of information transparency and the willingness to be profiled online for personalization. *MIS Quarterly, 30*(1), 13–28.

Barnes, J. S. (2003). Known by the Network: The Emergence of Location-Based Mobile Commerce. In E.-P. Lim & K. Siau (Eds.), *Advances in Mobile Commerce Technologies,* (pp. 171-189). Hershey, PA: Idea Group Publishing.

Bellavista, P., Kupper, A., & Helal, S. (2008). Location-Based Services: Back to the Future. *IEEE Pervasive Computing / IEEE Computer Society [and] IEEE Communications Society*, 7(2), 85–89. doi:10.1109/MPRV.2008.34

Buckley, R. (2007). *Location Based Advertising - Theory and Practice*. Available online http://www.mobiadnews.com/documents/lbs_buckley.pdf

Culnan, M. J., & Armstrong, P. K. (1999). Information Privacy Concerns, Procedural Fairness and Impersonal Trust: An Empirical Investigation. *Organization Science*, 10(1), 104–115. doi:10.1287/orsc.10.1.104

Culnan, M. J., & Bies, R. J. (2003). Consumer Privacy: Balancing Economic and Justice Considerations. *The Journal of Social Issues*, 59(2), 323–342. doi:10.1111/1540-4560.00067

Dinev, T., & Hart, P. (2006). An Extended Privacy Calculus Model for E-Commerce Transactions. *Information Systems Research*, 17(1), 61–80. doi:10.1287/isre.1060.0080

Eddy, R. E., Stone, L. D., & Stone-Romero, F. E. (1999). The Effects of Information Management Polices on Reactions to Human Resource Information Systems: An Integration of Privacy and Procedural Justice Perspectives. *Personnel Psychology*, 52, 335–358. doi:10.1111/j.1744-6570.1999.tb00164.x

Edmunds, A., & Morris, A. (2000). The Problem of Information Overload in Business Organisations: A Review of the Literature. *International Journal of Information Management*, 20, 17–28. doi:10.1016/S0268-4012(99)00051-1

Eppler, M. J., & Mengis, J. (2004). The concept of information overload: A review of literature from organization science, marketing, accounting, MIS, and related disciplines. *The Information Society*, 20, 325–344. doi:10.1080/01972240490507974

Gidari, A. (2000). *No 'L-Commerce' Without 'L-Privacy': Fair Location Information Practices for Mobile Commerce*. Paper presented at the L-Commerce 2000-the Location Services & GPS Technology Summit. Available online: http://www.airbiquity.com/downloads/Privacy-Airbiquity.PDF

Haag, S., Cummings, M., & Phillips, A. (2005). *Management Information Systems for the Information Age* (6 ed.). New York: Irwin/McGraw-Hill Higher Education.

Herther, N. K. (1998). Push and the Politics of the Internet. *The Electronic Library*, 16(2), 455–461. doi:10.1108/eb045624

Junglas, I. A., & Watson, R. T. (2003). *U-Commerce: An Experimental Investigation of Ubiquity and Uniqueness*. Paper presented at the Proceedings of 24th Annual International Conferences on Information Systems (ICIS 2003), Seattle, USA.

Kendall, E. J., & Kendall, E. K. (1999). Information delivery systems: an exploration of Web pull and push technologies. *Communications of the AIS*, 1(1), 2–42.

Kendall, E. J., & Kendall, E. K. (2000). Individual, Organizational, and Societal Perspectives on Information Delivery Systems: Bright and Dark Sides to Push and Pull Technologies. In R. Baskerville, J. Stage & J. I. DeGross (Eds.), *Organizational and Social Perspectives on Information Technology* (pp. 179-194). Amsterdam: Kluwer Academic Publishers.

Klopfer, P. H., & Rubenstein, D. L. (1977). The concept privacy and its biological basis. *The Journal of Social Issues*, 33, 52–65.

Kobsa, A. (2007). Privacy-Enhanced Personalization. *Communications of the ACM*, 50(8), 24–33. doi:10.1145/1278201.1278202

Kourouthanassis, P., & Roussos, G. (2003). Developing consumer-friendly pervasive retail systems. *IEEE Pervasive Computing / IEEE Computer Society [and] IEEE Communications Society, 2*(2), 32–39. doi:10.1109/MPRV.2003.1203751

Laufer, R. S., & Wolfe, M. (1977). Privacy as a concept and a social issue: A multidimensional developmental theory. *The Journal of Social Issues, 33*, 22–41.

Levijoki, S. (2001). *Privacy vs Location Awareness*. Helsinki University of Technology.

Roussos, G., Tuominen, J., Koukara, L., Seppala, O., Kourouthanasis, P., Giaglis, G., et al. (2002). *A case study in pervasive retail*. Paper presented at the Proceedings of the 2nd international workshop on Mobile commerce, Atlanta, GA.

Shiels, M. (2008). Privacy worry over location data. *BBC News*. Retrieved Aug 28, 2008, 2008, from http://news.bbc.co.uk/1/hi/technology/7559731.stm

Unni, R., & Harmon, R. (2007). *Perceived Effectiveness of Push vs. Pull Mobile Location-Based Advertising*. Retrieved from http://www.jiad.org/article91

Waldo, J., Lin, H., & Millett, L. I. (2007). *Engaging Privacy and Information Technology in a Digital Age*: National Academies Press.

Westin, A. F. (1967). *Privacy and Freedom*. New York: Atheneum.

White, T. B. (2004). Consumer Disclosure and Disclosure Avoidance: A Motivational Framework. *Journal of Consumer Psychology, 14*(1 & 2), 41–51. doi:10.1207/s15327663jcp1401&2_6

Zeithaml, A. V., Parasuraman, A., & Malhotra, A. (2000). *A Conceptual Framework for Understanding e-Service Quality: Implications for Future Research and Managerial Practice,* Report No. 00-115, Marketing Science Instituteo.

Zimmermann, A., Specht, M., & Lorenz, A. (2005). Personalization and Context Management. *User Modeling and User-Adapted Interaction, 15*(3), 275–302. doi:10.1007/s11257-005-1092-2

ADDITIONAL READING

Ackerman, M. S. (2004). Privacy in pervasive environments: next generation labeling protocols. *Personal and Ubiquitous Computing, 8*(6), 430–439. doi:10.1007/s00779-004-0305-8

Barkhuus, L., & Dey, A. (2003). *Location-Based Services for Mobile Telephony: A Study of User's Privacy Concerns*. Proceedings of the INTER-ACT, 9th IFIP TC13 International Conference on Human-Computer Interaction, Zurich, Switzerland.

Beresford, R. A., & Stajano, F. (2003). Location Privacy in Pervasive Computing. *IEEE Pervasive Computing / IEEE Computer Society [and] IEEE Communications Society, 1*, 46–55. doi:10.1109/MPRV.2003.1186725

Bruner, C. G. II, & Kumar, A. (2007). Attitude toward Location-Based Advertising. *Journal of Interactive Advertising, 7*(2). http://www.jiad.org/article89.

Clarke, R. (2001). Person location and person tracking: Technologies, risks and policy implications. *Information Technology & People, 14*(2), 206–231. doi:10.1108/09593840110695767

Easton, J. (2002). Going Wireless: Transform Your Business with Mobile Technology. New York: HarperBusiness.

Galanxhi-Janaqi, H., & Nah, F. (2004). U-Commerce: Emerging Trends and Research Issues. *Industrial Management & Data Systems, 104*(9), 744–755. doi:10.1108/02635570410567739

Galanxhi-Janaqi, H., & Nah, F. (2006). Privacy Issues in the Era of Ubiquitous Commerce. *Electronic Markets, 16*(3), 222–232. doi:10.1080/10196780600841894

Hoadley, M. C., Xu, H., Lee, J. J., & Rosson, M. B. (2010). (forthcoming). Privacy as Information Access and Illusory Control: The Case of the Facebook News Feed Privacy Outcry. *Electronic Commerce Research and Applications.*

Junglas, I., & Watson, R. T. (2006). The U-Constructs: Four Information Drives. *Communications of AIS, 17,* 569–592.

Junglas, I. A., & Watson, R. T. (2008). Location-Based Services: Evaluating User Perceptions of Location-Tracking and Location-Awareness Services. *Communications of the ACM, 51*(3), 65–69. doi:10.1145/1325555.1325568

Kaasinen, E. (2005). User acceptance of location-aware mobile guides based on seven field studies. *Behaviour & Information Technology, 24*(1), 37–49. doi:10.1080/01449290512331319049

Lederer, S., Mankoff, J., & Dey, K. A. (2003, April). *Who Wants to Know What When? Privacy Preference Determinants in Ubiquitous Computing.* Proceedings of Conferences on Human Factors in Computing Systems (CHI), Fort Lauderdale, Florida, USA.

Lyytinen, K., & Yoo, Y. (2002). Research Commentary: The Next Wave of Nomadic Computing. *Information Systems Research, 13*(4), 377–388. doi:10.1287/isre.13.4.377.75

Miller, A. I. (2002). Einstein, Picasso: Space, Time, And the Beauty That Causes Havoc. New York: Basic Books.

Rao, B., & Minakakis, L. (2003). Evolution of Mobile Location-Based Services. *Communications of the ACM, 46*(12), 61–65. doi:10.1145/953460.953490

Rittenbruch, M. (2002). Atmosphere: A Framework for Contextual Awareness. *International Journal of Human-Computer Interaction, 14*(2), 159–180. doi:10.1207/S15327590IJHC1402_3

Sheng, H., Nah, F., & Siau, K. (2008). An Experimental Study on Ubiquitous Commerce Adoption: Impact of Personalization and Privacy Concerns. *Journal of the Association for Information Systems, 9*(6), 344–376.

Wallace, P., Hoffmann, A., Scuka, D., Blut, Z., & Barrow, K. (2002). *i-Mode Developer's Guide.* Boston, Mass: Addison-Wesley.

Watson, R. T., Pitt, L. F., Berthon, P., & Zinkhan, G. M. (2002). U-Commerce: Extending the Universe of Marketing. *Journal of the Academy of Marketing Science, 30*(4), 329–343. doi:10.1177/009207002236909

Xu, H., Oh, L. B., & Teo, H. H. (2009). Perceived Effectiveness of Text versus Multimedia Location-Based Advertising Messaging. *International Journal of Mobile Communications, 7*(2), 154–177. doi:10.1504/IJMC.2009.022440

Xu, H., Rosson, M. B., & Carroll, J. M. (2008). *Mobile Users' Privacy Decision Making: Integrating Economic Exchange and Social Justice Perspectives.* Proceedings of 14th Annual Americas Conference on Information Systems (AMCIS 2008), Toronto, Canada.

Xu, H., & Teo, H. H. (2005). Privacy Considerations in Location-Based Advertising, In C. Sorensen, Y. Yoo, K. Lyytinen, and J. I. DeGross (Ed.), *Designing Ubiquitous Information Environments: Socio-Technical Issues and Challenges,* Springer, 71-90.

Xu, H., Teo, H. H., & Tan, B. C. Y. (2005). *Predicting the Adoption of Location-Based Services: The Roles of Trust and Privacy Risk.* Proceedings of 26th Annual International Conference on Information Systems (ICIS 2005), Las Vegas, Nevada, 897-910.

Xu, H., Zhang, C., Shi, P., & Song, P. (2009). *Exploring the Role of Overt vs. Covert Personalization Strategy in Privacy Calculus,* Best Paper Proceedings of 69th Annual Meeting of the Academy of Management (AOM 2009), Chicago, Illinois, 2009.

KEY TERMS AND DEFINITIONS

Information Privacy: refers to the ability of the individuals to control over how their personal information is collected and used.

Locatability: refers to the ability of mobile hosts to determine the current physical location of wireless devices.

Location Commerce (L-Commerce): refers to commercial location-based services that utilize geographical positioning information to provide value-added services to mobile consumers.

Location-Based Service (LBS): refer to the network-based services that utilize the ability to make use of the geographical position of the wireless devices so as to be accessible with wireless devices through the mobile network.

Personalization: refers to the ability to provide content and services that are tailored to individuals based on the knowledge about their preferences and contexts.

Pull-based LBS (reactive LBS): is the location-sensitive content sent to the wireless subscriber's mobile device only when the subscriber explicitly requests for. Such pull-based LBS may be seen in some 'on demand' services where the user dials or signals a service provider for specific information / service such as the nearby points of interest. In this approach, location information is ephemeral and useful only to complete the transaction requested.

Push-based LBS (proactive LBS): is the location-sensitive content sent by or on behalf of service providers to a wireless mobile device at a time other than when the subscriber requests it. In the push-based LBS, service providers send relevant information or content to users based on users' previously stated product preferences, and by background observation of their behaviors through tracking physical locations of their mobile devices.

Chapter 79
Mobile Gaming:
Perspectives and Issues

Krassie Petrova
Auckland University of Technology, New Zealand

INTRODUCTION

Mobile gaming (mGaming) belongs to the category of mobile entertainment applications. It is widely adopted in some countries –for example in Japan (Baldi & Thaung, 2002; Chan, 2008) and is fast becoming a popular and profitable mobile commerce service (Kleijnen, de Ruyter, & Wetzels, 2003; Paavilainen, 2004, p. 133). In 2006, the revenue from phone games in Europe alone reached US$6 billion (Fritsch, Ritter, & Schiller, 2006). It is predicted that worldwide mGaming revenues will continue to grow with Asia-Pacific markets contributing significantly to the growth (Paul, Jensen, Wong, & Khong, 2008).

Past research results indicate that both customer perceptions and attitudes, and mGaming supply chain factors may play a critical role as determinants of mGaming business model success and mGaming

adoption (Barnes, 2003; Carlsson, Hyvonen, Repo, & Walden, 2005; Kuo & Yu, 2006; Macinnes, Moneta, Caraballo, & Sarni, 2002; Peppard & Rylander, 2006; Petrova, 2007; Siau, Lim, & Shen, 2001; Soh & Tan, 2008). Following up on prior findings the study presented here develops further the proposition that customer adoption of mobile gaming services and products is linked to:

i) User perceptions about the value of playing a mobile game in the context of their lifestyle, and

ii) User expectations about the quality of the mGaming service in the context of the environment.

The main objective of this chapter is to identify the determinants of mGaming success, to highlight the most important issues related to mGaming adoption, and to suggest recommendations for mobile game design and mGaming service pro-

DOI: 10.4018/978-1-61520-611-7.ch079

visioning. The chapter is organized as follows: First, definitions and background information are provided, and mobile gaming demand and supply are discussed. The sections following introduce mGaming adoption drivers and factors derived from studies using adoption models. mGaming determinants are proposed and discussed. The chapter concludes with an overview of future trends and research directions.

BACKGROUND

A mobile game is a video game played on a hand-held device such as a mobile phone, by a player with a connection to a mobile data network. A game may require a permanent connection, or may be a standalone one ('download once'). Actively connected players may be moving and frequently changing their geographic location. Mobile games may involve groups of competing and/or collaborating participants. Using location-awareness features, mobile games may superimpose features of the real world into the game space and create an augmented reality environment (Bell et al., 2006; Broll, et al., 2008; Finn, 2005; Koivisto, 2006; Maitland, van de Kar, de Montalvo, & Bouwman, 2005; Rashid, Mullins, Coulton, & Edwards, 2006). Pervasive mobile games involve players in interaction with another and with the physical environment, and may be played by geographically dispersed groups of players (Segatto, Herzer, Mazzotti, Bittencourt, & Barbosa, 2008).

As a service, mGaming uses the communication channel provided by the private mobile data network, which may also connect to the public Internet (the 'mobile Internet'). Only mobile network subscribers or prepaid customers may play mobile games which require a permanent connection. However some games may be played within an ad-hoc network formed by the players implementing a short range connection technology such as Bluetooth.

Most mobile games are designed and offered to be played for entertainment, with NTT Do-CoMo (Japan) the best known case of a mobile entertainment provider. DoCoMo users access the mobile Internet via iMode – the DoCoMo access platform. Mobile entertainment activities and specifically mGaming are seen by DoCoMo as a key growth driver (Barnes, 2003; Chan, 2008). However mGaming is also deployed in other contexts as a motivational strategy, or as a knowledge building facilitator. Examples include testing student knowledge (Wang, Øfsdahl, & Morch-Størstein, 2008), or encouraging 'sedate' players to exercise and thus improve their wellness (Bell et al., 2006; de Freitas & Griffiths, 2008; Wylie & Coulton, 2008). There is a current rise in the number of projects exploring location-based educational mobile games (Cogoi, Sangiorgi, & Shahin; 2006; Schwabbe & Goth, 2005), games involving 'sightseeing' or 'touring' (Spikol & Milrad, 2008), and virtual reality games (Doswell & Harmeyer, 2007) – all of them designed to be played by players actively moving in the physical space.

MOBILE GAMING: SUPPLY AND DEMAND PERSPECTIVES

Prior results in the area of user adoption of mGaming indicate that customer demand could be uncertain (e.g. Maitland et al., 2005) and therefore the business models deployed could be unstable. However even back in 2002 Anckar and D'Incau considered interactive mGaming as one of the top applications consumers were likely to adopt. Confirming this earlier prediction in the last five years the mGaming market has shown significant growth with an increasing supply of new games including multiplayer environments and situation-aware scenarios (Soh & Tan, 2008). In order to uncover the issues related to the future development of mGaming and the potential for

Table 1. Mgaming supply: A reference model. (Adapted from Petrova & Qu, 2006)

Mobile Industry Players	
Service Supply	
Mobile Business Service Provision	Content aggregators
Mobile Service Aggregation	Mobile portal providers
Mobile Data Service Provision	Mobile network operators; second tier providers
Application Supply	
Mobile Application Development	Mobile application developers; mobile content developers
Mobile Platform / Middleware Development.	Platform / middleware developers and vendors
Infrastructure Supply	
Mobile Device Supply	Mobile equipment vendors and retailers
Mobile Network Supply	Technology platform and infrastructure vendors, mobile network operators

its wider adoption, in this section mGaming is investigated from two general perspectives: Supply (the service provision perspective) and demand (the customer perspective).

A Reference Model for Mobile Gaming Supply

Adapting the reference model proposed in (Petrova & Qu, 2006), the key players in the mGaming supply chain are classified in Table 1 according to their operational areas: infrastructure (networks and devices), application (platforms and applications), and service (business and data services, and service aggregation).

Network operators occupy the key position in the infrastructure supply area as access enablers; they also ensure the quality of the mGaming service when a permanent network connection is maintained, e.g. in real-time interactive games which may need greater bandwidth, connectivity across operators, and location information (De Souza e Silva, 2008; Paavilainen, 2002; 2004, p. 65). On their part device manufacturers provide devices with functionality and configuration supporting game playing such as 3G/4G and Java capability, a color screen able to display 3D imagery, large memory, and a fast processor (Leavitt, 2003).

The major players in the application supply area include game and platform developers. Currently used game development middleware platforms are iMode, SMS, WAP, J2ME, BREW. Windows CE and Symbian OS are examples of mobile operating systems. Technologies deployed to provide location information for location-aware games are typically Cell ID (where location information is supplied by the mobile network), and GPS or A-GPS (the mobile handheld device needs the ability to process data provided by the global Geo Positioning System, maintained by the USA Department of Defense). At present, game developers encounter challenges when trying to ensure game compatibility across technologies, platforms and contexts including language (Baldi & Thaung, 2002; Bhatia, 2005; Buellingen & Woerter, 2004; Finn, 2005; Paavilainen, 2004, p.68; Rashid et al., 2006).

Finally the service supply layers of the reference model comprise content aggregators such as I-play (http://www.iplay.com/) and eamobile (http://www.eamobile.com/Web/). The business model deployed may involve subscription-based payment (e.g. VodafoneLive!, at http://games.vodafone.co.nz/), or a third party payment gateway (e.g. In-Fusio, at http://www.in-fusio.com/start.php).

Industry players tend to operate across areas: For example the global telecommunications company Vodafone acts as a mobile network operator, as a mobile data service provider, and as a game portal. The decisions a company makes about their business model may also depend on the legislative environment which differs between the European and the Japanese, or the European and the American markets (Henten, Olesen, Saugstrrup, & Tan, 2004; Maitland et. al, 2005). A detailed profiling of market players and description of their roles can be found in (Kuo & Yu, 2006).

Mobile Gaming Adoption and Demand Drivers

Mobile entertainment application and services including mGaming have been studied using existing information technology adoption models (e.g. Carlsson et al., 2005; Pagani & Schipani, 2003). Other studies focus on social factors (e.g. Barnes & Huff, 2003; Pedersen, 2005), and on user role preferences (Pedersen, Methlie, & Thorbjornsen, 2002). Key influences derived both from prior work and from empirical studies were reported in (Baldi & Thaung, 2002) and in (Moore & Rutter, 2004). Kleijnen et al. (2003) studied specifically mGaming adoption by applying the diffusion of innovations theory and considered complexity, compatibility, relative advantage, and communicability as factors influencing user decision. Further, Kleijnen, de Ruyter and Wetzels (2004) found that game players perceived navigation, communicability, risk, and payment options as the most important adoption factors. More recently Soh and Tan (2008) classified adoption and use factors into three main groups: mobile device penetration, mobile device enhancement, and mobile network enhancement. A list the potential drivers of mGaming adoption from a mobile entertainment services perspective derived from the studies selected for this literature review and extending the summary found in (Petrova & Qu, 2006) is presented in Table 2.

Linking mGaming Supply and Demand

While separate investigations of the mobile gaming industry and the consumer market allow identification of industry roles and relationships, and drawing conclusions about customer attitudes and intentions, it is not always clear how findings about adoption factors may be used to influence the design of mobile games and mGaming services, and to link mGaming demand and supply.

Analyzing further the approaches to modeling adoption deployed in the empirical studies reviewed it can be seen that the potential drivers identified above underpin some of the independent variables used in the empirical models. These variable have been subsequently found to be factors influencing positively intention to use and / or adoption (Table 3, last two columns).

Mapping the factors onto the mGaming reference model as shown in the first column of Table 3 may help address the gap identified above and create a framework linking mGaming supply and demand. It is proposed that there are two important determinants of mobile gaming supply and demand, each related to the role of the mobile gamer as a customer in the business and interface/infrastructure supply areas:

i) Requirements related to customer personal, professional and social lifestyle as the demand is not only for a useful mGaming service but for games and a related service which are lifestyle compatible and may enhance its quality ('Lifestyle').

ii) Expectations for the quality of the service as customers are already sufficiently experienced in the use of the new technology, and demand not just easy to use, but more adaptable, transparent and personalized services ('Quality of Service').

It is proposed that mGaming supply chain players may need to consider customer lifestyle

Table 2. Potential drivers of mGaming adoption. Sources: a) Baldi & Thaung, 2002; b) Pedersen et al., 2002; c) Barnes & Huff, 2003; d. Kleijnen et al., 2003; e) Pagani & Schipani, 2003; f) Moore & Rutter, 2004; g) Carlsson et al., 2005; h) Pedersen, 2005; i) Soh & Tan, 2008. (Adapted from Petrova & Qu, 2006)

Driver		a	b	c	d	e	f	g	h	i
1	Fun / "killing time" application	a			a	a	a	a		
2	Usefulness	a	a	a	a	a	a	a	a	a
3	Economic environment	a		a					a	
4	Technical environment	a	a	a	a				a	a
5	Cost	a		a	a	a	a	a	a	
6	Social status	a	a	a	a	a	a	a	a	
7	Personalization	a	a			a				
8	Owners' identity	a	a	a	a		a	a		
9	Culture	a		a						
10	Subjective norms		a	a	a	a			a	
11	Attitude to new technology		a	a	a	a		a	a	
12	Age, gender	a		a		a	a			
13	Simplicity of use	a	a	a	a	a	a	a	a	
14	Privacy risk				a	a	a			
15	Security risk			a	a	a	a		a	
16	Accessibility, mobility	a		a	a		a	a		a
17	Saving time	a						a	a	
18	Interactive innovation	a		a	a					a

requirements and quality of service expectations as decision making factors influencing the design of their respective business models. While mGaming service providers need to focus predominantly on lifestyle requirements, network operators need to consider expectations about the quality of service. On the other hand intermediary industry players such as game developers and publishers may need to consider both determinants in decisions about mGaming application design and development.

Player Requirements and Game Design

Some recent empirical studies have investigated the lifestyle and quality of service perspectives of mGaming, including their social, demographic and technical aspects. This section provides a brief commentary and suggests recommendations for mobile game and mGaming service design.

Socializability

Petrova and Qu's (2007) study of attitudes towards mobile gaming among tertiary students (New Zealand) showed that the attitude to mobile gaming was closely related to the social lifestyle of players. 'Expressiveness' was perceived as the most significant motivator in playing. Being observed to play was construed as a way to communicate to others the player's identity. The authors suggested that player motivation could be enhanced by games designed to create societies of players.

Table 3. Mobile gaming demand and supply determinants. (Adapted from Petrova, 2007)

Determinant	Factor	Value Proposition
Business: Requirements related to lifestyle suitability and enhancement ('Lifestyle')	**Compatibility** (drivers 1, 2)	Playing a mobile game as an activity may meet the needs of a specific consumer group – for example commuters with time to spare.
	Facilitating conditions (drivers 3, 4)	Payment options, billing and support options may impact on users' willingness to adopt. Increased network capability supports adoption.
	Trialability (driver 5)	As playing games has generally a level of addictiveness, free trials may lead to "addiction" and subsequent adoption.
	Observability/communicability (driver 6)	Refers to the ability to communicate within a peer group and be observed playing which may be of social importance.
	Image (drivers 7,8)	The personalized use of a mobile phone may lend its owner status-related features..
	Normative beliefs (drivers 9,10,11)	Playing the same game as one's friends may facilitate social acceptance; social pressures influence customer perceptions and decision making, and facilitate building a critical mass of customers.
Infra-structure & interface: Expectations for navigation, speed, imagery, reliability ('Quality of Service')	**Self-Efficacy** (driver 12)	Technical services need to match the requirements and needs of different customer segments For example a large group of relatively older potential gamers may not be able to play due to device limitations.
	Complexity (driver 13)	The ease of use of an entertainment application is important as an enjoyable experience is expected. In mGaming clear navigation and simplified game structure influence positively response time and may have implications for the decision to play.
	Trust (drivers 14, 15)	Perceived fear of privacy invasion (e.g. in location-based games) and/or lack of security may influence consumer choice.
	Relative advantage (drivers 16, 17, 18)	The ubiquity and accessibility of mobile entertainment may satisfy the demand for a "killing time" and relaxing "fun" service – for example interactive and multi-player games.

Paul et al. (2008) studied the effect of social interactions on players of mobile games (Malaysia) and identified socialization factors in multiplayer online games including collaboration, competition, communication, and recommendation. The participants in the study were asked to design and then evaluate mobile games with enhanced socializing. The authors concluded that games which focused on social lifestyle (i.e. social status, peer acceptance, and sharing experiences) may enjoy a longer life-cycle and thus could be more profitable.

Player Background

In the empirical studies already cited authors have indicated that a correlation may exist between the type of the game and the player background.

For example, Paul et al. (2008) pointed out that socializing in the context of mobile games may make it necessary to design games fine tuned to meet the needs of the specific target group such as teenagers, or female players. Hashim, AbHamid and Wan Rozali (2007) established that both male and female students (Malaysia) were interested in playing while older students (at a higher level of education) were less likely to play an educational game. Petrova and Qu (2007) reported that male players were more likely to download games and play (and pay for) multiplayer games with contexts such as strategy, sports and action while female players were more likely to play simple games (e.g. puzzles and card games). Ha, Yoon and Choi (2007) found that gamers from different gender and age groups had different preferences with respect to enjoyment while playing, and that gamer behavior may have been was affected both by the attractiveness of the game played, and by demographics such as age and gender.

Mobile Game Design

Ha et al. (2007) found that games needed to be simpler rather than more complex in order to be widely accepted. However once players were satisfied with their game choice they would expect the infrastructure to support gaming seamlessly. The findings by Duh, Chen and Tan (2008) were similar. Their study of mobile gamers' preferences (in Singapore) with respect to the relationship between mobile game design and mobile phone interface identified issues with mGaming provision related to a 'mobile lifestyle'. For example games requiring significant level of eye-hand coordination were not always convenient to be played while moving; games designed with a hierarchy of difficulty levels may last too long to be completed within the time limits of a journey. The authors suggested that rather than supplying more advanced features, both mobile game and mobile phone design needed to fit in with players' usual behavior. Other issues related to quality of service included the lack of mobile devices with better display screens and navigation pads, and games in need of better visual controls.

In summary there is a need for a higher level of cooperation between game designers and phone manufacturers as phone design needs to meet the usability requirements of different games while game design need to consider the mobile phone form factor. With respect to customer requirements for mobile games and the related services there is a need to target a well defined market segment or a group of customers, with a design that is compatible with the group's demographic parameters, social norms and usual behavior. The service provided needs to be perceived as valuable in its context (e.g. entertainment, education, tourism).

FUTURE RESEARCH DIRECTIONS

The research reviewed earlier allows the creation of a picture of the future trends in mGaming supply and demand. Trends in mobile game development include games designed to be played on a smart phone with enhanced video and audio features, a smart navigation pad, intelligent game controls, and incorporating the use of the built-in camera. Future mobile games will facilitate communication within gaming groups and the building of social mobile networks. Massively multiplayer mobile online games utilizing high bandwidth (4G) technology, and location-aware augmented reality and pervasive games operating both in a virtual and the real world will be offered to socially connected mobile gamer communities. Mobile games are also likely to become very prominent in educational models.

The independent portal provider's role in the future is not certain as mobile network operators and mobile data service providers will continue to collaborate with game developers and offer both downloadable and online games as part of the overall service package. This may lead to changes in the mGaming value chain and may ultimately make mGaming more affordable. However content aggregators may start specializing in context-related games such as educational or tourism oriented ones and retain their position as publishers of specialized gaming software.

Directions for further research in the area include usability studies of mobile games, and empirical studies based on lifestyle and quality of service as independent variables influencing the adoption of next generation mobile games. Results from such studies may inform game and device design research by highlighting the specific requirements of mobile game players and the dynamics of their acceptance and user behavior.

CONCLUSION

The chapter explores mobile gaming from supply and demand perspectives. A reference model is used to classify the key participants in the mGaming supply chain. mGaming adoption drivers and factors identified in prior work are used to construct the global determinants of mGaming demand: Customer life style requirements, and customer expectations about the quality of the service. It is suggested that mobile game life cycle and mobile gaming profitability would improve if mobile game design addresses the specific lifestyle needs of the targeted customer group, with mobile devices and networks seamlessly supporting game features and providing transparent but efficient services including location identification and connectivity. Further empirical research in the area may include in-depth studies of next generation mobile game adoption and spread from the perspectives of lifestyle and quality of service and involving both customers and industry players as participants.

REFERENCES

Anckar, B., & D'Incau, D. (2002). Value-added services in mobile commerce: An analytical framework and empirical findings from a national consumer survey. In *Proceedings of the 35th Hawaii International Conference on System Sciences,* (pp. 1087-1096). New York: IEEE Press.

Baldi, S., & Thaung, H. P.-P. (2002). The entertaining way to m-commerce: Japan's approach to the mobile internet - a model for Europe? *Electronic Markets, 12*(1), 6–13. doi:10.1080/101967802753433218

Barnes, S. J. (2003). The mobile commerce value chain in consumer markets. In *m-Business: The strategic implications of wireless technologies,* (pp. 13-37). Burlington, MA: Butterworth-Heinemann.

Barnes, S. J., & Huff, S. L. (2003). Rising sun: iMode and the wireless Internet. *Communications of the ACM, 46*(11), 79–84. doi:10.1145/948383.948384

Bell, M., Chalmers, M., Barkhuus, L., Hall, M., Sherwood, S., Tennent, P., et al. (2006). Interweaving mobile games with everyday life. In *Proceedings of CHI 2006 - Games and Performances* (pp. 417-426). Perth, Australia: Murdock University Press.

Bhatia, S. (2005). Any port in a storm? Retrieved June 1, 2005, from http://mobenta.com/analysis/

Broll, W., Lindt, I., Herbst, I., Ohlenburg, J., Braun, A.-K., & Wetzel, R. (2008, July/August). Towards next-gen mobile AR games. *Computer Graphics and Applications, 28*(4), 40–48. doi:10.1109/MCG.2008.85

Buellingen, F., & Woerter, M. (2004). Development perspectives, firm strategies and applications in mobile commerce. *Journal of Business Research, 57*(12), 1402–1408. doi:10.1016/S0148-2963(02)00429-0

Carlsson, C., Hyvonen, K., Repo, P., & Walden, P. (2005). Asynchronous adoption patterns of mobile services. In *Proceedings of the 38th Annual Hawaii International Conference on Systems Sciences* (pp. 189a). New York: IEEE Press.

Chan, D. (2008). Convergence, connectivity, and the case of Japanese mobile gaming. *Games and Culture, 3*(1), 13–25. doi:10.1177/1555412007309524

Cogoi, C., Sangiorgi, D., & Shahin; K. (2006, November). mGBL – mobile game-based learning: perspectives and usage in learning and career guidance topics. *eLearning Papers, 1.* Retrieved December 2008, from http://www.elearningpapers.eu

De Freitas, S., & Griffiths, M. (2008). The convergence of mobile gaming practices with other media forms: What potential for learning? A review of the literature. *Learning, Media and Technology,* *33*(1), 11–20. doi:10.1080/17439880701868796

De Souza e Silva, A. (2008, Spring). Alien revolt (2005-2007): A case study of the first location-based mobile game in Brazil. *IEEE Technology and Society Magazine,* 18–28. doi:10.1109/MTS.2008.918036

Doswell, J., & Harmeyer, K. (2007). Extending the 'serious game' boundary: Virtual instructors in mobile mixed reality learning games. In *Proceedings of the Digital Game Research Association (DiGRA 2007) Conference* (pp. 524-529). New York: ACM Press.

Duh, H. B.-L., Chen, V. H. H., & Tan, C. B. Y. (2008). Playing different games on different phones: An empirical study o mobile gaming. In *Proceedings of the 10th ACM International Conference on Mobile HCI,* (pp. 391-394). New York: ACM Press.

Finn, M. (2005). Gaming goes mobile: Issues and Implications. *Australian Journal of Emerging Technologies and Society,* *39*(1), 32–42.

Fritsch, T., Ritter, H., & Schiller, J. (2006). User case study and network evolution in the mobile phone sector (A study on current mobile phone applications). In *Proceedings of the 2006 ACM SIGCHI International Conference on Advances in Computer Entertainment Technology,* (Article No. 10). New York: ACM Press.

Ha, I., Yoon, Y., & Choi, M. (2007). Determinants of adoption of mobile games under mobile broadband wireless access environment. *Informational and management,* *44*9(3), 276-286.

Hashim, H. A., Ab Hamid, S. H., & Wan Rozali, W. A. (2006). A Survey on mobile games usage among the institute of higher learning (IHL) students in Malaysia. In *Proceedings of the First IEEE International Symposium on Information Technologies and Applications in Education (ISITAE '07),* (pp. 40-44). New York: IEEE Press.

Henten, A., Olesen, H., Saugstrup, D., & Tan, S.-E. (2004). Mobile communications: Europe, Japan and South Korea in a comparative perspective. *Info,* *6*(3), 197–207. doi:10.1108/14636690410549534

Kleijnen, M. D., de Ruyter, K., & Wetzels, M. (2003). Factors influencing the adoption of mobile gaming services. In B. E. Mennecke & T. J. Strader (Eds.), *Mobile commerce: Technology, theory, and applications* (pp. 202-217). Hershey, PA: Idea Group Publishing.

Kleijnen, M., D., de Ruyter, K., & Wetzels, M. (2004). Consumer adoption of wireless services: Discovering the rules, while playing the game. *Journal of Interactive Marketing,* *18*(2), 51–61. doi:10.1002/dir.20002

Koivisto, E. M. I. (2006). Mobile Games 2010. *Proceedings of the 2006 International Conference on Game Research and Development* (pp. 1-2*).* New York: ACM Press.

Kuo, Y.-F., & Yu, C.-W. (2006). 3g telecommunication operators' challenges and roles: A perspective of mobile commerce value chain. *Technovation,* *26,* 1347–1356. doi:10.1016/j.technovation.2005.08.004

Leavitt, N. (2003). Will wireless gaming be a winner? *Computer,* *36*(1), 24–27. doi:10.1109/MC.2003.1160050

Macinnes, I., Moneta, J., Caraballo, J., & Sarni, D. (2002). Business models for mobile content: The case of m-games. *Electronic Markets,* *12*(4), 218–227. doi:10.1080/101967802762553477

Maintland, C. F., van de Kar, E. A. M., de Montalvo, U. W., & Bouwman, H. (2005). Mobile information and entertainment services; business models and service networks. *International Journal of Management and Decision Making, 6*(1), 47–64. doi:10.1504/IJMDM.2005.005965

Moore, K., & Rutter, J. (2004).Understanding consumers' understanding of mobile entertainment. In K. Moore & J. Rutter (Eds.), *Mobile Entertainment: User-Centred Perspective,* (pp. 49-65). Manchester, UK: ESRC CRIC (University of Manchester).

Paavilainen, J. (2002). Consumer mobile commerce. In *Mobile business strategies: Understanding the technologies and opportunities* (pp. 69-121). London: IT Press.

Paavilainen, J. (2004). *Mobile games: Creating business with Nokia N-Gage.* Boston: New Riders.

Pagani, M., & Schipani, D. (2003). Motivations and barriers to the adoption of 3G mobile multimedia services: An end user perspective in the Italian market. In M. Khosrow-Pour (Ed.) *Innovations through InformationTtechnology; Proceedings of the 2003 Information Resources Management Association International Conference (IRMA'03)* (pp.957-960). Hershey, PA: IRMA.

Paul, S. A., Jensen, M., Wong, C. Y., & Khong, C. W. (2008). Socializing in mobile games. In *Proceedings of the 3rd International Conference on Digital Interactive Media in Entertainment and Arts* (pp. 2-9). New York: ACM Press.

Pedersen, P. E. (2005). Adoption of mobile Internet services: An exploratory study of mobile commerce early adopters. *Journal of Organizational Computing and Electronic Commerce, 15*(3), 203–221. doi:10.1207/s15327744joce1503_2

Pedersen, P. E., Methlie, L. B., & Thorbjornsen, H. (2002). Understanding mobile commerce end-user adoption: a triangulation perspective and suggestions for an exploratory service evaluation framework. In *Proceedings of the 35th Annual Hawaii International Conference on System Science* (pp. 1079-1086).New York: IEEE Press.

Peppard, J., & Rylander, A. (2006). From value chain to value network: Insights for mobile operators. *European Management Journal, 24*(2-3), 128–141. doi:10.1016/j.emj.2006.03.003

Petrova, K. (2007) Understanding the success factors of mobile gaming. In D. Taniar (Ed.), *Encyclopaedia of Mobile Computing & Commerce", Vol. 1, Part M-Entertainment.* Hershey, PA: IGI Global.

Petrova, K., & Qu, H. (2006). Mobile gaming: a reference model and critical success factors. In M. Khosrow-Pour (Ed.), *Emerging Trends and Challenges in Information Technology Management: Proceedings of the 2006 Information Resources Management Association Conference (IRMA 2006),*(pp. 228-231). Hershey, PA: IRMA.

Petrova, K., & Qu, H. (2007). Playing mobile games: consumer perceptions. In J. Filipe, D. A. Marca, B. Shishkov, & M. van Sinderen (Eds.), *Proceedings of the Second International Conference on e-Business(ICE-B)* (pp. 209-214). New York: IEEE Press.

Rashid, O., Mullins, I., Coulton, P., & Edwards, R. (2006, January). Extending cyberspace: Location based games using cellular phones. *ACM Computers in Entertainment, 4*(1), Article 3C.

Schwabe, G., & Goth, C. (2005). Mobile learning with a mobile game: design and motivational effects. *Journal of Computer Assisted Learning, 21,* 204–216. doi:10.1111/j.1365-2729.2005.00128.x

Segatto, W., Herzer, E., Mazzotti, C. L., Bittencourt, J. R., & Barbosa, J. (2008). Mobio threat: A mobile game based on the integration of wireless technologies. *ACM Computers in Entertainment, 6*(3), No. 39.

Siau, K., Lim, E., & Shen, Z. (2001). Mobile commerce: Promises, challenges and research agenda. *Journal of Database Management, 12*(3), 4–13.

Soh, J. O. B., & Tan, B. C. Y. (2008). Mobile gaming. *Communications of the ACM, 51*(3), 35–39. doi:10.1145/1325555.1325563

Spikol, D., & Milrad, M. (2008). Combining physical activities and mobile games to promote novel learning practices. In *Proceedings of the Fifth IEEE International Conference on Wireless, Mobile, and Ubiquitous Technology in Education (WMUTE'08)* (pp. 31-38). New York: IEEE Press.

Wang, A. I., Øfsdahl, T., & Morch-Størstein, O. K. (2008). An evaluation of a mobile game concept for lectures. In *Proceedings of the 21ˢᵗ Conference on Software Engineering Education and Training* (pp. 197-204). New York: IEEE Press.

Wylie, C. G., & Coulton, P. (2006). Exergaming. In *Proceedings of the 2008 International Conference on Advances in Computer Entertainment Technology* (pp. 338-341), New York: ACM Press.

ADDITIONAL READING

Dholakia, R. R., & Dholakia, N. (2004). Mobility and markets: emerging outlines of m-commerce. *Journal of Business Research, 57*(12), 1391–1396. doi:10.1016/S0148-2963(02)00427-7

Funk, J. L. (2003). *Mobile Disruption: The technologies and applications driving the mobile Internet*. New Jersey: John Wiley & Sons.

Lee, C.-w., Hu, W.-C., & Yeh, J.-h. (2003). A system model for mobile commerce. *23rd International Conference on Distributed Computing Systems Workshops (CDCSW'03)*, p. 634.

Natsuno, T. (2003). *I-Mode strategy*. Chichester, England: Wiley.

Nysveen, H., Pedersen, P. E., & Thorbjornsen, H. (2005). Intention to use mobile services: Antecedents and cross-service comparisons. *Journal of the Academy of Marketing Science, 33*(3), 330–346. doi:10.1177/0092070305276149

Sarker, S., & Wells, J. D. (2003). Understanding mobile handheld device use and adoption. *Communications of the ACM, 46*(12), 35–39. doi:10.1145/953460.953484

Shchiglik, C., Barnes, S., Scornavacca, E., & Tate, M. (2004). Mobile entertainment service in New Zealand: An examination of consumer perceptions towards games delivered via the wireless application protocol. *International Journal of Services and Standards, 1*(2), 155–171. doi:10.1504/IJSS.2004.005694

Van de Kar, E., Maitland, C. F., de Montalvo, U. W., & Bouwan, H. (2003). Design guidelines for mobile information and entertainment services: Based on the Radio 538 ringtunes I-mode service case study. *Proceedings of the 5th International Conference on Electronic commerce (ICEC '03)*, 413-417.

Varshney, U., & Vetter, R. (2002). Mobile commerce: Framework, applications and networking Support. *Mobile Networks and Applications, 3*(7), 185–187. doi:10.1023/A:1014570512129

Venkatesh, V., Morris, M. G., Davis, G. B., & Davis, F. D. (2003). User acceptance of information technology: Toward a unified view. *MISQ, 27*(3), 425–478.

KEY TERMS AND DEFINITIONS

4G (4th generation): An advanced wireless communication technology offering high quality of service, to become a future standard gradually replacing the currently considered best 3G technology.

Location Information: Information about the geographical position of an active mobile device which can be obtained independently of the mobile network via technologies such as GPS (Global Positioning Service), or can be supplied by the mobile network itself (e.g. using the Cell ID technology).

Location-Based Service (LBS): A mobile data service which needs and relies on location information, and which customers can access via a mobile devoice connected to a mobile network.

Mobile Application Development Platform: Software (middleware) which enables the development of applications supporting mobile connectivity (e.g. BREW, J2ME, WAP).

Mobile Commerce (mCommerce): A term referring to commercial transactions conducted over mobile access networks, including transfer of ownership of goods and the provision of services.

Mobile Game: A video game played on a mobile phone.

Mobile Gaming (mGaming): Playing a mobile game by one or more players.

Mobile Phone Form Factor: refers to the size, style, and other features of the mobile phone as a hardware object.

Mobile Platform: An operating system designed for and installed in a mobile device (e.g. Symbian OS, Windows CE).

Chapter 80
Role of Personal Innovativeness in Intentions to Adopt Mobile Services:
Cross–Service Approach

Sanna Sintonen
Lappeenranta University of Technology, Finland

Sanna Sundqvist
Lappeenranta University of Technology, Finland

INTRODUCTION

Because only a fraction of new service ideas are successful, and due to the turbulence and dynamics in mobile business markets, a thorough understanding of factors underlying mobile service adoption decisions is necessary. Use of mobile communications has been increasing extensively (Watson et al., 2002). Today, an extensive selection of mobile services is available to consumers. However, consumers use mobile devices mainly for simple services, like text messaging (Nysveen et al., 2005a). In order to better understand the acceptance of mobile services, it is necessary to study behavioral intentions (i.e. antecedents of actual adoption behavior) of consumers adopting new mobile services.

Consumer adoption behavior as a research topic has been given considerable notice, and several models have been provided to explain the behavioral intentions related to innovation adoption – also in the field of mobile communications. The background for these models exists in different fields of research and the theory base is rich: like the theory of planned behavior (TPB), technology acceptance model (TAM) and the diffusion of innovations (DOI) theory. Although these models have been useful in explaining behavioral intentions, several extensions have been proposed as it has been suggested that these basic models are too parsimonious. The present study follows this notion, and highlights the role of personal innovativeness in predicting consumers' adoption intentions. Personal innovativeness describes partly the personality of consumers, but is also attached to the technological

DOI: 10.4018/978-1-61520-611-7.ch080

domain. Personal innovativeness thus captures attitudinal influence toward adoption behavior, and may play a significant role in predicting adoption behavior.

The proposed model is based on TPB, TAM and DOI models as it investigates usage intentions via three overall influences: attitudinal influence (innovativeness), motivational influence (status image), and perceived control (willingness to pay). As mobile services differ in their characteristics (Hoffman & Novak, 1996), customers' intentions should be studied across service categories. Additionally, innovativeness should be seen as an individual characteristic which is invariant across different types of technology (Schillewaert et al., 2005). A cross service approach was chosen and the focus is on three sets of mobile services: mobile entertainment services, mobile services for everyday activities, and mobile notification services.

The purpose of this article is to contribute to the research on behavioral intentions to use mobile services. Key role is attributed to innovativeness in predicting mobile service adoption. The present study follows Nysveen et al.'s (2005a) proposition and integrates and updates TPB, TAM and DOI models. We hope to be able to provide a more nuanced understanding of consumers' motives for using mobile services by (1) studying motivational and attitudinal influences and consumers' perceived control, and (2) by studying the issue across three different mobile service categories. Additionally (3), we pay attention to the dual role of hardware (mobile phone) characteristics in adoption of related software (mobile services).

BACKGROUND

The theory of planned behavior (Ajzen, 1985), technology acceptance model (Davis, 1985) and the innovation diffusion theory (Rogers, 1983) are perhaps the most often applied models in predicting adoption behavior, as they provide a good starting point in investigating individual-level factors affecting the adoption of last-mile technology (Oh et al., 2003). Comparison of these theories (Figure 1) reveals that TPB and TAM both focus on predicting behavioral intention and actual behavior, whereas DOI and TAM share in common innovation related perceptions that are formed by the individual, and which are critical for the innovation adoption. Thus, further focus is given on three sets of variables: attitudinal, motivational and behavioral.

Attitudinal Influences: Personal Innovativeness

Literature in marketing suggests that a key success factor of new product introduction is identification of those people who are the first to buy the product or service launched into markets (Flynn & Goldsmith, 1993). It is necessary that the innovation is adopted by these first individuals who have a characteristic that has come to be known as innovativeness. Innovativeness can be seen as a psychographic characteristic of individuals. Midgley and Dowling (1978) define consumer innovativeness as the degree to which an individual is receptive to new ideas and makes innovation decisions independently of the communicated experience of others (p. 236). Yi et al. (2006) describe innovative adopters in their study as follows:

You buy into a new product's concept very early in its life cycle. You find it easy to imagine, understand and appreciate the benefits of a new technology and base buying decisions on this belief. You do not base these buying decisions on well established references, preferring instead to rely on intuition and vision. (Yi et al., p. 403)

Innovativeness thus reflects the consumers' openness toward new ideas and their willingness to be among the first ones to adopt innovations. Innovativeness is considered to be domain specific

Figure 1. The main concepts in the ground models

Theory base	Main concepts and their definitions
Theory of planned behaviour (TPB)	*Attitude toward the behaviour* The degree to which a person has a favourable or unfavourable evaluation or appraisal of the behaviour in question
	Subjective norm The perceived social pressure to perform or not to perform behaviour
	Perceived behavioural control The perception of the ease or difficulty of performing the behaviour of interest
Technology acceptance model (TAM)	*Perceived usefulness* The degree to which a technology is perceived as providing benefits in performing certain activities
	Perceived ease of use The extent to which a technology is perceived as being easy to understand and use
	Attitude The degree of evaluative affect that an individual associates with using the target system in his or her job
Diffusion of innovation (DOI)	*Relative advantage* The degree to which an innovation is perceived better than the idea it supersedes
	Observability The degree to which results of an innovation are visible to others
	Compatibility The degree to which an innovation is perceived as being consistent with existing values, past experiences, and needs of potential adopters
	Complexity The degree to which an innovation is perceived as difficult to understand and use
	Trialability The degree to which an innovation may be experimented with on a limited basis

(Agarwal & Prasad, 1998). Domain-specific innovativeness has been successfully used for detecting innovation adopter categories (Goldsmith, 2001; Goldsmith et al., 1998). Prior research (Yi et al., 2006) has shown that domain specific personal innovativeness predicts well innovation adoption behavior. As domain specific constructs (both at product and product category level) are highly associated with concrete behaviors (Goldsmith et al., 1995), it is hypothesized that:

H1: Personal innovativeness is positively related to the adoption of mobile services.

Rogers' (1983) original definition of innovativeness which was based on time of adoption view, offers a possibility to approach the adopter categories. In this view innovativeness was seen as the degree to which an individual is relatively earlier in adopting new ideas than other members of a system. According to Rogers' (1983), the compelling reason to buy for innovators and early adopters is either technological novelty or the real benefits. Price is not critical to them and they are often said to be willing to pay more. In a recent empirical study, Hsu and Shiue (2008) found that in computer software industry novelty seeking behaviors, i.e. innovativeness is positively related to consumers' willingness to pay. Thus, we can also propose an indirect influence through willingness to pay:

H2: The higher the personal innovativeness the higher the willingness to pay more for new mobile services.

Motivational Influences: Image

The role of mobile phone has changed as the penetration rates have risen. The phone is no more acquired just for phone calls, instead it provides multiple purposes for use. The mobile phone is a highly personal medium (Barwise & Strong, 2002), and is a kind of status symbol that represents one type of motivational influence (see Nysvenn et al., 2005a). Innovation literature very often discusses perceived innovation characteristics, and several concepts related to perceived innovation characteristics have been introduced over the time. For example, Moore and Benbasat (1991) extended the work of Rogers and added image construct. Perceived image represents the degree to which an individual believes that an innovation will bestow them with added prestige or status in their relevant community (Plouffe et al., 2001, p.68). Considering the nature of mobile communications and the stage of its diffusion, the spectrum of mobile phone models turns our focus on the image status that the mobile phone brings. It is not uncommon that new mobile phone models are launched in fashion shows together with new clothing designs. Lu et al. (2005) reported that in many Asian countries young people treat smart phones as new fashions items. However, innovation adoption studies have not paid much attention to the role of image. Few researchers have included the perception of image in their research models. For instance, image was found to be a positive determinant of perceived usefulness (Chan & Lu, 2004), and to increase the adoption intentions of internet banking. An indirect positive effect of image on virtual banking adoption has also been proposed by Liao et al. (1999). As image represents one type of relative advantage and thus reflects adopters' motivational state, it is proposed that

H3: The more important the innovation's motivational influence (i.e. image), the stronger the adoption intention.

Innovation adoption may follow belief-attitude-intention causal flow. Innovativeness represents consumers' attitudinal level toward adopting innovations, and in relation to this causal flow, it is assumed that image is one kind a 'belief' of an innovation. We thus follow the notion of Nysveen et al. (2005a), who suggested that motivational factors' effect on intention may be mediated by attitudinal factors, like innovativeness. Therefore we propose:

H4: Motivational influence has a positive effect on attitudinal factors (here consumer's personal innovativeness).

Perceived Control: Willingness to Pay

Perceived behavioral control is related to the extent to which consumers believe that skills, resources, and opportunities are present to perform the required behavior (Mathieson, 1991). Nysveen et al. (2005a) have also highlighted the role of individual user's economy in perceived control issues. In technology-mediated environments, consumers are concerned about the amount of control that can be exerted (Kang et al., 2006). Consumers face different control issues when adopting mobile technology and new mobile services. These concerns are particularly fed by consumers' apprehension about financial costs of using such services. Besides ensuring that the phone model meets the needs for advanced mobile services, the individual must have necessary financial resources to prepare for increasing costs. Hence, perceived control is related to the general assessment of whether or not the entire costs of using mobile services can be controlled by the consumer.

Willingness to pay (WTP) has been utilized by economists, psychologists, and marketing researchers in evaluating the demand for innovations (Wertenbroch & Skiera, 2002). In recent studies, Kim et al. (2007) considered the financial aspect of the consumer perception of the costs related

Figure 2. Research model

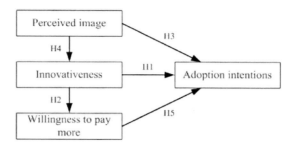

to mobile internet, and Shih (2004) compared the user acceptance of physical and digital products and online services, and suggested that the access cost influenced negatively only in the case of online services. When it comes to mobile services, WTP concept is multifaceted as the necessary financial sacrifice is binary: the device related costs and the continuous costs depending on the service usage. Following the main studies in the field, we hypothesize:

H5: The more a consumer is willing to pay for the innovation, the more likely he/she is to adopt it.

The research model (Figure 2) examines motivational, attitudinal and behavioral factors and suggests that innovativeness has a central role in predicting the adoption behavior.

UNDESTANDING INTENTIONS TO ADOPT MOBILE SERVICES

Data and Measurement

The data was collected in Germany, and 1454 eligible responses were obtained (see descriptive information in Figure 3).

The statements that reflected innovativeness and image were measured with a six point Likert-scale ranging from 1="that is perfectly applicable to me" to 6="that does not apply to me at all". The willingness to pay more for services was reflected with two indicators. The first captures how much the customer is willing to pay for mobile phone usage including new services and the second measure captured the absolute upper limit of mobile phone usage costs. The target variables in the interest were future intentions to use different mobile services. A six point Likert-scale ranging from 1="very interested" to 6="not interested at all" measured individuals' intentions to use new services. Confirmatory factor analysis was

Figure 3. Descriptive information of the respondents

Age	(%)	Level of education	(%)	Gender	(%)	Income	(%)
Under 20 years	25.4	Primary school	24.2	Male	51.5	< 2000 DM	5.7
20 to 35 years	31.4	Further schooling	38.0	Female	48.5	2001 – 3000 DM	12.1
36 to 50 years	31.2	High-school diploma	21.6			3001 – 4000 DM	17.3
Over 50 years	18.0	Study at a university	15.7			4001 – 5000 DM	19.3
						5001 – 6000 DM	14.9
						> 6001 DM	30.6

Figure 4. Scale statistics

Items*	Confirmatory factor analysis		Summated scale statistics				Error variance
	Loading	Error variance	CR	AVE	Mean*	Std dev*	
Intention: entertainment services							
entertainment1	.729	.469	.822	.540	4.494	1.382	.339
entertainment2	.762	.420					
entertainment3	.589	.653					
entertainment4	.838	.298					
Intention: services for everyday activities							
everyday1	.653	.574	.803	.404	3.759	1.427	.309
everyday2	.630	.603					
everyday3	.647	.582					
everyday4	.63	.603					
everyday5	.648	.58					
everyday6	.607	.632					
Intention: notification services							
notification1	.651	.576	.689	.428	2.670	1.246	.484
notification2	.750	.438					
notification3	.546	.702					
Innovativeness							
innovativeness1	.692	.522	.773	.461	3.761	1.144	.298
innovativeness2	.662	.562					
innovativeness3	.607	.631					
innovativeness4	.747	.442					
Image							
image1	.661	.562	.570	.400	4.165	1.458	.914
image2	.601	.639					
Willingness to pay more							
paymore1	.709	.498	.791	.657	115.580	112.850	.190
paymore2	.901	.188					
*The full items are available from authors on request.			*Computed from unstandardized values.				

conducted to verify the measurement model (see Figure 4). Future services included three separate categories: entertainment services (e.g. music downloads), services related everyday activities (e.g. banking) and notification services (e.g. location based alerts). The suggested research model was tested with structural equation modeling. In order to simplify the modeling procedure, summated scale were computed for each latent variable from its indicators. The error term variance for each was retrieved from the summated scale variance and latent variable's construct reliability (Fisher & Price, 1992; Bagozzi & Heatherton, 1994; Childers et al., 2001).

Path Analytic Assessment of Intention to Adopt Mobile Services

Figure 5 summarizes the results for the path coefficients and goodness of fit statistics for the models. The goodness of fit statistics were the same for all three model, and they suggested that the

model had an excellent fit to the data (χ^2=.6565, p=.418, df=1, NFI=.999, NNFI=1.003, GFI=1.00, AGFI=.998).

Based on the results, the hypothesized models succeeded rather well in explaining the intentions to adopt mobile services in the cases of entertainment and everyday activities. Considering the hypotheses, innovativeness was a significant predictor of intentions, thus H1 can be accepted. This relationship between innovativeness and adoption intentions is well established also in prior studies. For example, Mort and Drennan (2005) found statistically significant relationship in innovativeness and intentions to use mobile life enhancers. The second hypothesis discussed the willingness to pay more for mobile services and whether innovativeness has a positive influence on it. Based on the structural model, it can be said that higher innovativeness increases consumers' willingness to make higher financial sacrifices, thus supporting the hypothesis H2. The negative path coefficient between innovativeness and

Figure 5. Path coefficients

Path	Intention: Notification services $R^2=.168$	Intention: Entertainment services $R^2=.302$	Intention: Services for everyday activities $R^2=.339$
H1: innovativeness → intention	.370*	.221*	.459*
H2: innovativeness → willingness to pay more	-.271*	-.271*	-.271*
H3: image → intention	-.035	.312*	.014
H4: image → innovativeness	.646*	.646*	.646*
H5: willingness to pay more → intention	-.142*	-.168*	-.242*
* p<.001			

willingness to pay more is caused by the coding, i.e. lower values indicate higher innovativeness. Rogers (1983) proposed already in early 80's that innovativeness (namely innovators) and willingness to pay (personal income) are positively related. This view is supported in a review by Martinez and Polo (1996). Our results thus strongly support previous research findings from other fields. Our results indicate the hypothesis H3 holds only for the entertainment services, i.e. the higher social prestige coming along with the mobile phone is important only with entertainment services such as music downloads and games. This inclusion of diffusion related variables into TAM model was also supported by a recent study (see López-Nicolás et al., 2008). However, contrary to expectations prior research on adoption intentions of wireless Internet services via mobile technology (see Lu et al., 2005) has not found a direct effect of social prestige to adoption intentions. Lu et al. (2005) proposed that the effect of social influences on adoption intentions are mediated through perceived usefulness and perceived ease of use. The hypothesis H4 suggested that the motivational influence of image related to the mobile phone has a positive influence on domain-specific innovativeness, and based on the results this hypothesis can be accepted. This result is inline with Nysveen et al. (2005a), who originally proposed this relationship. Results reveal that consumers' willingness to pay more increased intentions to adopt all three types of services; the hypothesis H5 is thus accepted. The negative path coefficient

between WTP and adoption intentions is here also caused by the coding of intention, i.e. lower values indicate higher intentions. Also this result is inline with existing studies. For example, Sultan (2002) found that consumers' willingness to pay for internet services was highest in the early phases of adoption life cycles.

FUTURE RESEARCH DIRECTIONS

Limitations and future research are considered collectively because the limitations of any study may be the most efficient method for identifying future opportunities for research. The present study examined three service categories, but for instance, the adoption rates of mobile internet were not yet available, and therefore more research is needed to cover the diffusion of mobile internet and different services that come along with it. Additionally, the present model focused only on a set of variables under each main theoretical model (TPB, TAM, DOI). Thus, future studies should also pay more attention to concepts like role of normative pressure (e.g. Ajzen, 1991; Lu et al., 2005) in adopting mobile services and the interplay between service and hardware characteristics. For segmentation purposes, it would be fruitful to assess the demographic influences on the adoption of mobile services. For instance, age, gender and income could be relevant background variables and have significant effects across different types of services (e.g. Hung et al., 2003;

Nysveen et al., 2005b). Also including person's technological readiness (see e.g. Parasuraman, 2002) might offer interesting results.

CONCLUSION

The business field related to mobile phones is currently turning from selling the subscriptions to the content site with a wide variety of mobile services. Thus, understanding the adoption intention of mobile services is crucial for companies operating in mobile communications industry. Our model assessed three set of factors: motivational, attitudinal and behavioral. They all are important predictors of the adoption of mobile services. However, when predicting the adoption of mobile entertainment services, motivational factors, like image, become crucial. Based on the empirical evidence, it can be seen that the phone model has a binary role in service adoption. First, it is a necessity as there is still divergence in their applicability for different purposes of use. Secondly, it might be that since mobile services might be invisible to others, the image characteristic of the hardware i.e. mobile phone becomes more important in reflecting certain lifestyles or other psychographics. Mobile telecommunication operators and service providers should take these findings into account if they want to distinguish themselves in a highly competitive market.

REFERENCES

Agarwal, R., & Prasad, J. (1998). A Conceptual and Operational Definition of Personal Innovativeness in the Domain of Information Technology. *Information Systems Research*, *9*(2), 204–215. doi:10.1287/isre.9.2.204

Ajzen, I. (1985). From Intentions to Actions: A Theory of Planned Behavior. In J. Kuhl & J. Beckmann (Eds.), *Action Control: From Cognition to Behavior* (pp. 11-39). Heidelberg, Germany: Springer.

Ajzen, I. (1991). The Theory of Planned Behavior. *Organizational Behavior and Human Decision Processes*, *50*, 179. doi:10.1016/0749-5978(91)90020-T

Bagozzi, R. P., & Heatherton, T. F. (1994). A General Approach to Representing Multifaceted Personality Constructs: Application to State Self-Esteem. *Structural Equation Modeling*, *1*(1), 35–67. doi:10.1080/10705519409539961

Barwise, P., & Strong, C. (2002). Permission-based Mobile Advertising. *Journal of Interactive Marketing*, *16*, 14–24. doi:10.1002/dir.10000

Boccaletti, S., & Nardella, M. (2000). Consumer Willingness to Pay for Pesticide-free Fresh Fruit and Vegetable in Italy. *International Food and Agribusiness Management Review*, *3*, 297–310. doi:10.1016/S1096-7508(01)00049-0

Chan, S.-C., & Lu, M.-T. (2004). Understanding Internet Banking Adoption and Use Behavior: A Hong Kong Perspective. *Journal of Global Information Management*, *12*(3), 21–43.

Childers, T. L., Carr, C. L., Peck, J., & Carson, S. (2001). Hedonic and Utilitarian Motivations for Online Retail Shopping Behavior. *Journal of Retailing*, *77*, 511–535. doi:10.1016/S0022-4359(01)00056-2

Davis, F. D. (1985). *A Technology Acceptance Model for Empirically Testing New End-User Information Systems: Theory and Results*. Unpublished doctoral dissertation, Massachusetts Institute of Technology, Massachusetts.

Fisher, R. J., & Price, L. L. (1992). An Investigation into the Social Context of Early Adoption Behavior. *JMR, Journal of Marketing Research, 19*(3), 477–486.

Flynn, L. R., & Goldsmith, R. E. (1993). Identifying Innovators in Consumer Service Markets. *The Service Industries Journal, 13*(3), 97–106. doi:10.1080/02642069300000052

Fu, T.-T., Liu, J.-T., & Hammitt, J. K. (1999). Consumer Willingness to Pay for Low-pesticide Fresh Produce in Taiwan. *Journal of Agricultural Economics, 50*, 220–233.

Goldsmith, R. E. (2001). Using the Domain Specific Innovativeness Scale to Identify Innovative Internet Consumers. *Internet Research, 11*(2), 149–158. doi:10.1108/10662240110695098

Goldsmith, R. E. (2002). Explaining and Predicting Consumer Intention to Purchase over the Internet: An Exploratory Study. *Journal of Marketing Theory and Practice, 10*(2), 22–28.

Goldsmith, R. E., d'Hauteville, F., & Flynn, L. R. (1998). Theory and Measurement of Consumer Innovativeness. *European Journal of Marketing, 32*(3/4), 340–353. doi:10.1108/03090569810204634

Goldsmith, R. E., Freiden, J. B., & Eastman, J. K. (1995). The Generality/Specificity Issue in Consumer Innovativeness Research. *Technovation, 15*(10), 601–612. doi:10.1016/0166-4972(95)99328-D

Hoffman, D. L., & Novak, T. P. (1996). Marketing in Hypermedia Computer-Mediated Environments: Conceptual Foundations. *Journal of Marketing, 60*(July), 50–68. doi:10.2307/1251841

Hsu, J. L., & Shiue, C. W. (2008). Consumers' Willingness to Pay for Non-pirated Software. *Journal of Business Ethics, 81*, 715–732. doi:10.1007/s10551-007-9543-9

Hung, S.-Y., Ku, C.-Y., & Chang, C.-M. (2003). Critical Factors of WAP Services Adoption: An Empirical Study. *Electronic Commerce Research and Applications, 2*(1), 42–60. doi:10.1016/S1567-4223(03)00008-5

Kang, H., Hahn, M., Fortin, D. R., Hyun, Y. J., & Eom, Y. (2006). Effects of Perceived Behavioral Control on the Consumer Usage Intention of e-Coupons. *Psychology and Marketing, 23*, 841–864. doi:10.1002/mar.20136

Kim, H.-W., Chan, H. C., & Gupta, S. (2007). Value-Based Adoption of Mobile Internet: An Empirical Investigation. *Decision Support Systems, 43*, 111–126. doi:10.1016/j.dss.2005.05.009

Liao, S., Shao, Y. P., Wang, H., & Chen, A. (1999). The Adoption of Virtual Banking: An Empirical Study. *International Journal of Information Management, 19*(1), 63–74. doi:10.1016/S0268-4012(98)00047-4

López-Nicolás, C., Molina-Castillo, F. J., & Bouwman, H. (2008). An Assessment of Advanced Mobile Services Acceptance: Contributions from TAM and Diffusion Theory Models. *Information & Management, 45*(6), 359–364. doi:10.1016/j.im.2008.05.001

Lu, J., Yao, J. E., & Yu, C.-S. (2005). Personal Innovativeness, Social Influences and Adoption of Wireless Internet Services via Mobile Technology. *The Journal of Strategic Information Systems, 14*, 245–268. doi:10.1016/j.jsis.2005.07.003

Martinez, E., & Polo, Y. (1996). Adopter Categories in the Acceptance Process for Consumer Durables. *Journal of Product and Brand Management, 5*(3), 34–47. doi:10.1108/10610429610126560

Mathieson, K. (1991). Predicting User Intentions: Comparing the Technology Acceptance Model with the Theory of Planned Behavior. *Information Systems Research, 2*, 173–191. doi:10.1287/isre.2.3.173

Midgley, D. F., & Dowling, G. R. (1978). Innovativeness: The Concept and Its Measurement. *The Journal of Consumer Research, 4*(4), 229–242. doi:10.1086/208701

Moore, G. C., & Benbasat, I. (1991). Development of an Instrument to Measure the Perceptions of Adopting an Information Technology Innovation. *Information Systems Research, 2*(3), 192–222. doi:10.1287/isre.2.3.192

Mort, G. S., & Drennan, J. (2005). Marketing m-services: Establishing a Usage Benefit Typology Related to Mobile User Characteristics. *Journal of Database Marketing & Customer Strategy Management, 12*, 327–341. doi:10.1057/palgrave.dbm.3240269

Nysveen, H., Pedersen, P. E., & Thorbjørnsen, H. (2005a). Intentions to Use Mobile Services: Antecedents and Cross-Service Comparison. *Journal of the Academy of Marketing Science, 33*(3), 330–346. doi:10.1177/0092070305276149

Nysveen, H., Pedersen, P. E., & Thorbjørnsen, H. (2005b). Explaining Intention to Use Mobile Chat Services: Moderating Effects of Gender. *Journal of Consumer Marketing, 22*(4/5), 247–256. doi:10.1108/07363760510611671

Oh, S., Ahn, J., & Kim, B. (2003). Adoption of Broadband Internet in Korea: The Role of Experience in Building Attitudes. *Journal of Information Technology, 18*, 267–280. doi:10.1080/0268396032000150807

Parasuraman, A. (2002). Technology Readiness Index (TRI): A Multiple-Item Scale to Measure Readiness to Embrace New Technologies. *Journal of Service Research, 2*, 307–320. doi:10.1177/109467050024001

Plouffe, C. R., Vandenbosch, M., & Hulland, J. (2001). Intermediating Technologies and Multi-Group Adoption: A Comparison of Consumer and Merchant Intentions Toward a New Electronic Payment System. *Journal of Product Innovation Management, 18*(2), 65–81. doi:10.1016/S0737-6782(00)00072-2

Rogers, E. M. (1983). *Diffusion of Innovations,* (3rd ed.). New York: Free Press.

Schillewaert, N., Ahearne, M. J., Frambach, R. T., & Moenaert, R. K. (2005). The Adoption of Information Technology in the Sales Force. *Journal of Marketing Management, 34*, 323–336.

Shih, H.-P. (2004). An Empirical Study on Predicting User Acceptance of E-Shopping on the Web. *Information & Management, 41*(3), 351–368. doi:10.1016/S0378-7206(03)00079-X

Sultan, F. (2002). Consumer Response to the Internet: An Exploratory Tracking Study of On-line Home Users. *Journal of Business Research, 55*(8), 655–663. doi:10.1016/S0148-2963(00)00206-X

Watson, R. T., Leyland, F. P., Berthon, P., & Zinkhan, G. M. (2002). U-Commerce: Expanding the Universe of Marketing. *Journal of the Academy of Marketing Science, 30*(4), 333–347. doi:10.1177/009207002236909

Wertenbroch, K., & Skiera, B. (2002). Measuring Consumers' Willingness to Pay at the Point of Purchase. *JMR, Journal of Marketing Research, 39*, 228–241. doi:10.1509/jmkr.39.2.228.19086

Yi, M. Y., Fiedler, K. D., & Park, J. S. (2006). Understanding the Role of Individual Innovativeness in the Acceptance of IT-based Innovations: Comparative Analyses of Models and Measures. *Decision Sciences, 37*(3), 393–426. doi:10.1111/j.1540-5414.2006.00132.x

KEY TERMS AND DEFINITIONS

Adoption Intention: individual's readiness to perform a given behavior. Here readiness to buy mobile services.

Attitudinal Influence: consumer's attitudinal stage towards adopting innovations. Is illustrated here via personal domain specific innovativeness.

Image: a type of perceived innovation characteristic and consumer's motivational stage and is assumed to have positive relationship with adoption intentions.

Innovation: an object (service) which is perceived as new by an individual consumer. Here mobile services.

Motivational Influence: motivational influence composes of several elements like expressiveness and is believed to encourage adoption intentions.

Perceived Control: a belief that one has on influencing on a certain event. Here belief of consumer's financial resources effect on adopting new mobile services.

Perceived Innovation Characteristics: consumer's beliefs concerning important attributes of an innovation. Here perceived image that consumer gets by using new mobile services.

Personal Domain Specific Innovativeness: reflection of consumer's openness toward new ideas and willingness to be among the first ones to adopt mobile communications innovations.

Willingness to Pay: consumer's perceived control towards adoption of innovations, namely mobile services.

Chapter 81
Service Discovery Techniques in Mobile E-Commerce

Nandini Sidnal
K.L.E.S. College of Engineering and Technology, India

Sunilkumar S. Manvi
Reva Institute of Technology and Management, India

ABSTRACT

With the rising number of web services in mobile E-commerce, service discovery has become an important feature in the future of E-commerce for mobile users. A service in the network can be any software or hardware entity that a user might be interested to utilize. Service discovery is the action of finding appropriate service provider for a requested service. When the location of the demanded service (typically the address of the service provider catering services such as shopping, auctions, edutainment, etc.) is retrieved, the user may further access the service and use it. Service discovery is an emerging field in the area of ubiquitous and pervasive computing owing to its mobile devices with limited resources. There are various service discovery techniques and protocols (proposed or/and already implemented) particularly tailored to specific set of objectives. With service discovery, devices may automatically discover network services including their properties, and services may advertise their existence in a dynamic way. This chapter discusses various mobile E-commerce issues with major focus on service discovery issue. It elaborates on syntax and semantic based various service discovery mechanisms and concludes with future directions to service discovery mechanism.

MOBILE E-COMMERCE

Mobile E-commerce is trading of goods, services or information irrespective of location, using hand held devices for communication between all necessary parties to complete the necessary transactions in a wireless environment mostly through the Web. Today's technology has advanced to a state, that hand held devices not only register the names and numbers but also track the user location and are a substitute for wallets and credit cards, in future they are bound to replace and go further, that they may

DOI: 10.4018/978-1-61520-611-7.ch081

very well turn into intelligent assistants capable of anticipating many of the wishes and needs, such as automatically arranging for taxis to come and pick after business meetings or providing with summaries of relevant news and messages left by colleagues. But, for all these changes to happen, key issues of interoperability, usability, security, and privacy, one need to be continuously updated. **Mobile e-commerce** facilitates mobile application services like banking, payment, auctioning, ticketing etc.

The attributes of **mobile e-Commerce** as discussed in (Varshney, 2003) are ubiquity, convenience, connectivity, personalization, localization, automation and adaptation. Ubiquity: easier information access in real-time anywhere anytime since user devices are portable and mobile. Convenience: devices that store data and have Internet connections. Instant connectivity: easy and quick connection to Internet and other mobile devices and databases. Personalization: preparation of information for individual consumers as per their needs. Localization of products and services: knowing where the user is located at any given time and match service to them and provide quality services. Automation: Proactive services to be provided. Adaptation and intelligence: **Context** aware operations to be handled in the changing market environment.

Quality characteristics as defined (Nandini &Sunilkumar, 2009) that model attributes of **mobile E-commerce** system are as follows.

- Reliability: refers to a set of attributes that bear on the capability of the software to maintain its performance level under stated conditions for stated period of time.
- Functionality: refers to a set of functions and specified properties that satisfy stated or implied needs. It also refers to the existence of these functions and services that support end users interaction via the mobile system.
- Efficiency: capability of the system to provide appropriate performance relative to the amount of resources used under stated conditions.
- Scalability: the performance of the system should be the same even with the increase in network traffic.
- Flexibility: The system must be able to accommodate the dynamism in the E-market.

Following is the list of the **mobile e-commerce** applications (B2B, B2C) (Manvi, 2003) Mobile financial applications, Mobile advertising, Mobile inventory management / Product locating and shopping, Proactive service management, Wireless re-engineering, Mobile auction, Mobile entertainment services and games, Mobile office and Mobile distance education.

ISSUES IN MOBILE E-COMMERCE

The major issues in **mobile E-Commerce** can be broadly classified with respect to mobile devices, Wireless middleware and communications infrastructure (Hawick & James, 2004; Peter et al., 2002). Some of the issues with respect to mobile devices (Samaras, 2002) are as follows:

- Ultimate (physical) form(s) of mobile client devices
- Personalization of information presented to the user on mobile device
- Design of user interfaces for mobile devices that convey better required information, get the feedback from the user, facilitate customization and personalization.
- Design of applications for use on different mobile devices
- Acceptance of protocols or systems for mobile device communication.
- Mobile device upgradeability.
- Reduce processing power with usage of better processors that have clock rates suitable for computing applications on mobile devices.

- Accommodate or adapt the applications to suit the memory requirements of mobile devices.
- Design of file systems in mobile devices with limited memory available in handheld portable mobile devices.
- Limited input/output interface (screens, keyboards, etc):
- Limited battery life.

Wireless middleware is extremely important for developing new mobile commerce applications. Wireless middleware should have ability to hide the underlying network details from applications while providing a uniform and easy-to-use interface. While developing the wireless middleware the following issues are to be considered (Evans & Sarkar, 2004; Lei, 2002; Kalevi, 2001).

- Atomic transactions and synchronization of data.
- Low memory and adaptable operating system.
- Low cost and low memory requirements of encoding of the m-Commerce transactions.
- Specially designed browsers for mobile devices with functionalities including secured m-Commerce transactions.
- Data management and retrieval for location dependent services.
- Identity verification for secured payments and amount transfers by using biometrics or any other suitable techniques.
- **Service discovery** mechanisms to facilitate mobile users and reduce latency.
- Data security from viruses and intruders especially the m-Commerce contents such as inventory control operations, trading data, customers list, financial transactions, etc.

In **mobile E-Commerce**, service quality primarily depends on network resources and capabilities. The following are the communications infrastructure issues in **mobile E-Commerce**.

- Efficient usage of currently available limited bandwidth.
- Difficulties with mobile devices interfacing with multiple communications environments.
- Interoperability among communication technologies.
- Intelligent network routing to optimize the power and bandwidth resources.
- Frequent disconnections leads to discontinuous data transfer. Hence it is required to maintain continuous and seamless data transfer while moving from one network to another.
- Providing bounded end-to-end delays with minimum delay variations.
- Security for wireless transactions in wireless networks is important for maintaining data integrity and privacy.

SERVICE DISCOVERY ISSUE IN MOBILE E-COMMERCE

The process of obtaining a set of services which can possibly fulfill a user request is called **service discovery**. The general architecture of any **service discovery** is as follows: A service advertises and registers itself to a service register that keeps track of networked services. Services can de-register at any point of time. Figure 1 describes the process of **service discovery** and the entities involved. Each **service discovery** protocol (Marin-Perianu et al., 2005) consists of at least two basic participating elements: Client (or user)- the entity that is interested in finding and using a service, and Server- the entity that offers the service. Protocols may use service repositories to facilitate service mappings. Therefore, it is common to find a third participating entity called as directory. Directory

Figure 1. Generic service discovery process and entities

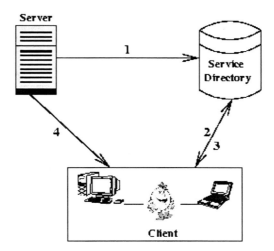

(or server, broker, central, resolver) is a node in the network that maintains service description information either partially or totally.

General **Service discovery** process can be explained in the following sequence:

1. The services are registered / deregistered in service directory.
2. The client requiring the service browses/queries to discover the services.
3. The client obtains the required service information from the service directory.
4. The client accesses the service from the server.

Web Services, by definition (Al-Masri & Mahmoud, 2008) are self-contained, self-describing applications that can be published, located and invoked remotely in a dynamic fashion over the Internet. This loosely coupled remote-service invocation capability has proven to be a particularly attractive proposition for e-commerce and business integration models. The introduction of software development via Web Services has been the most significant web engineering paradigm, in the recent years. The widely acknowledged importance of the Web Services' concept lies in

the fact that they provide a platform independent answer to the software component development question. The dependence on internet has increased as the number of internet enabled applications in **mobile E-commerce** is rising; proportionally the number of requests from the clients to access these services has also relatively increased. For any given **mobile E-commerce** application the requests from the clients are to be processed in shortest amount of time, with efficient use of available resources by the service provider, for which the web services need to be structured to reduce the service access time and increase the throughput of the system. **Service discovery** mechanisms are equally important as they have turned out as a challenging task in **mobile E-commerce**.

To access the web services through the mobile devices, services are to be mined in the network environment and placed in an appropriate database for flexible and adaptable accessibility. Mobile users are rarely aware of available web services that fulfill their current needs. Therefore, enhanced **service discovery** mechanisms are required, besides category or organization based search which are redundant in the mobile environment. **Service discovery** needs to find an appropriate service provider for every client request. Due to

Figure 2. Taxonomy of service discovery mechanisms

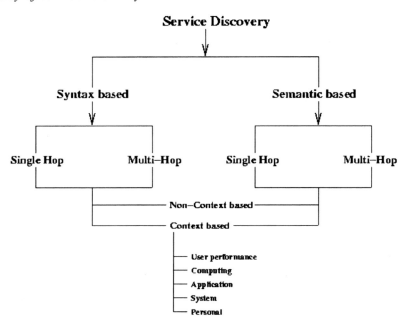

the limitations like processing and memory capabilities of the hand held devices, as the clients cannot keep the log of web services and requests, hence **service discovery** plays a vital role.

SERVICE DISCOVERY MECHANISMS

Service discovery plays a major role in the development and deployment of **mobile E-commerce** applications as they are web enabled. The two closely related tasks involved in a web **service discovery** are web service descriptions and techniques that are used to match service descriptions against the user requirements. The process in which the tasks are carried out gives rise to various **service discovery** architectures. The **service discovery** architectures depend on types of network, as each network is based on the assumptions suitable to them, the most important being the mobility and rate of joining and leaving of devices from the network. In the wired network, both the servers and the clients do not move at all and hence are not suitable for

mobile E-commerce. The classifications of the various **service discovery** mechanisms as per the taxonomy are as shown in Fig. 2.

One of the key objectives of the **service discovery** mechanisms in **mobile E-commerce** is to reduce the number of transmissions necessary to discover services in the users' devices so as to enhance the battery charge utility. This can be achieved by using aforesaid **context**s in matching process (Broens, 2004). In this section, first, **syntax** based **service discovery** mechanisms are elaborated and next the need and importance of **semantic service discovery** mechanism for **mobile E-commerce** are presented. Discussions on works or protocols for **service discovery** which are **context** aware for single hop networks, **semantic** based **service discovery** in non **context** based single hop networks and mechanisms under **Context** based single hop networks are not carried out as the contributions are not significant.

Syntax Based Service Discovery Mechanisms

In **syntax** based **service discovery** mechanisms, string matching technique is used to match the keywords in the user's query with service descriptions. These mechanisms are used when the number of web services are limited and the discovery process is manual. When there is an explosion in number of web services, matching with only keywords will not be adequate to get the desired results.

Non-Context Based Single Hop Networks

This section gives overview of some of the **syntax** based single hop **service discovery** mechanisms without considering the **context** in wireless networks. The DEAPspace group (Nidd, 2001) has proposed a solution to the problem of **service discovery** in pervasive systems without using a central server. A list of all known services called "world view" is present on all devices. Each device periodically broadcasts its "world view" to its neighbors, which update their "world view" accordingly.

Simple **service discovery** protocol (SSDP) (Goland, et al., 2009) is a lightweight discovery protocol for the Universal Plug and Play (UPnP) initiative, and it defines a minimal protocol for multicast-based discovery. SSDP can work with or without its central directory service, called the Service Directory. When a new service is to be added to the network, it has to multicast (one-to-many communications) an announcement message to notify its presence to the available devices including service directory. The service directory, if present, will record the announcement. Alternatively, the announcement may be sent through unicast (one-to-one communications) directly to the service directory. When a client wants to discover a service, it either searches in the service directory or sends a message through multicast.

Non-Context Based Multi-Hop Networks

The multi hop (also called as ad hoc networks) wireless category of **service discovery** mechanisms are compiled from (Outay et al., 2007), the ones where the service providers and clients are both mobile.

Overviews of some of these mechanisms are described in this section. Lightweight Overlay for **Service Discovery** in MANET (Lanes) is application layer overlay to discover services offered in a mobile ad hoc network (Klein et al., 2003). They offer a fault-tolerant and efficient structure, which can be used for **semantics**-based **service discovery**. Lanes are based on the Content Addressable Network (CAN). The basic concept of Lanes is a two-dimensional overlay structure, called lanes, where one dimension of the overlay propagates service advertisements; the other one distributes service requests.

Distributed **Service Discovery** Protocol (DSDP) is a distributed **service discovery** architecture which relies on a virtual backbone for locating and registering available services within a dynamic network topology (Kozat, 2003). Konark is a **service discovery** and delivery protocol designed specifically for mobile ad hoc networks and targeted towards device independent services (Helal, 2003). Konark assumes an IP level connectivity among devices in the network. To describe a wide range of services, Konark defines an XML-based description language, based on web **service discovery** language (WSDL), that allows services to be described in a tree based human and software understandable form. Service advertising and discovery can be done at any level of the tree, thus enables service matching at different stages of abstraction, from generic to very specific at the leaf of the tree. The service advertisements contain name and URL of the service, as well as time-to-live (TTL) information to help self-healing of the systems. The client peers can cache this service information to use it later so that they do not have to locate the services again. If no service information is cached for a desired service, a distributed pull method is used to retrieve the service location.

Secure **Service Discovery** Protocol is a dynamic **service discovery** infrastructure for small or medium size MANETs (Yuan & Arbaugh, 2003). The protocol allows finding, locating and evaluating services in vicinity required by client and fit for high dynamic environment without directory **agent** or central registry.

Context Based Multihop Networks

Context-aware **service discovery** has been addressed lately by several research initiatives that have proposed following enhanced discovery mechanisms. The work of (Robinson, 2005) describes a novel **context**-sensitive approach to **service discovery**, whereby queries and advertisements can be issued in a **context**-sensitive manner by using techniques such as query completion, query relaxation, preferences and query persistence.

Geography-based Content Location Protocol (GCLP) is a protocol for efficient content location in location-aware ad hoc networks (Tchakarov & Vaidya, 2004). The Protocol makes use of location information to lower proactive traffic, minimizing query cost and achieve scalability. GCLP assumes that all devices in the network know their own location. It makes use of this information to periodically advertise content to nodes along several geographical directions. Nodes that attempt to locate content need only contact one of these nodes to become aware of the presence of the desired content. A node can advertise its services by sending periodically update messages that follow a predefined trajectory through the network. This significantly decreases

the amount of proactive traffic as it is limited to nodes along the trajectories. Nodes along these trajectories cache the information received from the update messages. A client that wants to locate a service on the network sends out a query message that similarly propagates along predefined trajectories.

Alliance-based **Service Discovery** for mobile ad-hoc networks (MANET) is a peer-to-peer caching based and policy driven **service discovery** frame-work to facilitate **service discovery** in MANET (Ratsimor et al., 2002). The approach adopts structured compound formation of **agent** (a software **agent** is an autonomous program which is embedded with proactive decision making, adaptation, and intelligence) communities to the mobile environment and achieves high degree of flexibility in adapting itself to the changes of the ad-hoc environment. An alliance helps in **service discovery** and the alliance formation does not have the overhead of explicit leader election.

Context based **service discovery** as described in (Nandini & Sunilkumar, 2009) is a distributed system that provides the user with the ability to obtain services and information according to the **context** (location, time, situation, users, etc.). **Context** plays the role of a filtering mechanism, allowing only transmission of relevant data and services back to the device, thus saving bandwidth and reducing processing costs. The approach adopted here is the combination of **context**-aware computing and **agent** oriented computing, in order to provide better user tailored services in pervasive environments. **Agent**s have the advantage of being able to assist users, to discover and compose services. This helps with fast and autonomous adaptation to **context** changes.

The Cooltown project (Broens, 2004), focuses on expanding the view of physical entities to a virtual world of web content, in which people, places and things are web-present. The bottom layer of the architecture consists of mechanisms for obtaining points of interest (i.e. people, places, things) via discovery mechanisms. Discovery can take place by sensing the location of the points of interest (i.e. URL or ID from which a URL can be derived) via beacons. Cooltown's **service discovery** is location aware.

The discovery mechanism used in the **Context** Toolkit is centralized and facilitates development and deployment of **context**-aware applications. It uses only a single discoverer (i.e. central registry). When started, all components register with the discoverer at a known network address and port. The discoverer "pings" each registered component at a pre-specified frequency to ensure that each component is functioning correctly. Applications can discover services by using yellow and white page lookup mechanisms (Dey, 2001).

CB-Sec is an architecture developed to allow **service discovery** and its composition to derive the benefits from available **context** (Most´efaoui et al., 2003). It is based on mobile devices that not only consume web services, but also publish their data through web services. **Service discovery** is done by the **Context**-Based **Service Discovery** module (CSD). The request of the client is decomposed into basic services using UCMs (ubiquitous coordination model) social laws. Then the broker **agent** (i.e. another part of the CSD) retrieves **context** information from the **context** database. This information is used to discover the requested basic services closer to the user location.

Semantic Based Service Discovery

The syntactic discovery mechanisms (keyword-based) do not consider the **semantic**s of the requester's goals and service. They retrieve objects with descriptions that contain particular keywords from the user's request. In most of the cases, this leads to low recall and precision. In **semantic** based approach classification of the objects are based on their properties. This enables retrieval based on object types rather than keywords. Furthermore, they can specify the interrelations among **context** entities and ensure common, unambiguous representation of these entities.

Non Context Based Multihop Networks

The work in (Chakraborty et al., 2002) explains a group-based distributed **service discovery** protocol for mobile ad hoc networks. It is based on the concept of peer-to-peer caching of service advertisements and group-based intelligent forwarding of service requests to reduce the broadcast storm problem. It does not require a service to register to a lookup server. For service description the **semantic** capabilities offered by the DARPA **Agent** Markup Language (DAML) are used to effectively describe services and resources present in the network. The services present on the nodes are classified into hierarchical groups. Each node advertises its services to its neighbors within a defined number of hops. An advertisement also includes a list of the several service groups that the sender node has seen in its vicinity. This group information is used to intelligently select and forward a service request to other nodes in the network where there are chances of service availability. Thus, the **semantic** features present in DAML are used to reduce network flooding.

The project work DReggie as discussed in (Chakraborty et al., 2001) is an attempt to enhance the matching mechanisms in Jini and other **service discovery** systems. The key idea in DReggie is to enable these **service discovery** systems to perform matching based on **semantic** information associated with the services. In the DReggie system, a **service discovery** request contains the description of an "ideal" service - one whose capabilities match exactly with the requirements. Thus, matching involves comparison of requirements specified with the capabilities of existing services. Depending on the requirements, a match may occur even if one or more capabilities do not match exactly. Service descriptions in the DReggie system are marked up in DAML. The **semantic** matching process that uses these descriptions is performed by a reasoning engine.

Service discovery mechanism as described by (Gu et al., 2005) announces the presence of services by which mobile users can locate these services whenever required. **Service discovery** in dynamic mobile environments poses many challenges such as service providers may create and delete services or servers anytime; mobile services may be deployed in various forms, etc. In this paper, a design is proposed for a Service Locating Service (SLS), which addresses some of these issues to provide a flexible **service discovery** mechanism for **mobile E-commerce** applications. The architecture adopts a dynamic tree structure for organizing SLS servers to meet the dynamic requirements of services and servers; introduces service aggregation for fast locating; and also proposes multiple service matching mechanisms, which contain an attribute matching engine and a **semantic** matching engine for different service interfaces.

The protocol presented in (Zhang et al., 2007) is based on the concepts of peer-to-peer caching of service advertisements and group-based intelligent forwarding of service requests. It does not require a service to be registered with a registry or lookup server. Services are described using the Web Ontology Language (OWL) that enables increased flexibility in service matching.

OWL-S recognizes that not only content but also services are offered by Web resources. Users should be able to discover, invoke, compose and monitor these services. OWL-S develops an ontology for services that makes this functionality possible. One of the big tasks OWL-S tries to enable is automatic **service discovery**. This involves the automatic location of web services that provide a particular service that adheres to requested constraints.

The Web Architecture for Services Platform (WASP) project creates a supporting platform for mobile **context**-aware applications (Ebben, 2002). It indicates why the platform provides a good opportunity to apply a **context**-aware, ontology based, **semantic service discovery** mechanism.

One of the characteristics of the WASP platform is that it should intelligently search (i.e. **service discovery**) for relevant services from a broad and dynamic range of services.

Chakraborty et al. (2002) have come out with Bluetooth **semantic Service Discovery** Protocol (SDP) that enables a client application on a device to discover information about services on other Bluetooth devices. Every service is represented by a profile that is identified by a 128-bit Universally Unique Identifier (UUID). Attributes associated with a particular service are also identified by UUIDs. **Service discovery** requests, sent by the client, must contain one or more UUIDs. A match occurs on a peer device if and only if at least one UUID specified by the client is contained in one or more service records. UUID-based matching ensures that the protocol is lightweight, both in terms of discovery time and memory, and makes it well suited to resource constrained devices.

Context Based Multihop Networks

The **context** based **service discovery** protocol (CBSDP) (Khedr, 2002) is a **service discovery** protocol developed to overcome the issues with **service discovery** in highly dynamic ad hoc communications. It tries to solve the problems with current **service discovery** mechanism that are not capable of enabling services in a spontaneous networking environment It provides mechanisms that supply initial service configuration and it enables service composition. CBSDP provides users with the possibility to obtain services and information according to its **context**. The services are automatically detected by sensors. CBSDP uses a common ontology for the different services that behave as a basic communication between the **agent**s existing in the environment. The ontology is used to interpret the data of the service into meaningful information for the lookup service that is invoked when a user requests a service.

A **context** aware, ontology based **semantic service discovery** as proposed by Chakraborty et al. (2001) focuses on the advantages of using **context** awareness with **semantic service discovery** resulting in an intelligent web **service discovery** mechanism.

CONCLUSION

There is a requirement for efficient web service discovery mechanisms in near future, as there would be an exponential increase in the number of web services especially with regards to mobile E-commerce. Due to this explosion, manual discovery of mobile E-commerce services becomes impossible and one needs to adapt to automation of discovery process. This automation has to be efficient with respect to search time and accuracy. The discovery mechanism should operate as an human brain, for which cognitive agent based belief desire intention (BDI) architecture is to be adapted. Better search results can be obtained by using semantic matching rather than syntax matching. As mobile E-commerce clients use hand held devices which have computing, memory and battery limitations, the discovery mechanisms should use intelligent agent technologies which will overcome the aforesaid limitations to a certain extent.

REFERENCES

Al-Masri, E., & Mahmoud, Q. H. (2007). Investigating Web Services on the World Wide Web. In *Proceedings of the 16th International Conference on World Wide Web,* (pp. 1257-1258). New York: ACM.

Broens, T. (2004). *Context-aware, Ontology based, Semantic Service Discovery.* Thesis for a Master of Science degree in Telematics from the University of Twente, Enschede, the Netherlands.

Chakraborty, D., Joshi, A., Finin, T., & Yesha, Y. (2002). GSD: A novel group-based service discovery protocol for MANETS. In *proceedings of 4th IEEE Conference on Mobile and Wireless Communications Networks,* (pp. 140-144).

Chakraborty, D., Perich, F., Avancha, S., & Joshi, A. (2001). DReggie: Semantic Service Discovery for M-Commerce Applications. In *Proceedings of Workshop on Reliable and Secure Applications in Mobile Environment, 20th Symposium on Reliable Distributed Systems.* Retrieved December 2001 from http://ebiquity.umbc.edu/get/a/publication/9.pdf

Dey, A. K. (2000). *Providing Architectural Support for Context-Aware applications.* Unpublished doctoral thesis, College of Computing, Georgia Institute of Technology.

Ebben, P. (2002). Blueprint and design of the WASP application platform. *Web Architecture for services platform /D2.2.* Retrieved December 2002 from https://doc.novay.nl/dsweb/Get/Document-55283/Context-aware,%20Ontology%20based,%20Semantic%20Service%20Discovery

Evans, E., & Sarkar, N. (2004). Mobile Commerce Implementation in the Hospital Environment: Issues, Challenges and Future Trends. *Bulletin of Applied Computing and Information Technology, 2*(1).

Gu, T., Pung, H. K., & Yao, J. K. (2005). Towards a flexible service discovery. *Journal of Network and Computer Applications, 28*(3), 233–248. doi:10.1016/j.jnca.2004.06.001

Hawick, K., & James, H. (2002). Middleware Issues for Mobile Business and Commerce. In *proceedings of world scientific and engineering academy and society International Conference on E-Activities,* (pp- 44-48).

Helal, Desai, Verma, Lee, & Konark. (2003). A service discovery and delivery protocol for ad-hoc networks. In *Proceedings of the Third IEEE Conference on Wireless Communication Networks*. (Vol. 3 pp. 2107-2113)

Kalevi, K. (2001). Mobile electronic commerce challenges for global cooperation. In *the proceedings of 9th European Conference on Information Systems*. Retrieved October 2001 from http://is2.lse.ac.uk/asp/aspecis/20010060.pdf

Khedr, M. (2002). Agent-Based Context-Aware Ad Hoc Communication. *Lecture notes in computer science*, (pp. 105-118). Retrieved from http://www.springerlink.com/index/90548ATLK0P248RQ.pdf

Klein, M., Konig-Ries, B., & Obreiter. P. Lanes a lightweight overlay for service discovery in mobile ad hoc networks. In *Proceedings of 3rd Workshop Applications and Services in Wireless Networks* (ASWN 03). Retrieved July, 2003, from http://hnsp.inf-bb.uni-jena.de/DIANE/docsASWN2003.pdf

Kozat and Tassiulas. (2003). Network layer support for service discovery in mobile ad hoc networks. In *proceedings IEEE INFOCOM, USA,* (pp. 1965-1975). Washington, DC: IEEE Press.

Lei, H. (2002). Mobile Commerce: Vision and Challenges. In *Symposium on Applications and the Internet,* (pp.36)

Manvi, S. & Venkatraman. (2003). Agent Based Electronic Trading. *Institution of Electronics and Communication Engineers Technical review, 20*(4), 349-359.

Marin-Perianu, R., Hartel, P., & Scholten, H. (2005). *A Classification of Service Discovery Protocols*. technical report series 05-25, Centre for Telematics and Information Technology. Retrieved from http://de.scientificcommons.org/raluca_marin-perianu

Most'efaoui, S. K., Tafat-Bouzid, A., & Hirsbrunner, B. B. (2003).Using Context Information for Service Discovery and Composition. In *the Proceedings of the fifth conference on information integration and web-based applications and services*, (pp 129-138).

Nandini, S., & Sunilkumar, M. (2009). *Auction Service Discovery Model - An Agent Based Approach*. Paper presented at Fifth international workshop on Mobile Commerce and services (WMCS), Qingdao, China, (pp. 399-406). Washington, DC: IEEE computer society press.

Nidd, M. (2001). Service Discovery in DEAPspace. *IEEE Personal Communications, 8*(44), 39-45. Retrieved from http://www.springerlink.com/index/NRM5C9M93DV43Q5X.pdf

Outay, F., Vèque, V., & Bouallègue, R. (2007). Survey of Service Discovery Protocols and Benefits of Combining Service and Route Discovery . *International Journal of Computer Science and Network Security, 7*(11), 85–92.

Peter, T., Robert, N., & Merrill, W. (2002). Issues in Mobile e-commerce. *Communications of the Association for Information Systems, 8*, 41–64.

Ratsimor, O., Chakraborty, D., & Joshi, A. Finin, T. (2002). Allia: alliance-based service discovery for ad-hoc environments. In *Proceedings of the 2nd international workshop on Mobile commerce*, (pp. 1-9). New York: ACM press

Robinson, R., & Indulska, J. (2005). A context-sensitive service discovery protocol for mobile computing environments. In *proceedings of International Conference on Mobile Business*, (pp. 565 – 572). Washington, DC: IEEE Press.

Sadeh, N. (Ed.). (2002). <u>*m-Commerce Technologies, Services and Business Models*</u>. New York: Wiley.

Samaras, G. (2002). Mobile Commerce: Vision and Challenges (Location and its Management*).* In *Symposium on applications and the Internet,* (pp. 43-45). Washington, DC: IEEE Computer Society, Goland, V.Y., Cai, T., Leach, P., & Gu, Y. (1999). Simple service discovery protocol/1.0. *IETF Internet-Draft.* Retrieved from http://www. ietf.org/internet-drafts/draft-cai-ssdp-v1-03.txt

Tchakarov, J. B., & Vaidya, N. H. (2004). Efficient content location in wireless ad hoc networks. In *proceedings of IEEE International Conference on Mobile Data Management*, (pp. 74).

Varshney, U. (2003). Issues, requirements and support for location-intensive mobile commerce applications. *International Journal of Mobile Communications, 1*(3), 247-263. Retrieved from http://www.csee.umbc.edu/courses/graduate/666/mobile_commerce.pdf

Yuan, Y., & Arbaugh, W. (2003). A Secure Service Discovery Protocol for MANETs. In *proceedings of IEEE symposium on Personal, indoor and mobile radio communications,* (pp. 502-506). Retrieved from http://www.imec.be/pacwoman/Deliverables/WP5/WP5-CPK-D5.2-High_Level_Specification-09-12-2003-V1.0.doc

Zhang, B., Shi, Y., & Xiao, X. *(2007). A Peer-to-Peer Semantic-Based Service Discovery Method for Pervasive Computing Environment. In* Proceedings of 4th International Conference on Ubiquitous Intelligence and Computing, *(Vol. 4611, pp. 195-204). Berlin: Springer.*

KEY TERMS AND DEFINITIONS

Cognitive Agents: Cognitive agents are kind of agents that use Belief-Desire-Intention (BDI) based architecture, which are recently becoming popular due to their human kind of reasoning. Cognitive agents are normally static agents that require higher computation and more databases. These support autonomic computing.

Context Awareness: information that can be used to characterize the situation of an entity where an entity is a person, place, or object that is considered relevant to interaction between a user and an application including the user and application themselves. **Context-awareness** is defined as: a property of a system that uses **context** to provide relevant information and/or service to the user, where relevancy depends on the user's task.

Mobile E-Commerce: M-Commerce is defined as any type of transaction of an economic value having at least at one end, a mobile terminal and thus using the mobile telecommunications network.

Multicast: is a type of communication where one server/client sends message to many clients.

Ontology: Ontology is a formal and explicit specification of a shared conceptualization that can be used for sharing and reasoning on knowledge

Service Discovery: The process of obtaining a set of services which can possibly fulfill a user request is called **service discovery**.

Software Agents: Software **agent** is an autonomous software entity that can interact with its environment. They are implemented using software. **Agent**s are autonomous and can react with other entities, including humans, machines, and other software **agent**s in various environment and across various platforms.

Web Service: A Service is a software entity provided by a Service Provider. It performs an action (based on inputs) on behalf of a Service Requestor and provides a result (output).

Chapter 82
Perspectives on the Viable Mobile Virtual Community for Telemedicine

Jan-Willem van 't Klooster
University of Twente, The Netherlands

Pravin Pawar
University of Twente, The Netherlands

Bert-Jan van Beijnum
University of Twente, The Netherlands

Chariz Dulawan
University of Twente, The Netherlands

Hermie Hermens
University of Twente, The Netherlands

INTRODUCTION

A *virtual community* is an electronically supported social network: it can be seen as a group of people who have regular social interaction, independent of time and space, because of a common interest such as a problem, task, or feeling exchange (Eysenbach, Powell, Englesakis, Rizo, & Stern, 2004; Rheingold, 1993). When independence of time and space is achieved through the use of mobile devices and wireless communication technologies, such a virtual community is called a *Mobile Virtual Community* (MVC). Existing research interests in the MVC domain are grouped into *technology-centered interest, user-centered interest* and *business-*

DOI: 10.4018/978-1-61520-611-7.ch082

centered interest (El Morr & Kawash, 2007). The technology-centered aspects include issues such as platform design, development framework, mobile network bandwidth limits and intelligent agents. The user-centered issues include user interface, behavior, personalization, privacy, data security and trust. Business-centered aspects include marketing, investment and business models.

In another paradigm known as *telemedicine*, information and communication technologies are being investigated and employed in applications such as health discussion & maintenance, alleviation, cure and prevention of diseases. In recent telemedicine scenarios, sensors attached to the patient's body collect patient's vital signs, transmit them to a mobile gateway device being carried by the patient, which in turn uses wireless communication technologies to transmit the data to a healthcare center, for purposes like vital signs analysis and offering emergency assistance to the patient if needed. The sensors and the gateway mobile device together form a so called *Body Area Network* (BAN). Konstantas, van Halteren, & Bults (2004) describe such a BAN for telemedicine purposes. Other supporting actors involved in such a scenario are the technicians, healthcare specialists, doctors and (informal) caregivers.

According to the definition, the telemedicine scenario may be viewed as a virtual community if the patient and other actors could communicate with each other for the purpose of providing medical assistance and counseling to the patient. In situations where patient and caregiver mobility exists, this virtual community, may be said to correspond to a MVC. Such a MVC is an aggregated kind of community as defined in Demiris 2006, where communities of healthcare professionals only, patients/informal caregivers only, combinations of them, and general public communities are defined. The technical system that supports the realization of MVC is referred to as MVC platform (Van Beijnum, Pawar, Dulawan, & Hermens, 2009).

Considering the architecture of the MVC platform, it can be argued that the MVC potentially revolves around a set of services based on the principles of Service Oriented Architecture (SOA) (Papazoglou, 2003; Pawar, Subercaze, Maret, Van Beijnum, & Konstantas, 2008).

Based on the findings of Broens et al., (2007) and Maloney-Krichmar and Preece, (2005) we argue that to be a viable MVC, it should have a tailored focus and robust technical platform: it should be of clear interest to the users and the technology incorporated should be reliable. This chapter contributes to this area in general and mobile patient monitoring and treatment in particular, by 1) analyzing in detail the robustness and other requirements to be fulfilled by the technical platform for MVCs, 2) providing guidelines for MVC platform development based on service

orientation, and 3) discussing the actors, front-end views and service components involved.

The reminder of this chapter is organized as follows. The second section of the chapter illustrates a possible telemedicine scenario focused on patient monitoring and treatment which help to elicit the specific requirements to be supported by the MVC platform. Based on the requirements and services elicited in that section, the third section of this chapter presents a possible graphical user interface (GUI) for the platform depicting the requirements to be fulfilled from an end-user perspective. The fourth section discusses the internal design of the possible MVC platform and conclusions are presented in the last section.

SCENARIO BASED REQUIREMENTS ELICITATION

Scenario analysis is the process of understanding, analyzing, and describing system behavior in terms of particular ways the system is expected to be used (Hsia et al., 1994). Drawing use cases from the scenarios and relating requirements to the use cases is a popular approach in the system design process (Whittle & Krüger, 2004). We use a similar approach here to elicit the requirements for the MVC platform based on a scenario.

Scenario Description

Herewith we present a visionary scenario showing the intended use of the MVC platform. On the MVC platform, a number of different sub-communities could function independent of each other. Member can join these sub-communities as well as the aggregate MVC. One of the sub-communities is used by the persons Bob and Alice in the following scenario.

Bob (patient) and Alice (caregiver) join a MVC. The local healthcare center creates a sub-community called as telemedicine community. The MVC community management service recommends Bob, Alice and other members to join the telemedicine community. Bob and Alice join the community by updating their profile with information specific to the telemedicine community (e.g. problems Bob is suffering from). The MVC matchmaking service recommends the members to be a part of each other's social network based on their telemedicine community centric profile (e.g. interest in the same health condition). Bob, Alice and other members of the telemedicine community, including patients and (informal) caregivers, socialize with each other for sharing their experiences after joining the same sub-community. Meanwhile, the health-care center announces offering of a mobile patient monitoring service for the patients suffering from epilepsy. To facilitate mobile patient monitoring, a number of BAN manufacturers recommended by health-care center offer their BAN to the patients. Using the MVC context-aware matchmaking service, the MVC platform recommends Bob a particular BAN which is compatible with his smartphone. Bob purchases the recommended BAN and subscribes to the mobile patient monitoring service via the community platform. On the day Bob suddenly suffers from an epileptic

seizure; the medical specialist at the healthcare center requests the MVC platform to search for the nearest caregiver. On this request, the MVC context-aware matchmaking service searches for the nearest caregiver service based on Bob's and caregivers' current locations. Fortunately, Alice is the nearest informal caregiver to Bob. The medical specialist instructs the MVC platform to notify Alice about Bob's critical condition. Alice receives the notification and reaches to Bob's location for providing assistance.

Use Cases

Based on the given scenario, the following use cases can be derived. These use cases not only show possible uses of the MVC platform, but also identify who are involved and what are the tasks in fulfilling the use case. As elicited from the scenario, Figure 1 identifies the uses cases and the involved actor role(s), being patient, caregiver, medical specialist, product provider or service provider. For further illustration, a particular use case in which a sub-community is created is described in detail in Table 1. In this use case, it is shown that parameters of the new sub-

Figure 1. Use cases derived from the scenario and corresponding roles

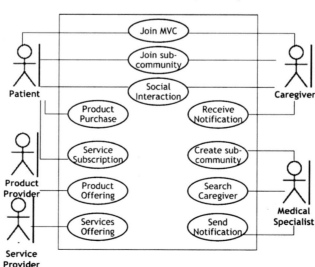

community can be set, including policy rules for the members and whether or not anybody can join the sub-community (public) or only on invitation (private) depending on e.g. the topic and privacy sensitivity of the sub-community.

Requirements Elicitation

In this section, the use cases derived in the above section are mapped to the high-level requirements to be fulfilled by the MVC platform. An overview of these requirements is provided in Table 2. As seen in this table, the platform should be able to perform various actions and provide various services. Afterwards, this section lists the services and policies necessary to meet these high level requirements.

Services and Policies

As described in the Introduction, the architecture and software design of the MVC can be made using SOA principles. A *service* refers to a unit of work which can be done by a service provider to achieve desired end results for a service consumer (Subercaze et al., 2009). In traditional virtual communities, services would refer to web-based (interaction) services. However, the impact of mobile technologies makes available a number

of mobile services, which are both produced and consumed using mobile devices. Based on the requirements listed above, we identify two groups of services: *mobile device services* and *MVC platform services*. Mobile device services run on the mobile device and platform services are those provided by the MVC platform.

Policies refer to the rules or constraints imposed on either the actor roles in the MVC or in the interaction with the services. In terms of the actor roles, there are specific guidelines about what an actor can do and can not do. For example, the product provider cannot search for caregivers. Thus, for the interactions between a role and a service, rules could be related to *permission constraints* and *prohibition constraints*. Permission constraints refer to the prescription that a certain interaction is allowed to occur. A prohibition constraint is the opposite as it describes an interaction that must not occur at all. Specifying policies is also based on the analysis of scenarios, because policies depend on the purpose and use of the MVC as well as on the roles and services that are present in the MVC.

The following listing provides required services in the MVC platform architecture:

- *Member Management Service:* This service includes the invited registration of

Table 1. Description of the use case create sub-community

Use Case Name	Create sub-community
Precondition	Medical specialist creating the sub-community is known to the MVC platform
Success End-condition	Medical specialist creates the sub-community with specific criteria
Failed End-condition	Medical specialist is not able to create the sub-community
Actor role	Medical specialist
Description	1. The medical specialist logs in to the MVC platform using his/her username and password 2. The medical specialist makes use of a module in the MVC platform that allows him/her to create a sub-community. 3. The medical specialist identifies and/or selects appropriate conditions for the sub-community to be created. Such conditions include which roles and services should be present; what policies govern the interactions between roles; and whether the sub-community is private/public. 4. The medical specialist saves information and creates the sub-community

the new members, editing and managing member profiles, the member type (e.g. patient, caregiver), logging in, session handling etc.

- *Directory and announcement Service:* This service provides functionality for the community support providers to post news, list the offered services, and listing of events such as those leading to improvement in the psychological and physical health of the patients.

- *Purchase Service:* this service allows the registration and acquisition of health-related products and services offered in the MVC. This process needs to be moderated by the healthcare center to assure relevance for the members and to avoid that the MVC becomes a brand-oriented advertising channel, therefore a *content moderation service* is required as well.

- *Content moderation service:* Certain types of contents, which negatively affect the psychological and physical health of the

patients, are discouraged. Hence, contents such as profile information, pictures posted by the members, product and services description are subject to publishing in the MVC after manual moderation. Automatic moderation techniques could be applied, for interactions such as instant chat. These features will be taken care of by the content moderation service.

- *Alarm Service:* This service enables the alarms, based on a predefined level of urgency. In case of an emergency, this service can be used to notify for example a caregiver.

- *Community Management Service:* This service consists of all the functionalities required to create, join, access and search sub-communities, (such as those of patients with a particular type of condition), publish, get and subscribe to information in the existing sub-communities.

- *Policy making and enforcement service:* To enforce the interactions between an actor

Table 2. MVC platform requirements and use case mapping

High Level Requirement	Use Case(s)
The platform should allow creation of a sub-community.	Create sub-community
The platform should allow management of a sub-community such that the preferences and constraints can be made regarding members, roles, and services.	Create sub-community
The platform should provide asynchronous and synchronous communications services such as email and instant messaging for inviting existing community members to join sub-community.	Create sub-community
The platform should allow creation and management of profiles.	Join MVC, Join sub-community
The platform should provide synchronous and asynchronous communication service such for inviting non-community members to join the main community and transmission of information.	Send notification, receive notification, Social interaction
The platform should allow product offering and product purchase.	Product offering, product purchase
The platform should allow service offering and service subscription	Service offering, service subscription
The platform should be able to identify who should be alarmed in case of an emergency.	Search caregiver
The platform should have information about the locations of the patient and caregiver	Search caregiver
The platform should be able to support multiple devices (e.g. smartphones) associated with multiple services.	Social interaction, social offering

role and a service, as well as to take into account the trust and privacy requirements in the MVC community, a set of policies need to be developed and enforced. The policy making and enforcement service takes care of the matters such as creation of a new policy and enforcing these policies during the MVC interactions.

- *Social Interaction Service:* This service handles the *one-to-one*, *one-to-many* and *many-to-many* interactions between the MVC members. This includes interaction functions such as instant messaging, group notifications, and subscription to the particular type of content (e.g. information posted by the medical specialist).

- *Context-Aware Matchmaking Service:* Semantic descriptions of the member profiles combined with description logic are powerful tools to perform matchmaking. The context-aware matchmaking functionality of this service could be used for example to recommend new members in the sub-community, or to search for the nearest available caregiver.

- *Content Exchange Service on the Mobile Device:* This service on the patient's mobile

device is aimed at sending the contents (e.g. text, images, and streams) generated at the mobile device to the community platform such that this content could be published in the community. Similarly, this service could also request/subscribe to the community content the user is interested in and present this content for user viewing.

- *Vital Sign Monitoring Service:* This service enables the monitoring of vital signs, such as blood pressure and oxygen saturation information.

- *Context Information Service on the Mobile Device:* This service obtains context information (such as location) of the patient and sends this information and subsequent context changes in real-time to the community platform. This information could subsequently be used by the context-aware matchmaking service.

- *Community Service:* This service indexes and allows modifications on what services are available to which sub-community.

- *Chat service:* As a sub-part of social interaction service, this service allows for instant voice, video or message chat amongst members of the MVC.

Figure 2. Specification of roles in a sub-community

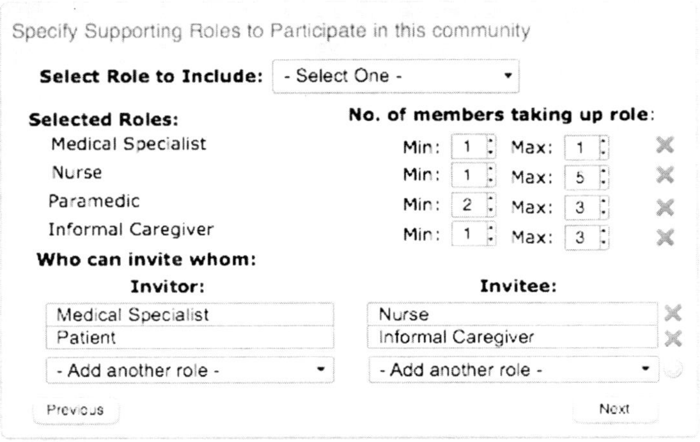

FRONT-END DESIGN OF THE MVC PLATFORM

To illustrate how the MVC platform supports the scenario presented in the above section, a design of how to specify some of the preferences is provided in this section. In Figure 2, the creator of a sub-community is asked to establish a set of policy rules related to the roles in the sub-community. As shown, different roles and cardinalities are entered, and rules for invitations to the sub-community apply.

Next to specifying roles, services available for the sub-community should be selected. *Alarm service, Chat Service, Location Service, Viewing Service, and Vital Sign Monitoring Service* are examples of services for the sub-community as applicable in the scenario. These are shown in Figure 3.

In a chat service or other similar social interaction services, policies exist such as who initiates contact to whom. These policies are related to the purpose of the chat session. Figure 4 shows how this can be specified.

Regarding the location service, not all actors are allowed to view the location of other actors. For instance, a service provider does not need to know the location of a medical specialist, but a medical specialist should be able to know the patient's location in an alarm situation. These policies define who is the provider of the location information as well as who are the authorized consumers of this information. Figure 5 shows how this concept can be specified.

INTERNAL DESIGN OF THE MVC PLATFORM

To support the desired functionalities of the platform described so far, a sound internal design is necessary. This section presents details on the possible internal design of the MVC platform. An overview of the high-level architecture of the MVC platform is presented in Figure 6. To ensure separation of concerns in the platform, three layers are identified:

- *Platform Services Layer:* The platform services layer is responsible for providing the MVC platform services, for example those described in the requirements elicitation section.
- *Mobile Services Layer:* The mobile services layer is responsible for making available the MVC platform services to the mobile

Figure 3. Specification of services in a sub-community

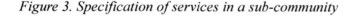

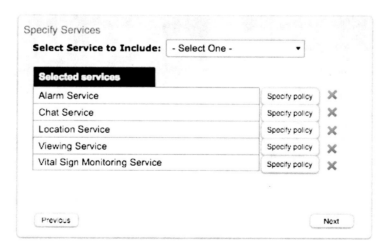

Figure 4. Specifying policies for a chat service

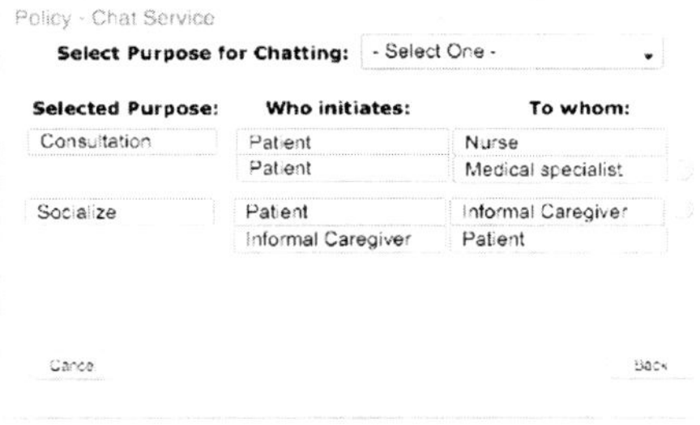

Figure 5. Specifying policies for a location service

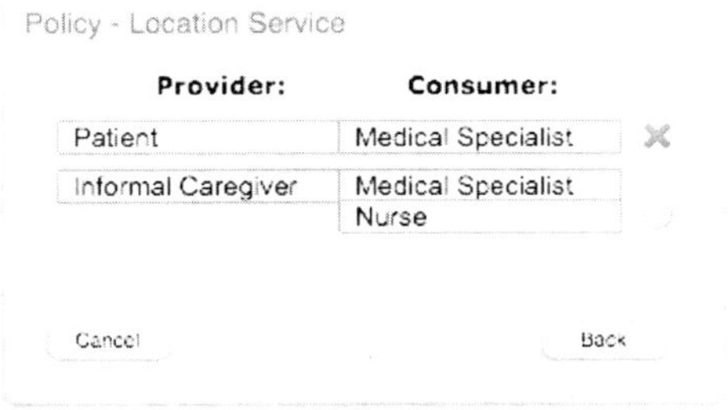

device and for providing services such as content exchange and context information service from the mobile device to the MVC.

- *Integration Layer:* Because of the use of different nature and technologies at the platform services layer and mobile services layer as well as to take into account the effects of the mobility, an integration layer is envisioned to support the mobile and platform services cooperation.

Internally, the detailed software architecture of the MVC platform could be represented using the Unified Modeling Language (UML). A UML class diagram is a type of diagram that describes the internal structure of a system by showing the system's classes, their attributes, and the relationships between the classes. One of the UML class diagrams for creating a sub-community is presented in Figure 7, with a description of the

classes and their relationships in Table 3. A design decision is made to show that parties (actors) have no direct access on the services. The services are linked to the sub-communities since the motivation for using these services should be to support the purpose of the existence of the sub-community was. In the same manner, not all roles have access to the sub-community services. Only authorized roles and parties as set in the policy for using the services are allowed to utilize the service.

CONCLUSION

Mobile virtual communities (MVC) are being explored in the telemedicine domain for the purpose of social interactions and monitoring to support tasks such as health discussion & maintenance, alleviation, cure and prevention of diseases. In this chapter, we present perspectives on the MVC for telemedicine.

Figure 6. Overview of the layers in the mobile virtual community platform

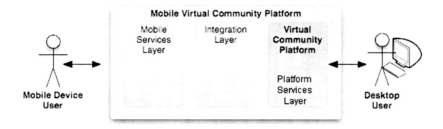

Figure 7. UML class diagram representing MVC internal structure for the creation of a sub-community

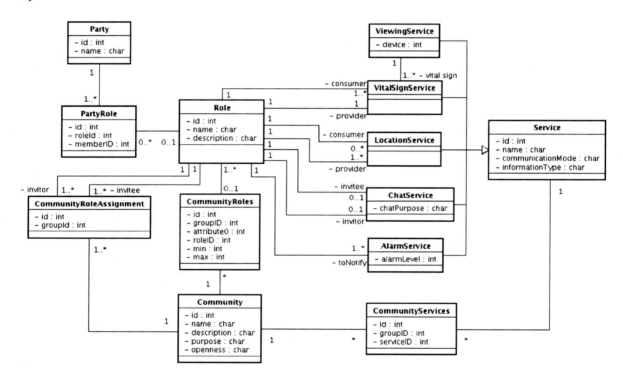

By means of presenting a possible scenario and scenario based requirements elicitation, we identify requirements and services for such a MVC. The chapter shows how the architecture and software design of the MVC revolves around service oriented principles. Illustrative policy-related interface components are discussed. It is necessary to be able to define rules for the platform users, due to the nature of the actors involved (e.g. healthcare professionals, patients and product providers).

To incorporate mobile services in the platform, a layered high-level architecture is presented that enables a clear separation of concerns between mobile and platform services. Finally, the chapter presents an internal design and an elaboration on the internals of such a platform.

In sum, the chapter provides perspectives on

Table 3. Description of the UML classes shown in Figure 7

Class Name	Description
Party	The party class refers to the parties (actors) of the MVC platform.
PartyRole	This model element shows the association type between a party and a role. The relationship shows that a party can take up multiple roles and that this is a requirement before a party takes up a role defined in a certain sub-community.
Role	The list of roles and its description are represented in this class.
CommunityRoles	This model element identifies the distinct roles that can only participate in the sub-community. These roles can be filled up by party roles.
Community	This model element refers to the sub-communities that are created in the MVC platform and which uses the services of the MVC platform. A sub-community may use multiple services in order to fulfill its goals. This class knows the name, description and purpose of the sub-community as well as the attribute related to the degree of openness of the sub-community.
CommunityRoleAssignment	The class contains the policy on role assignments in the sub-community CommunityServices. This model element refers to the services that are to support the goal of the sub-community.
Service	This class refers to the related Telemedicine services that can be utilized by certain sub-communities and is a generalization of various concrete services.
CommunityService	This class refers to the related community service that maintains the mapping of Service elements to Community elements.
AlarmService	This class contains the policy on whom to notify depending on the alarm level.
ChatService	This class contains the purpose of the chat as well as the policy on who initiates the chat and to whom it was initiated.
LocationService	This class contains the policy on who provides location information and who can consume the provided information.
VitalSignService	This class identifies the vital sign that will be collected from the provider as well as the policy on who consumes the vital sign information.
ViewingService	This class contains the device that will be used for viewing the vital sign information. This service is used in conjunction with the VitalSignService, wherein the consumer role makes use of the device preference defined in this ViewingService in order to view the vital sign.

how the viable MVC for telemedicine can be developed, based on extensive scenario analysis and using service oriented design principles.

ACKNOWLEDGMENT

This work is part of the IOP GenCom U-Care project (http://ucare.ewi.utwente.nl), sponsored by the Dutch Ministry of Economic Affairs under contract IGC0816, and the Freeband AWARE-NESS project (http://awareness.freeband.nl), sponsored by the Dutch government under contract BSIK 03025.

REFERENCES

Broens, T., Huis in 't Veld, R., Vollenbroek-Hutten, M., Hermens, H., van Halteren, A., & Nieuwenhuis, B. (2007). Determinants for successful telemedicine implementations – a literature study. *Journal of Telemedicine and Telecare, 13*(6), 303–309. doi:10.1258/135763307781644951

Demiris, G. (2006). The diffusion of virtual communities in health care: concepts and challenges. *Patient Education and Counseling, 62*(2), 178–188. doi:10.1016/j.pec.2005.10.003

El Morr, C., & Kawash, J. (2007). Mobile Virtual Communities Research: A Synthesis of Current Trends and a Look at Future Perspectives. *International Journal of Web Based Communities*, *3*(4), 386–403. doi:10.1504/IJWBC.2007.015865

Eysenbach, G., Powell, J., Englesakis, M., Rizo, C., & Stern, A. (2004). Health Related Virtual Communities and Electronic Support Groups: Systematic Review of the Effects of Online Peer to Peer Interactions. *British Medical Journal*, *328*(7449), 1166. doi:10.1136/bmj.328.7449.1166

Hsia, P., Samuel, J., Gao, J., Kung, D., Toyoshima, Y., & Chen, C. (1994). Formal Approach to Scenario Analysis. *IEEE Software*, *11*(2), 33–41. doi:10.1109/52.268953

Konstantas, D., Van Halteren, A., & Bults, R. (2004). Mobile Patient Monitoring: The MobiHealth System. *The Journal on Information Technology in Healthcare*, *2*(5).

Maloney-Krichmar, D., & Preece, J. (2005). A multilevel analysis of sociability, usability, and community dynamics in an online health community. *ACM Transactions on Computer-Human Interaction*, *12*(2), 201–232. doi:10.1145/1067860.1067864

Papazoglou, M. P., & Georgakopoulos, D. (2003). Service-Oriented Computing. *Communications of the ACM*, *46*(10), 25–28. doi:10.1145/944217.944233

Pawar, P., Subercaze, J., Maret, P., Van Beijnum, B. J., & Konstantas, D. (2008). Towards Business Model and Technical Platform for the Service Oriented Context-Aware Mobile Virtual Communities. *IEEE 13th Symposium on Computers and Communications (ISCC'08)*, Marrakech, Morocco.

Rheingold, H. (1993). *The virtual community: homesteading on the electronic frontier*. Reading, MA: Addison-Wesley Pub.

Subarcaze, J., Maret, P., Calmet, J., & Pawar, P. (2009). A Service Oriented Framework For Mobile Business Virtual Communities. In *9th IFIP Working Conference on Virtual Enterprises*, (PRO-VE 2009) Poznan, Poland.

Van Beijnum, B. J. F., Pawar, P., Dulawan, C., & Hermens, H. (2009). Mobile Virtual Communities for Telemedicine: Research Challenges and Opportunities. *International Journal of Computer Science & Applications*, *6*(2), 38–49.

Whittle, J., & Krüger, I. H. (2004). A Methodology for Scenario-Based Requirements Capture. In *Proceedings of the ICSE 2004 Workshop on Scenarios and State Machines (SCESM)*.

KEY TERMS AND DEFINITIONS

Body Area Network (BAN): A BAN is a network of devices around the body, consisting of multiple devices such as sensors and a gateway device.

Mobile Virtual Community (MVC): A virtual community (VC) is an electronically supported social network: it can be seen as a group of people who regularly interact because of a common interest, problem or task assignment. When independence of time and place is achieved through utilizing mobile devices and wireless communication technologies, such a VC is called a Mobile Virtual Community.

Permission And Prohibition Constraints: Permission constraints refer to the prescription that a certain interaction is allowed to occur; whereas prohibition constraints refer to permissions of interaction that are not allowed to occur.

Service Oriented Architecture (SOA): A SOA is an architectural principle based on the services concept, in which services performed by a services provider can be reused as a standalone component in a web-based architecture. A SOA can for example be implemented by web services technology.

Service: A service refers to a unit of work which can be performed by a service provider to achieve desired end results for a service consumer. Services are produced and consumed by both fixed and mobile devices.

Sub-Community: A sub-community is a subset of an VC, and refers to a community within the virtual community.

Telemedicine: In telemedicine, information and communication technologies (ICT) are researched and employed in medicine areas such as health maintenance, alleviation, cure and prevention of diseases. Originally, telemedicine is a combination of 'tele', meaning (geographical) distance, and medicine. However, next to distance, also time can be bridged using ICT.

Unified Modelling Language (UML) Class Diagram: A UML class diagram is a diagram following the rules of the UML, and used to represent the detailed internals of an information system.

Use Case: A use case defines a use of a system. It is generally used to concretize instantiated behavior of the system.

Chapter 83
Socio–Economic Effects on Mobile Phone Adoption Behavior among Older Consumers

Sanna Sintonen
Lappeenranta University of Technology, Finland

INTRODUCTION

Aging is one of the major trends that is about to change the structure of consumer markets. As people age, they face changes in their health and functioning, that make them differ from their younger counterparts. Retiring is one of the changes that people face when they age, it clearly gives them more opportunities to make choices and more time for decision-making, and therefore their consuming power shouldn't be overlooked. As electronic services are continuously developed, it is important to analyze aging people and identify the typical characteristics that affect their mobile phone usage.

The present chapter pursues to evaluate what influences the usage of mobile phones among the aging consumers. It is important to take a look at the

DOI: 10.4018/978-1-61520-611-7.ch083

typical characteristics related to aging. Technology itself may be strange to people that have retired a decade ago, when the diffusion of mobile phones was accelerating, and it is therefore considered important that technology related fears aren't overlooked. Technology related perceptions have been found to be important determinants of technology usage, and they should also be assessed when the aging consumers are analyzed. For the purposes of identifying relevant future users for mobile services, it is essential to analyze the effects of socio-economic characteristics on mobile phone adoption.

BACKGROUND

Aging has psychological, biological, social and economic influences on consumers (Pak & Kambil, 2006). For marketers the biological issues create challenges for product and service designs and communication methods. Changes in memory and information processing result in declining rate of learning and avoiding situations that aren't familiar. Economic situations change due to retirement, but it is considered that elderly have high discretionary income (Lunsford & Burnett, 1992). People age differently and aging itself is a multidimensional process, therefore differences in consumer responses among older people are not likely to be the result of any specific factor (Moschis, 1992), it is thus necessary to become familiar with aging related characteristics. Health has been considered important, when aging consumers have been segmented. Perceptions of health vary among different social groups and depend very much on age and experience and thus self-assessments can be very individual and eccentric (Blaxter, 1990). According to Leinonen (2002), self-rated health is determined by the existence or absence of chronicle diseases, level of functioning, way of living, psychological well-being, socio-demographic and socio-economic factors and adaptation to changes emerging through aging.

According to Czaja and Lee (2007), age-related changes in cognition have important implications for the design of technical systems, because human-technology interaction is an information-processing task. Learning is closely tied to memory functioning and even a normal decline of memory through aging renders difficulties in learning (Suutama, 2004). Cognitive abilities are thus related to technology adoption, because new technology requires new learning, which relies heavily on component cognitive abilities underlying fluid intelligence (Czaja & Lee, 2007). Fluid intelligence includes abstract thinking, reasoning, some of the memory functions and quick problem solving capacity in new situations (Suutama, 2004). This is why the complexity of innovation becomes important for aging consumers decision-making. Theory of planned behavior suggests that perceived behavioral control influences behavioral intentions and refers to people's perception of the ease or difficulty of performing the behavior of interest (Ajzen, 1985, 1991). The effort expected to bring a course of behavior to a successful conclusion is likely to increase with perceived behavioral control (Ajzen, 1991). The greater the perceived behavioral control the stronger should be the intention to perform the behavior and it will more likely occur. The harder the person tries, and the greater is his control over personal and external factors that may interfere, the greater is the likelihood that he will attain his behavioral goal (Ajzen, 1985).

Typical for elderly adopting innovations is the fear that it will not perform as desired (Lunsford & Burnett, 1992). Among older consumers and technology, a common issue under research is the fear for technology, i.e. technology anxiety. According to Meuter, Ostrom, Bitner and Roundtree (2003), technology anxiety focuses on the user's state of mind regarding their ability and willingness to use technology-related tools. Anxiety related to technology originates from computer anxiety, which has been studied rather widely (see Brosnan, 1998). Computer anxiety has been defined as emotional fear, apprehension and phobia felt by the individuals towards interactions with computers or when they think about using computers (Chua, Chen, & Wong, 1999), i.e. anxiety refers to the negative attitudes toward using the computer. It is a kind of state anxiety, which can be changed and measured along multiple dimensions (Chua et al., 1999). Likely the anxiety rises from the inability or lack of self-confidence in effectively managing or controlling the technology (Oyedele & Simpson, 2007). According to Moschis (2003) older consumers prefer avoiding complexity when buying services or products, and also when using them. Offerings are accepted if they are beneficial and they need to match the expectations of the consumer in functioning and quality. Consuming is risk averse and the decisions are mainly based on previous experiences.

Figure 1. Research model

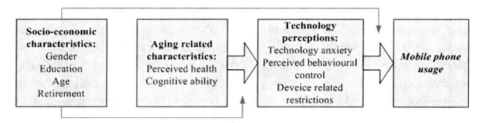

SOCIO-ECONOMIC EFFECTS AND MOBILE PHONE ADOPTION AMONG AGING CONSUMERS

Research Model

A multitude of variables could potentially influence the beliefs and attitudes people hold: age, gender, ethnicity, socioeconomic status, education, nationality, religious affiliation, personality, mood, emotion, general attitudes and values, intelligence, group membership, past experiences, exposure to information, social support, coping skills and so forth (Ajzen et al., 2005). The present paper suggests that gender, age, education and retirement all impact the mobile phone usage among aging consumers. The basic model behind the analysis is presented in Figure 1. Perceived health is suggested to influence the device related restrictions. Cognitive ability on behalf is proposed to influence on all the introduced technology perceptions: technology anxiety, perceived behavioral control and device related restrictions. The device related restrictions are also suggested to increase technology anxiety. Anxiety and restrictions are suggested to decrease the perceptions of behavioral control and all the technology related perceptions are proposed to influence mobile phone usage. This model will be tested with a multi-group analysis in order to evaluate differences caused by age, gender, education and retirement. It is proposed that socio-economic characteristics might operate as homologizers, indicating that the relationships between the constructs differ based on socio-economic status in the model.

Several researchers have found gender effects on computer anxiety indicating that females have less positive attitudes toward computers (Dyck & Smither, 1996; Gilbert, Lee-Kelley, & Barton, 2003). Gender – anxiety relationship however has been also studied with psychological gender revealing that there is a positive relationship between anxiety and femininity and a negative relationship between masculinity and anxiety (Todman & Day, 2006). Females have many times been later adopting new technology than males (e.g. Vishwanath & Goldhaber, 2003), and males have been found to feel more at ease with technology (Gefen & Straub, 1997). Therefore, when considering the older consumer segment, it is suggested that females are more sensitive to changes in different background factors. The first proposition is:

Proposition 1: The relationships between different constructs are stronger for female consumers.

In earlier studies, education has appeared to have influence on computer anxiety (Igbaria & Parasuraman, 1989). Considering mobile phone adoption, lower education consumers have been later adopters (Vishwanath & Goldhaber, 2003). It could be assumed that people with higher level education are more familiar with new technology from their past work experiences, therefore it is suggested:

Proposition 2: The relationships between different constructs are weaker for higher educated consumers.

Finally, it is also suggested that age influences mobile phones usage. Age has been found to be a moderator in technology adoption (Morris & Venkatesh, 2000), and Vishwanath and Goldhaber (2003) studied cellular phone adoption, and their results indicated that the non-adopters where distinguished also by older age. Considering the whole aging market, it is here assumed that younger part of older consumers isn't that prone to changes in the factors that affect mobile phone usage, and therefore it is proposed:

Proposition 3: The relationships between different constructs are stronger for older consumers.

Retirement is one of the cut points in life. It could be that part of those people still involved in work life, have had no choices but to adopt and start using mobile phones on behalf of their work status. There has not been much research considering the point of retirement and its relationship to technology adoption, but analogous to age it is here proposed that:

Proposition 4: The relationships between different constructs are stronger for retired consumers.

Methodology

The empirical evidence was collected with a traditional mail survey from a middle sized city in Finland. A sample of 1000 consumers aged between 55-79 years was stratified with age in order to form a representative sample, and it covered more than 10 percent of the relevant population. The response rate was rather high, 55.6 percent, and the responses followed the true age distribution of the relevant population. Females covered 56.8 percent of the respondents, which is also congruent with their proportion in the population.

The concepts included in the modeling were mainly measured with statements having five response alternatives ranging from 1=totally disagree to 5=totally agree. The measurement items selected to cover the level of cognitive capacity were drawn from the cognitive factor of Zung Self-Rating Depression Scale (Passik et al., 2000). Perceived health was measured with a global measure for self-rated health (Jelicic & Kempen, 1999) with five response alternatives varying from poor to excellent. This measure was complemented with three additional statements in order to form a multi-item scale and increase the measurement reliability.

Perceived physical restrictions for mobile phone usage were reflected with two statements that discussed the small buttons and small screen size in mobile phones. The measurement of computer anxiety has been extended to measure anxiety related to technology in general (Meuter et al., 2003), and a similar extension was made here for mobile phones. The indicators of computer anxiety included such elements as fear, uncomfort and embarrassment that have been part of the scales used in previous research (e.g. Cohen & Waugh, 1989; Loyd & Loyd, 1985; Selwyn, 1997). Perceived behavioral control items were based on previous literature (Morris & Venkatesh, 2000; Taylor & Todd, 1995). Revisions were made to match the present context, and four statements where used to reflect perceived behavioral control.

As mobile phones are almost at the position of everyday consumption commodity due to the high penetration rates, the traditional measurement for behavioral intention to adopt them was out of the question. In order to cover mobile phone usage, two items were developed for the purpose. One item discussed usage skills and the other captured the range of purposes to which mobile phones are used for. The summated scale composed from these captures the mobile usage from 1=low level users to 3=advanced users of mobile phone.

Figure 2. Scale statistics

Concept (abbreviation)	N of items	Mean	Std Dev	Construct reliability	Average variance extracted
Cognitive ability (ca)	2	3.574	1.224	.866	.767
Perceived health (ph)	4	3.325	.951	.853	.510
Physical restrictions (pr)	2	2.850	1.376	.902	.822
Technology anxiety (anx)	4	1.720	.803	.843	.521
Perceived Behavioral control (pbc)	4	3.681	1.087	.904	.705
Mobile phone usage (mp)	2	2.097	.540	.758	.613

The measurement model was verified with confirmatory factor analysis. The reliability coefficients for latent constructs were rather high and the average variance extracted was over 50 percent for each construct (Figure 2). Measurement invariance was also confirmed for all the subgroups that were analyzed.

Empirical Assessment of Socio-Economic Differences

Before testing socio-economic differences, the full research model was tested with the whole sample structural equation modeling (Figure 3.). The model fit indices suggested a good fit to the data (χ^2=6.868, p=.141, df=4, NFI=.989, NNFI=.981, GFI=.995, AGFI=.971). R square for mobile phone usage was .498, indicating that the model succeeded rather well.

Nearly all paths were significant, only two paths making an exception. Cognitive ability had no effect on the perceived device related physical restrictions. Additionally, these restrictions had no direct effect on mobile phone usage. It thus seems that health influences the perception of how much the small size of mobile phones bothers its usage. Good cognitive functioning decreases technology anxiety and increases consumers' perceived control related to mobile phones. Physical restrictions increase technology anxiety and together with anxiety they decrease perceived behavioral control. Direct influencers on mobile phone usage were perceived behavioral control and technology anxiety.

After the full model was tested and found to be eligible, four subgroup analyses were conducted in order to detect the effects of gender, education, age and retirement. The first subgroup analysis was conducted based on gender (Figure 4). Unrestricted model means that the path coefficients were allowed to be freely estimated for both groups. In restricted models, each path coefficient one after each other was forced to be the same across the groups. Thereafter, khi square difference

*Figure 3. Empirical validation of the ground model (*indicates a statistically significant path coefficient)*

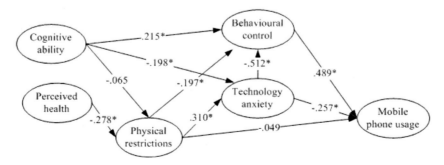

Figure 4. Gender differences in path coefficients

Relationship	Men N=193	Women N=235	Unrestricted χ^2 (df=15)	Restricted χ^2 (df=16)	Difference χ^2 (df=1)	p-value
ph → pr	-.171*	-.407****	10.91	12.78	1.87	
ca → pr	-.099	-.040	10.91	11.01	0.1	
ca → arx	-.235***	-.266***	10.91	10.97	0.06	
ca → pbc	.173**	.148**	10.91	11	0.09	
pr → arx	.319****	.519****	10.91	12.97	2.06	
pr → pbc	-.093	-.018	10.91	11.36	0.45	
arx → pbc	-.775****	-.740****	10.91	10.97	0.06	
pr → mp	**-.186****	**.133**	**10.91**	**15.38**	**4.47**	**<.05**
arx → mp	-.193	-.503**	10.91	11.56	0.65	
pbc → mp	.523**	.418*	10.91	11	0.09	
****p≤.001, ***p≤.010, **p≤.050, *p≤.100						

was measured to clarify whether the decrease in model fit was significant or insignificant. Only one path differed significantly between genders. Completely different from what was assumed; physical restrictions coming along with the size of the device had a different effect on mobile phone usage between male and female consumers. For males, the path coefficient from restrictions to usage was negative and significant, and for females the same coefficient was insignificant.

The second proposition suggested weaker path coefficients for highly educated consumers. Only one path indicated a significant group-wise difference (Figure 5). This was attached with the physical restrictions but this time the influence of it toward perceived behavioral control differed between higher and lower education. Surprisingly, the perception of physical restrictions had

a positive effect on perceived behavioral control among lower education consumers. For higher educated consumers, this relationship was totally the opposite, a negative path was found, which is consistent with the model estimated from the complete sample (Figure 3). It could be that the less educated persons facing stronger restrictions through the device size prefer that they have higher control and enough learning and knowledge concerning the usage of the phone, i.e. they have been able to pass the difficulties that the size of the device causes.

For the third proposition, the sample was divided in two groups; 55-64 year old consumers and 65-79 year old consumers (Figure 6). Age appeared to cause differences in one path. The direction was the same as suggested: cognitive ability had a stronger negative effect on perceived technology

Figure 5. Educational differences in path coefficients

Relationship	Lower education N=298	Higher education N=123	Unrestricted χ^2 (df=15)	Restricted χ^2 (df=16)	Difference χ^2 (df=1)	p-value
ph → pr	-.128	-.327***	11.77	12.88	1.11	
ca → pr	-.160	-.054	11.77	12.02	.25	
ca → arx	-.329***	-.257***	11.77	12.02	.25	
ca → pbc	.232***	.097*	11.77	13.05	1.28	
pr → arx	.503****	.386****	11.77	12.40	.63	
pr → pbc	**.142***	**-.113***	**11.77**	**16.01**	**4.24**	**<.05**
arx → pbc	-.745****	-.778****	11.77	11.58	-.19	
pr → mp	.121	-.040	11.77	12.65	.88	
arx → mp	-.408*	-.451*	11.77	11.76	-.01	
pbc → mp	.499**	.383*	11.77	11.77	0	
****p≤.001, ***p≤.010, **p≤.050, *p≤.100						

Figure 6. Age differences in path coefficients

Relationship	55-64 year old N=230	65-79 year old N=191	Unrestricted χ^2 (df=15)	Restricted χ^2 (df=16)	Difference χ^2 (df=1)	p-value
ph → pr	-.207**	-.391***	12.57	13.67	1.1	
ca → pr	.032	-.059	12.57	12.85	0.28	
ca → anx	**-.126***	**-.408******	**12.57**	**16.73**	**4.16**	**<.05**
ca → pbc	.115**	.142	12.57	12.6	0.03	
pr → anx	.509****	.324***	12.57	14.26	1.69	
pr → pbc	.049	-.012	12.57	12.77	0.2	
anx → pbc	-.826****	-.781****	12.57	12.69	0.12	
pr → mp	.072	.011	12.57	12.63	0.06	
anx → mp	-.692***	-.448	12.57	12.77	0.2	
pbc → mp	.140	.457	12.57	13.08	0.51	

****$p \leq .001$, ***$p \leq .010$, **$p \leq .050$, *$p \leq .100$

anxiety among older consumers. A small decline in cognitive functioning increases technology anxiety more among the older group.

Considering the analysis of age, the majority of the younger group had already retired, although 65 years is the general retiring age in Finland. Therefore, the analysis of based on working status is also considered important. Figure 7 summarizes the results from the multi-group analysis concerning retired and not retired people. It now seems that working life status differentiates the paths more than any other socio-economic characteristic analyzed. The results indicate that the last proposition was in the right direction supporting the notion that retired would have stronger path coefficient in the model. This was true for three paths. First, cognitive ability causes no anxiety for aging still

working but for the retired, decrease in cognitive functioning increases anxiety toward mobile phones. The second significant difference between groups was found in the relationship between anxiety and perceived behavioral control. This path is significant for both groups, but stronger for the retired. Among retired people, technology anxiety had a more negative path suggesting that the higher level of anxiety has stronger negative effect on behavioral control, which thus suggests that they are more insecure users of mobile phones. The last difference concerns the effect of perceived control on mobile phone usage. For those still in working life, the path is insignificant and for the retired, the path is positive and significant. This could indicate that the non-retired are very used to using the mobile phone and the control over

Figure 7. Differences in path coefficients by working status

Relationship	Working N=142	Retired N=273	Unrestricted χ^2 (df=15)	Restricted χ^2 (df=16)	Difference χ^2 (df=1)	p-value
ph → pr	-.220*	-.231**	13.79	13.78	.01	
ca → pr	.088	-.186**	16.47	13.78	2.69	
ca → anx	**-.086**	**-.351******	**17.5**	**13.78**	**3.72**	**<.10**
ca → pbc	.120**	.105	13.78	13.78	0	
pr → anx	.505****	.372****	14.76	13.78	.98	
pr → pbc	-.055	.03	14.31	13.78	.53	
anx → pbc	**-.617******	**-.872******	**18.47**	**13.78**	**4.69**	**<.05**
pr → mp	.121	-.092	15.59	13.78	1.81	
anx → mp	-.632****	-.063	16.11	13.78	2.33	
pbc → mp	**.083**	**.708***	**17.55**	**13.78**	**3.77**	**<.10**

****$p \leq .001$, ***$p \leq .010$, **$p \leq .050$, *$p \leq .100$

the device is rather self-evident, and among the retirees, them who have made effort for learning are higher level users of mobile phones.

FUTURE RESEARCH DIRECTIONS

The current research was conducted among aging consumers, but a similar research would be useful for other age cohorts. As the focus here was mobile phone usage in general heedless of the wide variety of mobile services available, the interests in the future is to aim toward identifying the adoption behavior related to mobile services and to assess the profitability of content services in advance. For the identification of target segments, it is important to evaluate how socio-economic characteristics discriminate consumers and therefore the current research method would provide useful insights if replicated to consumers of a wider age range. Considering the aging market potential for mobile services it would be of great importance to assess how the phone manufacturers and service providers develop their actions to match the needs of the changing market demographics in developed welfare states where age structures will become distorted.

CONCLUSION

The effects of socio-economic variables have been studied rarely, and when studied, the effects have been rather minor. Their influence has been mainly assessed in regression type research arrangements, and their true effect has remained unsolved. The purpose of the multi-group analysis was to display how the socio-economic indicators discriminate the influences of different factors behind mobile phone usage. Although, there didn't exist multiple diverging relationships in the models, results clearly indicate that gender, age, education and retirement change the nature of the relationship

between background characteristics and technology perceptions and between technology perceptions and rate of mobile phone usage. It can also be conjectured whether there would have been additional differences if the sample would have been composed differently.

Gender revealed differences between the technology characteristics and mobile phones usage. Education on behalf caused differences in attitude formation related to technology perceptions. The opposite direction of the coefficient between physical restriction and behavioral control compared with education level is rather interesting. It can be assumed that consumers with lower education place extra effort on behavioral control when the physical restrictions increase. Males and also higher education consumers appear to form a group that suffers from the small size of the mobile phones. This will be one of the future challenges that should be answered by the device and content designers. Age distinguished consumers when the aging related characteristics were concerned. Along with aging people face changes in cognitive functions caused by multiple reasons. The results clearly suggest that the decrease in cognitive ability turns against technological development by increasing technology anxiety. Including the working life status for the analysis pointed out that age truly isn't reasonable distinguisher in consumer behavior related to technology. In recent years, along with high investments on the infrastructure, mobile communication is present in many industries, thus making it familiar. Therefore, the aged consumers already retired even a decade ago don't benefit the influence coming along with technology utilization in working situations. Problems related to technology anxiety are treatable, courses are nowadays organized for senior citizens related to internet and mobile phones, and with training and peer support, the perceived control over the device is also expected to increase and change over time as positive experiences take place. In addition, the design of mobile phones should meet the requirements of elderly as well as the design of services provided through mobile communications.

REFERENCES

Ajzen, I. (1985). From Intentions to Actions: A Theory of Planned Behavior. In J. Kuhl & J. Beckmann (Eds.), *Action Control: From Cognition to Behavior* (pp. 11-39). Heidelberg: Springer.

Ajzen, I. (1991). The Theory of Planned Behavior. *Organizational Behavior and Human Decision Processes, 50,* 179. doi:10.1016/0749-5978(91)90020-T

Ajzen, I., Beauducel, A., Biehl, B., Bosniak, M., Conrad, W., & Wagener, D. (2005). Laws of Human Behavior: Symmetry, Compatibility, and Attitude-Behavior Correspondence. In *Multivariate research strategies.* Maastricht. Germany: Shaker Publishers.

Blaxter, M. (1990). *Health and Lifestyles.* London: Tavistock/Routledge.

Brosnan, M. J. (1998). *Technophobia: The Psychological Impact of Information Technology.* London: Routledge.

Chua, S. L., Chen, D.-T., & Wong, A. F. L. (1999). Computer Anxiety and Its Correlates: A Meta-Analysis. *Computers in Human Behavior, 15*(5), 609–623. doi:10.1016/S0747-5632(99)00039-4

Cohen, B. A., & Waugh, G. W. (1989). Assessing Computer Anxiety. *Psychological Reports, 65,* 735–738.

Czaja, S. J., & Lee, C. C. (2007). The Impact of Aging on Access to Technology. *Universal Access in the Information Society, 5*(4), 341–349. doi:10.1007/s10209-006-0060-x

Dyck, J. L., & Smither, J. A.-A. (1996). Older Adults' Acquisition of Word Processing: The Contribution of Cognitive Abilities and Computer Anxiety. *Computers in Human Behavior, 12*(1), 107–119. doi:10.1016/0747-5632(95)00022-4

Gefen, D., & Straub, D. W. (1997). Gender Differences on the Perception and Use of E-Mail: An Extension to the Technology Acceptance Model. *MIS Quarterly, 21*(4), 389–400. doi:10.2307/249720

Gilbert, D., Lee-Kelley, L., & Barton, M. (2003). Technophobia, Gender Influences and Consumer Decision-Making for Technology-Related Products. *European Journal of Innovation Management, 6*(4), 253–263. doi:10.1108/14601060310500968

Igbaria, M., & Parasuraman, S. (1989). A Path Analytic Study of Individual Characteristics, Computer Anxiety and Attitudes toward Microcomputers. *Journal of Management, 15*(3), 373–388. doi:10.1177/014920638901500302

Jelicic, M., & Kempen, G. I. J. M. (1999). Effect of Self-Rated Health on Cognitive Performance in Community Dwelling Elderly. *Educational Gerontology, 25,* 13–17. doi:10.1080/036012799267981

Leinonen, R. (2002). *Self-Rated Health in Old Age: A Follow-up Study of Changes and Determinants.* University of Jyväskylä, Jyväskylä, Sweden.

Loyd, B. H., & Loyd, D. E. (1985). The Reliability and Validity of an Instrument for the Assessment of Computer Attitudes. *Educational and Psychological Measurement, 45,* 903–908. doi:10.1177/0013164485454021

Lunsford, D. A., & Burnett, M. S. (1992). Marketing Product Innovations to the Elderly: Understanding the Barriers to Adoption. *Journal of Consumer Marketing, 9*(4), 53–63. doi:10.1108/07363769210037097

Meuter, M. L., Ostrom, A. L., Bitner, M. J., & Roundtree, R. (2003). The Influence of Technology Anxiety on Consumers Use and Experiences with Self-Service Technologies. *Journal of Business Research, 56*(11), 899–906. doi:10.1016/S0148-2963(01)00276-4

Morris, M. G., & Venkatesh, V. (2000). Age Differences in Technology Adoption Decisions: Implications for a Changing Work Force. *Personnel Psychology, 53*(2), 375–403. doi:10.1111/j.1744-6570.2000.tb00206.x

Moschis, G. P. (1992). Gerontographics: A Scientific Approach to Analyzing and Targeting the Mature Market. *Journal of Services Marketing, 6*(3), 17–26. doi:10.1108/08876049210035890

Moschis, G. P. (2003). Marketing to Older Adults: An Updated Overview of Present Knowledge and Practice. *Journal of Consumer Marketing, 20*(6), 516–525. doi:10.1108/07363760310499093

Oyedele, A., & Simpson, P. M. (2007). An Empirical Investigation of Consumer Control Factors on Intention to Use Selected Self-Service Technologies. *International Journal of Service Industry Management, 18*(3), 287–306. doi:10.1108/09564230710751497

Pak, C., & Kambil, A. (2006). Over 50 and Ready to Shop: Serving the Aging Consumer. *The Journal of Business Strategy, 27*(6), 18–28. doi:10.1108/02756660610710319

Passik, S. D., Lundberg, J. C., Rosenfeld, B., Kirsh, K. L., Donaghy, K., & Theobald, D. (2000). Factor Analysis of the Zung Self-Rating Depression Scale in a Large Ambulatory Oncology Sample. *Psychosomatics, 41*(2), 121–127. doi:10.1176/appi.psy.41.2.121

Selwyn, N. (1997). Student's Attitudes toward Computers: Validation of a Computer Attitude Scale for 16-19 Education. *Computers & Education, 28*(1), 35–41. doi:10.1016/S0360-1315(96)00035-8

Suutama, T. (2004). Kognitiivisest toiminnot. In T. Raitanen, T. Hänninen, H. Pajunen & T. Suutama (Eds.), *Geropsykologia: Vanhenemisen ja vanhuuden psykologia* (pp. 76-108). Porvoo, Finland: WSOY.

Taylor, S., & Todd, P. A. (1995). Understanding Information Technology Usage: A Test of Competing Models. *Information Systems Research, 6*(2), 144. doi:10.1287/isre.6.2.144

Todman, J., & Day, K. (2006). Computer Anxiety: The Role of Psychological Gender. *Computers in Human Behavior, 22*(5), 856–869. doi:10.1016/j.chb.2004.03.009

Vishwanath, A., & Goldhaber, G. M. (2003). An Examination of the Factors Contributing to Adoption Decisions among Late-Diffused Technology Products. *New Media & Society, 5*(4), 547–572. doi:10.1177/146144480354005

KEY TERMS AND DEFINITIONS

Adoption: A decision to buy and start using an innovation.

Cognitive Ability: The degree of the ability to learn and take care of normal matters.

Innovation: Idea, product or service that is new to the adopting consumer.

Perceived Behavioral Control: The degree to which the innovation is understandable and easy to use.

Perceived Health: The degree to which individuals perceived one's own well-being in terms of health conditions.

Physical Restrictions: The degree of problems arising from the size of the mobile phones.

Technology Anxiety: The degree to which the usage or idea of using the technology in question arouses unfavorable feelings and fear.

Chapter 84
Mobile Agents in E-Commerce

Bo Chen
Michigan Technological University, USA

INTRODUCTION

A **mobile agent** is a composition of computer program, data, and execution state, which is able to move from one computer to another autonomously and continue its execution on the destination computer. Mobile agents provide a new programming paradigm for building agile distributed systems. The ability to travel allows a **mobile agent system** to move computation to data source systems. This decentralized approach improves network efficiency since the processing is performed locally. For example, in an **e-commerce** application shown in Figure 1, mobile agents are used to search and purchase products. Once the *Buyer Server* receives a buyer's purchase request, it generates a mobile agent and sends it to the *Information Server* to search retailers who sell the product. Having a list of retailers, the *Buyer Server* dispatches a mobile

agent visiting these retailers. The mobile agent negotiates with retailers' local seller agents and reports the offers to the *Buyer Server*. The *Buyer Server* evaluates all the offers, and sends a purchase mobile agent to the best offer retailer to make the final purchase.

Some advantages which **mobile agents** possess over conventional computing paradigms are follows.

- Reduce network traffic and overcome network latency. Mobile agents can move to remote computers that contain objects with which the mobile agents want to interact, and take the advantage of being at the same host.
- Work in heterogeneous network hosts if a run-time support environment is installed on these hosts.
- Tolerant to network failures and support disconnected operation. Mobile agents are able

DOI: 10.4018/978-1-61520-611-7.ch084

Figure 1. Mobile agents migrate over networks searching and purchasing products

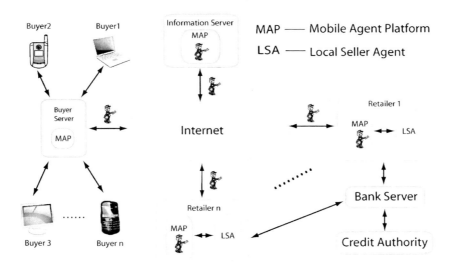

to operate without an active connection between the destination and the home host.

- Work autonomously.
- Flexible to change an agent's actions. Only the agent program rather than the computation hosts must be updated.
- Applications become in-situ reprogrammable using mobile code in mobile agents.

Mobile agents have received a diverse range of applications in information retrieval, network management, e-commerce, transportation systems, distributed control systems, and manufacturing. The advantages of mobile agents, such as reducing network traffic, supporting disconnected operation, overcoming network latency, and roaming ability in heterogeneous platforms, have great value to build ubiquitous e-commerce/m-commerce systems. Most **e-commerce** applications involve a large amount of information exchange and intensive data processing. Mobile agent approach scales effectively as the size of data to be processed and the number of data servers increase (Patel & Garg, 2005). Compared to the conventional **client-server** paradigm, mobile agents provide fast and efficient interaction with

remote services and save network bandwidth (Zhao & Blum, 2000).

M-commerce is an emerging e-commerce model, which conducts commerce using mobile devices such as mobile phones and PDAs (Personal Digital Assistant). Due to physical and network constraints (low CPU speed, small memory size, poor network connectivity, and limited bandwidth), the implementation of client/server approach in m-commerce systems faces significant challenges. The mobile agent paradigm offers an appropriate solution to reduce network traffic and tolerate poor network connectivity in m-commerce systems (Li, 2007).

This chapter attempts to highlight good features of the mobile agent paradigm for the applications in e-commerce. A number of selected mobile agent-based e-commerce systems and the agent platforms are introduced. The major security and privacy concerns in mobile agent-based e-commerce systems and the commonly used approaches to address these issues are discussed. The future research directions are recommended in the conclusions.

MOBILE AGENT-BASED E-COMMERCE APPLICATIONS

E-commerce is the greatest potential application area for mobile agents where the agents facilitate the phases of brokering, negotiation, payment, and delivery of a transaction (Zhao & Blum, 2000). A survey conducted by Kowalczyk (Kowalczyk, et. al., 2003) showed that the research community had made effort of using mobile agents to advance e-commerce. Mobile agent technology has been applied to e-commerce to provide functions, such as **e-trading** (Chen, et. al., 2007; Dasgupta, et. al., 1999), **brokering** service and **e-marketplace** (Du, et. al., 2005; Hu, 2007; Wang, et. al., 2002), **auction** (Lee, et. al., 2003; Shih, et. al., 2005), **electronic payment** (Guan, et. al., 2004; Patel & Garg, 2004), mobile stock investment decision-making (Wu, et. al., 2008), and global logistic services (Trappey, et. al., 2004). Typical mobile agent tasks include searching product information, making routing purchase, and conducting negotiations. In this section, several selected mobile agent-based e-commerce applications are briefly introduced.

The **electronic marketplace** provides a platform to facilitate buyers and sellers exchanging information about goods and services, match buyers with sellers, and make payments. To provide autonomy and independence for participating parties, Du, et. al. (2005) propose a mobile agent-based marketplace, which allows corporate data to be maintained by local buyers and sellers and transferred to the marketplace only when orders are matched. The **e-marketplace** consists of buyers, an intermediary server, and suppliers. Buyers send the request information to the intermediary server. The intermediary server aggregates demands, filters unqualified buyers or suppliers, generates the itinerary of the mobile agents for visiting potential suppliers, matches orders, keeps information about suppliers, and manages agents in the marketplace. When a mobile agent inquires product information in a supplier's server, a sta-

tionary agent residing in the supplier's server is activated. The local stationary agent searches the inventory database and reports to the mobile agent about the availability of the product.

MAGICS (Business-to-consumer mobile agent-based Internet commerce system) (Chen, et. al., 2007) is a mobile agent-based commerce system to facilitate the consumer buying process: search, evaluation, and purchase. The MAGICS allows customers to provide buying requirements to a proxy/agent server through a Web interface or a wireless terminal. Once the server receives a customer's request, mobile agents will be generated for the customer to get offers from merchants, evaluate offers, and even complete purchases.

Electronic payment is a critical step in e-commerce. An electronic payment system for agent-based e-commerce (Guan, et. al., 2004) employs Secure Electronic Transaction (EST) protocol and E-cash for online payment. The payment system includes entities such as Agent Butler, Merchant Host, Payment Gateway, Financial Institutions, and Trusted Third Party. The Agent Butler represents the cardholder who makes payment using a payment card through the EST protocol and dispatches mobile agents to Merchant Hosts for collecting product information. During the purchasing process, the Merchant Hosts invoke Payment Authorization request to the Payment Gateway for checking the credentials of the cardholder. If the cardholder is verified, the Merchant Hosts will receive payment capture token from the Payment Gateway and use it for actual payment.

A mobile reverse **auction** agent system (MoRAAS) (Shih, et. al., 2005) uses collaborative mobile agents to mediate between a buyer and sellers. The MoRAAS system consists of three components: a buyer agent, a broker agent, and a bid agent. When a mobile user wishes to make a purchase, he/she connects to a buyer agent server in the wired network through a mobile device. On the other hand, a broker agent chooses mobile sellers who agree to make a sell. Selected mobile sellers connect to bid agents and send information about the goods. As soon as the buyer agent has been created, it moves to the hosts of the selected sellers to negotiate with them. At the end of the negotiation and auction, the buyer agent sends the results to the user.

MOBILE AGENT PLATFORMS FOR SUPPORTING E-COMMERCE APPLICATIONS

A number of mobile agent platforms have been developed for e-commerce applications. Nomad (Sandholm & Huai, 2000) is a mobile agent-based **auction** system consisting of distributed auction servers – eAuctionHouse. Nomad allows mobile agents to travel to the eAuctionHouse site and actively participate in auctions on the user's behalf even when the user is disconnected from the network. The main components of the Nomad system include an interface for agent generation, an agent dock, an agent manager, and an agent database. The *Concordia* agent system is used as the basis of the Nomad agent dock. The agent manager notifies agents when the auction information they are interested in is altered. Nomad allows users to program their own agents or lunch predefined template agents from a web interface.

MAgNET (Dasgupta, et. al., 1999) is a networked **electronic trading** system that is implemented based on a mobile agent system called *Aglets*. If a buyer wants to find suppliers who provide the component parts required for manufacturing a product, the buyer creates a mobile agent with an itinerary of supplier sites and criteria for the acquisition of the product and dispatches the mobile agent to the potential suppliers. The buyer's subsystem consists of the buyer's stationary agent and a graphical user interface (GUI). The buyer's stationary agent creates and manages the buyer's mobile agents, and interacts with a human buyer through the GUI. The supplier's stationary agent in the supplier's subsystem interacts with the buyer's mobile agents.

MASISS (Wu, et. al., 2008), a Mobile Agent-based Stock Intermediary Services System, provides ubiquitous and seamless transaction activities for financial institutions. The MASISS framework is developed by the integration of J2ME and J2EE environment, consisting of mobile agent layer, business application layer, and resource layer. The mobile agent layer includes communication manager, agent gateway, and mobile server channel. The mobile agent layer is built on an agent platform, *Tahiti*, supported by IBM's Tokyo laboratory. It creates, clones, and dispatches mobile agents. The business application layer consists of service manager to provide services to investors, and data mining engine to find optimal association rule. The resource layer includes a user subscriber database, a stock price historical database, and a category stock association rule database.

IMAGO (Intelligent Mobile Agent Gliding on-line) system (Li, 2007) allows consumers to dispatch mobile agents from their handheld devices to visit E-stores for searching, comparing, evaluation, buying, and making payment. The IMAGO m-commerce framework defines three types of agents: device agents, stationary agents, and mobile agents. A device agent is installed on the handheld device allowing a mobile user to locate its home server, communicate with the home agent to invoke an m-commerce application. A stationary agent resides at its host to provide a bridge between the mobile users and the m-commerce applications, discover services, and act as the representative of the seller. A mobile agent represents the user roaming the Internet to visit vendors that may carry product desired by the customer, look for a special service, and conduct the transaction according to a specific trading policy. A simplified IMAGO IDE is implemented as a mobile portal on the handheld devices.

SECURITY ISSUES AND TECHNIQUES IN MOBILE AGENT E-COMMERCE SYSTEMS

Due to the open nature of the Internet, security and privacy issues are major concerns in e-commerce scenario where two unfamiliar parties engage in a trade. Strong encryption and authentication are commonly used approaches to build the trustworthiness of transactions over the Internet (Zhao & Blum, 2000). The protection of privacy includes the identities of customers and vendors, customer's bank account details, and exchanged information such as the integrity of bids, negotiated issues, and transaction details.

The most obvious security issues that a mobile agent security infrastructure must handle include host security and mobile agent security. In addition, a secure channel is needed over which a mobile agent can migrate. The host security is concerned with protecting a host from harmful behaviors of malicious mobile agents, while the agent security is concerned with protecting a mobile agent from malicious hosts. A **malicious agent** is an agent that performs harmful actions, such as unauthorized access and alteration of local resources (data, system calls), or an overuse of a host's local resources. A **malicious host** is an agent server that attempts to spy out and manipulate agent code or data and control flow, provide fake system calls, and execute agent code incorrectly, or to reverse engineer and manipulate agent code and trade secrets (Zhao & Blum, 2000). The commonly used approaches to address the host security include a secure runtime environment, runtime checking and access control, authenticating the owner of an incoming agent, code signature to prove that the agent has not been tampered with, and authorizing request services based on security policy. The problem of protecting a mobile agent from malicious hosts is challenging since it is difficult to protect an executing program from the host or interpreter, which is responsible for its execution.

There are several approaches to address this challenge. One possible approach is to employ host authentication to prove that the agent moves to the intended host. Software-based approaches are mainly based on cryptography.

Some of these security approaches have been used to implement secure mechanisms in mobile agent-based e-commerce systems. For example, Corradi et. al. (Corradi, et. al., 1999) propose a MH (Multiple-Hops) protocol to preserve the agent integrity. The MH protocol has the goal of detecting whether the collected data in the agent state portion has been maliciously modified and/or deleted by any visited e-commerce service providers. For the protection of information exchange, Zhang et. al. (Zhang, et. al., 2004) proposed an agent-based fair signature exchange protocol, which allows a party to delegate a mobile agent with the power to digitally sign a document on its behalf without disclosing its private key. Secure mobile agent-based E-negotiation (Al-Jaljouli & Abawajy, 2007) propose a security protocol that protects the information exchanged between the mobile agents during e-negotiations. Trust-reputation approach (Gan, et. al., 2008; Zhao & Blum, 2000) is also used to mitigate transaction risk by deriving the trustworthiness of certain agent from its transaction history.

Song and Korba (Song & Korba, 2003) propose a secure communication architecture for the mobile agents. Every agent must register and get its certificate from a Certificate Authority in the agent platform. All agents store their private key in their home platform. When an agent wants to move to other host for its e-business, the agent clones a representative mobile agent, signs and sends the mobile agent to the remote host with its certificate but without its private key. The representative agent communicates with other agents. When the communication involves important information exchange or needs to be signed with their private key, the representative mobile agent will build a secure channel and forward the messages to their home agent. The home agent then processes the messages with its private key.

With the roaming capability, mobile agent-based e-commerce systems raise significant new security threats from malicious agents and hosts. As an agent needs to move among external hosts to perform its tasks, the data collected by the agent may be modified, the credit carried by the agent may be stolen, and the mission statement of the agent may be changed during transport (Guan & Yang, 2002). The commonly used methods for protecting a mobile agent in transit include: bundling an agent in a secure envelop such that only the destination host will be able to read it or use cryptographic network protocols, such as secure socket layer. SAFE: secure agent roaming for e-commerce (Guan & Yang, 2002) proposes three transport protocols: supervised agent transport, unsupervised agent transport, and bootstrap agent transport, to provide a secure roaming mechanism for agents. Under supervised agent transport protocol, an agent has to request roaming permit from its owner before roaming. The owner decides if the roaming request is approved, which provides a mechanism to prevent its agent from roaming to undesired hosts. During roaming, the sensitive code/data of the agent are frozen. The host protection mechanisms include inspecting agent's credentials and authenticating incoming mobile agents.

CONCLUSION

Mobile agent technology has received an increasing interest in e-commerce applications. A numerous research efforts have been made for the implementation of e-commerce functions using mobile agents, design secure mechanisms to protect mobile agents and agent hosts, and the development of mobile agent platforms to support agent communication and migration. The research results clearly demonstrate the potential of using

mobile agent technology to improve the flexibility and efficiency of e-commerce systems. Despite the accomplished achievements, the application of mobile agent technology in e-commerce is still at infant state. The future research directions are recommended to promote standardization, enhance security, reduce footprint of agent platforms, and incorporate new technologies.

- Most reported mobile agent e-commerce systems are built on general purpose mobile agent systems, such as Aglets and Concordia. These agent systems are not compliant to two major **agent standards**, the IEEE FIPA (Foundation for Intelligent Physical Agents) standards and the MASIF (Mobile Agent System Interoperability Facility). The compliance with agent standards is important for the interoperation and cooperation among agents and agent systems.

- As the PDAs and mobile cellular phones widely spread, the m-commerce that combines e-commerce with mobile devices is likely to become a major business model in the near future. The physical constraints in mobile devices require agent platforms having very small footprint.

- XML (extensible markup language) is a recent standard recommended by the World Wide Web consortium for encoding information and their structures. XML is more flexible than HTML (Hypertext Markup Language) and less complex than SGML (Standard Generalized Markup Language) for Web-based applications. Using XML to encode agent communication language messages and represent different types of data facilitates the practical integration with a variety of Web technology and leverage Web-based tools and infrastructure.

REFERENCES

Al-Jaljouli, R., & Abawajy, J. H. (2007). Secure mobile agent-based e-negotiation for on-line trading. *2007 IEEE International Symposium on Signal Processing and Information Technology*, (pp. 610-615).

Chen, H., Lam, P. P. Y., Chan, H. C. B., Dillon, T. S., Cao, J., & Lee, R. S. T. (2007). Business-to-consumer mobile agent-based Internet commerce system (MAGICS). *IEEE Transactions on Systems, Man and Cybernetics. Part C, Applications and Reviews*, *37*(6), 1174–1189. doi:10.1109/TSMCC.2007.900653

Corradi, A., Cremonini, M., Montanari, R., & Stefanelli, C. (1999). Mobile agents integrity for electronic commerce applications. *Information Systems*, *24*(6), 519–533. doi:10.1016/S0306-4379(99)00030-7

Dasgupta, P., Narasimhan, N., Moser, L. E., & Melliar-Smith, P. M. (1999). MAgNET: Mobile agents for networked electronic trading. *IEEE Transactions on Knowledge and Data Engineering*, *11*(4), 509–525. doi:10.1109/69.790796

Du, T. C., Li, E. Y., & Wei, E. (2005). Mobile agents for a brokering service in the electronic marketplace. *Decision Support Systems*, *39*(3), 371–383. doi:10.1016/j.dss.2004.01.003

Gan, Z., Li, Y., Xiao, G., & Wei, D. (2008, 24-26 April). A novel reputation computing model for mobile agent-based e-commerce systems. In *2008 International Conference on Information Security and Assurance (ISA '08)*, (pp. 253-260), Busan, South Korea.

Guan, S.-U., Tan, S. L., & Hua, F. (2004). A modularized electronic payment system for agent-based e-commerce. *Journal of Research and Practice on Information Technology*, *36*(2), 67–87.

Guan, S.-U., & Yang, Y. (2002). SAFE: secure agent roaming for e-commerce. *Computers & Industrial Engineering*, *42*(2-4), 481–493. doi:10.1016/S0360-8352(02)00042-6

Hu, H. Y. (2007). A reliable and configurable e-commerce mechanism based on mobile agents in mobile wireless environments. In *2007 International Conference on Intelligent Pervasive Computing*, (pp. 7-10), Jeju City, South Korea.

Kowalczyk, R., Ulieru, M., & Unland, R. (2003). Integrating mobile and intelligent agents in advanced e-commerce: a survey. In R. Kowalczyk, J. P. Muller, H. Tianfield & R. Unland (Eds.), *Agent Technologies, Infrastructures, Tools, and Applications for E-Services. NODe 2002 Agent-Related Workshops. Revised Papers*, (pp. 295-313). Erfurt, Germany: Springer-Verlag.

Lee, K. Y., Yun, J. S., & Jo, G. S. (2003). MoCAAS: auction agent system using a collaborative mobile agent in electronic commerce. *Expert Systems with Applications*, *24*(2), 183–187. doi:10.1016/S0957-4174(02)00141-0

Li, X. (2007). The role of mobile agents in M-commerce. In *The sixth Wuhan international conference on E-Business*, (pp. 403-408).

Patel, R. B., & Garg, K. (2004). Distributed banking with mobile agents: an approach for e-commerce. *WSEAS Transactions on Computers*, *3*(1), 98–102.

Patel, R. B., & Garg, K. (2005). A comparative study of mobile agent and client-server technologies in a real application. *Advances in data management*, (pp. 176-182).

Sandholm, T., & Huai, Q. B. (2000). Nomad: Mobile agent system for an Internet-based auction house. *IEEE Internet Computing*, *4*(2), 80–86. doi:10.1109/4236.832950

Shih, D.-H., Huang, S.-Y., & Yen, D. C. (2005). A new reverse auction agent system for m-commerce using mobile agents. *Computer Standards & Interfaces*, *27*(4), 383–395. doi:10.1016/j.csi.2004.10.006

Song, R., & Korba, L. (2003). Security communication architecture for mobile agents and E-commerce. In *Proceedings of the 2003 international workshop on Mobile Systems, E-commerce Agent Technology*.

Trappey, A. J. C., Trappey, C. V., Hou, J. L., & Chen, B. J. G. (2004). Mobile agent technology and application for online global logistic services. *Industrial Management & Data Systems*, *104*(1-2), 169–183. doi:10.1108/02635570410522143

Wang, Y., Tan, K.-L., & Ren, J. (2002). A study of building Internet marketplaces on the basis of mobile agents for parallel processing. *World Wide Web (Bussum)*, *5*(1), 41–66. doi:10.1023/A:1015798306889

Wu, W.-H., Ko, P.-C., Lin, P.-C., & Su, M.-H. (2008). Applying mobile agent to a mobile stock intermediary services system development. *International Journal of Smart Home*, *2*(2), 1–12.

Zhang, N., Shi, Q., Merabti, M., & Askwith, R. (2004). Autonomous mobile agent based fair exchange. *Computer Networks*, *46*(6), 751–770. doi:10.1016/j.comnet.2004.06.005

Zhao, J., & Blum, T. (2000). Next-generation e-commerce: XML+mobile agent+trust. *CG topics*, (pp. 26-28).

KEY TERMS AND DEFINITIONS

Client-Server: one type of network architecture in which the client system makes service requests to the server system.

E-Commerce: buying and selling products or services over electronic systems such as the Internet.

Malicious Agent: an agent that performs harmful actions.

Malicious Host: an agent server attacks mobile agents to achieve a malicious goal.

M-Commerce: conduct commerce using mobile devices.

Mobile Agent System: provide mechanisms to support agent management, migration, execution, communication, and directory maintenance.

Mobile Agent: a piece of software that is able to move from one computer to another in a network.

Chapter 85
Mobile Telephony as a Universal Service

Ofir Turel
California State University Fullerton, USA

Alexander Serenko
Lakehead University, Canada

If we cannot end now our differences, at least we can help make the world safe for diversity. -- John F. Kennedy

INTRODUCTION

The opening quote nicely conceptualizes one of the most difficult challenges managers and regulators in the telecommunications sector face. While such individuals are not, for the most part, concerned with world-safety, they do need to address similar diversity issues in order to be profitable and to provide true universal services (i.e., reasonably priced, high quality telecommunication services to everyone who wishes to use them). Similarly to John F. Kennedy, managers and regulators understand that one-service or set of regulations that fits all

may not be a wise strategy. Rather, their offerings and regulatory mechanisms are always flexible, and they cater to a heterogonous subscriber market. While wireless service providers do try to cater to different market segments by offering a variety of service packages, regulators often employ a single set of regulations that serve the entire market. On the one hand, organizations offering mobile services to individuals attempt to segment the market to maximize various performance factors, such as usage airtime, revenues, and customer base. On the other hand, policies should be in place to avoid the discrimination of specific less profitable customer categories. In fact, in the 21st century, mobile telephony has become so critical for the well-being of millions of people that it is vital to ensure the fairness of mobile services delivery.

DOI: 10.4018/978-1-61520-611-7.ch085

OVERVIEW

The Need For Market Oriented Policies

Market segmentation is an obvious concept for wireless service providers. Its importance is further emphasized in today's networked society. Currently, many telecommunication service providers cater to a much broader market than the one they had initially targeted. For example, twenty years ago, expensive handset and service charges led to the adoption of wireless services by mostly high-income individuals. In today's markets, however, the penetration of mobile telephony has reached lower-income individuals as well (Jain, 2006). Thus, in modern heterogeneous markets, businesses continuously investigate demographic and psychographic profiles that affect subscriber interaction with telecommunication services (e.g., Chaudhuri, Flamm, & Horrigan, 2005; Rice & Katz, 2003). Their objective is to identify a number of distinct user groups and to serve them differently. For this, regulators utilize behavioral research to understand how subscribers, belonging to different market segments, develop perceptions and form behavioral outcomes of service usage, resulting in company revenues (Schejter, Serenko, Turel, & Zahaf, 2010). Therefore, mobile service providers may potentially discriminate against specific less profitable customer segments, for instance, low-income households who mostly subscribe to inexpensive basic plans, avoid premium services, live in remote regions, or are located in infrastructurally challenged areas.

To emphasize the importance of this issue, we may recall Hurricane Katrina, one of the deadliest natural disasters in the US history. Throughout this tragedy, wireless services were the only public communication means that remained intact. Thus, the potential use of mobile phones by lower-income individuals in the New Orleans area may have saved lives. Therefore, one may ask – 'would things have been different had the Federal Communications Commission (FCC) enforced affordable access to wireless services for low-income families?,' or 'would things have been different had the FCC enforced certain quality standards (e.g., maximum number of disconnected calls) in low-income areas?' It is believed that this argument conveys that both regulators and service providers should not only concentrate on differences in market segments to maximize their profits, but also on the facilitation of universal services.

Universal Services

Universal service is a key desirable objective for many regulators. It is broadly defined as providing reasonably priced, high quality telecommunication services to everyone who wishes to use them (Melody, 1997). This is an important concept because access to such services enables full participation in modern society (Blackman, 1995). To ensure the universality of telecommunication services, regulators typically define 'Universal service obligations' (USO) that are implemented through coverage constraints (Valletti, Hoernig, & Barros, 2002) and price-capping (Baake, 2002). Financing the nationwide provision of services in the US is done through a Universal Service Fund (Prieger, 1998) that subsidizes for telephone service in areas with no business-justification for service provisioning.

The term "universal service" has emerged in the early 20th century for describing the need for interconnecting the thousands of local phone companies that existed in the US (Mueller, 1997). Given the myriad of new communication bearer technologies, however, one of the ongoing debates relates to the scope of services included under this umbrella (e.g., broadband, cable, and cellular communications) (Pitt & Levine, 2004). For example, the 1996 Telecommunications Act in the US is pretty vague with regards to this scope. The

FCC states that the goal of universal service is to "increase access to advanced telecommunications services throughout the Nation; [and] advance the availability of such services to all consumers, including those in low income, rural, insular, and high cost areas" (Federal Communications Commission, 2006). The definition of "advanced telecommunications services" is left for a "joint board on universal service" that operates under the auspices of the FCC.

MOBILE TELEPHONY AND UNIVERSAL SERVICES

Currently, universal service policies do not explicitly deal with the wireless market. At the same time, it may be desirable to consider universal service policies that ensure various market segments have access and use wireless telephony services. That is, mobile services should be part of the "universal service" concept because they provide an invaluable service that puts those who cannot afford them in a disadvantage socially, economically, and even physically. Similar expansions of the universal service concept were suggested by several academics (Barrantes & Galperin, 2008; Burkart, 2007; Frieden, 1997; Navarro, 1996; Xavier, 1997) who call for the inclusion of 'essential' and 'socially desirable' telecommunication services (e.g., Broadband) under the universal service umbrella, and in the 'Universal Service Obligations' as defined by regulators. Some studies even suggest practical ways to estimate the essentiality and desirability of services to be included under this umbrella.

The recent years have brought additional criticism of the current American universal service regulations and the way they are implemented through regulations aimed at increasing competition while enforcing coverage. For example, it was argued that in contrast to government expectations, universal service regulations have not led to a significant increase in telephone penetration because of the associated implementation cost (taxation) which distorts the market (Rosston & Wimmer, 2000). Furthermore, the FCC's objective of increased competition for enhancing service penetration has been criticized. It was suggested that greater competition is a dubious goal; consumer satisfaction is a better objective that can more effectively promote service penetration and use (Shugan, 2003). The notion that customer satisfaction is a central concept worth studying by regulators was further supported in other investigations (Turel & Serenko, 2006; Turel, Serenko, Detlor, Collan, Nam, & Puhakainen, 2006).

It may be socially just and desirable to include mobile telephony services in the "universal service" basket. The first step for regulators, however, would be to expand the universal service basket to include mobile telecommunications services. This may either be enforced by regulators or self-imposed by operators, should they understand the legal and ethical implications. With respect to legal outcomes, the elimination of customer discrimination based on their demographic or psychographic characteristics may potentially reduce future legal actions taken by individuals, consumer organizations, or authorities. For example, people living in areas with no or poor quality mobile services may sue service providers. With regards to ethical outcomes, providers may be held morally responsible if they deprive individuals their basic right for communication.

CONCLUSION

So where should we go from here? The inclusion of mobile telephony in a more general definition of universal services is the first step that both businesses and regulators should take. This will allow individuals from different market segments to gain access to this important; some may say life-saving, technology, which allows individuals to become active contributing members of our society. This suggestion is in line with recent findings. For example, it has been found that (1) the poor typically use more expensive (prepaid) services to control their costs, and (2) affordability is an important predictor of mobile penetration, especially in the poor market segment, and as such, it has been suggested that priority should be placed on policies aimed at reducing the cost of mobile telephony for low-income groups (Barrantes et al., 2008). We echo these recommendations, but also provide a discussion about the means through which such recommendations can be implemented, namely market oriented universal service policies.

In terms of the Hurricane Katrina example discussed in beginning of this chapter, it is believed that if mobile telephony was offered as a universal service in New Orleans, more lower-income families may have had access to communication and more lives would have been saved during the disaster. In fact, wireless telephony requires less infrastructure than other communications means, including the Internet. Thus, it is infrastructurally efficient. It is a truly ubiquitous technology, available 24/7 that may be utilized for both every-day and emergency communication. Therefore, it is critical to ensure that people from various market segments may utilize it. This is why this issue has been perceived as important by academics and practitioners, as evident by the many papers that discuss this topic. It is hoped that further research will be conducted on this issue, and that regulators start embracing the idea of universal mobile telephony services.

REFERENCES

Baake, P. (2002). Price caps, rate of return constraints and universal service obligations. *Journal of Regulatory Economics*, *21*(3), 289–304. doi:10.1023/A:1015312531833

Barrantes, R., & Galperin, H. (2008). Can the poor afford mobile telephony? *Evidence from Latin America. Telecommunications Policy*, *32*(8), 521–530. doi:10.1016/j.telpol.2008.06.002

Blackman, C. R. (1995). Universal Service - Obligation or Opportunity. *Telecommunications Policy*, *19*(3), 171–176. doi:10.1016/0308-5961(94)00020-S

Burkart, P. (2007). Moving targets: Introducing mobility into universal service obligations. *Telecommunications Policy*, *31*(3-4), 164–178. doi:10.1016/j.telpol.2007.01.002

Chaudhuri, A., Flamm, K. S., & Horrigan, J. (2005). An analysis of the determinants of internet access. *Telecommunications Policy*, *29*(9-10), 731–755. doi:10.1016/j.telpol.2005.07.001

Federal Communications Commission. (n.d.). *Universal service*. Retrieved August 20, 2006 from http://www.fcc.gov/wcb/universal_service/

Frieden, R. (1997). Widespread deployment of wireless telephony - Business, legal, regulatory and spectrum challenges. *Telecommunications Policy*, *21*(5), 451–459. doi:10.1016/S0308-5961(97)00020-7

Jain, R. (2006). Interconnection regulation in India: Lessons for developing countries. *Telecommunications Policy*, *30*(3-4), 183–200. doi:10.1016/j.telpol.2005.11.005

Melody, W. H. (1997). Policy objectives and models of regulation. In W. H. Melody (Ed.), *Telecom reform: Principles, policies and regulatory practices*, (1st ed.), (pp. 13-27). Lyngby, Denmark: Technical University of Denmark.

Mueller, M. L. (1997). *Universal Service: Competition, interconnection, and monopoly in the making of the American telephone system*. Cambridge, MA: MIT Press and AEI Press.

Navarro, J. (1996). Access technology for universal mobility. *Alcatel Telecommunications Review,* (3), 176-183.

Pitt, D., & Levine, N. (2004). Universal service and the future of regulation. *Telecommunications Policy, 28*(3-4), 227–232. doi:10.1016/j.telpol.2004.01.003

Prieger, J. (1998). Universal service and the Telecommunications Act of 1996 - The fact after the act. *Telecommunications Policy, 22*(1), 57–71. doi:10.1016/S0308-5961(97)00057-8

Rice, R. E., & Katz, J. E. (2003). Comparing internet and mobile phone usage: digital divides of usage, adoption, and dropouts. *Telecommunications Policy, 27*(8-9), 597–623. doi:10.1016/S0308-5961(03)00068-5

Rosston, G. L., & Wimmer, B. S. (2000). The 'state' of universal service. *Information Economics and Policy, 12*(3), 261–283. doi:10.1016/S0167-6245(00)00011-1

Schejter, A., Serenko, A., Turel, O., & Zahaf, M. (2010). Policy implications of market segmentation as a determinant of fixed-mobile service substitution: What it means for carriers and policy makers. *Telematics and Informatics, 27*(1), 90–102. doi:10.1016/j.tele.2009.05.002

Shugan, S. M. (2003). Marketing perspectives on federal communications commission policies. *Journal of Public Policy & Marketing, 22*(1), 35–40. doi:10.1509/jppm.22.1.35.17617

Turel, O., & Serenko, A. (2006). Satisfaction with mobile services in Canada: An empirical investigation. *Telecommunications Policy, 30*(5-6), 314–331. doi:10.1016/j.telpol.2005.10.003

Turel, O., Serenko, A., Detlor, B., Collan, M., Nam, I., & Puhakainen, J. (2006). Investigating the determinants of satisfaction and usage of Mobile IT services in four countries. *Journal of Global Information Technology Management, 9*(4), 6–27.

Valletti, T. M., Hoernig, S., & Barros, P. P. (2002). Universal service and entry: The role of uniform pricing and coverage constraints. *Journal of Regulatory Economics, 21*(2), 169–190. doi:10.1023/A:1014387707275

Xavier, P. (1997). Universal service and public access in the networked society. *Telecommunications Policy, 21*(9-10), 829–843. doi:10.1016/S0308-5961(97)00050-5

KEY TERMS AND DEFINITIONS

Federal Communications Commission (FCC): The FCC is an independent agency of the United States government, created, directed, and empowered by Congressional statute, which regulates the telecommunications sector in the US.

Government Regulation: Government control over companies and consumer behaviors through rules, in order to produce outcomes which might not otherwise occur.

Market Segmentation: The process of classifying a collection of consumers into distinct sub-groups (segments) that behave in similar manners, share the same characteristics, or have similar needs.

Mobile Phone: Mobile phones are is a long-range, non-stationary, electronic device used for mobile voice and/or data communication over a wireless network which is comprised from a collection of transmission receiver base stations.

Universal Service: A legal and business concept used mostly in regulated industries.

Originating in the telecommunications sector of the United States, universal service refers to the practice of providing a baseline level of services to every resident of a country.

Index

N